David Pond offers up a broad sweep from the universal to the particular. His experiences as a counselor, family man, spiritual seeker, and philosopher wrap in an effortless embrace his very specific and practical explanations and exercises. Actual cases from his real-life clients put a human face on the symbols for me. As a professional astrologer myself, I applaud his masterful use of the astrological model in which he fits the many aspects of relationships so brilliantly. Also, what a gift for the non-astrologer to find the astrological archetypes in layman's language.

Diana Stone
Author of *The United States Wheel of Destiny*

One of astrology's most charismatic speakers, David Pond now demonstrates that he also writes lucidly and profoundly. Using astrology as a lens, *Astrology & Relationships* is David's distillation of decades of whole-hearted spiritual practice and day-to-day commitment to creating a wealth of loving relationships in his own life. His simple but wise exercises and illustrations will help you open to more love as well. This is a book to work with and to savor.

Donna Cunningham

As humans, we're on an eternal quest to find the right one—our "missing half." Some folks find their soul mates in high school, while some of us search forever. Here, finally, is a book to help us understand all that, through one simple credo: "You can have what you're willing to give." Why do you attract who you attract? How do you go about maintaining quality in a long-term partnership? How do you change your relationship status for the better? The answers to these questions and so much more are contained in this delightful book, presented in an easy, comforting, helpful style that belongs to only one astrologer I know. David Pond walks this talk, and I count myself blessed by knowing him.

There have been almost as many books written about relationships as there have been on the subject of The Soul. This one, however, is full of quiet wisdom. This is the one you should have.

Kim Rogers-Gallagher

Astrology needs a book like this, which explores the reality of relationship and suggests inner work, exercises, and meditations that can shift energies and bring back communication. David Pond's insights and experiences have coalesced into a wonderful and valuable work that I have used in my own life and will use with my clients.

A. T. Mann, author of *The Round Art*,
Sacred Sexuality, and *Millennium Prophecies*

About the Author

David Pond (Washington State) has been a professional practicing astrologer for twenty-five years. He has worked with thousands of people through counseling and workshops, field-testing the ideas and exercises in this book. He has also been a yoga teacher and guide for spiritual journeys to sacred sites around the world. He holds a Master of Science in Experimental Metaphysics, and is the author of *Chakras for Beginners* and, with Lucy Pond, *The Metaphysical Handbook*.

To Write to the Author

If you wish to contact the author or would like more information about this book, please write to the author in care of Llewellyn Worldwide and we will forward your request. Both the author and publisher appreciate hearing from you and learning of your enjoyment of this book and how it has helped you. Llewellyn Worldwide cannot guarantee that every letter written to the author can be answered, but all will be forwarded. Please write to:

David Pond
℅ Llewellyn Worldwide
2143 Wooddale Drive, Dept. 0-7387-0046-0
Woodbury, MN 55125-2989, U.S.A.

Please enclose a self-addressed stamped envelope for reply, or $1.00 to cover costs. If outside U.S.A., enclose international postal reply coupon.

Many of Llewellyn's authors have websites with additional information and resources. For more information, please visit our website at:

http://www.llewellyn.com

Astrology & Relationships

Techniques for Harmonious Personal Connections

David Pond

Llewellyn Publications
Woodbury, Minnesota

First Edition
Fourth Printing, 2005

Book design and editing by Michael Maupin
Cover art © 2001 by Masao Ota/Photonica.com
Cover design by Gavin Dayton Duffy

Library of Congress Cataloging-in-Publication Data

Pond, David.
Astrology & relationships : techniques for harmonious personal connections / David Pond. — 1st ed.
p. cm.
Includes bibliographical references and index.
ISBN 0-7387-0046-0
1. Astrology. 2. Planets—Miscellanea. 3. Interpersonal relations—Miscellanea. I. Title: Astrology and relationships. II. Title.

BF1724 .P66 2001
133.5'3—dc21

2001029602

Llewellyn Publications
A Division of Llewellyn Worldwide, Ltd.
2143 Wooddale Drive, Dept. 0-7387-0046-0
Woodbury, MN 55125-2989, U.S.A.
www.llewellyn.com

Printed in the United States of America

Other Books by David Pond

Chakras for Beginners

Western Seeker, Eastern Path

Mapping Your Romantic Relationships

with Lucy Pond

The Metaphysical Handbook
(Reflecting Pond Publications, 1984)

To Laura, my teacher of the heart

Contents

Acknowledgments

A BOOK THAT IS finally born after a seventeen-year gestation period has had many influences. In the beginning, there was friend and healer Brenda Leona's Aries excitement about the seed ideas that flamed the inspiration for initiating this book. My sister, Lucy Pond, collaborated with me as a coauthor during the first stage of the book's development, and many of the good ideas come from Lucy. To her, I give my undying loyalty. Beyond being my sister, as a fellow seeker on the path, she's been there for the most important passages in my life. I wish to thank Kris Rodrigues, who took on the unenviable task of editing the first rough, rough draft. Friends and fellow astrologers, Lynn Mitchell and Tina Summers, read the early work and offered helpful assistance.

I would also like to acknowledge the many clients, friends, and workshop attendees who provided the material of the book itself. By sharing their joys and sorrows, their desires and disappointments, and being willing to work with this material, they have shaped and refined the work.

Although nearly complete in 1991, I took a hiatus from the project and for this I would like to thank my four sons. I was at a point in the writing that took a great deal of focus to bring the work to its next level. My children were at a stage in their lives that also required a great deal of attention. It became clear to me that I could experience family while the kids were at home, and I could write later . . . but I couldn't write now and experience my children later—they'd be gone! I had faith that putting the book on hold for a few years and dedicating quality time to being with my family was the right path. I'll never regret this choice as it has been the greatest blessing in my life.

I would like to acknowledge Jeff Jawer for first believing in the book and steering me onto the path of publication. I would especially like to acknowledge Maria K. Simms from ACS who performed the main editing of the text. I stand in awe and appreciation of her talent for empowering my confidence as a writer, while simultaneously rephrasing a paragraph to more clearly express my intention. I'm also thankful for the friendship that grew between us through the process of my surrendering to her patient and personal guidance.

My appreciation is deeply felt for Laura, my wife and life partner. We celebrate twenty-seven years together at the time of this publication. We've been through it all, and have more than survived. All that is in this book has been "tried, trued, and tested" in our relationship. Her role in bringing this book into manifestation could not be overstated. From facing life issues with me and being willing to experiment, to believing in the book and supporting the many months of impossibly late nights, to suggesting to Jeff Jawer that he look at the manuscript, to reading and rereading constantly new revisions and sharing her oh-so-clear insights—and doing it all right from her loving heart.

I want to thank Michael Maupin at Llewellyn for his work as final editor and layout artist. Working with such a supportive editor, with enthusiasm for the material, creates an atmosphere of trust where the otherwise stressful experience of final editing flows to completion. I would like to thank my Gemini friends Sherrie Schouten and Ira Stollack for their timely help with the final proofreading.

I would like to express my appreciation for seekers on the path everywhere. Feeling connected to other beings who are doing what they can do to improve the quality of life on our planet gives me an inner strength to draw upon.

To the growing light that we are all awakening into, to the still quiet voice within, to the source of the guidance that comes to us during prayer and meditation, my eternal gratitude.

Introduction

WE ARE AT the dawn of an emerging global community. Individuality is certainly an important stage of development, but this is a planet with a population of more than six billion people, and it would seem this is an inappropriate place to be if your main lesson is to learn independence! More than independence, relating skills are essential for learning to get along on such a crowded planet. We are now entering a social period possessing the theme of an evolving global consciousness. We are each individual cells of consciousness within the larger body of Mother Earth, and it is how we interact, relate, and connect with one another that will be more important to survival and well-being than how we defend our individual space. At this point of planetary evolution, the path to the divine is through relating with others. It is in this spirit that this book is written.

As above, so below. This phrase is the basic premise of astrology and is likely to be found in most every book that has ever been written on the topic. Yet, too often, this is not what these very same astrology books teach. The universe is an exquisite example of harmony within change. By looking up into the evening sky, one cannot help but be inspired by the ever-changing patterns that always are in harmony. If harmony is the above, why do astrologers teach that certain signs are not compatible with others? Is that what we see in the heavens? Certainly not. I take the saying "As above, so below" as a mandate of what astrologers can teach by observing the heavens. My premise is that all relationships can improve and that we are all compatible with one another once we learn to accept and compensate for our differences. We have outgrown the luxury of not being able to get along with each other on our crowded planet.

As elusive as a butterfly, yet as delightful to behold, harmony in relationships is difficult to maintain, yet an absolute delight to experience. To be in harmony is to cooperate with the unfoldment of your life, to enjoy the partnerships, romances, and alliances along the way; to feel as if you and life are on friendly terms. This is not the submissive path of constant acquiescence. It is the deepest yearning of the soul to find peace and joy, and when relationships proceed from harmony, the full potential of all involved is actualized.

As an astrologer, I get the opportunity to listen to many people tell of their experiences, disappointments, and dreams. From this experience, I have noticed an evolutionary trend. Current astrological cycles suggest that this is a time for everyone to take their next evolutionary step. It is as if there is a crack in the structure of each of our lives. Due to the growth in consciousness that has occurred in each of our lives, the old form and way of relating to the world is no longer adequate. There is a general awakening occurring in the collective consciousness reflected through increased dissatisfaction with lifestyles and relationships that do not reflect the true essence of the self. It is as if the soul has returned for each of us and is demanding that we not sacrifice its integrity in any area of our lives. There is a hunger for intimacy in the modern world. People are not satisfied with what they have already experienced in relationships, and are expressing a desire to move beyond mediocrity in involvements with others into more expansive, growth-oriented relationships.

Why Astrology?

Astrology is a wonderful model for understanding harmony within complexity and change. When you go out into the evening sky and observe the ever-changing patterns of the planets in their movements through the heavens, you are always left with a feeling of harmony. The patterns, just like your life experiences, are ever changing, never to repeat themselves, and yet harmony exists.

To use astrology is to pattern your awareness of life after this model of harmony. Each of the planets, the Sun, and the Moon represent different centers of consciousness within you. These centers already exist; astrology does not cause them, but instead, represents these centers within you. The planets provide a reference map to experiences you are already experiencing, and astrology teaches the path of integration. In order to operate as an integrated system, harmony must be experienced at each center of consciousness autonomously, as well as within their relationship to each other. This is a tall order, to be sure. But harmony does exist in the solar system, and it can exist in our lives as well, when we apply the principles of balance to any given situation.

The beauty of astrology is that it can be learned from the inside out and affirmed by genuine experience. The astrological descriptions could be thought of as a finger pointing, but what the finger is pointing to in you is by far the most important issue. Don't try to cram your experiences into the model. Instead, let the model trigger your genuine experience related to each center of consciousness. Let the descriptions and exercises be as symbols that provoke your awareness of each center within, like characters in a play you are directing in the performance of your life.

Astrology is a very complex science that has grown out of a very simple truth: observing the heavens, with any degree of appreciation at all, always brings a deep breath of clarity within. In the moment of appreciation, all falls into perspective. Sunsets, moonlight reflected on water, sunrises—all have the tendency to pull us out of our many life concerns and inspire within us a sense of tranquillity. When we use astrology to understand human behavior, we are assuming that the planets in the heavens correspond to the various centers of consciousness within as well. As above, so below: outer reality reflects inner reality, the basic building blocks of metaphysical theory.

Many of the exercises you will encounter in this book are designed to awaken individual skills and heightened self-understanding. You may wonder what they have to do with your personal relationships. Again, the mystics admonishment: "Seek ye not in the world for that which you have not found within yourself." The metaphysical perspective on life is that the first relationship you have is with yourself. If you have not developed a particular part of your character, you will not find healthy involvements with others in this area of life. The exercises lead you to first identify a particular quality within yourself, and then to relate to it in others.

It would be wonderful if both people in a relationship would go through these exercises, but even if your mate is not interested, the relationship will benefit through your work. Be creative with the exercises and adapt them to suit your own needs. If you already have integrated a particular planet into your personality, the exercises likely will seem too obvious to be of any use. They are not for you—go ahead and skip them. However, if the planet in question is not operating in your relationships in a healthy way, these simple exercises are exactly where you need to start.

Our solar system is a wonderful model of harmony within change. Our lives can be more like that, too, if we listen to the lessons the planets teach.

THE SUN

The Center, the Heart

A WOMAN WENT to her guru with the question that had been burning in her heart. "Dear teacher," she began, "The same situation keeps happening to me over and over again. I fall in love and all of life is wonderful, and then the relationship invariably falls apart and I'm lonely, gloomy, and life seems terrible. This goes on until I fall in love and again, life is grand, only to be followed by the darkness of disappointment when it doesn't work out. This keeps happening to me, can you help me?"

The teacher thought for a moment and then responded, "Dear lady, love is a rare and precious thing. What you keep falling in, must be something else!"

Yes, true love is a rare and precious thing, and falling in love seems to be easy, but maintaining it—now that is something else. Sustaining the feelings of love is an art and can be cultivated. In this chapter, awakening the power of love from within, so that it is not dependent on outer circumstances, will be explored through the Sun in your birthchart. Learning how to relate to the world from this vital center allows for love to be the norm in your life, instead of something that you occasionally fall into.

This chapter is arranged in three sections. The first section is dedicated toward identifying and actualizing the Sun within you, regardless of what sign it was in at your birth. The second section focuses on identifying and interacting with the Sun in others—again, regardless of the particular sign. Both sections are filled with exercises and activities designed to bring your attention to the Sun aspect of your character. The third section explores the Sun through each of the signs, first for you, and then others. This describes the specific needs, strengths, and challenges of each Sun sign, particularly in regards to relationships.

Every birthchart has a Sun in it, and every person has a source of strength, purpose, and power that animates his or her life. Here resides the pure, radiant, essential self. The planets represent the questions, the subtleties of distinction that make up the complete you and your connections to the world around you. But within, just pure you. In the center of the solar system, as in the core of your being, lies the heart of the matter. Power, light, love—the source.

Love is a personal resource; not something that is found in the world. I remember the first teacher I had concerning this principle. This happened when I was a young man, just starting my family. I did the grocery shopping and regularly went to a large supermarket and, as these places tend to be, it was quite impersonal. However, there was one grocery checker that eventually caught my attention. He was always so sunny and playful with the customers, and I enjoyed watching him, as he was noticeably different from all of the other workers. It got to the point where I would stand in his line even when shorter lines were available! It always lifted my spirits just to interact with him.

One day my curiosity got the best of me, and I asked him how he was able to always be so happy. He did not have to think to come up with his reply. He smiled, a twinkle could be seen in his eye, and he said, "It's easy, I just figure that my love and happiness are the only things in life that nobody can tax or take away from me!" I was stunned by the simplicity and clarity of his philosophy on life. Here was a person who knew that the true power of love was his personal resource, not dependent on variables in the world or other people's actions.

Awakening the Sun from Within

The Sun is the core spark that animates the heart's natural urge for the experience of life: to reach out, touch, and embrace experiences with a sense of wonder and awe. To live life from this center is a true blessing that is available to everyone. However, the ability to maintain the state of heartfulness becomes more and more difficult with the pressures, responsibilities, and experiences of adulthood, but this is the path to the Sun; the center, the heart, the child within.

It is amazing to me how easy it is to love a young child. Interacting with a child tickles our hearts and brings joy to our life. We are not so enchanted with everyone as they get older; why is it so easy to love a child? It is because, at this early stage of development, the child is pure essence, all heart, the Sun. As they mature, the complications of integrating all the other planets and all the questions this creates veils the light of the Sun. To reawaken to the original essence of self is the path.

To be in loving relationships one has to be a loving soul. This starts with the self. Self-love is not possible if you simply wish for it. It can be a grand idea, but without action, it is just futile. As with loving another, self-love must be demonstrated in some way. It is like doing the dishes in this sense. You could wish that they were not dirty, wonder why, trace it all the way back to your childhood and experiences with your parents, or even contemplate as to whether or not it is a residual past-life experience that has created the condition. But in truth, action is required—you have to wash the dishes to have them clean.

It is the same with self-love. All the wishing, wondering, and questioning will not fill the void. Activity will. Cultivate the experience by creating disciplined time in the daily schedule. Just five minutes is enough—more is great—but a few minutes helps you to move out of the questions and into the experience of present time. Be Here Now: perhaps the simplest and most direct teaching of all.

Exercises for Being in Present Time

1. *Breathing:* Simple breathing exercises are excellent for pulling attention back to the moment. Focus on the in-breath and then on the out-breath. Whether you are walking or sitting, just focus on your breath. The in-breath and the out-breath. No thinking. Become so aware that you can even hear the subtle *click* as the breath changes from one phase to the next. This is a technique of entering into present time. The focus is on what is, not what could be or could have been.

2. *Daily Walks:* A daily walk with the intention of being fully aware of the experience, the sights and sounds of nature, would be another excellent technique to practice the art of living in the moment. If you live in an

inner city, you will have to look for it, but even one flower, a bird, a cloud against the sky can do the trick. Stay in the moment and surrender totally to the beauty of nature. Notice the trees, birds, and clouds, along with drinking in all the sights, smells, and sounds that surround you. It is amazingly refreshing to not think.

There are countless other ways to connect with the eternal now. Great peace can be achieved through listening to music with the sincerity of becoming the music. Remember, no jumping backward or forward in time. Stay in the present. Dancing, t'ai chi, yoga, and gardening are also satisfying ways to connect with the inner self, but then, so is doing almost anything that you fully enjoy. The trick is having the discipline to integrate these exercises in a schedule that seems already too full. It is exactly when you haven't the time to do these types of exercises, that you need them the most.

There are many paths to awaken the heart, depending on your personality type. What do you love to do? The importance lies not with which path you choose to connect yourself to the vital core within, but that you do, indeed, find a path.

Exercise

Do something good for yourself the first thing every morning.

This could be physical, emotional, mental, or spiritual, depending on your inclinations. A physical workout, yoga, meditation, a morning walk, journal writing, reading or listening to inspirational wisdom, and numerous other activities with the same intention of doing something good for yourself will work. By treating yourself with loving kindness and nurturing your self-development, you are cultivating self-love.

This helps create a more loving and lovable you. Cultivating the ability to experience love, even when new romantic love is not available, is an art that, once developed, can be the single most important thing that you can do for your health. It is not just coincidence that when people fall in love, they rarely experience ill health—love stimulates the thymus gland and activates the immunity system of the body. It works. It would be grand if the passion of new love continued at the same level as in the courtship stage of a relationship, but that is not the way things are. Love may be blind, but time isn't. When it is not available through romantic love, you must find a way to cultivate this same feeling in other ways.

Exercise

Spend ten minutes a day celebrating and appreciating your life.

On good days, bad days or in-between days, it is always possible to be thankful for something. Even if you cannot find anything that you appreciate, make something up! The effect that it brings is certainly worth the effort. The classic story of two friends walking down the street together is illustrative. One person looks down during the entire walk, noticing the litter and garbage. He inwardly grumbles at the mess of life. The other person looks up, noticing the clouds, the birds, the trees, and the beauty of nature. At the end of their walk, they each feel differently, even though they just were together experiencing the same time and space. Each is surprised at the other's perception of the experience.

It is really a matter of attention, isn't it? What are you paying attention to? Are you seeing what is there or what is not there? It makes a difference. For at least ten minutes a day, focus on the beauty of your world. If you can't find it, you're not looking hard enough!

You get what you look for in life. For a person skilled in the art of finding the highest good in others, there is no one they cannot reach. For a person who is skilled in the art of finding the lowest in others, there is no one they cannot criticize. The highest and the lowest are to be found in each of us.

The world of experience calls and the cycles of life pull us out of this center and into life with others. We get caught up in trying to fit into other people's expectations of us, drift far away from self-acceptance and self-love, enter into all types of questioning of who we are or should be, and eventually resolve the questions by returning to our center, incorporating our experiences into an expanded awareness of the self. The cycle repeats itself forever. We start from innocence, have experiences, create difficulties and imbalances in our lives, and eventually return to our innocence, hopefully. It is like one of my favorite sayings—somewhat crude, but to the point: "Enlightened today, asshole tomorrow." Doesn't this happen to all of us—often? Thus the cycle of the natural state, the questioning state, and the resolution—over and over again.

The natural state of the heart is open to the essential goodness of life, excited about opportunities to reach out and take in the delight of experiences. These very experiences, however, trigger the questioning state. Self-doubt and insecurities take the place of self-love. Measuring self against others, the confusion from broken dreams and difficult times, and just some of the harshness of life throw us into questioning ourselves at each and every turn. Ideally a healing occurs when we integrate our experiences, come back to our center and enter into the resolution stage—reconnecting with the eternal child within, forever open to the wonder and awe of life.

The natural state of your Sun is the easiest part of you to know because it is the one element that is always with you. One way to identify this core identity is to reflect back on your life and note which of your qualities have always emerged, have always returned, regardless of the ups and downs of life. Through all of the experiences, the successes, and the failures, which traits have been eternally you? These qualities and traits are the core level of truth about who you are and represent your natural state.

The questioning state arises because the Sun is part of a system—the other centers of consciousness represented by the planets and the Moon, ultimately must be integrated into the system as well. Each of these planets creates various situations and scenarios that draw attention into the many facets of being. When you expand consciousness to include each of these centers, the experiences connected to the next layer of consciousness at first seem to be external. With experience and awareness, the planet gets incorporated into self-awareness. Thus, the soul evolves with an ever-expanding awareness as more and more of what at first seems to be external to self at the questioning stage becomes integrated within the self at the resolution stage.

The Sun of your self-identity is the strongest message that you send to the world about who you are. When you project incompleteness or uncertainty about who you are to the world, you will obviously attract incomplete and uncertain relationships to you. When you project need, as in "I need a relationship," you attract relationships that reflect this state of need, and there will always be something lacking. The sad truth is that many who are searching for happiness outside of self would not recognize it even if they fell into it, because they have not yet found it within themselves.

An important question to ask yourself is: where is the source of your happiness and love? What are the conditions that you place on experiencing the power of love in your life? If your conditions are external, so that you focus on achieving the perfect conditions in the world, you have the cart before the horse. You are deferring responsibility for your experience of love to others. It is easy to assume that your partner is the source of the love that you are experiencing. But what is closer to the truth is that this other person is getting you in touch with your power of love. It is *your* love that you are sharing. This awareness leads to the resolution of the questioning state.

The Sun, the radiant self, continually burns brightly in the center of each of us. There are times when it gets pushed pretty far down inside, and other times when so much armor gets put around it to protect its vulnerability, that it becomes a task just to experience life from this center, even occasionally. The soul urge calls, however, and this is felt as a deep hunger, a hunger to experience life from the heart, the spirit of life itself. *Return* and *accept* are the strategies that work with the heart, rather than *attain* and *acquire*.

Additional Techniques for Activating the Sun

The following techniques are methods of integrating the power of the Sun into your life. Make it your responsibility to lead a positive, loving life and when you have accomplished this, your happiness and love will not be dependent on the actions of others. Joy becomes your resource that no one can tax or take away, and you will have contributed in making the world a more loving environment.

- A friend tells of his morning run, what he calls his "tune-up." After he has settled into the run, and has a steady aerobic pace, he then begins to integrate visualization into the activity. He first visualizes each of the chakra centers and feels their energy. Next, he focuses on the heart chakra and creates what he calls his love circle. While focusing on his heart and the warm feelings of love, he thinks of each of the people that he loves and brings their image into his love circle. As the heart is pumping away in the body, he pictures that all the love he is visualizing comes into his heart and then is distributed through the body, filling every cell in his body with love.

- Even something as common as eating your meals can become a ritual of experiencing life's fullness. Prayers and blessings at the meal can be integrated with a reverent attitude throughout the meal. Experience each bite, each taste, each texture: be thankful, and allow the experience to resonate with a deep level of satisfaction within you.
- Any activity that cultivates the attitude of thankfulness as a regular discipline works. To open up the emotional heart, count your blessings and set regular time aside each day for enjoying your heartfelt joys. Living in an environment that affords the splendor of nature is especially beneficial. Feel the sunset, the waterfall, the sunlight shimmering on a leaf dancing in the wind. Also, being with children and totally experiencing their reality certainly awakens the heart.
- The mind tends to be the dominant tool that most of us make decisions with in life. We analyze the potentialities like a business person, then weigh the alternatives in terms of plusses and minuses and make a rational decision. These decisions *think* good, but they do not always *feel* good. Learning to make decisions concerning important life path decisions from the heart, rather than the mind, can alleviate the tendency to be doing everything right and still not enjoying it.

We found a wonderful quotation in *The Sun* magazine by Mary McCarthy on this issue. "If someone tells you he is going to make a 'realistic decision,' you immediately understand that he's resolved to do something bad!"

Essentially, you learn to use the mind and heart as a team. The mind becomes involved, focuses on the question, gathers the information relevant to the question, and brings this before the heart to be the final judge. The trick is to awaken the glad heart before the question, make your decision, and then observe if you can stay in your heart with the decision made. If the decision pulls you out of the heart, assume that acting on the decision would do the same. If you are able to feel good about the decision, so that it is both mentally and emotionally a strong, positive affirmation of the question, then the omens are good for your ability to live with the decision in a heartfelt way.

The Sun in Relationships

Imagine this scenario: the Day of Judgment is upon us. The big guy comes down and makes a proclamation: "Some of you will go to heaven and experience eternal bliss. Some of you will go to hell and experience eternal damnation. Who goes where will be decided by a simple test. Those who pass the test go to heaven and those who fail will go to hell. The test is as follows: tomorrow, you will have to spend at least fifteen minutes in total harmony with the person closest to you." In this scenario, where the stakes are so high, each and every person could pass the test. It is not a question of whether we could get along with each other, it is a question of will we do what it takes.

The first section of this chapter focused on skills and techniques to help you find the Sun within yourself. The following section focuses on the skills required for relating to this core level of vitality within others. The sequence is important because the amount of self-esteem and self-love you develop will directly impact the quality of experiences you have with others. So, of course, the relationship you have with yourself, your inner partner, still has to be considered the most important and influential relationship that you have, for it is from this center that you set the tone for the quality of the relationships that you will have with each and every person you meet.

Being in touch with your inner partner at one time in your life is not enough—it is an ongoing process that requires daily participation. Neither is pure introspection enough to give you the awareness and sensitivity that are needed to form the bonding required for easy communication between the inner and outer you. Contrast is needed, and is provided by others in your life who will form this necessary contrast for definition of self. It is easy to define yourself as loving, forgiving, easy-going, and generous when you live alone, but bring in a close relationship and you will put that definition to the test! Your relationships, all of them, are necessary ingredients on your path to wholeness as you are given the opportunity to know more about yourself with each of them. They will mirror back to you the quality, or lack of quality, that you are projecting.

When you meet someone who recognizes the core within you and relates to your essential dignity, you feel very special and often associate the feeling with a sense of magic. When you recognize this in others, they feel the same thing—that someone has seen their real face. Let's call this soul recognition. When two people simultaneously recognize this special part of potentiality within the other, love occurs. The spell of territoriality is broken and trust allows each of the individuals to move closer to the other, giving birth to the highest manifestation of the relationship. At this stage, the fears of closeness or rejection begin to fall away, your defenses are dropped, and your face softens as you let go of the armor that has protected your vulnerability. When this simultaneously happens between two people, you revitalize and empower each other.

Exercise

Make it a daily habit to find, nurture, and bring out a sense of power, love, and joy in another person.

1. Ask your friend what he currently enjoys most in his life. Never assume that you already know the answer to this question, as this is a focus that frequently changes. This is an exercise of listening, and is your opportunity to make your friend feel special. All too often people end up in counseling or therapy, simply to have an hour a week when someone really listens to what they have to say. Encourage your partner to share the deepest, innermost thoughts, and you will find the more you listen, the more trust your friend will feel and the easier it gets for both of you to open up and communicate.
2. Develop empathy for your partner by trying to see life through her eyes and supporting the highest image she has of herself. Praise the light in your friend whenever you see it. This is most needed in trouble situations when you feel certain that everything that person does is wrong, bleak, or boring. What you see is what you get, and you have the power to emphasize whichever points of another person's character that you choose. The good and the bad are always present within the personality, just waiting to be watered so they can grow into full expression. Which side of your friend do you want to emphasize?

Exercise

Make it a habit to set aside at least ten minutes a day to celebrate the beauty and the joy of the love that you share with your partner.

This exercise is enhanced if both individuals in the relationship partake in the joy of their relationship together, but positive effects can even be attained if only one person does the work inwardly. This exercise is easy to do when the relationship is going along beautifully and not so easy when it is on shaky ground. When couples polarize on various issues, both people are locked into a "this and only this" reality, and from a spiritual perspective, we know that this is quite impossible. This exercise requires you to rise above the polarity to see a larger reality that encompasses both polarities, at least for ten minutes.

Allow for honoring the differences—agree to disagree. Keep in mind, as the first two exercises have shown, it is always possible to find the positive when you take the time and responsibility to look for it. Even on your darkest days, set aside the challenges just for ten minutes and remember what it is like to feel the love and peace in your relationship with each other. This will greatly help keep the problems in perspective.

Through this daily celebration of joy, you will be empowering your relationship with love and vitality, constantly renewing the strength of your bond and affirmation that you have chosen to experience your lives as a team. You are energizing your relationship to the degree that even challenges and problems will be a source of continued learning and growth instead of potential material for a break-up.

This series of exercises for activating the Sun are probably the simplest and easiest to perform of all the exercises presented in this book. They are also the most important and the ones that you will want to come back to whenever you or your relationship enter into troubled waters. Remember to always test yourself at this first level before you seek to make any other adjustments in your relationships. Are you in touch with your center so that your observations are not altered by an imbalanced perspective?

The Sun in Your Horoscope

The Sun in your horoscope represents the core of your astrological self. Activities related to your Sun sign are essential for your well-being and sense of vitality in life. So it follows that relationships that reflect this quality of your being will be the most empowering to you. The symbol of the Sun in astrology tells the story. It is a circle with a dot in the center. The circle describes the full potential of expression. The dot is where you begin, a seed of your potentiality, which often takes most of a life to fully actualize.

Your basic life lessons, the purpose of your life, are encoded in your Sun sign. If your relationship does not bring out the qualities of your Sun sign, the relationship will be missing an important ingredient—you. For you to bring your best to a relationship, the qualities of your Sun sign have to be appreciated by your mate. Conversely, when you relate to a person through the qualities of his or her Sun sign, you are relating to the core of that person's being. You have a wonderful opportunity to bring out the best in the other person.

It is important to remember that these descriptions are not ironclad tendencies. The Sun is but the center of your total identity—each of the other planets will describe different characteristics, which could strengthen or undermine those of the Sun.

Sun in Aries

Your Natural Essence At the core of your being lies excitement, intensity, and the quest for experience. You were born to act on your instincts and the sudden prompting of inspiration, for yours is the sign of action and you learn through primary, direct involvement with life. You naturally lean towards the future, and tend to be inspirational and hopeful for others. As the first sign of the zodiac, you are the pioneer, the initiator that gets the ball rolling. Not known for completing projects, you would rather leave that for others as you are most inspired when a project or relationship is new and fresh. Whether you constantly jump into new experiences, or approach familiar situations with a new approach, this quest for newness and adventure is central to your character. You are meant to be guided by instinct, so trust your impulses. Let enthusiasm be your guide. Your search for wholeness demands that you follow your heart, and then later stop and figure things out. This impulsiveness leads to making a few more careless mistakes than others, but it also allows for making many more gains.

You become more effective through the years as you learn to harness and direct your energy. Early in life your energy is like a flamethrower, but with experience it becomes more like a laser light—just as intense, but with more focus. Physical exercise is one of the paths that can help to keep you centered. Rigorous forms are good, but you will find that calming forms of exercise that center on breathing, such as yoga and t'ai chi, are especially beneficial. These disciplines help you focus and take responsibility for being in your center and not in a state of reaction to the world. You are a catalyst that can bring out the best and worst in others.

Relationship Skills and Needs In relationships, the sign of independent action gets tested in its ability to stay balanced with the needs of others. How to maintain independence within balanced relationships is your special test. The secret for maintaining long-term satisfying involvements for you is to challenge yourself to always find new avenues of personal growth within the relationship. The ram is going to butt its head against something, and you get to decide what. Impulse serves you well, so trust your inner voice. You seem to function best in relationships that respect and encourage this part of your character, but simultaneously help you harness and direct your energy so that it is not dissipated through initiating too many experiences at once.

You might periodically wish you didn't always have to be the one who gets things started in your relationships, but then again, you are good at it. You are at your best with a dynamic partner who can keep up with you. When you are lost in the shuffle of a relationship, which translates into not getting enough attention, you can be miserable. You crave adventure and thrive on excitement, so a relationship that becomes predictable bores you.

Areas to Work On How to maintain the intensity and pace of life that you enjoy and still be patient with others is the main focus here. Your zest can be interpreted as pushy by others. You are often in some form of competition with yourself, but those around you can interpret this as competition with them, which of course, leads to problems. Be mindful that your over self-involvement can keep you from being sensitive to the needs of others. By cultivating your listening skills you can overcome your tendencies to personally react to everything.

Understanding Sun in Aries in Others These people need lots of elbow room, so don't crowd too close. The paradox is that they want attention at the same time they are fighting for their freedom, so it's going to be tricky to find a point of balance. They learn best through their own experiences and like to make their own decisions so there's no sense in trying to direct them. Just stand back and watch or participate when you can. Their spontaneous and fresh responses do have a childlike magnetism of innocence, and you will likely find this to be their most attractive quality.

Aries people operate well on the spur of the moment, so leave some of the details of planning for the last minute and be open to the spontaneous changing of plans. They can become impatient when there is too much talk and not enough action—these people thrive on momentum. They can also get irritable when they feel too hemmed in.

When appropriate, ask their advice as they love to share their personal opinions. They are more insecure than you would think, and often their boastfulness is a cover-up for self-doubt. When they have inspired you, let them know; they need the feedback. Ask them some very personal questions about themselves, offering constant reassurance that you are personally interested in their life. They are not so fragile that you will have to agree with all that they do, but they do need your support. Express it often if you want them to know that you care.

Aries is the first sign of the zodiac and is thought of as the most primal and the most driven by instincts. Knowing that their actions are not premeditated will help you excuse some of the brashness that you may experience. This is a sign of action. Don't expect this sign to eventually outgrow its restlessness and settle down to routines—it won't. Your Aries partner will always crave the excitement of new experiences.

Sun in Taurus

YOUR NATURAL ESSENCE You are the connoisseur of the zodiac. You know and appreciate quality. This taste for the best will be reflected in all areas of your life, but perhaps your greatest gift is your ability to fully appreciate this quality. An enjoyable, comfortable and even luxurious life is often the result of your secret ability to attract people, resources and situations to you. Venus is the planet that has the greatest affinity with Taurus. Venus, the goddess of beauty, is the attraction principle in life. When you fully enjoy an experience, you encode your experience with magnetism. When you enter into the feelings of enjoyment and security, instead of seeking them outwardly, you send forth a tone of appreciation into the world. You attract that which you enjoy and which reflects your true feelings of security.

You came here to develop and rely on your skills, talents, and abilities to provide for your security needs at much more than just survival level. Abundance and prosperity are more to your liking, although you greatly appreciate the most simple and direct experiences of the sights, tastes, and smells of life. Simplicity is a requirement to your world, and you have the ability to perceive the obvious, so trust the obvious. When you find your life being pulled into the realm of mental complexity, you are out of your area of expertise and need to stop and reduce the situation to its basic parts. Trust your most innate sense of intuition, and you will remain right on course.

Relationship Skills and Needs Your need for security, comfort, and stability is reflected in your involvements with others, and as long as that is intact, you are easy to get along with. Your key word is comfort and this is experienced through emotional situations and through your physical surroundings. You need to feel appreciated in your involvements with others. When centered, you share a most earthy and warm self with those around you, and seem to be able to bring others back to present time. Your patience, your sense of the natural amount of time that projects take to complete, can be very soothing and comforting to others. Touch is so important that you need affectionate, hands-on relationships.

Clarifying personal values is an integral part of your search for self. The expression of these is certainly of utmost importance to you, but so is it for others, so remember to allow them this same right of expression. Cultivate tolerance of opposing values and opinions, as without this consideration, you can be overbearing and may find yourself pushing away the very people you want to draw closer. The compromising that is often part of relating, is not something that you are cut out to do, but you can cooperate, without compromising your values.

Areas to Work On When you are stretched past your comfort zone, you tend to be stubborn, demanding, and overbearing. At this point, almost everything is an obstacle and you will notice people are not so eager to spend time with you. Recognize these times as a need to be alone, and either take a walk or meditate, or just sit quietly until you return to your center. When you are feeling out of your center, spend time in a favorite spot in nature, and you will be immediately revitalized.

Taurus, the bull, is able to dig its hooves in and resist change. This is your strength, but it is also your weakness when you resist inevitable change. Consequently, your susceptibility to resistance pulls you out of the harmony that you crave. Always remember the simple path. Return to your *feelings* of comfort and security. With Taurus, there is always the danger of attachment: the risk of becoming overattached to the conditions and objects of your enjoyment and security, instead of experiencing the emotional feelings themselves.

Understanding Sun in Taurus in Others These people are strong, stubborn, and certainly capable of being exquisitely delightful. Comfort and security are the key issues here, so don't press too far past these when you are working through a stressful issue together. Be willing to move slowly, as only time and patience will enable you to build a strong and reliable foundation of emotional security with this Taurean Bull. They may be attracted to you in the moment, but winning the heart of a Taurus is a long process. Trust is the reward at the end of much hard work. A Taurus friend will make you earn it.

What your Taurus friends want from you is to be involved with the most basic part of your life. They enjoy feeling that they are a part of the practical decision making. They want to be useful. If you are reliable in the quality and substance of your friendship, then you will receive equal support from them. They can get bossy, so learn to just listen and not take it too personally, for that is not their true intention. They truly believe that they are sharing the truth with you which is why they take themselves so seriously. If you wish to influence Taureans, don't push. Present the practical and attractive qualities of your ideas and let them work with these concepts at their own pace. If you are perceived as pushy, the heels will dig in and no sign is better at resistance than Taurus.

The special gift of being with Taurus friends is that they will introduce you to the love of planet Earth. Through their heightened senses, you will perceive sights, smells, tastes, and experiences that you won't forget. They have great appreciation for the comforts in life. Spend some quiet time enjoying life's simple pleasures with them, and your ability to appreciate life will be enhanced.

Sun in Gemini

Your Natural Essence Gemini is an Air sign, the element of the intellect, and this arena is your strong suit. Lively, witty, and charming, you were born with the gift of gab—you can communicate with anyone. Every sign has a special gift to share with the rest of the zodiac. Gemini's gift is communication—you can find something of interest in every person you interact with, for it is not just the content of communication that is important, but the process itself of interacting and exchanging ideas that you find refreshing.

You are meant to be a bit of a dilettante and a dabbler. You live by the adage "variety is the spice of life." You perceive life as a brightly lit kaleidoscope of many opportunities that titillate your curiosity, and are meant to be a true mental gymnast in the world of polarities. As Gemini is the least-pretentious sign of the zodiac, you have the capacity to relate to intellectual highbrows and street people, as well. Freedom of choice, thought, and action are your basic needs. With an air of versatility, you compulsively jump into your new mental pursuits and stay with them until they no longer hold fascination. When bored with routine, you seek out some new form of excitement or challenge. Routines are boring. Mental stimulation is a must, and harmony for you is experienced within change.

Relationship Skills and Needs Communication is the key for successful relationships for you. A lively exchange of ideas, talking, enjoying the media and all other sources of information, these are all important qualities that you need to be appreciated for. You are at your best with open-minded individuals who give you the freedom to express the full range of your mental versatility. If relationships become too closed in, you get bored. You need a relationship that is open enough to allow for spontaneous exchanges with the wide variety of people you find interesting. You have a natural flirtatious character that is more interested in enjoying the moment than in being seductive.

Gemini likes to keep its options open, thus commitments might not be as easy for you as others. The haunting question of "What if something better comes along?" can make it difficult to fully surrender to any given situation. You have a knack for staying fascinated by life and you need to be with a partner that enjoys the busy life that you likely live. The key to your heart is through your mind, so if you are with someone who is lacking mental magnetism, you'll likely lose interest.

Areas to Work On Words are very important to you. Talking is often weighted more heavily than listening in your communications. This can be tiring for your audience. Instead of being a chatterbox who monopolizes the conversation, you might want to make sure that you are allowing others to also say what is on their mind. Other people can experience you as superficial if you continually change topics and dart back and forth from one idea to another. You have the ability to talk yourself in and out of trouble—don't let this skill degenerate into evasive techniques for dealing with issues at depth. This tendency to talk your way through most situations is probably what keeps you from totally experiencing them, so check to see that your words aren't getting in the way of your feelings.

Variety shifts into chaos when you allow yourself to get overly distracted. How to make good decisions can become a real dilemma for you as information always comes to you in pairs. Do you often say, "Then on the other hand . . ."? You need to work on sinking to a deeper level of perception to complement your naturally inquisitive character. By doing so you complement your mental attributes with your personal feelings, and avoid all of the pitfalls connected to being excessively mental.

Understanding Sun in Gemini in Others Geminis are lively, witty, and charming, and are great conversationalists as they are hardly ever at a loss for words. Their constant need for change and stimulation can make them impossible to pin down, so in order to hold their interest, you will have to be spontaneous and open to changes in your plans on a moment's notice. You won't get bored with your Gemini friends, but it is likely that you can get irritated in their lack of follow-through with what they say they are going to do. They forget and get distracted! They also reserve the right to change their minds, as consistency holds very little interest to them. All considered, if you want to engage a Gemini in a serious conversation, you would be advised to arrange a setting that is not filled with distractions that can easily grab the attention of your friend. This spontaneous person is also a delight to spend time with socially. There is very little that you could think of doing that a Gemini friend would not respond to with a "Sure."

Gemini people typically pride themselves on being informed and are often walking resource directories. If they don't have the information you are looking for, they know where you can find it. If you ever want an open-minded conversation to help you explore your options, these are the people to seek out. They need freedom to talk to others throughout the day, so if you are the jealous type, be forewarned, but rest assured that it is typically talk that they are going after. They are the least pretentious of the signs which is another refreshing quality to their personality.

Sun in Cancer

Your Natural Essence Your center is found within your emotional nature. You are meant to feel your way through life, rather than think your way through. Consequently, to experience harmony, you must first become fluid with your emotional nature. As the tides of the ocean, your moods also have an ebb and flow, and as you increase your ability to accept these, you learn to gently float with the tides and currents of your emotional nature. Once your emotions become safe territory to you, your warm, loving expression helps others open up to their feelings as well.

Your personal life and that which emotionally nurtures you are of the utmost importance to you. Within your secure boundaries, you are an expressive and fun person to spend time with. You need to be needed, and your natural caring tendencies allow you to nurture and give much from your vulnerable loving center. Your emotional sensitivity is such that you are easily influenced by the close company you keep. This even extends to the environment, so choose wisely where you live and with whom you spend time.

Home, family, friends, food, and money are typically the building blocks of your life. These security issues give you boundaries and a sense of belonging, both essential for you. Once you have decided who is in your family and who you can trust, you will defend them with great loyalty. Sentimental and nostalgic, you cherish your memories, and reminiscing with friends can be a favorite pastime. When you choose a lifestyle outside of home and family, you still demonstrate this strong emotional attachment to whatever you identify with. It might not be the traditional image of Cancer with 2.3 kids and a white picket fence that suits you, but your personal touch in home and family life is still the greatest resource you have.

Relationship Skills and Needs Cancer's role in the zodiac is to teach others that it is safe to feel. In order to teach this, you must first learn it yourself, so practice the art of surrendering to your emotional cycles rather than resisting them. The secret for fulfillment in relationships for Cancer is the principle of nurturing. You need to be needed, and being with someone who appreciates this, without taking advantage of you would be ideal. This need to nurture others can indeed bring out the best in them, but it can also foster dependence. Once you commit to a partner, you are a loyal and protective mate. Being in a relationship that focuses on the personal life, home, and family is a must, as this brings out the best in you.

For the most part, you avoid all forms of confrontation, but especially when someone has an issue with you. You are deft at the famous crablike sidestepping to avoid serious issues. The greatest paradox that you experience in your relationships with others deals with how you express your emotional sensitivity. The more sensitive you feel, the more volatile and harsh you become, even to the extent of pushing away the people whom you are trying to draw closer to you. Let the soft side of your nature show more; it is what others like most about you. Let down your defenses and experience a real flow of emotion between you and others, as that is where you will discover the love you seek.

Areas to Work On Yours is the astrological sign of the Crab, whose physical description probably fits you—tough on the outside and vulnerable on the inside. Most of your friends define you as sweet and nurturing, and certainly you are capable of this form of expression, but you can get crabby. Learning to surrender to your emotional cycles is the cure-all. Give yourself permission to be one with your emotions, to honor them. When you feel outward, go ahead express and project yourself into the world, but when your cycles pull you inward, give yourself permission to retreat in order to define your boundaries.

Not one to risk your security, you can be defensive in the protection of your established boundaries, resisting change and growth for yourself and others. When you are not open to growth, others can feel your care and concern for them as smothering. Consider the paradox that you continually deal with in this life as contrasting urges of the soul force and the ego. On the one hand, you have the need of the Cancer ego to establish and maintain your pre-existing identity, resisting change. On the other hand, you have the need of the soul, as in all of us, to expand and embrace new experiences. Until you come to resolution in the dealing with this dichotomy, your life can be rather turbulent from the build-up of pressure that comes from resistance. Once you expand your identity to include the needs of both the soul and the ego, the struggle subsides and you become more fluid, allowing for both needs so that your life becomes more rhythmic. Both phases of the cycle are equally important: outward growth followed by inward consolidation in a never-ending cycle of growth and integration. When you learn to satisfy your emotional needs by taking part in the process of nurturing, you are a much freer person. When you identify a personal need, give that to another. When you need a hug, give a hug. The process satisfies the need and you feel great.

Understanding Sun in Cancer in Others Plan to take a long time to get to know these people, because what you see on the surface is only the beginning. They are very cautious about opening to new people and situations so you will feel the shell of the crab if you approach too close, too fast. Cancers are warm, loving, and nurturing to those they trust, and to become close to a Cancer is to become as family. They relate to the most personal side of your character. Though Cancer is as tough as they come on the outside, on the inside they are sensitive and easily hurt. It is pointless to assume that Cancers will not take your communications personally; they will. They can react quite defensively when they feel threatened and become incredibly loving when they feel safe.

These people can help sharpen your emotional communication, as you'll soon learn that they are responding to your feelings instead of whatever words are being spoken. Allow them their moods, as their natural emotional state is tidal and flows outward and inward. If you ask them why they feel the way they do, they will likely come up with reasons, but in truth, their moods do not need reasons; they just simply exist. Cancers are very security conscious and protective of their current lifestyle. Keep this in mind when presenting them with decisions and give them time to sort through their feelings, as this is a necessary step in their decision making process.

Activities centering around the home, family, and the personal side of life are their favorites. Private time together is preferred over large social gatherings. When you want to sort out your personal feelings, they can be the most comforting of friends.

Sun in Leo

YOUR NATURAL ESSENCE Your path is to celebrate life, to go for the gold and to become all that you can become. Like the Sun that rules Leo, you are here to shine brightly in all that you do. Your great strength is your heartfulness, and you will be most successful with projects and people that you can pour your heart into. Your personality itself is one of your main resources. You are a high impact player—people notice and are affected by you.

To be at your best, you have three essential needs: (1) As the Sun, you function best when you are the center of attention. It is important that your relationships, career, and all involvements with life, revolve around you. Don't worry about being selfish. We do not complain when the Sun is out, nor do we complain when Leo is at its best; you give as much as you receive. (2) The second need deals with the heart, both the physical and the emotional. The heart is the source of your strength. Physical, aerobic activity is important for your physical well-being, and heartfelt relationships are essential for your emotional well-being. Your first law of success is to get involved with people and experiences that you can pour your heart into. (3) Just as important as the first two needs is your need for a life with fun, play, and celebration to bring out your full potential. When these three needs are met, your generous nature pulls all that is around you into the light of your being. You are dramatic, expressive, and a natural entertainer.

Relationship Skills and Needs Your generous and loving nature fits very well within relationships as you pamper and readily give to loved ones. To be ignored is just awful, but you won't stand for that, so it is seldom an issue for you. However, your reluctance to share the stage with others can become an issue, and if unchecked, your constant need to outshine everyone else can lead to an undesirable competitiveness in all of your interactions. Your passions run deep and strong and you will not settle for a complacent relationship. Therefore, you appreciate and are desirous of romantic partners that are creative and even flamboyant in their courtship. You can be the most loyal and supportive, or the most unforgiving of the signs when someone crosses you or a loved one. You have to learn to forgive and let go rather than carrying resentments.

You are here to celebrate life and an ideal relationship for you would include plenty of opportunity to enjoy the good life. Take responsibility for finding a relationship that revolves around you. As self-centered as this might seem, be assured that it is when you have the full attention of your partner that you are able to give the most of your generous, loving character. You simply do not do well as an appendage to someone else's life.

Areas to Work On Your willpower is commendable and you take great personal pride in all that you do. These two qualities, when excessive, are also the root of all your challenges and greatest difficulties. Your need to outshine others can lead to competitiveness and even blind ambition, where winning at everything is all important. You have an abundance of love and power, but need to ask yourself: how are they arranged in my life? Is it the power of love or the love of power that most animates your behavior? As you grow to respect that your true power comes from following the path of the heart, your successes are welcomed by others.

The other area that Leo typically needs to work on to improve their interactions with others deals with your defensive attitude when challenged. Pride is a two-edged sword for you. When you pour your heart into someone or something, you deserve to feel proud. But when you react defensively because your pride gets wounded, it stands in the way of your growth. Developing your listening skills and learning to be truly empathetic to others certainly improves all areas of your life.

UNDERSTANDING SUN IN LEO IN OTHERS Treat Leos with honor, respect, and as much admiration as you can throw in. A natural sense of royalty surrounds them, and when treated appropriately, they play their part splendidly. To make the biggest impact on them, come from your heart, for that is the language they best understand. They need to feel special and unique, and cannot bear being overlooked. Leo is ruled by the Sun and they certainly can be the sunshine of your life if you will give them the opportunity. Even though they can seem demanding and even selfish, remember they have just as much to give as they ask for. Allow them full reign and know that when you push or make demands on them, it will only provoke resistance and stifle the same illumination that you so much enjoy in Leo.

Leos love to celebrate and enjoy life, so don't hold back. Never take any of your time together for granted and you will stay in their good favor. Like the lion, they are lazy and easygoing until pushed. Then the beast will come out. Leos make powerful allies, but equally powerful foes, so it is definitely to your advantage to stay on their best side. To move beyond difficulties with these people, always appeal to the heart as this brings out the best in them and the Sun will return.

Sun in Virgo

YOUR NATURAL ESSENCE You are naturally refined and well-thought-out in your personality expression. Known for your attentiveness to detail, you are very discriminating by nature and typically hold very high standards of expectation for yourself. As an earth sign, you are here to demonstrate your philosophy of life by integrating it into all that you do. You are more of a doer than a talker. Your considerate nature and your attentiveness makes you a very here-and-now kind of person and you have a natural ability to pull other people back to the moment. The symbol of the Deer is appropriate for Virgo: sleek, trim, agile, and peaceful in its natural habitat. When something new is introduced to your environment, or you are out of your natural habitat, then you have the "deer-in-the-headlight" syndrome—Virgos are wound tight. Health, hygiene, and cleanliness are high priorities for you. Also, a Zen-like quality is demonstrated in you by focusing on the essence of life; by doing away with all that is nonessential. By keeping your life simple, you project a genuineness that others admire.

As the perfectionist, you are thorough and do not like to make mistakes. Since you like a well-maintained, orderly life, chaos is intolerable to you, and it seems to be your role to bring order to life. You have a knack for focusing on what is relevant in the moment, and it is this innate practicality which allows you to be a natural problem-solver. By taking the time to plan how to create the best quality with the least waste of resources, you try to find the most effective and efficient path available for any task. A job worth doing, is worth doing right, is a Virgo creed. Consequently, your life improves through the years by this constant attention to details. At times, you can be too hard on yourself, but you are most comfortable when you are working on something. Learn to balance that by creating time to appreciate the work done, and your life will become much more enjoyable. Your keen eye for simplicity and the integrity by which you live your life is most refreshing to others.

Relationship Skills and Needs In relationships, as in all of life, you are a discriminating person. You know what you like, and you know what you do not like, and it becomes very important that you focus on what works for you. In relationships you like to be useful. You do not seem to need to be the center of attention, but it is essential that your efforts are appreciated. You will certainly do your part to pitch in and usually, you work yourself into an indispensable position. Feeling best when you are needed, you enjoy giving to others and find it easier to promote the underdog than those who already have it good in life. You are delightfully sensual and responsive when you allow yourself to be so; however, you typically demonstrate your feelings for others by doing things for them. This utilitarian part of your character needs to be involved in a relationship that appreciates your abundant ability to assist others.

Areas to Work On In your striving for perfection, your naturally analytical character can become excessive; leading to worry at a mild level, and when extreme, a critical, fault-finding nature could develop. Paralysis via analysis results when you have not learned to restrain this natural gift to situations where it is useful. Learn to be kind to yourself, to do something good for yourself everyday to help balance out a naturally self-critical character. It would also be wise to organize your time spent with the critic in you, perhaps at the end of the work day. Assess your day, evaluate it, be tough on yourself, analyze it right down to the detail, and then move on. Learn to discipline this time to a quality ten minutes and you will be freed from its constant droning on in the background all day long.

You also need to learn to build completion into your daily schedule, or you will always see more that needs to be done. Set realistic goals for what can be achieved in a healthy workday, and when you reach the goal, stop, celebrate the accomplishment. Feel the completion. This would help compensate for that endless sense of "There's just a few more things that I need to do."

You certainly have no more faults than others, but you are likely more aware of yours, leading to feelings of insecurity. You can fall prey to the feeling that you have a little more work to do on yourself before you will allow yourself to fully enjoy life. You can't wait to enjoy life until this feeling leaves, because it doesn't; it is part of the Virgo experience. Learn to tame and accept this voice of uncertainty, instead of assuming that it will one day go away, and you will become a much more peaceful person.

Understanding Sun in Virgo in Others Virgos appreciate life's simple pleasures and are not ostentatious whatsoever. If you want to impress these folks, do so with sincerity and genuineness as extravagance in any form holds little value to them. Known for their perfectionist tendencies, Virgos are detail-oriented people who enjoy going through all of the specific parts that make up the whole. Don't rush them through this process or you will just frustrate them. In their task-orientation to life, you will find them always wanting to help you improve existing situations. Remember, this does not mean they are looking for things to criticize; they are just sharing their gift of seeing the small details that may have been overlooked. Likewise, they may seem to be overly cautious about approaching new situations, but it would be more appropriate to say that they are being thorough in their investigation, considering all of the details in any given situation.

These people will teach you patience. You, on the other hand, can help them by creating a safe place for them to express their feelings, as they are naturally more of the doers than the speakers in life. Take the time to listen as their thoughtfulness is often expressed in a painstakingly deliberate manner. Virgos don't mind you expressing your problems to them, so don't fear that you are burdening them. Instead let them know you need them and they have made a difference by being in your life. They can feel left out and unappreciated if you only share the good with them. Shy and reserved, they are more comfortable with a small circle of friends rather than big social doings.

In business dealings with Virgos, be thorough and have your facts together, and they will certainly appreciate your preparation. They will rarely jump into new situations without first analyzing all of the potential ramifications, but once they agree to a task, expect them to do their best. They are naturally refined by character, so you might want to tuck in your loose ends around Virgos and certainly save crude behavior for other situations. Any activities that involve nature will certainly bring out the best in your Virgo friends. Also, activities that are task oriented, working on mutual projects together, and all health-related activities are favorite relationship activities for these people.

Sun in Libra

Your Natural Essence Libra is the sign of agreements, partnerships, and relationships, and you will certainly learn about yourself through your involvement with others. At the highest level, you reflect the beauty, charm, and grace of all that you experience, and it is this appreciation of the aesthetics of life that allows you to demonstrate a keen sense of style and design in all that you do. Yours is the sign of the scales, and you have a special sensitivity for balance, fairness, and equality. You try to be rational in your behavior, are excellent at understanding the thoughts and values of others, and can always stretch another's present perspective with a new angle on any given situation. Because Libras possess an exciting use of language, and seem to never tire of hypothetical problem solving situations, there are many times when you would rather talk about a situation instead of actually experiencing it. You are intrigued by the infinite variety of choices in life, and your inclinations towards cooperation certainly make you a skilled team-builder.

You have a keen appreciation for beauty in all of your surroundings and social interactions. Finding the perfect harmony in your social situations, which is important for you, leads to the development of a naturally diplomatic character. Remember, to harmonize you must first be in tune yourself. When you take the time to tune yourself to your standards, you function as a tuning fork for others, helping them lead a more balanced life. When you fail to take responsibility for the state of balance that you crave, you become like the teeter-totter, constantly trying to balance the issues in your life.

Relationship Skills and Needs Your natural intuitiveness and responsiveness to the needs, values, and opinions of others bids very well for your potential in relationships. Just as you are not to take advantage of others, you are also not to allow others to take advantage of you. You have a keen eye for design and harmony and often hold an ideal of a perfectly harmonious relationship, which can lead to a "peace at any cost" syndrome. Win-win situations are a must for you, but be cognizant that the cost can be too high if peace requires you to sacrifice your own ideals. At worst, you can throw away your own self-identity by overresponding to the expectations of others. Because almost everything in your life is up for negotiation, you can appear to others as wishy-washy and lukewarm concerning your commitments. When trying to convince someone of your intention, be sure that you first have convinced yourself.

Your natural refinement and appreciation for style can bring out the best in others. Being with a partner who also enjoys a bit of elegance in life would be ideal. Social activities and cultural events can be favorite shared experiences.

Areas to Work On You are often caught spending too much time trying to make the perfect choice, when your time could be better spent just making some choice and then getting on with it! Your dilemma is that information often comes to you in polarities so that you see both sides of any issue. The endless weighing of alternatives is only overcome by coming to your center, seeing both polarities, and recognizing that the point of balance for which you seek is within you. When you seek for it externally, your reality can become a house of mirrors, and the real you is difficult to identify. You like to be liked, but learn to trust that people will naturally like you, even without you trying to please them.

Your focus on appearances can lead to disappointments when others do not live up to your ideal of them. Learn to relate to the genuine person behind the appearances and presentations to deepen your connections with others.

UNDERSTANDING SUN IN LIBRA IN OTHERS These people are refined and primarily intellectual. Talk about books, movies, art, social events, and even other people, and you will keep their attention. Ask their opinion, truly listen to what is said, and notice how they have designed their life and how they participate in their relationships. Just talk about their relationships, and you will have them opening up to you because Libras often spend a great deal of time thinking about the important people in their lives. They make wonderfully attentive partners as they genuinely are concerned about you, but can often feel lost behind the personality of the people who make up their lives. Take time to see them as individuals in their own right and they will feel special.

Cooperation is a keynote for them. Don't expect them to make a decisive stand without considering others; they can't. They like to share their decision-making process and will want your input. Libras most enjoy spending pleasant time together, but have a strong distaste for emotionally confronting issues. When working out differences, they respond best to a calm, rational approach, and you can always trust in their sense of fair play.

Sun in Scorpio

YOUR NATURAL ESSENCE You are intense, magnetic, and powerful enough to get the things that you want when you put your mind to it. "Still waters run deep" best describes your temperament for there is always more going on beneath the surface than meets the eye. Your emotional nature is very strong and often you are more expressive in silence than with words. Even in its natural state, Scorpio is an extremely complex psychological sign. This complexity is reflected in the five different totems associated with your sign. All the other signs have one, but Scorpio has five. At the lowest level, the Scorpion represents the ability to defend yourself with a stinging sarcastic wit that intuitively knows the weaknesses of others, and can even take advantage of them. The Serpent represents the well-known Scorpio sexual magnetism and fascination with the dance of the sexes. The Eagle represents your piercing vision; you don't miss much, if anything. The Dove is yet another symbol for your sign which represents the descent of spirit to Scorpio, once it has learned how to surrender and present its vulnerability to others. To do this, you must be able to enter into the forgiveness of self and others from the prisons of past hurts and pains. Only then will you be allowed the trusting of others, probably the most difficult task of all for Scorpios. The fifth symbol is the Phoenix. From out of its own ashes, the Phoenix is said to have risen again, in a higher more glorious form. This is symbolic of your regeneration capacity. Never count a Scorpio completely out; you always have the capacity to come back.

In view of these complexities, you can see why you are encouraged to spend some necessary private time to get in touch with your center, and feel comfortable in your life. You have a knack for reading the motivations and intentions of others, which could lead to a shrewd businessperson, a counselor, healer, analyst, or very intense romantic partner. Not fooled by presentation, you do not suffer fools. Your natural inquisitive and slightly suspicious character allows you to see beneath the surface of whatever is going on around you. Seeing the best and worst of others could lead to a cynical or a compassionate character, all depending on your skill at forgiveness. Being controlled by others is a fear that can stop you from the final surrender required for the deep levels of intimacy that you crave.

Relationship Skills and Needs There are so many layers to your personality and decision-making process that you may project this complexity onto others, making it difficult for you to accept them as being exactly who they say they are. As you learn to trust yourself more, it becomes easier to trust others. The paradox of your sign is that you crave intimacy, but you fear exposure, so you often give mixed messages to others. If you are willing to look at the hidden aspects of your psyche as revealed through the challenges and difficulties that arise with others, your relationships will be a continual source of growth in consciousness for you. You like a little intrigue and mystery in your life, and this is reflected in the types of relationships that you attract.

Avoid relationships that trigger jealousy in you, as this brings out the worst. Holding on to old grudges and pains can be your downfall. Remember, the jailer and the prisoner are in the same building. By holding others to past mistakes you are also holding yourself to your past. You tend to be excessive in your attitudes about sex: either too much or too little can be the issue. Your sexual relationships can improve considerably once you allow this part of your expression to become natural and easy. The psychological aspects of sex are as important as the physical aspects for you, and you are at your best with a partner that appreciates the intimate and passionate person that you are.

The beauty of Scorpio is in your ability to lose yourself so deeply in union with another that both individuals are transformed and what is experienced is far greater than what either of you could have been individually.

Areas to Work On Your Achilles' heel is your emotional entanglement from the past. Forgiving, letting go of the past, and trust are the central issues here. In your true desire to get to the bottom of issues, you hold on to old issues past the point that is advisable or even healthy for your emotional well-being. Your memory is long standing, and it is only the power of forgiveness that can release you from the past. You need to develop the strength of character to see what you needed to learn from all of your past pains, identify your role in the process, and determine why it was appropriate. The learning is always there—outer reality always reflects inner reality—however, in your attachment to the pain, the learning can be overlooked.

Issues of control over sex, money, and power are likely to present themselves in relationships. All require trust. Outer trust reflects inner trust. Scorpios have more capacity for growth in consciousness than any other sign but it takes strength to look at the darker parts of your personal character, and it is not always flattering! But with character strength, you begin to see that this outer mistrust reflects a mistrust of yourself. If you are always willing to evaluate your own motivations when you question the motivations of others, you will see where you need to work on your character development. When you learn to live up to your moral standards and let others live up to theirs, you become much freer. Having seen the best and worst of human behavior, you possess a guarded and suspicious approach to life. You seem to have a need to work through some of the darker aspects of the human experience, which would scare most people away. A fascination with intrigue can keep you from enjoying life's simple pleasures. Scorpio is the best sign at protecting its vulnerability—they say you can never hurt a Scorpio twice—but the armor that you build to protect yourself also prevents you from experiencing the deeper levels of intimacy that you crave.

Understanding Sun in Scorpio in Others "Still waters run deep" is a good description of these people. Know that there is always more going on beneath the surface than what appears, and allow them to open up when and how they choose. As they feel comfortable, they will share deeper parts of themselves, but this will take time. These people have a wonderful sense of humor, very dry and black, and they can see life in refreshingly honest terms that can be very funny. Just don't rush your Scorpio friends and don't ask too many personal questions as they are cautious with new people. Once they are secure, they will get down to the real nitty-gritty and they will help you be honest with yourself as they notice every nuance of emotional variation.

There is no sense in lying to Scorpios; they read what is going on beneath the surface better than anybody else. Although they are excellent at knowing the secrets of others, they always remain somewhat mysterious themselves, which is not to say they have anything to hide, but simply that their comfort zone requires that they keep a few parts of their life private. Always remember that Scorpios are responding to the emotional message you are sending, instead of the words.

Sun in Sagittarius

YOUR NATURAL ESSENCE You are the true optimist and it is this positive attitude that allows you to attain goals that others only wish for. Equally physical and mental, at the core of your being is a fire that propels you into an ever-expanding reality. Whether it be physical as in travel, or mental as in philosophy, you are here to expand your boundaries as an adventurer in life. Your happy-go-lucky temperament permits a jovial, enthusiastic approach to life, which at best, leads to an inspiring personality that motivates others. At its worst, however, this can promote an impatient and intolerant attitude towards others. You like to be direct and to the point.

As you develop your higher mind by studies in philosophy, religions, foreign travel, etc., the teacher in you comes out, and you seem to enjoy encouraging people past their biases, prejudices, and narrow points of view. This higher mind perspective allows you to always see the point of synthesis whenever you are presented with conflicts. Seeing the positive in all situations is what attracts others to you—your enthusiasm for life is infectious, and can be very persuasive. Not a dabbler, you either jump in with both feet, or you don't bother. Once you select an activity, you like lots of excitement and get bored as soon as the action dies. Consequently, you are at your best when you aspire to a goal, a dream, a vision.

The archer needs something to aim at. Your far-reaching intellect needs freedom to consider the realm of possibilities, but the tendency to say yes without considering the implications can lead to a scattering of the life force. You simply have too many arrows in flight simultaneously. When you are in touch with your center, the excitement of living naturally emanates from you.

Relationship Skills and Needs Your happy-go-lucky attitude can be very inspiring to others and this is bound to win you many friends. Typically good-natured, you most enjoy spending time with others who look for the positive in life. Your bluntness is legendary and you don't deal well with extremely sensitive types. You like to say it like you see it. To nobody's surprise, you expect—even demand—honesty in your relationships, and do best with those who don't try to curtail your need for freedom and experience. You get excited about life! It's best to be with someone who also enjoys and appreciates an expansive lifestyle. You do tend towards "pal" types of relationships, and your need for exploring new frontiers makes you a wonderful travel companion, fellow student, or friend.

Communication is very important to you, so you do not deal well with strong silent types. Your far-reaching intellect enjoys relating with others on a wide range of abstract, philosophical issues. You need to respect the morals and ethics of those with whom you become close, as you are known for being a truth seeker.

Areas to Work On Extremist tendencies are the main source of difficulties for you, which can lead to various problems. You might be an indulgent character: "If one is good, ten must be better!" Or, you could have dogmatic beliefs that can appear quite judgmental: "holier than thou." An impatience with life can catch you racing for the future, passing up the here and now. Since all these behaviors have their roots in excessiveness, the number one trait to develop to balance your natural tendencies is the virtue of temperance.

In your anticipation for the future, you can look right past your present involvement in the here and now reality. This impatience can be felt as pushy by others. You will also have to find healthy outlets such as sports and outdoor activities to express your natural competitive character. Otherwise, your competitive spirit will manifest as an argumentative and defensive character leading to a need to win at everything. You need a goal, that is clear, but you get lost in the world of potentialities. You will become more successful in life when you learn to shoot one arrow, follow it, pick it up, and shoot it again until it has reached its mark. Your tendency is to shoot as many arrows as possible, to keep your options open.

In relationships, your positive nature is most often uplifting, but your inability to deal with negativity can make you lopsided. Cultivate your ability to listen intently to others. Without compassion for the challenges that others face, your enthusiasm can easily turn to an idealistic judgment of others, such that they begin to feel "should" upon.

Understanding Sun in Sagittarius in Others The Sagittarian's cheery disposition is truly uplifting as they can find the positive in most anything. These enthusiastic souls will certainly brighten up your life, but they will also test your ability to keep up with them. As they always seem to be on the go, give these people lots of room to roam. They are ruled by the Centaur, half-rider and half-horse, and you will get far with them if you keep that basic imagery in mind. Encourage them to spend time out of doors, and you will see the best that they have to offer. Act inspired when they share their ideas with enthusiasm, and you will win their heart. Take them on a trip that proves to be a real adventure, and you have seriously won them over. Offer them the ordinary and the stable, and you will lose their attention.

Their far-reaching mind loves philosophical, political, and spiritual discussions. Once engaged in conversation, however, don't ask questions of them unless you are prepared for their blunt response. These people are certainly not known for their tactfulness. Sagittarians, quite unintentionally, tend to promise more than they can deliver. They really do believe that there will be enough time to fulfill all of the promises they make, and they are always amazed when things take more time than they thought should be the case. These people typically need someone in their life to help restrain their enthusiasm and develop the capacity for sustained activity. Remember, Sagittarians need to dream; sometimes they are just looking for the sport of dreaming.

Sun in Capricorn

Your Natural Essence Yours is the sign of the Mountain Goat, surefooted and ambitious. You were born to climb, have high standards, and are at your best when you are aspiring towards an accomplishment. You demonstrate a competence in all that you do, and others can feel secure under the umbrella of your protection. It is your knack for order which gives you the ability to organize your world—you have a innate sensitivity to systems and how each of the parts must work together to best operate. These skills are rewarded in business and career—very natural places for your self-expression. But it is important to remember that Capricorn is not just a business sign. You are a Capricorn in all areas of life. When you include the personal in the structure of your life, you can have it all! Even with family life, you will have a natural sense of the roles of each of the members so that the family unit, as a system, functions at its highest potential.

It is said that Capricorn starts life old and grows young, and typically, the second half of life is much more enjoyable than the first. It takes you that long to get everything in your life organized just the way you like it. Your patience and endurance are legendary however, and you have a knack for getting involved with projects that pay off through time. Even though you may appear to be the ultraconservative, you are certainly not against taking calculated risks, if the odds are in your favor. The paradox of your sign is that how you feel about yourself and how others see you are often very different. You always appear strong, in control, on top of things, but just like the rest of us, you also have your insecurities and fears. They just don't show. Professionally, this is to your advantage. Personally, it does not work so well.

Success and approval are significant issues and they will continue to consume your attention until you realize that you are the person who can either give or take these away from yourself. You are extremely resourceful, and your serious nature allows you to learn from all of your experiences. You are paying attention. Early in life, you are likely frustrated by the incompetence of others, but through the years you begin to develop compassion. You understand that it is your role to help others organize their lives and become more effective. Consequently, you serve quite naturally in roles as the leader, teacher, manager, coach, etc., as others tend to defer to your authority.

Relationship Skills and Needs In relationships sincerity, loyalty, and commitment are key themes. You take your responsibilities seriously, and you expect others to be as accountable for their actions as you are with yours. Mutual respect is an important prerequisite in all of your interactions with others. If you feel another is looking down at you, or if you don't respect the other, the relationship will not proceed as you'll have nothing to do with others without respect. You admire competence and are not known for indulging the emotional issues of others. Your serious, hardworking temperament does best with those that appreciate a quality of excellence in all areas of life, including relationships, and you need to be with someone who is willing to aspire to these heights with you.

Capricorn might seem to focus entirely on business, but you definitely have a romantic side to your character as well. In romance, as in all of life, you have very high standards, but you also have the good sense to know when you have achieved your standards and how to celebrate the success. To be involved in a love relationship with someone who respects your roles in the world, but sees right through them at home, is ideal. You love it when someone relates to the soft side of your character and, indeed, a very tender side of your character does come out when appreciated by another.

Areas to Work On You too often get caught up in the task at hand and forget about your heartfelt relationships. Be mindful, there are times when your priorities for personal and professional values will be tested. Is success so important to you that you are willing to sacrifice close emotional bonds with others? You are someone who periodically needs to redefine your value system—where did it come from, and why are you supporting it? You are so responsible, but to what? To pick up the expectations of others and accept them as your own without question fulfills your desire to climb mountains, but the success will have little personal significance until you learn to climb your own mountains. You intend to be successful; why not select aspirations that reflect your true values and enjoyment of life?

In youth, you tend to give away your personal power by excessively seeking the approval of others. When you grow to realize that your power lies in the strength of your character, and the recognition you seek must first come from yourself, then your strength and wisdom will attract others. Also, growth in self-respect will enable you to soften and become a more likable and friendly person. Once you have attained the standard of living for which you have been striving, and your life is organized to your very high standards, then you are more able to enjoy your close emotional bonds with others.

Understanding Sun in Capricorn in Others Sun in Capricorn people are hardworking, down-to-earth, and exceedingly pragmatic. Their serious nature often leads to an all-work, no-play attitude, and you might have to remind them not to take life so seriously. Organization and responsibility are their great strengths so if you are in a working relationship with them, you'll truly appreciate these qualities. But if you are in a love relationship with Capricorn, you'll likely feel that romance is put on the back burner. They do love it, however, when you break through the structure with wine and candles to court their romantic side. The Capricorn standards of excellence, when expressed through romance, brings out an aristocratic quality to a love relationship. These people are definitely a class act.

If you are looking for practical information on how to better organize your life to take advantage of your skills and resources, these are the ones to seek out. Capricorns are so dependable that you will never have to worry about them following through on commitments and responsibilities. Count on them, but at the same time, keep in mind that they are much more sensitive than they may appear.

Sun in Aquarius

YOUR NATURAL ESSENCE To be in your center, you need to feel free to explore your uniqueness and individuality. In relationship to the other signs, Aquarius represents the voice of the future. This keeps you slightly ahead of your time. You are not bound by the rigid conditioning of your culture. Born to be a free spirit, you need to experiment with life, to soar above the ordinary and be free to actualize your abundant mental abilities. Your character traits preclude predictability and your progressive, idealistic temperament keeps you always open to change and growth. Your love of friendships and social activities needs to be balanced with alone time, lest you get lost in the world of others. Being a highly independent character, you have a preference to go your own way in life rather than follow the crowds. Consequently, it is not always easy to be an Aquarian because you cannot rely on social approval to substantiate your identity. Therefore, you have to be much more self-affirmed than most in order to actualize your uniqueness.

Your keen intellect functions equally as well in rational, scientific realms as it does in abstract, theoretical realms. This enables you to rise above personal concerns and see things from a detached, universal perspective. Because you feel most centered when your far-reaching intellect has unlimited opportunities, you need to take responsibility for creating a lifestyle that allows for your abundant interests. Don't expect your culture to provide a tailor-made life for you. More likely, you will have to invent it . . . give yourself permission to do just that.

Typically altruistic, your high degree of social consciousness leads you into the role of being the rebel or the reformer. Rarely interested in the conventional, you are most often found on the leading edge of whatever interests you, and you feel most secure when you have a cause or a purpose beyond yourself to advocate. You are not here to conform to the current social systems; you are here to help them change and evolve to meet the ever-changing needs of the future.

Aquarius is one of the most paradoxical signs of all. On the one hand, it is said to be the sign of groups, yet Aquarians are usually too independent to be joiners. It is also said to be the sign of friendships, yet it is also the most impersonal of all the signs. These paradoxes are what make you such a puzzle to others; you just do not seem to fit into anyone's mold or expectations.

Relationship Skills and Needs Your friendly, open nature functions very well in relationships of all kinds. Your way of expressing yourself is not as the goopy romanticist, but instead, through caring friendship. Freedom is an important component to your self-identity. You encourage and celebrate the uniqueness of your friends, and are most impressed with those who have created a lifestyle that reflects their individuality. Your friends love this about you and feel free to express their truest self in your presence. There is often something unusual about your relationships as your need to experiment with life does not stop with yourself.

Easy-going friendships are often easier for you than commitment-based relationships. It is not that you can't stay in long-term relationships. It's just that committed involvements cannot be felt as limiting, or they will not last long. Since you have to see your relationships as an opportunity for the expression of your individuality, instead of a denial of it, you are at your best with a partner that is also willing to grow and evolve within the relationship.

Not one for sentimentality, you rarely indulge emotional sensitivities, and your ability to detach from personal feelings can be very liberating for others. You help them laugh at their situation instead of taking things so personally. You prefer to objectify emotional situations and deal with them through distance and rational thinking. To gain this perspective, you detach from the moment, essentially rise above your personal feelings, and see things from a higher, universal vantage point. This detachment can be felt as aloofness by others. You feel most at ease with those that understand and accept this as part of your character. You strongly resist attempts to change you. The mind is too precious a resource to waste and you will often be found helping others to actualize their abilities.

Areas to Work On Your uniqueness, your greatest gift, is also the source of most of your problems. Remember, one of the side effects of being unique is that your point of view is original—don't expect others to always agree with you. Until you accept yourself as being independent and free, you tend to attract people and situations that challenge this need. You then rise to the occasion and resist the controlling force. Ultimately, though, you ask yourself, "To whom am I trying to prove my independence?" Once you have accepted yourself, you realize that you do not have to be justified in the eyes of anyone else, and you begin to attract a different set of friends and situations—ones that encourage and accept your uniqueness.

Your detached manner can make you appear insensitive to others. Even though talking about personal feelings and concerns will likely seem petty to you, it does help others to feel more comfortable with you, so oblige them periodically. The other area that you can work on to improve your involvements with others deals with how quickly you process information—considerably faster than others. Slow down. Your "know-it-all" tendency has a difficult time letting others complete their thoughts. Truthfully, you often do know more than others, but this can alienate others by one-sided communications. Others will feel more comfortable with you the more that you develop your listening skills, although this will require restraint on your part.

Like a messenger of the future, you function as an alarm clock, helping others to awaken from a culturally conditioned view of reality. Your perceptions can even be shocking to others, creating a "delayed gratification syndrome" in your communications. Since your perspective is often unique, it is often, at the moment, unsettling to others. You stir up thought. Still, you will find that when people have time to digest the information, they begin to appreciate the perspective you offer.

Understanding Sun in Aquarius in Others What you will first notice about relationships with Aquarians is that they are very mentally stimulating.

There seems to be an electrical quality to these people that sparkles with excitement when they are enjoying themselves. Bright, clever, and alert, they will keep you on your intellectual toes. Friendship is their forte so if you are lucky enough to be in this select circle, you will see the best that this sign has to offer. There always seems to be something unique about these individuals. It is best to reserve your expectations of them, as they typically do not fit into any mold other than their own. These are free-spirited souls who resist restraint but will encourage as much freedom and independence in you as they demand for themselves. If they feel constrained, they will often do something other than what is expected of them just to demonstrate their right to act as they choose. Very progressive thinkers, these people enjoy a lively exchange of ideas and will most value your true thoughts on any topic, instead of what you think you should say.

There are two sides to Aquarians: the rebel and the reformer. The rebel takes delight in shaking things up just for the sake of it. The reformer takes a responsible role for initiating changes in the world to keep up with the ever-changing needs of the future. Both types resist traditions that restrain the rights of the individual. Aquarians are altruistic and idealistic, and when you appeal to this side of their character, you are sure to meet a willing partner. They make wonderful conversationalists, yet they often feel unsure of themselves. As confident as they appear socially, they are just as insecure about the private, personal side of their lives. Don't let their aloofness fool you as they are much more sensitive than appearances may lead you to believe. They are often awkward in demonstrating their personal feelings so don't expect them to gush out their emotions for they are not likely to indulge your sensitivities. Instead, they prefer to help you rise above what they see as the muck and the mire of personal emotions into the clear light of rational objectivity.

Very mental in their approach to life, they need to intellectually explore possibilities that they have no intention of acting upon, and they often talk a much more radical and experimental life than they actually live. Still, Aquarius is a sign of evolutionary growth, and they do need freedom to experiment with themselves and with life. Periodically, they need time and space by themselves as this is a source of their strength. Don't make too much of it if you feel them pulling away from the relationship. They will wind their way back to you when they are ready. A fuller life, lived closer to the edge, is possible with your Aquarian friends.

Sun in Pisces

Your Natural Essence Yours is the most complex path of all. Being the final sign, Pisces is essentially an accumulation of all the previous signs all rolled up into one! Because you see a little bit of yourself reflected through everyone, one of your greatest traits is your compassionate and understanding character. You feel inside yourself what others are going through. This relates to your first task: learn to distinguish between your feelings and others by spending quality time alone each and everyday to connect with the deepest, private part of your character. Your core is a moving, fluid, sensitive reality, meant to feel your way through life. Consequently, others will rarely totally understand you. Consider the symbol of the two Fish to better understand the range of your emotional experiences. One of you is on the surface, interacting with others just as everyone else, while the other part of you is swimming in deeper waters, only known to you and God. Self-acceptance for you includes accepting a reality that embraces the entire range of human emotional experiences. Thus, you are here to teach the power of faith, which transcends the limited reality of the ego. It is when you have cultivated a faith in a larger reality that encompasses your life, that your power grows.

Relationship Skills and Needs In relationships, the romantic in you comes to full expression to the point of literally getting lost in relationships, for better or for worse. Your sensitivity to others is your greatest gift, but the source of most of your problems as well. You are truly able to adapt to another person's lifestyle, and it is natural for you to do so in your relationships. You are absolutely responsive to the emotions of your partner. This empathy is certainly a wonderful quality, but it also leads to you being very vulnerable, allowing others to take advantage of you. There is very little that your forgiving character cannot accept in others, so naturally, this gets tested. Your emotional reality can embrace and accept the experiences of others, seemingly as if you are here to offer understanding, and to help others find a deeper meaning in their lives.

There are times, however, that you hunger to be understood and want someone to extend a compassionate hand to you as well. Somewhat disappointing, but true, you find you are more understanding of others than they are with you. Understand that it comes with the territory, and disappointment for you is essentially a frustrated God search. It is a calling from the inner fish whose needs cannot be met by others—only by you and your relationship to the divine. This is why you need time alone: to cultivate your relationship with the inner you. It is essential. Your feelings run so deep that words cannot always convey your experiences, and, therefore, it is best to be with someone who does not press you to put into words that which cannot be spoken.

Areas to Work On Self-pity in all of its many guises is responsible for most of your difficulties. This is not an open embrace, but a self-sacrificing feeling of resignation, of having to accept the burdens of the world. Worry, moodiness, and loss of self-identity are all characteristic of a need to get back in touch with the inner you. Your Achilles' heel is guilt—you can't bear the thought of hurting another, and since this is your bottom line, you inadvertently teach others how to take advantage of you! When you give in to being manipulated by the lower part of another's character, you are encouraging this behavior. This is indeed exactly opposite of what you want, but the tendency can surface to make excuses for the ones you love, rather than truly helping them become the best they can be. You will stay in difficult situations far too long. Deal with the unpleasant situation directly, without hesitation, and realize that compassion for the human experience has to start with you. Ask for more from your life—you are worth it.

Understanding Sun in Pisces in Others A Pisces friend can be a true blessing, for this sign is devoted and intensely personal. Since this is the most private sign of the zodiac, you will have to dig long and deep to encourage your friend to open up to his or her true feelings. Your efforts will be returned with great sincerity and devotional friendship, but it will take time and a persistence to peel away the layers of protection. This is a complex, emotional, hidden sign. Your Pisces friends will always try to make you feel comfortable to the degree that it appears they are not taking care of themselves. Relating takes so much out of them that they need periods of alone time to recover from all of the intensity they experience when they are close to someone.

It is wise to keep in mind the symbol of the two fish when relating to Pisces. One is right there with you, interacting, nodding in agreement, responding. The other is in a completely different realm. Remember your Pisces friend can be in both realms simultaneously, and it is wise to call attention back to the moment when you have something important to say. These people hear with their ears, and their heart. What you say stirs up such inner personal feelings that their attention is often split between trying to listen to you and being aware of their own churning feelings. These images, stirred up from memories, often pull the Pisces out of the moment to re-experience a past emotion. Consequently, their responses can seem inconsistent or even illogical to the situation of the moment.

THE MOON

Emotional Fulfillment

OF ALL THE celestial bodies, the Moon goes through its cycles the fastest. From New Moon to Full Moon and back again in just twenty-eight days, it represents that which is most cyclic and changeable in us as well—our emotional character. Where the Sun represents the conscious self-identity, the Moon represents the ever-changing cycles of emotional responses to the Sun's light, thereby necessitating the first great balancing act in the development of consciousness. Since Sun and Moon rule different phases of the daily cycle, they represent essentially different realities. The Sun rules the day, where all is visible and the conscious mind is in charge, while the Moon rules the night of the subconscious where emotions dominate.

Having emotions is part of being human. How we each respond, adapt, and interact with this part of our character is a matter of personal choice, but the fact that everyone feels is as unmistakable as the fact that everyone breathes. Emotions cover a wide variety of experiences. They give capacity for love, happiness, joy, compassion, and all that has meaning in life. They also represent anger, disappointment, sentimentality, and despair. With emotions, there is the capacity to feel, and the range is from joy to sorrow and everything in between. It is when emotions are not allowed expression, in spite of their overwhelming presence, that they become problematic. This chapter will explore the source of negative and positive emotions and provide exercises for establishing healthy outlets. It is an art. It takes training and practice, but the rewards are certainly worth the effort.

It could be said, with little argument, that emotions are the least-understood aspect of the human experience. Our school systems focus primarily on intellectual training, which is understandable, as mental pursuits tend to be rational and logical to the degree that they can be measured. You can study algebra, and your teacher can design a test and easily measure your degree of competence. Emotions, on the other hand, are subjective in nature and, therefore, cannot be measured. Perhaps this is why emotional fulfillment is not part of our educational curriculum. How could you be tested and graded on your competence? How can something be measured that has no shape of its own?

Our culture is just emerging from a time when emotions have been considered second-class citizens compared to rational thought. Men, particularly, have been trained to overcome their feelings and emotions. Overcome usually means repress. Women are taught that too much emotional expression makes people, and especially men, define you as weak and needy. So, who is left with skills for dealing successfully with emotional expression? And then ask: who has been prepared for meeting the emotional challenges of creating relationships?

The image of a strong person in our culture is often associated with one who has learned to control his emotions. Indeed, this is one type of strength, but it is hardly sufficient in achieving emotional fulfillment. Emotional strength deals with adaptability and responsiveness, which allows a person to flow and gently ride upon the tides of emotions. Emotions are cyclic in nature. In order to be successful in dealing with them, you must be able to move with the tides. Trying to stop the movement of your emotions is like trying to stop the tides of the Pacific Ocean, or wishing that the Moon was always full. Both are equally futile endeavors, and will only prove to be a source of frustration.

Emotional Cycles

Just as our view of the shape of the Moon and the tides of the ocean are in a constant state of change, so, too, are your natural emotions. Our culture overemphasizes constancy as a virtue where business goes on as usual, regardless of personal feelings. Even the labels we use to describe our moods, "up" and "down," implies that half of our feelings are considered bad. This fear and resistance of negative emotions leads to control and repression, rather than to the more desirable, always-sunny disposition. When one learns to surrender to the ebb and flow of one's emotional character, a graceful natural rhythm emerges.

Experiment with identifying your emotional cycles as outward and inward, instead of up and down. In the inward phase, you learn to retreat from the outer world to reflect and contemplate the meanings of the outward experiences. Create proactive experiences for yourself for the inward-turning time and you will benefit, rather than just get through the low tides. When your inward cycle is resisted, emotional issues can erupt, becoming problematic and difficult, and finally pushing to the surface where they are usually blown way out of perspective and out-of-balance.

When you adapt to your natural rhythm, emotional experiences become integrated into your daily life which enables you to become more responsive to all of life's situations. You feel sad when sad is appropriate and joyful when situations tickle your heart. You become more graceful in all of your emotional responses so that instead of becoming an annoying distraction, they become a source of enrichment, woven throughout the fabric of your daily life. Canceling appointments and retreating within yourself every time you feel a mood shift is not suggested. Instead, you are encouraged to fulfill your responsibilities, while being aware of your mood shifts throughout the day. Think of the outward and inward phases of the cycle as relative, instead of absolute. Much of the stress of life can be avoided by listening and responding to your emotions rather than trying to overcome them. The following exercises are designed to help you identify these cycles.

Exercise

Chart the ebb and flow of your emotional cycles on a calendar or daily journal.

1. Use of scale of -3 to +3 to evaluate your emotional state on any given day: -3 is the pits, 0 is ambivalent, and +3 is ecstatic. The numbers between -3 and +3 are the shades between melancholy and joy.
2. When you first get up in the morning, before you begin interacting with the world, take stock of your emotional state and record your rating.

3. You might wish to use an astrological calendar for this purpose. This type of calendar has the signs and cycles of the Moon recorded for each day. In and of itself, this calendar will not figure your cycles for you. But because it charts the Moon cycles, after a few months of recording your emotional status, you can begin to notice the correlation of your cycles with the Moon phases and signs.

Through the above method of recording, you can familiarize yourself with your natural emotional rhythm. At first it takes in-depth searching to decode your feelings and to become aware of the subtle differences. It is easy to get caught in a trap of making excuses for your feelings. "Of course I feel upset, look at what I have to deal with." The point being, which occurs first? In your emotionally low cycles, almost anything will serve as a reason to explain why you are not feeling well.

Using this information will allow you to more effectively plan your time and maximize your energy. Ideally, during the low cycles, you would disengage from outer attention and turn your focus inward. You can still do everything you need to do, but in a more passive, reflective way. High-energy times are when you are able to handle more activity and naturally express more enthusiasm. If a life is filled with expansion and expression exclusively, there is no opportunity to integrate and find meaning. Appreciate these inward cycles as a time that allows you to internalize your experiences.

Emotional Nurturance

The secret of emotional strength deals with nurturing. With physical strength and assertive force you can win obedience, and that's all. But with emotional strength and nurturance, you can win love. Real nurturing forms bonds with others. Imagine the situation where the parents of a family decide that it would be most cohesive if the whole family would eat together on Sunday nights. One approach would be to discipline the family members to the degree that you show up at dinner or find yourself on the outs with your parents for the whole week. In this case, fear is the motivating factor, and that works. Everyone obediently shows up for dinner. Another approach would be the path of nurturance by providing a great dinner with favorite treats. The parents could create an atmosphere of love and acceptance through these ritual dinners. This could be the time when each of the members had the opportunity to share what is going on with them. On the surface it would look like dinner, but it is so much more. Feeling loved and a part of the whole family would be the shared experience. Both approaches meet the parents' goal of cohesiveness. The difference: empty obedience holds the family together through fear of discipline; nurturing holds them together through the power of love.

Remember this rule when you are dealing with emotional relationships: That which you nurture, grows. Whether it be the "is-ness" or the "isn't-ness," the choice is always yours. You can either see what is there or you can focus on what is missing.

Exercise

Make it a daily habit to nurture the aspects of your relationship that you wish to see grow.

1. This is an exercise in preperformance visualization. Just before you go to sleep at night, think about your relationship and one quality you wish to see grow. Let it be something you see as in the best interest of everyone involved. This is the seed you are nurturing. With your eyes closed, see this aspect of the relationship blossoming. Picture what it would be like if your wish were to come true. Continue on in your imagination and allow yourself to feel what it would be like if this aspect were real. Enter into the emotions of what it would feel like—feel it in present time as if it were already true. Allow yourself to fall asleep with this feeling.

2. When you first wake up in the morning, remember your feelings from the night before. Take a moment to enjoy them. Now, vow to nurture that part of the relationship you have been visualizing.

3. Throughout the day, periodically connect with your visualization, and experience the positive feelings you associate with this growth. From this positive state, bring your mate's image to mind and see him or her enjoying this feeling too. When you again spend time with your mate, consciously become aware of even the slightest growth in the desired direction. Allow the growth to take place in steps. Stay with this until the momentum of the growth is self-maintaining, which can take one night, or one week, or one month. It will work.

Ask yourself honestly, "When I am away from my partner, what is the quality of my emotional feelings towards that person?" If the answer is that it is mostly negative, with a focus on the frustrations, irritations, and disappointments of the relationship, then what are you nurturing? What is going to grow? Obviously, your frustration is going to grow because that is what you are investing in. On the other hand, if the quality of time spent away from your mate is positive, with a focus on that which you enjoy about the relationship, then that is what you are nurturing, and that is what will grow.

This lesson will teach you a very simple truth about you and your relationships: that which you nurture, grows. Create an inner nest of warmth and love for your mate to return to, and most assuredly, the fruit of your labors will improve your relationships.

Emotional Withdrawal

It is surprising how many people think their feelings are obvious to those around them. Though you don't expect your friends to be mind readers, when it comes to interpreting your feelings, you might wish they were. After all, your feelings are so apparent to you, others would have to be totally insensitive to not know what is going on with you! A typical scenario might progress like this: something is very important to you, and you are quite aware of your feelings concerning this issue. Your husband comes home with other things on his mind. You know what your feelings are, so you feel no need to communicate the obvious. But he doesn't notice . . . *aha!* Since he doesn't notice, that means he doesn't care! Because if he did care, he would talk about the issue without you having to bring it up. Right?

How many times have you assumed that your partner should be psychic? This scenario always leads to emotional withdrawal. It is as if the other person is tried, convicted, and sentenced for a crime that he didn't even know he committed . . . and the fact that he didn't know is the evidence to convict him. If this situation sounds familiar, ask yourself, "Is it really fair to hide something from others, and then judge them for not finding it?" As you work on expressing your emotions with ever-more deftness, you will be surprised how often you discover that what appeared obvious to you is not so apparent to the people around you.

Exercise

Make it a daily habit to express your feelings, even if they seem totally obvious.

1. Start with positive emotions—they are safer! At least once a day, tell a child, a lover, a friend, or a mate about your good feelings towards them. It may seem redundant or obvious, but you'll be surprised how this simple exercise influences a relationship.

2. After you have developed a positive emotional rapport with a selected person, try sharing a sensitive feeling. Make it something not connected to your friend's behavior. You are sharing a personal feeling, so begin setting the stage by establishing a positive emotional rapport. After you feel comfortable, ask your friend's permission to discuss a sensitive issue. This is certainly a very cautious approach, but many people have a tendency to take the flower of their sensitivity down to the freeway of morning rush-hour traffic, and then feel bruised because they were not treated delicately. Be respectful of the vulnerability of the inner you by first making sure the person with whom you have chosen to share your feelings is open to receive them with the same sensitivity you are feeling. Just because you are ready to share something does not mean that someone is ready to receive it.

3. Remain aware of the positive emotional rapport you have with your friend, and hold this awareness throughout the discussion of your sensitive issue. Feelings easily color one's perceptions, yet you can position yourself in a place from which you can watch your emotional involvements with a degree of detachment. This is the vantage point of the witness. Essentially, you allow your attention to be in two places at once. Part of you is involved with the activity in front of you, and another part of you is watching and observing your involvement from a place inside yourself.

   When you are monitoring your reactions, it is easier to see how you can slip into overidentification with the sensitive part of your character, perceiving everything as a potential threat. When this happens, you run the risk of having all your protective defenses pop up right in front of you, with your friend looking at you from the outside, suddenly appearing to you as an adversary. You have to be in two places at once, within your consciousness, in order to overcome this tendency.

4. After you have been successful at both positive and sensitive emotional expression, try this biggie: express a negative emotion that was caused by your friend's behavior. This would be something that has been bothering you about your friend. This is big-league stuff, and not many are truly successful at this type of communication. The greatest danger now is that of triggering the other person's defenses. After all, you will be challenging his behavior. Since these types of emotional expressions typically carry a negative charge, the communication can easily become intense. If your true intent is to neutralize or change the negative polarity to positive, you can—but realize that emotions color perception.

The trick here is to express the negative emotion in such a way as to not create a new problem. Techniques that help are:

1. Use a preperformance visualization of seeing and feeling the union of you and your friend after the emotional communication. Know your intent. If you cannot visualize closeness at the other end of the emotional expression, then why bother trying to achieve it? You already know you will fail. Allow yourself success, by first imagining renewed closeness and then being relentless until you experience it. With this type of intensity of commitment, you will never fail.
2. Describe the situation from your feelings, instead of projecting blame. "I feel . . ." instead of "You caused . . ." or "You made me feel . . ."
3. Be aware of the tone of your voice. Remember, when communicating your emotions, it is not just the words that others will respond to. Facial expressions, body language, and accompanying feelings will also have their impact.
4. You are asking your friend to be willing to make adjustments in reasoning. Be just as willing to adjust your own. Then you can be assured that your sharing is a true exploration of each other's feelings rather than a blaming session. Can you trust your senses when you are experiencing anger, jealously, or depression? No, absolutely not. The senses are colored

by the feelings and gather information from the objective world to justify the feelings. You will lessen the risk of this occurring when you realize that you, yourself, are subject to misperception.

Past Experiences

Most long-term relationships have a certain amount of energy locked up, but not forgotten. All too often, the attitude of "no sense in crying over spilled milk," is used in dealing with the past. This attitude is most unfortunate as it cuts you off from the resource of many of your life experiences and valuable lessons. The future is filled with maybes, could bes, and might bes, but the past is filled with the actual content of your life, and it is not dead. It is the living foundation of your present life.

Considering the past as being alive has certain benefits, the most important being that it represents a storehouse of information about yourself. For most, the past is a vast field of experience, whether it be pleasant or unpleasant, from which meaning has yet to be fully harvested. Where you have walked away from a challenge, considering it best to simply drop it and move on, you have left part of your total available energy locked up in the discarded experience. The following exercise will help you to reclaim that energy.

Exercise

Through memory and visualization, learn to harvest the meaning from your forgotten past.

1. This exercise needs to be done privately, in a quiet and relaxing environment. Pick a time when you know you will not be interrupted. Then, either lie down or sit in a comfortable position that you will be able to maintain for at least ten minutes. Close your eyes and regulate your breathing so that it is slow, steady, and calm. After a few minutes of relaxing, affirm your intent by telling your higher mind you are interested in gaining meaning from significant past experiences. You would like its assistance, first through finding the appropriate memories through which you can learn, and then through facilitating the growth that can be integrated into the now. Do not be afraid to talk to your higher mind—it is there to help you. Talk to your higher mind as if it were a friend, an ally from whom you are seeking help.

2. Now ask your higher mind to help you recall an actual memory that is unresolved. There are usually more than enough of these to choose from, so you should not have any difficulty finding one for review. When the memory comes, simply accept it.

   Some people have a difficult time accessing their memories. For these people, deep body work, like massage and rolfing, can release the memories that have been stored in the muscle tissue of the body. While being worked on, certain points get touched and the memories stored in the muscle tissue get released.

3. Try to maintain the vantage point of the "spiritual detective." You do not necessarily want to engage all the hurt and confusion of the memory. That's not the point. Stay detached so you can view it with the intent of gathering information that you previously missed. If you believe everything has a reason, your soul had some lesson in mind for you when it allowed this experience.

4. This step is the most important of the process. Before you leave your memory, ask your higher mind, "What am I to learn from this situation?" Be open to learning. Know that the learning is there—it always is, just not always identified. All of your challenges are there for your growth, and now you are seeking to understand the situation in a new light. What were you to learn? An answer will come to you, and all you have to do now is accept it, without too much questioning or fabrication of excuses. Sometimes you see that you brought this on yourself through actions you had initiated (karma). Sometimes you see that you were being asked to develop a strength or quality you just were not quite ready to accept at that time. You can always learn something. Know in your heart that all of your experiences in life were authored by your very soul itself, and there is a lesson to be learned from all of it.

The question is often asked, "If you had a chance to do it over again, what would you do differently?" Well, you never really get to change the past, but you can always change the meaning of the past, as this last exercise has shown you. When you change the meaning, you change the living foundation of the present.

Vulnerability

Along with the celebration that love brings, also comes the vulnerability to pain. With love there is a risk—no, let's say a guarantee—that with love comes pain. In the process of coming to know another person, there are the inevitable bruised feelings and misunderstandings. They hurt, but the wounds are healed through the love shared. However, another type of pain that is not so easy to heal is the pain of isolation that comes when you are too good at protecting your vulnerability. The natural hurts and pains involved with getting to know another are nothing compared to the pangs of loneliness that result from walling yourself up in protection.

A requirement of experiencing emotional intimacy is that you be willing to present your vulnerability to another by opening your heart and feelings. Know that life comes with its share of emotional pains and disappointments, and direct your attention to the way you handle and process them. It makes all the difference in the world as to how healthy a relationship stays. If a person has the belief pain and disappointment should not happen in a good relationship, all types of problems are created, stemming from unrealistic expectations. This naiveté and inability to accept pain as a natural part of a healthy relationship leads to protecting one's vulnerability by shielding the heart, making it impenetrable. It works, but the heart impervious to pain is also inaccessible to love.

Emotional Comfort Zones

One of the characteristics of the human critter is that it is comfortable with that which is familiar. Emotional habit patterns, whether they are satisfying or painful, make up your comfort zone. Your comfort zone is defined by your past experiences. To expand your comfort zone means that you will feel uncomfortable until you adjust. All this has to be understood if you are to work with your emotions.

Too often, people wait for the exact right time or the right set of circumstances to grow and expand, and it never comes. By definition, if it is a new and unfamiliar experience, even a positive one, it is uncomfortable. Unless you want to stay somewhat the same, you will have to keep stretching beyond what is comfortable. This is how growth occurs, and growth is a part of the human condition.

Let's call this an exercise of emotional stretching. Notice, this is not a request to simply get over your feelings or to repress them. The lesson is one of adapting to your feelings through acceptance. Become aware of what you are trying to accomplish. Familiarize yourself ahead of time with the process you will be going through.

Exercise

At least once a month, force yourself to try a new experience that you have been wanting to do "as soon as it feels right."

1. The trick here is not to wait for any specific right set of circumstances to emerge. Many clients voice that there must be something wrong with them because they do not feel at ease in new situations. Apparently, no one told them that such feelings are part of the human condition—welcome to the club! In time, you will welcome the feeling of not knowing exactly how some event will most likely turn out. Perhaps you have wanted to get out and interact with people more often, but every time the opportunity arises, it doesn't feel quite right, so you decline. Know that is your tendency and compensate for it. When you find yourself saying it doesn't feel right, remind yourself you always say that, and then force yourself to go out.
2. When you have forced yourself to try a new experience, visualize in advance what to expect. Tell yourself it is healthy and normal to be feeling uncomfortable. Talk to your emotions and let them know that it is all right to feel insecure. Soon this new situation will become familiar, and once again they will feel comfortable. Try it, it works.

Silent Emotional Communication

One of the genuine frustrations in working through emotional difficulties with a partner is the inadequacy of words to accurately describe your intent. How frustrating it can be to know your intent so clearly and then to hear how poorly your words describe your feelings. There are also many emotional states and feelings that cannot be put into words. How often have you wanted to express a feeling to a friend, and you just could not begin to find the appropriate words?

Instead of being facilitative, words can actually inhibit that which you are trying to express. Consequently, learning to express yourself without words can lead to a tremendous feeling of accomplishment and relief. In this next exercise you will need a willing partner who is also interested in this type of work.

Exercise

Set aside five minutes of quiet time for you and a partner. Stare deeply into each others' eyes and experience your emotions. Silently, share your feelings.

1. This is silent communication, so the ground rules are no talking before, during, or after the experience. No fair asking the other person what he was feeling when you saw him twitch! This is an exercise in developing your ability to know from your emotional feelings what your partner is experiencing. Feel safe in sharing your inner emotions, knowing they will not be judged or even discussed by your friend.
2. Quite naturally, silent communication is always uncomfortable at first, even with loved ones. We are not used to others looking deeply into the windows of our soul, but as you move beyond your own resistance and stay with the feelings, you will begin to notice that your partner is going through the same experiences. The degree of difficulty you have in staying with this exercise is the measure of how strong your defenses are operating.
3. Stay with the emotions as they pull your attention to the depth of your being. Simultaneously, stay attentive to the gaze and your awareness of your partner's experience. You will experience a strong sensation of energy. Try not to freeze in resistance to the energy, or to get stuck on one sensation. Emotions are fluid, let them move through you with nonattachment.
4. You will note in a very short time, you and your friend develop a strong emotional bond. You begin to feel not only the separate emotional fields of you and your partner, but also the combined energy, forming a third energy field. Allow this rapport to be felt throughout the day as you take note of both yours and your friend's feelings. It will become easier and easier to silently communicate with a knowing glance.

The gulf that most often separates couples in their emotional relating is regrettable. Settle for nothing less than close emotional bonding, and alienation will disappear. Demand that your closest relationships be of the highest order of love and satisfaction, and they will be. Always give love from your deepest center, and you will not be disappointed.

Emotional Openness

Most people understand the concept of open-mindedness. It is not always practiced, but at least it is understood. There are different mental perspectives to all situations, and everyone has an independent view of life. Open-minded individuals welcome stimulating thoughts whether they synchronize to their own or not. They are able to appreciate different ways of thinking as a natural facet of life and realize they are expanded through alternative perceptions. The same openness is possible at the emotional level, although considerably harder to attain.

In any situation, there can be many right ways to feel, and no wrong ways. This certainly sounds easy enough to understand, but it is immensely difficult to live. To learn to allow others their emotional truths without feeling personally responsible for how they feel is a true freedom. In order to achieve this, you have to learn to overcome the defensive reaction that responds to polarities as conflict. The difficulty stems from the ego-defense mechanism. Wouldn't it be wonderful to be so secure within your own emotions that you could be around people with different feelings without feeling threatened? You can, but it is an art, and usually needs to be consciously developed.

The secret is in finding your emotional center and then staying there, even though it is constantly changing. Everyone has an ego that functions as a sentinel, patrolling the boundaries of their comfort zone and protecting the fortress against any challenging emotions. The ego's job is to help maintain your self-identity, but it is often overprotective and does not allow you to experience any feelings that are not part of the preexisting emotional structure. If you were as guarded mentally as you are emotionally, you would never learn anything because you would not allow new thoughts into the mind. This would be a sorry state of affairs. No growth. The same applies with emotions; if you never allow new emotional experiences into your life, there will be no growth.

There is always clarity in your center. Learn to reside here during emotional interactions, and you will be emotionally open. Know that the sentinel will be there, sounding the alarm when real invasion occurs. Be aware that when you allow your attention to be fully placed on the sentinel, your defenses will immediately go up to protect against the perceived invasion. Instead, immediately retreat to your center where you are the safest and the clearest. Retreat is often thought of as a sign of weakness, but when you are returning to your strength, it is anything but weakness.

Emotional fulfillment in relationships does not just happen. It takes clarity of intent to ride the ever-changing tides of your own emotional cycles. It takes even more clarity of intent to learn the emotional patterns of your partner. To gently ride the currents of the combined emotional energy of both individuals requires still greater clarity, but settle for nothing less. Stay diligent and be willing to teach each other along the way—you will get there and the rewards are well worth the effort.

The Moon Through the Signs

The sign your Moon was in at your birth describes your habits and comfort zones, the way you respond to your emotional needs, and how you express yourself emotionally. In relationships, the Moon is just as important as the Sun. These two parts of your character must be integrated for you to experience the best with others. The sign of your Moon gives definition to the unconscious habit patterns that are expressed through the personality as a response to what is going on around you.

Consider the needs of your Sun sign and think of your Moon sign as the emotional support system you need to sustain the strength of the Sun. While your Sun sign describes how you project yourself to the world, your Moon sign describes how you retreat to rejuvenate yourself and what habit patterns of comfort you develop. Knowing the Moon sign of others will give you clues as to how to better understand and relate to their emotional needs.

Moon in Aries

YOUR EMOTIONAL NATURE Your emotional center is dynamic, intense, and inspirational. Spontaneity best describes your response to life. You are a strong, assertive person, with a fiery emotional temperament. Your impulsive nature propels you into action, eliminating any chance of "sitting on" emotional issues. The benefit of this tendency is that you can quickly move through issues and rarely harbor resentments from the past. You are also a lot of fun to be with. You portray a very idealistic attitude concerning emotional experiences—you like to be up, at high tide all the time.

You provide an eternal spark that can keep relationships dynamic and alive. As a catalyst, you help draw others out of themselves to deal with issues as they arise in the moment. How to experience the intensity that you crave in a world that settles for complacency is an issue. This might even make it difficult for others to relax and be themselves around you for, oddly enough, they sometimes translate your inspiration as insensitivity. To harmonize with others at the emotional level, you must learn to read their reactions for clues as to when your intensity is becoming overwhelming. Slow down, and be cognizant of the other person's inability to handle intensity on the same level. Emotional relationships improve tremendously when you have other outlets for your abundant energy. You definitely do best in relationships that do not try to curtail and limit your enthusiasm.

Areas to Work On The difficulty of this placement is that it is almost impossible for you to surrender to the moment without feeling that you must act on it in same way. Your direct manner can be perceived as demanding or pushy when you let your focus become extreme as to how your emotional needs should be met. Positive idealism makes it difficult for you to adjust to low cycles, but when you resist this natural inward movement, and react defensively, you become crabby and irritable. Your fire never need die out, but your life becomes more graceful when you start allowing rhythms in your life, not needing every moment to be the most intense. This makes it easier for you to accept other people's emotional cycles without needing to "fix" them.

Understanding Moon in Aries in Others These people have a bright, intense emotional character that responds to the moment. You will always know how they feel and will need to learn to deal with issues right when they come up. They prefer the "intense confrontation and then be done with it" approach to emotional encounters, rather than any drawn-out solution. Their feelings can be easily hurt, and to protect themselves, they usually become defensive. Allow them to vent pent-up anger and frustration. Venting is healthy. Just don't allow yourself to be a target.

Moon in Aries individuals are very inspirational and motivational. They possess a "can do it" philosophy about life that will motivate you to become all that you can become. They are at their best in a very active relationship, so passive activities are usually not tolerated. They love to be surprised by spontaneous plans you might present. However, there are times when it is best just to leave them alone, and let them go at their own pace. These people change moods very quickly, so be prepared. They need to be recognized and appreciated, and yet, they want you to support their independence.

Moon in Taurus

Your Emotional Nature When you rely on your genuineness, your emotional expression is like a clear mountain stream. It refreshes others with its naturalness. Your common sense is uncanny in providing for your security needs, which are of primary concern with this placement. Like the bull, you are strong, sensual, and stubborn, but like Venus (ruler of Taurus) your expression is soft, and shows a knack for creating a comfortable, if not luxurious, lifestyle. Once you have overcome your fear of not having enough, you shift from acquisition to appreciation of the material world. Some involvement with nature or the arts is usually required to give you the greatest sense of abundance, so when you need to be comforted and return to your center, take a simple walk in nature. You need to feel a rapport with the land, climate, and vegetation of where you live. You draw a great deal of strength from interaction with nature. Because you are highly sensitive to your environment, your home will likely reflect your personal touch. Your possessions will be important for you, and with your eye for quality, it is best for you to live in prosperity. Taurus comforts can get expensive.

In relationships, you seek out steady, uncompromising, emotional involvements. Your stability comes through a secure emotional involvement with your home and a partner. When these are in order, you are easy-going, nurturing, and express your feelings with affection. Simple touch, like holding hands and hugging with your partner, gives you a sense of grounding and soothes your emotions. Life with you can be delightful when you have a secure base of operations. Once you have developed a secure foundation you share your uncomplicated ability to enjoy life's simple pleasures.

Areas to Work On Where stability is your forte, adaptability is likely to be your weakness. When challenged, your tendency is to resist first, and dig your heals in to see if you can outlast the challenge. Any threat to your security base puts you on the defensive, and you lose the ability to rationally deal with the situation. To overcome this tendency, first watch the action. Observe the point at which you resist the inevitable. Remind yourself that life is change—change is law. The Moon represents your ability to adapt to necessary changes in an ever-changing reality. Watch where your resistance costs you in the needless expenditure of energy. Your life becomes more graceful as you become more aware of when it is in your best interest to adapt rather than resist.

Understanding Moon in Taurus in Others Moon in Taurus individuals have a down-to-earth practicality about the way they respond to life. They usually know where they stand on emotional issues and are not easily influenced. You can rely on these sturdy individuals, as they like to follow through on all commitments. Realize ahead of time that their first response to change is resistance. You cannot force these individuals to change; if they are going to make a change in their lives it will be because they have already decided it was the right thing to do. Continuity allows them to steer a steady course in life, but also makes it difficult to adapt to disruptions in their plans. Give them plenty of advance notice and don't expect spontaneous changes in plans to be appreciated. Along with wanting a comfortable life, Moon in Taurus individuals want an uncomplicated emotional life. Not at ease with the uncertainty of intrigue, they prefer to relate to those who are clear and direct.

In intimate relationships, these people need to feel secure about your love and concern for them. They know how to enjoy life, and through their heightened awareness of the senses, you can become much more appreciative of life's simple pleasures as well. Highly affectionate, these individuals are soothed through simple touch, like holding hands, hugs, and massage. No need for pretense with Moon in Taurus individuals—they appreciate genuineness and naturalness above all else.

Moon in Gemini

Your Emotional Nature Your adaptability and responsiveness to the moment are your gifts. With a lighthearted, breezy approach to your emotions you easily slip into a very friendly stature. Also, the love of variety and the ability to find something of interest in every person you meet makes you a fascinating conversationalist. You require a great deal of mental stimulation to hold your interest in any project or person, and it is the prerogative of Gemini to reserve the right to change whenever you seem fit. Not only do you easily adapt to change, you are emotionally attracted to exciting and even confusing situations. Your feelings become real when you put them into words. The distance from your feelings that words give is comforting and gives you the perspective you crave to make sense of your world.

Your easy-going temperament is most comfortable in relationships that are congenial and friendly. Not known for sentimentality, you prefer a relationship that has a lively exchange of ideas as its foundation. Communication revitalizes you, so you wouldn't do well with the strong, silent type. You need interaction, and do best in a relationship that does not restrict an open exchange with many and diverse friends. Although you would likely resist, your ideal could be someone who helps you toe the line and follow through on your current commitments.

Areas to Work On When excessive, your openness to the moment leads to an easily distracted character. You do need room for spontaneity in your day, it's true, but your energy gets scattered. You get caught spinning your wheels until you establish some priorities and follow through on them. Your ability to use words and your adaptability can lead to a sidestepping tendency in dealing with important emotional issues. This makes it difficult for others to pin you down. It can lead to superficiality until you learn to move out of your mind and into your feelings. Your tendency is to try to make emotional situations rational, and you become quite confused when they are not. The need to realize emotions exist without reasons is crucial, because when you rely exclusively on your intellect, you deprive yourself of other meaningful resources like intuition and feelings. Develop your faith in an intelligence greater than logic, and then you can enjoy those issues in life that do not make sense as sources of wonder and awe.

Understanding Moon in Gemini in Others Be prepared to listen to what is going on with these individuals. They need to talk, share, and relate endless details about their lives, even to the extent of talking their way through emotional situations as a way of coming to terms with their feelings. The interaction is what they find exciting and satisfying. Keep your expectations of how they should respond or react to a minimum, and they will trust you. Your mental rapport is going to have to be very strong for bonding to occur, and you will have to understand their need for variety and change. You may feel that their many interests come before their feelings for you, but try not to read too much into their spontaneous reaction to life. It's just their nature; they don't want to miss anything. You will not get bored with these inquisitive souls, but you will certainly be tested in your flexibility, as they will change plans often.

Moon in Cancer

YOUR EMOTIONAL NATURE You are emotionally sensitive and reserved. Strong family ties, especially to your mother, play a significant part in your life. These ties and past emotional patterning have formed the basis of how you now react to what is going on around you, which is with caution. You are very wary of any threats to home or family security, as this is most likely where you are seeking emotional fulfillment. Your emotional nature responds to the pull of the Moon's cycles just as the oceans do: high tide, low tide, in an ever-changing cycle is the way. Gently surrender to these emotional currents instead of resisting their natural flow, and you will attain harmony with your emotional nature.

You are at your best in relationships when you feel you are needed and can channel your abundant emotional nature in a positive way. When you focus on yourself, you can feel needy, but when you focus on meeting the needs of others, you feel needed. This nurturing quality is indeed your gift, but when you become excessive in its expression you can unwittingly create emotional dependence in others. When your emotional world is safe and nurturing for you, you help others become more secure with accepting the cyclic nature of their emotions as well. Since you respond directly to what people are feeling, and not what they are saying or doing, you are excellent at silent emotional communication.

AREAS TO WORK ON It is wise for you to periodically review your emotional habit patterns to see if they are current with how you actually feel in the moment. You can hold onto the past with such tenacity that you close yourself to new experiences. This causes you to be excessively defensive whenever you feel challenged. When fear is motivating you, you may be exceedingly cautious about forming new emotional relationships. Allowing for the cyclic nature of your emotions, learning to adapt to, rather than resist their pull, makes all the difference in the world.

Letting go of loved ones is especially difficult for you. Whether it be leaving home, the children leaving the nest, or a friend moving to a different town, letting go of your attachment to the existing form of your relationships is anything but graceful for you. Although these types of experience are not wounds, they still hurt until you adjust to the new form of bonding. Endings like parting with a lover, divorce, or death of a loved one are wounding to you—you simply do not say goodbye easily. It does take time for you to heal—be patient with yourself and have faith that you will once again establish nurturing ties with others.

Understanding Moon in Cancer in Others Emotional security is likely to be much more of an issue with these people than first appears. Expect to move slowly in establishing your bonds of friendship and trust. They are cautious and reserved, but that does not mean that they do not care about you. They will stand back and observe you and feel out where they can best fit into your world. Much of how they relate to the world, and to you, is through their feelings that can overwhelm them, so they pull back and again watch and wait. Encourage them to talk about their feelings, and yet, know that much of what is going on for them is not easily translatable into words. Their insecurities will surprise you. They appear strong on the outside, but on the inside, they are extremely sensitive. They will protect their vulnerability until they trust your loyalty, and then express tremendous warmth and caring for you. Realize that they are likely to respond to the emotional undercurrents of any situation, not just the presentation; they are responding to how you feel, not what you say. Once accepted into their close circle, you become as family and their loyalty is unfaltering.

Moon in Leo

Your Emotional Nature When you feel secure, you express your emotions affectionately and easily. When you feel emotionally unsure, you express with much more decorum and control. The regal in you expects to experience the best in life, and you have the spirit to back it up. At best, your love of life seems to turn up the light wherever you are. Your personality is compelling and persuasive, and you are not to be taken lightly. There is a strong need for recognition in you that leads to creative bursts of activity. This draws the attention to you, and you blossom within. This is not arrogance; it is your natural place in the world, and you will be most comfortable once you have established a lifestyle that revolves around you. Your generous nature gives back all that you receive, so everyone benefits when your life is order.

You are very selective with whom you share the warm and friendly side of yourself. You have a big heart and need to be with others who also express through their heart. You are most at ease with those who know how to enjoy life. You are likely a work-hard, play-hard personality who likes to do everything with a bit of gusto. You do best in relationships that go at life head-on, rather than settling into complacent comfort. In love relationships you are extremely loyal, although you reserve the right to flirt for the fun of it. You like to feel proud of those you love, and set high standards of expectations for them. An ideal relationship would focus on the personal, fun, creative side of life, as much as on achievements.

Areas to Work On Your pride is a two-edged sword. When it helps you become more heartfully connected to all that you do, it is as a gift. When it prompts you into defensive reaction because you cannot bear to be wrong, it works against you. This can lead to emotional responses that seem arrogant and excessively self-centered to others. As you become more self-affirmed and secure with yourself, you become less defensive to perceived threats.

Your winning personality can easily get swept up in the spirit of competition. If you do not find healthy, creative outlets for this natural part of your character, you will develop a tendency to compete with inappropriate people at inappropriate times. You like to win, but when it goes beyond fun and becomes compulsive, realize that this will drive others away from you. You must learn how to direct your abundant will power and to restrain yourself, so as to share the stage with others. As you do, you find that others enjoy your successes all the more.

Understanding Moon in Leo in Others These people can be fun, warm, and lovable. They express their emotions with heartfulness and dignity. There always seems to be something royal and regal about these individuals. They are big-hearted folks and if they are secure in the heart, you will see the best of them. However, if their heart requirements are not being met, their tremendous need for attention and recognition are likely to lead to a strong competitive nature. Then they can seem self-serving and demanding. They do not want their relationships to be ordinary in any way. They feel they are special people and they want their relationships to reflect this; they want the very best. Moon in Leo individuals are likely to be just as proud of you as they want you to be of them. In intimate relationships, they need to be the center of attention; they do not deal well as an appendage to someone else's life. They will give just as much as they expect in love relationships, which is considerable. They do not adapt to change well, so always introduce changes in plans slowly.

Moon in Virgo

YOUR EMOTIONAL NATURE When you are at ease, you express yourself with sincerity and an absolute attentiveness to the needs of the moment. With your Moon in Virgo there is a high degree of self-awareness, sometimes too much so. You are emotionally high-strung and alert because of the exacting standards to which you hold yourself. Since you are not comfortable with chaos in your life, your emotional comfort zone requires predictability and routine. The analytical nature of Virgo and the emotional nature of the Moon creates a dilemma for you. The Moon's role is to adapt to the many changes throughout the day, and Virgo's need is for order and predictability. The dilemma is that emotions are not predictable by nature. As you simplify your life by reducing the number of unpredictable events, you create more order in your life and resolve the dilemma.

Since you naturally spend much time analyzing your feelings, you become quite good at analyzing others' feelings as well. You feel best when you are being useful and you likely enjoy helping others. Your need to be busy and productive also leads to a strong need to feel solid about your work or your position in the world as a condition of self-worth. When these conditions are met, you reflect more confidence and comfort with yourself. You seem to be most at ease when you are tending to the details of your life which can lead to an excessively practical approach. Don't become too busy to have fun!

You easily become totally involved with those you love. Your emotional security with another is based on your usefulness. This utilitarian approach is how you are most comfortable expressing your feelings, and it is wise to develop relationships with those that appreciate this quality in you. You are uncomfortable with those that demand you verbally express your feelings. You prefer to demonstrate your feelings in action, rather than put them into words. Your attentiveness to the moment is often refreshing to others, as it pulls them into present time.

Areas to Work On Areas to work on deal with your self-critical nature. You tend to worry too much about yourself. This excessive self-awareness can become quite inhibiting and you need to get out of thinking about yourself and what might possibly go wrong. Learn to direct your attention into right activity. Are you working to overcome problems or to maintain perfection? Your answer makes all of the difference in the world as to how difficult you will make your life. If your model for living life is overcoming problems, then there will be a perpetual stream of challenge/solution situations before you. When you learn to change your modus operandi to maintaining perfection, then you start the day with a feeling of life being in a perfect state to begin with. Essentially, this is a philosophical shift—you accept the Divine perfection of life, even if this might not be apparent. You still will be busy making adjustments all through the day, but from this perspective, the adjustments are to maintain, rather than achieve, equilibrium in your life.

It can be challenging for you to simply feel right and good about yourself, which keeps you trying too hard, too much of the time. You almost always need to remember that to slow down and relax is all right. The solution for most of your challenges lies in finding right activities that involve both your mind and your feeling nature.

Understanding Moon in Virgo in Others These people are very rational in their emotional expression, or at least they try to be. They hold themselves to very exacting standards, are very thoughtful, and rarely act out of character. Moon in Virgo individuals seek appreciation for their efforts, and this is one area you can't overdo it. They need a great deal of reassurance about the role they play in your life. They want to be adding something significant to its overall quality, and seem to always work themselves into a position of being indispensable. This placement leads to a tendency to look at life through the lens of a current problem. Problem sharing and problem solving can be techniques for closeness between you and a Virgo Moon friend. They crave interaction and involvement on their work issues, so don't be afraid to get involved. Conversely, don't be afraid to remind them that there is more to life than work. They are typically overcoming their excessively self-critical nature. Your feedback and support will speed along this process, as their primary emotional need is to feel appreciated. If you value sincerity and integrity more than flamboyance, this is the type for you.

Moon in Libra

Your Emotional Nature Harmonious social interacting is essential to your emotional well-being. You have natural charm and you bring out refinement in others. Skilled at diplomacy, you seem to be able to get what you want in life without having to be forceful. There is gracefulness that accompanies your emotional relating along with a certain removed distance that protects you from overinvolvement. It is easy for others to like you. The aesthetics of life are quite important for your emotional well-being. Your living and working environments should reflect your appreciation for beauty.

With your Moon in Libra, the sign of relationships, much of your emotional fulfillment will come through your involvement with others. The give and take that is required to cooperate in relationships is something that comes quite naturally to you. Appearances are important to you and you pay a great deal of attention to the thoughts, attitudes, and values of your partner, as you like to please your mate. The ideal of perfect equanimity leading to emotional serenity is quite attractive to you as well, and you prefer to work out difficulties in a calm, rational manner (or not at all), rather than deal with emotional unpleasantness.

Areas to Work On Your desire for serenity and tranquillity can all too easily lead you to the "peace at any cost" syndrome, which you eventually regret. You are extremely responsive to the needs, values, and thoughts of your partner, sometimes too much so. When this becomes excessive, you develop a people-pleasing character that lacks depth and genuineness. The question arises, do you respond to the genuine emotional needs in front of you, or do you ignore all that is unpleasant in favor of the ideal? How you respond to this question will determine how deep, or how superficial, your relationships will be. You need to remember that to bring your best to a relationship you have to be balanced in your own right, rather than just adapting to the needs of the relationship.

Learning to be more direct in your emotional interactions with others is a skill that you need to develop. Your tendency to consider how others will respond to your expression makes it difficult for you to speak your mind. This leads to a tendency to say what you think others want to hear, rather than how you genuinely feel.

Understanding Moon in Libra in Others There is a certain sense of style and class in these people that will motivate you to put your best foot forward. Their natural refinement is also expressed in the emotional realm and they are quite uncomfortable with unpleasantness of any sort. You can expect them to be fair, just, and diplomatic in all of their dealings with others. Moon in Libra individuals think before they act, so give them time to go through their evaluating process, rather then push for immediate decisions. Do not expect them to be overly emotional and syrupy, as they are more comfortable with some distance from their feelings. This does not mean that they do not care about you, they are simply concerned about refined expression. They probably do not handle anger well, so you will have to watch for the subtle signals and help them express their real feelings. They really do believe that emotional issues and differences could best be solved if people would simply deal with differences in a clear, calm, and rational way. Of course this is unrealistic, but realize that it is their ideal nonetheless, and you will be better able to understand them.

Moon in Scorpio

Your Emotional Nature Moon in Scorpio leads to a psychologically complex and intense emotional nature. “Still waters run deep” likely describes your feelings, as more is going on beneath the surface than you reveal to others. You have a knack for responding to the hidden message in communications, since you respond more to what others are not saying than to the actual words they use. This leads to a skill at reading the intentions and motivations of others—you are not easily fooled. The complexity of your sign comes from your need for both intimacy and privacy. You seem to be drawn to intriguing, even complicated, relationships with others, because when life gets too simple and obvious, you get bored.

To be in a relationship with someone who is willing to work through the rough spots would be ideal. You are not interested in spending time with people who live on the surface. Trust is essential. Very tenacious in your feelings, you prefer to work through emotional issues and get to the bottom of the matter, rather than drop them unresolved. However, without trust, you can hold onto resentments and hurts privately, creating a gulf between you and loved ones. You are excellent at silent emotional communication and your best relationships are with those who are able to read your feelings without words. You can overwhelm others with the depth of your passion and feeling nature, unless you balance your intensity by cultivating the ability to enjoy peaceful, easy feelings as well.

AREAS TO WORK ON In relationships, issues concerning sex, joint resources, and control issues invariably arise. Trust in others is the main test. You have likely experienced some of the darker aspects of the human experience and, because of this, it takes effort for you not to become cynical and jaded. Once you have learned to forgive yourself and others for past misdeeds, you are free. This is not as easy as it sounds, as jealousy, grudge, and resentment have more of a hold on you than you would like to believe. Consider these old issues as siphoning off your energy—it takes energy to hold on to resentments with others. There is less and less of you available to experience the fullness of life when there are more and more of those old issues to maintain. To experience the depths of intimacy that you crave, you must set aside your fears of rejection and learn to trust and surrender. This might be the most difficult task imaginable for you, as you are skilled at protecting your vulnerability.

It is not uncommon for Moon in Scorpio people to report that their early childhood environment was perceived as emotionally unsafe, leading to a very guarded approach to emotionally trusting others. But trust is the path, as you crave an intimacy which can only be experienced by removing the armor protecting your vulnerability. Trust in your own strength of regeneration—you are a survivor and you always bounce back.

UNDERSTANDING MOON IN SCORPIO IN OTHERS Emotions for these people run strong, deep, and intense. There is a mysterious quality about their souls that keeps you feeling that more is going on with them than meets the eye. Moon in Scorpio people are excellent about getting you to reveal your secrets, but you will realize they share their innermost feelings only after trust has been established. As they begin to share their private side with you, treat it as special, privileged information, not to be shared with others. They are uncanny at knowing your true motivations and intentions and are not easily fooled by presentations. They are often much more expressive in silence than they are with words. Silent looks and glances to and from these individuals can communicate volumes of information.

The paradox of these individuals lies in their craving for emotional intimacy, yet their emotional world is often guarded and protected with the barbs of past memories. Forgiveness does not come easy to these psychologically complex individuals. Never assume that time itself will heal wounds with them. It doesn't. It is best to deal directly and in the moment with emotional issues to keep the air clean between you and them. Those with Moon in Scorpio have a need for some privacy and prefer one-to-one, intimate sharing over large social functions. Trust is something that you will develop together. Your own emotional growth will be speeded up through the closeness of this friendship.

Moon in Sagittarius

YOUR EMOTIONAL NATURE You have a friendly, jovial temperament which leads to popularity and a life of much adventure. Your naturally expansive tendencies propel you beyond home and family for emotional experiences. Your love of learning leads to interests in social issues, travel, education, politics, religions, philosophy, and all that can expand your experiences. Since you feel good while contributing to expanding the perspective of others, you make a natural teacher. You love diversity and are rarely limited by biases and prejudices. The Sagittarian temperament is idealistic and hopeful in the way that you deal with problems. You prefer to be blunt and direct while working through issues. You respond to changes in your environment or emotional world in a direct and immediate way, and are usually quite independent. You have very high moral and ethical standards and attempt to mold your emotional nature towards your ideal. With your assertiveness, you can become defensive and even competitive, but usually your positive nature prevails, and you try to gain a philosophical perspective on any conflict. This gives you the ability to learn from your experiences, once you overcome your reactionary tendencies.

Your positive, upbeat nature allows for many friendships and you would find a relationship that focused exclusively on personal issues as restrictive. Some of your emotional satisfaction comes from exploring abstract, philosophical issues with a partner. It is not that you are impersonal. No! You are quite warm and friendly, but the lofty goals of Sagittarius need room to roam, both physically and mentally. Others are positively affected by your enthusiasm, as you are quite expressive and persuasive. Honesty is a quality that you demand in your relationships. You prefer those who are blunt and direct, rather than discreet and controlled in their emotional expression.

Areas to Work On The high-minded nature of Sagittarius can easily become moralistic, dogmatic, and even self-righteous in your attempts to educate others. Your inclination is to expand other people's perspective, but first make sure you've done that yourself by exploring the religions and philosophies of other cultures. Your ideals do not include the down side of life, and you can find yourself quite lost when your flame of inspiration cyclically burns low. You have such a distaste for the negative, that during your low cycles, you can spend the entire time trying to get out of them! This can lead to periodic burnout if you ignore the need to rest and rebuild during your low cycles.

It can be difficult to accept other people's emotional cycles as well, because you tend to think it is your responsibility to make everyone around you feel good and positive all the time. Mostly this is a wonderful quality and comes from altruistic motives, but it can be interpreted as intolerant by others. When you realize that you are not responsible for other people's happiness, then you share your natural enthusiasm without expectations, and others feel more comfortable around you.

Other challenges hinge around the principle of freedom. This is a primary need of yours, and until you find a positive, creative way of expressing this in your life, you can find yourself resisting intimacy for fear that it might trap you. Remember, you are an emotionally free spirit and your right to be free does not need permission from others.

Understanding Moon in Sagittarius in Others These people are optimistic, outgoing, and fun-loving. Decidedly positive, they want to believe in the best. They like a fast-paced life with plenty of mental stimulation. The enthusiasm of Sagittarius is infectious and it is easy to feel more positive in their presence. The excitement of anticipating future potentialities is one of the main types of emotional experiences they enjoy, so indulge their dreams, plans, and goals, as this keeps them at their best.

Moon in Sagittarius is looking for an adventure, an opportunity to grow and expand and, if that can happen through you, you will win your companion's love. Allow lots of room to change, as these people need a variety of forms through which to express. They are honest and sincere, so you will not have to be threatened by their need to occasionally spend time by themselves. They need to occasionally connect with their urge for freedom by following their own momentum without considering other people's expectations. Give them this freedom and you have won a warm-hearted, enthusiastic friend. Although good natured naturally, these fiery folks can turn competitor and occasionally need a good philosophical argument just for the sport of it. Without an adventure to plan or a goal to pursue, they can feel quite hemmed in.

Moon in Capricorn

YOUR EMOTIONAL NATURE You are likely known for your emotional strength, as you respond to your emotions in a controlled and responsible way. Your great strength is dependability—you can be trusted to follow through on commitments. You prefer not to indulge your emotional sensitivities, instead choosing to be productive and busy at bringing more order in your life. You feel most at ease when you are in control of your life, and are not comfortable at all when things get out of hand. You are at your best when you are pursuing a clearly defined ambition which you can organize your entire life around.

Your ability to control your emotional expression gives you an air of authority and competence that casts you into leadership roles, as others also feel quite comfortable with you in charge. You are most at ease and open with your feelings when you clearly understand the role you are playing. Career issues can even dominate relationships and you need to be in relationships that support and encourage this basic part of you. As you learn to celebrate your successes along the way, your life becomes more enjoyable. Your patience and persistence ultimately pays off and your life seems to improve with time.

Mutual respect is essential for you to even consider allowing closeness with others. When respect is lacking, you respond in a controlled, professional manner. With respect, your loyalty is such that you are there for others through thick and thin. Your strength is that you can weather the hard times, which greatly improves your ability for long-term relationships. Sincerity, loyalty, commitment, and honor are important in your emotional dealings with others. Since you do not surrender to emotional commitments easily, when you do, you are extremely loyal in honoring them. You expect this same reliability and accountability in others and are not afraid to call others to task when they do not follow through with commitments.

Areas to Work On Your love of order and organization can inhibit you from the spontaneous enjoyment of life. You will typically defer your emotional needs to career and other responsibilities. This leads to all work and no play; not much fun for others to be around. You usually need to remember to lighten up and be easier on yourself. You have no difficulty taking responsibility for others and you likely need to learn more about taking care of yourself.

It can be a challenge for you to express your emotions spontaneously, as other people's reactions to you and your feelings are not always one and the same. This makes it difficult for you to get an accurate mirror of your emotions. Others respond to you as if you were rock steady, even when you are feeling quite the opposite. Professionally, this is to your advantage. In love relationships, however, this trait becomes a problem. Here, your presentation of character strength betrays you when you want to share your sensitivities. You need to learn that it is all right to be weak once in awhile. Your world will not fall apart and you will feel refreshed for having dropped your barriers, at least for a breather.

Understanding Moon in Capricorn in Others For these people, the theme of respect is of central importance in all of their relationships. Moon in Capricorn individuals are responsible to the nth degree. Trust them—commitment is like a solemn bond for them. If they promised something, they will deliver. Of course, they will expect the same accountability from you. They want your recognition for their accomplishments along with the person behind the work. You will have to respond to both of these needs. They identify with their work so much that they need to share this part of their life with their partners.

They need their relationships to take some definite form, so the more clearly you can define your expectations, the more comfortable they will become. When they are in one of their broody, introspective moods, it is best to leave them to their work. They want your support concerning some of the hardships and difficulties they have endured. These people respect competence, yet, they need to feel useful in your life to feel secure, so don't fear asking them for assistance. They are comfortable in a providing role. They are not sentimentalists, but when they have someone in their life who sees through the mountain of strength and recognizes their sensitivity, they become very loyal and loving friends. Their appreciation for quality and their high standards of excellence are just as important to them in relationships as everywhere else in life.

Moon in Aquarius

YOUR EMOTIONAL NATURE You are an emotionally idealistic person who has the courage and strength of your convictions. You need to be more self-affirmed than most, because your unconventional temperament will not always gain the support of others. You have a natural knack for gaining objectivity and perspective on emotional issues by rising above them and seeing life from a larger perspective. You are naturally independent and free spirited and you grant this same freedom to others. Friendships are important to you. You are sometimes the rebel, sometimes the reformer, but never conventional, nor interested in maintaining the status quo. Your tendency is to think first and then make emotional adjustments based on how you have assessed the situation.

Words become the bridge that allows you to reach your emotions, which are fairly buried, since you tend to rationalize and intellectualize your feelings. Lofty emotions, like altruism, you can understand, but you may treat personal emotions as if they were foreign intruders. You like to rise above petty emotional concerns to see things in a larger perspective. Your tendency is to respond to situations through your ideals, or even theories, on what should work.

You do best in relationships that support and encourage the autonomy of both individuals. Also, your highly intellectual temperament would function best with a partner who did not exclusively focus on personal issues. These seem petty to you in light of larger social concerns and to be with a partner that shared your social interests would be ideal. Friendships are often easier for you than intimate personal relationships until you recognize that your freedom is not dependent upon the approval of others. Once you accept your uniqueness, you no longer need to fight for it and instead, you share your originality with others. Respect for each other's freedom and individuality is a priority to maintain a quality relationship. There is something truly unique about you and when you accept that, you encourage originality in others as well.

AREAS TO WORK ON You need to develop skills for quieting your mind to respond to the deeper calling from your emotions. Otherwise your predilection towards intellectualizing will have you thinking about, rather than feeling your emotions. This can lead to others interpreting your behavior as aloof and insensitive. How to maintain your detached perspective and simultaneously empathize with the sensitivities of others is the trick. Other challenges deal with your independent streak that rebels against the expectations of others. You have to do things your own way and for your own reasons. This can make all forms of cooperation difficult for you until you find a positive, creative way to demonstrate your uniqueness rather than just being the nonconformist.

Understanding Moon in Aquarius in Others These highly independent individuals are sure to keep you guessing as to how they will respond next, as they refuse to conform to convention or expectations of others. They are friendly, outgoing, and open to share their ideas. Often altruistic and inclined towards larger social issues, they love to deal with abstractions. They question authority at every turn and are advocates for individual rights. Don't expect them to pamper your emotional sensitivities—they won't. It is not their expertise, nor their interest. It is not that they are hiding their emotions, it's just that they are mistrustful and completely unsure of that arena of expression.

To bring out their best in working situations, give them the freedom to fulfill their responsibilities in their own way. They view life from a far removed vantage point, which gives them a unique perspective. They will provoke your thinking, as the clarity of their insights is often shocking. Keep things light, friendly, and impersonal to best get along with these people. Share your ideals and hopeful thoughts on how life could be improved. Encourage them to talk about their ideals, and frankly let them know when they have walked on your feelings. Tell them how that feels to you. They really do not know unless you confront them with it. Their matter-of-fact-ness can be annoying and you will need to let them know when they are being insensitive. They have an abstract sense of humor that is a true pleasure to share. Expect a fresh original point of view when you ask their opinion.

Moon in Pisces

Your Emotional Nature You are a deep feeling and very complex person. Your sensitive nature even absorbs the emotions of others, which can lead to confusion as you try to understand why you feel the way you do. With time, you begin to sort out your true feelings from others, and greater clarity comes to your emotional life. To do this, you need some time alone each day to identify the real you. You are impressionable and are very good at reading the significant personality and character traits of others, even those you have just met. Poetry, music, and art are natural channels for your emotional needs for expression. When you allow yourself to feel in the moment, you are sweet and responsive.

You are very compassionate, sympathetic, and understanding of others, and seek love in which you can be devotional. Your idealistic nature is easily disappointed when those close to you do not live up to your high expectations. The two Fish in the symbol for Pisces describes the two layers of your emotional needs. One fish is swimming on the surface interacting with others just as we all do. This part of your character needs involvement with others for fulfillment. The second fish is swimming in deeper waters known only to you and God. This part of you needs to go to the well within for fulfillment. Meditation, prayer, artistic involvement, and a mystical attunement with nature can provide for these needs. Think of the downward side of your cycles as the calling for you to turn your attention inward. Once you have accepted the depth of your emotional feelings and learned to harmonize with them, you help others get in touch with their deeper feelings as well.

Areas to Work On You are a tremendous source of comfort for others, as it is natural for you to be sympathetic. This is your gift. When you carry it too far and absorb the emotional burden of others, it is your test. This can make you a target for those who would take advantage of your inability to hurt others. Your Achilles heel is your susceptibility to feelings of guilt and self-pity. This can lead to the emotional martyr, always deferring your emotional needs to others. It seems as if you understand everyone and no one can understand you. This fosters various forms of self-denial and indulgences in self-pity until you learn to surrender gracefully to your emotional cycles. You are a naturally humble person, but you need to learn that humility does not call for self-denial. True humility is standing out of the way by trusting in the power of faith, allowing the divine to become successful through you.

Understanding Moon in Pisces in Others These deep feeling individuals are most often governed by their emotions. They will react to even the slightest emotional shift in your feelings toward them, so be aware that your nonverbal communications will be more loudly heard than your verbal ones.

They are naturally compassionate and have a knack for drawing out your deepest personal feelings. Move slowly with them, because much of who they are is hidden, and only time will bring it to the surface. They will respond to the purest and deepest spiritual connection from you. They are understanding and caring by nature and you can trust that any revelations that you care to share with them concerning your sensitivities will be handled in the gentlest of ways.

Moon in Pisces people enjoy the poetic, romantic approach. The imaginative, the magical, and the mystical holds their interest. Their emotional cycles may appear confusing to you, as they periodically need to go to a place inside themselves that words cannot convey. When you have their attention, there are none more sensitive and understanding, but there are times when they need to be alone to connect with the depths of their emotional character. Without quality alone time, they become overwhelmed by the worries and concerns of others. When you establish an emotional bond with these people, the reward is a truly caring and compassionate friendship.

MERCURY

Mind and Communication

AT THE SUN level of consciousness, you become aware of your identity and purpose as a separate, distinct personality. At the Moon level, you become aware of the cyclic pattern that reflects the many facets of your emotional character. Mercury acts as the messenger between the two, helping us make sense of our world with the capacity to think and communicate those thoughts.

In the astrological model of understanding relationships, Mercury represents your communication skills. It includes all that goes into making up the ideas and beliefs you wish to share with others, your ability to express yourself, and your listening and interactive skills. This chapter explores each of these facets of communication with exercises and examples for developing the many sides of Mercury's communication skills. Many of the exercises are necessarily basic by design and may appear totally obvious, but it is my experience that the simple truths are often the most profound.

The importance of good communication in relationships could never be overstated—it is the hub that connects every other aspect of the relationship together. It is that vital. Whether it be the expression of love, anger, or working out business agreements, communication is what allows you to interact with others. Some are born with a natural ability to interact with others, others have inhibitions. Success in all aspects of life is enhanced by your ability to communicate with others, and it is a skill everyone can improve upon.

Thinking and knowing your own thoughts is one thing, but effectively communicating those thoughts to others is another. We moderns pride ourselves in the high technology of a worldwide communication network with satellites, computers, television, radio, and telephones, allowing us to receive and transmit communications almost instantaneously to and from anywhere in the world. But still, Mercury's puzzle often remains an enigma for even the simplest types of communications within relationships. After sorting through the difficulties that arise over and over again with communication, it finally sinks in—what you think you have said, and what another person hears you say, are not always one and the same. That is the puzzle. The solution is in taking communication skills seriously, paying attention and working with the puzzle.

In all relationships, it is the quality of the communication that is unique and special, or not so special. To improve the quality of communication requires that you first contemplate the techniques you are currently using. This takes a great deal of honest self-analysis. Communication, in general, can be separated into several important skills that lead to quality interaction. The following sections are designed to help you understand and activate the Mercury level of consciousness.

Knowing Yourself

The individuation process of becoming separate and distinct from all others involves knowing who you are. This requires that you learn to speak out for yourself, pull away from the mainstream of thought, and speak from personal experience instead of repeating what others have said. Each and every encounter you have is an opportunity to delve a little deeper into the hidden recesses of the self, an opportunity to confront how you really think, as opposed to how you think you should think. Eventually, you rely on yourself, more and more, and stop needing others to support your ideas. Imagine the benefits of being so secure in your self-awareness that you never feel threatened or intimidated by opposing or differing thoughts of others. Imagine the freedom! That is the goal.

In order to be a good communicator it is important that you know how you stand and what your beliefs are concerning the important issues in your life. It is the big killer to a conversation when someone asks your thoughts about a given topic and you respond, "I don't know." This first exercise is designed to help you develop a stronger self-awareness.

Exercise

Start a journal of your thoughts, attitudes, and beliefs about the various aspects of your life.

1. Pick a time of the day you can be assured of twenty minutes of uninterrupted solitude. Affirm to yourself that communication with your journal is your opportunity to pull hidden parts of yourself up to the surface. Vow not to hold anything back. Your writing is not for public viewing and will be like talking to a most private and special friend, so you can be as personal and intimate as you choose. Get to know yourself through your journal.
2. Use this as a session for communicating with yourself—carry on dialogues, ask and answer questions. You will quickly learn to communicate with the many parts of your self. With time, you may wish to divide your journal into various areas of interest: dreams, goals, relationships, philosophy, fears, and magical experiences. Most of all, your journal writing should be fun.
3. Periodically, read your journal. Get to know the person who wrote it (you). This is the stuff that individuality is made of. The truths and the inconsistencies are the total package of you. Read without judgment, and you will grow faster in your love and acceptance of yourself.
4. Sometimes there are no words to express how you feel, and at these times, try drawing a picture. Notice the colors that you choose to work with, and above all, don't judge your work. Just let what is on the inside come to the outside. This is an exercise of getting to know who you are, and the nonverbal has just as much need for expression as the verbal.

As you get to know yourself, learn to distinguish the difference between your preferences and your judgments. Preferences are statements of your individuality and reflect your taste. Judgments are psychological resistances and are felt much stronger. Knowing your preferences enhances your communication skills, while expressing your judgments blocks the free flow of information.

You can always identify a judgment by its accompanying psychological reaction. If you simply do not like the way another person is behaving, that is a statement of your preference. But, if you find another person's behavior intolerable to the point that it upsets you, that is a judgment. It is beneficial to ask yourself: "Why am I experiencing such a strong reaction?" "What is being triggered within myself?" If you are willing to answer yourself honestly, you will always find something you needed to learn about that behavior. Preferences are flexible, changeable, reflecting the changes in you. Judgments are harsh and unmoving, and resist change. No new information can get past them. Consequently, no growth will occur.

A good exercise to deepen your awareness of your preferences and judgments would be to write a page pertaining to each in your journal. Think about the things you like and dislike and then try to ascertain the strength of its psychological impact on you. From your analysis of your various likes and dislikes, you would either put them on the "preference" list or the "judgment" list. It would be interesting to look at the judgment list and see if it couldn't really be called your "need to work on self" list.

The Buddha said, "You are what you think, having become what you once thought." With this in mind, a great tool for any of us might be a computer printout delivered at the end of each week, with all thoughts tallied and ranked by category of what was most thought about during the previous week. It would be startling for most! It would be an even greater tool if that computer printout was available for all to read at the library! Then we would start taking more responsibility for what we think! We do not have that tool yet, but we do have the ability to monitor our thoughts and ask ourselves periodically throughout the day, "Is this really what I choose to think about?"

Everyone has a mind and the capacity to think. What we choose to think about, however, is a matter of individual choice. I like to say it this way: "Your capacity to think is God's gift to you—what you choose to think about is your gift to God."

Expressing Self

Communication is the art of sharing information—"I'll show you mine if you show me yours." If you want more intimacy in your relationships, then be willing to take the first step by expressing yourself. Sometimes this is frightening, as you will not always know how your ideas will be received. Be proud of the information you have to share and be equally secure about any ignorance you may have on a certain topic. You do not have to know everything to be a good communicator, although the bottom line here is self-knowledge, so you must be aware of what you do and do not know. Confidence that your perceptions are, at the very least, valid to you is also necessary. Next, you throw them out for others to examine and they will either support your ideas or reject them. That is what communication is all about.

The ego will typically present reasons for not being totally honest in expressing yourself. These rationalizations are the outcome of a fear of being rejected. Be brutally honest with yourself, and examine all the reasons you come up with for not expressing your truth. Assume any reason is probably a false, limited perspective, and not worth the sacrifice of your truth. The ego is tricky, however. It will manufacture all kinds of benevolent reasons for protecting "others" from the truth. People involved with relationship difficulties often express a fear of telling their mates exactly what is going on inside of them, and furnish a variety of rationalizations. "But he would be destroyed if he knew how I really feel." This kind of reasoning constructs barriers and initiates the beginning of the communication gap.

At this stage, isolation enters the picture, you start feeling bad when you are together, and inhibitions rise. But who is at fault? Is your partner really keeping you from saying what is on your mind, or is it your fear of what others might think of you? By "saving" your partner from what is really going on inside of you, you are responsible for holding the relationship back from its ultimate growth. No two people grow at the exact same rate, and you both have to take turns being the one to instigate growth. Being willing to speak your truth is the beginning point.

Listening Skills

Ranking right up near the top in learning to be a good communicator is knowing how to listen effectively. This is just as important as knowing your own thoughts. There are two types of listening: passive, simply listening and absorbing the information; and active, entering into the dialogue by both listening and interacting. This next exercise is aimed at developing your passive listening skills.

Exercise

The next time you are conversing with someone, practice totally letting go of your thoughts. Listen attentively with an absorbing mind. What is being communicated to you? How does this person feel about his or her communication?

With this exercise you want to allow yourself to be imprinted with the information being shared. Not thinking of how you feel about what is being said and not simply waiting to share your thoughts, you are just listening. This is passive listening. Your friend is transferring information to you, and your job is to receive it. You do not have to comment on it or judge it. You only have to receive it. It might be helpful for you to picture yourself as standing in the speaker's shoes to assist you in gaining absolute empathy for his point of view. At the end of the communication you should know what he knows. Do you?

The Art of Interviewing

Passive listening is simply not interrupting. It's a one-way street of allowing the ideas of another person to be expressed before you jump in and share your ideas. It is not true communicating, which always implies interaction. To be listening and interacting simultaneously is the art of interviewing.

A skilled interviewer not only draws out the other person's thoughts on any given topic, but also sharpens the conversation by asking incisive questions. It is fun to be asked questions about yourself by a person who is really listening. When you assume you know what others think or feel about a topic and thus do not bother to ask their opinion with great attentiveness, you have missed an opportunity for growth in the relationship. This kind of "type-casting" is the first rung of the ladder of feeling isolated from your mate. Think about the people you enjoy spending time with and notice, do they "type-cast" you, or are they truly interested in your current thoughts?

Wouldn't it be nice to clearly know what your friend thinks about a certain topic? The following exercises will help you develop this talent.

Exercise

Set up an appointment with a friend to conduct an interview.

1. It might sound corny, but the skills you develop as an interviewer are directly transferable to improving your skills at drawing out others in all relationships. Let your friend know what you are up to. Tell her you would like to sharpen your interviewing skills by asking her opinion on some topic of interest. Most people would be flattered by this invitation, so you will not have trouble finding a willing partner.
2. Create an atmosphere of openness and trust. Remember, your friend will be cautious about sharing true thoughts, as we all are until we feel it is safe. You can tell your friend you will be open to her true perceptions, but ask her to inform you when you miss the point or stray from the clarity of her communication. Make your first intention that of responding to her inner truths. This is not the time for you to express your opinions on her thoughts.
3. Maintain your role throughout the interview. Your friend has some thoughts, ideas, and opinions on a topic, and it is your task is to find out what they are. Draw your friend out by asking lots of questions. Get involved with her thinking process and extend yourself to understand as much as you possibly can.

Developing your talents as an interviewer is one the primary keys to the enhancement of more satisfying relationships. The more you practice, the better you will become at entering the world of other people's thoughts. The age-old axiom of each man being an island unto himself is quite true, but bridges can be made to span the gap.

Open-mindedness

Being open-minded is one of those great concepts that most would subscribe to, but few achieve. There exists in all of us a natural tendency to screen information that is not consistent with our belief systems, thereby initiating defensive reactions. Psychologists call this "selective reinforcement." It is easy to hear information that is consistent with your beliefs and difficult to hear information that is not. The psychological reaction most people go through when confronted with opposing points of view is not conscious; it is a reaction that operates with or without your permission and absolutely deters open-mindedness. You can train yourself to avoid this reaction, but it takes work.

The defensive reaction has a functional value during the early developmental stages of youth, as it protects the immature mental structure from having to incorporate too many divergent thoughts. But with maturity, the mind becomes strong and develops the cohesiveness of individuality, making it possible to listen to opposing points of view without worry of these ideas becoming your ideas. Once this strength is accomplished, there is a noticeable hunger for other ideas. It is unfortunate, however, that the defensive habits of the past may linger into adulthood, and can surface whenever you feel challenged. This defensiveness blocks the free flow of ideas and will be felt as closed-minded by others.

The following exercise is designed to help you track down, identify, and overcome your defensive reactions.

Exercise

At least once a week, read information that is exactly opposite of what you believe to be true.

1. This exercise challenges your defensiveness by seeking it out, tracking it down, and confronting it face-to-face. It is not hard to find points of view that differ radically from yours, and the stronger your reaction against the person or writing, the better it is for this exercise. These might include issues such as abortion, capital punishment, or political viewpoints, and can be found in magazines, newspaper editorials, and in books.

2. While you are confronting yourself with this information, take note of your reactions and feelings. What is happening? Watch the process that your mind is going through. Remain in the role of the detached observer while simultaneously surrendering to your reactions. You do not want to change the reactions at this point, so simply watch the process of rejecting the information, discounting it and believing it to be false. This firsthand glimpse of your defensiveness at work is the same psychological reaction that prevents people from being open-minded.

3. Once you have the ability to recognize your defensiveness, you can start to overcome it. Breathe deeply and tell your mind you can see what it is doing. Let it know your thoughts are perfectly safe and there is absolutely no threat in allowing an open attitude concerning this different point of view.

4. Now, refocus on the information that triggered the alarm. Force yourself to entertain the challenging information. This time, try to understand its point of view by imagining how someone can think this way. Practice this exercise weekly until you have overcome the knee-jerk reaction.

This exercise shows you how strong the tendency is to screen information. It has also shown you this process can be overcome. But it is not magazines and newspapers you wish to improve your relationships with, it is people. Realize the defenses you have had to overcome exist in everyone else as well, and you will likely have to deal with the closed-mindedness of others at times. As you are able to become more open you can help others in dealing with close-mindedness. Although this concept is easy to grasp intellectually, its hard to put into action. The following exercise will help you in broadening your perceptions.

Exercise

With a partner, choose a book that has different front and back covers. Hold the book between the two of you so that one person sees only the front cover and the other person sees only the back cover. Now each of you describe exactly what you see.

1. Be honest as to your perceptions; describe only what you see with your eyes. Now, ask your partner to describe only what he sees with his eyes.

2. What is happening? It is just one book that you are describing, yet you are both seeing something very different. One of you can only see the front cover, and the other person only sees the back. Now stage a mock argument over the differing points of view. Try to convince the other person that what you are seeing is the only true perception available because it is what you are seeing. Ridiculous, isn't it?

3. Now enter into cooperative discussion with each other. Know that what you are seeing is correct. Know also that what your partner is seeing is correct. Both of you should be sharing your perspectives with total confidence. Though different, both are absolutely correct.

This exercise may seem obvious, but it is effective in teaching your subconscious that differing points of view are equally valid and offer yet another perspective on life, not a challenge. Remember this exercise the next time you get into an argument with another person. Of course there are differing points of view! The more you can accept that fact, the more open-minded you will become. There is a saying in the Eastern tradition of spirituality: this and that too. In your dealings with others, apply this same principle. Instead of "this or that," try the attitude "this, and that too."

Thoughts as Energy

Thoughts carry an energy with them. Communication is a medium of energy exchange between people, and when it proceeds freely, unimpeded by resistance, the exchange revitalizes both individuals. When there is resistance to the flow of communication, it is a double blitz on the energy field. First, there is no opportunity for being revitalized by the interaction with the other person's energy field, and second, energy is expended on the resistance itself. This is why some people get exhausted by working with the public and why others experience increased energy from the same interactions.

From this view, we all need each other's mental energy in order to activate greater levels of potentiality. Einstein and other great thinkers have approximated they had only actualized a small portion, 10 to 20 percent, of their mind's potential. Isn't that a rather haunting legacy? It makes you wonder what portion of the mind's potential the rest of us are using? It does provoke questions: "What is the purpose of the other 80 percent of the mind?" "Are we in some form of regressive evolution in that we are losing more and more of the mind's capacity?" "Or, have we simply not learned how to actualize the rest of the mind as yet?"

Our individual energy fields are only able to generate enough energy to animate a small portion of the mind's potential. By interacting with the thoughts and ideas of others in a nonresistant way, you open up to the expanded energy, and doors opening to the unexplored 80 percent of mind begin to open too.

The t'ai chi of daily living is learning how to have an open mind all day long, which allows for the removal of needless resistance and facilitates merging with the ideas of others.

Mercury Through the Signs

Mercury's sign at your birth represents how your mind tends to operate—how you gather information, analyze it, and make it useful in your life. It shows how you learn best, and indicates your tendencies in communication. Topics that relate to the sign of your Mercury will be natural strengths for you, and can hold the greatest interest for you. Remember, you can work with your Mercury—if you do not like some its characteristics, you can use your will to compensate for your tendencies so that you might better understand differing views.

Mercury in Aries

YOUR MENTAL MAKE-UP The Mercury in Aries mind is bright, enthusiastic, and impulsive. You prefer to trust your first impressions rather than labor through decisions. Yours is an adventurous type of mind that enjoys challenging conversation and thought. One of the secrets of your mental vitality is momentum. When you are on a roll and involved in situations that require you to think on your feet and trust your instincts, you are at your best. Your attention with specific topics is typically short-lived, as there is a continual craving for new mental interests. You may leave projects half-finished, as your mind is directed towards new experiences. Your staying power increases as you work on changing the flamethrower of Aries intensity into a laser light of steadfast consciousness.

Your great strength in relationships is your zest for adventure. Your enthusiasm provides a spark and serves as a catalyst for growth and exploring new avenues of mental interest. You need a very active, spontaneous relationship to hold your interest. Being around you and your ideas is exciting and fun. You are a "can-do" type of person and you definitely have the ability to motivate and inspire others to push beyond their limits. It is actually quite difficult for you to be around the whimpering type of person who moans, "I don't think I can do that." You are the idealist when you are at your best, and hope is something that you offer others. You are typically very good at expressing your anger—almost too good—although you are equally quick to forgive and forget and to leave the past behind.

Areas to Work On To some, your directness and impulsiveness can seem pushy. Mercury in Aries is notorious for jumping to conclusions before all of the needed information is in. What you need to develop to complement your impulsiveness is patience and diplomacy. In the general skills section on Mercury, you need to pay particular close attention to the listening section. Listening to others with an ability to truly understand their perspective is not your forte, but it is a skill that you can develop.

Since you tend to speak on impulse, you will likely experience "foot in mouth" disease—Aries will invariably say the wrong thing at the wrong time. As with the other fire signs, Mercury here will require you to overcome your defensive tendencies to improve relationships. With practice you learn the art of social grace, learning to respond, rather than react, to the ideas of others. Then your fiery enthusiasm is experienced as inspirational instead of irritating.

Understanding Mercury in Aries in Others You will not be bored by these people! Their spontaneity with life can actually be quite refreshing. This same impulsiveness can also be exasperating, as these people will be forever seeking new avenues of expression and you might tire of this forever newness. Spontaneity is the key of this sign. Unbridled, this tendency leads to impulsiveness, but when tempered and directed, the energy leads to pure inspiration, the vital spark of life that animates action. That is one of the true benefits of relating to these individuals, their energy will invariably rub off on you.

The Mercury in Aries mind is like a spark plug and is likely to ignite whatever has been lying dormant and inactive in you. Sometimes you will like this catalytic action and sometimes it might feel too aggressive. They are more innocent with their words than it appears.

One of the characteristics of Mercury in Aries people is that they learn through primary, direct, personal experience. This means that they are not meant to listen to the advice of others, they really do have to go their own way. This is likely to seem excessively headstrong to you, but that is how these people's minds operate.

Mercury in Taurus

Your Mental Make-up You have a steady, thorough, practical mind that has tremendous endurance and holding power. Your value system is closely related to your mental processes and because of this, you are likely to express innate common sense. Your mind likes to deal with tangible, down-to-earth, practical matters and your need for security protects you from taking risks. Venus rules Taurus, and this influence softens, refines, and typically brings an interest in art, music, and good literature. There is a notable love of luxury and comfort, which can also bring a bit of mental laziness.

You make your best decisions while not in the presence of others. This gives you time to work with the ideas that you are considering. It is good for you to have the following rule of thumb concerning your business decisions or matters relating to your personal security: sleep on it. When you give your mind the time that it takes to go at its own natural pace, it will rarely fail you. Your strength lies in knowing yourself and then communicating this with great honesty and simplicity.

Areas to Work On You are meant to learn to rely on yourself, which leads to challenges in cooperation and in the making of agreements with others. One of your dilemmas is this: you are meant to be a strong-minded individual who knows what you value and what you like, so why compromise? This will come up as a real question in many of your dealings with others. Where your strength is your mental staying power, this same tenacity can lead to a resistance of new ideas. You do not like to compromise, and yet, in order to truly share with others, some give and take is required.

Mercury in Taurus gives you endurance, or you could call it coping abilities—you do not sway from your path easily. The advantages of this are obvious, you demonstrate a thoroughness in all you do. The disadvantages are not just the obvious stubbornness, but also the potential for missing the magic moment. There are times when you are just too set and practical to make needed changes, so you tend to endure hardships rather than change. After a few experiences of coping with situations far longer than was necessary, you begin to realize that it is wise to ask yourself, "Is it truly in my best interest to resist change, or am I only doing this because I always resist?"

Understanding Mercury in Taurus in Others The Mercury in Taurus mind is steeped in common sense, insists on thoroughness, and is resistant to change. These people will demonstrate all these qualities. Their communications are direct and to the point and they will appreciate this same quality in you. They give a great deal of thought to their security and all decisions that they make will get filtered through their current security system. You will grow to appreciate that when Mercury in Taurus individuals make an agreement with you, they will do all that is possible in order to fulfill that commitment. It is getting them to change when change is required that is the test.

You will learn quickly that you cannot get pushy in your dealings with these people. Force will never work when it comes to getting them to change their mind. It only makes things worse, as the Taurus Bull will just dig in a little deeper in the face of intimidation. Your best hope for persuading these people is to inform them of the practical reasons for a change that you wish to see, and then give them time to make their own decisions.

If you are ever feeling a little flighty and you need some down-to-earth practical assistance, talk to a Mercury in Taurus. When these people feel comfortable, even the tone and quality of their voice can be soothing and calming. The highest types of these individuals have a quality of genuineness, refreshing as a clear mountain stream.

Mercury in Gemini

Your Mental Make-up You are great fun to talk to. Versatile, witty, charming, and naturally communicative, this is a strong placement for inquisitive Mercury. Variety has to be a keynote in your life, as you tire of repetition and are exhilarated through lively exchange of new ideas. Your communication skills and breadth of interests keep you very current with information. You are a mental gymnast in your ability to leap from one idea to another with absolute agility. Emerson once said, "Consistency is the hobgoblin of little minds." It is probably a statement you would like to have said, as ideally, you would always give yourself the prerogative of change. Why stay with something that is no longer stimulating?

Your inquisitive nature leads to your greatest gift, a natural open-mindedness. Curiosity about how others think, as well as a naturally wide base of interest, makes you a very good conversationalist, if you can stay on track. Your mind is like a many branched tree, and the way that you learn is likely to reflect this. There are usually several open books that you are simultaneously reading, along with opened magazines and newspapers, all lying conveniently at hand in what other people might consider a mess, but you consider an information nest. You might feel guilty about not staying with one mental interest, but essentially that is not your role. Your great strength is connecting ideas together, so being a bit of a dilettante is appropriate.

Areas to Work On Your openness to the moment, when excessive and undisciplined, leads to a scattering of your mental energy. Your effectiveness in all aspects of life depends on how efficiently you change from one mental concern to another throughout your day. "Time lags" build up when you are not effective at closing one project before opening another. A time lag is created when you leave a project at an inappropriate point in its process. The next time you approach the project, it takes time to get back to where you left off. It is really appropriate for you to be doing several things at once, you have the kind of mind that thrives on this type of stimulation. The question is whether you are accomplishing your tasks or just chasing something new. If, even to you, your life seems chaotic, you need to practice the art of focusing. Stay focused on a particular project or idea until you feel progress, then go ahead and change your focus to another interest.

This mental curiosity of yours is going to be both an asset and a liability in relationships. On the one hand, you keep a relationship interesting with the addition of your current mental pursuits, which are ever changing. On the other hand, you can exhaust your listeners with your ramblings and your quick dropping of one form of mental fascination for another. Your breezy nature can drift into superficiality without mental discipline. You were born with adaptability. Add depth to your thinking and you will add wisdom to your knowledge.

Understanding Mercury in Gemini in Others Those with Mercury in Gemini are lively, witty, and open to new ideas. Conversation is often their forte, and if you do not have anything to say, they will have enough ideas for both of you! These people are informed on a wide variety of topics and they will find genuine interest in just about anything you have to offer. Connecting ideas, people, and situations together is their fascination and they often become walking resource directories. They like to have open, friendly conversations with many people, so you will have to curb any possessive tendencies you might harbor in dealing with these mental gymnasts.

One of your issues with these people is likely to center around reliability, as this placement leads to an easily distracted mind. Their words may "trick" you, and it would be wise for you to not accept any casual statements as deep truths. Sometimes they are "just talking." Their attention is as playful as a spring breeze, and as changeable. Give these people lots of room to change their mind, because they probably will.

Mercury in Cancer

YOUR MENTAL MAKE-UP Your great gift is your ability to connect with the personal lives of others—you care about people's feelings. A natural nurturer, you like to be helpful and the helping professions hold opportunity for your natural talents. Yours is a dreamy, highly subjective type of mind. Your feelings strongly influence your interactions with others as you communicate with two levels simultaneously—with words and with emotions. You are also excellent at reading other people's feelings behind the words they are expressing. Matters concerning the home, family, security, relationships, and the personal side of life are your forte, so, of course, these tend to dominate your conversations. Because of your highly sensitive nature, you have developed a noticeable knack of sidestepping issues that will confront your emotions.

Your mind tends to reflect upon past issues and, until you have some distance on situations, it is hard to make good decisions. You need the time it takes to know how you feel, and not just think, about important decisions. You have a very retentive mind and it is probably not true if you ever say, "I forgot." Money matters, along with all security issues, are prevalent in your thinking patterns and conversation. Usually a voracious reader, you are a good conversationalist about literature, favorite authors, or periods in history. You love simply reminiscing with friends and family.

AREAS TO WORK ON Thoughts and emotions can quite easily get mixed up for you. You learn through experience that it is not wise for you to make important decisions while you are emotionally charged—just know ahead of time that your emotions distort your perceptions. It is best to wait to make important decisions until you feel emotionally balanced. Your nurturing tendencies lead to a need to be needed and this can easily lead to codependent relationships. Need-based relationships are limited in their potential—wounded sensitivities become the dominate topic of communication and the nature of their bond. Be careful of those who say, "You are the only one who can help me." This is an unhealthy attitude for anyone and giving in to it continues to foster the illusion.

The other area to work on deals with your defensiveness—the crab shell. It is so easy for you to take everything you hear personally, that it is difficult to maintain objectivity in your communications. Remember that this part of your character is malleable. Although you naturally will listen through your personal emotions—that's the way you are wired—you can compensate with your will. You can literally will yourself out of your personal feelings and pour your attention and your empathy into the other person. This allows you to feel where they are coming from. Now Cancer understands—when you feel the other's view. Call this empathetic listening. As you develop this skill, it does miracles for all your communications.

Understanding Mercury in Cancer in Others Mercury in the emotional sign of Cancer indicates thinking will be strongly influenced by current emotional issues. It is wise for you to take this into account in your interactions. It is first important to establish emotional rapport and trust before attempting other types of relating. Remember it is hard to fool Mercury in Cancer people—they have an ability to know how you feel, not just how you think, and they notice the slightest discrepancies.

These people will show an interest in the personal side of your life and once you have gained their trust, you will have gained a most caring friend indeed. They tend to take everything personally. Being naturally cautious and defensive, they are slow at opening up to new people and situations, but it is worth the wait. Talk about mutual friends, home, money, or dining experiences and you will slowly win over a Mercury in Cancer friend. The more history you have with these people the more they will trust you.

They have excellent minds and even better memories. Give them room for their emotional cycles, including some silent periods. Don't assume that something is wrong when they are not particularly verbal. Sometimes they just have nothing to say. Expect a "cautious first" approach to new ideas and plans.

Mercury in Leo

Your Mental Make-up One of your true resources in life is your personality itself—you have a knack for expressing yourself in such a way that makes anything more enjoyable. Your warm-hearted humor is ever present and invariably gets other people laughing. Yours is a warm, proud, and stubborn type of mind. Your mental strength is such that once you set your mind at something, there is very little that you cannot accomplish. You can be a lot of fun or overbearing, all depending on your ability to share the stage with others. Your mind is fueled by the ambition to creatively express yourself and you can function equally well in the arts, business, or education. The Leo "king of the jungle" syndrome also gives you natural leadership and managerial abilities. You are at your best when you involve yourself in activities into which you can pour your heart and mind. You are a straight-ahead communicator, with a distinct flair for the dramatic in your expression.

In relationships, your best decisions are made from the heart. Nothing else really works for you. You can bring out the fun in any situation and laughter from the heart is your greatest gift to share with others. You take pride in honesty in communication and you are quite insulted if anyone even questions your intention. Your thoughts on any topic are backed by a powerful will, thus it is almost impossible for anyone to coerce you into changing your opinions. You do need a partner that pays full attention to you, but you give as much as you demand.

Areas to Work On Your challenges in relationships are likely to stem from the traits of being too self-centered. When challenged by differing points of view, your pride is easily wounded and you tend to defend your position first. You may need to literally teach yourself to overcome your pride in order to gain empathy and understanding of other people's perspective. The communications you enjoy best are those that agree with your perspective. Not argumentative by nature, you simply discount people who have opposing viewpoints to yours! As you become secure within yourself you realize that you do not need to relinquish your point of view to understand another's and with this understanding, your defensiveness begins to drop away.

The natural sunny disposition of Leo can give way to stormy skies when you are not getting your way. You don't do "humble" real well—but life has its way of humbling all of us occasionally. You probably won't handle these periods gracefully, but they pass, and if you allow yourself to admit it, there was something to be learned from the experience. Don't let your pride stop you from growing from your life experiences.

Understanding Mercury in Leo in Others You will likely notice Mercury in Leo people right from the start, as they have a way of expressing themselves that attracts attention. You do not want to take these people lightly because they are as equally powerful foes as allies. They are fun to be with, when you stay on their good side. They tend to dominate, it's true, but there is something natural about their "take charge" attitude that makes this dominance seem appropriate. These individuals demand a great deal of attention—again, true—but they have just as much to give, so it is usually worth your investment.

Appeal to their sense of humor and you'll have your best chance for establishing a good rapport. They have very high moral standards and you will have to rise to your best to be on strong footing in their lives. With Leo, the quickest way to the mind is through their heart, and if you are willing, they can make any situation seem more fun. Favorite activities to share with these people are anything that is just for the enjoyment of the experience—sports, games, recreation, entertainment. All these are activities that bring out their best. They have playful minds that turn to fierce competitors when the desire to win at everything gets the best of them. Allow your Mercury in Leo friends to save face whenever they stumble—they hate public exposure of their mistakes.

Mercury in Virgo

Your Mental Make-up Yours is the conscientious, detail-oriented type of mind—you notice the small things that others overlook. Mercury in Virgo is a mind that tends towards the practical. Your analytical abilities are highly developed, leading to a very discriminating and discerning intelligence. You have a knack for simplifying issues and focusing on the relevant information in the moment. Virgo has a task-oriented view of life and you are at your best when you are being productive. When you do not feel useful, you tend to turn your critical eye inward and begin to worry about needless details. Your incisive wit is most often appreciated by those of an intellectual orientation.

Relationships in which you feel appreciated bring out your best, as you like to help. You can then be experienced as a most loving, attentive, and considerate partner. You typically do not enjoy psychological complexity in your communications and most appreciate those who are sincere.

Areas to Work On One trait that you will have to watch is the tendency to be overly critical. Virgo is called the sign of the perfectionist and thus, there is a tendency to see the flaws or imperfections in others, and then offer suggestions as to how to refine or improve. This is not always welcome advice. How you present your perceptions will have a great deal to do with how they are received. Are you being critical or informative? The different methods you have of sharing your views will make all the difference. Remember, criticism erodes and information builds.

You can get caught in cycles where it is hard to break free of worrying about needless details and insignificant matters. Your mind is going to be busy analyzing, evaluating, and considering—you need to decide on what. When you find yourself being overly worrisome and critical, it is a sure sign that you need another task into which you can pour your mental attentiveness. It can be a creative project, professional or self-improvement, but you are at your best when your mind is busy with constructive tasks. Otherwise it will drift towards petty concerns about your health and well-being and you will be stuck in the "paralysis via analysis" syndrome.

Understanding Mercury in Virgo in Others These people's minds are analytical, sharp, and crisp. Mercury in Virgo has the legendary eye for detail. These people like to be sure before they will boast of some talent, but if they agree to do something, be assured that they will put their best into it. One important thing to remember is that Mercury in Virgo people are not quite as critical or negative as they might sound. Their attention is drawn to the practical and realistic, and they often see the flaws in a plan or situation that others miss. They have a refined type of mind with a distinct distaste for the crude and rude.

Mercury in Virgo people are not known for making abstract jumps. They like to have all of the steps, down to the slightest detail, spelled out specifically. They like a clear plan of operation, so when you are presenting something new to them, have it worked out in your mind first. Be very patient and go through each of the steps in sequence, and you will have your best chance at success. Conversation dealing with the down-to-earth, practical aspects of life is often of interest to them. Their approach to new situations is cautious. If you are looking for support of a new idea or plan before all the bugs have been worked out, these are not the people to choose. If you are looking for practical insights into some of the details that you might have overlooked, there is no one better for you to talk with than a Mercury in Virgo friend.

Mercury in Libra

YOUR MENTAL MAKE-UP Yours is an adaptive, social type of mind that actually functions best in the presence of others. You will adapt to the level of intelligence that you associate with, so choose your friends and associates wisely. The opposite sign, Aries, projects self-awareness from a base of instincts. In Libra, the awareness of others enters into the picture and you focus a great deal on their values, thoughts and attitudes. You are learning about yourself through your social interactions. You have a need to weigh the alternatives before declaring your opinion. You have a theoretical type of mind that enjoys the mental gymnastics of, "But what if . . . ?" The scales of Libra also give you an innate sense of justice, balance, and fair play, making you a natural arbitrator and diplomat.

In relationships, you need to be with someone who is willing to talk over ideas and decisions together. You do not need others to make decisions for you, but you do like to consider their input. Your greatest natural skill as a communicator is that of the interviewer. You are like a mirror for others, ideally tilted in such a way that reflects the best of the other. Your social skills come not from knowing what you want to say, but rather from knowing how to ask great questions and be as a sounding board on which others can bounce off their ideas.

AREAS TO WORK ON Your lack of straightforward decision making gets in the way of building honest rapport. As a peacemaker, there are too many times that you settle for momentary peace at any cost, rather than deal with an unpleasant issue. That is a win-lose situation. In your agreements and dealing with others you are at your best when you settle for win-win situations that work out best for both parties. The one quality in the general skills section to which you must pay close attention is "knowing yourself." This could help offset your tendency to define yourself by others' opinions of you. When you overrespond to the expectations of others, you are not bringing your true self to the relationship. Ask yourself, "Are my agreements with others based on cooperation or compromise?" Be willing to stand up for your needs and interests as well as those of others. Then, and only then, can the balance that you seek be achieved.

Understanding Mercury in Libra in Others These people are the natural diplomats of the zodiac. They prefer to cooperate rather than make an independent stand, so they are very enjoyable to spend time with. When you talk with them, you will get the feeling they really are interested in your thoughts and opinions. Their keen sense of fairness makes them very trusted individuals. They will often wait for your lead, and then adapt to your position. Manners and social grace are important to these people. Mercury in Libra individuals have a keen appreciation for the elegant and eloquent in life. Relating to them will likely bring out the refined in you. They believe that any issue can be worked out in a rational, calm way and strongly resist emotionally unpleasant communications. Literature, the arts, theater, music, or the other people in their life, are typical favorite topics of discussion.

It is hard for these people to make an independent stand, and this might be frustrating for you. It is also hard for them to make decisions by themselves, they really want your opinion and even approval before acting on important matters. They truly would rather share responsibility for important decisions rather than go it alone. These people are in a constant state of evaluating the various alternatives in their life. When they are caught in the "indecision blues" by the endless teeter-tottering back and forth of trying to balance other people's expectations of them, they are at their worst. This is when they need to be helped by asking them what is important to them. When encouraged to share their ideas, they will, in a most creative way.

Mercury in Scorpio

Your Mental Make-up Yours is a deep, intense, and penetrating type of mind. You suffer no fools, as you always seem to know what is going on beneath the surface with whomever you are interacting. No one can really deceive you, as your instincts sense the motivations of others. Part of this is due to instincts and part is due to extremely acute perception. Not much passes your eye. Yours is the mind that goes to the essence of the matter. You have a powerful way with words, which either pushes people away from you or magnetically draws them closer. You do need some privacy and even a few secrets—it's part of the mystery of life that you so dearly love.

Silent emotional communication is a talent that is your trademark. Some may say that you are not expressive of your emotions because you do not always verbalize them, but in your silence, others get the message. The communication is effective. You can help others become more aware of their silent messages as well by gently revealing your perceptions as to what is going on with them. There will be many times when you understand others more than they do themselves, and tact is necessary to effectively share such awareness. You need to sink your teeth into a few psychologically complex situations in life. Anything too simple and direct will ultimately bore you.

Areas to Work On Your tendency to hold on to old issues is the key here. The memory of old hurts and wrongdoings can have such a hold on you that it prevents you from being fully open to present opportunities. Forgiveness of the past, for yourself and others, is necessary; otherwise, the Scorpio attitude of "never forgive, never forget" can take over. You have a sharp, cutting wit with a talent for sarcastic humor, but this can go too far into a cynical attitude. That is when others can feel stung by your remarks. Mercury in Scorpio is drawn to the shadows. Your love of mystery and intrigue can inhibit the sharing of life's simple pleasures with others. Give your mind a creative outlet for your love of mystery and what is going on beneath the surface. Study psychology, the occult, or mysticism as an outlet for this part of your character and you will find that your dealings with others will become more direct.

Understanding Mercury in Scorpio in Others Still waters run deep and the currents of thought going on within a Mercury in Scorpio person are likely to be much stronger than they appear on the surface. These people are extremely insightful and are rarely fooled by appearances. There is something mysterious about them, and they like it that way. It is both very difficult to hide anything from these people and equally difficult for you to find out something that they do not want you to know. It's all part of the mystery. The intensity of this placement makes these individuals formidable as either allies or foes.

Those with Mercury in Scorpio can be shrewd in business dealings and often have investment plans for joint resources. In any way they choose to engage their mental resources, you will see a steel trap of a mind that goes right to the important issues. They are not prudish and do not necessarily enjoy niceties. It would not be unusual for them to incorporate sexual imagery into their discussions.

This type of mind has a need to uncover the facts, see people for who they are, and see a situation exactly as it is.

Scorpio is one of the hardest signs of the zodiac to pinpoint because its range of expression, from the highest to the lowest, is tremendous. On the downside is the Mercury in Scorpio person who has not yet learned to let go of the past. This leads to a suspicious mental outlook and constant emotional entanglements with others. At worst it can lead to the revengeful type of mind that plots methods of getting even. On the other end of the continuum is the shrewdness and analytical nature of mind that, when applied in positive ways, can lead to tremendous insight. Research, depth psychology, money management, and even mysticism are areas of potential interest.

Mercury in Sagittarius

Your Mental Make-up With Mercury in Sagittarius you are the eternal optimist, a forward-thinking person whose sense of humor and openness can go a long way toward overcoming your inability to tend to details. This is the adventurer mind that gravitates toward travel, education, philosophy, travel, religion, politics, and travel. You are able to frame most anything in a positive light and your enthusiasm can be infectious. A natural teacher, you love to share your ideas with others, and feel compelled to help others move beyond their biases, prejudices, and narrow points of view. Therefore, it is your responsibility to first expand your own mind and make sure that you are not being narrow or dogmatic.

In relationships, you are the truth seeker. You prefer blunt, open, and direct dealings, rather than beating around the bush with subtleties. It would be wise for you to include at least a few very down-to-earth friends in your circle to balance your enthusiasm with some practical perspective. You don't deal with "down" very well and like to be with others who match your sunny disposition. You need to be appreciated for your dreams and goals—they are an important part of who you are. Sagittarius without a dream is the soup without the spice.

Areas to Work On Excessiveness, in all of its many guises, is the source of most of your difficulties with others. You tend to promise the Moon and say yes to just about anything, assuming there will be time and energy for it. Your intentions are always sincere, but a tendency to promise too much can become a problem for people who depend on your follow-through. This is the placement of the storyteller. In creative endeavors, this is indeed a gift, but it might also make it difficult for you to stick to the facts without exaggerating. Impatience is another issue that is likely to come up in your relationships. Your sense of time is not quite the same as others—you want everything to happen right now. You will push and prod, but ultimately, it is not other people's sense of time that will adjust. It is you learning to be patient with others, that will bring more harmony into your relationships.

There is not just one arrow in the quiver of the Centaur Sagittarian. Consequently, you are likely to get spread very thin when you pursue too many interests simultaneously. When you learn to shoot one arrow, track it down and then shoot it again until it reaches its goal, your effectiveness improves considerably. As with all the fire signs, you may need to improve your listening skills. Fire is quick to react, but did you really hear what the other person said?

Understanding Mercury in Sagittarius in Others At best, this placement leads to inspirational, idealistic individuals who genuinely desire to see things in a positive light. If you ever need a pick-me-up, a shot of enthusiasm, these are people to seek out. On the down side, their communication focuses on the hypothetical, the potential, and the ideal of situations, without much compassion for everyday reality. They need a goal and a dream to pursue and will want to share their enthusiasm with you. At best, this can ignite the positive in you, and you can find your relationship with this person inspirational. At worst, you can find this mind unyielding and intolerant of anything other than the positive.

Favorite topics for these people are philosophical, religious, political, and abstract issues. The Higher Mind is a type of sport for them and they can love a good challenge or debate. They enjoy it, but sometimes do not realize how, in the heat of competition, they become aggressive, assertive, and even insensitive to your point of view. The intentions of individuals with Mercury in Sagittarius are most often honorable, but they are likely to promise more than they can actually deliver. They can be very convincing, even to the point of persuasive, so keep your wits about you. They will always attempt to convince you that right now is the best time to make a decision.

Mercury in Capricorn

Your Mental Make-up With a serious, ambitious mind, you typically need a major project to give your organizing capabilities room to operate. Your mind tends towards the practical application and utility of ideas. If you can not see the practical worth of information, you will not bother taking the time to learn it. With a busy and productive mind, you lean towards task-oriented mental activities. You have a special sensitivity for the organization of ideas and how they fit together as a system. You have the natural authority type of mind and people usually respond to you as if you know what you are talking about. You are the natural boss, or bossy, as the case may be. You always appear to know what is going on and to be in control. There are some areas of life where this tendency is an attribute, such as professional pursuits, but there are other areas, such as personal relationships, where this same tendency becomes a detriment.

In relationships, commitment, loyalty, and respect are musts. You have very high standards and you expect others to be as accountable for their actions as you are with yours. Irresponsibility is something that you can not tolerate in others. You have good ideas that can be helpful in organizing other's lives to make them more productive. Your frustration with others comes in their failure to recognize what is so obvious to you. This is actually where you came to be a teacher, so don't begrudge them allowing you to do your work. You require a relationship that demonstrates a respect for each other's career ambitions. You are willing to work patiently toward your goals and would benefit by a relationship that jointly worked at building success and security from the ground up.

Areas to Work On You can be excessively serious and are likely to catch yourself with a knitted brow more often than you would like to believe. This comes from being overly task oriented and forgetting all about your other needs to enjoy life. It is good for you to be around lighthearted people who remind you not to take life so seriously. At worst, you become more sensitive to a system of operation than to the people involved with it. Be mindful of that. Try not to take your tasks so seriously that you alienate those with whom you are emotionally involved. They count too. When you are sensitive to other's needs and sensitive to the needs of the task at hand, then the leader comes out in you.

The other area to work on deals with your susceptibility to the conventions of your time. You can overly respond to the expectations of others until you learn to define your own goals. You will be successful, you will climb mountains, but are they your mountains?

Understanding Mercury in Capricorn in Others You will grow to appreciate the responsibility and follow-though of your Mercury in Capricorn friends. If they say they are going to do something for you, bank on it. Their inner commitment to following through on agreements is something in which they take pride. Make sure you are prompt in your appointments with these individuals. Time is a resource and Capricorn is not one to waste it, nor do these people appreciate time wasted by tardiness in others. If you ever need a practical perspective and want help getting organized, a Mercury in Capricorn friend is the person to talk to.

Approval is more important to them than is likely apparent. They always seem strong and in control, but they have just as many insecurities as the rest of us. Sincerity, loyalty, commitment, honor, integrity, excellence, accountability—these are all big themes with Mercury in Capricorn people. They tend to be task oriented and rely on others in their life to come up with fun plans. Don't expect snap decisions with these people, they like to consider all plans thoroughly before making a decision. But once the decision is made, count on it. These serious-minded individuals much prefer quality to frivolity—take them to the symphony, a play, or a lecture, rather than out drinking and dancing.

Mercury in Aquarius

Your Mental Make-up Mercury is very strongly placed in Aquarius and your intellect is likely to be a dominant aspect of your personality. You pride yourself in your independent thinking and have likely created a unique worldview. You are not as prone to following conventions as others and definitely resist following orders or stupid rules. Your mind is anything but conventional and your perspective can often be shocking to others because of this. You seem to function as a messenger, or an alarm clock, helping others wake up from their slumbers. A bit of a futurist, you are open to considering alternative points of view and yet must get used to "delayed gratification." Since your ideas are not common, others likely resist some of your ideas in the moment and then later express appreciation. Sometimes aloof and detached, your mind likes to soar above the issues at hand and see things in a larger perspective. That is what you offer ideally—the big picture. Your mind is backed up by a powerful will and you will not be intimidated. This resistance serves you well when it is appropriate to hold your ground, and it will get in the way when the situation requires flexibility.

Aquarius is either the rebel, the revolutionary, or the reformer, but never the conformer. As the rebel, you enjoy being the pot stirrer that resists the status quo. As the revolutionary, social activism can be your form of expression. As the reformer, you get involved in a humanitarian cause or higher purpose. When you have found a way to serve others with the use of your often brilliant mind, you are at your best. Friendships are your natural strength and you would want this quality to be in all of your relationships, whether they be professional or personal.

Areas to Work On Your independent mind might have a difficult time cooperating with others and you might even periodically be the nonconformist just to demonstrate your right to be free from social convention. As you become secure with your uniqueness as your birthright, you no longer need to fight for your right to be free—you simply accept and express it. Your role changes from being the rebel to becoming the reformer.

The key phrase for Aquarius is "I Know," and if you really listened you would probably be surprised just how many times you use those very words. And most often, you truly do know, but still you have to be careful of the "know-it-all" attitude that most find offensive. The difficulty is that your lightning-quick mind actually does process information at a much faster pace than others. What do you do in the meantime, while your mind has already seen the whole picture, and the person who is talking to you is still laboriously drawing out the point? You will have to slow down your mind and be patient with others in order to enhance your communication skills.

Understanding Mercury in Aquarius in Others You will have to keep on your toes to stay in touch with these fast-thinking individuals. These people have a very strong mind and it is likely to influence your relationship with them. Expect them to offer a unique and original point of view on any topic. Progressive ideas, self-actualization, science fiction, topics that stretch the mind, social concern—all are topics likely to interest your Mercury in Aquarius friends. They typically get frustrated with slow, labored speaking, so you might want to pick up the pace a bit in talking to these people.

Expect the unexpected from them as their minds resist social conventions. When you want a unique perspective, or are seeking information as to how to make changes in your life, these are the people to seek out. If you want someone to understand your personal emotional needs, don't count on them—they typically like to rise above the personal to attempt to see things in a larger, universal perspective. That is well and good, but sometimes this perspective can seem cold and impersonal. Give these people the freedom to fulfill their responsibilities in their own way. They do not work well with someone looking right over their shoulder and having specific expectations of them.

Mercury in Pisces

YOUR MENTAL MAKE-UP Yours is a dreamy poetic, highly sensitive type of mind. Your mind is creative and feeling oriented, rather than logical. Your imagination is tremendous, and, when harnessed through creative expression or spiritual development, brings out the best in you. Compassion is the way for you, for you listen to stories that irritate others, always having an ear for those who are not heard elsewhere. This gives you a special sensitivity for the disadvantaged and downhearted. You are highly impressionable and this is certain to play a role in your relationships. Your mind and thoughts are influenced by the emotional climate that surrounds you, and it is definitely to your advantage to know this. You are so sympathetic to others that you risk losing yourself, unless you also allow for quality alone time to connect with the innermost you.

There are two Fish in Pisces: one swimming on the surface, interacting with the rest of us; and the other swimming in deeper, inner, spiritual waters. With your Mercury in Pisces, you will have to tend to both aspects of your character. You need some time alone to involve yourself with the inner world of personal feelings, daydreams, and rapport with the divine—a time for quality introspection. Meditation would be great for you. When you have developed this inner connection, you are able to help others find the meaning of what is going on in their lives as well.

Areas to Work On It is not easy for your mind to stand up and defend yourself, as Pisces has a definite tendency to yield to pressure. At most you are accommodating; at worst, self-sacrificing. Humility is natural for you, but all too easily leads to self-denial. The feelings connected to self-pity do get you in touch with your inner world, but there is pain associated with this approach. It works, but it hurts. As you develop the discipline of quality time with the inner world through creativity or spirituality, you satisfy the need to feel in a healthy way.

Pisces is an emotional sign and your mental perceptions will be influenced by your current feelings. This can lead to confused or inspired thinking, all depending on your ability to compensate for the emotional influence. This requires you to transcend your immediate experience—to be in the world, but not of the world. As you develop this discipline, you add depth to your thinking. Remember to keep your life simple. When you start getting overinvolved in the problems and concerns of others, you get lost in a sea of emotions that aren't yours.

Understanding Mercury in Pisces in Others When you want to be heard and understood in a compassionate and caring way, these are the people to seek out. They might not always have great practical advice for you, but they do have an unending amount of acceptance and openness. These are people to whom you can tell your stories, even your problems. They are great listeners. The highest types demonstrate compassion and understanding, and add depth to any discussion. Realize that they are responding just as much to your feelings as to what you are saying. There's no sense in trying to hide your feelings. But you can feel safe in the revelation of your feelings, as acceptance is the way with these people.

There are times when Mercury in Pisces people seem to be lost in a dream world. They are. Remember, if you have something important to say, draw their attention to it first. Do not assume that just because they are nodding their heads in agreement, they are really listening. Sometimes it is difficult for these complex individuals to separate thoughts and feelings, as the mind and emotions are linked together. At times confused, at times compassionate and wise beyond comparison, and always kind, these sensitive souls appreciate gentleness in their interactions with others. Their ability to respond to the silent message of what is going on beneath the surface can help you connect to your deeper feelings concerning any topic.

VENUS

Magnetism, Sexuality, and Intimacy

A YOUNG BOY AND girl were walking home from school one day. The boy, being at an age where he was interested in impressing the girl, says to her, "I have a new puppy at my house. Would you like to come over?" She responds, "No thanks, I just got a new pony, and I want to go ride her." Undaunted, the boy continued his efforts, "Well, I also just got a new bicycle, maybe you can come over later, and I'll let you ride it." Unimpressed, she replies, "No thanks, I just got a new four-wheeler motorbike, and I'll be riding that." Finally, out of frustration, the boy pulls down his pants and says, "Well, I know you don't have one of these!" As nonchalantly as ever, the girl then pulled down her pants and said, "Yes, but with one of these, I can get all of those I want!"

Although obviously not in its highest manifestation, this joke illustrates the law of attraction—Venus. This chapter explores what it is you can do to enhance your ability to attract people, situations, and resources into your life, and how to receive greater enjoyment from them once you do.

Venus relates to your values concerning love, pleasure, relationships, art, and the enjoyment of life. The range of expression goes from the base to the refined. At the physical level, Venus first focuses on experiences in the sensory, material world and seeks that which delights the senses. This seeking of pleasure is satisfied only when one has learned the art of appreciation of enjoyment, for experience without appreciation keeps the elusive goal of satisfaction just out of reach on an ever-expanding search for sensory gratification.

The sexual revolution and the feminine revolution have evolved and merged into a revolution of the understanding of love. In the patriarchal, "It's a man's world" culture from which we are emerging, possessive love was the dominant theme. Love was thought somehow finite. You had a set amount, and if you gave it away elsewhere, there would be less available for your mate. All jealousy comes from this belief—there isn't enough love to go around. In contrast to this, is the process of the feminine heart—the more you love, the more your capacity for love grows.

Mothers have always known this. When you have one child and your heart is just filled to the brim with love, do you have to divide your love to make room for another child? Certainly not. Your capacity for love grows, and you are able to love both children fully. As this truth is recognized, the status quo of relationships will be shaken. A new model for sharing with others is emerging with a theme of "monogamous of body and polygamous of spirit."

Venus represents your capacity to enjoy experiences and attract needed resources, opportunities, and people into your life. The following is an exercise in cultivating your ability to appreciate your experiences, thus adding to your ability to attract abundance into your life.

Exercise

Focus on the sensation of enjoyment for at least five minutes every day.

With this exercise you shift your focus from the experience at hand to your appreciation of the experience by focusing on the emotional feelings of enjoyment in their own right. This directly activates your Venus, and can be done in a variety of ways. While you are eating something you enjoy, close your eyes for a few moments. Notice, first of all, that it tastes good. Now let your focus shift from the sensory delight to the appreciation of the feeling of enjoyment itself. Do the same while listening to a favorite piece of music, looking at a beautiful sight, or hugging a friend. All of these provide opportunities to experience enjoyment and appreciation to the fullest extent.

When my wife read about this exercise, her comment was, "Often, I just stop for a moment in a day and realize 'I am happy,' a spontaneous acknowledgment in the moment, and I am thankful." Instead of purposefully setting aside five minutes for this, she has integrated this into her awareness throughout the day.

Each time you complete the search for pleasure with the awareness of the pleasurable feeling, you complete the circle of experience to appreciation and send this tone of energy into the world. This activates your magnetism and attracts more of that which you truly enjoy. It seems almost too easy to be true, but give it a try and see if it doesn't bring more enjoyment into your life.

Exploring Your Magnetism

To explore your sexual magnetism, represented by Venus, you must first have an understanding of magnetism itself. As we know from observing a magnet, polarity both attracts and repels. White/black, male/female, day/night, good/bad, yin/yang, positive/negative—each of these has magnetism through the polarity of opposition. Many a passionate love affair begins with intense attraction, but ends in total separation. What happens to the intense flames of the fire? If one does not learn how to balance and maintain the intense attraction, it will inevitably flip to repel and the relationship may end.

Your attitudes concerning sexuality strongly influence all aspects of your relationships, not just physical. First, know that you are magnetic—you are constantly attracting or repelling people and experiences to you. Venus is always operating at some level. The degree of conscious awareness you have of its operation will be the degree of control you have over the quality of these experiences. To become consciously aware of how your magnetism is currently operating, observe your life with detached awareness and note what you are currently attracting to you in all areas. And when you have attracted something to you, how receptive are you to the experience? Do you allow yourself to appreciate gifts, compliments, and assistance? Or do you dodge, deny, and deflect any attempts of others to give to you?

If you have difficulty receiving simple compliments, favors, and offers of assistance from others, consider the message that you are energetically giving out to the world—"I don't receive, I only give." What type of relationships will you attract to you? You know it—ones that are all giving on your part with not much coming back from the other. To remedy this, practice being gracious in receptivity.

Say thank you to the compliment and allow yourself to feel good about it. Allow return favors and offers of assistance graciously. Try the affirmation, "Joyously I give and joyously I receive."

Maintaining Magnetism

To live a life of sustained magnetic energy is quite a balancing act. The polarities have a stronger pull as your energy increases and it is easier to respond with extremist behavior. Think of being young and in the throes of a new passionate relationship—the highs and lows, the extremes. A reactionary person cannot handle the pull of the polarities and is bounced out of the relationship. To stabilize the extremes and yet stay in the energy is the balancing act, and as with any act of balancing, you must first find the center point. Are you in touch with your center? Go back to an activity with the Sun to regain your center.

To maintain a balance, there needs to be an equal amount of giving and receiving in order for you to be revitalized through your interactions, instead of feeling drained. This is the ultimate teaching of the Chinese yin and yang as energy complements.

This concept is illustrated in the example of two counselors I know. One sees three clients a day and is exhausted from giving, giving, and more giving. With each client, she is in control and believes these sessions rely solely on her giving and directing, exclusively. She is not aware of what she receives from her clients, and thus, there is no magnetism through these exchanges. If she is not talking and directing the sessions, she feels she has not given enough. This is not an energy exchange, it is a one-way street and the only way for her to replenish the loss of energy is through sleeping or some other form of complete rest.

Compare this to another counselor who sees between five and six clients a day, but is revitalized through a giving and receiving with each one. She feels there is something for her in the experience with every client she sees. She is there for them, but knows that she benefits and grows through her involvement with her clients as well, so there is give and take. Consequently, instead of being exhausted at the end of her sessions, she is revitalized. It is the interaction, the constant exchange, that allows her to benefit through synergy.

All who work with the public are aware of the feeling of being overwhelmed by the demands of others. But herein lies the answer: when you are only identifying with the giving, energy problems will arise. The polarity of magnetism is not working for you. The wise person understands this, melts resistance with acceptance, and finding the meaning in each encounter, is revitalized through the exchange. It's still the same situation, the same public, the same you, but with a shift in your attention, you have been revitalized, rather than drained. You still get tired at the end of the day, but not exhausted.

Energy Flirting

Sometimes the spark of energy needed to activate magnetism needs to be jump-started. I call this energy flirting, to distinguish it from the undesirable come-on. Playfulness is required to keep the spark of magnetism alive in a relationship. There are times in our life cycles, such as when we have two or three children under five-years old, that it might be more difficult to keep the energy of magnetism alive. But even then, it is still important to maintain playfulness in the relationship, or everyone starts taking things too seriously. It is the glad heart that keeps the fires of the romantic heart burning. Flirting is a way to keep the fun in a relationship, like tickling the other person's aura.

Flirting is a playful way of experimenting with your magnetism, yet it is often the root cause of many hurt feelings and potential arguments. There is great social pressure, especially if you are married, to avoid flirting. Let's get this straight from the start. There are healthy and unhealthy forms of flirting, the key being in your motives. You must always be clear in your intent, because other people are certainly going to question it!

To flirt means to risk. By definition, it is an experience of playful amorousness, a situation that mocks courtship. Flirting can be fun, but the danger in this type of relating is that it can lead to situations more intense than bargained for. There is a fine line (all too often crossed over) between playful acknowledgment of another and the undesirable come-on, an invitation to some greater sport. This seductive type of flirting always has an ulterior motive connected to it, but energy flirting has no such motive. Flirting for the sake of a playful enjoyment of the moment with another person, but not as a prelude to seduction, is what is being encouraged. It is an open expression of magnetism and a method of establishing nonsexual, yet magnetic, rapport with others.

Even when you are clear in your motivations, how do you respond when someone misinterprets your playfulness? Do you tend to get flustered and retreat? Do you get angry or hurt over the misinterpretation? Rather than get frustrated over this, learn to simply redirect the energy back to your intention. Your motives remain clear and unchanged to you, and that is what is important here. You wouldn't feel guilty about pushing down a young puppy that was jumping up on you, nor should you feel guilty about redirecting the miscommunication when someone overresponds to your playfulness.

You can learn how to generate energy with others, and yet remain discriminating, so that hurt and chaos are not the end result. Confusion results when energy flirting gets misinterpreted. The other end of the spectrum is total avoidance of interacting with people you do not know well, whether it be because you are fearful of taking risks with others, or simply because you are shy. This is very safe, but a life void of magnetism is a drab existence and soon loses its spark.

The following is an exercise in purposefully increasing your magnetic field.

Exercise

Practice energy flirting with the people in your daily life. These could be the grocer, the postal clerk, or the children who make up your world.

1. Practice with the people and situations who are least likely to misinterpret your intentions. Smile, interact, and take the opportunity to singularly relate to each of these people in an open and honest fashion. Make all of your exchanges personal. Heartfully express warmth and openness through your eyes. Sometimes there will be a response and other times not, but experiment.

2. Become aware of the way you feel in the presence of different people. With energy exchanges, you are learning how to recognize the chemistry in all of your relationships. You will grow to realize that each and every person you interact with brings out a slightly different response in you.

3. Learn to refocus on your intent when you run across a misinterpretation. You are in control, you initiated the contact, and you can guide its course. Be assured, they will follow suit with your intention. If your intentions are pure and heartful, it will be returned to you.

As you increase your magnetism, you will attract more attention—it always happens. Be prepared for this. The energy and light in you has increased through your openness. Know it is the light within you that others are attracted to, and you will minimize the difficulties of integrating the increased attention.

Dealing with Increased Magnetism

Maintaining the increased energy you have generated through flirting is more challenging than it first appears. As your magnetism increases and you attract more attention and opportunities, your comfort zone is going to be stretched. Dealing with the increased magnetism, so that it can be integrated into your life without disruption, not only continually tests your abilities to use discrimination, but also requires constant examination of your values. A barrage of opportunities, not previously available, can all of a sudden appear quite enticing, and the lure of the senses becomes stronger as well.

Which opportunities you allow, and which ones you do not, is completely up to you and your values. When unbridled, the Venus function entices you into new traps of indulgence. Consequently, a person may be quite temperate in behavior at one level of magnetism, but when it is increased, could become quite excessive in behavior. Remember, each situation you attract is not necessarily a call to participation. With experience and discrimination, you learn to decline unhealthy opportunities and enjoy them simply as evidence of your magnetism. With time, your value system expands and governs your choices, thereby permitting true enjoyment of the experience, instead of chasing a whim.

Developing Your Sexuality

We are in the middle of a cultural revolution concerning sexual attitudes and mores. From the Victorian era, to the expulsion of restraints in the '60s, and finally, to the present threat of health risks, the social transformation of sexual values has been a dominant theme of our era. In my astrology practice, I have also noticed a trend with my clients concerning the need to experience a deeper, more satisfying type of love, especially with their sexual partners. Sex, even good sex, when exclusively physical, is rarely enough to sustain a relationship. Sex, as part of an intimate relationship that has deep sharing on many levels, is what brings satisfaction.

Developing a healthy sexual identity in these times is quite a challenge. There is a great deal of cultural conditioning concerning sexuality to sift through, but ultimately, your role with sexuality is something that you must discover for yourself. Cultural training gives so many mixed messages. There are rules, codes of conduct, morals, ethics, and explicit expectations taught, but there is also a tremendous undercurrent of implicit information on the topic. From movies, to books, to selling cars, sex is a theme that bombards the visual environment.

Even Madison Avenue and the marketing agencies have had a strong impact on attitudes to which you become conditioned concerning your sexuality—"With this product, you can look like this, and then you'll get your man," or "Use this product to become strong in the marketplace," etc. Is it any wonder few have emerged into adulthood with healthy sexual attitudes? A great deal of deconditioning is required just to define your own personal attitudes and needs.

Sexuality is so much more than how much, how often, how many. More than just the physical act, sexuality deals with all aspects of the magnetism between people. This magnetism either attracts you to someone, repels you from someone, or leaves you feeling neutral. Those are the options. Sex is one of the most instinctual urges of humankind and is a major function in all of life, whether you are experiencing sexual relations or not. Nature provided the body with instinct to assure the survival of the species. That you will feel the urge and desire to form sexual union is a fact of life, but it is the response to this stirring within you that becomes the issue of sexuality.

Mostly, developing a healthy attitude concerning sex is simply learning how to allow your instincts to operate. This isn't easy, because along with instincts comes a tremendous amount of cultural conditioning seeking to repress or mold the instincts into whatever is considered proper. To children, it is usually presented as a taboo—you are not supposed to know too much too soon. Since sex represents the very core of life itself and is the basic spark of all creativity, it would seem the more you know, the better prepared you will be for life. But, this isn't always the case. One way or another, everyone has had to experiment with sexuality.

Sexual union not only offers the greatest opportunity for complete intimacy with another, but is the only opportunity that allows for all levels of sharing to take place simultaneously. And that is the great worth of merging the sexual and spiritual in your relationships—it is the one opportunity to put it all together.

Sexuality is a form of creativity. When two people come together a third entity is created. To begin with, they each have their own separate identities, but now they also have the identity of who they are as a couple. Likewise, sex is the most obvious way that two become one, but for this transformation to occur and become complete, total surrender is required. Whether it be for purely sensual gratification, or for a transformational spiritual experience, you will find the more you become one with your partner, the more satisfaction you will experience.

The sexual act itself is a dance of paramount alchemy. Is it any wonder that many confuse sex with love? It is a rare undressing of the facades. This union provides the opportunity to become as close as one can come to another person. Sweating, breathing, touching, sights, smells, and sounds that would usually seem embarrassing, are shared with another. Such is a moment of intense closeness and opportunity for transformation.

The sperm of the man is a representation of his entire being, and this is why, after sex, the woman is so emotionally open to her partner. She carries a portion of his soul within her, and when both partners are sensitive, they are quite aware of this connection. This concept makes a good argument for being selective and responsible with your sexual partners! Choose wisely, for on a karmic level, a bond is being formed.

Cycles of Sexuality

The couple that has successfully maintained a long relationship can vouch for the fact that there are times when the sexual energy is just not there. When this inevitable situation occurs in your relationship, how do you respond? Many people try to fix a bad back by changing their shirt, so to speak. They become anxious over the lull in sexual energy and, fearing that it is going, or gone, react by assuming they are with the wrong person, and change the person. It never works. You are still taking the same you to the new relationship, and you are still going to go through your cycles. Wouldn't it be more fruitful, and a whole lot easier, to learn more about these cycles?

Women typically know more about cycles than men. From learning how to adapt to the cycles of emotion that accompany the menstrual cycle, women simply have more experience with high and low cycles as a natural rhythm in life. But, just because they have grown up with these cycles does not mean that they have any easier time understanding them.

There is a common fear that if you cannot sexually please your mate, you will lose him or her. If this has been part of your conditioning, it is certainly a challenge for you to learn how to stand up for your own sexual rhythm of expression. So often, it is much easier to just adapt to your mate's cycle, instead of talking about your ever-changing needs. But this lack of honoring your energy does not lead to magnetism. It actually leads to a depletion of the energy field.

Educating each other as to personal style, needs, desires, and turn-offs requires honesty and communication, the foundation of any good relationship. Routines are a sure-fire way of killing the spontaneity required for magnetic relating, and the subversive techniques of "Not tonight, I have a headache," simply do not face the real issues. Understanding your sexual cycles and learning how to educate your partner to these cycles is the way. When you can deal with this issue, which is as much of a communication issue as anything else, realize you are greatly helping your partner understand you better, and this will strengthen the foundation of your relationship.

Men are virile, potent, and sexually always ready to go—at least that is what is taught in the locker rooms of America. It takes gentle guidance to educate this insecure male into the awareness of sexual cycles as a natural function of relating. Most men have an innate fear that when their sexual drive is low, it might be dying—we must press forward! Many need to learn that these cycles do not impede sexual relating, but instead, facilitate potency. In weight training, you are advised not to exercise the same muscle groups every day. After the day of rest, you come back even stronger than before. Activity—rest—activity. Align with the cycles of life—honor the down time and come back stronger.

Women, on the other hand, are naturally more aware of their cycles of sexuality. Regardless of how much they love their mate, there are times when they are simply not sexually attracted to him, and they are able to accept this without judging the relationship. However, women have just as much implicit cultural conditioning to decipher as men. Where man is taught virility, women are often taught through "Barbie-doll consciousness" that they are the object of man's desire. Many women fear abandonment if they are not always available to receive their mate's sexual advances. Women are not typically encouraged to teach their man how to be their ideal sexual partner, but it could improve many marriages if they would assume that role.

Eventually you realize you go through these cycles, with or without, another person. Your partner is not "causing" your cycle. He or she just happens to be there with you. Age and experience are the best teachers for this lesson, and once you understand this, you have learned a great deal.

Intimacy and the Moment

Is there any greater treasure in life than the experience of intimacy with another—complete merging, where both drop their separate selves and merge into one? This is the great reward for mastering relationship skills. Intimacy would not be held in such high regard if it was such an easy accomplishment. To be truly intimate with another requires complete honesty, attained only through sharing the fears, the lacks, and the truth of the self with another. It is dropping into the soft spot in your being and sharing from there. Through intimate exchanges, you are communicating beyond the realm of the persona, and it is noticeably satisfying and often stark in its openness. The facades are gone, and you feel relieved and comfortable with sharing even more parts of the self.

Intimacy requires complete surrender to the unfolding moment. Holding back in any way cuts off the magic. So why hold back? Old wounds are the answer. We have all been hurt along the way in life—it happens. When we get hurt, we naturally build armor to protect ourselves. Much like if you cut yourself, the body naturally forms a scab. Just like the body, which will maintain the scab until the wound is healed, our emotional wounds need their armor until healed as well. If you are carrying around old wounds, you've got armor. That's fine, as far as protecting your vulnerability is concerned, but this same armor blocks you from the intimacy you crave.

There is a chain of command concerning intimacy. To experience intimacy you must be able to present your vulnerability. To do this you must first be able to trust. To trust, you must first be able to forgive. We are all stumbling along on our path of awakening—we have all been hurt and hurt others, abandoned and been abandoned, betrayed and been betrayed—life happens. Can you accept the essential humanity of yourself and others? Can you forgive and learn something from it? If so, you can trust opening to your vulnerability and allowing intimacy.

The great twist is that there are no guarantees in this type of investment. The man who allows himself to be ruled by the woman is thought of as henpecked. The woman who surrenders her ego to the man is thought of as being repressed. For alchemy to take place, there must be a complete mixing of the two energies. Both surrender their independent sense of self for the experience of something greater than was possible through simply being alone. This is surrender without sacrifice—synergistic relating.

The experience of intimacy is not limited to sexual union. One can learn to totally surrender to an intimate experience through a conversation, a meditation, a walk in nature. To surrender is to let go of control. The following exercise will facilitate this.

Exercise

Stay five minutes longer.

Imagine this scenario: you have a little extra time and decide to stop by a friend's house for a visit. You both share your recent stories and what is currently on your minds. What happens when you reach the awkward zone where no one has anything to say? Do you tend to look at your watch, exclaim that it is getting late and you must be going? That seems to be the universal response.

This is the magic moment—your feelings of being out of control are the source of your comfort zone feeling stretched. Stay five minutes longer. Stay in the void, surrender. Something will happen, and it was not born out of your control. Ah, the intimate moment. Now translate this to your relationship with your lover, your spiritual practice, your creative expression—stay five minutes longer.

Sacred Sexuality

Sacred sexuality is making love with all levels with your partner simultaneously—the physical, emotional, mental and spiritual. This is learning how to celebrate the divine in sexual union, bringing sacredness to the sharing.

Spirituality and sexuality have long been divorced by many of the world's religions and teachings. Chastity, obedience, and poverty, remember? Chastity was a worthy attempt to get in touch with the spiritual nature by denying the physical, but it didn't always work. What most often happens is that denial and repression create just as much of an imbalance as overindulgence. Or as one teacher said, "You become a horny celibate." Spiritual sexuality certainly need not exclude physical sexuality, nor is it limited to physical relationships. A successful merging of these two worlds can be a true experience of heaven on earth.

The following is an exercise from tantra yoga.

Exercise

While in the passion of sexual union, slow down the rush to orgasm. Focus on your breath and move your attention to the emotional, mental, and spiritual aspects of the embrace as well as the physical.

1. After the fire of the sexual embrace has begun, stop all movement of your bodies. Take note of the rush to physical sensation that is occurring, however, override it with your spiritual will. Focus on each other's breath. Put your mouths together, and as one breathes out the other breathes in so that your breaths are merging into one and recycling through each other.
2. With your eyes closed, both visualize the energy moving up your spines, away from the genitals. See your spine as a thermometer of your love and visualize a flame starting at the genitals and rising through your spine and out the top of your head.
3. Visualize the two fires merging into one flame. Feel this taking place at the physical, emotional, mental, and spiritual levels. Calmly share your images, visualizations, and feelings with each other.
4. Gently move your bodies to keep the fire of passion animating the flame of your love. You can maintain this for as long as you like. When the rush to orgasm takes hold, slow it down by deepening your breath. Feel your body and soul merge with the body and soul of your mate.

Through experimentation you will be able to adapt this exercise to your own style. Don't be afraid to experiment. You will notice that instead of being exhausting, this type of lovemaking is exhilarating. To engage the spiritual dimension of any involvement brings sacredness to the experience. There is a whole level of joy that can be experienced through your spiritual relating. To embrace another spiritually, to celebrate the divine within others, is infectious and inviting. Synergy takes place through your close-bonded friendships, as you allow yourself to merge into their being and welcome the same through them.

Venus leads the sweet nectar in life—follow its lead and you will find life offers a bounty of opportunities to enjoy. In the following section learn more about how Venus leads to the garden of delight through each of the signs.

The Planet Venus in Your Birth Chart

Venus is the planet that rules how you attract others into your life and what you need to feel loved and appreciated. It represents how you enjoy what you have—your experience of either being satisfied or not satisfied. When you understand what you are specifically looking for in these regards, it is easier to set up your life so that you will have a fair chance of having your needs met.

The sign your Venus is in describes the way you are most open to receiving love. When you are out of touch with your Venus function, you may be trying too hard without receiving enough satisfaction for your efforts. If you do not understand the Venus function in others you are trying to please, you may try to give them the kind of support or recognition you would appreciate, but still be off base in your relating with them. Astrology helps.

Venus in Aries

YOUR MAGNETIC MAKE-UP The spark of Aries is born right out of the self as instincts. Your values are deeply rooted in the instinctual and you might not even be able to consciously identify them. They are just part of who you are. You do value independence, for yourself and for others, thus you need relationships that honor this. What sets you apart from others is your willingness to jump into activity on a moment's notice—you are an exciting person! When you turn on the charm, others experience you as sunny, spirited, and lots of fun. You are action oriented, restless with routine and need a relationship that explores something new—forever.

You go after what you want with total conviction and then can leave with just as much fanfare when the thrill is gone. The person who surrenders too quickly does not hold your attention, as you enjoy the chase. This placement leads to a very idealistic nature concerning love and with your spirited nature—there is no reason your ideals can not be attained. Others enjoy spending time with you as you seem to bring a quality of being alive to all that you do.

With the Venus in Aries need for constant newness in life, this could work out in one of two ways for relationships. One, a lifelong series of short, intense relationships. You do tend to attract dynamic individuals. Enjoy them while they are exciting and fresh, and as soon as routine sets in, end it and go on to the next exciting person. The modern world does not judge this as much, so this could work. Or, two, if you found yourself in a relationship that you want to last, it is going to be up to you to keep the relationship fresh with constant new growth.

AREAS TO WORK ON Difficulties in relationships arise over your impatience. Aries seeks immediate action and you tend to want what you want, and want it now. Others can even consider you selfish and inconsiderate as the Aries impulse comes right from within. This makes it very difficult to truly understand the needs and values of others. Cooperation is essential in relationships and, for this to occur, you must first develop sensitivity for others. Developing diplomacy as the balance point to your enthusiasm helps others to share your excitement. Your endurance will get tested if you wish to establish long-term relationships.

UNDERSTANDING VENUS IN ARIES IN OTHERS These people most value spontaneous involvement with life and often crave a lifestyle with a tremendous amount of activity. They most appreciate direct, up-front dealings, so save your tact for others—Venus in Aries prefers your gut level, in the moment, response every time. They like to be surprised by spontaneous opportunities and bore of routine rather quickly. Very idealistic in love, they love the newness of romance. To keep their interest and maintain a long-term relationship, you will always have to find new avenues of expression.

These individuals will have no difficulty knowing what they want in any negotiations with you. However, you might have to remind them of your position, or the agreement will turn out decidedly one-sided. You may periodically need to completely pull away to avoid being consumed with the intensity of their life. When you want to be with someone who can enjoy the moment and always find something exciting to do, these are the people to call.

Venus in Taurus

YOUR MAGNETIC MAKE-UP Your values include beauty, quality, stability, and security, and your lifestyle is likely to reflect this. Your heightened sensual awareness gives you a connoisseur's eye for surrounding yourself with beauty. Your love of luxury is complemented by an equal ability to enjoy life's simple pleasures. Good food, good music, a nice home life does not need to be complicated for you. Affectionate, loving relationships are a must. Your values are perhaps your greatest resource and you will not have to compromise them to achieve the quality of life that you envision, but you do have to cooperate.

You are devoted in romance once you feel safe and comfortable. Your love really begins to blossom once there is a solid ground from which the relationship operates. You cannot and will not be pushed. You will move or act when you are ready. You reach for what is safe and secure when it comes to affairs of the heart.

The long-shot chance that may interrupt your routines of security is not of interest to you.

You are very dependable and appreciate this quality in others as well. You prefer stability and security in relationships, and have a distaste for complexity and psychological intrigue. Patience is your forte, thus you are willing to wait for the right kind of love. To be comfortable is of the essence. You are a nester and must have a comfortable home. When you are secure, others experience you as refreshingly genuine.

Areas to Work On An excessively rigid adherence to your values leads to stubbornness, and you might find that this placement makes it difficult to let go of resistance when change and adaptation are required. Another potential difficulty to watch for is a tendency to become materialistic to the degree that you are more concerned over money and possessions than people. You might also have a tendency to become quite possessive of those you love and you periodically need to be reminded that people are not objects that can be owned.

Understanding Venus in Taurus for Others Security, comfort, and quality are key issues with these people. Kind, generous, and sweet, these people like to cuddle, and touching is a most important form of communication with them. Regardless of how fast they come on to you, it will take a considerable time to win them over, so don't rush them. Always listen to the clues as to what they value most in relationships. Just listen—they'll give you all the information you need to have a successful relationship.

They can be equally stubborn and impossible when they feel threatened or pushed, so don't try unless you are willing to risk the whole relationship. Gentle coaxing, subtle bribing, and simplicity work best. Eating, drinking, and casual socializing are the activities that make these people comfortable. They have expectations as to what constitutes a good time and what does not. Your job is to discover what these are before you are forced to randomly trip over them. Don't try to change them. Just relax and get comfortable with their habits, their routines, and their friends.

Venus in Gemini

Your Magnetic Make-up You are versatile, friendly, and flirtatious, and thrive in open-minded relationships. You like to talk about almost anything, especially love. Mental stimulation is a must for you and you pride yourself in being informed. When you flirt, it is most often out of innocent joy of the moment, rather than for seductive purposes. You crave what is new and bore easily with anything once it becomes routine. Excitement is usually more important to you than stability, and this shows up most in the type of people you find attractive. You are involved in relationships that prove puzzling to others. You need interactions with others, but are often thought of as independent, because you never limit yourself to the confines of a dependent relationship. Too much time alone is boring—you need many people in your life. This keeps you from trying to have any one person meet all of your needs.

Areas to Work On Because of highly changeable values, Venus in Gemini is accused of being fickle and superficial. You form quick infatuations and enjoy the diversion of building whole fantasies around people you barely know. You are an extremist and have been known to fall in and out of love very quickly. The fantasy is usually more important to you than the reality of building something concrete. If this is beginning to wear you out, you might try slowing down the whole process.

In relationships, you will likely need to develop empathy for the emotional needs of others. The Gemini attitude of "just change" is rarely appreciated by someone caught in the throes of emotional turmoil.

Understanding Venus in Gemini in Others These are friendly, freedom-oriented people who like new and exciting experiences. Their life is an adventure, and they will be drawn to people who are as curious as themselves about the wonder of life. Take time to ask them about what they want to do, but realize that for them, part of the pleasure of getting to know someone is sharing in that person's life and experiencing things that they would not on their own.

They crave playful and even childlike forms of relating. Pursue them with curiosity, and they will readily share. They will not back down from intense relating, and yet they fear commitment. Being a pal and truly sharing in each other's lives will be the most satisfying.

You are dealing with a highly changeable personality, so you will have to stay in present time. These people can change quickly and they are looking for someone who can keep the relationship exciting and fresh. Shared learning experiences are helpful—perhaps taking a class together, or a trip to a new place. Most of all, keep involved in a life of your own that stretches past what the two of you share. Give Venus in Gemini people lots of time to talk about themselves, as this is an activity they thoroughly enjoy. They need the freedom to talk and interact with a wide variety of people, but you will not need to be jealous, as it is most often only talking they are after.

Venus in Cancer

Your Magnetic Make-up You are warm, caring, and nurturing with those in your inner circle and extremely cautious with others. It might take longer to win you over as a friend than most, but once friendship is established, there are none more loyal than you. When you accept somebody into your life, that person becomes as family. You become very attached to those you love and break-ups are harder on you because of that. If you are cautious in opening up to others, know that it is appropriate. Traditional family values work just fine for you and you seek a sincere, loving companion with whom to share your life. You are sweet and nurturing and do love to take care of the people in your life.

The right choice of relationship is essential for you, as your feelings get hurt easily and you need a mate who is sensitive to that. Naturally affectionate and devoted, you are wary of newcomers or totally new situations. People have to prove themselves to you, since you are not naturally trusting without an established history to fall back on. Comfort and familiarity are essential. It is difficult for you to talk about your feelings until you feel completely safe. Family activities are an extremely important and influential part of your life and you'll never forget a birthday, anniversary, or other important event. Your love life must be totally secure, or you will have a difficult time feeling centered. Your love gets better with time.

Areas to Work On You can be overly cautious and so focused on security that you fail to allow new experiences and people into your life. Another area to be aware of is your tendency to be overly protective of those you love. Along with a smothering tendency, this can inadvertently promote codependency-based relationships. Your hypersensitivity can lead to getting your feelings hurt when no hurt was intended, as you have a strong tendency to take everything personally. It would be wise for you to identify your emotional cycles and learn to gracefully respond to them by creating healthy activities for your down and inward turning time. This can help you avoid your tendency to sabotage situations in your life, creating problems where none exist in order to justify getting off by yourself to work it out—which you needed to do anyway! Learning to be proactive with your cycles is the message. When you do, your inward turning time becomes enriching, instead of simply the working-through of a bad mood.

Understanding Venus in Cancer in Others These people are sweet and caring. You will be attracted to their warmth and sincerity. In developing ties with them, be willing to start out and continue slowly. What you say is not as important as what you feel. They respond to your emotional message, not just the words. Their family is going to be a part of your life together. If you are prepared, this won't push you off course. It's not a choice for them but a given, so do not interfere, but support them.

Those with Venus in Cancer require some private time to sort through their complicated emotional life. They are moody, so let them decide when they can move forward and when they will need to retreat. They are also ultrasensitive and get their feelings hurt easily, so be gentle. Their feelings can overwhelm them and they cannot always talk about what is going on with them. Don't push, remain patient and loving, and you will have developed a lifelong companion.

Venus in Leo

Your Magnetic Make-up You are high spirited, warm and loving. Heartful involvement makes up the core of your life. You are here to celebrate life and this is genuinely shared with others. You require loyalty, total devotion, and honesty from your partners, and you willingly give this back in return. You are so strong that your moods and feelings get broadcast without words. You have to be with someone that you are proud of and you must feel that you play a central part in their life.

Your relationships are laced with integrity, honor, and respect. Learn to say what you want, rather than being hurt when it just doesn't magically happen. You are not as easy to read as you believe yourself to be. You are attracted to drama and intensity, and these are necessary components to any of your important relationships. You are fun to be with, but you are stubborn and will not be pushed. Once you have made up your mind, you won't change. You demand to have your own way and you will not spend time with people whose values you do not respect. You like knowing that you have enriched someone's life through your involvement with them.

Areas to Work On Pride is a two-edged sword for you and gets in the way whenever you feel slighted—and Venus in Leo can feel slighted if it is not being adored! To say that you expect a great deal out of relationships is an understatement, to say the least. Not that this is wrong for you, but you will certainly want to pick your partners wisely because of this. Everyone starts their relationships off with a great deal of romantic attention toward the other, but for you this not just for courtship. You would like this kind of attention as a way of life. You do not have to change or compromise who you are, just know that many people would find this tiresome. Yet with the right person, it can be special. So again, choose wisely.

This is not the most cooperative placement for Venus and you will have to do some work on yourself to allow for the values of others when they run contrary to your own. You can be so idealistic in love that you become impatient with the down cycles in a relationship and can appear quite demanding to your lover.

Understanding Venus in Leo for Others These people are passionate and magnetic. You can't push them into anything, so don't even try. Gentle coaxing works best. They want their life to be special and they will do all they can to make this a reality. Join in where you can. These people are very strong and have hearts of gold. They truly enjoy giving and will feel challenged when this is expected of them, rather than their gift to give. They like a lavish display of love and it is not an exaggeration to say they like to be adored. Although somewhat demanding in their expectations, they have just as much to give in return.

These people are charming and well informed in some area of the arts or entertainment, and this may prove to be your thread of mutual interest. Their "offspring," be it business, children, or some form of artistic expression, is something they value. They will appreciate your participation, so don't overlook this. Be careful what you choose to joke or kid around about with these individuals, as they will not tolerate being slighted in any way. If you bruise their egos, even by accident, it will be quite difficult to work your way back into their favor. They prefer private one-on-ones to larger social gatherings, as they want all of your attention. Plan to share in the good life with each other.

Venus in Virgo

YOUR MAGNETIC MAKE-UP You are very specific about your likes and dislikes and are very discriminating in love. Health issues, diet, nutrition, and neatness are core issues in your values. Since you like to be of service, you will feel most secure in relationships when you are clearly needed. You tend not to be a gushy romantic, preferring to express your feelings for others in action—you want to pitch in and contribute to your partner's life. Uncomfortable with adoration, you feel best when your efforts are simply appreciated. Actually, you value simplicity in all ways. Naturally suspicious of extravagance, your tastes run toward simple elegance. For this same reason, you value genuineness in others. You are not a complex person in your relationship needs, just specific. This applies to gifts as well and you likely appreciate simple and useful gifts more than gifts you cannot use, which become dreaded clutter.

You are delightfully sensual when all the conditions are just right, discrimination being one of your virtues. You have a critical eye and it is important for you to be with someone who appreciates this quality in you. Actually, the more you care, the more you are likely to share your perceptions on how others can improve their life. You are not being critical just for its own sake. It is because you want to be of assistance, and you notice the details that others miss.

AREAS TO WORK ON You need to turn off your thinking cap in order not to miss the playful and frivolous joy of love. Virgo is naturally modest, but you likely go too far with this and fail to speak up for your own needs, limiting your opportunities for joy. Your perfectionist tendencies can easily degenerate into simply worrying too much, which dampens your magnetic energy. Venus is your magnetism and if you worry constantly, what will you attract? Your self-esteem in love is likely not all that it could be and you would benefit by having a partner that supports your expression of love.

You can become so comfortable with routines that your relationships run the risk of becoming mechanical, like one of the items on your checklist. Although wonderfully affectionate when the conditions of right time, right place, and right person are met, there is still a tendency to be perfect technically in lovemaking, without bringing your emotions into the experience.

UNDERSTANDING VENUS IN VIRGO IN OTHERS Virgo is the sign of the helper in the zodiac and these people want to be just that in your life. There is a gentleness here that is not readily seen—Virgo has the reputation of being hypercritical. You might see this aspect of Venus in Virgo if you get close enough, for they only share their critical eye with those they care about. But, they are as sweet as they come as well. Use the image of coaxing a deer out of a cave if you want to draw them out. Although it is not openly apparent, their self-esteem needs to be bolstered—they will thrive if encouraged. All they really need is your appreciation for their efforts—they will work hard to earn it. There is something marvelously genuine about these souls, so drop all pretentious airs to reach them. Their refined and sensitive nature also has a strong distaste for the crude and the rude. They know how to enjoy life's simple pleasures, so they are really not hard to please. If you want to impress them, just be real. They shy away from extravagance, preferring thoughtful and meaningful gifts.

Sincerity is another virtue you will grow to appreciate about your Venus in Virgo friends. If they said it, particularly concerning matters of the heart, they meant it. Caution is the way with Virgo, so don't expect them to jump into new experiences or feel comfortable with your friends right away. Allow them their natural readiness cycles. Their ability to find meaning in tending to the everyday tasks of life is inspiring to be around.

Venus in Libra

YOUR MAGNETIC MAKE-UP Beauty and relationships are the twin anchors of your values and you hold the ideal of the beautiful relationship. Constantly aware of these ideals, you have very high standards of what is possible in relationships. With your natural gift for diplomacy and your strong dislike for arguments, you much prefer cooperation over coercion. When you focus your eye for beauty on others, you reflect the best in them and people enjoy spending time with you. You have a distinct charm as you seem to instinctively know what other people value. You are a very romantic soul, but for you, romance is not just a bedroom issue. You would like a partner who likes to get dressed up once in awhile, go out to a fine restaurant, take in some culture, go for a walk on the beach, read poetry to each other—ah, *romance!* For you, sexy is just as much a mental issue as anything else—you have to be attracted to your partner's mind to feel the magnetism.

You have a keen sense of fairness, and when you have developed this quality, people trust you. You also have a keen sense of design and harmony, thus, appearance is important in all aspects of your life, including relationships. You can be both eloquent and elegant and have a noticeable sense of style about you.

Areas to Work On Your difficulties lie in the fact that your real-life relationships often can't live up to the ideal you hold in your mind. When your relationships are operating at best, you have the ability to enjoy them like no other. However, you have a definite tendency toward avoidance when unpleasantness reveals itself. You tend to compromise your values in the name of peace in the moment. When your emotions are involved, clarity is lost as you become uncomfortable. You have a mental image of the right relationship and you treat your emotions as if they fogged the picture. When you settle for your life looking good on the surface without confronting the real depth, your relationships become superficial. You ultimately learn that avoiding the small issues only leads to bigger issues, and to establish the tranquillity you desire, it is best to come to balance, even with the minor issues.

Understanding Venus in Libra in Others These are naturally refined individuals. Manners and social decorum count with them, so dust off your social graces and plan to put them to use. Your dates might consist of attending art openings, film festivals, concerts, and the theater if you want to remain high on the list of favorite friends. They are communicators and will want to stay informed on all aspects of your life. These mental exchanges are an important aspect of their sexuality, so don't slight this area of the relationship.

Cooperation is very important to them and they will value your input on any decisions they are going to make. It is not that they need you to make decisions for them, they just feel more comfortable with shared decisions, rather than taking independent action. Appearance matters, so look your best and never embarrass them in public, as that will be inexcusable. All private dealings should be handled in private and then left there. Their tendency to avoid the unpleasant can have them glossing over sensitive issues until it is too late. Encourage them to dig a little deeper when you sense something is wrong or you will get the "everything is fine" answer to your inquiries. Their tastes lean to the aesthetics in life more than function, so when you want to give them a gift, skip the appliance section and look for art or jewelry, or plan a special elegant night out. They make wonderful companions, who are really good at doing anything together.

Venus in Scorpio

Your Magnetic Make-up You are secretive, intense, and somewhat shy. You do not like your private life discussed with others, yet, it's something others are curious about. You are reserved and controlled with your emotions and it takes great provocation to get you visibly upset. You need total devotion from those you care about, as this alleviates self-doubt and fear of rejection. It's best for you to stay away from relationships that provoke your jealousy and mistrust. You are too vulnerable to these issues, so choose partners wisely.

You are continually working on yourself, wanting to purge old, unwanted parts of your character. You are deeply complex and difficult for others to figure out. You are passionate and devotional with your love once it is given. Your sex life is often very important to you, yet it is not the purely physical aspects of sex that you find most intriguing. It is the psychological aspect of the sexual union that you find most rewarding, and you are fascinated with the transformations that your partner undergoes through your shared passion.

Areas to Work On You tend toward jealousy and suspicion of your partner, as you are dealing with a fear of rejection. This can be a poison to your relationships with which you must come to terms. The person you really doubt is yourself. There is often a haunting fear that, somehow, you are going to be made a fool of, and this can prevent you from totally surrendering to a relationship.

There are so many hidden aspects to you that you assume it is the same for others. You will have to develop faith and trust in your partners. You question whether others are being fair with you. But again, what you may be questioning is yourself. The three things you could work on to improve all of your relationships are forgiveness, forgiveness, and more forgiveness.

UNDERSTANDING VENUS IN SCORPIO IN OTHERS These people are magnetic and intense. Secretive and private, these folks are easy to misread, and what you see is not always what you get. They have parts of their character that even they are not comfortable with. Even if you notice these, don't confront them. They fear revealing too much or being taken advantage of. If they are only comfortable showing you their most polished sides, you are going to miss out on their real self, which is quite complex, hidden, and not so idealized. These people are gutsy and perceptive, and your awareness of people will increase by spending time with them. Their sense of humor is often laced with sexual innuendoes.

Trust comes slowly to them. When they do show themselves, they may feel that they are revealing a deep secret and you will have to appreciate it accordingly. You might try to get them to talk about their past emotional hurts, but don't expect them to open up too quickly. Their old wounds won't go away until they are openly dealt with. They help you to understand more about yourself, always forcing you to deal with the most hidden parts of your character. You will grow quickly around these people.

Venus in Sagittarius

YOUR MAGNETIC MAKE-UP You are outgoing and adventurous, and will enjoy relationships that broaden your perspective on life. You are most attracted to people who are different from you, or have vastly different experiences to draw from. You want to learn and continually expand, so adventure is more exciting than intimacy. You are an escape artist when it comes to being pinned down, and can talk your way out of anything when you are put to the test. Freedom is what you are seeking and what you are most committed to maintain. You want to be in charge of your relationships and thus you have no problem taking the lead. Relationships become real when you start planning a future together. Having shared goals is an integral part of your bonding with others. To maintain long term relationships, you will have to create new goals within the relationship once previous ones are met. Your idealism can be quite inspirational for others.

You have high moral standards concerning social behavior and this is likely to be an important issue in your relationships. Honesty and blunt discussions are your natural way and you may have difficulty with people who have difficulty speaking their minds. Naturally philosophical, topics on religion, politics, and the wisdom teachings can hold interest for you. Perhaps your greatest gift is your ability to frame things in a positive light, thus you typically are joyous and playful with friends.

Areas to Work On Unless you have expanded your value system to include the rights of others, you can appear quite judgmental and even evangelical. When you are at philosophical odds with your partner, you can hold to your position with dogmatic zeal. This can lead to competitiveness.

Another area for you to work on deals with your restlessness. It does keep you on the move and open to new experiences, but it can make it difficult to fully enjoy the experiences and people with whom you are currently involved. There can be a subtle fear that you might be missing something and, paradoxically, this fear creates the reality of you missing the potential in the moment by always looking to the future.

Understanding Venus in Sagittarius in Others These people want to grow and learn, so be willing to tell them about life as you know it. Introduce them to your world, but remember to respect and treat them as individuals. Share books, movies, and travel. Whenever possible, take a trip together. These people crave new experiences and thoroughly appreciate the times that you ask their advice on your situations. They are almost always ready for a good philosophical debate—which can escalate too quickly if you are not careful.

When they are not being judgmental, these folks have an excellent sense of humor and your life can be much more exciting just through spending time with them. They are very warm and outgoing. Many people are drawn to spending time with them, yet they are selective about who becomes their close friends. Don't let the pace slow down, as they need excitement. They will find it with you or someone else. What they fear most is stagnation and missing life's opportunities.

Venus in Capricorn

Your Magnetic Make-up Sincerity, loyalty, and commitment are hallmarks of your personality and you will filter out all involvement with others that does not meet these standards. Obviously, this will limit your options and that is just fine with you. You also possess a fair amount of patience and discernment, so if you seem cautious in forming new ties with others, it is because that's how you are meant to be, and it is worth the wait! You tend to be pragmatic in terms of the heart. "Pragmatic heart" might very well be an oxymoron—ultimately, for love to blossom, we all must take some risks. Risk and Venus in Capricorn might be an oxymoron too! This is the puzzle of your heart involvements.

You likely surrender to close relationships in measured steps. Since you do not take your commitments lightly, you are inclined to think about the long-term ramifications of your actions before you jump into anything. Capricorn is task oriented. You like to stay focused on projects, take pride in excellence in all that you do, and you need to feel respect from your partner with these concerns. These very same qualities allow you to shine in pursuing your ambitions, but can hinder your closest of ties. Intimacy is born out of vulnerability and if you confuse vulnerability with weakness, you won't risk what it takes to surrender to intimacy.

You want a relationship that focuses on building a life together and it would be best to choose a partner with similar priorities. You are delightfully sensual when you allow yourself the opportunity. Once you have given yourself to another in love, you remain extremely loyal through the thick and thin of it all.

Areas to Work On Your standards of performance are so high for yourself in every area of life that you can always feel that you are under pressure. This overfocus on outcomes, rather than the process, makes it difficult for you to truly enjoy where you are and what you have accomplished. Your cautious reserve can be interpreted by others as standoffish, but then, you tend to earn the object of your affection through time. Your tendency to put romance on the back burner once you are secure in a relationship, as if commitment itself were enough, could lead to dry, businesslike involvements. To balance this tendency, remember to create time for the personal side of your relationships.

Understanding Venus in Capricorn in Others It will take some time to get to know these people as they are naturally cautious about opening up to new situations. They pride themselves in being capable and competent, so you can trust that they will follow through on any commitments they make. Of course, they will expect the same of you. To stay on their good side, follow through on all of your agreements and treat them with respect. They will certainly respect sincerity above flamboyance in you.

Venus in Capricorn people work at their relationships and pride themselves in the way that they carry through with their commitments. They are primarily attracted to people who are almost overly involved with their work, or at least decidedly serious about life in general. Don't be afraid to talk about your work issues with them. They prefer to deal with matters exactly as they are, so honesty and frankness will work best. They detest being patronized. Confusion or vagueness will make them shut down, so try to completely carry through with your agreements. Nothing will go unnoticed. Although slow to win over in love, once they give their heart, they stay committed.

Venus in Aquarius

Your Magnetic Make-up You are friendly, outgoing, and mental about your love concerns. To you, love is an ideal, something to reach for, something abstract. Your idealism is most apparent in your choice of companions. You can admire, enjoy, or be attracted to one specific quality in a person and ignore others parts that you don't want to deal with. This kind of compartmentalization is rare. It may have you forming relationships only with specific parts of people, which is why you need a large circle of friends. Good mental rapport is essential, but you are just as likely to spend time with someone with whom you share only a small, quirky interest. Your friends love you because you seem to recognize and appreciate that which is most unique about them. You are not one to value convention, thus you secretly enjoy the eccentricities of others, and there is usually something different and unique about close relationships that you form.

You cannot tolerate people being possessive of you and are comfortable allowing others their freedom. Infatuation comes easy, but deeper love is more rare for you. It would have to be with someone who accepted you just the way you are, and the relationship would have grown from a friendship inward towards personal love. Platonic relationships that are open and honest are also comfortable.

Areas to Work On You value freedom and independence to such a high degree that commitment-based relationships can seem a threat to you. You need to learn that it is possible to express your individuality through your commitments. You are more comfortable with friendships and loosely defined relationships than you are in one-to-one encounters, until you learn to become more at ease with the personal side of life. You understand altruism and other lofty emotions, but you can appear quite insensitive to the personal feelings of others.

Understanding Venus in Aquarius in Others These are friendly and open people. They will like you if they are curious about you, and they can appreciate that you are an independent person with a life of your own. They are seeking the truth and will appreciate your concern for clarity, so you can be brutally honest with them. There always seems to be something experimental about their relationships, as they are not cut out for following the expectations of others. Since they place a high value on uniqueness, there is no need for being anything other than your own true self with these people.

In one sense, it will feel like you know these people very quickly, but you may also feel you never quite understand them. Don't try. Their need to communicate will be immense, so words are going to be a key to your connection. The path to their heart is through the mind. Ask them about their dreams and fantasies and plan to share many of yours. Be prepared for them continuing their relationships from their past into the present. No relationship is ever completely over for them. Their honesty and impersonal approach to life will be refreshing. If you are looking for a nonjudgmental relationship with someone who accepts you with all of your quirks and idiosyncrasies, a Venus in Aquarius person may be the right one for you.

Venus in Pisces

Your Magnetic Make-up You are the romantic idealist and devoted in love. You are also very difficult to pin down. You are easily swayed by the emotions and expectations of others. When you bond with someone, it is through the heart and your feelings run deep. You try to keep your relationships centered by not dealing directly with issues. Your sympathetic nature is easily manipulated by loved ones. This is draining, and is probably why you choose a small circle of friends. It would be exhausting for you to be involved with too many people. Relationships that involve the spiritual or creative aspect of you offer the greatest opportunity for fulfillment.

You are a very sweet, caring, and nurturing partner and it is wise to choose relationships with those who appreciate this, without taking advantage of you. Your compassion for the feelings of others is such an integral part of your character that you are usually found in some profound helping or healing profession. Your sensitivity can also find healthy outlets through the arts and creative expression.

Areas to Work On Susceptibility to self-pity can lead you to martyr yourself to the ideal of love—it is as if feeling, itself, is the intoxicant for you. Your sensitivity is often overwhelming, which can lead to great personal upsets when you are confused or disappointed. You often feel bad in a relationship, yet, you don't make the necessary changes. You have a distinct tendency to make excuses for those you love, thus it is difficult for you to break away from someone once you are involved.

Your biggest challenge lies in your inability to defend yourself, which often leads to allowing yourself to be taken advantage of by others. It would be wise for you to remember that when you allow the lower part of another person to take advantage of you, you are encouraging and supporting the behavior which ultimately helps no one.

Understanding Venus in Pisces in Others These people are sweet, nurturing, and very easy to like. They appear to be easygoing, but often there is much tension running just beneath the surface. There is great magnetism, but also an apparent wall that separates them from others. These people may readily feel misunderstood, so be willing to move slowly and don't make assumptions about them. You will be wrong more than you imagine. Since their emotional life is quite complex, it will simply take much time and patience to fully know them and allow them to feel comfortable with you. If you keep your time with them pleasurable and trouble-free, you will see them more frequently.

Venus in Pisces people are incurable romantics in love, so poetry, music, and candlelight dinners go a long way towards winning their favor. They love to please, so you will not have to defend your interests with them. However, you might have to help them stand up and defend their own interests, as they do tend toward self-sacrificing behavior. Their emotional world is extremely complex and can appear like a quagmire when they get overinvolved with worrying about people. If you are looking for a kind, gentle, and compassionate friend, one who has Venus in Pisces is ideal.

MARS

Power, Passion, and Anger

MARS IS THE dynamic, action-oriented aspect of your personality that allows you to go out and get what you want out of life. It represents how you apply yourself, initiate action, defend and protect yourself, and how you act on your passions and frustrations. It is the warrior within—it represents your honor code, what you are willing to stand, and even fight for. And if you do engage battle, at one level or another, Mars represents your style of combat. It is the complement to Venus and, ideally, goes out and initiates experiences that Venus values, completing the circuit of magnetic energy.

Power, passion, and anger, all related to Mars, are easily the most intense of human experiences. For good or for ill, how you handle these will directly impact the quality of your relationships. Whether your experiences here lead to action, passion, and intensity, or to frustration, irritation, and anger is up to you. To be in control of your power you have to be able to deal with each of these polarities. These are the vehicles through which you coordinate thought and action. Whether you fear or crave these experiences, your relationships will reflect and even magnify your ability, or inability, to deal with the intensity of life. Can you be both loving and powerful? Assertive and receptive?

This chapter will help you explore these questions of integrating your personal power so that you can be initiating when you need to assert yourself and confident enough to flow with situations when that is what is required. The separate topics of power, passion, and anger will be explored in their role within relationships. With each of these main expressions of Mars-related activities, the underexpression, overexpression, and balanced expression of energy will also be explored. Activities and exercises to facilitate the integration of the assertive energy of Mars in a healthy way in your life will be presented. The second half of the chapter will interpret Mars through each of the astrological signs, for you and for others.

The Nature of True Power

Personal power is the ability to initiate, define, protect, and defend yourself. This type of power has very little to do with actual physical strength. True power is an inner strength that is characterized by being self-assured. In relationships, the self-assured person is not dependent on his or her mate. How do you go about getting what you want? When you are good at this, you feel effective and perhaps lucky. When you are not, you can feel weak or out of control.

The power to initiate gives you the tool to reach for what you want. It is through your words and actions that you become effective in your world. Without initiative action, all you can do is want and wait. You can choose to withhold your passions, but by doing so you also choose to avoid complete representation of yourself. If you do not express anger when you feel it, how is anyone to know of your values? How are they to know when they have hurt or offended you? How do you express yourself when someone has trespassed your comfort zone?

When you disengage from your power, you become passive and remain at the mercy of your world. You are not properly educating others as to your limits and boundaries and your choices are restricted to waiting for life to come to you.

There can be an underexpression, an overexpression, or a balanced expression of power.

Underexpression of Power

This is exemplified by the person who typically feels quite vulnerable in personal relationships. Saying "no" is difficult. While interacting with this type of person, you often receive mixed messages—they are saying "yes," but you are feeling "no." When you ask, "What's wrong?" the reply is most often, "Nothing." So then what do you do? Not much, because nothing is wrong, at least that is what they are telling you. Still, the energy is not right, either. If you are the underexpression type, you too often are acting in response to others without feeling that you are in control of the flow of your life. Your relationships may lack the magnetism that comes from polarity. By always saying "yes," the energy has nothing to bounce off of, and it dissipates.

Another underexpression of power is the bleeding-heart type. These people cannot define and defend their space with conviction, and it is not uncommon for others to take advantage of this. They are always there for a friend who needs them, but they would never ask for assistance themselves. These people seem to be at the bottom of their own totem pole in terms of whose needs come first. They truly enjoy giving strength and support to others, but they easily fall into a trap of volunteering to sacrifice their own needs. They seem to believe that standing up for their own rights might displease others.

Most people who suffer from underexpression of their will are very kind and gentle souls. They care for others and feel selfish if they stand up for their own needs, thus allowing their energy to run down. If this sounds like you, you need to examine your beliefs in this regard. You might ask yourself, "Am I really offering other people my best when I am not standing up for my own needs?"

Overexpression of Power

The overexpression of power conjures up images of the brute, always controlling and domineering. Indeed, this can be part of the syndrome, but it is often more subtle than that. The need to always be in control is the keynote of the person overexpressing the use of power. The subtle art of persuasion is magnified into outright manipulation. The force or threat of physical violence, psychological power trips, and the excessive need to compete are all different types of one-upmanship that dominate the control of a situation.

Physical violence, whether real or held out as a threat, is the harshest form of overexpression. It presents a difficult and very real situation. If you are involved in a relationship where violence exists, it is advisable not to try to solve the problem yourself—seek professional help. People who get involved with physical violence carry an excessive energy charge. The surge of adrenaline becomes a sensation of tremendous impact. Some become addicted to such intense states of energy. Even though they are not aware of it happening, they are drawn to situations that will provide that sensation. The same rush can be provided without the negative charge of physical violence through thrill-seeking and dangerous sports like skydiving, skin-diving, mountain climbing and motorcross bike racing. Pushing yourself to take on activities that require courage, like public speaking, is also a healthy way to challenge yourself.

Psychological power trips, although not physically threatening, are just as troublesome in relationships. This can range from the threat of, "Don't get me mad, I don't know what will happen," to the withholding of love as punishment for not getting one's own way. People who pull psychological power trips always have a gift of persuasion. They know how to use their power so well that they can persuade you to do their bidding, against your own will.

The task of recognition of the situation falls on the one being manipulated, as the person who is doing the manipulation is usually quite unaware that it is occurring at all. Typically, it is a subconscious behavior. If this is a situation with which you are familiar, then you will have a responsibility to help your mate see it. Subconscious motivations exist in everyone and by definition, you cannot see your subconscious, as this is beneath conscious awareness. So how do you become aware of your subconscious motivations?

One of the beautiful things about being involved in a relationship is the mirroring that takes place. If you have overcome defensiveness, you can learn about your subconscious motivations through the response of other people to you. The relationship with your mate is the best possible reflection of this part of your character. It takes cooperation, however. First off, you must be willing to see your mate beyond your habitual responses in order to maintain a freshness of response. If you become locked into routine responses to your mate, then the mirror aspect of the relationship is gone. You can only see yourself through your mate's eyes if you look. Secondly, it takes a partner who is open enough to express true feelings and share his or her responses with you.

Excessive need to compete is probably the least problematic of these three main types of overexpression of power, but it is still troublesome in many relationships. The need to compete, to be the best, is honorable in some situations and tiresome in others. This is the easiest one to see and the easiest one to translate into appropriate channels. Friendly competition can turn to a battleground all too easily. The best answer for a competitive nature is competition. Rather than trying to stop the behavior, channel it into a healthy expression like sports or chess, where competition is the agreed-upon mode of exchange.

Overcompetitiveness also influences one's professional life. "Too many roosters in the barnyard" is an all-too-familiar scenario in the work world where the competition for success brings out the worst in some people. Learn to compete with yourself, rather than against others and you'll enjoy your victories more. There's a well-known saying in sports: "It is not whether you win or lose the game that is important, it's how you play the game." It is interesting that this is usually said to the losers, not the winners! However, it is just as important to learn how to win graciously as it is to lose graciously. To enjoy success without gloating seems to be the balanced expression.

Balanced Expression of Power

The balanced expression of power is experienced as confidence and in being self-assured. This type of person is able to initiate activity when appropriate, and to cooperate with others when that is appropriate. A balanced expression of power is shown by those who would not settle for the mediocrity of a life void of power, yet have learned not to let this become disruptive. Balanced types have learned how to reach deep into themselves and into life, as well, without being ruthless or insensitive. In relationships, these people can always be counted on to say "yes" when they mean yes, and "no" when they mean no. You get no mixed messages from them and you never feel as if they are trying to take advantage of you.

One of my golfing partners is an example of a person with a balanced expression of power. He is competitive—no doubt about that—but he is also absolutely encouraging to those he competes with. Once I asked him about this and his reply was simple, "There is no honor in defeating someone other than when he is performing at his best." This is in sharp contrast to those who compete by wishing the worst to their opponents. My friend's attitude brings honor to competition.

Those who are balanced in their power have learned to sidestep many of the conflicts that others get drawn into. This is not to say that power conflicts will not periodically emerge in your life. They will. But if I throw a ball to you, we are not playing catch unless you catch the ball and throw it back. The same principle is true in power conflicts. As you grow in power, those who are still insecure in their power will periodically take issue with you in order to test their own power. But it is not a power conflict unless you take it personally and feel a need to defend yourself. Then it becomes your issue, too, even if they initiated the conflict. You also have the option of sidestepping the issue and removing yourself from the conflict by retreating to your place of power in your center.

In the Eastern martial arts like t'ai chi, aikido, and karate, practitioners learn to stay in their center in the face of conflict, rather than getting pulled away from their source of power. If you lose your center while in combat, your opponent will be able to use your lack of balance against you, and you will soon find yourself on the mat. The first rule in staying balanced with your power is staying in touch with your center at all times.

The following is an exercise for awakening the sense of power in you.

Exercise

Breathe a deep power breath. Energy follows breath. As you breathe in, feel power coming into you. Pull your breath deep into your abdomen, the center of your power. Hold this power breath and feel your power radiate from your solar plexus. Do this five times.

This exercise is a method of breathing power into your body. Whenever you have a major test in front of you, try this exercise. Mystics know that on the wings of breath you can breathe anything into the body. Picture the Sunday morning comic strips. The character has a dialogue box issuing from his mouth. Picture this in reverse and put what you want in the dialogue box and then breathe it into your center. This power breath can be translated into a revitalization breath quite easily. Try it at a time when you are feeling somewhat depleted and you will notice wonderfully effective results. Simply visualize energy, rather than power, and proceed exactly the same as in the above mentioned exercise.

Varieties of Passion

Passion is the ability to engage totally with an experience. It is a loosening of control and surrendering to the ensuing emotional experience of a situation. Passion is most often thought of in bedroom terms. However, the intensity of abandoning yourself in the moment can be found in a wide variety of experiences from the most carnal to the most spiritual. Sensations are a strong aspect of passion; you can feel them as a physical experience that ranges from amorous to wrathful. The key is the intensity of the emotional reaction that accompanies loss of ego control.

In most mystery schools, ashrams, and centers of consciousness, initiates are encouraged to avoid passion. They are taught to overcome the association with the animal instincts of character in order to establish a strong foothold in higher-mind consciousness. But if one has already established a strong base in the higher mind, engaging one's passions with consciousness can be one of life's most fulfilling rewards. In the most refined and evolved of individuals this is not dangerous, but rather, pleasurable. The integration of mind, body, spirit, and emotion that expresses itself in passion can lead to a divine rapport with the universal. The trick is the integration of all parts of the character. In the person who is neither developed nor integrated in all aspects of life, passion can lead to very unpredictable situations.

Just as with power, we can explore the underexpression, overexpression, and balanced expression of passion.

Underexpression of Passion

When passion is denied, one is cut off from much of the vitality of life. Capacity and tolerance for passion, however, are very individual matters. For some, passion is not experienced as a problem, but rather as something for which they are consciously striving. For others, a lack of passion is a problem they wish to overcome. This is usually caused by a fear of losing control. The ego has such a firm grip on the attention that it refuses to abandon its position. This makes for an impossibility of experiencing the kind of passion which comes from letting go of conscious control and fully merging with the situation at hand. It is not unusual for people who deny passion to have grown up in homes with strict moral teaching, which causes guilt to be associated with passion. Other causes of underexpression can range from traumatic experiences such as abuse, rape, and molestation, to a subtle fear of the unknown.

Frigidity and impotence are illustrative of underexpression of passion. The experience of deep sexual intimacy is blocked by a psychological reaction that makes it difficult for the person to surrender. These psychological reactions can stem from a variety of causes, and professional help through counseling is often required. Nonetheless, I would still like to offer my experience as to what has worked for some of my astrological clients.

These suggestions are directed to the partner of someone who is experiencing a difficult time in their sexual expression. Be patient. Be tender. Be gentle. Be reassuring that you would value their abandoned release of passion—that it can't be wrong. These seem to be the main ingredients required to coax your partner back into a healthy sexual relationship. Be compassionate—try to accept the situation as it is, rather than focusing on any frustration that you might be experiencing. Your frustration is understandable, but if you are trying to help your mate you do not want to complicate the situation. Although it seems that underexpressing individuals are afraid of experiencing their own sexuality, it is often the case that the fears are based in not being able to please their partners. Fear of being unable to please or satisfy their partners can lead to avoiding sex altogether.

If you are the lover of a person who has difficulty in surrendering to the sexual experience, ask yourself, "Do I allow myself to experience satisfaction in my sexual life?" It seems an odd question considering the nature of the problem at hand, but in healing a sexual relationship, you want to consider the roles of both people.

Ask yourself these questions: "Have I gently taught my partner how to please me? Do I enter into satisfaction after a sexual embrace? Or do I always feel hungry for more?" If you tend towards the hungry answer, imagine what your mate experiences. It is likely that your partner does not often get to enjoy your satisfaction. If this is the case for you, learn how to cultivate gratification. This requires the ability to shift from the desire mode to the enjoy mode. Desire is healthy, especially if it can be enjoyed. It is more of a trick than it seems for many people. To desire without enjoying can be painful—it leaves you in a state of want.

Notice that while mentioning satisfaction, descriptions like "allow" and "enter into" are used. To enjoy requires a shift of your attention from desire. To desire is to want something that you are not experiencing, and to enjoy is to enter into something that you are experiencing. Start from where you and your mate are now. Try not to wish for experiences other than that which are available in the here and now. Court, tease, and play with your mate to make sexual intimacy a safe, enjoyable experience for both of you. Enjoy whatever warmth the two of you share and cultivate the sense of satisfaction.

Overexpression of Passion

This type is the sensationalist. The excitability of the senses becomes addictive, and the overfocus on the senses often leads to drugs, alcohol, and excessive sexual appetite. The losing of control becomes so desirable to the individual that escapism becomes a problem. Whenever pressures mount in the personal life, this person seeks release through involvement in some type of passionate experience.

All types of sexually deviant behavior fall into this category. This is a difficult area to discuss because there is such a variety of human sexual experience that the terms "healthy" and "unhealthy" really must be ascertained at the individual level. What is healthy for one person may not be for another, and vice versa. Healthy could be described as that which brings joy, happiness, and satisfaction for everyone involved in the experience. Unhealthy sexual habits that do not bring deep satisfaction can be retrained, but it takes a willing, dedicated effort.

Masochistic sexual behavior, rape, molestation, and abuse are extreme examples of unbalanced passion. These are only mentioned as examples, and advice will not be offered concerning these activities other than encouraging professional help. Quick cures or a simple attitude change is rarely strong enough medicine to cure these ailments. The causes are much more deeply rooted in the subconscious and assistance is required to break free of these types of addictive behavior.

Excessive focus on pleasure can also be a problem. Although most of us are working on learning how to bring more pleasure into our lives, too much of a good thing can be bad when it leads to hedonism. Again, this has to be judged at an individual level, but when pleasure-seeking disrupts other aspects of a healthy life, you can assume that it has gone too far and moderation would be advised. Sex, drugs, and alcohol are typical vehicles for one prone to excessiveness. The body itself is a beautiful barometer of how you are doing with excessive behavior. Hangovers and the like are the body's alarm system that your lifestyle and its needs are in conflict. Learn to listen to your body as you would a trusted physician and it will teach you all you need to know about your limits.

Thrill-seeking and a reckless lifestyle are also subconscious behavior patterns that signal an overexpression of passion in one's life. Examples are reckless driving on the verge of danger, illegal activities that put one in the company of a dangerous crowd, and all lifestyles that tempt disaster.

Balanced Expression of Passion

The ability to move in and out of passionate experiences is the keynote of the person who is balanced in the expression of passion. Rather than a total abandonment of control, this is a directed and conscious movement into the sensation of a particular experience.

In sexual sharing, you are able to fully merge with your partner. Before balance, sexual passion is completely surrendering to the sensations that are occurring within the self. With balance comes the ability to observe the sensations simultaneously while experiencing them. Since you can observe your sensations, you will also be able to observe those of your lover. The more evolved person will even be able to observe the combined sensations of the two individuals as they lose control and merge into one. This is the highest type of sexual union, and is the intent of tantra yoga. Rather than denying the sexual expression, it courts it. The tradition teaches that if one can detach from the pure physical sensations and the rush to orgasm, the sensation can be transmuted and experienced through each of the chakras. This is the kundalini serpent energy that rises up the spine into the higher regions of consciousness.

Sex is not the only avenue of this type of passion. Rituals, competitive sports, skydiving, downhill skiing, dramatic theater, dance, and many forms of artistic expression are also methods of evoking and directing the passionate experience. Those balanced in the expression of passion typically do not try to sterilize their life by removing themselves from all that is unpleasant. The home birth and conscious dying movements are reflective of cultural evolution towards reintegrating meaningful rituals and putting some of the guts and passion back into life.

When our five-year-old nephew was dying of cancer the entire process from diagnosis to death took about eighteen months. This was enough time for the parents to go through the entire range of reactions from anger and sadness to the hope for success of the medical treatments. In the last week of his life, it became apparent that he was actually dying and the doctors at the hospital had the wisdom to suggest the child be taken home and allowed to die in his natural environment. The night before he died, we had a slumber party at his house. Our children, his other cousins, and many of the important people in his life all camped out on his living room floor, with him resting on the couch. It was such a meaningful experience to watch him consciously say goodbye to the loved ones in his life. It seemed so healthy and even natural to watch the children playing with him and, in their own ways, saying goodbye. I slept very little that night. I kept waking up and looking at the situation with awe and reverence. Young Jacob sleeping on the couch, on what was likely to be his last night with us, the children and adults scattered about the floor in sleeping bags—it all seemed so surrealistic.

In the morning, we all awoke and said goodbye. It was so very powerful. The children knew exactly what was happening and the experience touched them deeply. When we got home, we received a call notifying us of Jacob's passing. Just after we left, he had asked for his father and told him that he had to go now. His father asked, "Where are you going Jake?" He replied that he did not know, he just had to go. He closed his eyes and death came quickly. I tell this story because of the impact it had on all of our lives. It was a conscious passing, and the ritual of the slumber party helped all of us face, with courage, one of life's toughest lessons. The children's witnessing of this natural phenomenon helped ease their fears and concerns about the mystery of death.

It takes courage to face life. It takes courage to face death. By sterilizing our lives to protect us from these deep emotions, we have robbed ourselves of the ability to experience the natural passion of life. Have the courage to show up for your life—you will be giving your Mars room to express itself.

Dealing with Anger

Anger is closely related to power and passion, and is an area of expression that causes great difficulty for most people whether they are in or out of relationships. A healthy alignment with your anger is a major contributing factor toward experiencing happiness in your relationships. You have to successfully deal with it before you can proceed to more satisfying types of emotional expression.

Working through angry states comes down to intent. If your true intention is to get past the anger and move on to a state of harmony, being honest with your anger can be very effective. However, to do this you must be very honest with yourself. If your true intent is just to have a target on which to vent your frustration, then your anger will only create more reasons for being angry, which can undermine even the best of relationships.

Anger itself is representative of how you deal with the larger concerns of power and passion. If you never get angry, then everything that happens around you is all right, all of the time. There are philosophies that subscribe to this, but is it your philosophy? If it isn't, you can get into trouble by sending out messages that all is well. Only you will know where the truth lies. If your insides are upset much of the time, there is a good chance that you have difficulty expressing your anger.

When you smile and act as though nothing is wrong, while on the inside you are churning over some unresolved situation, you are misrepresenting yourself.

Anger is one of the emotions that people go through and, just like the others, it needs expression. Anger can be terrifying, especially when it is not understood, and it can ruin relationships when it is expressed in an inappropriate way. Anger might very well be one of the hardest aspects of relating you will ever have to deal with. If you have repressed anger for many years, then it can be even more challenging to get comfortable with its expression. Proper expression of anger is an important part of any successful relationship.

Anger is an ally of power, passion, and your drive to be strong. The way that you deal with anger is probably akin to your effectiveness in your total life expression. Stretched out in a long continuum, anger and joy will be the two extremes. Imagine a pendulum swinging between the two poles of anger and joy. Now imagine placing your hand in the path of the pendulum so that it cannot swing toward anger. What happens to its movement? Can it swing only toward joy, stop at the bottom of its arc and swing back to joy? If you block one end of the continuum, the other will be inhibited as well.

Underexpression of Anger

There is a saying: "As a man thinketh, so he becomes." If you subscribe to this, then you know that your thoughts count, whether you act on them or not. Underexpression of anger leads to an inward turning of its expression. This introversion never dismisses or dissolves the intensity of anger, it simply implodes rather than explodes. It is as if you got angry at yourself and your body responded with tension problems. Your thoughts are powerful motivational forces.

People who suffer from underexpression of anger often have a moral conflict with anger itself, feeling that it should not be there to begin with. Guilt is usually the source of the conflict. There is often a correlation between people who have difficulty in expressing their anger and people who have had strong religious, moral, or spiritual backgrounds. This is somewhat understandable since obedience is one of the religious vows of many spiritual paths. Often, these are peaceful souls who just plain wish they didn't have to deal with anger at all!

Wishing anger was not there leads to the "oh, it's not worth the hassle" syndrome—an honest attempt at dismissing the force of the anger. It does not work. The energy gets dismissed only in its expression—it is still there, only now it operates beneath the surface. In the long run, subliminal anger is just as destructive as overt anger, and is often more damaging because no one can deal with it. It is not out in the clear light.

When anger is repressed, it often leads to the "kick-the-cat syndrome": the boss yells at the man, who comes home and yells at his wife, who yells at her child, who kicks the cat! When not dealt with directly, anger can also come out in passive-aggressive ways like lacing your speech with barbs at the person with whom you are angry. These barbs never deal with the true issue you have with the person, rather they become generalized into a overall frustration with that person.

Another variation of underexpression is expressing your anger with the wrong person. An example that most people are familiar with is a situation similar to this: your coworker makes you angry, but you sidestep the issue. Still, you stew inside yourself. You just can't think of anything else other than how this person has offended you. You call a friend and just talk and talk about your angry concerns. The next time you see your coworker, you again act like nothing is wrong, but you hold a grudge and begin to withhold your friendship. The sad part of this is that the coworker really does not know what is going on, other than that you have started to pull away. You have released the motivation for clearing the air by venting your anger in the safe haven of your friend on the phone.

If anger could truly be dismissed, that would be one thing, but more often the energy is still there, just not dealt with. Emotions can be like water passing under a bridge. It successfully passes one point only to build up at the dam downstream. This clog of pent-up anger can be quite destructive when the dam finally bursts. This is when it is easier to get a divorce, rather than confront your feelings. But there was a time when confronting your hurt feelings would have been a more effective way to deal with the situation.

Honesty is an issue in underexpression of anger. On the surface you appear to be one kind of person, but inside you are quite different. You may give off the image of being easy-going, but if you are experiencing inner turmoil, you are not sharing the reality of yourself. In this state, you typically attract people and situations that are somewhat confusing—the result of giving out mixed messages in the first place. The ego will often justify lack of honesty with statements such as, "I do not want to hurt my partner with the truth." When you find yourself justifying lack of honesty for the benefit of your partner, ask yourself if it is not lack of courage that you are experiencing, rather than the altruistic desire to protect your partner.

Overexpression of Anger

This type of person represents the hair-trigger personality. Even the slightest provocation, real or imagined, is enough to set him off. He feels a need to defend, control, and manipulate others before they manipulate him. The chip-on-the-shoulder is always taunting others to knock it off, and, of course, they do! Overexpression of anger typically stems from an insecurity concerning personal power. The person fears that he does not have it, so he is always fighting for it. Remember, you never have to fight for what you already have. Rather then being angry at the world and trying to control it, the balance comes from learning self-control. When you can control yourself, you do not need to control others.

It sounds easy: why not just quit fighting with others? Why not relax and let your guard down? Because it becomes addictive. Anger triggers the release of adrenaline—it can be felt in the body as a rush of energy. Many people become addicted to this rush and need a fix of anger each day to feed their habit. Yes, it certainly is energy, but more often than not, it is destructive. Many people fall prey to this negative form of energy as if they need it to fuel their drive. Before they can really apply themselves to the job at hand, they need to get a fix of anger. To get their energy up to accomplish their tasks, they manifest some petty annoyance in their lives, generating angry energy.

What you pay attention to grows. Realize this when you are overexpressing anger—you pay attention to your frustrations and they grow. You get trapped by the word "because"—whatever you say after because, justifies your anger and frustration. When anger is overexpressed, it becomes an investment of your attention on what triggered the anger, and the situation grows.

It is interesting that we have the phrase "pay attention." We truly do pay, as an investment of our energy, to wherever our attention goes. There are only twenty-four hours in a day and there are only so many things that you can think about. What you choose to think about is a payment of your life force. Be careful what you think, as life coalesces around your thoughts. Always remember that you are the person who has control over how you think. If you are always in a state of angry reaction to the world around you, you have given all of your power away.

When you overexpress anger, you can be heard saying such things as, "Well, I have a right to be angry. Do you know what just happened?" A situation arises that elicits an angry response from you, like someone running a red light and almost hitting you. The anger of the moment is appropriate, but if it is carried around for the next three hours, you have gone overboard. Now your anger has control of you, rather than you having control of it. You have fallen prey to justifiable anger. If somebody else acted like a jerk, why should you feel bad? Here the attitude concerning anger is revealed—it is seen as a reward, and there is just cause for it. Is this really the reward you want for your energy?

One of the difficulties in dealing with the overexpression of anger is the apparent rewards it brings. You often get your way, as others see there is no limit to your willingness to escalate your anger until they back down. Our modern world seems to reward this "win at any cost" attitude. At worst, you use your anger as a bullying technique and intimidation becomes a way of life for you. If this describes you, you would have to assess the cost of this behavior on your personal happiness. You are winning, but are you happy?

If you are the person who is overexpressive with your anger, it behooves you to find healthy, constructive ways for releasing your excess fire energy. Aerobics, running, swimming, weight-training, and dancing are just as effective and certainly less destructive than volatile anger.

Balanced Expression of Anger

With a balanced expression of anger, you know how to maintain your power and can clearly define your personal space. You speak your truth with conviction, rather than hostility. You have become conscious of the impact of your anger on others when unchecked. You have learned to express anger when it is appropriate and hold it in check when it is not appropriate. It is not unusual to see balanced types involved in social activism of one type or another. There are many issues in the modern world to which anger is an appropriate response, and when you have learned to translate the anger into action, you can be a catalyst for change.

I know a woman in her mid-thirties who appears to have a good handle on this. She is married and has three children. She grew up in a family with four sisters and one brother. She learned at an early age that she had to speak up or get lost in the pack. Life was fast, and there was no time to go back and deal with issues from the past. She developed a wonderful ability to express her anger in the moment and then be free of it. Others knew exactly where they stood with her, because she told them.

Her husband was of the underexpression type. He mistrusted her expression of anger during their early years of marriage. He tried to change her ways, but she stood her ground. He confided that he eventually learned a great deal from her about a balanced expression of anger by watching the effect her expression of anger had on their children. This had initially caused him concern. When the children would do something that would make her angry, she would heat up and express her anger in the moment at the behavior. In the next moment, though, her obvious love would return and he could see that the children were not threatened, scared, or hurt by her behavior. Quite the contrary, they seemed to benefit by learning which actions caused anger in her. She was naturally uninhibited in the expression of her anger and fortunately, she was also uninhibited in the expression of her love, which is not always the case with overexpression. She expressed both love and anger with ease and forthrightness. The children learned that it was their behavior, and not themselves that caused the anger.

Not all are naturals at this type of expression but everyone can learn to acquire balance. Parents with young children typically learn that it is possible to simultaneously express their love of their children and their anger over specific behavior. It helps to treat children like they are big people in little bodies, and adults like they are little people in big bodies.

Exercise

The next time that you are angry at your mate, specifically state which behavior triggered your anger.

For a healthy expression of anger, the most important distinction to make is between the behavior itself, and the person who created the action. Can you focus your anger only at the behavior and not the person? If you can, you have a balanced expression of anger and others will benefit from your expression rather than be hurt by it. Anger can hurt others only when they feel it is directed at them, instead of what they did. Learn to take the flamethrower of anger and focus it into a laser light of preciseness.

When this is accomplished there is no confusion in its expression. So instead of statements such as "You make me angry!" learn to be more specific with your expression with such statements as, "When you said or did such-and-such, that made me angry." The specific message is not as threatening to others and their defenses are not aroused as easily. This allows for a discussion of the anger rather than a reaction to it.

Creative Frustration

Frustration creates energy and fuels anger. What happens next is up to you. Everyone experiences frustration and has a different threshold of how much of it they can handle before the energy turns into anger. When frustration is transformed into action it becomes drive.

If you walk into your kitchen and become frustrated over the dirty dishes, there is a choice involved as to what happens next. You can either stew in the frustration until it becomes anger and then yell at somebody to clean it up, or you can silently transform the frustration into action and clean the kitchen. Anger or action, it is your choice. The alchemists of old were said to be able to change base metals like lead into gold. Spiritual alchemists transform base human emotions, like frustration and anger, into their golden potential of creative drive.

How frustration enters your life appears to be a matter of destiny—it just happens, but how you respond to frustration is up to you and your free will. How long it takes you to translate the energy from frustration into creative action seems to be a valid measure of the health of your responses to it. The sooner that you translate frustration into constructive action, the more it plays a positive role in your life. If you sit and stew with your frustrations for long periods before you act on them, you are just hurting yourself by directing the negative energy inward upon yourself, often leading to health complications.

Exercise

Practice the art of creative frustration by joyously performing your daily tasks and chores.

Recognize that much of the fuel to accomplish your daily chores comes from frustration. You are doing a task because you are not happy with the way things are—that is frustration. But once the energy comes in through frustration, then it is yours—you can do with it what you please. Just buy into the energy. Learn to disassociate from the source of your frustration and instead, vest your energy on the process of accomplishment.

We hear about nonattachment as an important aspect of spiritual life. Often this is translated as not having possessions or things, but it is even more important in being an alchemist of transmuting angry, frustrated energy into positive, creative drive. Energy is energy. It just is, and is neither positive nor negative in itself. It is your experience with the energy that creates the positive or negative feelings. Frustration and anger are experienced as negative energy. If you remain attached to whatever apparently caused the frustration or irritation, then all of the energy you receive from the experience will be given back to whatever triggered it.

If you can get to the point of nonattachment in dealing with frustration, then when you become frustrated you will immediately detach from whatever brought on the frustration. Then it becomes just you and your energy. It is still negative energy, but at least you have control of it now. The alchemist then breathes deeply to fuel the inner fires, and transmutes the energy from the base level of frustration into creative, positive energy. Now, what you do with the energy is up to you and your creative choice!

Androgyny: Mars and Venus United

Both men and women are experiencing more inner wholeness than ever before. In the past, the image of a successful relationship was of two halves coming together to create one whole. The current image is of two whole people coming together to experience the synergistic possibilities of union on a higher plane. Neither party truly needs the other person to feel complete, at least in the ideal. Both partners have learned how to involve themselves with life so that they are happy, fulfilled individuals in their own right. Yet, the desire for relationship and connecting with one's lifetime mate remains a goal, regardless of whether or not this is a necessary function of life. The truth is that marriage, or other forms of relationship commitment, are not essential for life to continue, but are extra, and enhance the quality of one's life experience.

Two separate images come to mind. The first is that of the half-full cup that needs to be filled by another, much the same as the romantic notion that it is somehow beautiful to need another. If we translated the image to money, it would be illustrative. If every time I saw you, I needed five dollars, you would soon tire of our friendship. The same is true in the half-full cup image. If you are truly using the other person to satisfy your needs, then you become a subtle drain to that person, the more so as your partner's experience with you becomes one of meeting your needs.

The other image is that of the full cup—you approach your relationships as if you were a full cup, looking to share your abundance. When two people both approach their relationship as full cups, all is possible. The energy of the relationship is not spent fulfilling each other's needs, and can be directed into more creative experiences. Both individuals have learned to fill their cups from the fountain of life. Allow yourself to pursue emotional, mental, and spiritual intimacy with others and life itself, and you will be more as a full cup to your "special" person.

Mars Through the Signs

Mars represents the desire function and Venus the ability to experience satisfaction. Ideally, the two work together in your life. With desire you are allowing your energy field to be awakened. With satisfaction, you focus on receiving, accepting, enjoying, and appreciating that which is before you. This completes the cycle that began in desire. Venus and Mars enter into a delightful dance as you learn to shift your focus from being the pursuer to giving yourself permission to fully enjoy that which you have experienced.

Mars in Aries

Your Energy Blueprint You assert yourself with complete abandon and throw yourself into all that you do with drive and intensity. You will do best in very active relationships that allow for your spontaneous nature to jump into action on the spur of the moment. Yes, you are impulsive, it is your most natural way of being. At best, this represents the ability to take decisive action when needed. You like to do what you want to do when you want to do it, and you can thrive only with a partner who supports your independence. You are a catalyst with a knack for stirring others up, both positively and negatively. Your passions ignite quickly and you will likely have to slow your impulses down for a mutually gratifying sexual life with your partner. You typically express your anger in the moment and then are done with it. The beauty of this is that it allows you to be fresh and not harbor feelings of resentment from the past. You would do best with an independent mate that can stand up to your apparent brashness.

You are at your best while initiating some new project. Ideally, you would have a job that took advantage of this pioneering part of your character that likes to forge ahead. Intense physical activity is a healthy outlet for using the abundant energy of this placement. Keeping the body healthy and vital also allows for the clearest level of instinctual guidance, a gut-level sense of appropriate action. With this placement, you want to consider your instincts one of your main resources.

Areas to Work On Cooperation is not your forte, as you are at your best when there is momentum in your life and you do not have to stop to consider other people. There can be a quite unconscious defensive reaction that has you protecting yourself against anything that appears to challenge you. At worst, this represents an aggressive, insensitive person who is always looking for someone to challenge. You can become very impatient with those who like to stop and consider an activity before plunging into it, yet this type of person can be very good for you in helping you acquire a balanced perspective. The challenge for Mars in Aries is that it can lead to volatile relationships. You can become very feisty in your dealings with others unless you create opportunities for initiating new experiences in your life. One of your main challenges will be in sustaining your efforts to bring your projects through to completion, and in maintaining long-term relationships.

Understanding Mars in Aries in Others Mars in Aries individuals are likely to be governed by impulses. This leads to action and these people need to lead very active lives. Thoughts immediately translate directly into action for them. When asked the question, "Why did you do that?" the likely response of, "I don't know, it just seemed right in the moment" is absolutely honest. You need not be worried about any hidden motivations with these people—you will know what their motivations are by observing their actions. Passion and anger both seem to run hot with this placement. Although volatile and aggressive in the moment, these people rarely hold grudges, so the air is usually cleared quickly, keeping the relationship fresh.

In relationships, these individuals thrive on spontaneous activity. Fun and unpredictable, they certainly can be great for keeping life rolling along. It is the excitement of new experience that drives them into action. When life becomes stable and predictable, the Mars in Aries personality gets restless. Whenever you need an initiating spark to get a project off the ground, these are the people to enlist. Your frustrations with them are likely to arise in two areas: their tendency towards not following through on projects and their tendency towards taking action without considering your needs or feelings. Be direct and assertive in your dealings with them, or their intensity will simply overwhelm you. Surprise them with periodic spontaneous plans and you will have the best chance of holding their interest.

Mars in Taurus

YOUR ENERGY BLUEPRINT The energy of Mars is funneled into practical, sustained efforts in Taurus. You assert yourself with determination and you are likely to be known for your endurance on the positive side and your stubbornness on the negative side. Taurus is the Bull, and the action of Mars in this sign leads to steady, strong, sure-footed behavior. The security needs of Taurus will be abundantly provided for by the action of Mars. You will likely find yourself focusing on practical, business, and financial issues, although as Taurus is ruled by Venus, you have great appreciation for beauty, as well. You focus on quality and whatever you do, your standards will by evidenced by your efforts. Your actions are filtered through your security needs and you work hard to build a comfortable life.

In relationships, your determination translates into loyalty and commitment. You are known for your follow-through in whatever you apply yourself to, and this trait also leads to the ability to sustain long-term relationships. The sensuality of Taurus makes for a very affectionate, loving way of expressing your passion. You also know how to make your life comfortable and secure, which is very attractive to others. You prefer not to express anger—you get your way by holding your ground and outlasting your adversaries. No one can badger or intimate you into anything.

AREAS TO WORK ON The tenacity of Taurus, when excessive, can lead to an unyielding temperament. Problems in relationships can erupt over your stubbornness, possessiveness, and excessive material concerns. Your first choice in adapting to changes and to the unexpected is most likely to dig in your heels. Your set ways lead to needless resistance, and it is wise for you to always ask yourself if the test in front of you is really something that you need to resist. Remember it takes energy to resist. Your stick-to-it-nature is an asset in business, but in relationships, you tend to be too practical for your own good.

Understanding Mars in Taurus in Others Mars in Taurus leads to stable, reliable, dependable action. These people are typically steady, as they consider the practicality of a course of action before embarking on it. You want to give them the time they need to make decisions about what course of action to take. You will find them at their worst when you rush them. "You can lead a horse to water, but you can't make him drink" applies to this type. If you want a Mars in Taurus individual to change a particular behavior, you must first present the practical advantage of an alternative, and then give them the time to mull it over, before it will be considered.

In relationships, Mars in Taurus is loyal, dependable, and affectionate. Surprises and sudden changes of plans are not advised as you will likely meet with resistance. In arguments, these people can become very stubborn. When you provoke resistance, the heels dig in and that is it. In terms of anger, this placement means a slow boil. Typically, Mars in Taurus is very sweet and gentle, but "mad as a bull" could also describe the temperament when pushed too far. Plan activities far ahead of time that relate to their desire for comfort and enjoyment of the senses in order to best fit in with their natural expression of energy. They prefer to fully experience the quality of an activity at a comfortable pace, rather than to rush through the experience to meet a fully packed agenda.

Mars in Gemini

Your Energy Make-up You assert yourself through your mind, and the versatility of Gemini propels the expression of your energy into many and varied projects. You can be known as a jack-of-all-trades type of person, as you typically dabble in many pursuits rather than postholing in a specific path of action. The energy of Mars gets dispersed through the realm of ideas in Gemini, and you can be known as an idea person. You are likely to be a very good conversationalist, as the expression of your energy through talking is very natural for you. Others may get frustrated over this part of your character, as merely talking about things to do is often more rewarding for you than actually doing them! Your energy is more like the short-distance runner than the marathoner. When you are forced to do one thing all day long, even if it is something that you love to do, it is exhausting. But when you have many changes of activity throughout the day, your energy stays fresh and responsive.

The intellectual aspect of a relationship is likely to be very important to you as you need to be able to communicate with your mate. A sexy partner for you would be someone with a dazzling intellect. Your passionate nature gets bored with routine, so you will want a partner who is open to variety in your lovemaking styles. Your adaptability allows you to sidestep arguments when you wish to, as you have natural ability to talk yourself in and out of trouble.

Areas to Work On You likely have challenges with following through on commitments, as you are very easily distracted. How to steer a steady course is most difficult for you, as you are always aware of alternatives. Fascination is a one word description of your type of happiness; thus when you say you are committed to a person it usually means as long as you are fascinated. Fascination is healthy for you, but this can easily flip into being infatuated and this is one of your downfalls. Your quest for variety can lead to superficiality unless you discipline yourself to fully experience what is before you.

Understanding Mars in Gemini in Others You will never be bored with these people! The intellectual nature of this sign directs their actions into a variety of pursuits and interests. Mars in Gemini is motivated by fascination and these people are easy to talk to and hard to pin down. On the one hand, this leads to a spontaneous, animated curiosity for life that you are likely to find delightful. On the other hand, their ability to follow through on commitments is hampered by an easily distracted nature.

Arguments are easily resolved with these individuals as they can just as easily see your point of view as their own. Not to say they do not argue. They do, and will likely change positions in the middle of an argument just to keep it going! But likely it is all in sport for them and no harshness or grudge will result. If you are working on projects with a Mars in Gemini friend, be prepared for them to change the plans—often. They continue to get fascinated with new possibilities and you will likely have to rein them back to the project at hand.

If you are open to allowing variety into your intimate sharing with these people, you have a treat in store. To engage their passion, the mind must be engaged, so plan activities that allow for mental stimulation to best fit into their natural expression of energy. Surprise them with tickets to the theater, or a lecture, or even both with coffee in between, to bring out the best in them.

Mars in Cancer

Your Energy Make-up You assert the forceful side of your character through your emotions. Activities connected to the home, family, and nurturing are all natural expressions for you. Security is such an important issue for you, that you choose to establish boundaries with friendships and activities, and then focus within that which you have defined as your circle. This leads to a close and small group of friends, rather than a large group of casual acquaintances. Friends become as family to you once you let them into your life. You also have an ability to defend yourself and fight the battles for loved ones that you feel are unable to defend themselves.

In relationships, you can be very loyal and committed—you tend to hold on tenaciously to that which gives you security and, ideally, you would be with people who appreciate this. Physical touching, holding, and hugging are natural and important for you. Your passionate nature is slow starting and long lasting. Your anger gets activated when your boundaries are threatened. Your anger is subjective and emotionally based, which can be troublesome in relationships because it is difficult for others to objectively deal with your issues. You are quite at home in the domestic environment and can be a natural nest-builder, creating living environments that are likely to be warm and cozy.

Areas to Work On Your moods are powerful and, at times, can control your actions. You are able to express your emotional warmth with those who you most care about, but you might seem cold and unapproachable to others. Your particular dilemma in relationships deals with how you express your anger—when you express it with others, it causes hurt feelings and if you hold it in, it causes stomach problems. When you are most hurt and in need of comforting, you tend to express yourself in the harshest way, driving away the opportunity for the tender loving care you need. This is resolved once you are able to express your sensitivities in a sensitive way. Also, it would be wise for you to ask yourself, "If I am overprotective of my boundaries, how will I ever grow?"

Understanding Mars in Cancer in Others This placement leads to a strong emotional nature. You can feel these individuals as they express themselves through emotions. If you are on the inside with this type, you will feel the graces of a warm, affectionate, nurturing character. They are loyal and committed to those considered close. If you are not on the inside, you can be treated with what may feel like cold indifference until they warm up to you. It is actually their insecurity with you that causes this appearance. Be patient, it is worth the wait. These individuals are cautious about accepting new emotional friendships, but once accepted by them, you will be treated as family.

Mars in Cancer retreats within a shell of defensiveness when threatened and then suddenly explodes with anger. Family members will receive the full force of Mars in Cancer's negative emotions. These people will only express anger where it is safe and they know they will still be loved when the explosion is over. Count on them to act in a way that protects that which makes them feel secure and safe in life. Activities such a day at the beach, shopping for personal items or furnishings for the home, an evening meal together, or family outings are certain to win their favor.

Mars in Leo

Your Energy Make-up Proud, strong, and assertive, you are not meant to take the back seat to anyone in this life. Your love of life and your willfulness creates quite a strong personality. This is a "work hard, play hard" combination—you have ambitions, but not just for worldly success. You also want a rich personal life with plenty of recreation, entertainment, creative expression, and just plain fun. When animated by your heart, you can be extremely joyful. When animated by a desire to win, you can become extremely competitive and driven. In both cases, you have a natural flair for life that is meant to be expressed and enjoyed. With Mars in Leo, "Passion be thy name" and you need to express this same dramatic flair in your romantic life. It is good for you to be with heartful, playful people as they bring out the most childlike part of your character.

In relationships, you are a catalyst for fun, as your ability to thoroughly enjoy life is best shared with others. It is essential that you are the center of attention in relationships and it is not an exaggeration to say that you need to be adored—you do not play the second fiddle graciously. Your pride extends to those you love and care for and you promote and protect them as well as yourself. You are a loyal, affectionate, and loving partner as long as you are not in competition with your mate.

Areas to Work On In arguments, your will to succeed will tend to be a problem, because you will always win. Always winning is never to anyone's advantage. When you are upset with others, it is almost impossible for you to put yourself in their position. So, of course, this is part of your homework. Your willful nature is that which allows you to succeed, but it is also that which makes you seem arrogant to others. You function well under the spotlight, but you will have to learn to share center stage with those you love to avoid the resentments that could build in your supporting cast.

The right use of will is your test and there are certain to be many power conflicts with others until you have learned to control your will, instead of being controlled by it. Direct your power creatively, right from the heart, and you are certain to be both successful and enjoy it as well.

Understanding Mars in Leo in Others These people can be formidable allies or foes, so know who you are dealing with right from the start. High spirited, they do nothing half-heartedly. When you are on their good side, you will see the most heartful, joyful, fun side of their character. They strive to be the best at whatever they do. At times, you will admire this creative intensity and winning attitude and other times you will feel as though they are always competing with you.

These people are passionate souls in all that they do. When you provoke their anger, you will know exactly where they stand, as they are not timid about expressing displeasure. Be prepared for a few issues of dominance, as this placement leads to staying in the driver's seat. By choice, these individuals would rather be having fun and laughing than in any type of argument, so appeal to their heart and you will soon see the brighter side of their character. When Mars in Leo people are enjoying life, no one does it better. Plan activities that center around fun and creativity and you will bring out the best in them.

Mars in Virgo

Your Energy Make-up You assert yourself in an exacting and precise manner. You need to be busy and productive and can love a task-oriented lifestyle. Your ability to master techniques often leads you to success, as you always find a more effective, efficient path to do whatever it is that you are doing. You like to be self-sufficient and able to personally care for all of the many details of the maintenance of your life. You tend to be highly discriminating and your analytical qualities make you an effective and efficient problem-solver. You pride yourself in not wasting anything: time, money, or resources.

In relationships, you often strive for an uncluttered rapport of a peaceful and simple lifestyle. Your sincerity and genuineness make you a caring and attentive partner. Your refined temperament does not rely on brute force to get your way. You are more of a finesse player, prefer to use your ingenuity to surmount obstacles. You have an incisive wit and appreciation for intellectual humor. When you do express your anger, it often comes out in sharp, critical ways. You appreciate people who are self-sufficient, but on the other hand, your security is based on your usefulness, so you would not want someone too independent. To be with a partner that enjoys working on tasks together would be ideal. As an earth sign, Virgo is marvelously sensual and affectionate and will be highly discriminating with choice of partners. You tend to shy away from the powerful, complicating emotions of deep passion, preferring the "life's simple pleasures" approach to your sexuality.

Areas to Work On Learning to be tolerant of other people's less than perfect ways will be one of your challenges in enjoying relationships. Try not to project your standards of perfection onto others, or you will be considered as nitpicky. It is not double-talk to say that you have to include human imperfection in your model of perfection to most enjoy life. Your tendency of being task oriented can squeeze out time for romance and you need to be reminded to build completion into your daily life or you'll always feel that there is more that you can do.

Your analytical mind sometimes gets in the way and you can tend to worry over endless details that might go wrong.

UNDERSTANDING MARS IN VIRGO IN OTHERS These refined souls temper their aggressive tendencies with their abundant intelligence and neither utilize, nor appreciate, the use of brute force. These are task-oriented individuals who like to stay busy and productive. Whatever they do will be done with diligence and a keen eye for perfection—if it is worth doing, they want to do it right. The Mars in Virgo standards of perfection are not taken lightly and this can make them sticklers for details. Don't assume they will overlook the small things. They won't. Power conflicts would be rare with them as they have little drive for dominance, preferring to focus on perfecting their own process. Not that there won't be arguments. They can be sharply critical of your efforts, but it is not about dominance—they just want you to get it right!

Mars in Virgo requires the time it takes to analyze a considered path of action. This is all part of their natural process—if you force them into spontaneous activity, you will experience strong resistance. They are extremely bright and clever and appreciate intellectual humor over pure slapstick. They appreciate quality and are not impressed with pretentiousness. Sometimes, those with Mars in Virgo forget to have fun, as their life tends to be filled with the business of maintaining all of their responsibilities. They are not given to their passions; however, this is a very caring and considerate placement.

Mars in Libra

YOUR ENERGY MAKE-UP The aggressive force of Mars is at its most refined in Libra and you rarely express yourself harshly. You are aware of appearances, not only in clothes, but also how you present your personality. This gives a natural sense of style and grace in all that you do. With your ability to be a team player, you steer a course far away from power conflicts. However, in your drive for peace and balance in your life, you may over respond to the demands of your partner and settle for "peace at any cost." The trouble is, the cost is often too high if you have to sacrifice your own integrity. You simply do not handle anger well, in yourself or others. The empty wish is that you will never have to deal with unfair people—empty because it is unrealistic. Your path of action is to be the diplomat, negotiating for peaceful settlements instead of accepting whatever is offered. Remember, it is cooperation that will work best for you, not compromise.

In relationships, you enjoy peaceful, easy time with your partner and have a strong distaste for unpleasant emotional encounters. Your refined temperament prefers the charm of romance to the depth of passion. You do have a knack for seeing the other person's point of view, so you tend to be very considerate of others rather than asserting yourself without regard. At best, this leads to a naturally cooperative temperament. You like to believe that all disputes could be worked out if people could only sit down and work out their differences in a calm, rational manner.

Areas to Work On Your concerns for how others think of you can lead to a "people pleasing" type of pretentiousness. You also have a marked distaste for all that is unpleasant, which leads to backing down in the face of conflict. Your test of courage deals with learning to be fair with yourself as well. To allow another person to take advantage of you violates the absolute balance that you crave, just as much as taking advantage of others would. It has to be win-win in all of your dealings with others. Physical exercises involving balance, like yoga postures, t'ai chi, and dance are excellent activities to help encode the sense of balance into the body. When you seek balance by trying to find it in the outer world, it creates the teeter-totter phenomenon of always overcompensating one way or another. Come from balance in your expression, rather than from seeking it.

Understanding Mars in Libra in Others Do not expect these people to jump into action on the spur of the moment. They won't. This placement leads to considered action. Everything has to be thought out and weighed against alternatives. These individuals strive to be fair in all dealings and agreements with others. Always diplomatic, the achievement of fairness, justice, and equality is a high priority for those with Mars in Libra. They appreciate, and demonstrate, a refinement of character.

This placement can also lead to procrastinators who think about doing, more than actually doing. It is best to approach these people as coolly and as calmly as you can when expressing your anger, because Mars in Libra would rather acquiesce in the moment, and then do what it pleases later, rather than stand there and argue. Not known for their passion, they are wonderfully romantic and their refinement will show here as well. Favorite activities can be getting dressed up and going out for a social evening together—they do appreciate style. Shopping for clothes, talking about the people in their life, and activities related to the arts are also enjoyable activities for them.

Mars in Scorpio

YOUR ENERGY MAKE-UP This is easily the most complex position for the planet of action because so much of the energy of Scorpio goes on beneath the surface. This placement gives you an extremely powerful will. You have a strong impact on others and you will be tested with the right use of your natural ability to influence others. You have tremendous psychological strength which is the power behind your endurance and your ability to be in control of most situations. This is also your biggest challenge, as it is difficult for you to reveal your vulnerability to others. This makes the intimacy that you crave an elusive goal. The shrewdness and the calculating nature of this sign are most beneficially expressed in business. In relationships, this same calculating nature doesn't allow closeness easily. Your tremendous endurance gives you excellent coping abilities and you can be counted on to follow through on commitments.

You are a passionate person and, for you, passion is more than a sensual experience. You also enjoy the psychological transformations that you and your partner experience. You function best in an intimate one-to-one relationship. Issues concerning control, money, and sex are likely to be hot spots in your relationships. It seems wise to always evaluate your motivations while you are in a conflict over these issues. Remember the basic metaphysical premise: "Outer reality mirrors inner reality." When conflicts arise with others, be willing to ask yourself why you have attracted this challenge to you. You are meant to be involved in using your power, and as long as you are willing to evaluate your motivations, you can effect deep change and transformation in others.

AREAS TO WORK ON Mars is where you can feel frustrated unless you are taking constructive, decisive action. Your frustrations run deep and likely affect those around you psychologically. Even when not expressed verbally, your buried resentments and hostilities are clearly felt by others. This psychological power you have can easily manipulate others, and the low road would be to take advantage of this. The impact of your energy field on others is to the degree that you can hurt or heal, all depending on how you dedicate your energies. In your intense desire to get to the bottom of issues, you often hold onto problems far longer than is advised. With Scorpio's attachment to old wounds, fueled by the warrior energy of Mars, you will have to watch your tendency for being vindictive, or at worst, revengeful.

Understanding Mars in Scorpio in Others These are strong-willed individuals that are tough negotiators and it is best to know that right from the start. Mars in Scorpio individuals have strong emotional energy fields that are usually charismatic. It is hard to pull a fast one on them, as they seem to have instincts into what your true motivations are. Sheer intensity and the ability to be self-controlled allows these individuals to maintain a constant, focused attention to their will. It is not likely that you would ever get those with Mars in Scorpio to do something against their will.

Trust comes slowly to them, as they have likely seen the best and the worst of human behavior. Once you have gained their trust, you have gained a profound loyalty. These people do not like to talk about their motivations, but at times, that is just what is needed. The intensity of this sign would much rather reach for the depths of the relationship rather than be superficial. Be prepared for a psychological involvement with these people, as much of their intensity exists beneath the surface.

There is a sweet side of Scorpio that is revealed to those they trust. They are likely to be fascinated by the unknown, so be advised to always keep something mysterious about yourself to hold their interest. The long memory of Scorpio can cause them to hold onto old grudges. Do not assume that time will wash away their memories—if there is an unresolved conflict in your relationship, it will stay unresolved until dealt with, so it is best not to side step issues. Plan private time together, rather than social outings, to bring out the best in them.

Mars in Sagittarius

Your Energy Make-up You assert yourself in a casual, easy-going way while pursuing your activities. You maintain a friendly disposition, but this masks a fierceness of character. You have the drive to be a winner in life, and you tend to come out on top in most situations, although you don't take glory in defeating others. You like to stay active and are at your best when you are pursuing a goal. You need lots of room to roam, literally, and it is good to have intense physical activity, even competition, with this placement. This gives your competitive spirit a healthy outlet. You tend toward bursts of enthusiasm, and like to have the freedom to follow your inspiration. You prefer to have many projects and interests going at once, instead of a singular focus.

In relationships, your friendly manner allows you to avoid much conflict. The physical side of passion holds strong attraction for you and you can be a playful and amorous lover. You are known for your direct and blunt character. Argument for you is a sport. Friendly debates over political, religious, or philosophical beliefs are fun for you, but you have to remember that not everyone enjoys debate as sport. You would like a partner who is willing to live life to its fullest, go on a journey on a moment's notice, enter into a philosophical discussion with you, and, do it all with a great deal of fun.

Areas to Work On Your tendency to focus on the big picture often has you overlooking the details of your plans. You like to do what you want to do when you want to do it, and this can make you appear quite impatient to others. You are friendly and view yourself as being a warm person, but your bluntness can offend the sensitivities of others. At worst, the warrior in you can become dogmatic and evangelical in your beliefs. You too often assume the moral high ground in arguments, giving you a "holier than thou" approach. Another dark side of your character can show itself as becoming a tyrant in insisting others keep a positive attitude. Your energy easily becomes scattered. Although you like doing many projects at once, always have one goal that you shoot your arrow towards, follow it, pick it up and shoot it again until it hits the eventual target. This can make you more effective in realizing your goals.

Understanding Mars in Sagittarius in Others These people typically have a very intense yet, at the same time, easy-going manner. Sudden bursts of enthusiasm are likely to get these individuals heading off in several directions simultaneously until they learn to control their goal-setting ability. Their upbeat approach is there in romance as well, and they are fun-loving, enthusiastic lovers. They appreciate bluntness, so be as direct and as open as possible in your dealings with them. This placement leads to high moral standards and a naturally honest character. Although typically fair in their dealings, they usually get their way, as they are quite persuasive and have a knack for talking people into coming along on their many activities. These people can be open-minded if you give them the chance, yet they can be fierce competitors if you happen to trigger their defensiveness.

Mars in Sagittarius needs a great deal of activity, so be prepared for anything if you plan on spending time with them. Life turns into an adventure on a moment's notice with these types. An expansive, optimistic attitude coupled with a "let's go for it" philosophy, creates room for a tremendous amount of potential activities. Talking about dreams, potential travel, and adventure is good fun for these individuals. Politics, religion, and philosophy can sometimes get them going on a rather dogmatic, evangelical train of thought. Be prepared for a bit of moralizing from this combination. Travel, adventure, outdoor activity, and any form of education are favorite activities of theirs to share with others.

Mars in Capricorn

YOUR ENERGY MAKE-UP You assert yourself with a tremendous drive for productivity and can organize your energies to actualize your goals. You tend to be very ambitious and have extremely high standards for yourself. You function best at the top of the ladder in whatever you do as you have a natural ability see the needs of the entire system and, thus, you are a skilled manager that can help others be more productive in their pursuits. You are not one for excessive talking about a project; you like to get on with the task at hand. You are a master organizer and, at times, this can go too far in directing the lives of others. Being competent in most things yourself, your frustration and anger get triggered by incompetence and lack of responsibility in others. Remember, we all have different talents, you just happen to be more competent than most.

You need to be in a relationship that supports your professional goals. If you are with someone who blocks or rejects your profession, certain conflict will result, as you have a need for industrious activities. You are very passionate, but only when deep commitment and loyalty is assured. You tend to hide your social shyness by being busy. Then you are either too busy for friendship, or are caught up in seeing people according to how they fit in with your ambitions. The ideal would be to be in a relationship with someone who respects your professional pursuits, yet also complements your natural tendencies by bringing more of the personal side of life.

Areas to Work On It is easy for you to get too caught up in pursuing your ambitions. This can lead to an opportunistic attitude that can result in a "projects before people" attitude. Your natural authoritarian nature can come off as bossy when you are involved in arguments. Disputes over responsibility and accountability are likely to arise in your relationships. The productive drive of this combination is excellent in business, but needs to soften in order to fully enjoy relationships. Otherwise, the relationship will become another cog in the machinery of your life and will be molded around your ambitions. Learning to relax with others and just hang out would be a good place to start.

Understanding Mars in Capricorn in Others Mars in Capricorn individuals are organized, ambitious, and productive in the way they assert themselves. Reliability, dependability, and responsibility are typical qualities. Of course they will be punctual, and demand this of you. These people tend to be very cautious about letting new people into their life, but once your are in, loyalty and commitment are guaranteed. They carry their responsibilities as a high priority and are comfortable as providers. Mutual respect is a prerequisite for effective dealings with them, so treat these people with respect and you will gain their friendship.

Mars in Capricorn people will definitely like to stay busy, and relaxing to them often means doing some favorite task. They will probably want you to be involved as well and will likely organize your life around their career. They appreciate competence in others, yet they feel secure in a relationship in which they are useful, so don't hesitate to ask for assistance. Recognition and acknowledgment are more important to them than what may appear, so don't hold back, assuming they already are getting plenty. To complement their industrious tendencies, they need to be with others who take charge in planning fun, social, and recreational activities. Of course, they will enjoy time with others working on mutual tasks, but they also would enjoy social activities that allow them to show their class, as there is a bit of the aristocrat in them.

Mars in Aquarius

Your Energy Make-up You assert your intensity through the mental realm, and have likely put together your own unique worldview. You like the freedom to act in your own way. This need for independent action can get you fighting for your rights, or expressing them, depending on where you are at with accepting your uniqueness. There is something unique about you and this requires more self-acceptance, because other people do not always understand your motivations and perspective.

Rebel or reformer? Aquarius represents both forms of not fitting into the status quo. If the rebel, then you are known for your obstinate disregard for traditional values. If the reformer, then you work for progressive changes within whatever you are involved. Either way, you are certainly not the traditionalist who likes to rely on tried-and-true methods. No, you seem at your best when expressing yourself in an innovative and sometimes unorthodox manner. You like to be on the progressive leading edge of whatever you do, and you tend to cast an eye to the future. Your warrior energy is at its best when fighting for a cause you believe in.

In relationships, friendship has to be an important base to build upon. The mental aspect of your relationships is very important, and sexy, to you, begins with the mind. You are not very patient with dull-witted individuals, nor with those who dote on their personal emotions, so you do best with those who are not overly sensitive. Somewhat of an experimentalist in love relationships, you definitely do best with a partner who does not bring a great deal of preconceived notions of what a relationship should be like.

Areas to Work On If you need to prove your right to be free, you will need someone or something to resist and will therefore attract people to you who try to control or restrict you in some way. This gives you another opportunity to prove your independence by resisting the expectations of others. At some point along the way, you finally prove your independence to the most important person, yourself, and start expressing your uniqueness, rather than fighting for it. Then, since there is no edge to your energy, you start attracting people into your life who enjoy your uniqueness and individuality.

Understanding Mars in Aquarius in Others These people pride themselves in their independent ways. Expect them to be highly original in all they do. They do not follow the pack. They will insist on doing things their own way, and they have very low tolerance for bossiness in others. Sometimes they will go out of their way just to demonstrate this right to be different. Give them room to act in their own way and you will find them very friendly. This is an intellectual placement and these people require an intense mental partner to hold their interest. Still, they will want to have friends and often feel a need to maintain a separate lifestyle outside the relationship to honor their precious freedom. Not jealous by nature, they will likely grant you as much freedom as they require themselves.

They seem to have a secret fear of being normal, so expect them to be somewhat experimental and unorthodox, including in their sexuality. These people value change and a dynamic, growth-oriented relationship. Their power is through the intellect and they will respect you all the more if you stand up for your views. Your best chance of influence with them is to put your point of view in the highest, philosophical, universal terms you can imagine. All intellectual activities, social time with mutual friends, and spur of the moment, wild-and-crazy activities are favorite ways of spending time with others.

Mars in Pisces

YOUR ENERGY MAKE-UP Your warrior energy is in one of the least-warriorlike signs, Pisces. On the one hand, this gives you a sweet and caring disposition with a tremendous amount of compassion for others. On the other hand, when your warrior energy is required to defend yourself or define your boundaries, you are ill-equipped to do battle. This is a very watery, emotional placement for the planet of action. Mars here usually leads to a convoluted expression of energy, as there is as much activity inward as there is outward. You need some time alone each day to allow for inner processing of all the outer activities of your life. Without this alone time, it is easy for you to feel overwhelmed. Pisces softens the aggressive spirit of Mars and you are most likely a sweet person that is easily influenced by others.

In relationships, you are a romantic and imaginative lover. When you are angry, you tend to implode rather than explode. This leads to indirect ways of asserting yourself and others might have a difficult time understanding what your issues are. Ideally, your life would be set up to allow for activities that connect you with your inner world. The softer forms of physical expression like dance, swimming, and t'ai chi, as well as all forms of creative expression and compassionate action, are most compatible with your energy. Your physical energy is likened to the tides of the ocean and harmony comes when you learn to go with these tides—time for outer activity, time for inner activity.

Areas to Work On Your natural compassionate nature can be an easy mark for those who might take advantage of you and play on your sympathies. You tend to feel guilty about your anger and you need to learn to stand up for yourself as much as you do for others. You are susceptible to all types of escapist tendencies when confronted with harsh reality. Without creative outlets, you likely create inner turmoil by repressing the expression of your feelings. Then you have to get off by yourself to work things out. But getting off by yourself was what you needed to do anyway. The choice of how you get there is up to you—with or without the turmoil?

Understanding Mars in Pisces in Others Mars in Pisces individuals are typically kind and gentle. You will more likely feel their frustrations rather than hear about them, as these people do not act directly on their anger and frustration, making it difficult to understand exactly what their issues are. They deal with their issues inwardly long before they express themselves to others. This delay makes it difficult to clear issues right in the moment with them. They need to get off by themselves to process the information before finally coming to resolution. This is appropriate for this sign. Power conflict would be unlikely—they are strong support people and often prefer anonymous roles behind the scenes.

More-evolved types have a definite charisma that comes from the successful merger of inner and outer activities. In relationships, their caring and compassionate nature has the best chance to shine, and their ability to fully surrender to a situation is a natural at romantic passion. Activities related to music and dancing can be enjoyable ways of spending time with Mars in Pisces friends. Do not be afraid to express your fears and insecurities with these compassionate individuals. They are more likely to feel good about your relationship if they feel they can support and be of assistance to you.

JUPITER

Growth Through Goals, Dreams, and Giving

> THE MOMENT ONE definitely commits oneself, providence moves too. All sorts of things then begin to occur that would never otherwise have occurred. A whole stream of events issues from the decision, raising in one's favor all manner of unforeseen incidents and meetings and material assistance which no one could have dreamed would come this way. Whatever you can do or dream, you can begin. Boldness has genius, power, and magic in it.
>
> —Johann Wolfgang von Goethe

It was surely a person who understood Jupiter that coined the phrase "All work and no play makes Jack a dull boy." Thank God for Jupiter, the planet that encourages us to reach for more of the abundance and rewards in life! Jupiter is the largest planet in the solar system. It relates to the expansive urge in you to reach out and improve situations in your life by taking advantage of the opportunities that come your way. Overcoming difficulties may be satisfying, but expanding into new areas of growth allows life to be more of a celebration—this is the path of Jupiter.

Jupiter relates to the optimism and confidence that allow you to reach for life's rewards. Your benevolent urge to give to others, your belief systems, and your personal philosophy of living also corresponds to Jupiter.

When you give the largest planet license, this can lead to excessive behavior of all types. In this chapter, the role of goal setting and following one's dream will be explored as techniques for improving your relationships. Giving as a means of sustaining growth in the relationship and using affirmations as a method of expanding your belief systems will also be presented. Jupiter through each of the astrological signs concludes the chapter, giving ideas of how you can unlock this expansive urge in yourself and others, specifically with regard to relationships.

The inspiration that comes from creating positive, growth-oriented goals helps you stay involved in your life and encourages the feeling of benefit from life's experiences. The difference between those who actualize their full potential and those who do not is decided by one's attitude towards growth and full participation in life. Many people were raised with the opposite of a Jupiter attitude: "Life's a bitch and then you die." This negative philosophy looks and prepares for challenge, and not surprisingly, finds life to be one! Not to say that life isn't challenging; it certainly is, but not exclusively. Developing your Jupiter function can help you to overcome negative attitudes so that you can experience the fullness that life offers.

Just as some people resist the new, there are people who suffer from a form of chronic goal-setting—always rushing off toward the dangling carrot of the future! They are missing the satisfaction of the here-and-now reality in favor of what might be next. Always rushing toward ever-expanding goals leads to a hyperextension of the energy field, rather than a balance of growth and consolidation, which is the ideal. To keep a healthy balance, treat the reaching of a goal as the out-breath and the appreciation of the achieved goal as the in-breath.

In relationships, Jupiter's goal to improve conditions in life becomes the animating fuel that stimulates growth and abundance. When couples first get together, there is a common scenario that relates to Jupiter: the two walk hand-in-hand on a beach and ask each other, "What are your goals and dreams in life?" The fuel for the relationship becomes where their goals and dreams overlap. One of the secrets for renewing long-term relationships centers around the ability to create new goals once previous ones have been realized.

The excitement of new growth and opportunity is natural and easy in the courtship stage of a relationship. Maintaining excitement deals with the art of staying in touch with the expansive goal-setting qualities of Jupiter once the euphoria of new love has worn off. Couples who see life as an opportunity, rather than as a challenge, and who continue to create goals that are mutually growth-oriented, have the best chance of maintaining an exciting relationship.

Pursuing goals and following your dreams are similar in that they both supply an animating force toward expansion. Goals and dreams stimulate a united vision that bring people together through working for a common cause. The more that both you and your partner become invested in common goals, the more closely your lives become intertwined. You become inspired with a vision of where to go from here. The true test, however, lies in your success in making your dreams come true. If none of your joint dreams materialize, there is great disappointment, and often the relationship begins to wane. The dreams and visions alone are not enough. They are simply the call for change. When they are not actualized, they are not satisfying. If you are "just a talker," you talk a good future, but that is where it ends. If you are "just a dreamer," you get lost in the fantasies of how life could, should, and might be, but you can't quite seem to actualize your dream.

Rule

Goals and dreams are empowering to the degree that progress is made towards their actualization.

It becomes quite apparent that goals and dreams in themselves are not enough to sustain a relationship. There must be movement toward the actualization of these aspirations if you are to truly benefit from the positive motivation that they can bring.

Goals and Cycles

The I Ching, a Chinese book of wisdom, teaches about adapting to the ever-ongoing cycles of change in life. Every situation in life, when viewed independently, is either increasing or decreasing in its actualization, and it is to your best advantage to know where you are in relation to your goal. Life is change. Every project, situation, and relationship has its peaks and valleys of increase and decline. Similarly, growth always follows decay and vice versa. One of the teachings in the I Ching is called "After Completion," and it teaches that the moment a goal is completed, decline begins. The teaching goes on to indicate that the only way to avoid entering into decline is to expand your goals, so that there can be a new outreaching.

The same principle holds true in relationships. A couple starts out with goals and dreams of what they want for their life with each other. Driven by a sense of purpose and direction, they set out to achieve these goals. During the spirit of the quest the relationship is fueled by this continual reaching for the united future, but what happens when the goals are completed? The relationship may run out of gas, and they can experience great unrest in their relating.

A common example is that of the empty nest syndrome, when a couple's children leave the family home to set up their own lives. As the family unit shrinks back to just the two parents, they often experience a crisis. When the goal of raising a family has been completed, the relationship begins to wane unless the couple is clever enough to initiate some new goals like travel, spiritual growth, a new home, or some other joint adventure.

Without goals, stagnation can easily occur with decay soon to follow. We often hear the story of a broken relationship that suffered from going nowhere: "We stopped growing together," "I lost interest," "We didn't inspire each other any more," or "It was boring and predictable"—a real killer to growth. A bottle of wine, a hot tub, and some dream-weaving could improve many a dull relationship. Taking a holiday away from the ordinary routines is also a way to rekindle some forgotten dreams.

Goal-Setting Techniques

A goal is not a wish. A goal relates to a specific activity, and a wish is typically related to a state of being such as "I just wish I were happy," or "I wish my marriage would improve." It would take a genie to bring such vague wishes into reality. What are the conditions that would make you happy? What are the conditions that would lead to improvement? Step one in the process of creating goals is to understand them to be specific and measurable.

Step 1

Translate wishes such as "I wish to be happy," into specific goals.

Your wish becomes realizable when you translate the desired experience into concrete activities. First, of course, you must determine what it is that would make you happy! What are the specific conditions that you can imagine would lead to happiness?

Just as important as creating specific goals is the necessity to choose goals you have some control over, which stems from accepting that your happiness is your responsibility. If your happiness is dependent on someone else's action, such as wishing that your husband would be more attentive to you, then you have given away your power to be happy. You cannot control how others choose to act. Consequently, to blame your partner because your life isn't what you want it to be is unfair. Create goals that are dependent only on you, such as exercising daily, losing five pounds, hugging everybody in your family at least once a day, or meditating for ten minutes before starting each day.

This next step is designed to sharpen your ability to create goals and experience the momentum they bring into your life.

Step 2

Create simple, short-term goals and then set about achieving them.

The purpose of this exercise is to watch the process of attaining goals and to notice the positive effect that this has on you. Your choice can be recreational, creative, task-oriented, or spiritual, but keep it simple and easily attainable, such as walking a mile, reading a book, going to an art opening, or even cleaning the garage. The process of creating a goal and following through in the most complete way possible is really the issue here, not the garage. When you have completed your goal, stop and acknowledge your success. By including the elements of completion and satisfaction into your goal setting, you complete the circuit and a general enhancement of the energy field can be felt.

Notice what starts happening by declaring your goal. First your attention becomes focused, and through this, you create a thread that connects you to the realization of that goal. If no progress is made toward achieving the goal, the thread remains taut and will drain you by reminding you of the unfulfilled goal. This is why you should be careful of how many things you declare as goals at one time—you create a thread of intent connected to each of these ideas or projects. When there is progress, you feel the sense of power—when there is no progress, you feel impotent and the situation drains your energy rather than replenishing it.

With long-term goals, the same process applies, but requires you to maintain your vision through time, and time has its cycles. There will be a waxing and a waning in the intensity of your goal as it influences your life. Will you be able to ride the currents of time and remain tenacious to your goal even through the droughts of inspiration? Try picturing a thread of energy between you and your goal and imagine that the goal is pulling you towards its actualization. Completion of long-term goals is one of the very basic steps to creating success.

Step 3

Create a long-term goal for self-enrichment, such as a special trip or completing a course of study. Write down your goal and place it in a conspicuous place.

1. When you write your goal, empower the writing with your vision of its completion. With each word imagine what it will feel like to achieve the goal. (Don't write it down if you do not intend to follow through.)
2. If it is a car that you have been wanting, you could hang a picture of the exact car you desire in a conspicuous place. If it is a trip that you are planning to take, place a picture of your destination where you will see it often. You might even want to augment this one with some travel brochures. If it is an amount of money that you want to start making on a monthly basis, write the figure down. The refrigerator is a convenient spot to place such goals—every time you open the door you will be reminded of your intention.
3. The goal reminder (picture, writing, etc.) is charged with your original intention. If a time comes when you feel you have lost sight of your goal, go to your reminder and hold it, contemplate it, and reconnect with the original vision that is encoded within it.
4. As an alternative reminder, you could encode a special crystal to be symbolic of the realization of your goal. As you meditate and visualize the completion of your goal, hold the crystal. Visualize your goal being absorbed into the stone. You can connect with the power of your vision by holding the crystal and feeling your original intent.
5. Above all, acknowledge movement towards the completion of your goal—settle for nothing less. Sometimes it takes imagination to see the

progress, but if you interpret all events as contributions and recognize that even the inevitable challenges will sharpen your skills, you become better prepared for the eventual completion.

Empowering Your Goals and Dreams

Have you ever noticed how some people seem to enjoy life much more than others? It is easy to say, "Sure, I'd enjoy life, too, if all of those wonderful things were happening to me!" But, perhaps, it is the other way around—all of those wonderful things happen to those people because they know how to enjoy life. It is the question of responsibility again: who is responsible for manifesting your goals and dreams? The more personal control you develop over these faculties, the more they become tools in your life. As Richard Bach's reluctant messiah in his book *Illusions* says, "To bring anything into your life, first imagine that it is already there."

Exercise

Create a goal or dream, imagine it as real, and then emotionally relate to the world as if it were already true.

The trick here is to enter into the emotional realm of experiencing your dream. Don't wait until it is actualized to enjoy it. Begin enjoying it now so that your emotions become as a seed around which life can coalesce. Imagine what it will feel like when you have achieved your goal . . . now, make those emotions a current reality.

The whole process of setting, moving toward, and attaining goals is empowering, but be sure that you are first setting appropriate goals. Much of the disappointment in life comes from unrealized goals that were not realistic in the first place.

How do you know if your goal is really attainable? In setting goals, first choose something that is a natural extension of who you already are—the goal has to be within the realm of possibility. If your goal is one or two steps beyond your current situation, your likelihood of achieving it is considerably greater than if your goal is ten steps. Second, don't be too stringent on the timing, and remember that patience is required, especially with goals that have the capacity to change your life. The purpose is to set goals and expand the boundaries of your capabilities. It is this simple—no goals, no growth. However, if you set goals beyond your reach, you set yourself up for failure and, once again, no growth.

Relationship Goals

After you have developed the skill of creating and achieving appropriate goals in your personal life, you can seek to develop the same in your relationships. All of the same principles apply. They have to be attainable, and at the same time, lead to growth. You attract people into your life to help you grow, but when the growth has stopped, so does the need to stay together. Consequently, people often suffer great guilt and pain when a relationship dissolves, and yet, why should you stay together if you are not growing through the process of your time spent with each other? Sentimentality is not enough to bond two people together into a meaningful tie, and relationships, particularly marriage, were never designed to be endurance tests. Change is a requirement of growth, and growth is required for life. Both partners in any meaningful relationship share this crucial responsibility.

Exercise

With your partner, create specific goals that are growth-oriented for both individuals.

For couples who want to refresh their relationships, it would be wise to initiate some joint activities in which both of you are novices. That way, you are exploring the new frontier together. Any two clever people can find mutual goals if they really look. These can include career, education, improvements in the home, personal development classes, sports, and creative endeavors. Taking a weekend trip to a nearby lodge is also refreshing, but if that is not financially possible, then plan to take a day trip by car, or consider hikes or bike rides. In maintaining any relationship, it is important to experience some out of the ordinary adventures. They simply require a little research, planning, and the willingness to move beyond complacency.

Although it is always possible to find mutual goals, it is also likely that many of your goals are not shared by your partner. Let's say that you want to entertain more and your mate does not like socializing. It doesn't mean that you have to sacrifice this desire in your life. It does mean, however, that you have to come to terms with this being an important aspect of your life. The two of you will have to communicate more, and come to new agreements on how to meet both of your needs. Perhaps you are feeling left out of social functions and wish to be invited out more often. To remedy the situation you will have to take the initiative and instigate some theater-going or movie outings with friends or family members. To sit home and not do anything other than wish you were with another partner is accepting defeat too readily.

Cultivating Dreams

Dreams and imagination fit, more appropriately, in the chapter on Neptune, but the way in which they relate to Jupiter and the enrichment of life will be presented here. Fantasy and imagination are much more important in life than is often believed. Dreams can come true, but you first must have the dream. Cultivating this aspect of growth makes life magical. Although following your dreams may lead to wanderlust, not following any dreams will certainly lead to boredom.

Dreams are to goals as popcorn is to food. Nutritious foods ideally form the backbone of your diet, but on occasion, you snack "recreationally." As long as you know which is which, they complement each other nicely. It is the same with dreams and goals. Many people sell their dreams short, thinking them unrealistic. Well, they are unrealistic! That is what makes them so special. If only that which is realistic and practical is allowed to be experienced, life becomes predictable and dull. When dreams are not acted upon, they become escapist fantasies of the inner world, but when they are acted upon, they enrich the power of living creatively.

Dreams are spun with imagination, that glorious sport that allows you to move beyond the confines of the rational, predictable world. They are tools of creativity. What you can imagine, you can become, but if you can't imagine it, you can't become it. It is that simple—without imagination and creative flair, you live your life in predictable patterns. Reach beyond the practical, and in the process you will add excitement and enrichment to your life.

Special trips, vacations, and experiences of the "once in a lifetime" sort are the stuff that dreams are made of. Not to include this aspect of life in a relationship is settling for less than life has to offer. Everyone has the power to integrate creative dreams into their lives. It is just that some do not bother to take the risk for fear of not being able to succeed.

It is curious to recognize how easily inhibitions can rule your thoughts. If you are not willing to bring your dreams and goals into your consciousness, then how can you ever hope to have them realized? The first step is to have the courage to ask yourself what you want, and then allow yourself to dream the picture. Set it up exactly how you would wish it could be. From that point you can lay a foundation of making those dreams come true.

Is it practical to be a dreamer in these times, when the necessities of life are often hard to come by? You bet it is—living life as a creative adventure is a necessity if you are to fully experience the bounty available! Learn to stretch your boundaries by cultivating dreams. First, of course, you have to find them, but be cautious in your selection, for just as with goals, appropriate dreams are critical. Unrealized dreams are just as disappointing as unrequited love, and you will want to safeguard against this. This next exercise is designed to help you select an appropriate dream to pursue.

Exercise

In your journal, label a section for "Dreams." Create three dreams and make a page for each. Next you will want to write about them.

1. Be creative. What situations can you imagine as greatly enriching your life? Be bold, forget about whether it is realistic or not. At this stage, you just want to develop your ability to dream. Create dreams that are fun to think about—dreams that would be wonderful—if only they could happen to you. Write them in your journal while you are in the spirit of imagining how exhilarating it would be to experience them in real life.

2. Now that you have a field of dreams, you are going to start narrowing the field by focusing on each one separately. This needn't be done all in one sitting—do it as your time allows. Rather than splitting your attention, aim to focus all of your daydreaming potential on one of these dreams at a time. Wear the dream as if it were a coat of reality. In your mind, experience the dream as already being true. How does this affect you? What does it bring out in you? Can you visualize it all the way through to completion, or does your imagination stop at some point along the way? Is it easy to remain focused, or does your imagination tend to wander?

3. After you have gone through the above steps, write down your experiences, reactions, and thoughts concerning this dream.
4. Follow these steps with all three dreams. After you have written your experiences in your journal, go back and read each one. Be analytical. Which dream fits you the best? Which one could you see through to completion? If your imagination stops halfway through in the dream, your experiences are likely to stop before completion. Which was the most enjoyable to imagine? Did one seem to excite you and empower you more than the others?
5. Select the one dream that seems best suited to you and create a special section, exclusively for it, in your journal. Now start using your journal as a means to focus your ideas, thoughts, and plans towards actualizing that specific dream. Begin collecting information. If your dream is a special trip, you can collect brochures, magazine articles, books, and pictures that relate to the trip or destination. Remember, the process of pursuing the dream is just as valuable as achieving it. Enjoy the courtship.

Pursuing dreams in a relationship is not necessary, at least if survival and getting by are your standards. Many relationships endure without having them, but how much more satisfying to lift a relationship above the mediocrity by the vitality of dreams. They empower the relationship with the energy of two dreamers. Once you are skilled in adding dreams to your own life, go through this same process for a shared dream in your relationship. Again, create three dreams together, and enter them into your journal. Together, review them one at a time. Record your shared thoughts. Choose a dream that you both agree on—no fair compromising. If you haven't found a dream that you can both pursue with equal vigor, you haven't looked enough.

The Art of Giving

When you find yourself wanting more from your relationships, you can feel frustrated unless you know the art of giving. Giving is an aspect of growth that is yours to control. In the early stages of relationships, there is nothing more natural than this expression, whether it be it affection, flowers, poems, gifts, or attention. It is what you want to do. When you stop giving, you break an essential flow of energy, and problems emerge. The dynamics of relating has been altered. Instead, a mutual utilitarian relationship is all that you can hope for, and this is a far cry from romance!

It is so common to see this happen: the beloved essentially changes into a work mate, and both settle into mutually facilitative roles for each other. The romance of goal-setting and dreaming is set aside at this point, as the two come together and analyze how far they have come, rather than where they can go with each other. Fantasy is exchanged for reality, as the two settle into the routine of making a living, tending to the chores, and taking care of business. Practical matters get accomplished, but where is the romance and the celebration of having found each other?

A functional relationship can be enhanced through the romance of giving. Work can still be conducted successfully, but with more celebration of your partner—not just on birthdays, anniversaries, and the like, but throughout the year. Consider that through your giving you are adding fuel to the flames of the original passion you felt for each other. Your giving becomes a tithing that you offer to your love. It is truly magical that your attitude toward your partner will improve, and you will become involved with current reasons for your sharing together.

Women are particularly sensitive to this display of affection, but there are a surprising number of men who like the little reminders that signify appreciation and adoration. Partners often stray from the marriage because of just this issue. They fall in love with someone else who they feel loves them, and verifies this with compliments and gifts, satisfying needs long ignored by their marriage partner. Surprise giving is highly romantic and fun, both when you are the giver and the recipient.

Jupiter Through the Signs

Jupiter is the largest planet in the solar system and represents all that is expansive. How you grow, expand, and improve conditions in your life by creating goals and pursuing opportunities are all related to Jupiter. Where you feel fortunate in life and want to give to others is described by the sign of Jupiter at your birth. Without discipline and restraint, however, following the path of Jupiter can lead to indulgences, and all forms of excessive behavior.

To most benefit from Jupiter in relationships, you would create mutual goals and dreams that are in harmony with both individual's Jupiter signs. Read the descriptions for Jupiter in your sign, and also in your partner's, to get a sense of what activities would be growth oriented for both of you. If the avenues of growth for each of your signs are radically different, then you will have to allow time for separate growth for each of you within the relationship.

Jupiter in Aries

YOUR GROWTH POTENTIAL This is a pioneering placement for the planet of expansion. You need to approach life as if it were a challenge, and an adventure, and go for it! Comfort does not hold nearly the reward for you as adventure. With Jupiter in Aries, to be in a relationship that periodically veers off in a whole new direction maintains your enthusiasm for growth. Since you are known for your positive vision and your courage in facing new and uncertain situations, it would be best for you to be in a relationship with a person who is equally as excited about your enthusiasm and, yet, adds a practical perspective as well. You can become blindly idealistic unless you have tempered your drive with a more realistic perspective. If you are naturally timid and have this placement, you could benefit with a partner who encourages you to take a few risks. The excessive tendencies of Jupiter in Aries can lead to rash behavior, just to keep things interesting. You may need to temper the Aries tendency to think of self first, if you are to keep the relationship fires burning as brightly as your own.

Your people skills operate best at the one-to-one level, where the abundance of enthusiasm you possess can be shared with another in a way that offers hope and inspiration. Your spirit for life is a natural extension of you that you can give to others. You project a "can do it" attitude—you can encourage others to believe in themselves as well.

UNDERSTANDING JUPITER IN ARIES IN OTHERS These individuals need to be singled out and recognized for their personal contributions to any endeavor in which they are involved. They like an adventure and are attracted to the "spark plug" type of person that keeps things happening. Reward for them is akin to excitement. They will soon bore of routine, so keep adding new, exciting plans to your relationship calendar to interest their future-oriented philosophy on life. When they are feeling generous, they will share of themselves, more often than giving gifts. They would also prefer your time sharing a joint activity, over material tokens.

Try not to take it personally, or as a slight to your relationship, if they periodically have goals that don't include you. It is natural for this placement of Jupiter. If they are allowed to pursue their individual growth, they will ultimately have more to offer their relationships.

Ideas for activities to bring a sense of reward to your relationships include surprising them—they will love it; plan trips and adventures; or even move to a new place together. Outdoor action-oriented activities are always well received. Taking a class in aikido or t'ai chi would be growth-oriented and appreciated.

Jupiter in Taurus

Your Growth Potential Your goals should include a high standard on the material plane, as mere survival does not offer enough for you—you want to experience luxury and prosperity in your life as well. Affectionate, sensual, and earthy, you do best in relationships where there is a mutual respect for the material world. Ideally, your shared goals would be aimed at improving your standard of living and bringing more beauty and luxury into your life. Your philosophy and religious beliefs are equally down to earth. You came here to enjoy the material plane, not to struggle with it, but beware of a tendency to become excessive in your search for wealth. With Taurus, there is always the danger that you might become more attached to the form than to the experience of enjoyment. Remember to include life's simple pleasures, such as walks in the park, and be mindful that the abundance of beauty nature provides is always available to further enhance your enjoyment of life.

When you are feeling generous, you like to give special gifts to special people. When you are invited to someone's house for dinner, you like to show up with a bottle of wine, a loaf of bread, flowers, or at least something to demonstrate your appreciation.

Understanding Jupiter in Taurus in Others Reward for these individuals includes all that leads to comfort and increased security in life. Since they appreciate quality, and even some luxury in their lives, material gifts as tokens of your affection will be appreciated. If you plan outings, remember they like to be comfortable, so make reservations ahead of time at fine hotels and restaurants to capture their interest.

Once they set their sight on a goal, they will pursue that one goal until completed, as they prefer not to scatter their energy by engaging many goals at once. Their pursuits will often center on material and financial rewards, but their appreciation for beauty can also find outlets in artistic expression and involvement with nature. Their philosophical nature is equally grounded in reality. They will shy away from pursuits that are excessively abstract, preferring to pursue knowledge that can be integrated into everyday life. If it cannot be demonstrated, it is not going to hold much interest for them.

Ideas for activities to bring a sense of reward to your relationship include landscaping the home together; taking a class in art appreciation together; taking a prosperity workshop; touring the local art galleries; starting collections of treasured objects; shopping; joining a gourmet club.

Jupiter in Gemini

Your Growth Potential An image of abundance for you might be being locked in a bookstore after hours! Your goals will be decidedly mental and, since life presents a panorama of learning opportunities for you, it is not likely that you will ever become stagnant. You feel abundant and generous in relationships that provide a stimulating intellectual environment where media, reading, current affairs and plenty of talking are the norm. Mutual goals that benefit the relationship focus on learning, writing projects and expanding the intellect. Your open-minded philosophical outlook leads to being bit of a dilettante and a Renaissance person. You thrive in a relationship of many and varied interests. This will lead to a busy life and you would not do well in a relationship with someone who hems you in.

When undisciplined, your excessive tendencies could lead to superficiality, flightiness, and idle gossip as the only means of connecting with others. Ideally, your relationships would be with open-minded and highly communicative partners who also have a depth of feelings. Your flexibility is indeed a great gift, but without depth, you can easily get lost in the puzzle of your own curiosities. Ideally, your partner would help pull you toward the personal meaning beneath your intellectual wanderings. Jupiter looks for a larger meaning and in its search for answers, Gemini often forgets the question.

Understanding Jupiter in Gemini in Others These naturally inquisitive folks are easy to please as long as you remember that they love variety and intellectual stimulation. They are definitely not picky and thus find plenty of opportunities to stay fascinated by life. Mutual goals related to learning and acquiring information are surely appreciated, as long as they are short-term goals. Those with Jupiter in Gemini shun goals that require long-term commitment. Pursuing several goals simultaneously with short bursts of energy is their natural style. Jupiter in Gemini individuals have a tendency to get distracted before completing goals; consequently, with shared goals, it will likely be up to you to keep the focus.

They will appreciate you for recognizing the worth in their interests, and they will want to share these with you. They will express their generosity by bringing you information—books, magazines, catalogs, videos, etc. This is what they think is rewarding and they will want to share this abundance with you. They will be hard to pin down in philosophical, political, or religious discussion; however, they will bring in points of view you have never considered before. Their eclectic and open-minded outlook will dazzle you, if not make you dizzy. They love to explore the many and tire of the one.

Ideas for activities to bring a sense of reward to your relationship include taking classes and workshops together; taking short trips to explore your area; playing word games, such as Scrabble, crossword puzzles, and Trivial Pursuit; touring a television studio and sitting in on a talk show or newscast; reading favorite books to each other. A dream date might be a freeform day—head out with no destination or agenda. Let the day unfold as your mutual interests move you.

Jupiter in Cancer

Your Growth Potential Your philosophy leads to a rich personal life and you will likely screen your relationships to those that enhance your existing lifestyle. A rewarding relationship for you would focus on nurturing each other's emotional needs particularly connected to the home and family. You would benefit from a relationship that has shared interests in all the rituals and celebrations that add to these most personal aspects of life. Planning a dinner party for friends might be a favorite shared activity. Issues concerning security, both emotional and material, are likely to be a high priority in your life and you will not be comfortable with others who always are encouraging you to expand beyond your current lifestyle. Religious and philosophical beliefs that support the role of the family as the main cornerstone for healthy life prove to be enriching for you. Other areas that you would like to share with others include developing nurturing abilities in the healing arts, enjoying good literature, gardening, interior decorating, food preparation, raising and educating children, or pets, or plants, or . . . ?

When excessive, Jupiter in Cancer leads to a lifestyle that overfocuses on security. Although you need a partner that honors your conservative nature, it would be ideal if your mate also encouraged you to embrace new growth. Otherwise, your relationships would run the risk of becoming islands onto themselves, cut off from the larger world.

Understanding Jupiter in Cancer in Others These security-minded individuals pursue goals that substantiate their current lifestyle. Their naturally cautious approach to life will have to be accounted for if you want to get on their good side. Take your time in getting to know them, they are not likely to rush into anything. Shared goals related to improving conditions within the home and family are rewarding for them. Once their own security is well established, they can be very charitable and would enjoy giving to civic-minded organizations. Reminiscing about times gone by while sharing a fine meal is an evening well spent as an opportunity to expand into the past. They love to entertain in their home as they are much more at ease and gracious on familiar turf. To help them extend their comfort zone, you could explore the cuisine from different countries.

In philosophical and religious matters, these individuals are typically conservative with a natural inclination for maintaining the traditional values of home, family, church, and country. More progressive types can find reward in the healing professions and all that deals with nurturing others.

Ideas for activities that would bring a sense of reward to the relationship include trips to the ocean and all water sports; taking a couples' massage class; going to psychic fairs; going to a home show; joining a dinner/book club; taking cooking classes; and catering a meal for special friends.

Jupiter in Leo

Your Growth Potential The planet of expansion in the sign of personal greatness promises grand opportunities for you. To win, to achieve, to celebrate and to have fun—these are the goals of Jupiter in Leo. You are a big thinker and, likely, a big doer as well. You value relationships that support a reach-for-the-stars approach to life. There is natural leadership ability with this placement, and you will require relationships that submit to your take charge attitude. However, you also know how to enjoy life, and your innate generosity inspires others to join in the good times. Sports, creativity, and recreation are all beneficial relationship activities. All activities that animate your heart and get you laughing, loving, and enjoying life are worthy of shared aspirations. There is nothing "halfway" about you, which tends to lead to either extravagance or generosity. Beware of the excessiveness of Jupiter that can lead to an exclusive self-orientation unless disciplined to a more compassionate view. On the other hand, the magnanimous proportions of this placement show a desire to be the giver, the benevolent ruler, who has so much abundance that one of your great joys becomes sharing life's bounty with others.

Your "go for it" philosophy would feel restricted by timid partners. You shine in relationships that allow you to live life as royalty.

Understanding Jupiter in Leo in Others Seeking the best that life has to offer, these enthusiastic souls set out to do everything in a big way. Once they set their goals, which are most often on a grand scale, they exercise no restraints. They are winners, and never settle for second best. This can be intimidating, and they can drift into competitiveness unless you always allow them to save face. They are impatient with those who are timid, so be bold in making plans with them to hold their interest. To win their hearts, keep your ear to the ground for cultural events, entertainment shows, or exciting sporting events, and get front row tickets. They are not spectators in life—they want to join in—and center stage is where they feel most comfortable! Their philosophy is "Life is meant to be lived and enjoyed," and they will certainly want you to join in with the best life has to offer.

Jupiter in Leo has strong convictions and beliefs and, at worst, intolerance of opposing views. Royalty doesn't bow down graciously. So stand your ground, they will respect your strength of convictions—they might not believe you are right, but they will respect strength. They can express their generosity in a lavish way, lucky you, but they will expect the same in return.

Ideas for activities that can bring a sense of reward to your relationships include all creative and recreational activities; planning a weekend skiing adventure; taking classes in some form of creative expression. For their birthday, book them an hour in a recording studio, or have their portrait painted! Make travel plans to the sun with recreational and entertainment opportunities and above all, fun!

Jupiter in Virgo

YOUR GROWTH POTENTIAL You like to pursue the type of growth for which you can find practical application in everyday life. You enjoy relationships that can share life's simple pleasures. You prefer to demonstrate your beliefs by the way you live, rather than to expound on them philosophically, and you tire easily with those whose beliefs are not supported by the way they live. Your perception of a rewarding life is one of order, with everything running smoothly and efficiently—but relationships rarely do. Your goal of self-sufficiency is fine in the material world, but, when excessive, can be stifling for your personal life. For this reason it would be desirable for you to be with someone who reminded you that all work and no play is no fun.

Personal health and hygiene can also be a cornerstone of your philosophy, and relationship activities that focus on improving health would be a natural. This is not a dreamer's placement. No, you are the realist, preferring not to look too far ahead of yourself. A complementary relationship for you would be someone who could help you expand your goals, to see beyond the immediate, and stay in touch with the big picture. To be in a relationship with a partner that enjoyed maintaining, fixing up, and improving the house or other projects would also be stimulating for you.

UNDERSTANDING JUPITER IN VIRGO IN OTHERS These refined individuals may appear too cautious and conservative in reaching for what life has to offer, but it would be more appropriate to say they are discriminating in their choice of activities. Their restraint often leads to an understated, rather than boastful approach to life. They are conscientious and meticulous in their attention to the details of completing their goals. What they lack in speed and spontaneity, they make up for in quality. The quality of their everyday reality is improved through application of all that is practical and well-ordered.

Their philosophical outlook is very grounded in practical reality. They are not much for enjoying the abstract, unless a practical application of the philosophy can be demonstrated—they are realists. When you are looking for a discerning eye to help you put the final touches on a project, they fit the bill perfectly. If you are looking for interaction on an abstract idea you are pursuing, you will both get frustrated. They also have an ability to find reward through life's simple pleasures. Being conservative, the Jupiter in Virgo person would be delighted with a single rose, rather than a dozen, as extravagance may cause anxiety. When they are feeling generous they often choose practical gifts, or more likely, roll their sleeves up and pitch in on any project you are doing. They like to be of service, and a rewarding activity for them often involves assisting others, with only appreciation required in return.

Ideas for activities to bring a sense of reward to your relationship include classes on diet, nutrition, and exercise; attending a yoga retreat; attending an alternative energy workshop; taking part in an environmentalist's club clean-up weekend; a backpacking trip; looking for bargains at garage sales; travel related to service such as the Peace Corps.

Jupiter in Libra

YOUR GROWTH POTENTIAL Relationships, partnerships, agreements, and social interactions are the arenas that you reach toward to experience abundance. Jupiter brings luck and you can expect to be fortunate in your involvement with others. You are looking for a person to share your refined interests, and with the confidence of Jupiter, you believe in the ideal relationship. Relationships that feed the mental part of your character are a must. If you find yourself with a strong, silent type of partner, you will have to invest in your social life for mental stimulation. You would feel abundant in a relationship where all decisions are discussed—you are a team player and would do best with another that appreciates this quality in you. Shared involvements with the arts or academic pursuits would fit your refined nature. You demonstrate a sense of style in all you do, but when excessive, this leads to pretentiousness, all presentation and no substance. The need for approval from others can also become excessive, and you can find yourself doing anything you can to meet the expectations of others.

Your faith and philosophy are built around a strong belief in justice. Essentially pragmatic, you have a firm belief that if people could simply be fair and just in all of their dealings with each other, life on this planet would improve immensely. Harmony is your gift, arbitration your talent, and fairness your way. These natural talents will, no doubt, be called on by others seeking a balance of perspective in their lives.

Understanding Jupiter in Libra in Others These refined individuals enjoy gracious living and appreciate style in life. They are delightful to spend time with socially, as they are genuinely interested in others and have a definite skill for bringing harmony to any situation. Activities related to the arts, as well as intellectual pursuits, hold special interest for them. Jupiter in Libra leads to keen appreciation for style and appearances, so put on your best to make a good impression with them. They can be charming and naturally diplomatic, but will often defer to others, choosing to be cooperative, rather than assertive in their choice of social activities. Trust their innate sense of fairness, but don't expect quick decisions, as they will likely weigh all the alternatives before making any decisions. Actually, they prefer to be in relationships, where there is a shared responsibility for making decisions and are most uncomfortable dealing with unpleasantness of any kind. Whatever they do, they like to do it with others, so plan on being included in their plans.

Ideas for activities to bring a sense of reward to your relationship include taking a relationship or a negotiations seminar; getting dressed up and going out for an elegant night on the town; taking dance classes; taking in a fashion, car, or boat show where the latest styles are presented; planning a trip to Greece to study the architecture and the roots of democracy; studying the metaphysical properties of color and sound.

Jupiter in Scorpio

Your Growth Potential Growth for you is more of an inner process than external. You are naturally fascinated by the profound, the mysterious, and that which lies just beneath the surface of normal perception. Thus, along with respect for your need for private musings, your ideal partner would also have the ability to pierce your veils and share the depths of your being. As you have a burning desire to see the underlying causes and motivations of behavior, you will need a partner who can handle being under your looking glass. Shared explorations in psychology, the occult, and the metaphysical can be valuable relationship activities.

You may seem like a loner at times, but in Scorpio, the drive is to blend and merge with your partner, to transform yourself, through the union. Even in sexual sharing, the experience is as much psychological as it is sensual for you, and with the right relationship, sexuality can be a door to the unknown as taught in tantra yoga. When this psychological/erotic aspect becomes excessive and burdensome, you can look exclusively to sex as a way of experiencing intimacy with your partner. Your philosophical outlook might be spiced with a healthy cynical attitude—just enough to keep you from being gullible.

This placement leads to natural financial skills and, ideally, you would be in a relationship that was interested in pooling resources and then making appropriate investments to take advantage of this talent. All types of shared business interests would be a natural.

Understanding Jupiter in Scorpio in Others These enigmatic individuals prefer to be private concerning their goals and ambitions, so consider it a statement of acceptance if they reveal their dreams to you. There is nothing superficial about them, as they prefer the profound and mysterious to the trite and common. One-to-one, in-depth encounters, rather than glitzy social gatherings, are their preference. Likewise, in relationships, they are intense and passionate, and find intimate time together to be more rewarding than casual chitchat. Since they are interested in exploring the depths of the human psyche, you might feel yourself being studied when you are in their presence. These individuals are rarely fooled by appearances, so there is no sense in trying to pull the wool over their eyes. Be clear in your motivations and intentions in all your dealings with them. Never assume they are not paying attention—they are.

The obvious and mundane rarely hold their interest, so don't count on them to join in activities that they deem trivial. They are especially keen in business and financial matters, and since Scorpio is the sign of shared resources, they will likely want you to get financially involved. This could be fortunate for you, because Jupiter is the planet associated with luck, so they tend to do well in shared investments.

Ideas for activities to bring a sense of reward to your relationship include taking a skin-diving class together; giving the *Kama Sutra* (and promise to be a willing partner!); taking an investment strategy class together and make an investment; planning a trip to take part in a traditional ritual, e.g., a Native American sweat lodge, fire walking, or medicine-wheel ceremony.

Jupiter in Sagittarius

YOUR GROWTH POTENTIAL The expansiveness of Jupiter in its own sign leads to an abundance of goals, dreams, and visions—you are the eternal optimist who approaches life as a grand adventure. You are looking for a partner to explore life with at all levels. Traveling with your mate, or exploring the religions, philosophies, and cultures of the world are ideal shared goals. This could be either actual physical travel, or vicarious travel through books and education. When disciplined, you maintain an expansive worldview and naturally encourage others to frame their experiences in a positive light. When excessive, you become the dream chaser, always wondering what is over the next hill and never fully surrendering to the moment. Your energy will certainly be scattered until you learn to focus your goal-setting ability. A relationship partner who gives you room to dream, but who also helps you to focus on the everyday world, would be ideal. You would also value a partner who enjoys philosophizing with you.

You look at life as a field of opportunities, so those who are overly cautious and timid will not likely capture your heart. Your positive outlook can be infectious and inspirational. Wealth for you can be found in the development of the higher mind. A relationship with mutual interests in philosophy, education and consciousness growth complements your restless physical nature. Your ability to theorize and to plan can lead to natural teaching abilities, and your natural generosity is expressed by helping expand the horizons for others.

UNDERSTANDING JUPITER IN SAGITTARIUS IN OTHERS These expansive individuals like to live their lives as an adventure, and pursuing goals is part of their natural expression. If anything, this placement can lead to pursuing too many goals. Naturally optimistic in their outlook on life, their tendency is to say yes to any opportunity that comes their way, without first considering the practicalities concerning the offering. High-minded and philosophical, they love to talk about abstract and lofty concepts. They are not just talkers, however, and will head off in pursuit of adventure at a moment's notice.

Travel holds special interest to them, and many of their goals will center on this theme. On the other hand, money concerns hold little interest, other than for providing the opportunity to fund experiences. They are risk takers and often will squander their resources believing there is always more where that came from. Intellectual pursuits including moral, ethical, political, religious, and philosophical topics will gain their interest. They also like outdoor and sporting activities. Because these are action-oriented individuals, any plans you offer that expand their experiential base are likely to be favorably received. Indulge their dreams and plans, as the considering of potentials is sport for them.

Ideas for activities to bring a sense of reward to your relationship include a day at the race track with a set limit of how much to bet; taking a class in comparative religions; studying a foreign language with the goal of going to that country; spending a day at the legislature watching politicians at work. Share outdoor activities, including hiking, horseback riding and sports, and, of course, travel, travel, and more travel.

Jupiter in Capricorn

YOUR GROWTH POTENTIAL The planet of growth and opportunity in the sign of worldly success shows that your career and status in the world are going to be very important to you. Relationships that mesh nicely with your worldly ambitions have a chance—relationships that potentially disrupt your security do not. You need to set your sights on important accomplishments in order to feel best about yourself and you will likely encourage your mate to get involved. You do best in relationships that support and respect your career ambitions. You take your responsibilities seriously and would want your mate to do so as well. When excessive, this leads to an exclusive focus on getting ahead and your relationship can take on the quality of a small business. It would be complementary for you to be in a relationship with someone who reminded you of other important aspects of life, like family, recreation, and creativity. Your organizational abilities are highly developed, and when you feel generous, you like to help others get their life organized and on track.

Outside of career, rewarding relationship activities for you might include the study of crystals and geology. With your respect for the land, gardening, and landscaping can also be enriching activities. You have a pragmatic philosophical outlook, thus you hold people accountable for their beliefs—if others cannot demonstrate their beliefs in their life, you will not have much interest in entertaining their views.

UNDERSTANDING JUPITER IN CAPRICORN IN OTHERS These ambitious individuals are the masters of calculated risk. They pursue goals that have risk involved, but first they want to be sure that the odds are in their favor. They are achievers and not much gets in the way of them accomplishing what they set out to do. You would be advised to know this if you are getting involved. If you are interested in building a life with a Jupiter in Capricorn, you have made a good choice. But don't count on them putting their ambitions on the back burner in favor of relationship needs. Shared goals related to business hold the most interest for them, but they can also enjoy major projects around the home and yard. They like to stay industrious and their idea of a good relationship is one that shares everyday tasks together with strong support for one another's career.

Their philosophical outlook is typically conservative and they won't even entertain philosophical discussions that cannot be demonstrated and integrated into everyday reality. Ideas that are presented to them are considered in terms of practicality and feasibility and are then pursued with their knack for organization. Relationship goals that enhance security, prosperity, and position are favored, and they often rely on their partner to come up with activities that are recreation and fun oriented.

Ideas for activities to bring a sense of reward to your relationship include taking a pottery class together; going on a geology field trip; attending a gem and mineral show; going to a museum or art gallery where the classics are exhibited; planning a home remodeling project with the intent of doing much of the work yourselves; attending workshops in far-away places that enhance their business (make sure the tickets are a tax write-off!); starting a small business together.

Jupiter in Aquarius

Your Growth Potential The expansiveness of Jupiter in the intellectual sign of Aquarius shows you to be the social visionary who has a strong humanitarian leaning. You are most comfortable in friendships where you live by the premise, "Don't judge me and I won't judge you." You need freedom to be who you are, so a relationship that restricted you with too many "shoulds" would be catastrophic, as you would always find yourself rebelling against the expectations. Your philosophical outlook is typically liberal, with a leaning toward alternative views. You would not do well with a partner who is overly cautious and conservative, you want to be with someone who is willing to experiment with lifestyle. You are most interested in people who represent the vanguard of their fields. It is better for you to be in a relationship that allows you to express your uniqueness and individuality, rather than having to defend it. You grant this same right of freedom to others, as you seem to instinctively realize that we are all in each other's best interests.

Shared goals that deal with participation in social change and evolution are particularly exciting for you. You are an information junkie and you would value a relationship that shared your interests in lofty, universal perspectives. When you are feeling generous, you share yourself by being a friend who wants to liberate others from constricting beliefs. When undisciplined, this would lead you to being the eccentric nonconformist who seeks to be different just to be different. When disciplined, you can be an effective leader and organizer of groups and help activate others toward a humanitarian cause.

Understanding Jupiter in Aquarius in Others Goals for these socially minded individuals are more often related to larger social issues than private concerns. Intellectual in their approach to life and somewhat eccentric, they are most appreciative of activities that are unique in some way. They are quite natural at friendship and awkward with intimacy, where they will need your help. They will need to be assured that experiencing intimacy is not the first step toward getting their wings clipped. They will often pursue goals that demonstrate their individuality and can seem to be nonconformists, as they rebel against conventional, socially conditioned thinking. Their abundant mental energy is utilized best when directed toward a purpose or cause. They are quite outspoken about needed social reforms and are often on the leading edge of their pursuits. You will find them intolerant of conventional thinking, so go ahead and take risks in your dealings with them. Impress them with any original thinking, no matter how outlandish, for you'll surely bore them silly if you pass along information that you have heard without thinking about it. Time spent with mutual friends, working towards social causes together, and all shared intellectual activities will hold their interest.

Ideas for activities that could bring a sense of reward to your relationship include attending film festivals which feature out-of-the-ordinary art flicks; visiting groups exploring alternative lifestyles; attending political rallies; joining international neighbor-to-neighbor organizations; going to electronic and computer shows; going flying or hang-gliding; just hanging out together as friends.

Jupiter in Pisces

YOUR GROWTH POTENTIAL Jupiter in the deep, mystical sign of Pisces leads to a natural altruistic temperament and compassionate, philosophical view of life. Your powerful faith and inner conviction define wealth as an inner phenomenon, rather than a worldly one. Your deeply romantic and caring nature is well suited for growth in the right relationships. Pisces is the sign that is least concerned with the personal ego, and growth for you is simply not personal. Your compassion and care extend toward others, and you would find a relationship rewarding that joined forces in some charitable activity to help relieve the suffering in the world. Excessive tendencies, however, lead to sentimentality and a martyring tendency, so it is wise for you to remember that it is self-transcendence that you seek, not self-denial. Excessiveness leads to savior/victim relationships where you find yourself making excuses for your partner.

It is far too easy for you to sacrifice your goals in favor of another's. A fine line of distinction must be drawn between serving others out of a sense of fullness in your life, and serving others because it is expected of you. Your greatest opportunity for being a benefactor for others is in your ability to help them see the deeper meaning in life. People are drawn to you because of your depth of understanding, not your worldliness.

Relationship activities that allow time for inner enrichment, such as yoga, meditation, nature, art, and all forms of creativity would be beneficial. An ideal relationship partner would also help you find practical applications for your abundant imagination, otherwise, your inclinations might lead to escapism.

Understanding Jupiter in Pisces in Others These naturally compassionate souls are typically self-effacing and prefer to contribute in silent, unobtrusive ways, rather than trying to grab the spotlight for their endeavors. You need not worry about being judged by these forgiving souls—you will feel like you can let your guard down with them and just be yourself. Artistic, humanitarian, and religious pursuits are natural arenas for their goals, but difficult for them to define, as it is rarely ambition that motivates them. The difficulty arises from the subjectivity of their goals: to be kind, loving, and compassionate are examples. When others are in times of need, Jupiter in Pisces individuals will drop their own pursuits to support them. These people are often found in profound roles of assisting others, and this provides their naturally charitable temperament a sense of reward. Their self-sacrificing ways seem to invite being taken advantage of, and the mettle of your honor and integrity will get tested in this regard. You are sure to notice one trait that is conspicuously different about them: they do not gossip or put others down—they respect others even in their absence. Their inner world is immense, thus they need to spend considerable time alone. Don't wonder if something is wrong, just allow them their inner musings and when they return they will have all the more to share with you.

Ideas for activities that could bring a sense of reward to your relationship include a spiritual retreat (near the water); a wine tasting club with the goal of visiting foreign wineries; theater, dance, and magic shows. To capture their love of fantasy, plan a trip to Disneyland, a romantic cruise ship adventure, or a day at the beach, topped off with a bottle of champagne and a hot tub.

SATURN

Challenges, Pressures, and Insecurities

In viewing our solar system with the naked eye, Saturn is the most distant planet that can be seen. In astrology, it represents the limits of the sensory world and deals with all kinds of limitations that must be faced in order to build strength of character. There would be utter chaos without the boundaries and limitations of Saturn, as there would be no definition of the self. Ideally, Saturn functions to provide form and structure through which the individual identity can express, thereby establishing clearly defined boundaries and responsibilities.

Saturn also deals with the types of challenges, pressures, and insecurities you must overcome to successfully build your identity. There are no simple cures for Saturn issues—it is the one planet for which benefit requires patience, persistence, and self-discipline. Of course, these are qualities that most of us are reluctant to develop, but Saturn has a way of forcing the issue.

Responsibilities are a central issue in everyone's life. These vary from culture to culture, but everyone assumes a role in maintaining the social structure of their time. This social-conditioning process begins very early in life as the parents offer guidance to the child as to the expectations of the family. This continues to evolve through the input of the schools, churches, and government, etc., as to the expectations society has on the individual. By the time the individual reaches adulthood, the obligations and responsibilities provide the cohesive structure which becomes the backbone of life, and ultimately gives individuals a role through which to express their identity.

Saturn is experienced within you as a sense of pressure to maintain self-identity—your response to this pressure determines the outcome. If rebellion is your reaction, you will certainly experience difficulties and challenges which are seemingly insurmountable. On the other hand, if surrendered to, this same pressure can be a tremendous source of character strength. Saturn only demands self-mastery, that's all!

Every life and every relationship has its share of challenges—that much is for certain. How each of us deal with these tests, however, is highly unique. Those who appear to have fewer challenges have simply learned how to deal with their stumbling blocks in a more graceful way, before they become major issues. Relationships provide a constant source of tests, as you must deal with your partner's expectations of you. Consequently, Saturn lessons will become either your weakest or your strongest link to your partner, depending on how well you handle pressure in your own life. Before you start dealing with relationship pressures, it is wise to develop skills in your personal life. This chapter will present techniques, exercises, and awarenesses to successfully deal with challenges in your own life and in your relationships.

Saturn lessons must be kept in the perspective of first knowing there are no irresolvable problems. In spiritual terms it is said this way: in the beginning all was one; then it split into its many forms so that we may experience the material plane, the plane of duality. For a problem to become so, it had to split from its solution. Accept the problem as appropriate, and the solution will be revealed to you.

The solution is intimately connected with the problem. When you try to push away your challenges, you unwittingly push away the skills that are necessary to overcome them. It is as if the entire reason for having challenges resides within prompting the new skills you need to develop in order to overcome the challenge. Your higher mind is sending you specific tasks when it deems it is in your best interest to learn the new skills required to surmount the challenge.

There is definitely an art to facing difficulties head on, and then extracting the skills they encase, but once you learn this, you have stumbled upon the golden egg of opportunity. From this point forward, you allow yourself to befriend the challenges as appropriate and grow from them, instead of viewing them as adversaries and backing away from them. Challenges become opportunities to test how far you have come, and they awaken your perception as to where you still need work. In each and every obstacle lies a lesson for you—look for it and learn from it.

One nice thing about Saturn issues is that they always come preannounced. Saturn issues do not come out of the blue, totally unexpected. When you get to the Uranus chapter, you will learn about the unexpected, but with Saturn, there is always a build-up of pressure first. Tend to the issue at this first subtle level, and a subtle adjustment is all that is required. Wait until it becomes unbearable pressure, and it will take hard work to resolve. That is how it is with Saturn—listen to the whispers, or listen to the shouts, but you will have to eventually deal with the issues it symbolizes. If you are driving down the highway in your car and you hear a strange noise coming from the engine, what do you do? If you tend to turn up the radio to deal with the situation, you are ignoring the whispers and soon you will have to deal with the shouts.

Discipline is required to deal with Saturn challenges. Whether it be self-discipline, or discipline imposed on you through confrontations with authorities, both require discipline. Individuals who practice conscious self-discipline have less outer challenges to face. They have consciously aligned with the work required from Saturn, and in doing so have removed the need for pressure from others to prod them along.

With Saturn challenges, you always have the opportunity to delay the process—you can put it aside and not deal with it, if you so choose. But the lesson always returns. Those who have not learned that all relationships will have their share of problems, have the habit of calling off relationships every time they reach a point of confrontation. It is easy to say the other person was wrong, and that the problems in the relationship resided within that person. The pattern is one of ending the relationship, and then once again beginning the search for a person who is more suited for your needs. This is like changing your shirt to fix a bad back.

It may be through a different time, a different face, or a different place, but one way or another, the same lesson will return to you. On the other hand, when you accept personal responsibility for the challenge and learn the lessons, they do not return. It's not that all lessons are over, but now at least you have the opportunity to move on to something different. Also, you will find the challenges become more subtle as you develop the capacity to perceive them sooner, while they are in a less-aggravating state, instead of waiting for them to become full-blown crisis situations in your life.

Learning Through Experience

"Boy, I really learned something this time." How often this is said when we pick ourselves up after falling flat on our face. But is that statement accurate? Learning takes place not simply as a realization, but as an active process, which occurs when you change behavior based on your experiences. It would be more appropriate to say, "Boy, I really became aware of how much I don't know this time." Experience will show you that lessons repeat themselves until behavior is changed. In the attitude of growth, after confronting a challenging situation, you become aware of what you need to do to avoid similar problems in the future. This information is stored within your memory bank to be used the next time you attract a similar type of confrontation—and there will be a next time. When this happens, remember your awareness from your previous experience and apply the information. Then you can say, "Boy, I really learned something this time."

Saturn wisdom is based on actual experience. It teaches you to learn and make adjustments in your life based on your direct experiences. Another nice thing about Saturn: the issues are always absolutely crystal clear as to what the problem is and what needs to be done. Not that we want to hear it, but Saturn always reveals the slow steady path to resolution—no quick cures here. It never calls for speculation. It demands you draw on your personal experience.

The following exercise is designed to help you become aware of all the factors involved in a challenge confronting you.

Exercise

At the moment you become aware of a challenge, stand back and be a detective. Notice everything connected to the moment: your thoughts, the setting, the sequence of the unfolding events.

1. Your experiences will serve as the laboratory for learning the lesson. Be as precise as possible as you thoroughly examine the details of the current challenge.

2. Sift through the information of the event by organizing it into a time sequence. When did you first start to feel that something could be problematic? This will be the clue as to when Saturn started sending you messages. How did the build-up proceed? Ask yourself, "What was I doing, thinking and feeling at the moment I became aware of the challenge?"
3. Now, the most important step. After you have contemplated the information, calm yourself by deep breathing. Ask your higher mind to reveal the lesson you are to learn from this situation. Just ask yourself: "Why am I being confronted with this challenge?" "Why is this appropriate for me?" and, "What do I need to learn from this?"

The answer is there. It always is; Saturn is anything but vague. Just calm yourself, but be diligent in your attentiveness to where growth can occur as a result of this challenge. Life is filled with guides, teachers, and messengers. If you have the presence of mind to ask yourself these honest questions, then you become the type of person who learns something from every test. It's a simple shift of focus, but an extremely important one, in order to break free of the "life as a challenge" syndrome.

Life can get very specific in its teachings when you really watch, and for me it is the little challenges that pop up in the moment that are great teachers. I became aware of this process while I was a cook at a restaurant. I remember cutting myself with a knife while chopping onions one day. The immediate question I asked myself was, "What was I thinking about?" It was shocking, but the honest answer was that I was thinking some very cutting thoughts about a coworker! Talk about "what goes around, comes around!"

The Role of Projection

Projection is the psychological process of seeing unintegrated aspects of yourself reflected through others. That which you most dislike, or become infatuated with, in another person represents some unintegrated part of your own nature. When you become critical of another person's shortcomings, look closely to see if it is exactly that which needs refining in yourself. This awareness sheds new light on why it is that certain people upset you the way they do. Perhaps it is a little like looking into the mirror for too long a time. Projection is not just a problem. Its natural function is a magical process that, when understood, represents a tremendous resource for getting to know what you need to work on at any given moment.

An analogy of the process could be described like this. There is a little person inside of you whose job is to edit all incoming information and constantly review the data of your experiences. When she or he comes across something that is not clear, she or he sends it to the projection booth within your consciousness. And then, just as a film projector sends the tiny images on the film to the big screen, your inner-projector sends these unintegrated images from your consciousness onto the big screen of life so that you can see them better. The characters on the big screen are the people in your life. The setting is your real life. It makes it all so easy—learn to watch what is going on around you—it is your screen, your script, and your lessons.

There is a difference between preference and projection that should be understood. Preferences are natural choices you have made, the likes and dislikes which reflect your values and tastes. Projections, however, are psychological reactions. A projection is measured by the strength of the psychological reaction you experience. If you are in a restaurant and notice you do not like someone's loud voice at the next table, that is a preference. But if that same loud voice gets you so upset that you cannot focus on anything else, that's projection. This would indicate some part of your character was unclear and unintegrated as you witnessed the loud social behavior. The range of possibilities stretches from having a fear that you are like that yourself, all the way to the possibility that you may be totally inhibited when it comes to expressing yourself in public. As you become skilled in the art of reading your projections, you will be able to recognize why the particular situations are there in your movie.

It takes a great deal of character strength to be able to look at the hidden aspects of your psyche because the revelations are not always flattering. Learning to recognize problems in a relationship as clues to projection will alter your awareness of these challenges. Instead of feeling the problem is exclusively the other person's fault, you become aware of a hidden lesson to be learned through this frustration. This insight gives you a greater sensitivity and respect for the challenge. With experience, you will handle these more delicately and even learn to welcome them.

Exercise

Make a section in your journal for "Projections." Now select a situation in your life that seems to fit this category. Write down your experiences surrounding the event.

1. There are probably many examples of projection that you will become aware of once you start looking, but for now, isolate just one instance. Perhaps you had a strong psychological reaction to how someone dressed, or maybe the way a coworker acts at work throws you into a tailspin. Focus on a particular incident that evoked an angry response, or caused you to become psychologically upset to the degree you suspect projection might be going on.

2. Make two subsections under Projections: one for "Objective Experience" and one for "Subjective Experience." Under Objective Experience, write down the setting and the people involved. Under Subjective Experience, write down all of your inner-awarenesses concerning the situation. This will include your feelings and reactions.

3. Now ask yourself the question, "What am I to learn from this experience?" If you are sincere in this question, you will see glimpses of the answer. The trick is to be genuine. Remember, there is a part of you that would love to believe it is someone else's problem! Your Higher Mind will reveal why you went through the reaction, but your lower self will reveal to you why the other person caused the problem. Listen to both voices. Write them both down. Now, you've got something to work with.

4. Document your progress in dealing with this challenge. Notice how the projections change as you work with the issue.

In the introduction to this book, it was stated that the first and foremost relationship that each of us develops is the relationship with our inner partner. When you are aware of the process of projection, you realize all your challenges in relationships are representative of challenges you are having with your inner partner. Instead of being hurt and frustrated when you come across difficulties, you become extremely attentive and start asking yourself: "Why is this challenge appropriate for me? Why have I attracted this particular situation into my life? Why do I go through such a strong reaction when it occurs?" With these honest questions will come honest answers. More of the magic of life becomes apparent as you realize the answer is always encoded within the problem. When you deny its existence as a problem, it will continue to crop up through projection.

Dealing with Rejection

Everyone has had to deal with rejection in their life—it is part of our curriculum. Those who have the greatest difficulty with this become the ones who limit their choices in life, fearing rejection or disapproval if they wander from the tried and true. There is a saying concerning love that is an understatement, if there ever was one: "Love is a risk, you might get hurt." It's not a risk—it's a guarantee! There is such a focus in the modern world upon not experiencing pain that many people are willing to suffer loneliness and isolation in order to avoid the pain of rejection. It's silly. Surely there will be some pain in either case, but along with the pain that comes from an intimate relationship, there's also the shared love to heal the wounds. However, this is not so with the pain that comes from loneliness. Love is worth the risk—even if the relationship ends not of your own accord and you are left loving and miserable. Even then, "It is better to have loved and lost then never to have loved at all."

A common response to the fear of rejection is to get out of the relationship before very much of your heart is on the line. People who keep changing partners before any real love can develop, or demanding so much control that they push the beloved out of their life, are prime examples. To totally confront your feelings and vulnerabilities with another takes time. It also takes courage, as there are no guarantees in the affairs of the heart, other than it is always a risk. Your beloved can turn away from you, seek out someone else, or in other ways reject you. You have to develop confidence and somehow trust that your partner will not walk away when you begin to confront relationship problems. Remember, great agility is required in the dance of life. To be graceful with both the wins and the losses is a true accomplishment.

Rejection hurts, but we do survive it. It always throws us back inward on ourselves. We do not like the blues connected with the experience, but what incredible work gets done! We re-evaluate our values, goals, desires, and with time emerge much clearer from the process.

Allowing Other People Their Challenges

One of the most obvious facts concerning individuality is that we are all different. Individual responses to the exact same situation can vary tremendously. Some things come naturally and easily for you, and other things are learned only through great effort. For example, one person might find adapting to change very easy, while sticking with a project until it's completed is difficult. Another person might be exactly opposite in this regard. One of the biggest challenges in relationships is accepting this simple truth: what is easy for you is not necessarily easy for your partner, and what is difficult for you is not necessarily difficult for him or her. It is unfair to assume how another person should perform. This is so simple, and yet, as always, the simple truths are the easiest to overlook.

No one can be responsible for another's actions, but this premise is often tested, particularly in the closest of relationships. You can feel so connected to the people closest to you that it can feel like they are representing you every time they speak or act. This is just too much responsibility for anyone to take, and yet, it happens all the time. A paramount lesson in dealing with others is to allow them to be themselves, even when their actions may be quite different from your own. For some people this comes naturally, and for those who have not had much experience in intimate relationships, it is a huge stumbling block. It takes much love and understanding to let people be who they are without this feeling of personal responsibility attached to it.

Shedding Expectations

Disappointments in relationships certainly do exist. There are great lessons involved with shedding unrealistic expectations in your relationships. More disappointment is actually caused by unrealistic expectations than by failed performance in and of itself. With an awareness of this basic difference in all people, you can begin to bring your expectations in line with what might actually occur. With time you may be able to dismiss expectations altogether, which is the highest art of all.

Exercise

Become aware of when you are being critical in your relationships and work on changing that into being instructive.

> Language is often the issue here—it is not just what is being said, but also how it is expressed. Imagine the scenario: you have a teenage child and it is her chore to wash the dinner dishes. She is busily performing her task and you notice that she has been using cold water to rinse the dishes, leaving them greasy. Here is the moment—are you going to be instructive or critical? Critical would sound like, "You are doing it wrong, don't use cold water to rinse with." Instructive would sound like, "Try using hot water to rinse with, it does a better job of cutting the grease."

Certainly it is a fine line that separates these two activities: instructing or criticizing. The difference is measured not only by your intent but by the impact it has on others. Where instructing always aims at improving, criticizing always erodes, as it is based on the assumption that the other person should have known better. Why should they have known better? Perhaps no one has ever instructed them, or informed them about what you accept as common knowledge.

It is so easy to assume that since something is obvious to you, it should be obvious to other people as well. Use the following rule of thumb concerning the obvious: assume that it isn't! Whether it be concerning emotions, or how something should be done, or what is important to you, never assume that others will know what that is until you have informed them. Much compassion is required to remember we are all students when it comes to loving and accepting. In the closest of relationships, there is a balance of teaching and receiving, no one has all of the answers all of the time! We each trade roles. Many teachers have said that to love God is easy—God is perfect. But to love man, with all his imperfections, that is difficult.

From Challenge to Solution, How Long?

There is no such thing as a relationship without challenges and difficulties, and no such thing as a life without problems. No matter how far along you are on you path of self-perfection, you will never get to the point of never making any more mistakes. As one teacher said, "It is easy to know if you still have work to do on yourself. If you are still in a body, you've got work to do!" When you truly realize this, it becomes absolutely apparent how futile it is to hold others in judgment for making mistakes.

One thing that helps in resolving relationship conflicts is shortening the amount of time it takes to restore your balance with each other. Say you have a falling out with your partner—nothing too unusual about that. How long does it take you to get back on solid ground? Some couples never get back on terra firma. They let the ground underneath them wash away until the foundation of the relationship essentially dissolves, and off they go seeking a new relationship that does not have problems. It is amazing how many people believe the presence of a problem in a relationship is a valid reason to contemplate throwing out the whole sharing. The truth is you are going to be working through a variety of situations and problems with those who are closest to you, and as you accept this as a very natural part of the territory of togetherness, you won't be so shocked when a problem appears.

Exercise

Work on shortening the amount of time it takes to get back to a healthy place of relating after a falling-out with each other.

1. Try working with the image of the relationship as a life raft floating on the ocean. A falling-out is a falling-off, for both people. During a crisis in the relationship, both partners are floundering around in the ocean, but eventually, one of you is going to get back onto the raft. Make a pact with your mate that whoever gets back on the raft first helps the other person also get back on board.
2. What stands in the way of this helping attitude during a problem is vindictiveness. This is a tendency to believe that others deserve to be floundering because they created the problem in the first place. Realize that, even if they are at fault, there will be other times when the fault is yours. Let go of blame, learn what you need to from the situation, and get the relationship back to a healthy place as quickly as possible.

My wife and I have been together for over twenty-seven years at the time of this writing. Our early years together were passionate and stormy. Over the years we have worked at the principles in this chapter and, although I believe we have just as many issues now as we ever did, we have shortened the time considerably that it takes to work through the rough spots. That is the other nice thing about Saturn: our ability to work with its lessons improves through time.

Saturn Through the Signs

In the following section Saturn through each of the signs will be presented. Information is given as to how your Saturn lessons will affect your personal growth and also, as to how it deals with your relationships, both for you and for those with whom you are relating.

Since Saturn lessons are easily the most difficult to integrate within yourself, it is not surprising that they will also represent the lessons that are the most difficult to accept within your partner. In dealing with Saturn, problems arise through two different responses to an issue. One is overcompensation, which happens when you place too much importance on the pressure of the Saturn issue, to the exclusion of other parts of your life. The other occurs through ignoring the challenge of Saturn in yourself, thus allowing it to occur through the process of projection. You cannot see the source of the problem within yourself, so you project its traits onto others. The nature of the challenge, overcompensation tendencies, projection tendencies, and a balanced integration of the challenge will be presented for each of the signs.

Saturn in Aries

THE CHALLENGE Your test is learning to take initiative in your life by acting on your best intuitive hunch, yet in a Saturn-approved, disciplined way. It's a bit of an oxymoron—disciplined spontaneity, but that is exactly your test. You can be very intense about your search for "who am I?" This question continually emerges for you, prompting you to throw yourself into some new challenge to test your identity. Saturn is restraint and you must learn from experience how to gain control of your will, so that you can call on it when you need it, and relax it when you don't. You are learning the responsibility of leadership, not by dominating and imposing your will on others, but by recognizing the need to take decisive action. You must face the need to act with confidence and courage.

In relationships, yours is the razor's edge test of maintaining individuality without violating the integrity of others. Your fear of losing yourself in a relationship has to be worked through in order to develop satisfying ties with others. If you think of independence and relationship as mutually exclusive, you will never get there. You will ultimately have to express your independence within a cooperative relationship, without violating the needs of either—the razor's edge.

Overcompensation If you go too far with your "need to lead," this will manifest as an overpowering personality. You make your life a battleground in which others easily become your competitors. Watch your blood pressure, as this approach can lead to a hot temper. You tend to get what you want in most situations, but the price is often the alienation of others. You need to learn to relax, not as a way of life, but simply as a counterbalance to your intensity. Try not to view so many situations as if they were personal tests. To always be the center of attention interferes with the development of good relationships.

Projection If you are projecting this quality, rather than identifying the challenge inwardly, you are likely to be irritated by other people's rash and impulsive behavior. Since you fear your own impulsiveness and spontaneity, you react negatively when you perceive these traits in others. If you are completely out of touch with the nature of this issue within yourself, you will tend to attract overpowering, intimidating, and forceful people into your life. As you learn to be more decisive, the projection diminishes and you attract less of the domineering type of people into your life.

Balanced Expression With balance, there is an equal expression of control and spontaneity. You avoid moving between the poles of rash, ruthless behavior and periods of apathy. The peaks and valleys of your life have smoothed as you have learned that it is best to restrain your impulsiveness in order to have sustained creative energy. You are very much in charge of your own life, acting out of choice rather than reaction—a true individual of your own making. In relationships you have learned to assert yourself when appropriate, and yet restrain your impulses when others are expressing themselves. Recognizing other people's needs for your leadership, you offer inspiration and motivation, rather than imposing your authority. You know when to control and when to let go.

Understanding Saturn in Aries in Others Courage, confidence, and learning to initiate action in a controlled manner are the main tests for these people. There are two types of expression: first, one that shrinks from the test and acts in an apparently unselfish way. The second type readily takes command and control. Realize that the apparent unselfish behavior of the first type is likely to be a mask for a lack of confidence in making an independent stand in life. This type is repressed, more than restrained, in the choice of action. These individuals might defer to you in making decisions, but then feel frustrated they did not get to do what they wanted. Encourage them to make their own choices and to learn how to stand up for themselves whenever they are being treated unfairly.

The second type of Saturn in Aries individuals are learning to express their individuality in a straightforward way without becoming overbearing. Appeal to their sense of humor to get around excessive defensiveness. Direct confrontation is not advised, as they are likely to meet force with force. Instead, divert their attention, and in a lighthearted way, let them know that you are not their adversary, nor in competition with them. They are likely to provoke your defensiveness also, so do not get caught in the "argument for the sake of the argument" syndrome with them. Their primary fear is that if they are not in absolute control, someone will take advantage of them. When integrated, Saturn in Aries leads to the decisive individual that is able to back off when everything is going smoothly in a relationship, and able to initiate appropriate action when that is required.

Saturn in Taurus

THE CHALLENGE Taurus represents your values, particularly concerning the material world—how you earn your money and how you spend it. Saturn here will pressure you to constantly work on defining these values. Security issues are likely to be the core of your main challenge. Your resourcefulness at providing for your security needs will certainly be put to the test, as will your relationship with your possessions—do you own them or do they own you? You tend to worry about not having "enough," and this has affected your capacity to enjoy the abundance of what you do have. The test is learning how to enjoy abundance and prosperity without all the worry of "what if . . . ?" This will require discipline and restraint.

Taurus issues are not particularly relationship oriented, and honoring the importance of your partner in your life can be overlooked. Worst-case scenario would be you relating to your mate as a possession! Or more likely, your partners can feel uninvolved in your life unless you include them in your process.

There is this paradox: Taurus issues truly do need to be resolved within the self—they are your values in question. But if you exclude your partner from some of your most important issues, you will certainly create problems in your relationships. Integration comes when you share your issues with your partner, receive his or her input, and ultimately make your choices based on your values.

OVERCOMPENSATION This occurs if you have an unrealistic fear of not having enough of whatever you desire. Perhaps you witnessed poverty in your early life, or perhaps your early conditioning focused on money and possessions as the primary symbols of security. That joke printed on T-shirts, "He who dies with the most toys wins," might be your philosophy. The trick to remember with Taurus is "to enjoy." When you are overcompensating, your money and possessions do not bring you enjoyment in and of themselves, but rather worry and anxiety about how to make them secure, or how to get more. Allow yourself to experience the comfort, abundance, and prosperity that you have worked for. Prosperity is as much an attitude as it is anything else.

PROJECTION Projection is your issue if you are constantly dealing with people who have issues with selfishness and stubbornness. If you are just mildly out of touch with this in yourself, then your projections manifest through your complaining of how other people's value systems are excessively materialistic. If you cannot see this issue at all in yourself, then you are in relationships with people who are extremely materialistic, stubborn, intolerant, and selfish. Once you identify your dislike of this trait in others as a projection of your fear of this in yourself, then you have a position of power to work with. You need to get clear about your own values and leave other people's issues to themselves.

BALANCED EXPRESSION By achieving self-mastery with the Taurus issues in your life, you have learned to be the connoisseur of the material world. Your possessions reflect your refined value system and your life is neither needy, nor cluttered with unimportant possessions. You have developed the discipline of experiencing security as a state of mind and have learned to enjoy life's simple pleasures. By trusting in your natural abilities, your genuineness shines through all you do. Your strength comes from believing in your values and knowing that you will not have to compromise what you believe in to be secure. People know where you stand and the nature of your personal opinions and since you easily accept these in yourself, others also easily accept them. You have an uncanny sensibility, which to you is just common sense, but to others, it seems like you are privy to the laws of manifestation.

Understanding Saturn in Taurus in Others These people are learning about developing a right relationship with the material world. Their insecurity relates to a deep fear that they will not experience enough prosperity. If you share resources with this person, realize that both of you will need to pay close attention to your agreements about how money is to be spent. You can help your Saturn in Taurus friends feel more secure by reminding them that their skills, abilities, and talents are the true source of their security, rather than money and possessions. Help them in learning how to enjoy that which is acquired, and the realization that money is no guarantee of happiness.

If you borrow anything from those with Saturn in Taurus, be mindful of returning it in the same condition that you received it in. They will grow in respect for you if you care for their possessions as they would. There is no point in trying to overpower them once they have made up their minds on any topic—it can't be done. If you wish to influence them, outline the practical reasons why your proposal is worthwhile, and then give them the time to make their decision.

The higher types with this placement are masters at manifestation. They know how to take an idea and, with disciplined attention to detail and follow-through, bring it into tangible form. They can be excellent advisors in business and financial dealings—they know what works.

Saturn in Gemini

The Challenge Yours is the test of staying open-minded and communicative. Given a choice, you would like to be recognized as a great communicator. Perhaps as a songwriter, a playwright, a journalist, or a poet—one way or another, you crave recognition, and fear rejection, through your use of words. At times, you feel that you cannot adequately express yourself—that your communication of who you are and what you think presents an insurmountable barrier. This is a fear that you must be willing to face, and then forge ahead in your attempt to make connections with the world around you. Realize that part of your test is to be informed, and this is realized through listening to others openly and attentively. You have a tremendous respect for learning, yet, apprehension concerning your ability to learn can be a problem.

Overcompensation You are likely to be a great speaker and poor listener. Perhaps fear of not appearing intelligent prompts you into commenting on everything, making it difficult for others to carry on an in-depth conversation with you. You demonstrate a bit of "salesman consciousness," always ready with a line. This leads to others doubting your sincerity. At worst, you become an intellectual snob and too readily judge others by how educated and informed they are. A tendency to rationalize and intellectualize everything in your life leaves little room for exploring the emotional side of your character—the side of you that you strongly mistrust. You have to learn that the world is not run just by logic, that the subjective, feeling side of life has just as much relevance as the rational.

Projection You are likely to be quite annoyed by know-it-alls and gossips. When extreme, you can even be critical of writers, teachers, and other intellectual authorities, thinking them pretentious. If you are irritated by those who comment on everything, it is a sure sign that you have issues with expressing yourself. A mild projection of the Gemini test leads to attracting superficial people who partially deal with issues, then quickly dart off to some other interest. Do you get frustrated with people who do not follow through on commitments because they got distracted along the way? A complete dissociation with the Saturn in Gemini test would lead to having relationships with those who make you feel intellectually inferior. If you are measuring your intelligence against others, you are missing the point. Take responsibility for learning what you need and want to know.

Balanced Expression You are mentally secure to the degree that you are unthreatened by the way others communicate, allowing you to totally merge with their thoughts and ideas. By openly entertaining the thoughts of others without judgment or defensiveness, and bringing your abundant information into the mix, you are constantly learning and teaching. You have learned to restrain yourself from idle gossip and have likely disciplined your intellect to become an authority in your chosen field of knowledge. You have taken on the responsibility of being informed about the issues on which you choose to comment, so others naturally turn to you as an important link on an information chain. You have become secure in your communications by knowing how to find something of interest in all the people that you meet. You are a good resource for introducing people of similar interests to each other.

Understanding Saturn in Gemini in Others For these individuals, issues concerning the intellect and communication are the sources of pressure from Saturn. You will know them by their expertise or ineptness in matters of the mind. Their test is to be informed, yet open to the views of others. Those who have not yet developed the discipline of Saturn will display the lower characteristics of Gemini: scattered, superficial, unreliable, and prone to gossip. The higher types are authorities in their field of expertise. They are informed, eager to learn more, and willing to share from their vast resources of information. Yet another type, somewhere in between the first two, are the intellectuals, who are the most slippery people imaginable in arguments and discussions. They are clever—you might have to work extra hard at pinning these mental gymnasts down. They are likely to be masters at evasive techniques in order to keep as many options open for themselves as possible. When this is overemphasized, the options become a burden by distracting them from the here-and-now reality. At best, they have taken on the responsibility of being informed and they can become a resource of useful, interesting information. They are important networkers, and if they do not have the information you seek, they know where you can find it.

Saturn in Cancer

The Challenge Cancer deals with personal emotions, how you feel about your life and involvements. Saturn here shows that your soul came into this life to be tested in its ability to create and sustain an emotionally nurturing environment—both externally through your physical home, and internally, as one who nurtures and provides for others. This may be easily enough said, but this is exactly where you are the most vulnerable. It is not unlikely that your early family life left much to be desired. The test is: will you let your insecurities and fears push away the closest of ties, or will you become an authority of what a nurturing environment is all about and set about creating it?

Knowing where you belong is important, and is discovered once you allow yourself to take on emotional responsibilities, without feeling them as a burden. This type of strength allows you to maintain your emotional sensitivity and at the same time build nurturing relationships. One of your difficulties in relationships is the push-pull nature of your emotional needs: "Come close, but don't crowd me."

Overcompensation When this is the case, there is either the fear of not having enough emotional closeness, or the fear that emotional bonding is restricting to personal growth. Both of these can cripple the development of forming intimate bonds. It is likely that you have built an impenetrable emotional fortress around you. Cancer is the soft spot deep within you, but Saturn fears "soft" and can restrict your safety zone for emotional intimacy so that you are starving for closeness and, at the same time, pushing away the very people that could provide it. When you go through a difficult passage in a relationship, you immediately redefine your emotional boundaries and the violating partner is expelled from your inner circle with such vehemence that the difficulty between the two of you becomes terminal.

The other form of overcompensation takes on such responsibility with immediate family concerns that there is no room for any growth outside of the family. By excessively tending to the needs of those already in your nest, you do not allow time for new people to find easy access into your life. Is this what you do out of choice, or is this a cover-up for simply being insecure about making new friends and expanding your personal boundaries?

Projection The thought of becoming emotionally dependent on another appalls you, yet you attract people who become emotionally dependent on you. That is the paradox of projection: you attract toward you exactly what you do not like in yourself. This leads to the "you know who you are by who needs you" syndrome. When you are completely out of touch with this within yourself, you form relationships with those who make excessive emotional demands on you, and then feel smothered. Once you identify these traits as projections, then you can see them as signals of your craving/fearing complex, related to anxiety about emotional responsibility. It is paradoxical, but when you enter into what you fear, it disappears! Taking on emotional responsibilities is actually just the cure you need.

Balanced Expression You have learned to be comfortable and secure with emotional closeness. This is expressed through having a committed love relationship, having a child, or even owning a pet. You have learned one of the secrets of fulfillment, which is not to undersell how much time and effort go into creating a secure and satisfying emotional relationship. You have moved beyond the fear of losing yourself through emotional surrender and you are understanding the process of defining personal needs and the effort required to satisfy these. You have learned how to share your vulnerabilities, because you know this is essential for experiencing intimacy. Intimate people in your life become as family and you are at ease in expressing your love and allowing others to love you.

Understanding Saturn in Cancer in Others Individuals with Saturn in Cancer express emotions with a strong push-pull tendency. Realize that they want and need emotional closeness, but at the same time, fear it. Be gentle, and move toward emotional bonding slowly with them, as their comfort zone is easily violated. They are likely to test you in various ways as to the depth and sincerity of your emotional commitment with them. It is worth passing the test. You eventually become as family, and that is the only way that Cancer knows how to let you into their life.

They are likely to be somewhat defensive until you have established some secure emotional bonds with them. When they are feeling uncertain, they readily retreat into the Cancer shell and respond to you as an intrusion that they must defend against. Realize this ahead of time and be willing to remove the emotional barbs that are often present in communications, as they are certain to react defensively to these hidden messages. Treat these people as family, and they will likely respond to you in kind.

Saturn in Leo

The Challenge Yours is the test of leadership and the right use of power. Leo deals with affairs of the heart, with the enjoyment of life, and with ego formation and expression. Saturn in this sign seeks to restrain, restrict, and limit this developing ego. However, Leo does not restrain easily. Your challenge might even be thought of as somewhat of a game. Why not be the best at what you do? Why not win whenever possible? You have probably learned that in your relationships, this success syndrome can undermine your happiness. If you always win, you lose respect for those you compete with, but then, you must always win. A right balance of ego strength is required. Knowing when to assert yourself and when to restrain your drive is what brings balance.

Is it the "Power of Love" or the "Love of Power" that most animates your behavior in relationships? The path out of these struggles lies in developing the presence of mind to ask yourself if your motivation is coming from your heart or not. You will know the answer by how much love and joy your behavior is bringing. If your successes are not bringing you increased happiness, do you have the character strength to restrain your ambition, or do you have to save face at any cost?

Overcompensation A fear of not being successful and important can lead to an excessively domineering, stubborn personality. Your pride is so important to you that you stubbornly adhere to a chosen direction in life, even if it is not satisfying, just to save face. Success can become so important to you that you overlook the development and enjoyment of your personality—who you are, not what you are doing. At worst, this can lead to the autocratic personality, demanding loyalty and subservience from others. In relationships, you are likely to be highly competitive and defensive. You need to learn restraint and self-control in order to maintain heartful connections with others.

Projection If you are easily annoyed with people who express themselves in an uninhibited way, or if you resent people who attract attention, and find yourself criticizing people who are successful—these traits are likely to be cover-ups for being excessively meek yourself. If you are completely out of touch with this aspect in yourself, then you get involved in relationships with those who could best be described as tyrants. Your perspective and point of view never seems to be as important as theirs. And although you do not like always giving in, the threat of overreaction from the tyrant in your life holds you back. You need to start taking responsibility for following your own heart. Royalty doesn't have to ask for permission or approval. Develop the discipline of coming from your heart. Experiment with pretending that you are confident, as a method for priming the pump of feeling stronger about yourself. It works. Put on a smile, take a deep breath, and project optimism. The world responds to you as if it were true, and so it becomes.

Understanding Saturn in Leo in Others When dealing with Saturn in Leo individuals, treat them as royalty, as special people, and you will get off on the right foot. Honor, dignity, and pride are all important issues with them. They seem particularly sensitive to any perceived challenge to their authority, and they can periodically puff up with defiance at the slightest hint of rebellion. When you feel that they are overstepping their rights and becoming too demanding, appeal to their sense of humor, and remind them that you are not in competition with them. Let them know that you appreciate them for being in your life, then their royal spirit will shine for you. Realize that approval is important to them, and that is why winning at whatever they do seems so essential.

They both crave and equally fear a life directed by the heart. Realize that they are being tested with learning how to love. Help direct them into first loving and appreciating themselves. From this they can learn to allow others into their heart. It is challenging for them to disassociate from their projects. If you don't like something they do, they are certain that you don't like them, because for them, there is no difference. You can help them become secure by letting them know that you value them as individuals, and not just their accomplishments.

Saturn in Virgo

The Challenge Yours is the test of learning moderation and discrimination in your search for perfection. You can usually think of something in your life that needs improving, and you set out to remedy the situation. This attitude works well in professional pursuits, but can be problematic in love. When this gaze of perfection falls on your relationships, you cannot help but notice some of the flaws. The trouble is, relationships are rarely perfect and it's easy to find faults when you look for them. Yours is the test of self-perfection and unless balanced, you can be inhibited in your own expression for fear of making mistakes, or critical of others' lack of perfection.

How you approach the process of perfection is all important. Is the focus on repair or maintenance? Both work for Virgo. If it is repair, you will always need to have problems to fix. If it is maintenance, you begin by viewing your life, as is, as perfection, and then you make subtle adjustments to maintain that state. You need to keep your life uncomplicated to avoid excessive worry over needless details. When you discipline yourself to take part in some form of daily self-improvement, you seem to give yourself permission to enjoy life more.

Overcompensation You are likely to have a strong dose of the Puritan work ethic and your drive for self-sufficiency can limit your ability to receive support from others. Fear of things not being perfect can make you excessively analytical and make it very difficult for you to accept that which is not logical and practical. You become the fussbudget, excessively worrying over the details of your life, especially with health-related themes. You may have a very difficult time accepting emotions at all, especially when expressed through a mate or partner. You have a fear that if you enter into the emotional state of your mate, you might drown from their overwhelming emotional needs. At worst, the perfectionist in you sees only the flaws in other people. With this as your focus, your ability to develop satisfying relationships would be severely inhibited. You are learning how to overcome a deep sense of insecurity that stems from being overly self-critical. You need to develop some restraint with this critical voice, both with self and others, and develop a regular program for self-improvement.

Projection You are overly aware of your partner's negativity and critical nature, to which you respond with negativity and criticalness. Now two people are negative rather than just one! You get irritated with people who are perfectionists, and become easily annoyed with those who criticize your actions. If you are completely out of touch with this inner process, you are likely to attract excessively critical people to you. This can lead to the henpecked personality. You are sensitive to criticism, yet the paradox of the projection is that you attract people who are very critical of you. As you develop the ability for self-analysis, your sensitivity to critical feedback from others lessens and you experience less and less of it.

Balanced Expression You have learned how to measure yourself on your own high standards of perfection and to allow others their standards. You enjoy the process of bringing situations to perfection without being too concerned when there is still work to be done. You have developed a daily habit of doing something for self-improvement along the lines of nutrition and exercise, and you have a technique for starting the day from a sense of perfection within yourself. You are extremely self-perceptive, yet not to the degree of inhibition. It is important that your efforts are appreciated, but you do not go overboard on this. You seem to know how to pitch in and help others without entering into "servant consciousness." You have become a master of details through persevering in your attitude of efficiency in all that you do. You have learned to be considerate of other people's processes and express your perceptions of how they can improve their lives with an attitude of helpfulness, rather than criticalness.

UNDERSTANDING SATURN IN VIRGO IN OTHERS Those with Saturn in Virgo are being tested with the challenge of overcoming a basic sense of insecurity by learning how to work through challenges piece by piece. They tend to be very self-critical, and can be stymied by "paralysis via analysis." Stand back and allow them the time to process their step-by-step approach to problem solving. Success comes to them through diligence of routines. Virgo is not a boastful sign and they tend to understate their ego needs. Your encouragement will be appreciated whenever it is expressed. Ultimately, their basic drive for perfection leads them to the discovery of how to effectively and efficiently deal with their challenges. Since there is already an overdose of critical self-analysis, they are exceedingly sensitive to critical feedback from others, so give them your praise to balance this tendency.

Standards of perfection lead them either to become exquisitely attentive to the details of their life, or to be highly critical of the details of your life. Realize that these times will exist and gently remind them, when you see them as being compulsive with the small matters. They want to somehow be helpful in your life as this translates into security to them. The reward that they most highly cherish is your appreciation when they do contribute and they will contribute, as this combination leads to a dedicated work ethic. They also need to be reassured that everything is all right in the bigger picture.

Saturn in Libra

THE CHALLENGE Yours is the test of cooperation with others, so fairness, justice, and equality are very important issues in your relationships. You crave peace, tranquillity, and serenity. These are available to you when you are willing to defend the scales of justice and relate from a place of balance within yourself. You tend to be preoccupied with comparing yourself to others. Before you can realistically share with someone, you must first know yourself—first self-definition, and then cooperation with others. First find balance within yourself, then balance in a relationship comes on its own. This is an important lesson for you. You can easily get caught into thinking that balance comes as result of your relationships, and that is not the case. Yours is the path of learning to negotiate for arrangements that are in everyone's best interest, and to settle for nothing less.

OVERCOMPENSATION This can happen in two different ways with Libra. In one sense, you might fear taking advantage of others to the degree that you do more than your share, just to make sure things are balanced. The trouble is, you likely go too far with this and actually tilt the scales in the other direction. If this is the case, you have to remember that compromising yourself in order to gain peace in the moment has to be considered just as much of a violation of balance as taking advantage of others—neither lead to equality.

Another expression of overcompensation is the legalistic point of view. Everything, including relationships, becomes evaluated strictly to the letter of the law. There is an excessive forcing of the issue of fairness with a rigid adherence to the issue, more than to the person in front of you. Doing yoga exercises of standing on one leg can be very good for you. These will encode the message of balance into the cells of your body. The process of learning these postures would be illustrative of achieving balance with others. At first, it takes big adjustments to compensate for the lack of balance and you teeter-totter back and forth from too much effort. As you continue to work with it, you start to sink into the experience of centeredness, rather than trying to achieve it.

PROJECTION When you are mildly projecting Saturn in Libra issues, you dislike unfairness in others. You attract people to you who have difficulty being fair in their dealings. You talk a lot about people taking advantage of you, and how you are defenseless against this. You are aware of these imbalances, but you take the attitude of "peace at any cost." The trouble is, the cost is too high, because when you compensate your perspective of fairness so as to not make waves, you are settling for less than you truly want.

If you are completely out of touch with this in yourself, you likely attract relationships that require total compromise on your part. Others seem to know that you readily back down from your original stand to avoid conflict. Through compromising your standards, you are teaching others to take advantage of this part of your character. This stems from taking too much responsibility for how other people might react to your perceptions. That is not up to you. The most that you can do is share your perspective, and then let others take the responsibility for how to use the information.

Balanced Expression You have learned to honestly share your perspective without adjusting it to fit how you assume others will react. By developing and trusting your negotiating skills, you have become an impeccable diplomat and others have learned to trust your fairness—your agreements reflect everyone's best interest. In relationships, you are not only concerned with the ideal form that looks right, you have also developed a deep appreciation for the process of the relationship and are willing to deal with the unpleasant aspects as well. You have come to grips with the disappointments that stem from searching for the perfect partner. This has led you to the understanding that the balance you seek is not to be found in the outer world, rather it is a state of being within you that allows you to accept polarities, disagreements, and contradictions as natural.

Understanding Saturn in Libra in Others Those with Saturn in Libra are learning how to effectively cooperate with others, and thus, relationships of all sorts become their main focus. You can always appeal to their sense of fairness, as this is a part of their character with which they most likely identify. They have an ideal of perfectly equitable relationships, but have a fear that they might be taken advantage of. Realize that they are extremely sensitive to any imbalances, whether imagined or real, in your interactions. It is best to be aware of this and not to assume that minor discrepancies will be ignored. They won't.

In their search for the ideal partner, they will tend to project perfection on their current love interest and feel devastated if problems erupt. This leads to a tendency of theirs to assume the partner was a poor choice, and they go off once again in search of the ideal. When problems do erupt in your relationship, help them through the troubled waters and encourage them to regain balance within the relationship. Once they gain this security of knowing that a relationship can improve and move beyond the occasional problems that occur, they become skilled diplomats themselves and can help others regain balance of perspective in their lives.

Saturn in Scorpio

THE CHALLENGE Scorpio represents the psychological impact of merging with another, and many of your challenges in life will come to you through your emotional interactions with others. You simultaneously crave and fear intimacy. There may be repeated emotional crisis in your relationships concerning attitudes around sex, money, and power. You fear losing control and your test lies in facing your insecurities concerning trust. The paradox is that you crave intimacy, and yet, for this to occur, you must surrender control, and that is the very thing you most fear. It is likely that you have had some painful experiences that seemingly justify your not fully trusting others. These memories form emotional scar tissue that creates a fear of being rejected, or hurt by your beloved. However, it is a deep transformational union that you crave with your partner, not the justification for maintaining your emotional isolation. Forgiveness or resentment—your choice, your test.

OVERCOMPENSATION In overcoming your fear of being controlled by others, you likely go too far and tend to be manipulative in your relationships. At worst, this leads to being very skilled in psychological warfare. You have likely had experiences in life that have shown you the darker side of human nature and your memories serve as justification for your perspective. This locks you into a cycle of suspicion and paranoia. When you hold on to judgments, jealousies, grudges, and resentments from the past, you are not available to receive the gifts of the present moment. Once you have figured this out, your keen sense of others' weaknesses can be used for their benefit (as in being a counselor, healer, financial advisor, etc.).

Excessive focus on sex as the primary vehicle for intimacy could also be a manifestation of overcompensation with Scorpio. In sexual union, there is the opportunity for both partners to go through an ego death and go beyond separateness. But without a flow of emotion between the sexual partners, the overcompensation leads to being a "performance jockey," with frequency, postures, and manipulations being the focus, rather than the sweetness that comes from a tender surrendering moment with your lover.

PROJECTION Your emotional relationships can erupt into battlegrounds until you are willing to look at the hidden aspects of your own character as revealed through your problems with others. Your tendency is to mistrust your partner. It can take many forms, but there is an undercurrent of doubt that pervades the development of true intimacy. A complete projection of this would lead you to attract a manipulative partner, somebody who is always pulling your strings, particularly with issues concerning sex, money, power, or emotions. You know that it is happening and you wish it would stop, but somehow you remain powerless. It is not easy to identify this projection, as the denial principle is likely to be embedded deep within the emotional structure. You need to develop the strength of character to look at the darker side of your own character first, before you start questioning the motivation of others. You don't have to necessarily identify with this darkness, just look at it. When you face the hidden aspect of your character and see it for what it is, simply the shadow, you break the spell of having to constantly deal with the darker parts of other people's character.

BALANCED EXPRESSION You have learned the power, and not just the virtue, of forgiveness. Your memories of past hurts have become a vehicle for you to improve your current relationships, rather than a jail that binds you with grudges and resentments. Instead of being suspicious of other people's motivations, you have become an astute observer of human behavior, and are likely fascinated by psychology, or the occult, to help deepen your insights. Your relationships are profound, rather than superficial, and you have learned to complement physical sex with emotional intimacy. You are precise in all of your money dealings, and have learned to benefit others as well as yourself with your shrewdness and understanding of finances. Emotional and psychological bonding are healthy aspects of your relationships. When you are hurt in relationships, or run across conflicts, you have learned to go deep within yourself to discover what you need to work on to improve the situation.

UNDERSTANDING SATURN IN SCORPIO IN OTHERS Saturn in Scorpio individuals will be powerful allies, or powerful foes. It is best not to get on their bad side, as they can have a strong drive for getting even. Holding onto grudges, that have been forgotten by others, is a recurrent theme in their relationships. You may have to openly work at checking in with them to clear the score card that you didn't know about. Theirs is the test of forgiveness, and periodically, they will have to be reminded of this. They have a rich inner life that keeps much of who they are hidden just beneath the surface. Problems concerning sex, power, and money are periodic visitors, as Saturn in Scorpio people have a very difficult time of letting go and simply trusting.

At times, they are intensely private souls who do not like to be drawn out. They need their privacy. If you have earned their trust, they will be very committed to you, although somewhat possessive. There are some personal issues that they simply refuse to talk about. You will quickly learn which issues these are, and understand why they are to be avoided. The degree of emotional control that you will surely notice on the surface does not accurately reflect the depth of their burning passions. Don't give up too early, their love is worth the wait.

Saturn in Sagittarius

The Challenge Saturn in this placement molds your philosophical nature with a strong focus on morals and ethics that become an essential part of your character. Your challenge is to put form and structure into abstract, philosophical issues. You seek out relationships based on honesty and understanding of your lofty mental wanderings. Challenges with others are likely to erupt over disagreements concerning philosophical issues. You are being tested with balancing two distinctly different forces: the limiting and restricting nature of Saturn, with the lofty and expansive Sagittarian ideals. When Saturn restricts these ideals to rigidity, there will be problems dealing with dogmatic beliefs that you defend with evangelical zeal. It is not uncommon for one with this placement to have been raised in an excessively rigid, moralistic family which would have been experienced as repressive. The challenge in adult life is in discovering your personal truth, without denying the rights of others.

Overcompensation If you have not first done your homework of expanding your philosophical outlook beyond your personal horizons, you might appear as the boring moralist. You think that you are expanding other people's perspective, when in actuality, you are only trying to indoctrinate them to your dogmatic point of view. In overcoming your fear of not being right, you sway to the point of becoming excessively argumentative. You can become so rigid in your adherence to the laws and rules of your religion that you completely ignore the spirit they were meant to foster. The solution to your challenge lies in developing respect for other people's point of view. You must understand that truth is relative to experience, and that everyone's experiences are unique. When you demonstrate respect for another person's point of view, they will naturally grow to respect you, and you can become a very successful teacher.

PROJECTION A mild projection of this is typified by a strong dislike of high-minded people who readily share their personal philosophy. Your dislike of this type of behavior is likely a cover-up of your own feelings of inadequacy in expressing your beliefs. This is often caused by the disillusionment of being raised in an excessively moralistic environment that stifled, rather than encouraged, spiritual growth. A stronger projection of this is evidenced by attracting dogmatic, narrow-minded relationship partners. Although you strongly dislike such people, they are in your life ever so ready to moralize and judge your behavior. They measure your character to theirs, and you most often come up short. If this is the case for you, then you will need to develop a stronger personal philosophy of your own. As you become better at understanding and expressing your own convictions, you will stop attracting this test.

BALANCED EXPRESSION Through your expanded philosophical perspective on life, you serve as a vehicle for others to grow past limiting perspectives. Teaching of some type, formal or informal, is natural for you. Through your inquiry into the philosophical workings of life, and your competitive drive with yourself to continually be more than you were in your past, you inspire others to reach for their goals also. You are a truth seeker, able to find a kernel of truth wherever you look. You have developed an ability to learn from your experiences and then to generalize your discoveries into the meaning of life. Your penetrating mind has an intuitive link with the divine, giving you direct experiences of the core meaning of life. Most importantly, you have learned to demonstrate your truth through the way you live your life.

UNDERSTANDING SATURN IN SAGITTARIUS IN OTHERS A difficult aspect of this combination is the self-righteous type of expression. Their philosophizing and moralizing is the banter of self-justification along with being judgmental of the morals and ethics of others. Their defensiveness can be threatening. If you are strong enough to avoid reacting yourself, you can deflect their arrows of incision by asking them questions that are out of their area of expertise. In the moment, you are likely to see only the ego reactions, but they will take the questions home and work on them as a step to expanding their perspective.

Saturn in Sagittarius individuals pride themselves with the definition of their moral and ethical character. Honesty and bluntness are the best approaches for communicating with them. Be bold with them—they want to know the truth. They like philosophical discussion and can even enjoy a good debate with you as if it were sport. At best, they are disciplined thinkers who enjoy contemplating the theoretical, higher aspects of life. The excessive exuberance and idealism of Sagittarius is tempered by Saturn's influence and these people try to find a constructive, practical approach to actualizing dreams. They can help you formulate realistic goals and a positive path to the future.

Saturn in Capricorn

The Challenge Saturn in its own sign of Capricorn is strongly placed. Worldly ambition and success are likely to be very important to you. You are learning the test of leadership and the right use of authority. Professionally, this is a very favorable placement, as you will surely know how to capitalize on the various opportunities that come your way. Being practical and pragmatic in business is certainly the best approach to clarity. Conversely, this placement is not as favorable for emotional relationships, as you may appear to be more interested in career than love. It is not easy for you to express your emotional sensitivities, as you view this as a weakness that you would like to overcome, rather than to indulge in. Those closest to you may complain of you being too cold and methodical about your approach to sharing love. Your challenge is in learning to be successful without having to sacrifice the personal side of life.

Overcompensation Success can become so all-important that your career concerns overshadow all other areas of expression. You become so disciplined and organized that you look at most forms of relating as some sort of a task rather than a pleasure. People in your life can become as cogs in a wheel of your ambition. At this point, rigidity can set in. You become the taskmaster wanting all the parts of your life to be part of a plan—spontaneity falls away.

Your drive for status can lead you to seeing people through their accomplishments, achievements, and social position, which can leave you missing the personal side of involvements with others. People are viewed in terms of how they may help you to accomplish something you are working on. It is your loss, as emotional closeness could be a wonderful balance point in your life. Your excessive focus on ambition masks an insecurity with the personal side of your life. Learning to reveal your insecurities to allow for personal time with others is the antidote.

PROJECTION A mild projection of Saturn in Capricorn issues would be a dislike of status-conscious people who measure their life by their worldly success. You can find yourself resenting people who have better cars, or better houses than you. You seem overly aware of who owns what. A strong projection of this would be attracting to you a relationship with a person who is all ambition and no love—a workaholic. Although you strongly dislike this quality, you are attracting people to you who do not have time for the personal side of their life. This might be masking your own fear of failure. Through watching these people be successful in business, but not in their personal life, you can see that the price of success is too high. It is something that you don't want, and thus, justifies not striving for success yourself. You will have to realize that your form of success will not be the same as it has been for anyone else. You must move on and discover what mountains you were born to climb.

BALANCED EXPRESSION You experience pride through the excellence and fulfillment of your achievements. You are involved in working relationships where there is equality through goals realized. Respect is a key ingredient in your significant relationships, defining a two-way street of approval. Loyalty and commitment are other important qualities that define your meaningful relationships. You understand the need for patience and persistence in creating the quality of life to which you aspire and, with time as your ally, you get to the top. You are willing to use your organizational talents to assume a position of authority in society and are fulfilled, rather than burdened, by the load. You like providing for others, but more than just money, you have learned to help others develop their natural skills and abilities.

Understanding Saturn in Capricorn in Others Saturn in Capricorn individuals take themselves seriously, and relationships of any type must be founded on mutual respect. Loyalty and commitment rank high on their list of important qualities, so if you make agreements with them, be sure that you plan to follow-through. Irresponsibility is intolerable. They can become excessively status conscious, and can measure people exclusively by what they have accomplished until they become secure in their own achievements. Their focus on accomplishments masks their insecurity with the personal side of life—thus, they are more likely to feel comfortable helping you with career issues, rather than personal. Emotional rapport with them must be developed slowly, and realize that they appreciate sincerity more than sentimentality as a form of emotional expression. They do not accept failure easily, so they will work hard to maintain a relationship once established. There is a certain dignity to the higher types and it is a polished reserve that they exude, rather than a rigid adherence to protocol.

Saturn in Aquarius

The Challenge You are learning how to be both responsible and independent at the same time. Wanting to be a free, innovative spirit, and still be accepted by the world, is going to force you into finding practical ways of expressing your uniqueness. Until you find a responsible way for expressing your independence, you will experience problems in your relationships. Your independent streak will pop up at inappropriate times, such as not following through with agreements. You express a need for closeness and yet you rebel when your partner has expectations of you. Your challenge lies in accepting your uniqueness, rather than fighting for it, and then finding a way of demonstrating that in the world by aligning with a social cause or purpose that you believe in. Once you learn the secret of fulfilling responsibilities joyously, you will feel the freedom that you long for.

Overcompensation Uniqueness at any cost can lead to some odd expressions of nonconformity. A fear of being ordinary underlies your resistance to all that is expected of you. This can lead to the "rebel without a cause" syndrome.

You attract people who confront your right to do things your way, then you rebel against this, almost as if your individuality itself was on the line. When you are spending too much time defending your choices, you might want to review just what you are trying to accomplish. This can be a clue that you have not yet accepted yourself and the full ramifications of individuality. When you come to realize that you need to prove your independence to yourself, and not to others, then you express your uniqueness, rather than fight for it. With this understanding, your commitments and relationships are no longer a threat and become welcome opportunities for you to express yourself.

Projection A mild projection of Saturn in Aquarius is a dislike of highly individualistic people. You likely view them as annoying nonconformists who just refuse to cooperate. A strong projection of this occurs when you attract people to you who have definite problems with commitment. Their freedom is so important that they fear losing it through commitment. It would not be out of character for them to periodically do something outlandish, just to demonstrate their right to do things their way. This you abhor, but still you seem timid about expressing your own uniqueness. You must learn to break this cycle by establishing a stronger independent stand yourself. Dare to be you, the *true* you, and then find a disciplined way of expressing this responsibly in the world.

Balanced Expression You have found ways to express your individuality and maintain responsibilities simultaneously. Your life demonstrates the principle of "freedom is a function of fulfilling responsibilities joyously." You are able to express uniqueness in all that you do without interrupting proceedings in order to demonstrate this. You have marshaled your rebellious tendencies into the qualities of the social reformer. You take some aspect of social change as a personal responsibility, which you express through a chosen social cause. You take your responsibility of informing others of your point of view seriously, and yet, you do not get caught up in the reactions of others. Since you have become secure with your individuality, you are secure with accepting the uniqueness of others as well. You have an ability to accept others on their terms, which gains you many friends who feel comfortable being themselves in your presence.

Understanding Saturn in Aquarius in Others There are two types of Saturn in Aquarius people: reformers and rebels. The first type are the responsible social visionaries, the consummate humanitarians who have found ways to contribute to improving life for others. These people appreciate social interaction with like-minded individuals. There are times when they can seem very aloof and impersonal. It's not that they are insensitive to your personal concerns, it's just that they like to keep things in perspective through detachment. These are the people to talk with whenever you want to see things in a bigger picture.

The second type are the nonconformists who express uniqueness by constantly rebelling against any type of conventionality. This type looks down upon humanity as a boring group of predictable people. They are defining themselves in terms of what they are not, but at this stage, have not yet developed what they are. The more that you are able to accept them on their terms, the more they will feel comfortable with you. Both types are highly individualistic and do best in relationships that have a strong friendship base.

Higher types with this placement are responsible social activists. They believe it is part of their responsibility to assist society in its evolution. They have an eye for the future and consider the ramifications of current social policies on future generations. They likely will motivate you to examine your life path in light of a larger universal perspective.

Saturn in Pisces

THE CHALLENGE Yours is the test of putting form and structure into your faith and beliefs. Do you believe in a greater intelligence that is somehow guiding the development of your life, or do you find despair and disappointment around every corner as things just do not seem to work out as you plan? This is precisely the challenge of faith and its flip side, fear. The more that you learn to be responsible for your inner life and set aside quality time for the development of your spiritual character, the more the chaos subsides in your life.

An important question that you must ask yourself is this: "Did I come here to suffer or celebrate my spiritual life?" It seems a ludicrous question, but it is relevant with this placement. When you are responsible to the Saturn in Pisces need for inner activity, then you find healthy spiritual or artistic activities that pull you into your inner world. If your spiritual life is not disciplined by Saturn, then it is likely that your relationships are chaotic and clouded by illusions. This creates disappointments and suffering that require you to go off by yourself to work through your pain in your inner world. So you get to your private, inner world one way or another—through celebrating or suffering—your choice, your challenge.

Overcompensation Self-pity, in all of its manifestations, is likely to be an issue that can undermine your happiness until you discipline this part of your character as if it were an indulgence that you must control. Any number of variations on the theme of the martyr are likely to come up for you in your relationships. You equate being a good person with caring for others and when you become excessive in this, you become the worrier. In overcoming your fear of not being compassionate, you become animated by guilt and seem compelled to take on the worries and problems of the world.

Another manifestation of overcompensating is becoming so devout and pious that you miss much of the adventure that life offers. Perhaps you were raised with the fear of a punishing God, leading to a moral rigidity—your faith becomes a set of rules instead of an enriching emotional experience.

Projection If you have a fear of being swallowed up in the chaos of your emotions, you are likely to protect yourself against this and tend to dislike emotional types, classifying them as unrealistic dreamers. You insist on a rational life and become irritated with others when they follow their feelings and instincts without a sound rational support. If you are going through a strong denial of this in yourself, you tend to attract the victim type of person as a relationship partner. This person always seems to be a victim of his or her moods, and goes through periodic bouts of guilt, suffering over concern for others. Although you do not like to do it, you get pulled in and seem to have to help organize this person's feelings toward getting a grip on reality. When you are spending an inordinate amount of time helping others build form and structure in their emotional life, it is a sure sign that you need to do just that for yourself. You need to become responsible for establishing emotional boundaries and creating disciplined time with your inner world so you can keep your emotions in perspective. Then you will not feel overwhelmed by the needs of others, and will be able to define your boundaries without being insensitive to other's needs.

Balanced Expression You have a disciplined spiritual life, and can help others find meaning in life beyond simply acquiring possessions. You have learned to take responsibility for your emotional character, and can get involved with the emotional life of others without becoming overwhelmed. You have become the epitome of the compassionate person, yet not to the degree of becoming "long suffering." You seem to know the limits of what you can realistically do for others, and have learned that it is not your responsibility to process the emotions of others. You have realized that the greatest gift that you have to give to others is becoming a pillar of spiritual strength in your own life. You have found ways to serve others without denying yourself. You have realized that you can passively feel the suffering that is in the world, or you can actively do something about it, and you have chosen the path of responsible action.

Understanding Saturn in Pisces in Others Saturn in Pisces people are extremely sensitive, and until they have disciplined themselves to gently float on the ever-changing tides of their emotions, they seem to be a victim of their moods. They are learning to take responsibility for their emotional character, and need to learn to define their boundaries without shutting others out.

These individuals might periodically drift into martyring behavior patterns. Whenever you suspect this is the case, ask them directly, "Is your life about suffering or celebrating?" If they are still facing the challenge of this placement, they are periodically overcome by the empathy they feel for the hurt in the world. When they have mastered this challenge, they have found ways to do their part of helping in the world by some type of compassionate service, without going through self-denial in the process. They can be a source of spiritual strength for you by helping you see the deeper meaning of the events of your life. When you feel a need to be listened to without fear of judgment, these are the friends to rely on.

Introduction to the Outer Planets

WHERE THE SUN, Moon, Mercury, Venus, and Mars represent the most personal aspect of a person's character, and Jupiter and Saturn represent the social levels of involvement, Uranus, Neptune, and Pluto represent transpersonal or collective forces. A good astronomer could point out the planets up to Saturn in the night sky, and you would be able to see them with the naked eye. This is not so with the final three planets—you would need an extension of the normal senses (a telescope) to see them. In astrology, they also represent forces that are beyond the normal range of perception. Rational thought is adequate to understand the operation of the planets up to Saturn, however, to understand the operation of the outer planets, one must go beyond rational thought and begin to use faith and intuition.

Due to the extended amount of time it takes for each of the outer planets to orbit the Sun (Uranus, 84 years; Neptune, 167 years; Pluto, 249 years) they will each spend many years in a given sign. This means that everyone born within a several year period will have the same outer planet arrangement in their charts, thus the themes of the outer planets relate to an entire generation.

How is it that cultures, relationships, and individuals evolve? Where does the new information come from? The answer can be found in outer planet correspondences to individual—and collective—awakening and growth into greater consciousness. Isn't this the purpose of life—to evolve, to awaken to consciousness, to grow in awareness of what one was not aware of before?

The final three planets could be pictured as our connection to the angelic level of consciousness, where information essentially descends upon the individual as if it were being sent by invisible forces of the universe. The role of free will is different with these outer planets than with the previous planets. Up to Saturn, the planets symbolize essentially malleable forces. If you want to enhance—or tone down—a certain characteristic, you can do that with your free will. But the outer planets symbolize forces beyond the influence of the ego identity. Call them divine influences, if you will. Here, free will takes on a different role. You can neither invite, nor stop this type of influence. Free will at this level represents how you respond to their uninvited messages. Your options are either to resist and struggle, or accept the callings and surrender to their evolutionary impact on your life.

Uranus, as the first of this triad, is experienced in our lives as the unexpected. Events connected to Uranus force us to change our view of the established order that has been built into our lives up to Saturn. The psychological urge connected to Uranus is felt as a drive to go beyond the conventional expectations that have been placed on us by our culture, and to establish our individuality and uniqueness. At the lowest level, Uranus corresponds to rebellious, eccentric, erratic behavior. At the highest level, the Uranian theme relates to speeding up the evolutionary process of the soul. It manifests as the awakening urge to discover new realms of potentiality.

Neptune relates to the imagination and all aspects of fear and faith. It represents how we incorporate the new information brought to us through the unexpected Uranus events. While Uranian events come crashing through the Saturnine boundary of the ego identity, Neptune dissolves the separate sense of self to allow a merging with a larger spiritual reality. At the lowest level, Neptune relates to all escapist activity such as drugs, alcohol, illusions, and escapist fantasy. At the highest level, Neptune relates to the creative inspiration and spiritual vision that comes to one who has learned to align with the calling for an inner life in a healthy way. Art, music, meditation, prayer, and surrendering to the beauty of nature are examples of healthy "escapes."

Pluto, as the final planet, represents the death and rebirth principle. The old view must die before a higher, more encompassing reality can be reborn. Pluto's theme is like a volcano, reaching deep into the realm of the subconscious and bringing new material to the conscious mind to be integrated into the self-identity. At the lowest level, Pluto represents an obsessive-compulsive urge for power to control and dominate others. At the highest level, Pluto is the capacity for self-transformation. By confronting and purging the darker, hidden aspects of self, the divine intent of one's life blossoms into consciousness.

The three outer planets together symbolize the spiritualization of consciousness and have more to do with collective issues than personal issues. Still, they have their personal effect in how you respond to collective issues. Each of these planets will be explored in the following chapters. Remember as you read that these issues are not strictly personal. Think of them as the agents of evolution, prompting the awakening of humanity to a larger, spiritual reality.

URANUS

The Urge for Freedom and the Expression of Individuality

> The sense of discovery, becoming aware of something that I hadn't noticed or put together in quite the same way before, that's the freedom I wish for. Freedom from anything that separates me from this moment. To think of each and every moment as an opportunity to learn and become more aware of God's wonder; that each and every person I meet might be another of Goddess' messengers; that each situation I enter into is individually tailored for my learning and benefit; this is what true freedom means to me . . ."
>
> —Anonymous

Uranus, the first of the three outer planets, is called "The Awakener." It represents our awakening to another dimension of reality and our urge to break free of limitations. The drive to live a life beyond the commonplace; to actualize hidden potentials that lie beyond the grasp of normal intelligence; to move beyond that which was taught by your culture and to emphasize that which makes you truly unique—these all relate to the Uranian level of consciousness. Where Saturn represents how individuals find a responsible role and fit within the culture they were born to, Uranus represents the drive to evolve beyond the constraints of that culture. The longing for freedom and the right to express the uniqueness of your individuality are the ways that you personally experience this planet.

Does your drive for independence and need for freedom stand in the way of your relationships, or enhance them? As a counselor I often hear variations on the theme of "Do I have to give up me to be a part of you?" A significant question to ask yourself is, "Are my relationships an expression of my individuality or a denial of it?" As you read this chapter, continue to ask yourself this question. Whether you feel trapped or free in a relationship is dependent on your answer. This chapter will explore the themes of freedom and individuality as they relate to relationships. We will take a look at some of the traps that stand in the way of achieving independence and offer potential solutions.

One of the beautiful aspects of astrology is that it teaches integration. Ultimately, each of us must find a way of incorporating all of the planetary functions into our lives in order to experience the elusive goal of fulfillment. At one level, adhering to responsibility and obligation seems to be in direct contrast to the needs for leading a free and independent life. As you grow and evolve, you find that they are not in contrast at all. Responsibilities do not limit individuality, they provide an opportunity to express your individuality—they become the arena for your individual expression. It is how you fulfill the responsibilities that is either an expression or a denial of the truth of who you are.

Finding True Freedom

Freedom, that elusive butterfly, is an experience that many seek and few ever totally achieve. As you develop a lifestyle, responsibilities come for maintaining that lifestyle. The balance between freedom and responsibility is a dilemma everyone must face. Many people seek freedom by constantly running from others, as if by making no commitments the desired liberty will be experienced. This creates an illusionary freedom at best, as then one is never free from having to run. Let's face it, there is no ultimate freedom as long as you are in a body—there are certain limits and restraints built into the system. True freedom is ultimately relative. The more you resist responsibilities, the more they are experienced as burdensome. The more that you accept your responsibilities as the maintenance of your lifestyle, the more they become opportunities to creatively express yourself in their fulfillment.

Is your life directed by free will or destiny? This perennial question, like all questions of polarity, contains two truths. The answer is not this or that. Instead, it is this and that. Free will and destiny both have to be accepted in order for freedom to be experienced. Destiny may bring you blessings such as a loving partner or a perfect opportunity for a life change, but destiny also brings you challenges, difficulties, inconveniences, and petty annoyances that enter into your day uninvited.

"Uninvited" is the tip-off that destiny is at work, as this signals something happening that is outside of your apparent control. Destiny can bring major situations and events, but it more often manifests in small ways. In these situations, your only position of power is in how you adapt to the situation. A certain skill is required to deal with the uninvited situation. Destiny unfolds as you develop the skill required to deal with the situation that appears before you. It could be diagrammed this way:

> Destiny ➔ brings challenges ➔ leads to skill development ➔ leads to using new skills ➔ leads to destiny ➔ leads to new challenges, etc.

Freedom is achieved as you learn to move directly to the skills required when you meet challenges, rather than simply venting frustration for having the challenge in the first place. As you learn how to be creative in your response to the unexpected you are rewarded by the experience of greater freedom.

Fulfilling Independence

To be independent is to take absolute responsibility for your life. This includes how you think, act, react, feel, and participate in your life. You realize that you cannot control your destiny, but you can control how you experience it. Carl Jung once said, "Free will? That's my ability to do gladly that which I must." A truly independent person understands this means not wasting time grumbling or resisting that which you must do anyway.

To be independent is to have access to fulfillment from within. No one else is needed for you to have this experience and no one can detract from it. You learn to draw from an internal source that is inexhaustible in its ability for renewal. When you are in touch with this, your fulfillment will be independent of what happens to you.

Ultimately, the meaning of your life will not be measured externally in the uncertain world of events and material things. This is not to suggest that you will start to live in a vacuum, only that you will have more control over how you respond to what goes on around you as you become less dependent on externals. People will not have to act in any certain way for you to love them, nor will things have to go in a certain way for you to be happy. This is the freedom that comes from independence.

Independence is not achieved by simply staying out of relationships, as this is quite impossible anyway. Whether they be intimate, casual, or circumstantial, relationships are the way of life. To experience relationships as a gateway to independence, rather than a obstacle to it, is the highest expression of personal freedom. To have a satisfying relationship both with yourself and with your partner brings both freedom and love.

When you are not independent, you seek out relationships based on mutual need. Need-based relationships, whether through friendships, work, or marriage, are typified by a feeling that you are not complete without your partner. At this stage of relating, you experience lack when your partner is not present—you have grown to need this person. What does your partner experience when you reconnect with him or her? A drain. Believe it or not, when you allow your batteries to run down when you are away from each other, your partner will experience your presence as a drain when you come back together. You are not bringing to the relationship, instead, you are taking. Maybe neither of you are conscious of what is occurring, but in time, you will eventually become a burden, because you are always needing something from this person. The mutual need syndrome leads away from an exciting, growth-oriented life.

Compare this to the type of relationship between two independent people. Each individual is fully involved with life and has taken personal responsibility for his or her own happiness. The two find stimulation and fulfillment whether they are with each other or not. They might miss each other when they are apart, and they may prefer each other's company to being alone, but they do not need each other to feel a fullness of life. What do they experience when they reconnect after busy and full lives away from each other? Fullness. There is much to share with the other. They each experience a completeness through the exchange, whether they are on the giving or the receiving end. Rather than being as half-filled cups needing something from each other, they have become as two full cups seeking to share their fullness.

It sounds so ideal, why are there not more relationships like this? Because it can be scary to be with someone who does not need you—where's the security?

How do you know that your independent mate will come home? These are the questions that will arise and challenge you. When you can identify this basic insecurity in each other and not get defensive, then you can help each other through the trouble spots.

Cultural Deconditioning

A philosophy professor of mine in college once said, "You cannot truly be free until you have broken free of all the cultural conditioning that you have received." I have since grown to believe this is impossible, but it does represent an interesting high-water mark to shoot for with Uranus. Before you can know about your individuality, you must first take the time to know what you have been taught about yourself through your upbringing. Are you simply a product of that conditioning, as if you were an empty bottle, and what your parents poured into you is your true self? Certainly not. There is an essential you that came into this life complete within itself, having its own agenda to work on. You cannot really know this essence without going through some questioning of the impact of your upbringing.

Parenting, the school years, peer pressure, and exposure to media all contribute a tremendous amount to forming your identity. This cultural process may or may not be consistent with your true nature, but you'll never know unless you spend time questioning this conditioning. Many never do of course. They have accepted the spoon-feeding entirely without ever raising an eyebrow. To this type of person, appearances and what other people might think are the main considerations when making decisions.

If you are longing for greater freedom and yet, make most of your choices based on what others expect of you, you need to ask yourself the question, "What would I do if it was my life to live?" This, of course, is a ludicrous question—obviously it is your life, but until you have awakened to the Uranus level, you might not be acting as if it were. Think about it! What if you had the freedom to make choices solely on what your authentic self dictates . . . what would this be like? How would your life be different? The degree to which you are not even able to imagine a life lived by your independent choices is a measure of how much you have compromised your authentic self to fit in with others.

Are you aware of how many times you make choices based on conditioned reactions rather than personal choice? Spend a few hours in a conversation and watch how many times you respond without really thinking. Every time you settle for this type of communicating, especially with yourself, you are selling yourself short. Cultivating individuality requires you to continuously make choices based on the information that you have in front of you at the moment. Every time you unconsciously make decisions, you are following old patterns. This is easy, and unfortunately, becomes easier with age. It is also very boring and inhibits growth.

Freedom from Opinions

Set opinions lock you into your past decisions and deny a current, on-the-spot, evaluation of the situation at hand. Wherever opinions, even positive opinions, overrule your ability to think in the moment, you have lost the opportunity for a fresh perspective. To be alive and on the edge of discovery is what freedom is all about. It is the opportunity to break free of cultural, and self-imposed, conditioning. This is a goal that will take work to accomplish.

Even a positive, healthy opinion, such as making a decision that you are never going to eat red meat or junk food again, can deaden your ability to respond to the moment. The truth of your experiences might be that every time either of these is offered to you, you choose not to eat them. But if you always decide in the moment, rather than parroting a decision made in the past, then these choices are alive, current expressions of who you are in this moment. This type of thinking brings a quality of aliveness to your life.

Honoring the Uniqueness of Self and Others

You can have as much individuality, freedom, and independence as you are willing to give to others. In the alchemy of relating, the two partners form opposite poles in the total process of becoming whole. At best, each should be able to develop further and faster because of their relationship—the electrical current is right for growth. The most successful and satisfying of relationships are the ones that encourage the individuals to express the most in their lives. It is not simply that two come together for the purpose of relating only to each other. That would be an inversion of energy and, with time, the relationship would become stale. In the most successful relationships, both partners encourage each other to be fully individuated beings.

Individuality, freedom, and independence are traits that you enjoy when they define you, and yet these same traits can feel threatening when they define your partner. Think back: aren't the traits that frustrate you about a person often the same traits that compelled you to get to know that person in the first place? Why is that? Upon first attraction, it is a person's uniqueness that makes him or her outstanding. And yet, at a certain point, too much individuality and "doing things my way" interferes with the bonding that is required to set up a foundation of trust. What is the answer? If either you or your partner begins sacrificing individuality in favor of the needs of the relationship, resentment can start to creep in. And even worse, if you begin playing a role, rather than being yourself, the relationship still suffers. There is a fine line between cooperation and sacrifice, and everybody has to define that line for themselves.

The motives for forsaking individuality are usually quite innocent. It sounds good in the marriage ceremony . . . "And from this point onward, this couple will forsake living for self, and begin to live for each other." This is not to say that it is the fault of the ceremony. The ceremony only sanctifies that which naturally happens. Actually, from this point onward there will be a continual negotiation process between commitment to the relationship and commitment to the self. Many couples enter into a magnetic, exciting relationship only to find themselves chipping away at their mate's uniqueness. Unfortunately, through time, this constant pressure begins to work, ultimately leading to a bland relationship with no magnetism. It is a wise person that encourages the independence of his or her mate.

Independence without the relationship would be easy—all you would have to do is think about yourself. Relationship without independence is also a way for many. But independence within relationship—now, that is a fine balance. Too much focus on the rights of the individual and the relationship suffers. Too much focus on the needs of the relationship and the individual suffers. To be in a satisfying, cooperative relationship without sacrificing the needs of the individual is indeed an art. If you let go of what empowers you for the sake of the relationship, the price is too high. A relationship is fed by the individuals within it, and will be as strong, exciting, and stimulating as those who make up the team.

The Authentic Self and the Persona

In each of us there is the authentic self, which is the source of your true individuality. There is also the persona, or mask of the self. These are both parts of yourself and it is helpful to know how they differentiate from each other. The persona is the mask worn to facilitate self-expression and it can be both cultivated and changed.

It is like your clothes—they are not the true you, but they make you comfortable in the world and facilitate the expression of the true you. Your authentic self is something else. You were born with it. Persona relates to your ego identity, the authentic self relates to your soul identity and is expressed as your individuality. Individuality is the eternal truth of your being and the persona is the current expression of your ego. The persona was adopted and cultivated as a vehicle of expression. To know more about your individuality, learn to distinguish it from your persona.

Exercise

In your journal, make two headings. Under "Persona," write about the current way you are presenting yourself to others (clothes and personality). Under "Authentic Self," write about the you behind the persona.

Persona is the current way that you are presenting yourself to the world based on how you would like other people to perceive you. Also included within this are your current activities and beliefs that you are cultivating. These are parts of your expression that change and make up your current style. It may just be a phase that you are going through or a necessary arrangement due to temporary circumstances, i.e., family circumstances, money, health, etc. The persona is also influenced by your response to the expectations of others—the "shoulds."

1. Under the heading of Authentic Self, write things about the deeper, core you that may or may not get expressed out into the world. List such things as the kind of person that you know yourself to be. These would be your deep-rooted beliefs and ideals concerning life. Be as honest as you can in your observation and recording. The purpose is to help you see the transitory nature of your persona and the eternal nature of your authentic self. This exercise may take some time to complete as these are parts of yourself that you usually clump altogether. Allow yourself the time that it takes to separate and define them.
2. After you have written a page or two on each, read the two sections and contemplate their similarities and differences. Are they very close so that one list is a reflection of the other? If they are, you are apt to be a happy and fulfilled person. Likely, there will be some discrepancies between the two lists.

3. Write your observations in your journal. Take note of problems you are having in your relationships because of these discrepancies. You will discover that where the two lists are radically different is where you are having difficulty in your relationships.

Both of the descriptions you wrote were truths about you. Where there are inconsistencies between them is where you are likely to be sending out mixed messages. This is why the saying "Be true to yourself" has so much validity in relationships. When you are not being true to your authentic self, for whatever reasons, you are not expressing your persona self with clarity. This is certain to manifest as confusion in your relationships. It is often that simple.

A common example of this is how people will often respond to in-laws. Fearing that their natural behavior would somehow be inappropriate, many people adjust to what they think is expected of them, when they are around their in-laws. This discrepancy creates the tension that is characteristic of this situation. Another example is of the genuinely friendly person who has an extremely jealous mate. The natural expression is curtailed for fear of the jealous response from the partner, thus creating a frustration.

Traps and Solutions Along the Way

Independence and freedom seem to be contrary to cohesive and close relating. There are many common traps along the way that make relationship and independence seem mutually exclusive. Are they opposite or complementary? Each of the following traps and solutions deal with the two themes: opposite and complementary. There are a few main motifs and thousands of variations that you will probably recognize in the following examples.

The Trap of Fighting for Freedom

Some people fight for the right to be free, others express it through a demonstration of that freedom. What is the difference? One has to do with words and one has to do with action. When you are secure in your individuality, you need not fight for it, as it is simply a function of who you are. You only have to fight for that which you do not have. The people who are making the most noise about freedom are usually the ones who do not have it. Granted, there are times when making noise is the appropriate first step. Examples are battered women, or any group of people who are defending their rights. In the context of your personal relationships, however, we are referring to situations when only you and your attitude are holding you back.

When you accept your uniqueness and individuality, you are living your life through your freedom and independence. You do not think about it, because it is simply a fact of your being. That is a clue about the trap of fighting for your independence. On whose permission is your independence based? Who is it you are trying to convince? You or someone else? When your freedom is based on permission or approval from others, are you really free in the first place?

An example of this is when you agree to something that you really do not want to do and you take on the task with a grudge. You wish you were doing something else. You might even feel a little put off that you were asked in the first place. You respond as if you are being forced into doing something that you really do not want to do.

The Solution

Until you can accept responsibility for your own actions, it will always appear that others are making excessive demands on you and that you must fight for your rights. Remember, just because others are asking you to do something, it doesn't mean you have to do it. They probably do not even know that you are against doing it because you said you would. True freedom requires you to acknowledge that you are the one who is absolutely responsible for everything that has happened and is happening in your life. Nothing has happened to you outside of your acceptance and agreement of it, consciously or unconsciously. If you accept this premise, then you can be absolutely free, or as Hemingway said: "Every damn thing is your own fault, if you're any good."

To be free, simply assume that you already are, and then you will begin to look at your responsibilities and so called "restrictions" in a different light. All that you do is the result of your choice. If you agree to do something, then do it with your best attitude, as it is your choice. If you do not want to do something, but you say yes, then you'd best do it with a positive attitude, as it is still your expressed choice. You always have the option to say no, and when that answer best supports how you feel, use it. All options become an opportunity to express your individuality. Your task becomes one of expressing that which you truly feel.

The Trap of the Backdoor

Many people are not consciously aware of their drive for freedom. Unconsciously, these drives get worked out through the cleverest of means, such as the "backdoor technique." This is a subversive method of undermining the relationship in small ways to keep the backdoor of escape open. With this technique, you can easily justify leaving the relationship at any convenient point. You keep just enough problems brewing to justify a lack of total commitment. You do not want to let the relationship get too secure and comfortable. This way you are always prepared to leave if you need to . . . just in case.

One execution of the backdoor technique is that of finding fault with your partner when you talk about him or her to your friends—accompanied by many a story concerning the problems of the relationship. This is a type of lobbying for support in case you choose to end the relationship. Imagine what it would be like if you were in a relationship that all your family and friends see as great. Everybody that you count on for feedback loves your mate. Now, how are you going to feel if you leave this person? Guilty, right? So, if you have any thoughts of getting out the backdoor, you better prepare your support group by slandering the relationship. Sound familiar? If you find yourself often discussing the negative aspects of your relationship with others, think about it. What are your motivations? Perhaps you will find a bit of this backdoor opening in yourself.

The Solution

If the backdoor is open, close it! It is never fair to evaluate a relationship when it is at its most awful, and if the backdoor is open, it is at its worst. It is amazing how many people are afraid of letting things get too good in a relationship for fear that it might trap them. Let it become its best! See it in its best light before making a decision. Take responsibility for your evaluation of the relationship and vow to get it at its best before you make a decision concerning its future. It takes strength of character to go out the front door if you choose to end the relationship. Do you have the courage to own up to the decision? Can you acknowledge that you need to leave because you are no longer growing in the relationship, not because there is something wrong with your partner?

The Trap of Rebellion

Independence is expressed by the urge to evolve and grow into all that you are capable of being and to break free of restraints. There is a basic tension between independence and the restraints that it seeks to break free of. This tension is the source of the energy that stimulates the urge to either rebel or reform. To rebel is to fight against, and to reform is to fight for. The reactionary path would lead to rebelling against a perceived, and always available, antagonist. The trap is that by rebelling against a given situation, you essentially dedicate your energy to exactly the conditions you detest. To resist is to persist.

This adversarial type of consciousness is always against something—it thrives on the energy of the polarity. In its full-blown form, injustices are constantly focused on and found. There are times when rebellion is the appropriate course of action (as Thoreau wrote in *Civil Disobedience*), but when someone thrives on adversarial energy, this person will inevitably find issues to rebel against. A subtler form of adversarial consciousness is looking at life as a constant challenge that must be overcome: here is the problem, where is the solution? Here is the difficulty, how do I deal with it? Here is the conflict that must be resolved, etc. This is ultimately an exhausting way to live and eventually takes its toll as one tires of the battle.

The Solution

The adversarial path can eventually give way to a visionary path, creatively chosen, if you can learn to draw on the subtle inspirational energy from creative choice. To fight for something you believe in as a reformer is part of the visionary path and is infinitely harder than following the path of rebellion. Why? The energy from polarity that is built into adversarial thinking has to be self-generated to pursue a visionary path. When you are fighting against something, the opposition provides the energy you need to work for your cause. But when you pursue creatively chosen paths, there is no opposing force to draw energy from—you have to learn to feed on the subtle inspirational energy. To creatively express individuality through personal choice, rather than through reaction, is to become the dreamer that lives out the dreams.

The Trap of Searching for Freedom from Responsibility

Those who are self-employed have undoubtedly heard this one: "I wish I were my own boss. Then I could do whatever I wanted, I'd be free of all these responsibilities." What a joke! To be successfully self-employed requires one to be more attentive to responsibilities, not less.

You either know this or you do not, and people who don't know it, don't know it with a passion! They firmly believe that it is responsibility that stands in the way of freedom. Fighting responsibilities simply doesn't work, and is at best, foolhardy. But until you've had enough experience fighting the windmills of "unfair expectations," you are trapped in thinking that you can somehow get free of them, rather than meet them.

The Solution

As always, take responsibility for everything in your life. Freedom is a function of joyfully fulfilling responsibilities in a way that does not compromise your individuality. Accept your challenges as the consequences of your choices. Handle your responsibilities with effectiveness and joy. The real you should be expressed through all of your various activities. Call it "getting one step ahead of your karma." Learn to trust your life. Instead of resisting the consequences of your choices and creating further complications, accept the obstacle on your path as if it were exactly appropriate for you. This prompts you to evolve into a higher level of consciousness through which you can resolve the situation at hand.

The challenges don't go away, you just handle them more gracefully. Extra time comes from removing the resistance to the challenges. Think of it, how much energy do you expend in "I wish I didn't have to do this, I shouldn't have to do this, and I don't want to do this"? Eventually you get to a point where you are handling your responsibilities in a fraction of the time that it used to take, and the extra time represents your freedom.

Evolving Relationships

The bottom line with Uranus is the need to evolve. All of the breaking free of the expectations of others, the need for independence and striving for individuality, are part of the same urge to evolve. To awaken to the Uranus level in relationships does not mean that one cannot maintain commitments, but it does mean that the relationship itself must continually evolve and grow beyond previous limitations. This allows the individuals within the relationship this same opportunity to discover more of what life's potential is all about. Growth, discovery, and excitement are the characteristics of an evolving relationship.

Uranus Through the Signs

The sign Uranus is in at your birth represents a dynamic area of life for you that stays in change. Uranus resists status quo. This is where you came to cast off the cultural conditioning you have received, and constantly reinvent this area of life so that it is more in line with your authenticity. With Uranus, everyone born within a seven-year period of time will have the same sign. This collective surge is the force that molds society and the evolutionary themes within civilization.

There are appropriate stages in this process. First, awaken to your individual truth, then contribute to cultural change by adding your fresh insights. Uranus starts off by awakening you to your individuality, but it does not stop with the ego. When outer planets get expressed through the ego, problems erupt. It is best to align with larger causes that your ego supports—causes that are not just about you. As rebels, revolutionaries, or reformers, this is an area of life that your generation came to transform.

Relationships can be a disruptive area, as Uranus awakens you to your independent self. If you see your freedom as pitted against relationship issues, a battle will result. Your relationships must constantly grow and evolve to new levels in order to satisfy the Uranian urge for a life of discovery.

All three of the outer planets are generational in nature. We will limit the discussion to the overall themes that your generation came to revolutionize and its likely impact on relationships.

Uranus in Aries

The urge for constant change and discovery that Uranus represents is certainly not wasted in Aries, the sign of spontaneous action. This pioneering placement leads to a generation that is not only willing to break free of tradition, but is compelled to do so. Since both Uranus and Aries deal with independence, count on these people to stand up and join the fight for individual rights within any system, whether it be the family, a business, or society. This combination is likely to be disruptive in relationships if the focus on independence is not complemented with attention to the rights and needs of the relationship. Until a Uranus in Aries person is able to see a relationship as an arena to express individuality within, the relationship may remain problematic. Causes such as Amnesty International can be meaningful for this group.

Uranus in Taurus

The evolutionary push from this combination leads to a group of people who are here to initiate changes in monetary and security related themes within a culture. Where Taurus typically leads to attachment to possessions and money, Uranus here will not tolerate limitations and, although these people are brilliant and inventive in ways of making money, they are not attached to accumulating it. Discovering new skills and talents for making money is part of the call. Not interested in manual labor, Uranus follows the inventive qualities of the intuitive mind into ways of providing security. On the down side, the disruptive influence of Uranus can keep relationships on edge concerning money and security issues.

As we move toward a global economy, this generation might very well play a significant role in reinventing economic policies. They could also find satisfaction working for change concerning land use, such as helping to create public land trusts.

Uranus in Gemini

This decidedly mental combination leads to a generation of inventive thinkers. They came here to explore new dimensions of the mind and its capacity. This revolutionary tendency pushes for reforms in education and how ideas are transferred. The Internet with its vast network of information, accessed electronically, would be particularly appealing to these folks. They resist conventional ideas and are willing to cast off their previously held beliefs in the light of new truth. In relationships, they will resist any rigidly held conventional beliefs and can be counted on for bringing fresh insight into any conversation. They would subscribe to Emerson's statement, "Consistency is the hobgoblin of little minds." The thrust of the evolutionary force behind this group leads them to revolt against any form of censorship. Radio Free Europe is an example of this mentality, and this group can also find meaning by supporting the drive to make education available to all.

Uranus in Cancer

This generation came to revolutionize attitudes concerning the home and family. The evolutionary push is in the personal aspect of life. Cancer is often aligned with traditional values, but with Uranus here, these souls will choose to break with tradition and pursue these most personal of issues in their own unique way. Many have had children outside of marriage and have been pioneers in the home birth and home schooling movements, supporting individual rights of choice in this regard. The traditional image of the nuclear family has been shattered by this group who have explored coparenting with the parents living in different homes, gay couples adopting children, and even alternative names for their children. Issues concerning the needs of homeless and hungry would be appropriate choices for social action. Also, issues dealing with water quality, pollution, and land use might stir these individuals to action.

Uranus in Leo

This dynamic dramatic combination leads to a generation that is seeking new ways to creatively express themselves. The liberating influence of Uranus will encourage the unrestrained flamboyant expression of Leo, thus the entertainment industry and the arts will continue to be revolutionized by their involvement. With Leo ruling matters of the heart, the revolutionary energy of Uranus here leads to a generation seeking new freedom in how they express their love. The free love movement is an example and with the advent of contraception, this group has been on the forefront of the sexual revolution. On the political front, Leo represents royalty and heroes, and Uranus here will constantly seek out new stars to glamorize. Causes that support veterans' benefits, or the arts, can be meaningful sources for social action.

Uranus in Virgo

The evolutionary surge behind this generation is not so much with sweeping global change as it is with specific issues and interests. The technological and health industries will provide opportunities for the revolutionary interests for Uranus in Virgo.

The fitness industry has been spurred on by this group with their research in high-tech vitamin supplements, the healing properties of herbs and organic foods, and new technology of fitness equipment. The computer and electronic industry has also seen many advances and inventions with these high-tech wizards leading the way. Virgo represents daily routines, and the disruptive influence of Uranus will keep this group constantly reinventing their daily schedule. They will need relationships that support their need for constant self-improvement.

Those with this placement can find appropriate outlets for their revolutionary zeal in the environmental movement. Also support of world health organizations such as the Red Cross, and support for scientific research on diseases, would also be appropriate. Workers' rights and benefits will also be a focus for their desire to initiate social change.

Uranus in Libra

Libra is represented by the scales of justice and this generation came to revolt against all issues of inequality. The feminist movement with its adage of "Equal pay for equal work," is a prime example of their influence. Traditional roles in relationships are undergoing radical change with this generation. Women in business suits pursuing their careers, and stay-at-home dads, in touch with their femininity, are examples. Libra is associated with the arts and you expect these people to break with tradition in terms of their tastes and interests. Libra holds the ideal of justice, not just for self, but for all and this generation will continue to revamp the legal system with the adage " . . . and justice for all." Support of the ACLU and conflict resolution groups could provide a healthy outlet for this group. Groups that promote literacy and exposure to the arts would also be natural.

Uranus in Scorpio

The rebellious nature of Uranus working through the sign of Scorpio is certain to have its impact on society's attitudes concerning sexuality. Expect this generation to break from tradition and flaunt their unconventional attitudes about sexuality even if—no, especially if this causes a reaction in the general public. The gay rights movement is a prime example— not just the fight for freedom of individual choices, but also a focus on changing the laws that do not support the basic legal rights for gays. Scorpio represents that which a culture considers taboo, and you can expect Uranus here to explore what was previously forbidden. Penetrating insights into the human psyche can come from this combination and you can expect them to contribute to advances in the fields of psychology, the occult, the healing arts, and crime investigation. Social causes related to uncovering and preventing of sexual abuse, or exposing corruption in business and government, can be outlets.

Uranus in Sagittarius

The thrust of the evolutionary force driving this generation will lead to religious and political reforms. Sagittarius rules all things foreign and this generation will be global in its perspective of where change needs to take place. Uranus leads to revolutionary activity and we can expect the Sagittarian generation to work at overthrowing and revamping the judiciary system of the courts. Religious freedom or fanaticism will also be in the balance for this group. At worst this could lead to "holy war" mentality, and at best a global acceptance of all religions. Philosophical, political, and religious arguments would not be unlikely in relationships where one or both partners have this placement.

Uranus in Sagittarius will likely be in the forefront of educational reforms. Social causes that promote religious and moral education would be natural outlets, as would be support of global political issues such as the "Free Tibet" movement.

Uranus in Capricorn

Uranus' liberating energy is somewhat held in check in Capricorn, which seeks to maintain existing order. The thrust of evolution here propels the formation of multinational corporations in the march toward a global community. You can look for this generation to revolutionize global economy by breaking down the barriers to free market enterprise. At the same time that companies are going global, workers will become increasingly independent, aided by inventions that liberate individuals from the restricting "9–5" office life. The very nature of how business is conducted will continue to evolve from this generation's inventiveness.

Capricorn issues are often at odds with the needs of a relationship and this is likely to be an issue. They will need partners who are not overly demanding to allow these souls to express their inventiveness in their careers.

Loftier souls with this placement would seek to tear down structures that support favoritism and elitism in government. Capricorn is inclined toward the lawful world of science, and involvement with the advancing of scientific knowledge would be rewarding.

Uranus in Aquarius

Uranus is at its strongest in its own sign of Aquarius and the impulse for revolutionary/evolutionary activity is nonfiltered here. We would expect to see a generation of social activists. Social causes supporting human rights and the rights of future generations would be natural areas of expression. It is as if this group came to us from the future and they are here to remind us how much our current policies will impact the quality of life for future generations. We can expect them to pioneer new types of relationships with their drive to break down all types of stereotypes. Individual rights will be necessary within their commitments.

Any and all forms of social activism would be appropriate outlets. The humanitarian theme of this placement is complemented by an equally strong interest in electronics and we can not even imagine what gadgets this generation will invent. Space exploration and alternative sources for energy would be likely areas for their inventiveness.

Uranus in Pisces

In the compassionate sign of Pisces, we can expect Uranus to revolt against intolerance in religious and spiritual beliefs. This is spawned by the Piscean belief in the unity of humankind and they will likely rebel against all that stands in the way of ultimate oneness. Expect major reforms in the care of the handicapped and disadvantaged as Pisces does the clean-up work after Aquarius and tends to the needs of those who are not making it in society. This generation will likely be more spiritual than religious, and will help break down the barriers between religions, favoring the view that we are all children of the same planet and the same God.

Where Pisces will often martyr itself in favor of others, Uranus is decidedly not self-sacrificial, and we can expect this group to tend to the suffering in the world without getting pulled down by it. Relationships will have to allow for their need to serve humanity.

Natural expressions for social action would be victim relief activities, as well as ministering to the needs of the downtrodden and those without faith.

NEPTUNE

Imagination, Illusion, and Spirituality

NEPTUNE IS A spiritual planet and must be understood as such to align with its energy. It is not worldly whatsoever—its pull is to take you out of worldly concerns and into a transcendent reality. Neptune is expressed through the imagination and the range of potential experiences, from the high road to the low road, including: spiritual inspiration, creative insights, faith, the still quiet voice within, fear, illusions, escapism, and deception. That is a lot of territory and not all of it seems spiritual! All of these experiences are related to the desire to lose yourself in a reality beyond the separate sense of self. If you do not create healthy outlets for its expression, it will manifest in unhealthy ways. As an outer planet, Neptune is more concerned with your soul's needs than those of the ego. If the ego latches onto it and claims its territory, trouble invariably results. Neptune's influence is subtle, but pervasive. Whether this is a benefit for you, or a source of trouble, it is up to you and your capacity to tend to this subtle giant.

When experiences happen to you that are outside of the rational mind's ability to comprehend, how do you respond? Do they trigger fear or faith? Do they inspire you, or cause you concern over your sanity? Does your imagination wander aimlessly, sometimes deluding you and sometimes inspiring you? Or have you harnessed this faculty and honed it to a tool for creativity, inspiration, and inner spiritual guidance? All of these questions will be explored in this chapter and considered in terms of how they influence relationships.

We will first explore the imagination itself as the main vehicle through which Neptune is experienced. We will then cover illusions as the low road, with Neptune and spirituality as the high road. Next, spirituality in relationships is explored, followed by tests along the way in becoming familiar with this subtle realm.

Imagination: The Vehicle

Although imagination is the seed from which reality flowers, it is often underrated. If it cannot be imagined, it cannot be done. The sequence is always the same in the creative process—first Buck Rogers and then NASA—first imagination, then reality. Many people do not think of themselves as creative, and yet, it is something that everyone takes part in throughout life. The trick is to identify how the creative process operates in your life and see if you can direct its course, rather than let it wander aimlessly. What do fantasy, illusion, spirituality, escapism, inspiration, and deception all have in common? Imagination. In each of these activities, imagination is the process that allows the experience. Such a resource! For the artist of relationships, just as with the painter or musician, imagination is what allows an experience to rise above the common and mundane and become truly creative.

Neptune was only discovered late in the nineteenth century, and as such, is still relatively new in terms of our awareness of its function. We are just beginning to understand the impact that imagination and visualization have in our lives. Many of us have been raised to believe that imagination means not real. How many times did you hear, "Oh, it's just your imagination," as if it were a dismissal? By not respecting what a tremendous resource it is, imagination is relegated to escapist fantasy. However, imagination is simply a vehicle and, as such, is neutral—what you do with it determines whether its impact on your life will be positive or negative.

The most common use of our imagination is through various forms of escapism. Drugs, alcohol, fantasy, daydreaming of a different life, or even surrendering consciousness to television or movies—all of these function as methods of escaping the pressures of everyday living. True, imagination is most often used as a method of temporarily taking a break from reality, and there is nothing wrong with this. But there is nothing right with this either, as these escapist wanderings never change reality, and they essentially waste creative energy that could be used in more positive ways.

The easiest and most direct way of capturing the energy that gets wasted on idle fantasy is to invest it back into your life. The following exercise can help.

Exercise

Start each day by imagining in your mind's eye that your life is exactly perfect for where your soul needs to be at this point on its path. Feel the resultant sense of harmony this brings.

Spend a few minutes alone in quiet before you start your day, closing your eyes and experiencing your breath with great attention. Try to imagine, and it takes imagination, that at least from the soul's perspective, everything in your life is exactly as it should be for what your journey is about today. Sink into the feelings of harmony that come from this acceptance.

Most people have a fear of accepting their lives as exactly perfect as is—there is still so much that could be improved on! This fear comes from the illusion that if you accept your life as perfect now, you will be stuck with how it is forever. Just the opposite is true. By imagining that your life would be better if you had more money, if you were in a better relationship, if . . . , you are essentially disengaging from the spiritual authority of your own soul. To live your life from a spiritual perspective is to believe that your soul has been the author of every experience of your life, including your current reality. By imagining your life as perfect, you are engaging the spiritual authority of your soul and essentially investing the imagination factor back into your real life, rather than spending it on idle fantasy. There are times when the loss of a loved one or a painful divorce put us into a place we really do not want to be in, but even then, healing begins once we can accept the appropriateness of our current situation. This exercise helps your imagination become rooted in the reality of your current here-and-now situation in life. Now it can operate throughout the day, interacting with your real-life situations, and your life starts moving forward as faith unfolding.

Most everyone agrees that they are looking for peace in their lives. Few realize that you have to start from harmony in order to experience it throughout the rest of your day. You cannot maintain something that you do not have. With spiritual concerns, you must be willing to first find within yourself that which you are looking for in the outer world. Just as in the myth of returning from a quest and finding the sought after treasure in your own backyard, the same is true in spiritual concerns. Find it first in your inner world and you will have no trouble finding it in the outer world. The above exercise returns the spiritual quest to you.

The imagination awakens us to the fourth dimension of reality beyond the normal senses. This is the magic kingdom where reality is not limited by time and space constraints. Train your imagination and it becomes the key to opening to inspiration, both creative and spiritual. Without training, your Neptune will be randomly generating these inspired states, but just as often this world of make believe leads to illusions.

Illusion: The Low Road

There are many expressions of Neptune that are not inspired, but not necessarily problematic either. This would include idle daydreaming and mild escapist activities such as television and movie watching. However, there are expressions that are problematic and chief among them is susceptibility to illusions. An unhealthy manifestation of Neptune in relationships stems from falling in love with qualities in another that are not there—they are just imagined! The imagination is working, but in problematic ways. Then, through time, reality sets in and disappointment always follows. Disappointment in relationships is just as often a function of illusionary expectations as a problem in performance. It is only through experience that one learns to separate the two.

There are at least two different causes to this type of behavior. One source stems from an inability to accept the painful or lower aspects of the human experience. Then the imagination works by distorting your view of reality to support that which is emotionally tolerable for you. This denial syndrome is resolved by learning to expand that which is emotionally tolerable. Philosophically, you should realize that each and everyone of us has a higher self and a lower self. This could also be said of every opportunity that comes your way—it has its best and worst possible scenarios as potentials. If all you see in any person or situation is the highest and the best, you might be setting yourself up for the blindspot of Neptune. It is not being negative to imagine a potential worst case scenario—it's simply protecting yourself from susceptibility to illusion.

Another source of illusionary expectations comes from the savior-victim complex. This happens when you fall in love with others with the illusion that you can save them. This type of love is based on pity and soon becomes pitiful love! A typical scenario is this: you meet a person who has a series of misfortunes in life. This awakens your compassion. You believe that his or her problems actually come from never being fully loved and understood. The savior in you steps forward and you take the person on as a project, believing that once this person experiences the type of love you have to offer, problems will disappear. Does it work? Rarely.

The solution to falling in love with "wounded birds" requires experience. Until you have experienced the pain of this type of relationship syndrome, you will not believe you are prone to it. With experience, you learn that it is wise to look before you leap. If you are susceptible to this type of relationship, watch a person with some detachment before you give yourself to love. Do you admire the qualities that this person has developed, before you both met? Do you love the person as is, or are you falling in love with a potential?

Included within the category of illusions are all forms of deception. Being deceived by others, or deceiving yourself are attempts to create an illusionary reality. These soap bubble realities eventually burst. Involvement with drugs and alcohol is a more serious form of living in illusion and will not be dealt with in this book. If you or someone you love is having problems in this regard, seek help. Suffice it to say here that this type of person hungers for a transcendent life above the mundane normal experience. This hunger can be met by cultivating the high road with Neptune—the spiritual quest.

Spirituality: The High Road

Spirituality is a loaded word for many people. It brings up images of Sunday school, church, and ideas of good and bad. An expanded view of spirituality is the search for the divine, wherever it can be found. There are many paths that lead to this awareness: some do find it through church and traditional forms of religious participation; others find it through more private contemplative methods such as meditation, quiet walks in nature, or the sight of a falling leaf; others find it through music or art; while still others find it through loving. Whatever the form, this search leads to the underlying spirit that animates all of life. It deals with the inner quality that you bring to whatever it is you are doing. The spirit of the involvement, rather than the form, is the significant factor.

It should be understood that religion and spirituality are not the same thing. Religion represents an external authority of the nature of the soul and always teaches a specific dogma. Spirituality honors an inner authority of the soul and contains no dogma whatsoever. Religions often are based on a set of rules of what not to do—"Thou shall not kill," etc. Spirituality is concerned more with what you do, rather than don't. The spiritual path is in all that you do to open your heart to loving life, and loving others. There is a revolution taking place now that has many people leaving the churches and searching for the divine within their inner being.

Spirituality has to be redefined or many will deny their spiritual nature for fear of not having any fun. That is what is wrong with our religious traditions—they are not much fun! The spiritual paths that lead to a denial of worldly pursuits have missed the tremendous joy that is available through being in a body on this lovely planet. The new wave of spiritual growth has attracted a group of people that came here to celebrate the gift of life. It is an important distinction; did you come here to suffer for your spirituality or to celebrate it? As one teacher recently said, "The days of the suffering saints are over, make way for the laughing and dancing saints!"

Traditional philosophies concerning spirituality always began with the premise that being in a body represented a fall from divine grace and was cause to lament. It is wise to consider this philosophy when embarking on your own spiritual path. Many of the traditions that you will be exposed to will point you toward the belief that if you are really good and do a good job of facing your karma and learning your lessons, you will not have to come back here to Earth. What kind of a philosophy is this? It makes one wonder about the originators of these philosophies and religions. Didn't they have any friends? Didn't they have flowers and clouds and birds and the delights of nature in their world? Didn't they have any days that they would not have missed for anything? Whether it be going to heaven, reaching nirvana, or escaping from the wheel of death and rebirth, each represent a philosophy that leads one out of the physical world, rather than into it. The spirituality that is being promoted here would have you celebrate your life and relationships, rather than escape them.

Be willing to experiment with spirituality. You will have to work hard and be courageous enough to find your own way when embarking on a path away from tradition. The big step comes from assuming control over your spiritual authority, which means personal acknowledgment of whether you are in a state of spiritual grace or not. Traditional religions taught this as blasphemy, rather than your birthright. To start a journey towards celebrating the gift of life is to join the spiritual revolution.

As you develop on your path, you become more and more aware that there is a sense of purpose in your life, that your life does have meaning and significance, not just for yourself, but also what you are contributing to the benefit of others. To get in touch with your essential spirituality is to get in touch with your transpersonal self. This is that place in you that is connected with others—all others. To become aware of your transpersonal identity is to feel yourself lifted up beyond self-importance, to start taking yourself less seriously, to take what you are offering the world more seriously. When you have opened to this aspect of your life, relationships take on a different quality. They do so because you no longer are looking for something from them—you accept them as part of the divine grace of your life and experience them as such.

The truly spiritual person is able to see the divine manifested in all of life—everywhere you go and every person you see is another aspect of God/Goddess. To feel your spirituality when you are in the grocery store, the bank, preparing dinner, or visiting with friends is the essence of the spiritual life. A spirituality that exists only in a certain building at a certain time and place is no spirituality at all. The real satisfaction comes from becoming aware of the divine presence that is everywhere.

Spiritual qualities can be developed . . . "And these and greater things ye shall do . . ." But how? What are the techniques and procedures? Although poets and romantics would chafe at such a description, spirituality could be called the "technology of consciousness." There are skills and techniques of consciousness and just as with all skills, they improve with training and use, and go into a state of atrophy without use. The following is a discussion of the resources, skills, and procedures that can be developed on the spiritual path. First work with these skills as if they were personal resources and then try working with them with others.

The Witness

All spiritual traditions teach the necessity for developing the witness part of the character. The witness is that in you that has the ability to rise above all of the roles that you play and simultaneously see yourself in action. It is just watching the show, your show. Krishnamurti referred to this as the "Detached Observer." To Christian mystics it is referred to as the witness, while Buddhists call it the point of mindfulness. Hindu tradition identifies it as the third eye, and in astrology it is the Neptune function. It is the ability to attend to a larger, spiritual reality, simultaneous to attending to your personal life. To be in touch with the witness is to be in the world, but not of the world.

To employ the witness is a subtle technique, especially when you are engaging your imagination. When you are daydreaming and fantasizing, you have stopped controlling your conscious attention. To monitor your daydreaming, you have to be able to maintain your attention while the drifting is occurring. The trick is to be aware of it, and simultaneously, allow it to continue. A certain delicacy is required to be able to be in both places at once, which is the point of the added awareness.

You first tell yourself that you are going to practice being the witness the next time that you start fantasizing. As it starts occurring, stand back and watch it happen. If you are not gentle in your awareness, you will snap out of the daydream, that is why you must be delicate in your shift of attention. If you are successful, you will activate the witness.

At this stage you are seeking a passive observance of the effects that the daydream, or any activity is having on your energy field. Is there a subtle enhancement or depletion? A constriction or expansion? What you will begin to notice is that some of your fantasies are energy drains, essentially excrement of the psychic energy field. After these involvements, you will notice a general state of overall depletion. The range of this can be from the most subtle to total exhaustion.

You will also begin to notice those inner reveries which empower you. Again, this can range from the mild to the ecstatic. There is no external authority in this, as everyone has to find out for themselves. The faculty that allows you to distinguish between draining and empowering fantasies is what is being developed. It is different for everyone and it is always changing. That is why you must be able to monitor your energy field as a technique. No pat answer will work.

The witness is passive observation and in and of itself will change nothing in your life. To actually edit your imagination and direct it toward healthy, inspiring material requires the spiritual will.

Spiritual Will

There is a center within you that controls the direction of your imagination. It strengthens with use and atrophies with nonuse. This is called your spiritual will. When strengthened through exercises such as meditation, prayer, and creative visualization, this resource becomes available for your creative direction. This affords you the opportunity to improve and enhance all aspects of your life, including your relationships. Without discipline, the imagination operates randomly, sometimes enhancing your life and at other times undermining your reality by false perception. The following is an exercise for strengthening your spiritual will.

Exercise

Set aside ten minutes a day to practice disciplining your imagination. Color visualization is a good place to start. Sit with your back straight in a relaxed manner and close your eyes. With your inner eye, see each color of the rainbow. Go from red, to orange, to yellow, to green, to sky blue, to deep indigo blue, to violet.

This type of exercise can be thought of as "psychic push-ups." We do physical push-ups not to just become better at the exercise, but also to tone and strengthen the body for other activities as well. The same holds true with learning to discipline your imagination. The point is not only to get better at seeing colors, but to strengthen and tone your spiritual will for other activities.

This exercise, or others that you develop for the same purpose, allows you to direct the course, not the content, of your imagination. If you are daydreaming, fantasizing, or lost in inner reveries about someone or something, first engage the witness function. Observe your energy field and note if there is a subtle enhancement or depletion. If you sense a drain, engage your spiritual will and redirect your inner wanderings to something that empowers you. You learn to use your own energy field as a code of ethics to monitor if an activity is appropriate for you or not.

Using Meditation

Meditation is the most important resource that you have on your spiritual path. Meditation sets the stage for divine rapport. It can be said that the divine will never turn its back on you, but when you fail to meditate, you turn your back on the Divine. Meditation has its traditional forms including posture and breath control. For some people, these forms work very well. For others, especially those that have not yet learned to tame their energy field, a moving meditation is better. This can be walking, gardening, arranging flowers, or just about any activity that allows one to fully surrender to the moment.

It is usually the case that the busier a person gets, the more that meditation is needed, and the harder it is to find the time for it. Yet, daily meditation is the key ingredient to a spiritual life and when exercised, the need for counselors, drugs, alcohol, and therapy go down considerably. It is hard to market meditation, however—it costs nothing and doesn't require you to join anything. It can be thought of as a daily enlightenment hit. Enlightenment is too often thought of as a perfected state—once achieved, that's it, you can forget about it, get your halo, and start walking on water. It is not that way. It is more common to bob in and out of divine awareness—to be enlightened one moment and searching the next.

Meditation gives you perspective. It offers you the assuredness of your ability to experience tranquillity and fulfillment at will. There are many books, tapes, and techniques of meditation available. It is not important which one you choose—it is only important that you find a technique that works for you.

It first takes discipline to establish a pattern of meditation, but soon you will look forward to it as a reward. It takes a different type of will power to initiate a meditation practice than most people are accustomed to. Rather than the denial of will that is used to fend off unwanted activities, this requires your spiritual will to include desirable activities. Knowing that you should meditate is different than integrating it into your daily life. Experiment with it for at least one month and you will likely find that you never let go of it. Meditation can make that much of a difference. Your capacity for dealing with stressful situations will markedly improve along with being more able to enjoy life's simple pleasures. Meditation is like cleaning the inner windows of the soul. The activity itself is nice enough, but the true benefit is that you get to see through clean windows!

Spirituality in Relationships

The hunger for spirituality is an innate drive in all of us. And, as everything else connected to the human experience, it has its positive and negative expressions. To be involved in a relationship that has a sense of purpose and spiritual direction is indeed one of life's sweetest rewards, but the quest for a spiritual life, if not integrated into one's everyday reality, can just as easily be a burden on a relationship. Like the pain of unrequited love, it is also painful to long for a spiritually based relationship and not have it.

A common complaint with many is that they wish to be more spiritual, but their mate is just not interested. We all learn that you cannot tell someone that they should be more spiritual. For those of you who have tried, you know what I mean—it doesn't work! I advise someone in this situation to be as a tuning fork, and to take responsibility for resonating at the tone that you wish in your relationships with others. It is never fair to ask another to become something that you are not. It is also helpful to simply imagine that your mate is becoming more interested in developing a spiritual integration for his or her life. It is wise to pretend that it is true and act as if it were true. You will be surprised at how effective this is.

Another technique that can be helpful in encouraging growth in another is that of asking questions, rather than lecturing. Through this technique, you encourage others to review their life and to begin to look at it with a fresh perspective. You will be establishing an interviewing technique that is satisfying for both you and your partner. Ask questions that motivate your mate to think. The trick is to ask your questions in such a way that it doesn't appear you already know the answers, even if you do. If your enthusiasm becomes like religious zeal, you will overwhelm and alienate the person you are attempting to encourage.

Though it may seem rather deceitful to ask questions for which you already know the answer, if you do so with the right intent and sensitivity, you can achieve the desired results. Remember that your mate has an ego, just as you do, and no one likes to appear uninformed. Let's say that you are frustrated because your husband won't talk to you about spiritual issues and thinks it's just a bunch of bunk. If you appear all-knowing and approach your husband like he is a spiritual klutz, he won't want to participate. Why would he enter into a humiliating experience? His ego needs will demand that he dismiss the whole ball of wax, rather than appear the dummy. Why set up failure? Why not be sensitive to his ego needs rather than putting them down? With the technique of interviewing, you allow him entrance into the topic without appearing as the all-knowing authority, and you are likely to get better results.

Spiritual relationships might take many forms, but reverence will always be present—reverence for life and reverence for each other. A spiritual relationship is one that supports the soul growth for one another.

Soul Mates

The idea of soul mates is a most attractive and alluring ideal. The image of a soul mate is presented in popular spirituality as if it were a relationship laced with flowers, sunsets, and peace for evermore. This popular concept of soul mate is what I call an "earth mate." This is the mate who loves you no matter what—whether you are growing, moving forward, or moving backward; whether you are coming from your highest place or your lowest; or whether you are even trying.

A soul mate reflects your need for evolution. To be in the presence of a true soul mate is to be stripped of illusion about yourself. It is not always flattering and certainly not always comfortable to be in such a relationship. This person sees the you that you are evolving toward. That's the catch that most are not prepared for, and that's why soul mate relationships are not as easy or as idyllic as they may appear in fantasy.

Another popular myth connected to the soul mate idea should also be addressed. Many believe that there is only one soul mate per person—out of the billions of people on this planet, there is only one that is correct for you. Again, it just doesn't work that way. Life after life, time after time, we experience intimacy with many people. Once a lover, once a child, once a friend once a sibling, etc. We have all been around the block many times with many people and the soul remembers all of these experiences. All of these people make up your soul family. For some, it is a small family and for others it is large, but for all there is more than just one person that is going to affect you at the soul level.

It is glorious to connect with members of your soul family, to have that sense of reconnection across the barriers of time and space. It is blissful, wonderful, and most often confusing! Imagine, you fall in love, get married or form a steady relationship, and all is wonderful in paradise. All goes along just fine until you meet another person with whom you have a deep sense of soul connection. You are not sure why, but there is a sense of familiarity, comfort, and even intrigue around this person. What do you do? The choice is yours, but it need not interfere with the relationship that you have chosen as primary. Acknowledgment of a soul tie makes the sharing deeper and certainly does not assume that any one particular type of relationship (i.e., sexual or marriage), is the proper next step of relating.

Understand that soul mates might be brothers, children, teachers, coworkers, etc. When you open yourself up to the spiritual level of life and become aware of the quality of your soul, you will be surprised at how many people are a part of your soul family. It is said that when you are ready for the next lesson, the right teacher appears. This is not because the teacher comes out of the Himalayas to find you. It is because there are teachers in all walks of life, including yours. Many of your soul family connections will be in your current life for just a short time. These people will enter your life to help you connect with an important part of your evolution. A specific lesson is learned and then the reason for the relationship is over. Others of these will be ongoing, lifelong relationships.

Imagine that you are happily married and you have children. You are satisfied in your life choices and basically your life is set. And then you meet someone who starts making you question soul mate ties. The confusion begins when you try to interpret what this relationship means. Soul mate relationships trigger love. You may be monogamous, but your soul is not! You can pledge your body to one person, but not your soul, it seeks to learn and grow and interact with many. The challenges seem to center around the question of intimacy. Love is felt, should affection be expressed? How about sex? These are the questions that often arise and this is where people start getting hurt, including yourself. Learning to maintain intimacy with members of your soul family, without gravitating toward the physical, is a way of sustaining these ties. Call it being monogamous in body, and polygamous in spirit. Whole new forms of relationships open up that can blossom into lifelong friendships.

The myth continues to teach us that through finding your perfect soul mate you will be complete—you have half a heart and your perfect mate has the other half. When the two of you come together, the two parts magically form one complete heart. Again, experience supports that it just does not work quite that simply. Soul evolution is a process of learning how to be complete within yourself, a coming together of the male and female parts of your inner being. Soul mates enter into your life not to be that other half for you, but to awaken that other half. Herein lies the critical point in these relationships. If you attribute that awakened quality to your mate, you missed the magic moment. Each of your soul mate ties will enhance greater expression and wholeness of the self.

Pursuing Spiritual Vision and Relationships

A vision of a life purpose is not like a contract that you receive in the mail and once signed, that's it. It is more subtle than that, but just as binding. Having a vision and sense of purpose in your life does not always help relationships. Once a person receives a calling, priorities begin to change and the relationship partner can begin to feel like a second fiddle unless effort is made to see that this does not happen. Actually, all spiritual work should carry a warning label that reads: "Danger, pursuing this path may be damaging to your relationships." This is said tongue in cheek, but still, awakening to your spiritual side of your character essentially limits the field of what is tolerable in relationships for you, as you become less dependent on others for a sense of meaning in your life.

You cannot compromise here—if you are going to open to receive vision, you cannot place conditions upon it. If your secret conditions are that you will open to vision so long as you can also stay married, keep your family, have a reasonable income, and . . . you get the picture. Conditions show lack of faith, and having faith is a prerequisite for receiving vision. Have faith that your higher self would never send you a vision that was anything less than in the best interest of you and those you love.

Having a shared vision, or being with a partner whose vision dovetails with yours, would be ideal. It could not be overstated that it is important to support each other's vision in life so that you do not pit yourself in competition with another's calling. Remember that a vision is like a marriage in that it becomes a major life commitment. When you feel second fiddle to your partner's vision, resist the temptation to feel in competition, as this will most certainly lower your status in the relationship, rather than elevate. The more that you can posture yourself in support of the vision, the more your relationship becomes part of the vision itself.

Applications or Tests Along the Way

Relationship with the Psychic Image of Others

The quality of time spent with the inner, psychic image of your mate does make a difference, especially when you are not together. This inner, invisible connection is the Neptune level of your relationship. This can be cultivated to enrich the quality of rapport, but first you must identify how it is currently operating in your life. It is important to realize that Neptune's function does not depend on your belief in the transcendent level of life. It is there and operating, nonetheless. However, your skill at working with it depends on your faith in the efficacy of this invisible realm.

Experiment with this and see if it is true. Sometime when you are apart from your mate, invest your attention to that which you most enjoy about your relationship. Hold your friend's image in your mind with the highest regard and imagine some of the best of what the two of you have shared. Now, see what happens when you first come back together. Subtle work, but oh-so-powerful in its impact. Watch how much efforts make it easier for the two of you to fall into rapport.

The converse of this is equally true. Notice what happens when you are apart and you spend your time in resentment, or when the mental image you hold of your friend is tainted with disappointment. See what happens when you reunite. Neptune symbolizes your relationship with your inner partner. Although you might believe this to be totally private, watch and you will see that it has impact on your relationships in the world.

What you pay attention to grows. A simple truth, but oh so powerful. Yogananda called attention your "lifetrons." You give life to what you direct your attention towards. It is interesting that we have coined the phrase "Pay attention." It implies that your attention is an investment. You can pay attention to what is desirable and delightful in your relationship and that will grow. Or you can pay attention to what your relationship isn't, and believe it or not, this "isn't-ness" will grow. The magic of positive creative visualization is such that if you can train your imagination to focus on that which you wish to see grow, it will.

Watch out for your "yeah, but" tendencies! When I teach this powerful truth of attention, people will often respond, "Yeah, but . . ." and what ever they say next is what they are really paying attention to, investing in, and, of course, manifesting in their lives.

Fear and Faith

Fear and faith are essentially the same force. One is the negative use of imagination and the other is the positive. But quite clearly, imagination is the key ingredient of both experiences. Are your relationships based on fear, or are they based on faith? If you tend to be dominated by fear, then you are not in touch with your faith. Conversely, if you have cultivated your faith, you are not likely to experience much fear. Fear is simply a reminder that you need to cultivate your faith. If you are caught up in fear, whether it be fear of losing your mate, divorce, or even fear of having to stay with your mate, keep in mind that your fear colors your world of experience.

Many people seem to have a Sunday-school view of what faith is all about. They seem to think that it is nice, and that good people should have faith. Faith is not simply nice—it is powerful! The power of faith is in knowing that light and love are the strongest forces in the world. Faith is what gives you the courage to live life to the fullest, to confront fear with the absolute assurance that you can dispel it. Fear is only a landmark that you bump into when you are not using your faith.

If you were on a boat journey and you came across a warning buoy of approaching danger, you would more than likely change your course toward a safer passage. To understand the relationship of fear to faith is the same—fear is the warning buoy that informs you to change your course toward a safer passage.

Compassion or Martyrdom

It is a fine line that separates the compassionate person from the martyr. Both deal with the sensitive part of yourself responding to the needs of others. The difference is that one brings pain, and one brings joy. Compassion is the one characteristic that distinguishes a spiritual person from all others. It is possible to grow in awareness, in psychic sensitivity and to expand your consciousness without growing one iota in spirituality. Compassion is the awareness that "there but for the grace of God, go you or I." Compassion is based on self-transcendence, and martyring is based on self-denial. Similar, yes, but martyring behavior is always at the expense of the self, while compassion never is.

Compassion is the mark of a person who is aware of the quality of grace. People who are not aware of divine grace think that their gifts were attained through their efforts. The person with compassion never takes spiritual gifts for granted—never.

People are often made aware that there is no greater spiritual gift in life than a relationship with a loved one. When an accident or mishap takes the life of a loved one, it is often heard: "I never really knew how much I loved him until he died" or "I never took the time to let her know how important she is to me, and now that she is gone I can't ever do that." These and countless other examples of waiting until it is too late to express your love should serve as a reminder that relationships are a divine gift and your partner should never be taken for granted.

The martyr, on the other hand, is forever forsaking the spiritual gift of life as if denying self is a tribute to spiritual character. Belittling self and denying the awareness of spiritual grace in one's own life is spiritual suicide. I call it false humility, a way of glorifying self by denying self. The martyr role is a denial of the divine gift. If God is truly everywhere, including within one's self, denying self is denying God.

Frustrated God Search

Why is it that some people only turn to God and prayer at a time of crisis? Why don't they see that if they would learn to turn their eyes to the highest without a crisis, perhaps they would not need crisis in their lives?

It has been said often in this book that the first and foremost relationship that each of us go through is that with our inner partner. Once you begin to open the spiritual doors in your life, you begin to develop needs that only your relationship with the divine can satisfy. It is quite common that when people begin to develop spiritually, their relationships begin to suffer. Why? These people are looking for something from their partners that only God/Goddess can provide. It is important to realize which is which. Call this a frustrated God search. Learn to look to the people in your life for your people needs, and learn to look to God for the needs that can only be met by the divine.

The Barometer of Harmony

There is an essential harmony in life and to know this is to accept a divine gift. You have been given an inner barometer that can measure when you are in a state of harmony and when you are not. If you have faith that you are meant to live in harmony with yourself, your loved ones, and the universe, then when you are not in that state, your barometer will inform you that adjustments are needed. It may sound simple, and it is. Everyone has the right to live in harmony, and just as observing the planets in their eternal changing patterns teaches us—harmony is the norm, conflict is the illusion.

To act on this would be to put such faith in harmony that you mistrust your perceptions when you are not aligned with it. When you are in harmony, your perceptions are clear and often inspired. When you are not in harmony, your perceptions are distorted by the imbalance and action taken from this distorted perspective will only further complicate issues. This does not imply that you should always be in harmony! You will drift in and out of this state of grace as we all do. However, the spiritual person knows of the futility of acting while in a state of imbalance and simply waits for harmony to return. It does return and the more that you practice faith in it, it returns with greater frequency and for longer duration.

Neptune Through the Signs

Neptune is most clearly experienced as your imagination which takes you beyond the rational mind and objective reality. Through your mind's eye you have the capacity to transcend your everyday view of life and experience another dimension of reality. The capacity to imagine is given to all of us through Neptune—what each of us do with this gift is up to us. The range of potential expression covers the entire spectrum from fear to faith, from illusion to inspiration, from escapism to creativity.

Neptune's job is to dissolve the separate ego identity so that you can become aware of the larger transcendent reality of which you are part. With spiritual discipline you can learn to direct your attention away from illusion and toward inspiration. If one is not aware or experienced in the transcendent realms, this dissolving function of Neptune simply creates an identity crisis. The sign of Neptune at your birth is where you can draw inspiration, or get lost in the famous Neptunian blind spot. Neptune spends approximately fourteen years in each sign, and links you to a generational theme that you share with all those born in the same time period. This is the sign that describes what your generation idealizes, glamorizes, and where it is prone to illusion.

Since Neptune's transit is so slow, we will limit our exploration of Neptune though the signs of people who are living at this time. Much of the information is not specific to relationships, but is offered to give you added insights into your generation's underlying motivations and those of different generations.

Neptune in Cancer

Neptune's influence in Cancer would lead to a generation of those seeking inspiration from family, community, and country. The watery, introspective nature of Cancer provides a perfect medium for which Neptune operates in this naturally mystical generation. The inward turning of vision and imagination led to Sigmund Freud's work in psychotherapy, Kahil Gibran's lyrical descriptions of the soul, Edgar Cayce's demonstration that we are all connected in ways the senses can not fathom, and Albert Einstein's theory of relativity which revealed the mystical side of science. On the down side, the blind faith of Neptune can, in the sign of Cancer, lead to blind loyalty with whatever this generation defines as "us." Neptune can also mean aligning with illusionary ideals, i.e., "the war to end all wars," which turned out to be just another in a long line of wars. This is a particularly strong empathetic placement, and the need-to-be-needed aspect of Cancer can tend all too easily to codependent relationships. This generation has a rich imagination. Cancer's penchant for honoring the past relates to "retrospective visionaries," believing in the ideal of the good ol' days.

Neptune in Leo

Neptune's penchant for glamour is certainly not wasted on the sign of Leo! This generation idealizes its heroes and stars. The '20s, with its flapper girls, the Charleston, and the burgeoning movie industry, was not short of glamorous people. Leo likes to live life to the hilt and this generation can be inspirational or delusional. The end of this era brought the Great Depression where all the Neptunian fantasies and Leo excesses were revealed for what they were. This generation still honors its stars and believes that a spiritual life will lead to joy.

These are not sacrificial spiritual types—Leo wouldn't begin to know how to play the martyr. Their path is seeking love, joy, and glory. This generation has a particularly strong ability for creativity, with both the imagination of Neptune and the urge for creative expression of Leo linked together. For this generation pride, and loyalty can be either a source of inspiration or the blind spot.

Neptune in Virgo

After the collapse of the glory days of Neptune in Leo, the Neptune in Virgo generation adopted a much more conservative and cautious collective identity. These people were born during the depression, or shortly after, and the impact of this is noticeable. The belief in being frugal, conscientious, and humble are the spiritual qualities that this group was raised with. This generation is more than willing to work hard for what they get in life—for these souls, the work ethic is akin to a spiritual path. This group lives by the spiritual saying, "Before enlightenment, chop wood, carry water. After enlightenment, chop wood, carry water." This leads to them having a difficult time understanding people who believe that life owes them something. Virgo's leaning toward service provides an outlet for the compassion of Neptune. No strong egos here. Where Leo aligns with royalty, Virgo is more at home with the peasants and the ideal of simplicity is alluring for this group. This generation lives by the creed of "selfless service." The blind spot is not seeing when being of service becomes being a servant, and this naturally humble group can be taken advantage of by those who would exploit the helpers in the world.

Neptune in Libra

Neptune in Libra, the sign of beauty and harmony, leads to the ideal of a world at peace. Born during, or shortly after the Second World War, this generation has the memories of war at its most brutal stored in its psyche. The United Nations was birthed from this combination, creating a global forum for the Libran topics of diplomacy and peace. Libra leads to refinement and this led to the Cold War era, where war became like a mental game of chess instead of a battlefield. As young adults, this group became actively involved in the peace movement with the banner slogan, "Make love, not war." The Neptunian urge for a spiritual and transcendent life is quite compatible with the Libran appreciation for aesthetics, and this group's hunger for a more refined and intellectual spiritual path opened the doors for Eastern philosophy, Zen, and Buddhism to be introduced to the West. The dream of this generation is the ideal relationship, perfectly equitable in all ways. The blind spot is believing that such a relationship exists. The low road leads to getting lost in love, while the high road leads to finding oneself through balanced relationships. More evolved souls with this combination pursue their relationships as a spiritual path.

Neptune in Scorpio

The refined sensibilities of Libra give way to the gutsy approach of Scorpio with its interest in the mystical side of sex and death. Neptune blurs the line of distinction between life and death and this era brought a resurgence of interest in reincarnation and the immortality of the soul. Scorpio is the "taboo reviewer" of the zodiac and is more than a little intrigued by the shock value of pursuing paths that the rest of the culture fears. Shamanism as well as neopaganism, wicca, magic, and tantra yoga have flourished with this decidedly mystical combination. The imagination of Neptune can lead to exploring the sacred and mystical side of sexuality for some, and to simply getting lost in sexual fantasy for others. This combination relates to a generation whose spiritual quest will lead them into the mystical realms of the soul, and for those who get lost, Neptune exposes the nefarious dark side issues of Scorpio. Deaths of rock stars through drug overdose and of charismatic political figures by gunshot brought to the public awareness how thin the veil is that covers the darker aspects of the human psyche.

Neptune in Sagittarius

In the pendulum swing of the zodiac, issues sway from inner directed to outer directed as Neptune moves through the signs. After the introspective depth of Scorpio, the expansive qualities of Sagittarius symbolize a generation pursuing an externalization of the search for consciousness growth. Popular music with phrases such as "Keep on Truckin'" and "On the Road Again," captured the spirit of this wanderlust combination. The high road of this placement has been a reconnection with philosophical and religious interests from around the world, and the low road has led many on a path of continually searching for themselves somewhere "out there." The potential for excessive idealism and blind faith can mean susceptibility to paths that do not lead to the promised land, as is evidenced by how many of this era left their homes and families in search of themselves. The abstract world of Sagittarius provides an abundant opportunity for Neptune to dream, and the stories and myths of far-away places are like spiritual food. The conventional side of Sagittarius can be seen in how many from this generation have returned to the traditional churches for their spiritual needs. The sense of purpose they feel to morally educate others can be a source of inspiration, or can lead to proselytizing a particular dogma. The positive idealism of this combination leads to the spiritual belief that things will always get better in the future.

Neptune in Capricorn

After its lofty romp through Sagittarius, Neptune is brought down to earthy practical concerns in Capricorn. This is a very conservative placement for dreamy Neptune, and this generation will certainly require a spiritual path that can be demonstrated in the here-and-now world, rather than in abstractions. This was the era of Reaganism, the "trickle-down" theory of economics and a return to "traditional values." The imagination tends toward practical matters with this generation—God helps those who help themselves. It is interesting that Neptune first went into Capricorn in 1984 and this is the generation that would place faith in George Orwell's "Big Brother." Neptune is faith and Capricorn is order, leading this generation to believe that firmly establishing rules and consequences is the way to bring order, and is ultimately in everyone's best interest. Law and order can easily become the stranglehold of the police state and this generation will have to stay mindful of their blind spot in this regard. The earthy nature of Capricorn's influence on the spiritual side of Neptune can be seen from the growing interest in the healing properties of crystals to a tremendous resurgence of Earth-based religions. Capricorn is a feminine sign and this influence manifests in a growing hunger to learn about the feminine face of the divine.

Neptune in Aquarius

Neptune reaches to its visionary heights in Aquarius. The imagination soars to universal concepts and the belief in a global community with a strong support of individual rights. This is a watchdog generation who will certainly blow the whistle if they sense human rights are being violated, or the needs of future generations are not being considered in public policies. This is a generation that places faith in the oneness of all humanity and this will likely lead to revolutionary activity, seeking to topple over systems that favor elitism and separatism. These are the social visionaries for whom working for humanitarian causes is akin to a spiritual path. While Neptune in Capricorn brought us more in touch with the feminine face of the divine, Aquarius is androgynous in nature, meaning integrated with both the masculine and the feminine. This generation will bring a faith in humanity itself, beyond any allegiances with gender, political, or religious ideologies. The blind spot would be a susceptibility to fanatical beliefs. Aquarius likes to rise above personal emotions to see things in the universal perspective. This disassociation with emotions must be accounted for, or the risk of getting passionate over a cause can blind one to compassion—and causes without compassion always lead to further suffering, regardless of the intent.

PLUTO

Death and Rebirth, the Dark Self, and the Soul's Purpose

IN THIS CHAPTER we will explore the nature of Pluto, its illuminating mythology, some of the difficulties in dealing with its themes, and how those themes manifest in relationships. We'll deal with the psychological process of how the subconscious becomes conscious, and experiment with techniques for aligning with the best that this dark planet has to offer.

Pluto is shrouded by fear. Not for the timid, Pluto is the gate to the final frontier for the explorer in consciousness. It is the doorway into the initiatory descent which takes you to the depths of your consciousness in order to root out past pains and clear the consciousness of all that is not self. Pluto is the furthest planet away from the Sun. As such, it represents that which is furthest away from the center of your self-identity, and is obviously the hardest to incorporate into self-awareness. It functions like a volcano in that it brings to the surface of conscious awareness that which was previously hidden. It represents subconscious drives and hidden motivations that must be purged for one to truly be open to intimacy with others and with life itself. Its highest manifestations lead to renewal, transformation, regeneration, and healing. Its lower manifestations include control and manipulation of others, destructive compulsive tendencies, and all forms of perversion of the spirit.

Pluto is called a transpersonal planet in astrology, meaning that it is beyond the purely personal realm. It represents the collective shadow that shrouds the human experience on this planet. Until a person is willing to look at his role in maintaining this shadow level of the human consciousness, it operates as subconscious motivations that distort your conscious choices. We talk a great deal about free will in modern astrology, but Pluto often seems to exist outside the realm of one's will. When we engage the issues of this most difficult planet and the alarm of fear sounds, we're most likely to go scurrying back to safer levels of consciousness.

Pluto issues are heavy by nature—it is impossible to put a lighthearted spin on the planet associated with death! This is not a realm for sissies, and the meek need not apply. But to the explorer in consciousness, Pluto is the final frontier. To stop in the face of fear would be to give up the quest, and you may feel compelled to push further, allowing yourself to see that which had previously been hidden. It takes strength of character to look into the face of Pluto where you will see the darker side of your own character and reconnect with painful memories.

Pluto's orbit is 250 years, thus it connects you to a cycle of time of that duration. This is why we associate past lives with Pluto—your current personality wasn't here 250 years ago, but the origins that make up the current you can be traced back this far. We could call Pluto your karmic account that you brought with you from previous lives. You do not have to believe in reincarnation to work with Pluto, but at minimum, it is an appropriate metaphor to consider. If we come into this life with a certain amount of fate, some destined experiences are going to happen, one way or another. Considering the possibility of past-life issues while dealing with Pluto helps to remove the defensiveness and the sense of injustice from your current situation.

If you do not work with Pluto, it works on you and manifests as obsessions and compulsions which drive your conscious choices from some unseen place. At the highest level, Pluto represents your destiny, your purpose in this life, at least in terms of what the soul came here to do. Most people want to know their purpose, but few are willing to accept Pluto's terms. It takes absolute surrender, requiring absolute faith, nothing less. You cannot barter with this part of your character. It takes a powerful faith to trust in surrendering to a force larger than the self. You must believe that your soul would never lead you to anything less than that which is in your highest good and best interest.

Pluto in Mythology

In mythology, Pluto's role was that of the ruler of the realm of the dead—the underworld. On one of his journeys to the surface world, Pluto cast his eyes upon Persephone, the Goddess of innocence and springtime, and he was overwhelmed by a desire for her. He abducted her and took her to his underworld home to be his queen.

Ceres (Demeter in Greek), Persephone's mother, after searching the world over for her daughter, eventually discovered her whereabouts. In Ceres' anger, she caused droughts and plagues upon the Earth. Eventually, Ceres petitioned Jupiter to persuade Pluto to return Persephone to her. Jupiter consented upon the condition that Persephone had not eaten any food in Pluto's domain. If she had, he would be powerless to intervene. Pluto was aware of these conditions and seduced Persephone into eating of a pomegranate seed he offered her. Since she had taken food, Jupiter was powerless to demand her complete return, but a compromise was arranged so that Persephone would return to her mother for part of the year and remain with Pluto for the remainder, thus the seasons were born.

This myth paints Pluto in a particularly unfavorable light—ruler of the dark world, abductor, seducer, and rapist of Persephone. It is easy to see from these associations why, historically, Pluto has been given such negative interpretations. The myth reveals why individuals have such a fear of surrendering to forces outside personal control where Pluto is concerned. There is a fear of losing one's innocence and being subjugated to the manipulative control of a dark force.

Earlier versions of this myth suggest that Persephone willingly went to Pluto's realm of her own accord. This simple shift in the story line changes the meaning altogether. The abduction, the violence, and the fear is missing in the earlier, and perhaps healthier, version of the myth. Here the feminine willingly sacrifices her innocence to embrace her passion and surrender to her transformation. Pluto is not to be feared—respected certainly, but not feared. It represents the final gate in one's surrendering to a life guided by a higher force. If we willingly surrender to the Pluto force, we can avoid the abduction.

The Pluto Initiation

It can be seen from these myths why one must descend into the Pluto realms to awaken to full consciousness. One must be willing to go deep within self, face one's fears, even face death itself to assimilate this level of consciousness. This confrontation with the dark night of the soul is necessary if one is to live a life free of fear. The more that you are susceptible to fear, the more you will shy away from the Pluto level, as fear is one of its guardians. You have to be able to confront fear and move past it. It is not that fear goes away; it is that you develop the courage to move through the fear.

We want to grow into the light. We picture the spiritual path leading to enlightenment. But just as the darkest part of the night precedes the dawn, confronting the dark side, the shadow of self precedes growing into light. The shadow contains all the parts of you that you have kept hidden from yourself. To become whole, to awaken to your full power, this shadow side of self must be embraced as well.

A Philosophical View

Pluto links us to issues we've been working on for many incarnations. Pluto represents a part of our character that has never incarnated into physical form, but it carries our purpose for this life within it. A big-picture view of our purpose on this planet is to heal ourselves, our relationships with one another, and to purge the world of fear and darkness so that we may all more fully appreciate the gift of spirit that life truly is. To heal our planet, we first must be able to accept human darkness as a condition to which we are born. This requires a courageous look into the darker recesses of character to identify and root out the darkness that is part of inner consciousness.

Since Pluto experiences are beyond the ego's ability to understand, there exists a natural fear in encounters with this part of our character. The fear is that of losing control, and we do lose ego control while engaging Pluto. The ego, which tends to dominate consciousness, sends forth the message that we are moving into dangerous territory.

There are two levels of the Pluto realm. One is personal, one is collective. We each have our personal share of the collective darkness of humanity within ourselves. Pluto brings with it our personal karma with particular dark side issues.

Some may need to work with jealously, while others work with addictive tendencies, or violence, lust, greed, or whatever—we each have personal shadow issues. After purging yourself of personal karma, you are still not free of the dark. You are no longer working on your personal shadow issues, but now you evolve to work on the collective shadow.

To apply this information in your life, take special note of the next time you are caught up in one of Pluto's lairs—jealousy, resentment, hostile anger, etc. If it is not your personal karma, you should be able to disassociate from the experience. If you are able to detach from the experience and see it as something you are experiencing—not you, but merely something you are going through—it is not your personal issue. Instead it is a collective issue. If you are not able to detach and disassociate from the experience, it is your personal karma. You are advised to plunge in to see what lessons need to be learned, until you become free to let go of the experience.

It takes considerably more work to deal with personal issues than collective ones. When the issue you are working with is collective, you can simply dismiss the issue. If you can see it, name it, and disassociate from the experience, you can dismiss it. Although it might sound a little odd, the following is a method for disassociating from a collective karmic issue. Say to yourself: "This is the experience of jealousy (hatred, greed, etc.) that we humans go through." Now, instead of identifying with the experience, dismiss it with absolute intention. You make a statement such as "Jealousy be gone." To facilitate this detachment, take note of your language. Instead of saying, "I am jealous," try saying, "I am experiencing jealously." This simple shift helps. In the former example, you are identifying the experience as self, I am ______ (you fill in the blank). In the later example, the experience is not your identity, it is something you are going through. This simple shift makes it possible to shed the experience altogether.

Death, Rebirth, and Regeneration

Although Pluto does deal with literal death as the final transformation (this will be covered later in the chapter), here we are referring to it in terms of the many deaths and rebirths we all go through. Death, rebirth, and regeneration are the cycles of life. To have the birth of the new there must be death of the old. Nature teaches this lesson so clearly. The trees that have not been cut back will not be the biggest producers of fruit in the following season. The grass that is not mowed will not remain fresh and green, rather it will turn to seed and die. It is the death of the old that leads to the rebirth of the new.

Each initiation we go through is preceded by a death. The wedding initiates us into the world of marriage, but also signals the death of one's single life. The inverse of this is equally true—getting fired from one's job is the death of that cycle, and the initiating of the next. Endings and beginnings, beginnings and endings—this is the way of life.

We speak poetically of the death and rebirth process and relate it to the chrysalis process of the caterpillar becoming a butterfly. Indeed, it is a beautiful sight to behold, but one wonders, how does the caterpillar feel about it? It is the one whose guts are being eaten out! Pluto processes often feel just like that—like your guts are being eaten out through the process. It takes a profound faith to courageously let go of a past identity and to believe that a higher form of existence awaits you on the other side. Since Pluto is beyond the ego's ability to control the experience, the ego must surrender its grip on reality to go through the process. As the caterpillar must surrender its life to become the butterfly, the ego must surrender its life to evolve to yet greater levels of reality.

Pluto's Wounds

Pluto's wounds can be the most horrific of all—betrayal, rape, murder, violence, etc. Steven Forrest, in *The Book of Pluto,* reminds us of the benign aspect of the subconscious in protecting us from horrible memories. Some of the harshest experiences we go through are pushed beneath the surface of conscious awareness. This is benign, and for most people it is fortunate that they do not have conscious memory of all their life's experiences.

But for explorers in consciousness, we want to reconnect with our memories so that we might come into full remembrance of our soul's purpose in this life. Our memories are our legacy and our power. To face Pluto's wounds with this attitude makes a huge difference. It is not until we come into full remembrance of our history that we awaken into conscious awareness of our life's purpose.

The Subconscious Becoming Conscious

The conscious mind is said to be like a cork floating on the vast sea of the subconscious. The cork represents the limited amount that you can consciously be aware of at anytime. The sea is the vast storehouse of all your experiences, even past-life experiences. Transformation and growth in consciousness could be described as the process of the subconscious becoming conscious. Pluto represents the subconscious motivations that influence your behavior, but if they are subconscious, how can you know them?

By definition, the subconscious is that which is unknown, beneath the level of conscious awareness. If you know it, you can be sure that is not your subconscious. This process of the subconscious becoming conscious is an infinite process—there is always more to absorb until you have reached Christ consciousness or Buddhahood.

Pluto's job is to bring information from the subconscious into conscious awareness—like a volcano bringing the molten lava from the depths of the earth to the surface. How is the ego likely to react in this situation? Threatened, of course. You have to assume that fear will be present when working with Pluto issues. The ego is always going to sound the fear alarm—something is happening outside of its control. This happens. What happens next is up to you. Do you align with the fear, pull back from the experience, deny it, hide from it? That would be normal. Or do you move into the experience, even in the face of the fear? This allows you to become conscious of influences from the unconscious that had been previously molding your behavior. Have courage, realize that whatever is now emerging into your conscious awareness has been influencing you all along from the subconscious realms.

To regain your memory is to regain your power. This is the power that initiates on the path of consciousness growth need. Your history is not complete when repressed material is just out of sight. The courageous explorer seeks out the subconscious behavior patterns that are the manifest symptoms of buried memories. When you find yourself behaving in a way totally inappropriate for what you are consciously trying to do, do not reject the behavior in disgust and guilt. Accept it as a messenger. Accept it as a perfect messenger of some forgotten memory that is animating the experience. Memories come on the heels of infantile behavior patterns when you ask yourself, "When was this inexplicable behavior the appropriate response in my life?" You will likely be brought back to a memory of when the current behavior was first begun. Concentrate your search here to facilitate the memories coming to the surface.

The Hidden Self Revealed Through Others

A tremendous amount of clues as to our subconscious motivations can be discovered through noticing how others respond to us. At one stage of growth, each of us defends an image of who we think we are. If someone offers an opinion about you that is inconsistent with your established self-identity, you reject the information, and likely the person, as well. As you continue to develop, your need to defend yourself gradually diminishes. You become more secure in who you are, and are not so threatened by the way others view you. This is when you can start seeing the clues to hidden parts of your character revealed in other people's reactions to you.

It is much easier to see other people's subconscious motivations, than it is to see them in yourself. You need the perspective of others in order to truly know who you are. It is not that their view of you is right and your view was wrong. It's only that their view is another reflection of the many facets of your being. Each person reflects their own slightly different perspective of the total you. You can benefit by watching other people's reaction to you—take it in. If your reactions are somehow screening you from this valuable data, learn to get out of your way and let the information in.

The first time that somebody tells you something about you that you don't already know or that you see differently, you're likely to discount that perception, preferring to believe the person just doesn't know you very well. The second and third times that other people in other situations give you the same feedback about yourself, you are still likely to discount the information. Eventually though, your attention will be captured. All of these people know you in different ways, but are telling you similar things. That is when you begin to suspect that you might not know yourself as well as you thought you did. That is the breakthrough moment! Let go of your defenses and truly see yourself reflected through others.

Often, the path to your destiny is revealed through other people's responses. Pay attention when people mention that you are particularly gifted or talented in one way or another. Try not to discount the information even if you don't believe you are as great as someone makes you out to be. Is there a consistency here? Have other people mentioned the same talent in you? Is it consistent with something to which you would aspire? This is where destiny is revealed. Even if you are not sure if you are able to live up to expectations, if other people are receiving benefit from you, step out of the way and let the good happen.

Power, Manipulation, and Intent

Pluto is collective power and to engage Pluto is to get tested with the right use of power. Simply said, can you engage the use of power in such a way that benefits self and others, and is at no one's expense? Influence, persuasion, manipulation, and intimidation differ only in subtle distinctions.

Many spiritual, moral, and ethical people shy away from the word manipulation. It touches a sensitive chord. The people without morals and a spiritual base in life have never been afraid of the concept of manipulation. To the contrary, they become masters in its use. Unfortunately, too many people without moral and ethical standards have had the power and influence in our culture. It is time for those with spiritual values to allow themselves to use power so that they might have a positive cultural influence.

The word "manipulation" is a red flag for most of us. It is time that spiritual people began looking at the concept of manipulation. Is it wrong? It would greatly depend on the intent, wouldn't it? A chiropractor is manipulative. So is a nurse, a counselor, a teacher, a performer, a gardener, and a lover. All of these people have learned how to manipulate others to bring out their best. Manipulation is not wrong if it brings out the best in everyone involved. How else are we going to heal this planet and bring about the changes that are necessary if we are not willing to be influential? This is an important question that the spiritually minded must ask themselves.

Our spiritual heritage is not our spiritual future. In past spiritual cultures, aspirants learned to renounce the world. It was an important tenet of all spiritual traditions. Usually there were vows that an aspirant would take dealing with the denial of earthly power in favor of divine grace. Poverty, chastity, and obedience; remember? This renouncing of earthly power has minimized the influence of those with spiritual values. But we have grown. We are now at a spiritual revolution, we are remembering who we are and what we came here to do—we are claiming our power and awakening to the collective purpose that unites us all.

Virgin warriors no longer, we now have a cause: a spiritual cause of bringing this planet to a state of peace and harmony. It is possible, as evidenced by how many of us have the same united vision in our hearts. As we awaken to our soul's purpose and our collective vision coalesces, we become spiritual warriors on the path of the bodhisattva, those who forsake individual enlightenment until all souls are free.

The spiritual warrior can never be defeated. Time is on your side. It may take a long time, it may take many lives. It already has. Contrary to what appears to be the case in our individual lives, time is one thing that this planet has an abundance of. *Eternity.* Act as if eternity mattered, as if your actions were going to impact your life for eternity. This will awaken you to your soul's purpose.

Be willing to have power and influence, but first make sure that your own house is in order. Always be willing to review your own motivations, always be willing to learn more about who you are and be willing to change to incorporate what you have learned. Be relentless in your attempts to heal yourself, your relationships, and the planet.

Pluto in Relationships

In relationships, the highest urge connected to Pluto is to be involved in absolute union with another. The ideal is to be in an ego-death relationship in which both individuals relinquish their separate sense of selves to be transformed in a union that goes beyond the experience of separateness. To achieve this type of healing relationship requires that one first be able to ferret out the negative manifestations of Pluto in relationships. This includes obsessive-compulsive behavior, the compartmentalization of thinking about yourself in one way and acting in another, habitual ways of relating, and control and manipulation games in the relationship—whether you are the victim or the perpetrator.

Although you can never see your own subconscious motivations, you can see them in others, and vice versa. This is why people involved in relationships can potentially grow faster in their search for consciousness growth than people not involved in relationships. You have always got a mirror around you that can reflect your true motivations.

In long-term relationships, couples hopefully have learned the art of adapting to each other's growth and transformation. Without this, your long-term relationship can actually block growth. It is shocking to wake up next to a person that you have been with for years and suddenly realize that you no longer know this person. You listen to him talk and you realize how deeply his values have changed. You look closely, and realize that he hardly even looks familiar any more.

It is even more shocking when you realize that you have gone through a major transformation and no longer are the same person that your mate knew years ago. As you grow, learn, and experience life, you incorporate the experiences and, at times, make radical shifts in consciousness. Perhaps your values about sex, money, recreation, or life itself are not the same as they used to be. These changes usually occur slowly through time, but your awareness of them is often quite sudden. What do you do then? Hopefully you will have the courage to trim back the deadwood and make way for the new growth.

Transformation that leads to growth in consciousness could be something that people celebrate in each other, but more often, it is a process that is feared, especially when it is occurring with your mate. With change comes the fear that the foundation of security that you share will be shaken up. There is no way that you can be sure that your partner will still be interested in sharing the same type of relationship once this transformation is complete. But as you learn to welcome change, rather than fear it, you can go through these changes together, rather than just standing back and watching it happen.

Couples have to face this fear in order to maintain their long-term relationship. When you truly love others, you help them on their path of growth. You support them while they take classes, read stimulating books, and experiment with new ways of being. You do this even when you do not share their enthusiasm, because to not support their efforts risks your being part of the problem rather than part of the solution to the growth they seek. Your fear in regard to your mate is that he or she may grow away from you.

If you are the one making the waves by seeking out change, then try to be compassionate and to understand that your partner's resistance to your transformation is not a rejection of you, rather it is a fear of losing you. With this awareness, you can reassure and educate your mate so that your changes will not be as threatening to your relationship.

Many of the changes that any of us go through are silent. They are slow building transformations that begin on the inner level. At first they are just thoughts, perhaps dreams, and ever so slowly they work themselves up to a point where you yourself can recognize that a change is occurring. Eventually, you are able to talk about it with your partner, but it takes time before you can share the experience. Most often, when it reaches the level where you can talk about it, it has already happened. Still, couples are often frustrated when their partner is not aware of what is going on within them. Before you pass judgment on your mate for lack of sensitivity, ask yourself what you have done to inform your mate of your transformation.

Looking at difficulties in relationships as symbolic of unintegrated aspects of self is the only powerful position to come from in working out relationship problems. There needs to be a willingness to face and accept the lower and hidden aspects of one's nature. Without a willingness to look within, you will only see these unintegrated aspects of self expressed in others, but never yourself. When the focus is on what the other person can do to improve, there is no power, as you are at the mercy of the other person as to whether or not they are willing to do the required work. It is simply too much of a risk to place your happiness and fulfillment on how another person lives his or her life.

Degrees of Obsession

Obsession is being compulsively preoccupied by an idea, a belief, or a person. There are many degrees of this behavior and if extreme anxiety accompanies the obsession, professional help is advised, and it is beyond the scope of what we will deal with here. There are other levels of obsession to which most people would be able to relate.

Being infatuated with another in the flush of new love is delightful. Thinking of your new love fills you with a warmth and a glow, so you often find yourself musing over your beloved. Obsessions are one stop further on the train of passion. The warm glow is replaced by the raw edge of hunger. It is no longer delightful—now, ache best describes the emotion. Not joy, not love for the other—if that were the case your heart would be joyous with the thought. With obsessions, joy is replaced by a dull ache in the heart that it seems only the object of your obsession can heal. You have lost yourself in the other, powerless to control even your own thoughts, because you've given your power to the object of your obsession.

Obsession comes from surrendering to the Pluto level of consciousness without maintaining balance in the areas symbolized by the personal planets. Obsessions manifest in relationships in various ways. We can imagine worst case scenarios such as the stalker or someone spying on another. Again, these terribly invasive and threatening obsessions are beyond the scope of this book. A more common experience is from having such a hunger for deep love that you lose yourself in a projected fantasy image of what you wish were true about another. Jealousy can trigger becoming obsessed with the idea of your lover with someone else.

Another source of obsession that should be considered is past lives. Pluto connects us to people whom we have known in many ways in many lives. Past-life ties are confusing if they open you to hunger that cannot be met by the person in this life. It is as if your subconscious memory of who this person was for you in a previous life awakens the hunger for what the relationship offered you in the past. It is doomed to fail because that past relationship is dead, and you will not be able to mold your current relationship to fill this hunger. It can be so strange—you want, crave, need something from the person, that he or she cannot possibly give. This most often creates deep confusion.

Obsession happens in deep passionate relationships that fully surrender to each other, but something keeps driving them apart. It is as if both souls arranged to meet each other again in this life to awaken a hunger in relationships. They bring out a quality in each other that had always been missing in previous relationships, yet fate keeps a major road block in front of them, making it impossible to truly come together.

Even in ill-fated relationships, destiny seems to be at work. If you get caught in the snare of obsession, try to examine just what it is precisely that you are so enamored with about the other. It just might be that this person came into your life to awaken that quality within you, rather than to be it for you. It is as if the two souls arranged to come into each other's lives to awaken something that has been missing in previous relationships. If there is a deep ache involved, this is one relationship from which you will eventually have to move on. The ache is the clue. Accept the gift of this newly awakened part of your character and move on.

Pluto always leads to the loss of individual control of a situation, for good or for ill. To work with Pluto you have to be able to direct this obsessive-compulsive energy. From psychology we think of obsessive behavior as unhealthy, but it can be directed into healthy channels. No great work of art or tremendous social achievement has ever happened other than through an obsessive-compulsive personality. Can you imagine painting the Sistine Chapel on weekends? No! Some things take the passion of total surrender to bring them into form. Now if you are washing your hands fifty times a day, maybe you need help, but if you can direct the obsessive energy of Pluto into some creative or healthy project, you get the best of what it has to offer.

Transformative Intimacy

Intimacy is the final skill that the artist of relationships learns to master. Intimacy is all inclusive and incorporates all of the other skills mentioned in this book. It is a state of being that two people can enter into that allows for complete merging and surrender into the moment of the relationship. Passion is there at the physical, emotional, mental, and spiritual levels. All defenses are down as a spirit of trust settles over the relationship.

To achieve this you must first be able to actualize all of the relationship skills within yourself. You must know what it takes to make you feel vital; how to align with your emotional nature; how to be mindful of your own mental patterns and how to communicate with others; to know what gives you pleasure and how to share that with another; to define your boundaries, initiate activities, and act on your passion; to reach for the rewards life has to offer; to develop self-control, self-restraint, and self-discipline and to create a responsible role for yourself within your culture; to maintain your individuality without fighting for it and continually awaken to evolutionary opportunities; to have trained your imagination toward inspiration and away from illusion; to be willing to face the shadow side of self and others. That is all that it takes to be in a sustained intimate relationship!

If the list seems daunting, have faith in the natural order of life. We would not have been given all of these parts of our character if we were not meant to develop them. The planetary map can provide guidelines, but have faith that it is in the evolutionary best interest of the planet that we learn to activate the highest potential possible in relationships. Trust that the same forces that guide the evolution of our planet will also be there guiding and assisting you.

Death: The Ultimate Transformation

Pluto confronts us with our ultimate mortality. Undoubtedly, the biggest challenge that most of us go through is the fear of death, or the test of losing a loved one to death. The mystics tell us, "Death is not a tragedy, we all die, but not living your life fully for fear of death, now that is tragic!" However, there is no more sensitive issue than death, and it is typically a test for which most are unprepared. Death is one of the few things that all of us share in common yet, it is something that no one wants to face. This can be the most devastating of all human experiences, and not just for the one who has died. It is devastating for the survivors. In the preceding chapter, we dealt with the concept of having a relationship with someone even when you are only dealing with their psychic image. This certainly applies in the situation of death. All aspects of the relationship continue, except for the physical. Emotionally, mentally, and spiritually, the relationship continues and thus deserves attention.

The grieving and the guilt that people experience when a loved one dies certainly attests to the difficulty associated with the death experience. Intellectually, we are sorely underequipped to deal with this process and even less prepared in how to understand it. What follows next is not from the intellectual mind. If you have not had to deal with death in your life, this might seem excessively abstract, but if you are dealing with the process, this section can help you.

I can not think of a more tragic situation than losing one's child to suicide. The following information came from a taped response to a women's request for help in understanding the suicide death of her sixteen-year-old son. It is being reproduced here in hopes that it can help others who are groping for understanding the death of their loved ones.

> "To understand what is going on in your life at this time and to try to help you with your process of dealing with the death of your son requires us to move out of the normal place in our minds that intellectually puts the world together. We cannot really understand the door between life and death intellectually. The information that we seek comes from the heart which is experienced through praying, asking, believing, and having faith that there is a design, a sense of purpose, and a meaning behind all of life. We are all students here, everyone of us, and what we are all doing is learning. We are all learning about the life experience, which includes the death experience.
>
> "Let's go right to this question, 'Are you no longer experiencing your son?' You know that is not so. Try to stop your relationship with your son. Try to say, "Okay, now he is dead, he's not here, I am no longer experiencing him." From your own experience, you will have to acknowledge that you cannot do this. Every aspect of your relationship with him is continuing, other than the physical. Understand this. Everything other than the tangible aspect of this relationship with your son is continuing. Go to the place where you know this to be true from your own experience. You are still experiencing your son. The relationship between you and your son is evolving and growing and changing and offering you both opportunities for love, for disappointment, for anger, for joy—so what has changed? Nothing, other than the sensory aspects—everything about the relationship is continuing other than its sensory counterparts. It is true, your relationship with him is still very much alive.

"And it will always change. Relationships with one another are continuous even after death. The relationship is still alive and you are both still involved. There is a part of you that is definitely benefiting from this experience and that is the hardest part for you to accept. There is a part of you that is learning and growing from your son's experience of voluntarily jumping into the death experience. We have moral and ethical values concerning death and we say that people shouldn't take their own lives. You're not supposed to jump. You've got to wait until it's time and then it just happens. Well, I believe that. I don't want to jump and I don't want my children to jump and I can understand your disappointment in your son's voluntarily crossing that line, rather than waiting for some other force.

"But we cannot really be the ultimate judges of that. How do we know? Because what is true is that you are learning, growing, and benefiting, and he is learning and growing and benefiting and life is going on as much now as ever before.

"Think of all the times your life has just been normal routine with no major growth happening. You come home from a day's work, go through dinner and clean-up, watch a little television, go to bed only to get up tomorrow and do it all over again and you think this is life. In comparison, right now you are evolving, growing, pushing, becoming, feeling, and experiencing much more than ever before—you have never been more alive. There is a part of you that has been trained to believe that this should give you cause to feel guilt. How could you possibly benefit from this experience? The mother in you would be ashamed of benefiting from such an experience.

"But that is the culturally trained part of you, that is not the real mother, nor what you are actually experiencing. At a deeper level, you have been forced to look at life, to reinterpret life, to push at your boundaries of the known world—to reach, to grope, to pray, to meditate. Through your son's death, you are becoming more alive. To start acknowledging this growth would help you at this time. But to do this without a sense of guilt requires you to be able to stand back and see the big picture.

"Consider the electromagnetic scale of the gradations of energy waves. Everything from color, to sound, to x-rays, to television and radio waves—are all different frequencies of energy. When something vibrates within a certain frequency, we see it and call it color. At a slightly different frequency, we hear it and call it sound. At the densest frequency, we call it matter and we can bump into and experience it with the five senses. All are different frequencies of energy. In this current era of the 'Age of Reason' from which we are just emerging, we label that which can be perceived by the five senses as 'reality,' but what can be perceived by the five senses is just a tiny part of the whole of reality. We can only assume that we are like the little ant trying to understand the elephant—all we are doing is perceiving a very narrow portion of total reality.

"We know this to be true because there are all kinds of energy waves that we can't see, but we can measure. In the arrogance of man we say, 'That which I can experience between this frequency and that frequency is truth. All else is not true.' What a vain and narrow way to view life! Such an unnecessarily constraining view! Mystics, poets, and artists have forever gone far beyond that perspective. We all have. We all have experiences that are not measurable, yet we do not deny them because we can't see them, touch them, feel them, hear them, nor taste them. They are not within that one narrow band on the electromagnetic scale. And that is all.

"Understand that human life is just a particular frequency of a wave of energy that is continuous. Some call it the voice of God, the original word, 'And in the beginning was the word. . .' That which is knowable by our consciousness is only the smallest of portions of that which is not knowable by our limited range of consciousness. Mystics learn what they can about the knowable and leave the rest to the sense of mystery and awe of creation. Death is beyond the knowable, do not try to make sense out of this, it is beyond the range of your mind's capacity to understand.

"Imagine a six-month-old child. What is the scope of the child's world? Only mother and the breast—that is comfort, that is life. The rest? Who knows what it is. Now imagine that the mother leaves the child with a friend for the very first time to go out shopping by herself. The child is left with this new experience. Mom is gone. The child starts to cry because mom is gone. We adults all know from our expanded, mature perspective, that mom is coming back. But you can't tell that to the young child. At another perspective we know that your relationship with your son is continuous, and it's going to be again, and again and again. It is going on right now too. But you can't tell that to a mother who has only lost her child six months ago.

"We can assure you that you will once again be with your son, and that the relationship will go on, but you are like the child first separated from mom. You can't reach out and touch your son and you get scared.

There is a part of you that needs to make that one next step of being able to understand the futility and the vanity of believing that somehow or another the relationship is now gone, particularly in light of the fact that you are experiencing your son on an ongoing basis right now. If your son had gone on a journey far away, you couldn't touch him, see him, feel him, but you would still have a relationship with him. It's really the same for you now and it is being verified by your experiences.

"Your son is now one of your ancestors. Isn't that curious? Your ancestors are those that have passed before you—your son has become your ancestor! In many cultures around the world, the ancestors are welcome as ongoing members of the family and treated as such. They are invited to important gatherings, they are counseled with making important decisions and are honored in all ways as family members. You might consider if there is something in these traditions for you.

"There is a part of you that would feel guilty if you make this into a growth experience for you. This is what you have to confront. To the degree that you allow yourself to not feel guilty is the degree that you'll benefit and grow from this experience. Your son's connection to you is so absolute. I think of the rather bizarre experiments that have been done in the name of science. One comes to mind where baby rabbits were separated from their mother and taken to the bottom of the ocean in a submarine, thousands of miles away from the mother. Then the experimenters killed the baby rabbits one by one. Although the mother was thousands of miles removed, the monitors hooked up to her revealed a shock through her system at the precise time of each death.

"The connection between mother and child transcends time, space, and death. Your son's system went through shock when he took his life; the mother rabbit in you has experienced the same shock. You can track with your son through all of his experiences if you allow yourself to stay connected. You are no less than a rabbit, and your connection with your son is certainly no less profound then the mother rabbit with her young. All that your son is experiencing now is also affecting you.

"I think in terms of an ultimate perfection. It is only our narrowness that gets us complaining about how things are working out. We look out into the world and we see war and we see hunger and we look up to God and we complain, 'Why have you allowed this to happen, it is not supposed to be this way.' And of course the vanity of this perspective causes a lot of confusion. In our criticism of God we can miss the Divine. In our criticism of someone else's choices we can miss the Divine. How can we criticize the path of another? Can you measure the quality of a person's life in years? No, it is not for us to judge another's life and to say it was wrong or right. What you can do is take responsibility for the quality of your relationship with that person, whether he is in the body or not. The relationship goes on. You now have to go to a deeper place than before to get in touch with that relationship, but it is certainly still there. The relationship has now moved from a sensory relationship to a heart relationship, but it is of no less importance. Do not turn your back on your child simply because you can no longer see him.

"Ultimately, you cannot say that his choices were any better or worse than yours. You can't say that. Just as if he were still in his body, you can only take responsibility for the quality of your involvement. Let it be a quality that you are proud of. Enter into a place of health with your son. It is available through the heart. Blessings."

Death as an Advisor

We have grown to appreciate that you can never measure the quality or meaning of a person's life by the length of time that they are alive. Some believe that it is wonderful if a person lives to be a ripe old age of 100 and tragic if a person's life is ended at five. Yet, if a person has not learned to love in a hundred years and the five-year-old touched people's hearts, how could we say that one was better because of the amount of time? It is the quality, not the quantity of time that is important.

There is nothing that contrasts life as much as death. They represent the two extreme poles of the same continuum of experience. Mystics, poets, saints, and teachers consistently leave us with the same message: use death as a constant advisor. Every moment that you live might very well be your last. Doesn't that make you want to get going with your life? Do what you want to do and have those experiences that make your life special and certainly worth living. If your life were to be taken suddenly, have you done the things that you would choose to do? Have you lived your life with the gusto and courage that you would imagine? If you have used the excuse that the time is not right to say what you have to say or take the chances that you would like, then you may be fooling yourself. You may wake up one morning and realize that time has passed you by.

It is interesting to read the last thing a person writes before dying. In many messages you will find a similar theme of wishing that they had not been so serious. There is one poem that comes to mind of a woman who wished that she had taken more chances. Given another go round, she would walk in the rain more often and splash in every puddle. She wouldn't have been so stingy with her love and she certainly would have poured out her heart to more strangers. She would make up for the sobriety of her youth by having a good time, all of the time. She would forget about "respectability" and never be concerned of what others would think.

If you knew you had a limited amount of time to live, your sense of appreciation of life today would certainly be heightened. You would not waste much time with petty issues. Your life would be a celebration. Undoubtedly you would start living your life to the fullest. If you knew that tomorrow was going to be the last day of life for your mate, lover, or friend, your sense of appreciation for that person would certainly be heightened as well. What would life be like if every time you said goodbye to someone, you said it as the last goodbye. Imagine the depth of connection that would come to all your interactions.

It is often said, "Live each day as if it were the first day of the rest of your life." The saying is more poignant this way, "Live each day as if it were the last day of your life." Never take a friend for granted. Enter into each relationship as if it were a rare and special gift and indeed it will be.

Pluto Through the Signs

The most significant thing about Pluto's transit is that it takes 250 years to go through the entire zodiac. Its orbit is elliptical, rather than circular, therefore it does not spend an equal amount of time in each sign. From as little as twelve years in some signs, and over thirty in others, it averages approximately twenty years in each. Due to its lengthy sojourn through each sign, an entire generation will share the same Pluto. This is key in understanding its influence by sign; its influence spreads out over an entire generation. This is so pervasive, it is likely not even experienced as a separate influence—it is part and parcel of an entire generation.

The sign of Pluto is reflected in the primary themes that animate the evolution of civilization itself. It reveals an underlying drive influencing the conscious choices of all the individuals with the same sign placement. The movement of Pluto through the signs gives credence to the concept of "a generational gap"—

there truly are different animating forces molding the behavior of each generation. At best, passion and desire are awakened that fully rejuvenate the quality of the sign Pluto is in. At worst, the shadow of the sign is revealed—some of the horrors connected to history at any given time can be linked to the darker qualities of Pluto's sign. Although everyone of a particular generation is not susceptible to worst-case scenarios, everyone will face the shadow one way or another.

The sign of Pluto describes your generation's role for transforming the world we live in, for good or for ill. The theme of death and rebirth can feel like a fight for survival, thus Pluto's sign describes your generation's survival instincts. Look to your Pluto sign to discover the underlying, animating drive that compels you and your entire generation toward certain areas of expression. In modern astrology we no longer use the word "causes" in relationship to behavior, but with Pluto, "compels" or "compulsive" are acceptable descriptive terms. The dates given are approximate, as Pluto will move in and out of a sign during the beginning and ending of its transit. Check the tables in the appendix for exact dates.

Pluto in Gemini (1882–1912)

Gemini is an air sign, a sign of intellect and ideas. With Pluto in Gemini, this generation has a compelling urge to push back the boundaries of the known world. Being connected to the world of ideas through communication and education are part of the survival instinct with this group. Gemini is breadth of knowledge, Pluto is depth—put them together and you have a generation with a tremendous range of intellect. Freud set about giving a language to the subconscious; Einstein was making discoveries of the connections between energy, light, matter, and time; both are examples of Pluto in Gemini's urge to map out new territory of the human experience and give us a language to facilitate further discoveries. The communications industry, particularly newspapers, had a tremendous impact on the era, for good and for ill. Being informed is the Gemini prerogative, and the media certainly rose to the occasion to feed that hunger. It was clearly evident in this era that the power of the written word can mold public opinion. However, this was also an era where the sinister quality of Pluto showed itself as yellow journalism, propaganda, and misinformation. The birth of propaganda machines, feeding information to the public to mold its opinions and attitudes, represents the shadow side of Pluto in Gemini.

Pluto in Cancer (1912–1937)

The survival instinct of this generation leads to strengthening the family—"As long as we're together as a family, we'll survive." Cancer issues center around providing security for home, house, and family, thus Pluto's influence here leads to a generation with a compelling need to establish roots and boundaries. There is a tremendous drive for solidarity and a willingness to sacrifice personal needs for the sake of the family, or the country as in the case of the Second World War. This is an isolationist combination—Pluto in Cancer will establish its loyalties with who is family and who is not. The shadow side brings out the smothering tendency of Cancer. The "need to be needed" of this placement can unwittingly cultivate codependency, keeping people in their security needs as a subversive method of maintaining power and control. Too much focus on security and safety can create a stifling effect on individual growth. The family, the community, the local football team, the country, the religion—loyalties are established and lines drawn. At each of these various levels, Pluto in Cancer will decide who is within the safety net and who is outside. The outsiders will be treated as potential threats. When this generation errs, it errs on the side of being overly cautious.

Pluto in Leo (1937–1956)

The drive associated with Leo is dramatic self-expression, and with Pluto here shows a generation compelled to express itself in dramatic creative flair. The selfless attitude of Cancer, family before self, flips around in Leo where it can become self before family. Where Cancer will err on the side of too much caution, Leo will err on the side of too much risk. The survival instinct animating the entire generation is "express or die"—to reach deep within the self beyond cultural taboos, and to creatively express what's been discovered. Leo is acting out the hero myth and this whole generation feels "here I am to save the day!" The urge to develop individual greatness has led this generation to radically impact the entertainment and sports worlds, where heroes thrive. Power and love go together with Pluto in Leo and those with this combination must ask this question, "Is it the power of love, or the love of power that animates my behavior?" The shadow side is glory at all costs—an entire generation struggling with inflated self-importance. A little bit of self love can easily obsess into a lot of self-love. The need for every experience to be special and magical beyond compare can make it difficult for this generation to enjoy life's simple pleasures. Pluto in Leo needs for everything to be on a grand scale, and this has contributed to the debt enhancing lifestyle of our modern world.

Pluto in Virgo (1956–1971)

Virgo always sobers us up after the Leo indulgences. Gone are the flamboyant ways of Leo and in come the modest, self-effacing ways of Virgo. This generation seeks to transform some of the play of Leo and direct that energy to the work of Virgo. Many with this placement were born during the '60s with Uranus conjunct Pluto and the revolutionary energy of that era is within the birth chart of this generation. Where will the revolution explode? Environmental issues are likely. Virgo is an earth sign and believes in economy and sustainability, thus this generation will be forced to deal with the support of our current economic policies in light of their impact on the environment. Health issues will certainly also be in focus—high-tech vitamin supplements, hormone enhancers, and the like will capture the interest of many. Yoga is growing in popularity. However, by far and away, the dominant focus of transformational energy of Pluto in Virgo has been with the computer and technological realms. The shadow side is that Pluto can never be perfected in some squeaky clean Virgo fashion. This can lead to a quasi-neurotic belief that if just this one last part of the self could be fixed, everything would be perfect. However, this just leads to one more thing to be fixed. This generation can get so busy tending to the details of maintaining their everyday life, they miss the meaning and romance of life, lost in the task.

Pluto in Libra (1971–1983)

Beauty and relationships are the twin issues on which Libra focuses. The aesthetics of life are important and there will be a compelling urge to transform the effective, but drab, world of Virgo and infuse it with a greater sense of style. Libra is the first of the social signs (Libra through Pisces), and it becomes more and more apparent as Pluto continues to move through the social signs that survival depends more on cooperation than on competition. Relationships, as we know them, will go through a tremendous transformation with this generation.

Traditional roles will be shattered as Pluto will flaunt its disapproval of superficial social protocol. We can expect traditional political alliances to die and new ones to form. Libra is the peacemaker of the zodiac, and at best, Pluto here will take off Libra's kid gloves and get down to the brass tacks of dealing with the underlying issues separating individuals, groups, and countries. The rules and strategies of diplomacy will certainly go through a major transformation. The shadow side of Libra is excessive intellectualism, ignoring the heart and its message—things either make sense or they don't. Bad decisions always come on the heals of ignoring feelings. Another shadow of Libra is in its indecisiveness. Always being able to see both sides of the coin is a tremendous talent in diplomacy, but it is a great difficulty when important decisions must be made. Will this generation rise to the task of facing the important issues of the time, or will they avoid the unpleasant task of facing tough issues? Global peace, or war, hangs in the balance.

Pluto in Scorpio (1983–1995)

Pluto operates at its strongest in Scorpio, the sign that it rules. Here we can expect to see its most extreme expressions for good or ill. The survival instinct must face death itself from this most extreme of combinations. AIDS and euthanasia are two examples of how death itself has raised its head and demanded to be dealt with. Scorpio represents the psychological content deep within the human psyche and Pluto will seek to delve into this buried material and bring it to light. I joke and say that while Pluto was in Scorpio, we were all in therapy or should have been! Psychologists were having a heyday as the drive to explore family origin issues and the wounded child within was at its peak. At its best, this combination leads to a generation of deep seekers who are willing to look at the darker aspects of life in their pursuit of truth. Pluto in Scorpio demonstrates the power of the will when guided by specific intent, as the renaissance of interest in rituals, shamanism, and witchcraft demonstrate. We would assume this generation will transform our culture's attitudes concerning sexuality—like a moth to the flame, Pluto in Scorpio will dive right into what the rest of the culture considers taboo, and if this shocks the rest of society, all the better. This combination will reveal the hidden, sordid aspects of a culture's sexuality. This was the era that unveiled the shocking discovery of widespread sexual abuse in our culture. On the dark side, this generation has been so desensitized to death and violence through the media, that a cavalier attitude about death has developed. The number of murders and massacres committed by young teenagers with this combination is chilling.

Pluto in Sagittarius (1995–2008)

The Scorpio era of therapy came to a close as Pluto moved into Sagittarius. This fiery sign refuses to be defined by its past or its wounds. It is the explorer sign, the adventurer seeking the dreams and goals that lead to the future. The survival instinct of this generation is uniting with others in philosophical, religious, and political ideology. Sagittarius is the abstract, philosophical part of our character and Pluto here will lead to a generation of philosophers considering global issues of politics, religion, and education. Sagittarius deals will all foreign and ethnic issues and most of this generation will also have Uranus and Neptune both in Aquarius. The planets of destiny in global humanitarian signs holds the promise of this generation melding together a cohesive global community. The dark side of Sagittarius can lead to rigidly held fundamentalist beliefs of "holier than thou" attitudes—the make-up of fanaticism. When we slander each other's name for God, we have the making of holy wars, crusades, and other ethnic cleansings. Sagittarius may appear happy-go-lucky, but it is a fire sign and those arrows can just as easily become weapons of war as arrows seeking truth.

Conclusion

AT THE TIME of this writing, there has been an outbreak of the worst-case scenarios of Pluto in Sagittarius. Wars, and even attempts at ethnic cleansing, have erupted on our planet. What type of world we leave for future generations hangs in the balance of how we handle the shadow side of Pluto, currently manifesting as growing conflicts of ideologies and religious beliefs. Attempting to interpret Pluto's influence in any of the signs beyond Sagittarius would be purely speculative and philosophical at this point. It is impossible for us to know what type of a world the Pluto-in-Capricorn generation will inherit beginning in 2008—let alone future generations. So much will be determined by how we handle our collective Pluto in Sagittarius issues at this time.

Now, perhaps more than ever before, it becomes imperative to stretch our beliefs to develop compassion and better understanding of others. Global communications have put us all right in each other's faces.

I once heard a saying, "If you knew the secret life of your enemy, he wouldn't be your enemy anymore." If this is true for our enemies, how much more true for the important people in our lives. It has been the intent of this book to provide tools for improving the quality of our personal relationships. If we are successful, perhaps this newfound understanding can radiate out into the world, with the hope that these insights gained for accepting others spreads and grows. With this in mind, we can close with the affirmation, "May there be peace on earth, and let it begin with me."

Appendix: Ephemeris (1900–2005)

To use the ephemeris, find the table for the planet you are looking for, and go down the list of years until you come to your birth year. Continue through the year until you find the date *before* your birthday. The entry in the first row is the symbol of the sign the planet moved into on that day (see key below left). The second row is the date the planet moved into the sign and the third row is the time of day this occurred.

All times are listed in GMT (Greenwich Mean Time), so you will need to adjust for the time zone of your place of birth. The table (below right) shows the adjusted hours for the main time zones in the U.S. Subtract the number of hours listed below from the time listed in the ephemeris to calculate the local time for your time zone. (Note: this is only important if your birthday falls *on the exact day* of the entry in the ephemeris.)

Key

♈	Aries	♎	Libra
♉	Taurus	♏	Scorpio
♊	Gemini	♐	Sagittarius
♋	Cancer	♑	Capricorn
♌	Leo	♒	Aquarius
♍	Virgo	♓	Pisces

Time Zone	Standard Time	Daylight Savings or War Time
Eastern	-5 hours	-4 hours
Central	-6 hours	-5 hours
Mountain	-7 hours	-6 hours
Pacific	-8 hours	-7 hours
Alaska/Hawaii	-10 hours	-9 hours

Sun Sign Changes 1900-2005

1900
♒ 1/20 11:33am
♓ 2/19 2:01am
♈ 3/21 1:39am
♉ 4/20 1:27pm
♊ 5/21 1:17pm
♋ 6/21 9:40pm
♌ 7/23 8:36am
♍ 8/23 3:20pm
♎ 9/23 12:20pm
♏ 10/23 8:55pm
♐ 11/22 5:48pm
♑ 12/22 6:42am

1901
♒ 1/20 5:17pm
♓ 2/19 7:45am
♈ 3/21 7:24am
♉ 4/20 7:14pm
♊ 5/21 7:05pm
♋ 6/22 3:28am
♌ 7/23 2:24pm
♍ 8/23 9:08pm
♎ 9/23 6:09pm
♏ 10/24 2:46am
♐ 11/22 11:41pm
♑ 12/22 12:37pm

1902
♒ 1/20 11:12pm
♓ 2/19 1:40pm
♈ 3/21 1:17pm
♉ 4/21 1:04am
♊ 5/22 12:54am
♋ 6/22 9:15am
♌ 7/23 8:10pm
♍ 8/24 2:53am
♎ 9/23 11:55pm
♏ 10/24 8:36am
♐ 11/23 5:36am
♑ 12/22 6:36pm

1903
♒ 1/21 5:14am
♓ 2/19 7:41pm
♈ 3/21 7:15pm
♉ 4/21 6:59am
♊ 5/22 6:45am
♋ 6/22 3:05pm
♌ 7/24 1:59am
♍ 8/24 8:42am
♎ 9/24 5:44am
♏ 10/24 2:23pm
♐ 11/23 11:22am
♑ 12/23 12:21am

1904
♒ 1/21 10:58am
♓ 2/20 1:25am
♈ 3/21 12:59am
♉ 4/20 12:42pm
♊ 5/21 12:29pm
♋ 6/21 8:51pm
♌ 7/23 7:50am
♍ 8/23 2:37pm
♎ 9/23 11:40am
♏ 10/23 8:19pm
♐ 11/22 5:16pm
♑ 12/22 6:14am

1905
♒ 1/20 4:52pm
♓ 2/19 7:21am
♈ 3/21 6:58am
♉ 4/20 6:44pm
♊ 5/21 6:31pm
♋ 6/22 2:51am
♌ 7/23 1:46pm
♍ 8/23 8:29pm
♎ 9/23 5:30pm
♏ 10/24 2:08am
♐ 11/22 11:05pm
♑ 12/22 12:04pm

1906
♒ 1/20 10:43pm
♓ 2/19 1:15pm
♈ 3/21 12:53pm
♉ 4/21 12:39am
♊ 5/22 12:25am
♋ 6/22 8:42am
♌ 7/23 7:33pm
♍ 8/24 2:14am
♎ 9/23 11:15pm
♏ 10/24 7:55am
♐ 11/23 4:54am
♑ 12/22 5:53pm

1907
♒ 1/21 4:31am
♓ 2/19 6:58pm
♈ 3/21 6:33pm
♉ 4/21 6:17am
♊ 5/22 6:03am
♋ 6/22 2:23pm
♌ 7/24 1:18am
♍ 8/24 8:03am
♎ 9/24 5:09am
♏ 10/24 1:52pm
♐ 11/23 10:52am
♑ 12/22 11:52pm

1908
♒ 1/21 10:28am
♓ 2/20 12:54am
♈ 3/21 12:27am
♉ 4/20 12:11pm
♊ 5/21 11:58am
♋ 6/21 8:19pm
♌ 7/23 7:14am
♍ 8/23 1:57pm
♎ 9/23 10:58am
♏ 10/23 7:37pm
♐ 11/22 4:35pm
♑ 12/22 5:34am

1909
♒ 1/20 4:11pm
♓ 2/19 6:38am
♈ 3/21 6:13am
♉ 4/20 5:58pm
♊ 5/21 5:45pm
♋ 6/22 2:06am
♌ 7/23 1:01pm
♍ 8/23 7:44pm
♎ 9/23 4:45pm
♏ 10/24 1:23am
♐ 11/22 10:20pm
♑ 12/22 11:20am

1910
♒ 1/20 9:59pm
♓ 2/19 12:28pm
♈ 3/21 12:03pm
♉ 4/20 11:46pm
♊ 5/21 11:30pm
♋ 6/22 7:49am
♌ 7/23 6:43pm
♍ 8/24 1:27am
♎ 9/23 10:31pm
♏ 10/24 7:11am
♐ 11/23 4:11am
♑ 12/22 5:12pm

1911
♒ 1/21 3:52am
♓ 2/19 6:20pm
♈ 3/21 5:54pm
♉ 4/21 5:36am
♊ 5/22 5:19am
♋ 6/22 1:36pm
♌ 7/24 12:29am
♍ 8/24 7:13am
♎ 9/24 4:18am
♏ 10/24 12:58pm
♐ 11/23 9:56am
♑ 12/22 10:53pm

1912
♒ 1/21 9:29am
♓ 2/19 11:56pm
♈ 3/20 11:29pm
♉ 4/20 11:12am
♊ 5/21 10:57am
♋ 6/21 7:17pm
♌ 7/23 6:14am
♍ 8/23 1:01pm
♎ 9/23 10:08am
♏ 10/23 6:50pm
♐ 11/22 3:48pm
♑ 12/22 4:45am

1913
♒ 1/20 3:19pm
♓ 2/19 5:44am
♈ 3/21 5:18am
♉ 4/20 5:03pm
♊ 5/21 4:50pm
♋ 6/22 1:10am
♌ 7/23 12:04pm
♍ 8/23 6:48pm
♎ 9/23 3:53pm
♏ 10/24 12:35am
♐ 11/22 9:35pm
♑ 12/22 10:35am

1914
♒ 1/20 9:12pm
♓ 2/19 11:38am
♈ 3/21 11:11am
♉ 4/20 10:53pm
♊ 5/21 10:38pm
♋ 6/22 6:55am
♌ 7/23 5:47pm
♍ 8/24 12:30am
♎ 9/23 9:34pm
♏ 10/24 6:17am
♐ 11/23 3:20am
♑ 12/22 4:22pm

1915
♒ 1/21 3:00am
♓ 2/19 5:23pm
♈ 3/21 4:51pm
♉ 4/21 4:29am
♊ 5/22 4:10am
♋ 6/22 12:29pm
♌ 7/23 11:26pm
♍ 8/24 6:15am
♎ 9/24 3:24am
♏ 10/24 12:10pm
♐ 11/23 9:14am
♑ 12/22 10:16pm

1916
♒ 1/21 8:54am
♓ 2/19 11:18pm
♈ 3/20 10:47pm
♉ 4/20 10:25am
♊ 5/21 10:06am
♋ 6/21 6:24pm
♌ 7/23 5:21am
♍ 8/23 12:09pm
♎ 9/23 9:15am
♏ 10/23 5:57pm
♐ 11/22 2:58pm
♑ 12/22 3:59am

1917
♒ 1/20 2:37pm
♓ 2/19 5:05am
♈ 3/21 4:37am
♉ 4/20 4:17pm
♊ 5/21 3:59pm
♋ 6/22 12:14am
♌ 7/23 11:08am
♍ 8/23 5:54pm
♎ 9/23 3:00pm
♏ 10/23 11:44pm
♐ 11/22 8:45pm
♑ 12/22 9:46am

1918
♒ 1/20 8:25pm
♓ 2/19 10:53am
♈ 3/21 10:26am
♉ 4/20 10:05pm
♊ 5/21 9:46pm
♋ 6/22 6:00am
♌ 7/23 4:51pm
♍ 8/23 11:37pm
♎ 9/23 8:46pm
♏ 10/24 5:33am
♐ 11/23 2:38am
♑ 12/22 3:42pm

1919
♒ 1/21 2:21am
♓ 2/19 4:48pm
♈ 3/21 4:19pm
♉ 4/21 3:59am
♊ 5/22 3:39am
♋ 6/22 11:54am
♌ 7/23 10:45pm
♍ 8/24 5:28am
♎ 9/24 2:35am
♏ 10/24 11:21am
♐ 11/23 8:25am
♑ 12/22 9:27pm

1920
♒ 1/21 8:04am
♓ 2/19 10:29pm
♈ 3/20 9:59pm
♉ 4/20 9:39am
♊ 5/21 9:22am
♋ 6/21 5:40pm
♌ 7/23 4:35am
♍ 8/23 11:21am
♎ 9/23 8:28am
♏ 10/23 5:13pm
♐ 11/22 2:15pm
♑ 12/22 3:17am

1921
♒ 1/20 1:55pm
♓ 2/19 4:20am
♈ 3/21 3:51am
♉ 4/20 3:32pm
♊ 5/21 3:17pm
♋ 6/21 11:36pm
♌ 7/23 10:30am
♍ 8/23 5:15pm
♎ 9/23 2:20pm
♏ 10/23 11:02pm
♐ 11/22 8:05pm
♑ 12/22 9:07am

1922
♒ 1/20 7:48pm
♓ 2/19 10:16am
♈ 3/21 9:49am
♉ 4/20 9:29pm
♊ 5/21 9:10pm
♋ 6/22 5:27am
♌ 7/23 4:20pm
♍ 8/23 11:04pm
♎ 9/23 8:10pm
♏ 10/24 4:53am
♐ 11/23 1:55am
♑ 12/22 2:57pm

1923
♒ 1/21 1:35am
♓ 2/19 4:00pm
♈ 3/21 3:29pm
♉ 4/21 3:06am
♊ 5/22 2:45am
♋ 6/22 11:03am
♌ 7/23 10:01pm
♍ 8/24 4:52am
♎ 9/24 2:04am
♏ 10/24 10:51am
♐ 11/23 7:54am
♑ 12/22 8:53pm

1924
♒ 1/21 7:28am
♓ 2/19 9:51pm
♈ 3/20 9:20pm
♉ 4/20 8:59am
♊ 5/21 8:40am
♋ 6/21 4:59pm
♌ 7/23 3:58am
♍ 8/23 10:48am
♎ 9/23 7:58am
♏ 10/23 4:44pm
♐ 11/22 1:46pm
♑ 12/22 2:46am

1925
♒ 1/20 1:20pm
♓ 2/19 3:43am
♈ 3/21 3:12am
♉ 4/20 2:51pm
♊ 5/21 2:33pm
♋ 6/21 10:50pm
♌ 7/23 9:45am
♍ 8/23 4:33pm
♎ 9/23 1:43pm
♏ 10/23 10:31pm
♐ 11/22 7:35pm
♑ 12/22 8:37am

1926
♒ 1/20 7:12pm
♓ 2/19 9:35am
♈ 3/21 9:01am
♉ 4/20 8:36pm
♊ 5/21 8:15pm
♋ 6/22 4:30am
♌ 7/23 3:25pm
♍ 8/23 10:14pm
♎ 9/23 7:27pm
♏ 10/24 4:18am
♐ 11/23 1:28am
♑ 12/22 2:33pm

1927
♒ 1/21 1:12am
♓ 2/19 3:34pm
♈ 3/21 2:59pm
♉ 4/21 2:32am
♊ 5/22 2:08am
♋ 6/22 10:22am
♌ 7/23 9:17pm
♍ 8/24 4:05am
♎ 9/24 1:17am
♏ 10/24 10:07am
♐ 11/23 7:14am
♑ 12/22 8:19pm

1928
♒ 1/21 6:57am
♓ 2/19 9:19pm
♈ 3/20 8:44pm
♉ 4/20 8:17am
♊ 5/21 7:52am
♋ 6/21 4:06pm

Sun Sign Changes 1900-2005

Sign	Date	Time
♌	7/23	3:02am
♍	8/23	9:53am
♎	9/23	7:06am
♏	10/23	3:55pm
♐	11/22	1:00pm
♑	12/22	2:04am
1929		
♒	1/20	12:42pm
♓	2/19	3:07am
♈	3/21	2:35am
♉	4/20	2:10pm
♊	5/21	1:48pm
♋	6/21	10:01pm
♌	7/23	8:53am
♍	8/23	3:41pm
♎	9/23	12:52pm
♏	10/23	9:41pm
♐	11/22	6:48pm
♑	12/22	7:53am
1930		
♒	1/20	6:33pm
♓	2/19	9:00am
♈	3/21	8:30am
♉	4/20	8:06pm
♊	5/21	7:42pm
♋	6/22	3:53am
♌	7/23	2:42pm
♍	8/23	9:26pm
♎	9/23	6:36pm
♏	10/24	3:26am
♐	11/23	12:34am
♑	12/22	1:40pm
1931		
♒	1/21	12:18am
♓	2/19	2:40pm
♈	3/21	2:06pm
♉	4/21	1:40am
♊	5/22	1:15am
♋	6/22	9:28am
♌	7/23	8:21pm
♍	8/24	3:10am
♎	9/24	12:23am
♏	10/24	9:16am
♐	11/23	6:25am
♑	12/22	7:30pm
1932		
♒	1/21	6:07am
♓	2/19	8:28pm
♈	3/20	7:54pm
♉	4/20	7:28am
♊	5/21	7:07am
♋	6/21	3:23pm
♌	7/23	2:18am
♍	8/23	9:06am
♎	9/23	6:16am
♏	10/23	3:04pm
♐	11/22	12:10pm
♑	12/22	1:14am
1933		
♒	1/20	11:53am
♓	2/19	2:16am
♈	3/21	1:43am
♉	4/20	1:18pm
♊	5/21	12:57pm
♋	6/21	9:12pm
♌	7/23	8:05am
♍	8/23	2:52pm
♎	9/23	12:01pm
♏	10/23	8:48pm
♐	11/22	5:53pm
♑	12/22	6:58am
1934		
♒	1/20	5:37pm
♓	2/19	8:02am
♈	3/21	7:28am
♉	4/20	7:00pm
♊	5/21	6:35pm
♋	6/22	2:48am
♌	7/23	1:42pm
♍	8/23	8:32pm
♎	9/23	5:45pm
♏	10/24	2:36am
♐	11/22	11:44pm
♑	12/22	12:49pm
1935		
♒	1/20	11:28pm
♓	2/19	1:52pm
♈	3/21	1:18pm
♉	4/21	12:50am
♊	5/22	12:25am
♋	6/22	8:38am
♌	7/23	7:33pm
♍	8/24	2:24am
♎	9/23	11:38pm
♏	10/24	8:29am
♐	11/23	5:35am
♑	12/22	6:37pm
1936		
♒	1/21	5:12am
♓	2/19	7:33pm
♈	3/20	6:58pm
♉	4/20	6:31am
♊	5/21	6:07am
♋	6/21	2:22pm
♌	7/23	1:18am
♍	8/23	8:11am
♎	9/23	5:26am
♏	10/23	2:18pm
♐	11/22	11:25am
♑	12/22	12:27am
1937		
♒	1/20	11:01am
♓	2/19	1:21am
♈	3/21	12:45am
♉	4/20	12:19pm
♊	5/21	11:57am
♋	6/21	8:12pm
♌	7/23	7:07am
♍	8/23	1:58pm
♎	9/23	11:13am
♏	10/23	8:07pm
♐	11/22	5:17pm
♑	12/22	6:22am
1938		
♒	1/20	4:59pm
♓	2/19	7:20am
♈	3/21	6:43am
♉	4/20	6:15pm
♊	5/21	5:50pm
♋	6/22	2:04am
♌	7/23	12:57pm
♍	8/23	7:46pm
♎	9/23	5:00pm
♏	10/24	1:54am
♐	11/22	11:06pm
♑	12/22	12:13pm
1939		
♒	1/20	10:51pm
♓	2/19	1:09pm
♈	3/21	12:28pm
♉	4/20	11:55pm
♊	5/21	11:27pm
♋	6/22	7:39am
♌	7/23	6:37pm
♍	8/24	1:31am
♎	9/23	10:49pm
♏	10/24	7:46am
♐	11/23	4:59am
♑	12/22	6:06pm
1940		
♒	1/21	4:44am
♓	2/19	7:04pm
♈	3/20	6:24pm
♉	4/20	5:51am
♊	5/21	5:23am
♋	6/21	1:36pm
♌	7/23	12:34am
♍	8/23	7:29am
♎	9/23	4:46am
♏	10/23	1:39pm
♐	11/22	10:49am
♑	12/21	11:55pm
1941		
♒	1/20	10:34am
♓	2/19	12:56am
♈	3/21	12:20am
♉	4/20	11:50am
♊	5/21	11:23am
♋	6/21	7:33pm
♌	7/23	6:26am
♍	8/23	1:17pm
♎	9/23	10:33am
♏	10/23	7:27pm
♐	11/22	4:38pm
♑	12/22	5:44am
1942		
♒	1/20	4:24pm
♓	2/19	6:47am
♈	3/21	6:11am
♉	4/20	5:39pm
♊	5/21	5:09pm
♋	6/22	1:16am
♌	7/23	12:07pm
♍	8/23	6:58pm
♎	9/23	4:16pm
♏	10/24	1:15am
♐	11/22	10:30pm
♑	12/22	11:40am
1943		
♒	1/20	10:19pm
♓	2/19	12:40pm
♈	3/21	12:03pm
♉	4/20	11:32pm
♊	5/21	11:03pm
♋	6/22	7:12am
♌	7/23	6:05pm
♍	8/24	12:55am
♎	9/23	10:12pm
♏	10/24	7:08am
♐	11/23	4:22am
♑	12/22	5:29pm
1944		
♒	1/21	4:07am
♓	2/19	6:27pm
♈	3/20	5:49pm
♉	4/20	5:18am
♊	5/21	4:51am
♋	6/21	1:02pm
♌	7/22	11:56pm
♍	8/23	6:46am
♎	9/23	4:02am
♏	10/23	12:56pm
♐	11/22	10:08am
♑	12/21	11:15pm
1945		
♒	1/20	9:54am
♓	2/19	12:15am
♈	3/20	11:37pm
♉	4/20	11:07am
♊	5/21	10:40am
♋	6/21	6:52pm
♌	7/23	5:45am
♍	8/23	12:35pm
♎	9/23	9:50am
♏	10/23	6:44pm
♐	11/22	3:55pm
♑	12/22	5:04am
1946		
♒	1/20	3:45pm
♓	2/19	6:09am
♈	3/21	5:33am
♉	4/20	5:02pm
♊	5/21	4:34pm
♋	6/22	12:44am
♌	7/23	11:37am
♍	8/23	6:26pm
♎	9/23	3:41pm
♏	10/24	12:35am
♐	11/22	9:46pm
♑	12/22	10:53am
1947		
♒	1/20	9:32pm
♓	2/19	11:52am
♈	3/21	11:13am
♉	4/20	10:39pm
♊	5/21	10:09pm
♋	6/22	6:19am
♌	7/23	5:14pm
♍	8/24	12:09am
♎	9/23	9:29pm
♏	10/24	6:26am
♐	11/23	3:38am
♑	12/22	4:43pm
1948		
♒	1/21	3:18am
♓	2/19	5:37pm
♈	3/20	4:57pm
♉	4/20	4:25am
♊	5/21	3:58am
♋	6/21	12:11pm
♌	7/22	11:08pm
♍	8/23	6:03am
♎	9/23	3:22am
♏	10/23	12:18pm
♐	11/22	9:29am
♑	12/21	10:33pm
1949		
♒	1/20	9:09am
♓	2/18	11:27pm
♈	3/20	10:48pm
♉	4/20	10:17am
♊	5/21	9:51am
♋	6/21	6:03pm
♌	7/23	4:57am
♍	8/23	11:48am
♎	9/23	9:06am
♏	10/23	6:03pm
♐	11/22	3:16pm
♑	12/22	4:23am
1950		
♒	1/20	3:00pm
♓	2/19	5:18am
♈	3/21	4:35am
♉	4/20	3:59pm
♊	5/21	3:27pm
♋	6/21	11:36pm
♌	7/23	10:30am
♍	8/23	5:23pm
♎	9/23	2:44pm
♏	10/23	11:45pm
♐	11/22	9:03pm
♑	12/22	10:13am
1951		
♒	1/20	8:52pm
♓	2/19	11:10am
♈	3/21	10:26am
♉	4/20	9:48pm
♊	5/21	9:15pm
♋	6/22	5:25am
♌	7/23	4:21pm
♍	8/23	11:16pm
♎	9/23	8:37pm
♏	10/24	5:36am
♐	11/23	2:51am
♑	12/22	4:00pm
1952		
♒	1/21	2:38am
♓	2/19	4:57pm
♈	3/20	4:14pm
♉	4/20	3:37am
♊	5/21	3:04am
♋	6/21	11:13am
♌	7/22	10:07pm
♍	8/23	5:03am
♎	9/23	2:24am
♏	10/23	11:22am
♐	11/22	8:36am
♑	12/21	9:43pm
1953		
♒	1/20	8:21am
♓	2/18	10:41pm
♈	3/20	10:01pm
♉	4/20	9:25am
♊	5/21	8:53am
♋	6/21	5:00pm
♌	7/23	3:52am
♍	8/23	10:45am
♎	9/23	8:06am
♏	10/23	5:06pm
♐	11/22	2:22pm
♑	12/22	3:31am
1954		
♒	1/20	2:11pm
♓	2/19	4:32am
♈	3/21	3:53am
♉	4/20	3:20pm
♊	5/21	2:47pm
♋	6/21	10:54pm
♌	7/23	9:45am
♍	8/23	4:36pm
♎	9/23	1:55pm
♏	10/23	10:56pm
♐	11/22	8:14pm
♑	12/22	9:24am
1955		
♒	1/20	8:02pm
♓	2/19	10:19am
♈	3/21	9:35am
♉	4/20	8:58pm
♊	5/21	8:24pm
♋	6/22	4:31am
♌	7/23	3:25pm
♍	8/23	10:19pm
♎	9/23	7:41pm
♏	10/24	4:43am
♐	11/23	2:01am
♑	12/22	3:11pm
1956		
♒	1/21	1:48am
♓	2/19	4:05pm
♈	3/20	3:20pm
♉	4/20	2:43am
♊	5/21	2:13am
♋	6/21	10:24am
♌	7/22	9:20pm
♍	8/23	4:15am
♎	9/23	1:35am
♏	10/23	10:34am
♐	11/22	7:50am
♑	12/21	8:59pm

Sun Sign Changes 1900-2005

1957
♒ 1/20 7:39am
♓ 2/18 9:58pm
♈ 3/20 9:16pm
♉ 4/20 8:41am
♊ 5/21 8:10am
♋ 6/21 4:21pm
♌ 7/23 3:15am
♍ 8/23 10:08am
♎ 9/23 7:26am
♏ 10/23 4:24pm
♐ 11/22 1:39pm
♑ 12/22 2:49am

1958
♒ 1/20 1:28pm
♓ 2/19 3:48am
♈ 3/21 3:06am
♉ 4/20 2:27pm
♊ 5/21 1:51pm
♋ 6/21 9:57pm
♌ 7/23 8:50am
♍ 8/23 3:46pm
♎ 9/23 1:09pm
♏ 10/23 10:11pm
♐ 11/22 7:29pm
♑ 12/22 8:40am

1959
♒ 1/20 7:19pm
♓ 2/19 9:38am
♈ 3/21 8:55am
♉ 4/20 8:17pm
♊ 5/21 7:42pm
♋ 6/22 3:50am
♌ 7/23 2:45pm
♍ 8/23 9:44pm
♎ 9/23 7:08pm
♏ 10/24 4:11am
♐ 11/23 1:27am
♑ 12/22 2:34pm

1960
♒ 1/21 1:10am
♓ 2/19 3:26pm
♈ 3/20 2:43pm
♉ 4/20 2:06am
♊ 5/21 1:34am
♋ 6/21 9:42am
♌ 7/22 8:37pm
♍ 8/23 3:34am
♎ 9/23 12:59am
♏ 10/23 10:02am
♐ 11/22 7:18am
♑ 12/21 8:26pm

1961
♒ 1/20 7:01am
♓ 2/18 9:16pm
♈ 3/20 8:32pm
♉ 4/20 7:55am
♊ 5/21 7:22am
♋ 6/21 3:30pm
♌ 7/23 2:24am
♍ 8/23 9:19am
♎ 9/23 6:42am
♏ 10/23 3:47pm
♐ 11/22 1:08pm
♑ 12/22 2:19am

1962
♒ 1/20 12:58pm
♓ 2/19 3:15am
♈ 3/21 2:30am
♉ 4/20 1:51pm
♊ 5/21 1:17pm
♋ 6/21 9:24pm
♌ 7/23 8:18am
♍ 8/23 3:12pm
♎ 9/23 12:35pm
♏ 10/23 9:40pm
♐ 11/22 7:02pm
♑ 12/22 8:15am

1963
♒ 1/20 6:54pm
♓ 2/19 9:09am
♈ 3/21 8:20am
♉ 4/20 7:36pm
♊ 5/21 6:58pm
♋ 6/22 3:04am
♌ 7/23 1:59pm
♍ 8/23 8:58pm
♎ 9/23 6:24pm
♏ 10/24 3:29am
♐ 11/23 12:49am
♑ 12/22 2:02pm

1964
♒ 1/21 12:41am
♓ 2/19 2:57pm
♈ 3/20 2:10pm
♉ 4/20 1:27am
♊ 5/21 12:50am
♋ 6/21 8:57am
♌ 7/22 7:53pm
♍ 8/23 2:51am
♎ 9/23 12:17am
♏ 10/23 9:21am
♐ 11/22 6:39am
♑ 12/21 7:50pm

1965
♒ 1/20 6:29am
♓ 2/18 8:48pm
♈ 3/20 8:05pm
♉ 4/20 7:26am
♊ 5/21 6:50am
♋ 6/21 2:56pm
♌ 7/23 1:48am
♍ 8/23 8:43am
♎ 9/23 6:06am
♏ 10/23 3:10pm
♐ 11/22 12:29pm
♑ 12/22 1:40am

1966
♒ 1/20 12:20pm
♓ 2/19 2:38am
♈ 3/21 1:53am
♉ 4/20 1:12pm
♊ 5/21 12:32pm
♋ 6/21 8:33pm
♌ 7/23 7:23am
♍ 8/23 2:18pm
♎ 9/23 11:43am
♏ 10/23 8:51pm
♐ 11/22 6:14pm
♑ 12/22 7:28am

1967
♒ 1/20 6:08pm
♓ 2/19 8:24am
♈ 3/21 7:37am
♉ 4/20 6:55pm
♊ 5/21 6:18pm
♋ 6/22 2:23am
♌ 7/23 1:16pm
♍ 8/23 8:12pm
♎ 9/23 5:38pm
♏ 10/24 2:44am
♐ 11/23 12:04am
♑ 12/22 1:16pm

1968
♒ 1/20 11:54pm
♓ 2/19 2:09pm
♈ 3/20 1:22pm
♉ 4/20 12:41am
♊ 5/21 12:06am
♋ 6/21 8:13am
♌ 7/22 7:07pm
♍ 8/23 2:03am
♎ 9/22 11:26pm
♏ 10/23 8:30am
♐ 11/22 5:49am
♑ 12/21 7:00pm

1969
♒ 1/20 5:38am
♓ 2/18 7:55pm
♈ 3/20 7:08pm
♉ 4/20 6:27am
♊ 5/21 5:50am
♋ 6/21 1:55pm
♌ 7/23 12:48am
♍ 8/23 7:43am
♎ 9/23 5:07am
♏ 10/23 2:11pm
♐ 11/22 11:31am
♑ 12/22 12:44am

1970
♒ 1/20 11:24am
♓ 2/19 1:42am
♈ 3/21 12:56am
♉ 4/20 12:15pm
♊ 5/21 11:37am
♋ 6/21 7:43pm
♌ 7/23 6:37am
♍ 8/23 1:34pm
♎ 9/23 10:59am
♏ 10/23 8:04pm
♐ 11/22 5:25pm
♑ 12/22 6:36am

1971
♒ 1/20 5:13pm
♓ 2/19 7:27am
♈ 3/21 6:38am
♉ 4/20 5:54pm
♊ 5/21 5:15pm
♋ 6/22 1:20am
♌ 7/23 12:15pm
♍ 8/23 7:15pm
♎ 9/23 4:45pm
♏ 10/24 1:53am
♐ 11/22 11:14pm
♑ 12/22 12:24pm

1972
♒ 1/20 10:59pm
♓ 2/19 1:11pm
♈ 3/20 12:21pm
♉ 4/19 11:37pm
♊ 5/20 11:00pm
♋ 6/21 7:06am
♌ 7/22 6:03pm
♍ 8/23 1:03am
♎ 9/22 10:33pm
♏ 10/23 7:41am
♐ 11/22 5:03am
♑ 12/21 6:13pm

1973
♒ 1/20 4:48am
♓ 2/18 7:01pm
♈ 3/20 6:12pm
♉ 4/20 5:30am
♊ 5/21 4:54am
♋ 6/21 1:01pm
♌ 7/22 11:56pm
♍ 8/23 6:53am
♎ 9/23 4:21am
♏ 10/23 1:30pm
♐ 11/22 10:54am
♑ 12/22 12:08am

1974
♒ 1/20 10:46am
♓ 2/19 12:59am
♈ 3/21 12:07am
♉ 4/20 11:19am
♊ 5/21 10:36am
♋ 6/21 6:38pm
♌ 7/23 5:30am
♍ 8/23 12:29pm
♎ 9/23 9:58am
♏ 10/23 7:11pm
♐ 11/22 4:38pm
♑ 12/22 5:56am

1975
♒ 1/20 4:36pm
♓ 2/19 6:50am
♈ 3/21 5:57am
♉ 4/20 5:07pm
♊ 5/21 4:24pm
♋ 6/22 12:26am
♌ 7/23 11:22am
♍ 8/23 6:24pm
♎ 9/23 3:55pm
♏ 10/24 1:06am
♐ 11/22 10:31pm
♑ 12/22 11:46am

1976
♒ 1/20 10:25pm
♓ 2/19 12:40pm
♈ 3/20 11:50am
♉ 4/19 11:03pm
♊ 5/20 10:21pm
♋ 6/21 6:24am
♌ 7/22 5:18pm
♍ 8/23 12:18am
♎ 9/22 9:48pm
♏ 10/23 6:58am
♐ 11/22 4:22am
♑ 12/21 5:35pm

1977
♒ 1/20 4:14am
♓ 2/18 6:30pm
♈ 3/20 5:42pm
♉ 4/20 4:57am
♊ 5/21 4:14am
♋ 6/21 12:14pm
♌ 7/22 11:04pm
♍ 8/23 6:00am
♎ 9/23 3:29am
♏ 10/23 12:41pm
♐ 11/22 10:07am
♑ 12/21 11:23pm

1978
♒ 1/20 10:04am
♓ 2/19 12:21am
♈ 3/20 11:34pm
♉ 4/20 10:50am
♊ 5/21 10:08am
♋ 6/21 6:10pm
♌ 7/23 5:00am
♍ 8/23 11:57am
♎ 9/23 9:25am
♏ 10/23 6:37pm
♐ 11/22 4:05pm
♑ 12/22 5:21am

1979
♒ 1/20 4:00pm
♓ 2/19 6:13am
♈ 3/21 5:22am
♉ 4/20 4:35pm
♊ 5/21 3:54pm
♋ 6/21 11:56pm
♌ 7/23 10:49am
♍ 8/23 5:47pm
♎ 9/23 3:16pm
♏ 10/24 12:28am
♐ 11/22 9:54pm
♑ 12/22 11:10am

1980
♒ 1/20 9:49pm
♓ 2/19 12:02pm
♈ 3/20 11:10am
♉ 4/19 10:23pm
♊ 5/20 9:42pm
♋ 6/21 5:47am
♌ 7/22 4:42pm
♍ 8/22 11:41pm
♎ 9/22 9:09pm
♏ 10/23 6:18am
♐ 11/22 3:41am
♑ 12/21 4:56pm

1981
♒ 1/20 3:36am
♓ 2/18 5:52pm
♈ 3/20 5:03pm
♉ 4/20 4:19am
♊ 5/21 3:39am
♋ 6/21 11:45am
♌ 7/22 10:40pm
♍ 8/23 5:38am
♎ 9/23 3:05am
♏ 10/23 12:13pm
♐ 11/22 9:36am
♑ 12/21 10:51pm

1982
♒ 1/20 9:31am
♓ 2/18 11:47pm
♈ 3/20 10:56pm
♉ 4/20 10:07am
♊ 5/21 9:23am
♋ 6/21 5:23pm
♌ 7/23 4:15am
♍ 8/23 11:15am
♎ 9/23 8:46am
♏ 10/23 5:58pm
♐ 11/22 3:23pm
♑ 12/22 4:38am

1983
♒ 1/20 3:17pm
♓ 2/19 5:31am
♈ 3/21 4:39am
♉ 4/20 3:50pm
♊ 5/21 3:06pm
♋ 6/21 11:09pm
♌ 7/23 10:04am
♍ 8/23 5:07pm
♎ 9/23 2:42pm
♏ 10/23 11:54pm
♐ 11/22 9:18pm
♑ 12/22 10:30am

1984
♒ 1/20 9:05pm
♓ 2/19 11:16am
♈ 3/20 10:24am
♉ 4/19 9:38am
♊ 5/20 8:58pm
♋ 6/21 5:02am
♌ 7/22 3:58pm
♍ 8/22 11:00pm
♎ 9/22 8:33pm
♏ 10/23 5:46am
♐ 11/22 3:11am
♑ 12/21 4:23pm

1985
♒ 1/20 2:58am
♓ 2/18 5:07pm
♈ 3/20 4:14pm
♉ 4/20 3:26am
♊ 5/21 2:43am
♋ 6/21 10:44am

Sun Sign Changes 1900-2005

Sign	Date	Time
♌	7/22	9:36pm
♍	8/23	4:36am
♎	9/23	2:07am
♏	10/23	11:22am
♐	11/22	8:51am
♑	12/21	10:08pm
1986		
♒	1/20	8:46am
♓	2/18	10:58pm
♈	3/20	10:03pm
♉	4/20	9:12am
♊	5/21	8:28am
♋	6/21	4:30pm
♌	7/23	3:24am
♍	8/23	10:26am
♎	9/23	7:59am
♏	10/23	5:14pm
♐	11/22	2:44pm
♑	12/22	4:02am
1987		
♒	1/20	2:40pm
♓	2/19	4:50am
♈	3/21	3:52am
♉	4/20	2:58pm
♊	5/21	2:10pm
♋	6/21	10:11pm
♌	7/23	9:06am
♍	8/23	4:10pm
♎	9/23	1:45pm
♏	10/23	11:01pm
♐	11/22	8:29pm
♑	12/22	9:46am
1988		
♒	1/20	8:24pm
♓	2/19	10:35am
♈	3/20	9:39am
♉	4/19	8:45pm
♊	5/20	7:57pm
♋	6/21	3:57am
♌	7/22	2:51pm
♍	8/22	9:54pm
♎	9/22	7:29pm
♏	10/23	4:44am
♐	11/22	2:12am
♑	12/21	3:28pm
1989		
♒	1/20	2:07am
♓	2/18	4:21pm
♈	3/20	3:28pm
♉	4/20	2:39am
♊	5/21	1:54am
♋	6/21	9:53am
♌	7/22	8:45pm
♍	8/23	3:46am
♎	9/23	1:20am
♏	10/23	10:35am
♐	11/22	8:05am
♑	12/21	9:22pm
1990		
♒	1/20	8:02am
♓	2/18	10:14pm
♈	3/20	9:19pm
♉	4/20	8:27am
♊	5/21	7:37am
♋	6/21	3:33pm
♌	7/23	2:22am
♍	8/23	9:21am
♎	9/23	6:56am
♏	10/23	4:14pm
♐	11/22	1:47pm
♑	12/22	3:07am
1991		
♒	1/20	1:47pm
♓	2/19	3:58am
♈	3/21	3:02am
♉	4/20	2:08pm
♊	5/21	1:20pm
♋	6/21	9:19pm
♌	7/23	8:11am
♍	8/23	3:13pm
♎	9/23	12:48pm
♏	10/23	10:05pm
♐	11/22	7:36pm
♑	12/22	8:54am
1992		
♒	1/20	7:32pm
♓	2/19	9:43am
♈	3/20	8:48am
♉	4/19	7:57pm
♊	5/20	7:12pm
♋	6/21	3:14am
♌	7/22	2:09pm
♍	8/22	9:10pm
♎	9/22	6:43pm
♏	10/23	3:57am
♐	11/22	1:26am
♑	12/21	2:43pm
1993		
♒	1/20	1:23am
♓	2/18	3:35pm
♈	3/20	2:41pm
♉	4/20	1:49am
♊	5/21	1:02am
♋	6/21	9:00am
♌	7/22	7:51pm
♍	8/23	2:50am
♎	9/23	12:22am
♏	10/23	9:37am
♐	11/22	7:07am
♑	12/21	8:26pm
1994		
♒	1/20	7:07am
♓	2/18	9:22pm
♈	3/20	8:28pm
♉	4/20	7:36am
♊	5/21	6:48am
♋	6/21	2:48pm
♌	7/23	1:41am
♍	8/23	8:44am
♎	9/23	6:19am
♏	10/23	3:36pm
♐	11/22	1:06pm
♑	12/22	2:23am
1995		
♒	1/20	1:00pm
♓	2/19	3:11am
♈	3/21	2:14am
♉	4/20	1:21pm
♊	5/21	12:34pm
♋	6/21	8:34pm
♌	7/23	7:30am
♍	8/23	2:35pm
♎	9/23	12:13pm
♏	10/23	9:32pm
♐	11/22	7:01pm
♑	12/22	8:17am
1996		
♒	1/20	6:52pm
♓	2/19	9:01am
♈	3/20	8:03am
♉	4/19	7:10pm
♊	5/20	6:23pm
♋	6/21	2:24am
♌	7/22	1:19pm
♍	8/22	8:23pm
♎	9/22	6:00pm
♏	10/23	3:19am
♐	11/22	12:49am
♑	12/21	2:06pm
1997		
♒	1/20	12:43am
♓	2/18	2:51pm
♈	3/20	1:55pm
♉	4/20	1:03am
♊	5/21	12:18am
♋	6/21	8:20am
♌	7/22	7:15pm
♍	8/23	2:19am
♎	9/22	11:56pm
♏	10/23	9:15am
♐	11/22	6:48am
♑	12/21	8:07pm
1998		
♒	1/20	6:46am
♓	2/18	8:55pm
♈	3/20	7:55pm
♉	4/20	6:57am
♊	5/21	6:05am
♋	6/21	2:03pm
♌	7/23	12:55am
♍	8/23	7:59am
♎	9/23	5:37am
♏	10/23	2:59pm
♐	11/22	12:34pm
♑	12/22	1:56am
1999		
♒	1/20	12:37pm
♓	2/19	2:47am
♈	3/21	1:46am
♉	4/20	12:46pm
♊	5/21	11:52am
♋	6/21	7:49pm
♌	7/23	6:44am
♍	8/23	1:51pm
♎	9/23	11:31am
♏	10/23	8:52pm
♐	11/22	6:25pm
♑	12/22	7:44am
2000		
♒	1/20	6:23pm
♓	2/19	8:33am
♈	3/20	7:35am
♉	4/19	6:40pm
♊	5/20	5:49pm
♋	6/21	1:48am
♌	7/22	12:43pm
♍	8/22	7:49pm
♎	9/22	5:28pm
♏	10/23	2:47am
♐	11/22	12:19am
♑	12/21	1:37pm
2001		
♒	1/20	12:16am
♓	2/18	2:27pm
♈	3/20	1:31pm
♉	4/20	12:36am
♊	5/20	11:44pm
♋	6/21	7:38am
♌	7/22	6:26pm
♍	8/23	1:27am
♎	9/22	11:04pm
♏	10/23	8:26am
♐	11/22	6:00am
♑	12/21	7:21pm
2002		
♒	1/20	6:02am
♓	2/18	8:13pm
♈	3/20	7:16pm
♉	4/20	6:20am
♊	5/21	5:29am
♋	6/21	1:24pm
♌	7/23	12:15am
♍	8/23	7:17am
♎	9/23	4:55am
♏	10/23	2:18pm
♐	11/22	11:54am
♑	12/22	1:14am
2003		
♒	1/20	11:53am
♓	2/19	2:00am
♈	3/21	1:00am
♉	4/20	12:03pm
♊	5/21	11:12am
♋	6/21	7:10pm
♌	7/23	6:04am
♍	8/23	1:08pm
♎	9/23	10:47am
♏	10/23	8:08pm
♐	11/22	5:43pm
♑	12/22	7:04am
2004		
♒	1/20	5:42pm
♓	2/19	7:50am
♈	3/20	6:49am
♉	4/19	5:50pm
♊	5/20	4:59pm
♋	6/21	12:57am
♌	7/22	11:50am
♍	8/22	6:53pm
♎	9/22	4:30pm
♏	10/23	1:49am
♐	11/21	11:22pm
♑	12/21	12:42pm
2005		
♒	1/19	11:22pm
♓	2/18	1:32pm
♈	3/20	12:33pm
♉	4/19	11:37pm
♊	5/20	10:47pm
♋	6/21	6:46am
♌	7/22	5:41pm
♍	8/23	12:45am
♎	9/22	10:23pm
♏	10/23	7:42am
♐	11/22	5:15am
♑	12/21	6:35pm

Moon Sign Changes 1900-2005

Sign	Date	Time
	1900	
♒	1/2	9:26pm
♓	1/4	10:09pm
♈	1/6	11:46pm
♉	1/9	3:26am
♊	1/11	9:37am
♋	1/13	6:06pm
♌	1/16	4:31am
♍	1/18	4:27pm
♎	1/21	5:07am
♏	1/23	4:55pm
♐	1/26	1:50am
♑	1/28	6:47am
♒	1/30	8:13am
♓	2/1	7:48am
♈	2/3	7:38am
♉	2/5	9:42am
♊	2/7	3:08pm
♋	2/9	11:50pm
♌	2/12	10:49am
♍	2/14	11:00pm
♎	2/17	11:37am
♏	2/19	11:45pm
♐	2/22	9:54am
♑	2/24	4:33pm
♒	2/26	7:16pm
♓	2/28	7:05pm
♈	3/2	6:02pm
♉	3/4	6:25pm
♊	3/6	10:05pm
♋	3/9	5:46am
♌	3/11	4:39pm
♍	3/14	5:04am
♎	3/16	5:39pm
♏	3/19	5:35am
♐	3/21	4:03pm
♑	3/23	11:57pm
♒	3/26	4:25am
♓	3/28	5:42am
♈	3/30	5:13am
♉	4/1	5:01am
♊	4/3	7:14am
♋	4/5	1:17pm
♌	4/7	11:11pm
♍	4/10	11:25am
♎	4/13	12:01am
♏	4/15	11:38am
♐	4/17	9:39pm
♑	4/20	5:37am
♒	4/22	11:06am
♓	4/24	1:59pm
♈	4/26	3:00pm
♉	4/28	3:34pm
♊	4/30	5:30pm
♋	5/2	10:24pm
♌	5/5	7:01am
♍	5/7	6:36pm
♎	5/10	7:10am
♏	5/12	6:42pm
♐	5/15	4:08am
♑	5/17	11:20am
♒	5/19	4:31pm
♓	5/21	8:02pm
♈	5/23	10:22pm
♉	5/26	12:21am
♊	5/28	3:06am
♋	5/30	7:55am
♌	6/1	3:45pm
♍	6/4	2:34am
♎	6/6	3:00pm
♏	6/9	2:46am
♐	6/11	12:06pm
♑	6/13	6:31pm
♒	6/15	10:38pm
♓	6/18	1:27am
♈	6/20	3:57am
♉	6/22	6:54am
♊	6/24	10:52am
♋	6/26	4:28pm
♌	6/29	12:19am
♍	7/1	10:43am
♎	7/3	10:59pm
♏	7/6	11:12am
♐	7/8	9:05pm
♑	7/11	3:27am
♒	7/13	6:41am
♓	7/15	8:12am
♈	7/17	9:38am
♉	7/19	12:17pm
♊	7/21	4:49pm
♋	7/23	11:20pm
♌	7/26	7:49am
♍	7/28	6:18pm
♎	7/31	6:30am
♏	8/2	7:09pm
♐	8/5	6:01am
♑	8/7	1:14pm
♒	8/9	4:32pm
♓	8/11	5:10pm
♈	8/13	5:09pm
♉	8/15	6:25pm
♊	8/17	10:14pm
♋	8/20	4:56am
♌	8/22	2:03pm
♍	8/25	12:57am
♎	8/27	1:13pm
♏	8/30	2:03am
♐	9/1	1:49pm
♑	9/3	10:27pm
♒	9/6	2:53am
♓	9/8	3:47am
♈	9/10	3:00am
♉	9/12	2:45am
♊	9/14	4:58am
♋	9/16	10:40am
♌	9/18	7:39pm
♍	9/21	6:53am
♎	9/23	7:19pm
♏	9/26	8:06am
♐	9/28	8:10pm
♑	10/1	5:57am
♒	10/3	12:04pm
♓	10/5	2:22pm
♈	10/7	2:06pm
♉	10/9	1:17pm
♊	10/11	2:02pm
♋	10/13	6:02pm
♌	10/16	1:53am
♍	10/18	12:52pm
♎	10/21	1:25am
♏	10/23	2:05pm
♐	10/26	1:50am
♑	10/28	11:47am
♒	10/30	7:02pm
♓	11/1	11:06pm
♈	11/4	12:27am
♉	11/6	12:25am
♊	11/8	12:50am
♋	11/10	3:32am
♌	11/12	9:49am
♍	11/14	7:48pm
♎	11/17	8:09am
♏	11/19	8:48pm
♐	11/22	8:09am
♑	11/24	5:26pm
♒	11/27	12:30am
♓	11/29	5:24am
♈	12/1	8:22am
♉	12/3	10:01am
♊	12/5	11:27am
♋	12/7	2:04pm
♌	12/9	7:19pm
♍	12/12	4:04am
♎	12/14	3:49pm
♏	12/17	4:34am
♐	12/19	3:54pm
♑	12/22	12:33am
♒	12/24	6:34am
♓	12/26	10:47am
♈	12/28	2:02pm
♉	12/30	4:55pm
	1901	
♊	1/1	7:54pm
♋	1/3	11:36pm
♌	1/6	4:59am
♍	1/8	1:04pm
♎	1/11	12:07am
♏	1/13	12:52pm
♐	1/16	12:43am
♑	1/18	9:30am
♒	1/20	2:48pm
♓	1/22	5:41pm
♈	1/24	7:45pm
♉	1/26	10:16pm
♊	1/29	1:54am
♋	1/31	6:50am
♌	2/2	1:12pm
♍	2/4	9:33pm
♎	2/7	8:18am
♏	2/9	8:56pm
♐	2/12	9:26am
♑	2/14	7:10pm
♒	2/17	12:50am
♓	2/19	3:06am
♈	2/21	3:44am
♉	2/23	4:41am
♊	2/25	7:22am
♋	2/27	12:20pm
♌	3/1	7:30pm
♍	3/4	4:37am
♎	3/6	3:37pm
♏	3/9	4:12am
♐	3/11	5:04pm
♑	3/14	3:56am
♒	3/16	10:56am
♓	3/18	1:52pm
♈	3/20	2:06pm
♉	3/22	1:41pm
♊	3/24	2:37pm
♋	3/26	6:15pm
♌	3/29	1:00am
♍	3/31	10:29am
♎	4/2	9:57pm
♏	4/5	10:38am
♐	4/7	11:31pm
♑	4/10	11:02am
♒	4/12	7:27pm
♓	4/14	11:56pm
♈	4/17	1:06am
♉	4/19	12:33am
♊	4/21	12:18am
♋	4/23	2:11am
♌	4/25	7:28am
♍	4/27	4:20pm
♎	4/30	3:54am
♏	5/2	4:44pm
♐	5/5	5:27am
♑	5/7	4:54pm
♒	5/10	1:58am
♓	5/12	7:55am
♈	5/14	10:43am
♉	5/16	11:16am
♊	5/18	11:07am
♋	5/20	12:03pm
♌	5/22	3:47pm
♍	5/24	11:18pm
♎	5/27	10:18am
♏	5/29	11:07pm
♐	6/1	11:44am
♑	6/3	10:43pm
♒	6/6	7:30am
♓	6/8	1:55pm
♈	6/10	6:01pm
♉	6/12	8:10pm
♊	6/14	9:10pm
♋	6/16	10:22pm
♌	6/19	1:23am
♍	6/21	7:41am
♎	6/23	5:42pm
♏	6/26	6:14am
♐	6/28	6:51pm
♑	7/1	5:31am
♒	7/3	1:34pm
♓	7/5	7:22pm
♈	7/7	11:36pm
♉	7/10	2:45am
♊	7/12	5:10am
♋	7/14	7:31am
♌	7/16	10:54am
♍	7/18	4:43pm
♎	7/21	1:55am
♏	7/23	2:00pm
♐	7/26	2:45am
♑	7/28	1:33pm
♒	7/30	9:09pm
♓	8/2	1:59am
♈	8/4	5:16am
♉	8/6	8:07am
♊	8/8	11:08am
♋	8/10	2:38pm
♌	8/12	7:04pm
♍	8/15	1:17am
♎	8/17	10:14am
♏	8/19	9:58pm
♐	8/22	10:54am
♑	8/24	10:18pm
♒	8/27	6:13am
♓	8/29	10:36am
♈	8/31	12:44pm
♉	9/2	2:17pm
♊	9/4	4:32pm
♋	9/6	8:11pm
♌	9/9	1:26am
♍	9/11	8:33am
♎	9/13	5:52pm
♏	9/16	5:31am
♐	9/18	6:33pm
♑	9/21	6:44am
♒	9/23	3:45pm
♓	9/25	8:43pm
♈	9/27	10:29pm
♉	9/29	10:47pm
♊	10/1	11:28pm
♋	10/4	1:54am
♌	10/6	6:52am
♍	10/8	2:28pm
♎	10/11	12:26am
♏	10/13	12:19pm
♐	10/16	1:22am
♑	10/18	2:01pm
♒	10/21	12:18am
♓	10/23	6:46am
♈	10/25	9:26am
♉	10/27	9:34am
♊	10/29	9:01am
♋	10/31	9:42am
♌	11/2	1:09pm
♍	11/4	8:06pm
♎	11/7	6:15am
♏	11/9	6:30pm
♐	11/12	7:32am
♑	11/14	8:09pm
♒	11/17	7:04am
♓	11/19	3:04pm
♈	11/21	7:31pm
♉	11/23	8:52pm
♊	11/25	8:24pm
♋	11/27	8:02pm
♌	11/29	9:44pm
♍	12/2	3:02am
♎	12/4	12:24pm
♏	12/7	12:38am
♐	12/9	1:45pm
♑	12/12	2:04am
♒	12/14	12:42pm
♓	12/16	9:12pm
♈	12/19	3:09am
♉	12/21	6:23am
♊	12/23	7:22am
♋	12/25	7:23am
♌	12/27	8:18am
♍	12/29	12:04pm
♎	12/31	7:56pm
	1902	
♏	1/3	7:30am
♐	1/5	8:36pm
♑	1/8	8:47am
♒	1/10	6:48pm
♓	1/13	2:40am
♈	1/15	8:44am
♉	1/17	1:06pm
♊	1/19	3:49pm
♋	1/21	5:21pm
♌	1/23	6:56pm
♍	1/25	10:16pm
♎	1/28	4:58am
♏	1/30	3:28pm
♐	2/2	4:17am
♑	2/4	4:38pm
♒	2/7	2:27am
♓	2/9	9:29am
♈	2/11	2:31pm
♉	2/13	6:26pm
♊	2/15	9:43pm
♋	2/18	12:37am
♌	2/20	3:37am
♍	2/22	7:44am
♎	2/24	2:18pm
♏	2/27	12:05am
♐	3/1	12:27pm
♑	3/4	1:04am
♒	3/6	11:22am
♓	3/8	6:16pm
♈	3/10	10:21pm
♉	3/13	12:55am
♊	3/15	3:13am
♋	3/17	6:04am
♌	3/19	9:54am
♍	3/21	3:12pm
♎	3/23	10:31pm
♏	3/26	8:20am
♐	3/28	8:24pm
♑	3/31	9:12am
♒	4/2	8:20pm
♓	4/5	4:03am
♈	4/7	8:11am
♉	4/9	9:50am
♊	4/11	10:37am
♋	4/13	12:04pm
♌	4/15	3:18pm
♍	4/17	8:57pm
♎	4/20	5:05am

Moon Sign Changes 1900-2005

♏	4/22	3:28pm
♐	4/25	3:36am
♑	4/27	4:26pm
♒	4/30	4:16am
♓	5/2	1:16pm
♈	5/4	6:30pm
♉	5/6	8:23pm
♊	5/8	8:21pm
♋	5/10	8:15pm
♌	5/12	9:54pm
♍	5/15	2:36am
♎	5/17	10:42am
♏	5/19	9:33pm
♐	5/22	9:58am
♑	5/24	10:47pm
♒	5/27	10:50am
♓	5/29	8:50pm
♈	6/1	3:35am
♉	6/3	6:46am
♊	6/5	7:10am
♋	6/7	6:26am
♌	6/9	6:39am
♍	6/11	9:44am
♎	6/13	4:45pm
♏	6/16	3:22am
♐	6/18	3:58pm
♑	6/21	4:46am
♒	6/23	4:37pm
♓	6/26	2:50am
♈	6/28	10:39am
♉	6/30	3:26pm
♊	7/2	5:14pm
♋	7/4	5:07pm
♌	7/6	4:54pm
♍	7/8	6:43pm
♎	7/11	12:16am
♏	7/13	9:56am
♐	7/15	10:17pm
♑	7/18	11:04am
♒	7/20	10:38pm
♓	7/23	8:24am
♈	7/25	4:15pm
♉	7/27	9:57pm
♊	7/30	1:16am
♋	8/1	2:34am
♌	8/3	3:06am
♍	8/5	4:43am
♎	8/7	9:15am
♏	8/9	5:43pm
♐	8/12	5:26am
♑	8/14	6:10pm
♒	8/17	5:38am
♓	8/19	2:51pm
♈	8/21	9:57pm
♉	8/24	3:20am
♊	8/26	7:13am
♋	8/28	9:50am
♌	8/30	11:45am
♍	9/1	2:13pm
♎	9/3	6:42pm
♏	9/6	2:26am
♐	9/8	1:25pm

♑	9/11	2:01am
♒	9/13	1:44pm
♓	9/15	10:53pm
♈	9/18	5:14am
♉	9/20	9:31am
♊	9/22	12:39pm
♋	9/24	3:23pm
♌	9/26	6:16pm
♍	9/28	9:58pm
♎	10/1	3:19am
♏	10/3	11:07am
♐	10/5	9:40pm
♑	10/8	10:06am
♒	10/10	10:19pm
♓	10/13	8:07am
♈	10/15	2:30pm
♉	10/17	5:56pm
♊	10/19	7:40pm
♋	10/21	9:10pm
♌	10/23	11:39pm
♍	10/26	3:53am
♎	10/28	10:14am
♏	10/30	6:46pm
♐	11/2	5:26am
♑	11/4	5:44pm
♒	11/7	6:22am
♓	11/9	5:16pm
♈	11/12	12:44am
♉	11/14	4:24am
♊	11/16	5:19am
♋	11/18	5:14am
♌	11/20	6:06am
♍	11/22	9:24am
♎	11/24	3:49pm
♏	11/27	1:01am
♐	11/29	12:12pm
♑	12/2	12:33am
♒	12/4	1:16pm
♓	12/7	1:01am
♈	12/9	10:03am
♉	12/11	3:11pm
♊	12/13	4:38pm
♋	12/15	3:55pm
♌	12/17	3:13pm
♍	12/19	4:40pm
♎	12/21	9:46pm
♏	12/24	6:39am
♐	12/26	6:09pm
♑	12/29	6:44am
♒	12/31	7:20pm
	1903	
♓	1/3	7:12am
♈	1/5	5:14pm
♉	1/8	12:09am
♊	1/10	3:19am
♋	1/12	3:28am
♌	1/14	2:27am
♍	1/16	2:32am
♎	1/18	5:47am
♏	1/20	1:14pm
♐	1/23	12:15am
♑	1/25	12:55pm

♒	1/28	1:27am
♓	1/30	12:55pm
♈	2/1	10:52pm
♉	2/4	6:36am
♊	2/6	11:27am
♋	2/8	1:25pm
♌	2/10	1:33pm
♍	2/12	1:41pm
♎	2/14	3:53pm
♏	2/16	9:43pm
♐	2/19	7:29am
♑	2/21	7:46pm
♒	2/24	8:20am
♓	2/26	7:31pm
♈	3/1	4:45am
♉	3/3	12:00pm
♊	3/5	5:16pm
♋	3/7	8:34pm
♌	3/9	10:23pm
♍	3/11	11:47pm
♎	3/14	2:18am
♏	3/16	7:26am
♐	3/18	4:01pm
♑	3/21	3:33am
♒	3/23	4:06pm
♓	3/26	3:24am
♈	3/28	12:13pm
♉	3/30	6:29pm
♊	4/1	10:50pm
♋	4/4	2:00am
♌	4/6	4:39am
♍	4/8	7:27am
♎	4/10	11:11am
♏	4/12	4:45pm
♐	4/15	12:56am
♑	4/17	11:49am
♒	4/20	12:15am
♓	4/22	12:01pm
♈	4/24	9:07pm
♉	4/27	2:55am
♊	4/29	6:07am
♋	5/1	8:02am
♌	5/3	10:02am
♍	5/5	1:08pm
♎	5/7	5:52pm
♏	5/10	12:26am
♐	5/12	9:02am
♑	5/14	7:46pm
♒	5/17	8:05am
♓	5/19	8:21pm
♈	5/22	6:22am
♉	5/24	12:40pm
♊	5/26	3:27pm
♋	5/28	4:10pm
♌	5/30	4:42pm
♍	6/1	6:45pm
♎	6/3	11:18pm
♏	6/6	6:28am
♐	6/8	3:46pm
♑	6/11	2:47am
♒	6/13	3:06pm
♓	6/16	3:42am

♈	6/18	2:43pm
♉	6/20	10:17pm
♊	6/23	1:46am
♋	6/25	2:12am
♌	6/27	1:35am
♍	6/29	2:04am
♎	7/1	5:19am
♏	7/3	11:58am
♐	7/5	9:31pm
♑	7/8	8:56am
♒	7/10	9:21pm
♓	7/13	9:59am
♈	7/15	9:36pm
♉	7/18	6:28am
♊	7/20	11:26am
♋	7/22	12:47pm
♌	7/24	12:06pm
♍	7/26	11:33am
♎	7/28	1:13pm
♏	7/30	6:27pm
♐	8/2	3:21am
♑	8/4	2:49pm
♒	8/7	3:21am
♓	8/9	3:50pm
♈	8/12	3:23am
♉	8/14	12:52pm
♊	8/16	7:15pm
♋	8/18	10:12pm
♌	8/20	10:37pm
♍	8/22	10:13pm
♎	8/24	11:01pm
♏	8/27	2:46am
♐	8/29	10:21am
♑	8/31	9:14pm
♒	9/3	9:45am
♓	9/5	10:07pm
♈	9/8	9:12am
♉	9/10	6:22pm
♊	9/13	1:11am
♋	9/15	5:27am
♌	9/17	7:30am
♍	9/19	8:20am
♎	9/21	9:28am
♏	9/23	12:33pm
♐	9/25	6:53pm
♑	9/28	4:45am
♒	9/30	4:59pm
♓	10/3	5:24am
♈	10/5	4:11pm
♉	10/8	12:34am
♊	10/10	6:41am
♋	10/12	11:00am
♌	10/14	2:03pm
♍	10/16	4:24pm
♎	10/18	6:49pm
♏	10/20	10:23pm
♐	10/23	4:15am
♑	10/25	1:14pm
♒	10/28	12:58am
♓	10/30	1:35pm
♈	11/2	12:36am
♉	11/4	8:36am

♊	11/6	1:39pm
♋	11/8	4:50pm
♌	11/10	7:24pm
♍	11/12	10:16pm
♎	11/15	1:55am
♏	11/17	6:41am
♐	11/19	1:06pm
♑	11/21	9:50pm
♒	11/24	9:09am
♓	11/26	9:55pm
♈	11/29	9:42am
♉	12/1	6:14pm
♊	12/3	10:56pm
♋	12/6	12:55am
♌	12/8	1:58am
♍	12/10	3:47am
♎	12/12	7:22am
♏	12/14	12:56pm
♐	12/16	8:19pm
♑	12/19	5:34am
♒	12/21	4:48pm
♓	12/24	5:35am
♈	12/26	6:08pm
♉	12/29	3:57am
♊	12/31	9:33am
	1904	
♋	1/2	11:24am
♌	1/4	11:18am
♍	1/6	11:23am
♎	1/8	1:25pm
♏	1/10	6:20pm
♐	1/13	2:03am
♑	1/15	11:58am
♒	1/17	11:32pm
♓	1/20	12:18pm
♈	1/23	1:10am
♉	1/25	12:09pm
♊	1/27	7:26pm
♋	1/29	10:32pm
♌	1/31	10:38pm
♍	2/2	9:45pm
♎	2/4	10:01pm
♏	2/7	1:08am
♐	2/9	7:49am
♑	2/11	5:41pm
♒	2/14	5:36am
♓	2/16	6:27pm
♈	2/19	7:10am
♉	2/21	6:31pm
♊	2/24	3:05am
♋	2/26	8:00am
♌	2/28	9:36am
♍	3/1	9:16am
♎	3/3	8:53am
♏	3/5	10:24am
♐	3/7	3:18pm
♑	3/10	12:03am
♒	3/12	11:47am
♓	3/15	12:43am
♈	3/17	1:13pm
♉	3/20	12:09am
♊	3/22	8:52am

♋	3/24	2:55pm
♌	3/26	6:16pm
♍	3/28	7:31pm
♎	3/30	7:54pm
♏	4/1	9:04pm
♐	4/4	12:41am
♑	4/6	7:57am
♒	4/8	6:49pm
♓	4/11	7:38am
♈	4/13	8:04pm
♉	4/16	6:31am
♊	4/18	2:31pm
♋	4/20	8:22pm
♌	4/23	12:27am
♍	4/25	3:10am
♎	4/27	5:05am
♏	4/29	7:07am
♐	5/1	10:36am
♑	5/3	4:58pm
♒	5/6	2:50am
♓	5/8	3:17pm
♈	5/11	3:51am
♉	5/13	2:12pm
♊	5/15	9:30pm
♋	5/18	2:21am
♌	5/20	5:50am
♍	5/22	8:49am
♎	5/24	11:48am
♏	5/26	3:08pm
♐	5/28	7:29pm
♑	5/31	1:53am
♒	6/2	11:13am
♓	6/4	11:15pm
♈	6/7	12:02pm
♉	6/9	10:50pm
♊	6/12	6:06am
♋	6/14	10:10am
♌	6/16	12:26pm
♍	6/18	2:26pm
♎	6/20	5:11pm
♏	6/22	9:09pm
♐	6/25	2:31am
♑	6/27	9:40am
♒	6/29	7:07pm
♓	7/2	6:58am
♈	7/4	7:55pm
♉	7/7	7:29am
♊	7/9	3:32pm
♋	7/11	7:41pm
♌	7/13	9:10pm
♍	7/15	9:48pm
♎	7/17	11:14pm
♏	7/20	2:34am
♐	7/22	8:10am
♑	7/24	4:01pm
♒	7/27	2:01am
♓	7/29	1:58pm
♈	8/1	2:59am
♉	8/3	3:13pm
♊	8/6	12:30am
♋	8/8	5:44pm
♌	8/10	7:30am

Moon Sign Changes 1900-2005

♍	8/12	7:25am
♎	8/14	7:25am
♏	8/16	9:12am
♐	8/18	1:51pm
♑	8/20	9:37pm
♒	8/23	8:02am
♓	8/25	8:16pm
♈	8/28	9:17am
♉	8/30	9:44pm
♊	9/2	7:59am
♋	9/4	2:46pm
♌	9/6	5:53pm
♍	9/8	6:18pm
♎	9/10	5:44pm
♏	9/12	6:05pm
♐	9/14	9:05pm
♑	9/17	3:45am
♒	9/19	1:55pm
♓	9/22	2:20am
♈	9/24	3:20pm
♉	9/27	3:33am
♊	9/29	1:59pm
♋	10/1	9:50pm
♌	10/4	2:38am
♍	10/6	4:36am
♎	10/8	4:45am
♏	10/10	4:43am
♐	10/12	6:25am
♑	10/14	11:31am
♒	10/16	8:39pm
♓	10/19	8:50am
♈	10/21	9:51pm
♉	10/24	9:44am
♊	10/26	7:38pm
♋	10/29	3:24am
♌	10/31	9:04am
♍	11/2	12:40pm
♎	11/4	2:27pm
♏	11/6	3:20pm
♐	11/8	4:54pm
♑	11/10	8:56pm
♒	11/13	4:47am
♓	11/15	4:14pm
♈	11/18	5:14am
♉	11/20	5:06pm
♊	11/23	2:25am
♋	11/25	9:17am
♌	11/27	2:26pm
♍	11/29	6:27pm
♎	12/1	9:33pm
♏	12/4	12:01am
♐	12/6	2:38am
♑	12/8	6:46am
♒	12/10	1:53pm
♓	12/13	12:30am
♈	12/15	1:19pm
♉	12/18	1:33am
♊	12/20	10:57am
♋	12/22	5:08pm
♌	12/24	9:04pm
♍	12/27	12:01am
♎	12/29	2:56am
♏	12/31	6:12am
	1905	
♐	1/2	10:08am
♑	1/4	3:20pm
♒	1/6	10:43pm
♓	1/9	8:57am
♈	1/11	9:29pm
♉	1/14	10:11am
♊	1/16	8:25pm
♋	1/19	2:56am
♌	1/21	6:13am
♍	1/23	7:46am
♎	1/25	9:09am
♏	1/27	11:35am
♐	1/29	3:44pm
♑	1/31	9:51pm
♒	2/3	6:08am
♓	2/5	4:39pm
♈	2/8	5:03am
♉	2/10	6:00pm
♊	2/13	5:17am
♋	2/15	1:05pm
♌	2/17	5:00pm
♍	2/19	6:05pm
♎	2/21	6:03pm
♏	2/23	6:42pm
♐	2/25	9:31pm
♑	2/28	3:19am
♒	3/2	12:05pm
♓	3/4	11:12pm
♈	3/7	11:46am
♉	3/10	12:42am
♊	3/12	12:35pm
♋	3/14	9:48pm
♌	3/17	3:19am
♍	3/19	5:18am
♎	3/21	5:03am
♏	3/23	4:26am
♐	3/25	5:26am
♑	3/27	9:40am
♒	3/29	5:47pm
♓	4/1	5:03am
♈	4/3	5:52pm
♉	4/6	6:44am
♊	4/8	6:35pm
♋	4/11	4:28am
♌	4/13	11:30am
♍	4/15	3:13pm
♎	4/17	4:04pm
♏	4/19	3:30pm
♐	4/21	3:28pm
♑	4/23	6:04pm
♒	4/26	12:41am
♓	4/28	11:15am
♈	5/1	12:03am
♉	5/3	12:52pm
♊	5/6	12:21am
♋	5/8	10:01am
♌	5/10	5:34pm
♍	5/12	10:40pm
♎	5/15	1:12am
♏	5/17	1:50am
♐	5/19	2:05am
♑	5/21	3:56am
♒	5/23	9:12am
♓	5/25	6:34pm
♈	5/28	6:53am
♉	5/30	7:41pm
♊	6/2	6:55am
♋	6/4	3:57pm
♌	6/6	10:59pm
♍	6/9	4:17am
♎	6/11	7:53am
♏	6/13	10:00am
♐	6/15	11:29am
♑	6/17	1:46pm
♒	6/19	6:33pm
♓	6/22	2:57am
♈	6/24	2:33pm
♉	6/27	3:16am
♊	6/29	2:37pm
♋	7/1	11:17pm
♌	7/4	5:27am
♍	7/6	9:53am
♎	7/8	1:16pm
♏	7/10	4:04pm
♐	7/12	6:46pm
♑	7/14	10:12pm
♒	7/17	3:29am
♓	7/19	11:36am
♈	7/21	10:39pm
♉	7/24	11:16am
♊	7/26	11:01pm
♋	7/29	8:00am
♌	7/31	1:47pm
♍	8/2	5:09pm
♎	8/4	7:20pm
♏	8/6	9:28pm
♐	8/9	12:24am
♑	8/11	4:45am
♒	8/13	11:00am
♓	8/15	7:34pm
♈	8/18	6:30am
♉	8/20	7:02pm
♊	8/23	7:18am
♋	8/25	5:12pm
♌	8/27	11:31pm
♍	8/30	2:32am
♎	9/1	3:32am
♏	9/3	4:12am
♐	9/5	6:04am
♑	9/7	10:13am
♒	9/9	5:02pm
♓	9/12	2:20am
♈	9/14	1:35pm
♉	9/17	2:05am
♊	9/19	2:40pm
♋	9/22	1:37am
♌	9/24	9:17am
♍	9/26	1:06pm
♎	9/28	1:54pm
♏	9/30	1:22pm
♐	10/2	1:35pm
♑	10/4	4:20pm
♒	10/6	10:36pm
♓	10/9	8:09am
♈	10/11	7:49pm
♉	10/14	8:25am
♊	10/16	8:59pm
♋	10/19	8:29am
♌	10/21	5:33pm
♍	10/23	11:03pm
♎	10/26	12:55am
♏	10/28	12:24am
♐	10/29	11:33pm
♑	11/1	12:37am
♒	11/3	5:19am
♓	11/5	2:05pm
♈	11/8	1:48am
♉	11/10	2:32pm
♊	11/13	2:54am
♋	11/15	2:14pm
♌	11/17	11:50pm
♍	11/20	6:47am
♎	11/22	10:29am
♏	11/24	11:18am
♐	11/26	10:47am
♑	11/28	11:03am
♒	11/30	2:11pm
♓	12/2	9:26pm
♈	12/5	8:24am
♉	12/7	9:06pm
♊	12/10	9:24am
♋	12/12	8:14pm
♌	12/15	5:19am
♍	12/17	12:30pm
♎	12/19	5:25pm
♏	12/21	8:01pm
♐	12/23	9:00pm
♑	12/25	9:53pm
♒	12/28	12:32am
♓	12/30	6:30am
	1906	
♈	1/1	4:16pm
♉	1/4	4:33am
♊	1/6	4:58pm
♋	1/9	3:38am
♌	1/11	11:57am
♍	1/13	6:11pm
♎	1/15	10:48pm
♏	1/18	2:07am
♐	1/20	4:36am
♑	1/22	6:59am
♒	1/24	10:26am
♓	1/26	4:13pm
♈	1/29	1:06am
♉	1/31	12:45pm
♊	2/3	1:17am
♋	2/5	12:21pm
♌	2/7	8:32pm
♍	2/10	1:50am
♎	2/12	5:07am
♏	2/14	7:34am
♐	2/16	10:08am
♑	2/18	1:32pm
♒	2/20	6:17pm
♓	2/23	12:52am
♈	2/25	9:45am
♉	2/27	8:58pm
♊	3/2	9:31am
♋	3/4	9:19pm
♌	3/7	6:16am
♍	3/9	11:33am
♎	3/11	1:53pm
♏	3/13	2:48pm
♐	3/15	4:01pm
♑	3/17	6:54pm
♒	3/20	12:06am
♓	3/22	7:38am
♈	3/24	5:10pm
♉	3/27	4:27am
♊	3/29	4:58pm
♋	4/1	5:20am
♌	4/3	3:31pm
♍	4/5	9:53pm
♎	4/8	12:25am
♏	4/10	12:29am
♐	4/12	12:08am
♑	4/14	1:23am
♒	4/16	5:39am
♓	4/18	1:10pm
♈	4/20	11:15pm
♉	4/23	10:56am
♊	4/25	11:28pm
♋	4/28	12:02pm
♌	4/30	11:09pm
♍	5/3	7:03am
♎	5/5	10:53am
♏	5/7	11:23am
♐	5/9	10:25am
♑	5/11	10:12am
♒	5/13	12:45pm
♓	5/15	7:06pm
♈	5/18	4:54am
♉	5/20	4:49pm
♊	5/23	5:27am
♋	5/25	5:54pm
♌	5/28	5:14am
♍	5/30	2:10pm
♎	6/1	7:38pm
♏	6/3	9:35pm
♐	6/5	9:15pm
♑	6/7	8:40pm
♒	6/9	9:55pm
♓	6/12	2:40am
♈	6/14	11:20am
♉	6/16	10:55pm
♊	6/19	11:35am
♋	6/21	11:51pm
♌	6/24	10:49am
♍	6/26	7:50pm
♎	6/29	2:13am
♏	7/1	5:43am
♐	7/3	6:53am
♑	7/5	7:06am
♒	7/7	8:12am
♓	7/9	11:52am
♈	7/11	7:12pm
♉	7/14	5:55am
♊	7/16	6:25pm
♋	7/19	6:37am
♌	7/21	5:09pm
♍	7/24	1:29am
♎	7/26	7:38am
♏	7/28	11:46am
♐	7/30	2:17pm
♑	8/1	3:58pm
♒	8/3	5:57pm
♓	8/5	9:36pm
♈	8/8	4:07am
♉	8/10	1:55pm
♊	8/13	2:03am
♋	8/15	2:23pm
♌	8/18	12:50am
♍	8/20	8:31am
♎	8/22	1:40pm
♏	8/24	5:10pm
♐	8/26	7:55pm
♑	8/28	10:38pm
♒	8/31	1:56am
♓	9/2	6:28am
♈	9/4	1:04pm
♉	9/6	10:21pm
♊	9/9	10:05am
♋	9/11	10:40pm
♌	9/14	9:37am
♍	9/16	5:18pm
♎	9/18	9:39pm
♏	9/20	11:53pm
♐	9/23	1:35am
♑	9/25	4:02am
♒	9/27	7:58am
♓	9/29	1:34pm
♈	10/1	8:56pm
♉	10/4	6:20am
♊	10/6	5:52pm
♋	10/9	6:38am
♌	10/11	6:27pm
♍	10/14	3:02am
♎	10/16	7:34am
♏	10/18	9:00am
♐	10/20	9:14am
♑	10/22	10:14am
♒	10/24	1:24pm
♓	10/26	7:11pm
♈	10/29	3:18am
♉	10/31	1:18pm
♊	11/3	12:56am
♋	11/5	1:43pm
♌	11/8	2:13am
♍	11/10	12:10pm
♎	11/12	6:00pm
♏	11/14	7:53pm
♐	11/16	7:29pm
♑	11/18	6:58pm
♒	11/20	8:23pm
♓	11/23	12:59am
♈	11/25	8:53am
♉	11/27	7:17pm
♊	11/30	7:15am

Moon Sign Changes 1900-2005

Sign	Date	Time
♋	12/2	8:01pm
♌	12/5	8:37am
♍	12/7	7:30pm
♎	12/10	3:00am
♏	12/12	6:31am
♐	12/14	6:55am
♑	12/16	6:02am
♒	12/18	6:03am
♓	12/20	8:48am
♈	12/22	3:17pm
♉	12/25	1:15am
♊	12/27	1:23pm
♋	12/30	2:11am
	1907	
♌	1/1	2:29pm
♍	1/4	1:19am
♎	1/6	9:41am
♏	1/8	2:55pm
♐	1/10	5:07pm
♑	1/12	5:21pm
♒	1/14	5:20pm
♓	1/16	6:55pm
♈	1/18	11:42pm
♉	1/21	8:21am
♊	1/23	8:04pm
♋	1/26	8:56am
♌	1/28	9:00pm
♍	1/31	7:12am
♎	2/2	3:10pm
♏	2/4	8:55pm
♐	2/7	12:34am
♑	2/9	2:35am
♒	2/11	3:50am
♓	2/13	5:41am
♈	2/15	9:39am
♉	2/17	4:58pm
♊	2/20	3:46am
♋	2/22	4:30pm
♌	2/25	4:41am
♍	2/27	2:28pm
♎	3/1	9:31pm
♏	3/4	2:26am
♐	3/6	6:04am
♑	3/8	9:03am
♒	3/10	11:50am
♓	3/12	2:56pm
♈	3/14	7:20pm
♉	3/17	2:10am
♊	3/19	12:10pm
♋	3/22	12:36am
♌	3/24	1:07pm
♍	3/26	11:10pm
♎	3/29	5:46am
♏	3/31	9:33am
♐	4/2	11:59am
♑	4/4	2:24pm
♒	4/6	5:35pm
♓	4/8	9:47pm
♈	4/11	3:16am
♉	4/13	10:36am
♊	4/15	8:24pm
♋	4/18	8:34am
♌	4/20	9:25pm
♍	4/23	8:17am
♎	4/25	3:22pm
♏	4/27	6:47pm
♐	4/29	8:02pm
♑	5/1	8:59pm
♒	5/3	11:07pm
♓	5/6	3:12am
♈	5/8	9:20am
♉	5/10	5:29pm
♊	5/13	3:41am
♋	5/15	3:50pm
♌	5/18	4:52am
♍	5/20	4:37pm
♎	5/23	12:54am
♏	5/25	5:03am
♐	5/27	6:05am
♑	5/29	5:54am
♒	5/31	6:26am
♓	6/2	9:10am
♈	6/4	2:46pm
♉	6/6	11:12pm
♊	6/9	9:55am
♋	6/11	10:16pm
♌	6/14	11:21am
♍	6/16	11:35pm
♎	6/19	9:05am
♏	6/21	2:43pm
♐	6/23	4:42pm
♑	6/25	4:30pm
♒	6/27	4:00pm
♓	6/29	5:07pm
♈	7/1	9:14pm
♉	7/4	4:56am
♊	7/6	3:41pm
♋	7/9	4:16am
♌	7/11	5:18pm
♍	7/14	5:29am
♎	7/16	3:34pm
♏	7/18	10:34pm
♐	7/21	2:11am
♑	7/23	3:06am
♒	7/25	2:46am
♓	7/27	3:00am
♈	7/29	5:37am
♉	7/31	11:53am
♊	8/2	9:56pm
♋	8/5	10:27am
♌	8/7	11:26pm
♍	8/10	11:16am
♎	8/12	9:07pm
♏	8/15	4:35am
♐	8/17	9:31am
♑	8/19	12:05pm
♒	8/21	1:00pm
♓	8/23	1:33pm
♈	8/25	3:28pm
♉	8/27	8:26pm
♊	8/30	5:19am
♋	9/1	5:22pm
♌	9/4	6:20am
♍	9/6	5:56pm
♎	9/9	3:07am
♏	9/11	10:01am
♐	9/13	3:07pm
♑	9/15	6:46pm
♒	9/17	9:12pm
♓	9/19	11:02pm
♈	9/22	1:25am
♉	9/24	5:55am
♊	9/26	1:49pm
♋	9/29	1:09am
♌	10/1	2:05pm
♍	10/4	1:49am
♎	10/6	10:39am
♏	10/8	4:38pm
♐	10/10	8:47pm
♑	10/13	12:07am
♒	10/15	3:13am
♓	10/17	6:20am
♈	10/19	9:57am
♉	10/21	3:00pm
♊	10/23	10:39pm
♋	10/26	9:25am
♌	10/28	10:14pm
♍	10/31	10:28am
♎	11/2	7:43pm
♏	11/5	1:23am
♐	11/7	4:25am
♑	11/9	6:24am
♒	11/11	8:38am
♓	11/13	11:52am
♈	11/15	4:24pm
♉	11/17	10:31pm
♊	11/20	6:43am
♋	11/22	5:24pm
♌	11/25	6:04am
♍	11/27	6:50pm
♎	11/30	5:09am
♏	12/2	11:35am
♐	12/4	2:28pm
♑	12/6	3:18pm
♒	12/8	3:53pm
♓	12/10	5:44pm
♈	12/12	9:48pm
♉	12/15	4:24am
♊	12/17	1:25pm
♋	12/20	12:31am
♌	12/22	1:09pm
♍	12/25	2:06am
♎	12/27	1:27pm
♏	12/29	9:26pm
	1908	
♐	1/1	1:28am
♑	1/3	2:25am
♒	1/5	1:58am
♓	1/7	2:03am
♈	1/9	4:24am
♉	1/11	10:05am
♊	1/13	7:10pm
♋	1/16	6:45am
♌	1/18	7:33pm
♍	1/21	8:23am
♎	1/23	8:03pm
♏	1/26	5:17am
♐	1/28	11:08am
♑	1/30	1:33pm
♒	2/1	1:32pm
♓	2/3	12:50pm
♈	2/5	1:31pm
♉	2/7	5:24pm
♊	2/10	1:23am
♋	2/12	12:48pm
♌	2/15	1:46am
♍	2/17	2:28pm
♎	2/20	1:48am
♏	2/22	11:14am
♐	2/24	6:15pm
♑	2/26	10:28pm
♒	2/29	12:04am
♓	3/2	12:05am
♈	3/4	12:20am
♉	3/6	2:50am
♊	3/8	9:13am
♋	3/10	7:39pm
♌	3/13	8:28am
♍	3/15	9:09pm
♎	3/18	8:04am
♏	3/20	4:52pm
♐	3/22	11:45pm
♑	3/25	4:48am
♒	3/27	7:57am
♓	3/29	9:33am
♈	3/31	10:41am
♉	4/2	1:04pm
♊	4/4	6:26pm
♋	4/7	3:43am
♌	4/9	3:58pm
♍	4/12	4:41am
♎	4/14	3:33pm
♏	4/16	11:44pm
♐	4/19	5:41am
♑	4/21	10:10am
♒	4/23	1:40pm
♓	4/25	4:25pm
♈	4/27	6:57pm
♉	4/29	10:16pm
♊	5/2	3:44am
♋	5/4	12:23pm
♌	5/7	12:01am
♍	5/9	12:46pm
♎	5/12	12:00am
♏	5/14	8:12am
♐	5/16	1:26pm
♑	5/18	4:44pm
♒	5/20	7:14pm
♓	5/22	9:49pm
♈	5/25	1:03am
♉	5/27	5:30am
♊	5/29	11:48am
♋	5/31	8:37pm
♌	6/3	7:59am
♍	6/5	8:42pm
♎	6/8	8:33am
♏	6/10	5:30pm
♐	6/12	10:52pm
♑	6/15	1:25am
♒	6/17	2:35am
♓	6/19	3:51am
♈	6/21	6:27am
♉	6/23	11:09am
♊	6/25	6:16pm
♋	6/28	3:44am
♌	6/30	3:14pm
♍	7/3	3:58am
♎	7/5	4:20pm
♏	7/8	2:23am
♐	7/10	8:49am
♑	7/12	11:40am
♒	7/14	12:07pm
♓	7/16	11:58am
♈	7/18	1:02pm
♉	7/20	4:46pm
♊	7/22	11:48pm
♋	7/25	9:44am
♌	7/27	9:38pm
♍	7/30	10:24am
♎	8/1	10:56pm
♏	8/4	9:53am
♐	8/6	5:47pm
♑	8/8	9:56pm
♒	8/10	10:53pm
♓	8/12	10:09pm
♈	8/14	9:49pm
♉	8/16	11:55pm
♊	8/19	5:48am
♋	8/21	3:26pm
♌	8/24	3:32am
♍	8/26	4:23pm
♎	8/29	4:47am
♏	8/31	3:55pm
♐	9/3	12:52am
♑	9/5	6:40am
♒	9/7	9:06am
♓	9/9	9:04am
♈	9/11	8:22am
♉	9/13	9:11am
♊	9/15	1:27pm
♋	9/17	9:57pm
♌	9/20	9:42am
♍	9/22	10:34pm
♎	9/25	10:46am
♏	9/27	9:30pm
♐	9/30	6:28am
♑	10/2	1:12pm
♒	10/4	5:16pm
♓	10/6	6:49pm
♈	10/8	7:01pm
♉	10/10	7:43pm
♊	10/12	10:55pm
♋	10/15	6:00am
♌	10/17	4:51pm
♍	10/20	5:32am
♎	10/22	5:43pm
♏	10/25	3:59am
♐	10/27	12:12pm
♑	10/29	6:34pm
♒	10/31	11:12pm
♓	11/3	2:10am
♈	11/5	3:58am
♉	11/7	5:43am
♊	11/9	9:00am
♋	11/11	3:18pm
♌	11/14	1:07am
♍	11/16	1:23pm
♎	11/19	1:44am
♏	11/21	12:04pm
♐	11/23	7:39pm
♑	11/26	12:55am
♒	11/28	4:40am
♓	11/30	7:39am
♈	12/2	10:26am
♉	12/4	1:37pm
♊	12/6	6:01pm
♋	12/9	12:33am
♌	12/11	9:52am
♍	12/13	9:38pm
♎	12/16	10:12am
♏	12/18	9:12pm
♐	12/21	5:02am
♑	12/23	9:38am
♒	12/25	12:01pm
♓	12/27	1:38pm
♈	12/29	3:48pm
♉	12/31	7:24pm
	1909	
♊	1/3	12:54am
♋	1/5	8:24am
♌	1/7	6:01pm
♍	1/10	5:34am
♎	1/12	6:11pm
♏	1/15	6:02am
♐	1/17	3:01pm
♑	1/19	8:09pm
♒	1/21	10:00pm
♓	1/23	10:09pm
♈	1/25	10:36pm
♉	1/28	1:02am
♊	1/30	6:22am
♋	2/1	2:32pm
♌	2/4	12:50am
♍	2/6	12:35pm
♎	2/9	1:10am
♏	2/11	1:30pm
♐	2/13	11:48pm
♑	2/16	6:27am
♒	2/18	9:08am
♓	2/20	9:00am
♈	2/22	8:08am
♉	2/24	8:44am
♊	2/26	12:33pm
♋	2/28	8:08pm
♌	3/3	6:41am
♍	3/5	6:48pm
♎	3/8	7:23am
♏	3/10	7:40pm
♐	3/13	6:37am
♑	3/15	2:46pm
♒	3/17	7:09pm
♓	3/19	8:08pm

Moon Sign Changes 1900-2005

♈	3/21	7:17pm
♉	3/23	6:50pm
♊	3/25	8:55pm
♋	3/28	2:55am
♌	3/30	12:43pm
♍	4/2	12:51am
♎	4/4	1:31pm
♏	4/7	1:33am
♐	4/9	12:17pm
♑	4/11	8:57pm
♒	4/14	2:44am
♓	4/16	5:25am
♈	4/18	5:51am
♉	4/20	5:43am
♊	4/22	7:02am
♋	4/24	11:35am
♌	4/26	8:02pm
♍	4/29	7:33am
♎	5/1	8:11pm
♏	5/4	8:04am
♐	5/6	6:16pm
♑	5/9	2:26am
♒	5/11	8:26am
♓	5/13	12:14pm
♈	5/15	2:13pm
♉	5/17	3:24pm
♊	5/19	5:13pm
♋	5/21	9:15pm
♌	5/24	4:36am
♍	5/26	3:14pm
♎	5/29	3:39am
♏	5/31	3:37pm
♐	6/3	1:32am
♑	6/5	8:54am
♒	6/7	2:03pm
♓	6/9	5:40pm
♈	6/11	8:21pm
♉	6/13	10:50pm
♊	6/16	1:53am
♋	6/18	6:28am
♌	6/20	1:32pm
♍	6/22	11:29pm
♎	6/25	11:36am
♏	6/27	11:52pm
♐	6/30	10:03am
♑	7/2	5:04pm
♒	7/4	9:14pm
♓	7/6	11:41pm
♈	7/9	1:45am
♉	7/11	4:29am
♊	7/13	8:30am
♋	7/15	2:07pm
♌	7/17	9:41pm
♍	7/20	7:32am
♎	7/22	7:26pm
♏	7/25	8:01am
♐	7/27	7:00pm
♑	7/30	2:32am
♒	8/1	6:21am
♓	8/3	7:42am
♈	8/5	8:22am
♉	8/7	10:05am
♊	8/9	1:55pm
♋	8/11	8:08pm
♌	8/14	4:29am
♍	8/16	2:42pm
♎	8/19	2:36am
♏	8/21	3:24pm
♐	8/24	3:16am
♑	8/26	12:01pm
♒	8/28	4:37pm
♓	8/30	5:45pm
♈	9/1	5:19pm
♉	9/3	5:27pm
♊	9/5	7:55pm
♋	9/8	1:35am
♌	9/10	10:11am
♍	9/12	8:54pm
♎	9/15	9:00am
♏	9/17	9:49pm
♐	9/20	10:11am
♑	9/22	8:13pm
♒	9/25	2:22am
♓	9/27	4:32am
♈	9/29	4:07am
♉	10/1	3:14am
♊	10/3	4:04am
♋	10/5	8:09am
♌	10/7	3:58pm
♍	10/10	2:42am
♎	10/12	3:01pm
♏	10/15	3:46am
♐	10/17	4:02pm
♑	10/20	2:37am
♒	10/22	10:13am
♓	10/24	2:09pm
♈	10/26	3:01pm
♉	10/28	2:27pm
♊	10/30	2:27pm
♋	11/1	4:57pm
♌	11/3	11:10pm
♍	11/6	9:04am
♎	11/8	9:19pm
♏	11/11	10:04am
♐	11/13	9:57pm
♑	11/16	8:09am
♒	11/18	4:05pm
♓	11/20	9:20pm
♈	11/23	12:02am
♉	11/25	12:57am
♊	11/27	1:31am
♋	11/29	3:26am
♌	12/1	8:17am
♍	12/3	4:50pm
♎	12/6	4:30am
♏	12/8	5:17pm
♐	12/11	5:01am
♑	12/13	2:31pm
♒	12/15	9:39pm
♓	12/18	2:48am
♈	12/20	6:25am
♉	12/22	8:57am
♊	12/24	11:04am
♋	12/26	1:45pm
♌	12/28	6:17pm
♍	12/31	1:49am
	1910	
♎	1/2	12:37pm
♏	1/5	1:19am
♐	1/7	1:20pm
♑	1/9	10:40pm
♒	1/12	4:53am
♓	1/14	8:50am
♈	1/16	11:46am
♉	1/18	2:38pm
♊	1/20	5:58pm
♋	1/22	10:02pm
♌	1/25	3:24am
♍	1/27	10:52am
♎	1/29	9:05pm
♏	2/1	9:33am
♐	2/3	10:05pm
♑	2/6	8:03am
♒	2/8	2:14pm
♓	2/10	5:13pm
♈	2/12	6:41pm
♉	2/14	8:20pm
♊	2/16	11:19pm
♋	2/19	4:03am
♌	2/21	10:28am
♍	2/23	6:41pm
♎	2/26	4:59am
♏	2/28	5:16pm
♐	3/3	6:10am
♑	3/5	5:12pm
♒	3/8	12:23am
♓	3/10	3:33am
♈	3/12	4:10am
♉	3/14	4:15am
♊	3/16	5:39am
♋	3/18	9:31am
♌	3/20	4:03pm
♍	3/23	12:57am
♎	3/25	11:46am
♏	3/28	12:07am
♐	3/30	1:06pm
♑	4/2	12:56am
♒	4/4	9:32am
♓	4/6	2:01pm
♈	4/8	3:05pm
♉	4/10	2:32pm
♊	4/12	2:27pm
♋	4/14	4:34pm
♌	4/16	9:56pm
♍	4/19	6:35am
♎	4/21	5:44pm
♏	4/24	6:19am
♐	4/26	7:14pm
♑	4/29	7:12am
♒	5/1	4:46pm
♓	5/3	10:50pm
♈	5/6	1:24am
♉	5/8	1:33am
♊	5/10	1:03am
♋	5/12	1:50am
♌	5/14	5:32am
♍	5/16	12:58pm
♎	5/18	11:46pm
♏	5/21	12:27pm
♐	5/24	1:17am
♑	5/26	12:57pm
♒	5/28	10:33pm
♓	5/31	5:31am
♈	6/2	9:37am
♉	6/4	11:19am
♊	6/6	11:40am
♋	6/8	12:16pm
♌	6/10	2:51pm
♍	6/12	8:52pm
♎	6/15	6:42am
♏	6/17	7:08pm
♐	6/20	7:56am
♑	6/22	7:14pm
♒	6/25	4:15am
♓	6/27	10:59am
♈	6/29	3:44pm
♉	7/1	6:48pm
♊	7/3	8:38pm
♋	7/5	10:09pm
♌	7/8	12:44am
♍	7/10	5:54am
♎	7/12	2:41pm
♏	7/15	2:35am
♐	7/17	3:25pm
♑	7/20	2:41am
♒	7/22	11:06am
♓	7/24	4:57pm
♈	7/26	9:08pm
♉	7/29	12:27am
♊	7/31	3:20am
♋	8/2	6:11am
♌	8/4	9:40am
♍	8/6	2:58pm
♎	8/8	11:13pm
♏	8/11	10:34am
♐	8/13	11:27pm
♑	8/16	11:05am
♒	8/18	7:31pm
♓	8/21	12:40am
♈	8/23	3:42am
♉	8/25	6:02am
♊	8/27	8:43am
♋	8/29	12:14pm
♌	8/31	4:48pm
♍	9/2	10:57pm
♎	9/5	7:22am
♏	9/7	6:29pm
♐	9/10	7:22am
♑	9/12	7:39pm
♒	9/15	4:53am
♓	9/17	10:12am
♈	9/19	12:30pm
♉	9/21	1:29pm
♊	9/23	2:49pm
♋	9/25	5:37pm
♌	9/27	10:26pm
♍	9/30	5:22am
♎	10/2	2:28pm
♏	10/5	1:45am
♐	10/7	2:37pm
♑	10/10	3:25am
♒	10/12	1:51pm
♓	10/14	8:22pm
♈	10/16	11:06pm
♉	10/18	11:27pm
♊	10/20	11:18pm
♋	10/23	12:26am
♌	10/25	4:08am
♍	10/27	10:54am
♎	10/29	8:30pm
♏	11/1	8:12am
♐	11/3	9:06pm
♑	11/6	10:01am
♒	11/8	9:19pm
♓	11/11	5:26am
♈	11/13	9:43am
♉	11/15	10:47am
♊	11/17	10:12am
♋	11/19	9:53am
♌	11/21	11:45am
♍	11/23	5:08pm
♎	11/26	2:17am
♏	11/28	2:12pm
♐	12/1	3:15am
♑	12/3	3:57pm
♒	12/6	3:17am
♓	12/8	12:20pm
♈	12/10	6:22pm
♉	12/12	9:13pm
♊	12/14	9:39pm
♋	12/16	9:11pm
♌	12/18	9:48pm
♍	12/21	1:25am
♎	12/23	9:10am
♏	12/25	8:36pm
♐	12/28	9:41am
♑	12/30	10:14pm
	1911	
♒	1/2	9:02am
♓	1/4	5:50pm
♈	1/7	12:33am
♉	1/9	5:01am
♊	1/11	7:17am
♋	1/13	8:03am
♌	1/15	8:50am
♍	1/17	11:31am
♎	1/19	5:47pm
♏	1/22	4:06am
♐	1/24	4:54pm
♑	1/27	5:30am
♒	1/29	3:57pm
♓	1/31	11:55pm
♈	2/3	5:57am
♉	2/5	10:36am
♊	2/7	2:03pm
♋	2/9	4:28pm
♌	2/11	6:33pm
♍	2/13	9:39pm
♎	2/16	3:22am
♏	2/18	12:39pm
♐	2/21	12:53am
♑	2/23	1:37pm
♒	2/26	12:17am
♓	2/28	7:51am
♈	3/2	12:49pm
♉	3/4	4:21pm
♊	3/6	7:23pm
♋	3/8	10:24pm
♌	3/11	1:45am
♍	3/13	6:04am
♎	3/15	12:19pm
♏	3/17	9:21pm
♐	3/20	9:05am
♑	3/22	9:53pm
♒	3/25	9:12am
♓	3/27	5:14pm
♈	3/29	9:52pm
♉	4/1	12:14am
♊	4/3	1:49am
♋	4/5	3:53am
♌	4/7	7:15am
♍	4/9	12:23pm
♎	4/11	7:36pm
♏	4/14	5:06am
♐	4/16	4:46pm
♑	4/19	5:34am
♒	4/21	5:33pm
♓	4/24	2:41am
♈	4/26	8:03am
♉	4/28	10:13am
♊	4/30	10:39am
♋	5/2	11:06am
♌	5/4	1:09pm
♍	5/6	5:50pm
♎	5/9	1:26am
♏	5/11	11:35am
♐	5/13	11:33pm
♑	5/16	12:20pm
♒	5/19	12:40am
♓	5/21	10:53am
♈	5/23	5:41pm
♉	5/25	8:48pm
♊	5/27	9:12pm
♋	5/29	8:37pm
♌	5/31	9:03pm
♍	6/3	12:14am
♎	6/5	7:07am
♏	6/7	5:21pm
♐	6/10	5:37am
♑	6/12	6:27pm
♒	6/15	6:44am
♓	6/17	5:27pm
♈	6/20	1:32am
♉	6/22	6:14am
♊	6/24	7:46am
♋	6/26	7:20am
♌	6/28	6:54am
♍	6/30	8:35am
♎	7/2	1:59pm
♏	7/4	11:27pm
♐	7/7	11:39am
♑	7/10	12:32am

Moon Sign Changes 1900-2005

♒	7/12	12:34pm
♓	7/14	11:04pm
♈	7/17	7:35am
♉	7/19	1:34pm
♊	7/21	4:42pm
♋	7/23	5:30pm
♌	7/25	5:24pm
♍	7/27	6:26pm
♎	7/29	10:32pm
♏	8/1	6:44am
♐	8/3	6:21pm
♑	8/6	7:10am
♒	8/8	7:02pm
♓	8/11	5:00am
♈	8/13	1:02pm
♉	8/15	7:12pm
♊	8/17	11:23pm
♋	8/20	1:42am
♌	8/22	2:54am
♍	8/24	4:26am
♎	8/26	8:06am
♏	8/28	3:16pm
♐	8/31	2:01am
♑	9/2	2:37pm
♒	9/5	2:35am
♓	9/7	12:17pm
♈	9/9	7:31pm
♉	9/12	12:49am
♊	9/14	4:47am
♋	9/16	7:47am
♌	9/18	10:18am
♍	9/20	1:05pm
♎	9/22	5:21pm
♏	9/25	12:17am
♐	9/27	10:21am
♑	9/29	10:39pm
♒	10/2	10:56am
♓	10/4	8:59pm
♈	10/7	3:56am
♉	10/9	8:12am
♊	10/11	10:55am
♋	10/13	1:12pm
♌	10/15	3:54pm
♍	10/17	7:41pm
♎	10/20	1:05am
♏	10/22	8:36am
♐	10/24	6:34pm
♑	10/27	6:37am
♒	10/29	7:14pm
♓	11/1	6:12am
♈	11/3	1:49pm
♉	11/5	5:54pm
♊	11/7	7:29pm
♋	11/9	8:11pm
♌	11/11	9:39pm
♍	11/14	1:05am
♎	11/16	7:04am
♏	11/18	3:28pm
♐	11/21	1:54am
♑	11/23	1:55pm
♒	11/26	2:40am
♓	11/28	2:32pm

♈	11/30	11:35pm
♉	12/3	4:43am
♊	12/5	6:18am
♋	12/7	5:55am
♌	12/9	5:39am
♍	12/11	7:27am
♎	12/13	12:36pm
♏	12/15	9:09pm
♐	12/18	8:08am
♑	12/20	8:24pm
♒	12/23	9:05am
♓	12/25	9:18pm
♈	12/28	7:36am
♉	12/30	2:31pm
	1912	
♊	1/1	5:28pm
♋	1/3	5:25pm
♌	1/5	4:17pm
♍	1/7	4:23pm
♎	1/9	7:42pm
♏	1/12	3:07am
♐	1/14	1:57pm
♑	1/17	2:28am
♒	1/19	3:07pm
♓	1/22	3:06am
♈	1/24	1:41pm
♉	1/26	9:52pm
♊	1/29	2:42am
♋	1/31	4:15am
♌	2/2	3:47am
♍	2/4	3:23am
♎	2/6	5:13am
♏	2/8	10:53am
♐	2/10	8:35pm
♑	2/13	8:52am
♒	2/15	9:33pm
♓	2/18	9:13am
♈	2/20	7:17pm
♉	2/23	3:26am
♊	2/25	9:15am
♋	2/27	12:30pm
♌	2/29	1:42pm
♍	3/2	2:14pm
♎	3/4	3:53pm
♏	3/6	8:25pm
♐	3/9	4:43am
♑	3/11	4:12pm
♒	3/14	4:50am
♓	3/16	4:28pm
♈	3/19	1:59am
♉	3/21	9:16am
♊	3/23	2:37pm
♋	3/25	6:22pm
♌	3/27	8:54pm
♍	3/29	10:58pm
♎	4/1	1:40am
♏	4/3	6:15am
♐	4/5	1:47pm
♑	4/8	12:24am
♒	4/10	12:47pm
♓	4/13	12:42am
♈	4/15	10:15am

♉	4/17	4:51pm
♊	4/19	9:03pm
♋	4/21	11:53pm
♌	4/24	2:22am
♍	4/26	5:18am
♎	4/28	9:15am
♏	4/30	2:48pm
♐	5/2	10:30pm
♑	5/5	8:42am
♒	5/7	8:50pm
♓	5/10	9:08am
♈	5/12	7:20pm
♉	5/15	2:04am
♊	5/17	5:33am
♋	5/19	7:04am
♌	5/21	8:18am
♍	5/23	10:40am
♎	5/25	3:00pm
♏	5/27	9:27pm
♐	5/30	5:54am
♑	6/1	4:17pm
♒	6/4	4:19am
♓	6/6	4:55pm
♈	6/9	4:03am
♉	6/11	11:46am
♊	6/13	3:32pm
♋	6/15	4:24pm
♌	6/17	4:16pm
♍	6/19	5:09pm
♎	6/21	8:33pm
♏	6/24	2:58am
♐	6/26	11:58am
♑	6/28	10:49pm
♒	7/1	10:57am
♓	7/3	11:40pm
♈	7/6	11:30am
♉	7/8	8:33pm
♊	7/11	1:34am
♋	7/13	2:55am
♌	7/15	2:16am
♍	7/17	1:49am
♎	7/19	3:37am
♏	7/21	8:52am
♐	7/23	5:34pm
♑	7/26	4:41am
♒	7/28	5:01pm
♓	7/31	5:40am
♈	8/2	5:40pm
♉	8/5	3:37am
♊	8/7	10:09am
♋	8/9	12:57pm
♌	8/11	1:00pm
♍	8/13	12:14pm
♎	8/15	12:48pm
♏	8/17	4:28pm
♐	8/19	11:59pm
♑	8/22	10:43am
♒	8/24	11:07pm
♓	8/27	11:40am
♈	8/29	11:21pm
♉	9/1	9:20am
♊	9/3	4:45pm

♋	9/5	9:06pm
♌	9/7	10:43pm
♍	9/9	10:51pm
♎	9/11	11:18pm
♏	9/14	1:54am
♐	9/16	7:58am
♑	9/18	5:42pm
♒	9/21	5:51am
♓	9/23	6:25pm
♈	9/26	5:44am
♉	9/28	3:04pm
♊	9/30	10:12pm
♋	10/3	3:09am
♌	10/5	6:11am
♍	10/7	7:55am
♎	10/9	9:25am
♏	10/11	12:04pm
♐	10/13	5:18pm
♑	10/16	1:56am
♒	10/18	1:30pm
♓	10/21	2:08am
♈	10/23	1:29pm
♉	10/25	10:15pm
♊	10/28	4:22am
♋	10/30	8:36am
♌	11/1	11:46am
♍	11/3	2:34pm
♎	11/5	5:32pm
♏	11/7	9:17pm
♐	11/10	2:44am
♑	11/12	10:48am
♒	11/14	9:45pm
♓	11/17	10:24am
♈	11/19	10:17pm
♉	11/22	7:13am
♊	11/24	12:40pm
♋	11/26	3:36pm
♌	11/28	5:34pm
♍	11/30	7:55pm
♎	12/2	11:26pm
♏	12/5	4:22am
♐	12/7	10:48am
♑	12/9	7:10pm
♒	12/12	5:51am
♓	12/14	6:26pm
♈	12/17	7:00am
♉	12/19	4:57pm
♊	12/21	10:51pm
♋	12/24	1:11am
♌	12/26	1:43am
♍	12/28	2:27am
♎	12/30	4:55am
	1913	
♏	1/1	9:49am
♐	1/3	5:01pm
♑	1/6	2:10am
♒	1/8	1:07pm
♓	1/11	1:38am
♈	1/13	2:36pm
♉	1/16	1:46am
♊	1/18	9:07am
♋	1/20	12:14pm

♌	1/22	12:26pm
♍	1/24	11:48am
♎	1/26	12:26pm
♏	1/28	3:50pm
♐	1/30	10:30pm
♑	2/2	7:59am
♒	2/4	7:25pm
♓	2/7	8:03am
♈	2/9	8:59pm
♉	2/12	8:47am
♊	2/14	5:38pm
♋	2/16	10:29pm
♌	2/18	11:47pm
♍	2/20	11:08pm
♎	2/22	10:37pm
♏	2/25	12:11am
♐	2/27	5:11am
♑	3/1	1:52pm
♒	3/4	1:21am
♓	3/6	2:10pm
♈	3/9	2:57am
♉	3/11	2:35pm
♊	3/13	11:59pm
♋	3/16	6:21am
♌	3/18	9:27am
♍	3/20	10:08am
♎	3/22	9:55am
♏	3/24	10:37am
♐	3/26	1:59pm
♑	3/28	9:09pm
♒	3/31	7:53am
♓	4/2	8:39pm
♈	4/5	9:22am
♉	4/7	8:32pm
♊	4/10	5:31am
♋	4/12	12:09pm
♌	4/14	4:30pm
♍	4/16	6:53pm
♎	4/18	8:02pm
♏	4/20	9:14pm
♐	4/23	12:03am
♑	4/25	5:56am
♒	4/27	3:33pm
♓	4/30	3:54am
♈	5/2	4:39pm
♉	5/5	3:35am
♊	5/7	11:49am
♋	5/9	5:43pm
♌	5/11	9:57pm
♍	5/14	1:10am
♎	5/16	3:44am
♏	5/18	6:14am
♐	5/20	9:38am
♑	5/22	3:13pm
♒	5/24	11:59pm
♓	5/27	11:47am
♈	5/30	12:36am
♉	6/1	11:45am
♊	6/3	7:42pm
♋	6/6	12:40am
♌	6/8	3:51am
♍	6/10	6:31am

♎	6/12	9:27am
♏	6/14	1:00pm
♐	6/16	5:31pm
♑	6/18	11:41pm
♒	6/21	8:21am
♓	6/23	7:45pm
♈	6/26	8:38am
♉	6/28	8:22pm
♊	7/1	4:47am
♋	7/3	9:29am
♌	7/5	11:40am
♍	7/7	1:00pm
♎	7/9	2:59pm
♏	7/11	6:26pm
♐	7/13	11:37pm
♑	7/16	6:39am
♒	7/18	3:48pm
♓	7/21	3:12am
♈	7/23	4:07pm
♉	7/26	4:29am
♊	7/28	1:57pm
♋	7/30	7:23pm
♌	8/1	9:25pm
♍	8/3	9:44pm
♎	8/5	10:13pm
♏	8/8	12:22am
♐	8/10	5:03am
♑	8/12	12:24pm
♒	8/14	10:09pm
♓	8/17	9:52am
♈	8/19	10:47pm
♉	8/22	11:30am
♊	8/24	10:03pm
♋	8/27	4:54am
♌	8/29	7:55am
♍	8/31	8:16am
♎	9/2	7:47am
♏	9/4	8:21am
♐	9/6	11:32am
♑	9/8	6:07pm
♒	9/11	3:56am
♓	9/13	3:57pm
♈	9/16	4:55am
♉	9/18	5:34pm
♊	9/21	4:35am
♋	9/23	12:45pm
♌	9/25	5:26pm
♍	9/27	7:02pm
♎	9/29	6:47pm
♏	10/1	6:31pm
♐	10/3	8:08pm
♑	10/6	1:10am
♒	10/8	10:09am
♓	10/10	10:07pm
♈	10/13	11:08am
♉	10/15	11:30pm
♊	10/18	10:13am
♋	10/20	6:45pm
♌	10/23	12:45am
♍	10/25	4:06am
♎	10/27	5:17am
♏	10/29	5:30am

Moon Sign Changes 1900-2005

♐	10/31	6:29am
♑	11/2	10:08am
♒	11/4	5:44pm
♓	11/7	5:01am
♈	11/9	6:02pm
♉	11/12	6:17am
♊	11/14	4:24pm
♋	11/17	12:17am
♌	11/19	6:18am
♍	11/21	10:40am
♎	11/23	1:30pm
♏	11/25	3:13pm
♐	11/27	4:54pm
♑	11/29	8:12pm
♒	12/2	2:42am
♓	12/4	1:01pm
♈	12/7	1:45am
♉	12/9	2:12pm
♊	12/12	12:09am
♋	12/14	7:12am
♌	12/16	12:09pm
♍	12/18	4:00pm
♎	12/20	7:19pm
♏	12/22	10:21pm
♐	12/25	1:28am
♑	12/27	5:36am
♒	12/29	12:01pm
♓	12/31	9:38pm
1914		
♈	1/3	9:58am
♉	1/5	10:43pm
♊	1/8	9:13am
♋	1/10	4:12pm
♌	1/12	8:13pm
♍	1/14	10:40pm
♎	1/17	12:53am
♏	1/19	3:44am
♐	1/21	7:40am
♑	1/23	12:59pm
♒	1/25	8:13pm
♓	1/28	5:54am
♈	1/30	5:57pm
♉	2/2	6:54am
♊	2/4	6:20pm
♋	2/7	2:16am
♌	2/9	6:26am
♍	2/11	8:00am
♎	2/13	8:37am
♏	2/15	9:55am
♐	2/17	1:03pm
♑	2/19	6:38pm
♒	2/22	2:41am
♓	2/24	1:01pm
♈	2/27	1:09am
♉	3/1	2:07pm
♊	3/4	2:14am
♋	3/6	11:34am
♌	3/8	5:03pm
♍	3/10	7:02pm
♎	3/12	6:57pm
♏	3/14	6:39pm
♐	3/16	8:01pm
♑	3/19	12:23am
♒	3/21	8:15am
♓	3/23	7:01pm
♈	3/26	7:30am
♉	3/28	8:27pm
♊	3/31	8:42am
♋	4/2	6:59pm
♌	4/5	2:06am
♍	4/7	5:36am
♎	4/9	6:12am
♏	4/11	5:27am
♐	4/13	5:23am
♑	4/15	7:59am
♒	4/17	2:31pm
♓	4/20	12:52am
♈	4/22	1:30pm
♉	4/25	2:28am
♊	4/27	2:29pm
♋	4/30	12:50am
♌	5/2	8:53am
♍	5/4	2:02pm
♎	5/6	4:13pm
♏	5/8	4:20pm
♐	5/10	4:04pm
♑	5/12	5:30pm
♒	5/14	10:29pm
♓	5/17	7:40am
♈	5/19	7:54pm
♉	5/22	8:51am
♊	5/24	8:37pm
♋	5/27	6:28am
♌	5/29	2:22pm
♍	5/31	8:13pm
♎	6/2	11:51pm
♏	6/5	1:30am
♐	6/7	2:12am
♑	6/9	3:40am
♒	6/11	7:47am
♓	6/13	3:44pm
♈	6/16	3:11am
♉	6/18	4:01pm
♊	6/21	3:44am
♋	6/23	1:07pm
♌	6/25	8:14pm
♍	6/28	1:35am
♎	6/30	5:32am
♏	7/2	8:19am
♐	7/4	10:25am
♑	7/6	12:54pm
♒	7/8	5:11pm
♓	7/11	12:33am
♈	7/13	11:14am
♉	7/15	11:49pm
♊	7/18	11:47am
♋	7/20	9:12pm
♌	7/23	3:42am
♍	7/25	8:00am
♎	7/27	11:05am
♏	7/29	1:45pm
♐	7/31	4:35pm
♑	8/2	8:14pm
♒	8/5	1:27am
♓	8/7	9:03am
♈	8/9	7:25pm
♉	8/12	7:46am
♊	8/14	8:06pm
♋	8/17	6:11am
♌	8/19	12:52pm
♍	8/21	4:30pm
♎	8/23	6:18pm
♏	8/25	7:43pm
♐	8/27	9:59pm
♑	8/30	1:57am
♒	9/1	8:03am
♓	9/3	4:26pm
♈	9/6	3:00am
♉	9/8	3:15pm
♊	9/11	3:53am
♋	9/13	2:56pm
♌	9/15	10:41pm
♍	9/18	2:42am
♎	9/20	3:52am
♏	9/22	3:53am
♐	9/24	4:36am
♑	9/26	7:34am
♒	9/28	1:36pm
♓	9/30	10:33pm
♈	10/3	9:38am
♉	10/5	9:58pm
♊	10/8	10:40am
♋	10/10	10:26pm
♌	10/13	7:36am
♍	10/15	1:02pm
♎	10/17	2:49pm
♏	10/19	2:21pm
♐	10/21	1:40pm
♑	10/23	2:55pm
♒	10/25	7:39pm
♓	10/28	4:13am
♈	10/30	3:34pm
♉	11/2	4:08am
♊	11/4	4:44pm
♋	11/7	4:33am
♌	11/9	2:36pm
♍	11/11	9:42pm
♎	11/14	1:10am
♏	11/16	1:36am
♐	11/18	12:42am
♑	11/20	12:42am
♒	11/22	3:42am
♓	11/24	10:53am
♈	11/26	9:44pm
♉	11/29	10:22am
♊	12/1	10:53pm
♋	12/4	10:19am
♌	12/6	8:13pm
♍	12/9	4:03am
♎	12/11	9:09am
♏	12/13	11:23am
♐	12/15	11:40am
♑	12/17	11:46am
♒	12/19	1:47pm
♓	12/21	7:25pm
♈	12/24	5:02am
♉	12/26	5:19pm
♊	12/29	5:53am
♋	12/31	5:01pm
1915		
♌	1/3	2:12am
♍	1/5	9:28am
♎	1/7	2:53pm
♏	1/9	6:25pm
♐	1/11	8:25pm
♑	1/13	9:52pm
♒	1/16	12:17am
♓	1/18	5:14am
♈	1/20	1:42pm
♉	1/23	1:13am
♊	1/25	1:48pm
♋	1/28	1:08am
♌	1/30	9:55am
♍	2/1	4:10pm
♎	2/3	8:32pm
♏	2/5	11:48pm
♐	2/8	2:33am
♑	2/10	5:25am
♒	2/12	9:09am
♓	2/14	2:40pm
♈	2/16	10:46pm
♉	2/19	9:37am
♊	2/21	10:05pm
♋	2/24	9:57am
♌	2/26	7:11pm
♍	3/1	1:03am
♎	3/3	4:15am
♏	3/5	6:05am
♐	3/7	7:58am
♑	3/9	10:59am
♒	3/11	3:40pm
♓	3/13	10:16pm
♈	3/16	6:55am
♉	3/18	5:38pm
♊	3/21	5:58am
♋	3/23	6:22pm
♌	3/26	4:38am
♍	3/28	11:13am
♎	3/30	2:10pm
♏	4/1	2:49pm
♐	4/3	3:05pm
♑	4/5	4:47pm
♒	4/7	9:03pm
♓	4/10	4:08am
♈	4/12	1:31pm
♉	4/15	12:38am
♊	4/17	12:57pm
♋	4/20	1:36am
♌	4/22	12:53pm
♍	4/24	8:53pm
♎	4/27	12:47am
♏	4/29	1:23am
♐	5/1	12:37am
♑	5/3	12:39am
♒	5/5	3:23am
♓	5/7	9:41am
♈	5/9	7:10pm
♉	5/12	6:40am
♊	5/14	7:09pm
♋	5/17	7:47am
♌	5/19	7:31pm
♍	5/22	4:47am
♎	5/24	10:16am
♏	5/26	12:02pm
♐	5/28	11:27am
♑	5/30	10:39am
♒	6/1	11:49am
♓	6/3	4:32pm
♈	6/6	1:06am
♉	6/8	12:30pm
♊	6/11	1:06am
♋	6/13	1:38pm
♌	6/16	1:12am
♍	6/18	10:53am
♎	6/20	5:39pm
♏	6/22	9:03pm
♐	6/24	9:45pm
♑	6/26	9:22pm
♒	6/28	9:54pm
♓	7/1	1:14am
♈	7/3	8:24am
♉	7/5	7:01pm
♊	7/8	7:30am
♋	7/10	7:56pm
♌	7/13	7:06am
♍	7/15	4:22pm
♎	7/17	11:21pm
♏	7/20	3:50am
♐	7/22	6:06am
♑	7/24	7:03am
♒	7/26	8:10am
♓	7/28	11:04am
♈	7/30	5:06pm
♉	8/2	2:40am
♊	8/4	2:43pm
♋	8/7	3:11am
♌	8/9	2:08pm
♍	8/11	10:42pm
♎	8/14	4:55am
♏	8/16	9:17am
♐	8/18	12:18pm
♑	8/20	2:38pm
♒	8/22	5:03pm
♓	8/24	8:35pm
♈	8/27	2:21am
♉	8/29	11:08am
♊	8/31	10:38pm
♋	9/3	11:12am
♌	9/5	10:24pm
♍	9/8	6:42am
♎	9/10	12:00pm
♏	9/12	3:14pm
♐	9/14	5:41pm
♑	9/16	8:20pm
♒	9/18	11:49pm
♓	9/21	4:32am
♈	9/23	10:55am
♉	9/25	7:35pm
♊	9/28	6:42am
♋	9/30	7:20pm
♌	10/3	7:13am
♍	10/5	4:04pm
♎	10/7	9:09pm
♏	10/9	11:20pm
♐	10/12	12:21am
♑	10/14	1:56am
♒	10/16	5:15am
♓	10/18	10:38am
♈	10/20	5:57pm
♉	10/23	3:08am
♊	10/25	2:15pm
♋	10/28	2:53am
♌	10/30	3:26pm
♍	11/2	1:30am
♎	11/4	7:29am
♏	11/6	9:37am
♐	11/8	9:36am
♑	11/10	9:34am
♒	11/12	11:22am
♓	11/14	4:05pm
♈	11/16	11:40pm
♉	11/19	9:29am
♊	11/21	8:56pm
♋	11/24	9:34am
♌	11/26	10:23pm
♍	11/29	9:33am
♎	12/1	5:09pm
♏	12/3	8:33pm
♐	12/5	8:47pm
♑	12/7	7:53pm
♒	12/9	8:01pm
♓	12/11	10:57pm
♈	12/14	5:30am
♉	12/16	3:14pm
♊	12/19	3:02am
♋	12/21	3:44pm
♌	12/24	4:23am
♍	12/26	3:51pm
♎	12/29	12:41am
♏	12/31	5:55am
1916		
♐	1/2	7:43am
♑	1/4	7:25am
♒	1/6	6:58am
♓	1/8	8:21am
♈	1/10	1:07pm
♉	1/12	9:43pm
♊	1/15	9:18am
♋	1/17	10:07pm
♌	1/20	10:33am
♍	1/22	9:32pm
♎	1/25	6:26am
♏	1/27	12:43pm
♐	1/29	4:18pm
♑	1/31	5:42pm
♒	2/2	6:09pm
♓	2/4	7:16pm
♈	2/6	10:45pm
♉	2/9	5:50am
♊	2/11	4:30pm
♋	2/14	5:12am
♌	2/16	5:38pm

Moon Sign Changes 1900-2005

Sign	Date	Time
♍	2/19	4:08am
♎	2/21	12:13pm
♏	2/23	6:09pm
♐	2/25	10:20pm
♑	2/28	1:13am
♒	3/1	3:18am
♓	3/3	5:27am
♈	3/5	8:56am
♉	3/7	3:08pm
♊	3/10	12:46am
♋	3/12	1:03pm
♌	3/15	1:41am
♍	3/17	12:12pm
♎	3/19	7:37pm
♏	3/22	12:26am
♐	3/24	3:48am
♑	3/26	6:43am
♒	3/28	9:47am
♓	3/30	1:18pm
♈	4/1	5:48pm
♉	4/4	12:11am
♊	4/6	9:19am
♋	4/8	9:11pm
♌	4/11	10:01am
♍	4/13	9:07pm
♎	4/16	4:40am
♏	4/18	8:48am
♐	4/20	10:52am
♑	4/22	12:34pm
♒	4/24	3:07pm
♓	4/26	7:05pm
♈	4/29	12:35am
♉	5/1	7:49am
♊	5/3	5:12pm
♋	5/6	4:53am
♌	5/8	5:51pm
♍	5/11	5:45am
♎	5/13	2:15pm
♏	5/15	6:42pm
♐	5/17	8:09pm
♑	5/19	8:30pm
♒	5/21	9:33pm
♓	5/24	12:35am
♈	5/26	6:03am
♉	5/28	1:54pm
♊	5/30	11:53pm
♋	6/2	11:46am
♌	6/5	12:47am
♍	6/7	1:15pm
♎	6/9	10:59pm
♏	6/12	4:40am
♐	6/14	6:40am
♑	6/16	6:33am
♒	6/18	6:16am
♓	6/20	7:39am
♈	6/22	11:55am
♉	6/24	7:26pm
♊	6/27	5:43am
♋	6/29	5:55pm
♌	7/2	6:57am
♍	7/4	7:32pm
♎	7/7	6:06am
♏	7/9	1:16pm
♐	7/11	4:43pm
♑	7/13	5:20pm
♒	7/15	4:46pm
♓	7/17	4:55pm
♈	7/19	7:32pm
♉	7/22	1:46am
♊	7/24	11:36am
♋	7/26	11:53pm
♌	7/29	12:56pm
♍	8/1	1:18am
♎	8/3	11:54am
♏	8/5	7:56pm
♐	8/8	12:56am
♑	8/10	3:08am
♒	8/12	3:28am
♓	8/14	3:29am
♈	8/16	5:02am
♉	8/18	9:45am
♊	8/20	6:27pm
♋	8/23	6:21am
♌	8/25	7:24pm
♍	8/28	7:29am
♎	8/30	5:34pm
♏	9/2	1:24am
♐	9/4	7:05am
♑	9/6	10:44am
♒	9/8	12:39pm
♓	9/10	1:42pm
♈	9/12	3:17pm
♉	9/14	7:09pm
♊	9/17	2:38am
♋	9/19	1:45pm
♌	9/22	2:41am
♍	9/24	2:46pm
♎	9/27	12:22am
♏	9/29	7:21am
♐	10/1	12:28pm
♑	10/3	4:23pm
♒	10/5	7:28pm
♓	10/7	10:00pm
♈	10/10	12:40am
♉	10/12	4:45am
♊	10/14	11:38am
♋	10/16	9:58pm
♌	10/19	10:40am
♍	10/21	11:04pm
♎	10/24	8:45am
♏	10/26	3:09pm
♐	10/28	7:07pm
♑	10/30	10:00pm
♒	11/2	12:50am
♓	11/4	4:04am
♈	11/6	7:59am
♉	11/8	1:07pm
♊	11/10	8:19pm
♋	11/13	6:19am
♌	11/15	6:44pm
♍	11/18	7:33am
♎	11/20	6:03pm
♏	11/23	12:48am
♐	11/25	4:12am
♑	11/27	5:45am
♒	11/29	7:06am
♓	12/1	9:29am
♈	12/3	1:34pm
♉	12/5	7:35pm
♊	12/8	3:40am
♋	12/10	2:00pm
♌	12/13	2:18am
♍	12/15	3:19pm
♎	12/18	2:50am
♏	12/20	10:52am
♐	12/22	2:58pm
♑	12/24	4:07pm
♒	12/26	4:05pm
♓	12/28	4:41pm
♈	12/30	7:25pm
	1917	
♉	1/2	1:04am
♊	1/4	9:39am
♋	1/6	8:35pm
♌	1/9	9:03am
♍	1/11	10:01pm
♎	1/14	10:04am
♏	1/16	7:32pm
♐	1/19	1:17am
♑	1/21	3:28am
♒	1/23	3:19am
♓	1/25	2:41am
♈	1/27	3:33am
♉	1/29	7:34am
♊	1/31	3:26pm
♋	2/3	2:31am
♌	2/5	3:16pm
♍	2/8	4:09am
♎	2/10	4:04pm
♏	2/13	2:06am
♐	2/15	9:23am
♑	2/17	1:24pm
♒	2/19	2:32pm
♓	2/21	2:06pm
♈	2/23	2:00pm
♉	2/25	4:19pm
♊	2/27	10:34pm
♋	3/2	8:52am
♌	3/4	9:36pm
♍	3/7	10:29am
♎	3/9	10:01pm
♏	3/12	7:40am
♐	3/14	3:18pm
♑	3/16	8:38pm
♒	3/18	11:33pm
♓	3/21	12:31am
♈	3/23	12:53am
♉	3/25	2:35am
♊	3/27	7:28am
♋	3/29	4:28pm
♌	4/1	4:39am
♍	4/3	5:32pm
♎	4/6	4:54am
♏	4/8	1:54pm
♐	4/10	8:50pm
♑	4/13	2:08am
♒	4/15	5:56am
♓	4/17	8:25am
♈	4/19	10:10am
♉	4/21	12:31pm
♊	4/23	5:04pm
♋	4/26	1:07am
♌	4/28	12:31pm
♍	5/1	1:19am
♎	5/3	12:52pm
♏	5/5	9:39pm
♐	5/8	3:44am
♑	5/10	8:00am
♒	5/12	11:18am
♓	5/14	2:11pm
♈	5/16	5:04pm
♉	5/18	8:38pm
♊	5/21	1:53am
♋	5/23	9:49am
♌	5/25	8:42pm
♍	5/28	9:21am
♎	5/30	9:20pm
♏	6/2	6:34am
♐	6/4	12:27pm
♑	6/6	3:45pm
♒	6/8	5:45pm
♓	6/10	7:42pm
♈	6/12	10:31pm
♉	6/15	2:48am
♊	6/17	9:02am
♋	6/19	5:33pm
♌	6/22	4:27am
♍	6/24	4:59pm
♎	6/27	5:26am
♏	6/29	3:37pm
♐	7/1	10:14pm
♑	7/4	1:25am
♒	7/6	2:25am
♓	7/8	2:53am
♈	7/10	4:25am
♉	7/12	8:13am
♊	7/14	2:47pm
♋	7/16	11:59pm
♌	7/19	11:17am
♍	7/21	11:51pm
♎	7/24	12:33pm
♏	7/26	11:40pm
♐	7/29	7:38am
♑	7/31	11:48am
♒	8/2	12:49pm
♓	8/4	12:20pm
♈	8/6	12:18pm
♉	8/8	2:36pm
♊	8/10	8:24pm
♋	8/13	5:39am
♌	8/15	5:19pm
♍	8/18	6:02am
♎	8/20	6:42pm
♏	8/23	6:16am
♐	8/25	3:28pm
♑	8/27	9:15pm
♒	8/29	11:27pm
♓	8/31	11:11pm
♈	9/2	10:20pm
♉	9/4	11:06pm
♊	9/7	3:19am
♋	9/9	11:40am
♌	9/11	11:13pm
♍	9/14	12:02pm
♎	9/17	12:33am
♏	9/19	11:55am
♐	9/21	9:32pm
♑	9/24	4:37am
♒	9/26	8:33am
♓	9/28	9:39am
♈	9/30	9:15am
♉	10/2	9:25am
♊	10/4	12:14pm
♋	10/6	7:06pm
♌	10/9	5:50am
♍	10/11	6:32pm
♎	10/14	6:58am
♏	10/16	5:53pm
♐	10/19	3:00am
♑	10/21	10:14am
♒	10/23	3:16pm
♓	10/25	6:03pm
♈	10/27	7:08pm
♉	10/29	7:59pm
♊	10/31	10:26pm
♋	11/3	4:09am
♌	11/5	1:42pm
♍	11/8	1:56am
♎	11/10	2:26pm
♏	11/13	1:13am
♐	11/15	9:36am
♑	11/17	3:55pm
♒	11/19	8:38pm
♓	11/22	12:04am
♈	11/24	2:35am
♉	11/26	4:55am
♊	11/28	8:13am
♋	11/30	1:48pm
♌	12/2	10:32pm
♍	12/5	10:07am
♎	12/7	10:42pm
♏	12/10	9:52am
♐	12/12	6:10pm
♑	12/14	11:35pm
♒	12/17	2:59am
♓	12/19	5:31am
♈	12/21	8:06am
♉	12/23	11:26am
♊	12/25	4:03pm
♋	12/27	10:29pm
♌	12/30	7:15am
	1918	
♍	1/1	6:23pm
♎	1/4	6:56am
♏	1/6	6:50pm
♐	1/9	3:57am
♑	1/11	9:27am
♒	1/13	11:55am
♓	1/15	12:54pm
♈	1/17	2:03pm
♉	1/19	4:48pm
♊	1/21	9:52pm
♋	1/24	5:17am
♌	1/26	2:45pm
♍	1/29	1:59am
♎	1/31	2:26pm
♏	2/3	2:52am
♐	2/5	1:15pm
♑	2/7	7:57pm
♒	2/9	10:46pm
♓	2/11	10:57pm
♈	2/13	10:31pm
♉	2/15	11:31pm
♊	2/18	3:29am
♋	2/20	10:50am
♌	2/22	8:53pm
♍	2/25	8:33am
♎	2/27	9:01pm
♏	3/2	9:32am
♐	3/4	8:47pm
♑	3/7	5:05am
♒	3/9	9:23am
♓	3/11	10:12am
♈	3/13	9:15am
♉	3/15	8:48am
♊	3/17	10:58am
♋	3/19	4:58pm
♌	3/22	2:37am
♍	3/24	2:30pm
♎	3/27	3:07am
♏	3/29	3:28pm
♐	4/1	2:47am
♑	4/3	11:59am
♒	4/5	5:56pm
♓	4/7	8:22pm
♈	4/9	8:19pm
♉	4/11	7:40pm
♊	4/13	8:37pm
♋	4/16	12:57am
♌	4/18	9:19am
♍	4/20	8:46pm
♎	4/23	9:25am
♏	4/25	9:37pm
♐	4/28	8:30am
♑	4/30	5:33pm
♒	5/3	12:12am
♓	5/5	4:07am
♈	5/7	5:40am
♉	5/9	6:05am
♊	5/11	7:06am
♋	5/13	10:31am
♌	5/15	5:31pm
♍	5/18	4:00am
♎	5/20	4:25pm
♏	5/23	4:38am
♐	5/25	3:08pm
♑	5/27	11:27pm
♒	5/30	5:38am
♓	6/1	9:53am
♈	6/3	12:37pm
♉	6/5	2:30pm
♊	6/7	4:36pm

Moon Sign Changes 1900-2005

♋	6/9	8:14pm
♌	6/12	2:35am
♍	6/14	12:10pm
♎	6/17	12:10am
♏	6/19	12:30pm
♐	6/21	11:04pm
♑	6/24	6:51am
♒	6/26	12:01pm
♓	6/28	3:26pm
♈	6/30	6:04pm
♉	7/2	8:44pm
♊	7/5	12:04am
♋	7/7	4:42am
♌	7/9	11:20am
♍	7/11	8:33pm
♎	7/14	8:09am
♏	7/16	8:41pm
♐	7/19	7:49am
♑	7/21	3:46pm
♒	7/23	8:19pm
♓	7/25	10:32pm
♈	7/27	11:59pm
♉	7/30	2:06am
♊	8/1	5:48am
♋	8/3	11:21am
♌	8/5	6:49pm
♍	8/8	4:17am
♎	8/10	3:45pm
♏	8/13	4:27am
♐	8/15	4:22pm
♑	8/18	1:17am
♒	8/20	6:11am
♓	8/22	7:48am
♈	8/24	7:56am
♉	8/26	8:35am
♊	8/28	11:19am
♋	8/30	4:50pm
♌	9/2	12:53am
♍	9/4	10:56am
♎	9/6	10:35pm
♏	9/9	11:19am
♐	9/11	11:50pm
♑	9/14	10:02am
♒	9/16	4:15pm
♓	9/18	6:26pm
♈	9/20	6:07pm
♉	9/22	5:27pm
♊	9/24	6:31pm
♋	9/26	10:45pm
♌	9/29	6:25am
♍	10/1	4:46pm
♎	10/4	4:43am
♏	10/6	5:28pm
♐	10/9	6:04am
♑	10/11	5:06pm
♒	10/14	12:54am
♓	10/16	4:41am
♈	10/18	5:14am
♉	10/20	4:20am
♊	10/22	4:10am
♋	10/24	6:40am
♌	10/26	12:54pm
♍	10/28	10:42pm
♎	10/31	10:45am
♏	11/2	11:31pm
♐	11/5	11:52am
♑	11/7	10:50pm
♒	11/10	7:25am
♓	11/12	12:52pm
♈	11/14	3:11pm
♉	11/16	3:26pm
♊	11/18	3:20pm
♋	11/20	4:46pm
♌	11/22	9:23pm
♍	11/25	5:50am
♎	11/27	5:25pm
♏	11/30	6:13am
♐	12/2	6:20pm
♑	12/5	4:41am
♒	12/7	12:52pm
♓	12/9	6:47pm
♈	12/11	10:33pm
♉	12/14	12:35am
♊	12/16	1:49am
♋	12/18	3:35am
♌	12/20	7:25am
♍	12/22	2:33pm
♎	12/25	1:10am
♏	12/27	1:49pm
♐	12/30	2:03am
1919		
♑	1/1	12:01pm
♒	1/3	7:15pm
♓	1/6	12:18am
♈	1/8	4:00am
♉	1/10	7:01am
♊	1/12	9:49am
♋	1/14	12:56pm
♌	1/16	5:16pm
♍	1/18	11:57pm
♎	1/21	9:43am
♏	1/23	10:00pm
♐	1/26	10:35am
♑	1/28	8:54pm
♒	1/31	3:44am
♓	2/2	7:38am
♈	2/4	10:02am
♉	2/6	12:22pm
♊	2/8	3:31pm
♋	2/10	7:46pm
♌	2/13	1:17am
♍	2/15	8:32am
♎	2/17	6:07pm
♏	2/20	6:04am
♐	2/22	6:57pm
♑	2/25	6:08am
♒	2/27	1:36pm
♓	3/1	5:14pm
♈	3/3	6:28pm
♉	3/5	7:14pm
♊	3/7	9:10pm
♋	3/10	1:09am
♌	3/12	7:18am
♍	3/14	3:26pm
♎	3/17	1:29am
♏	3/19	1:25pm
♐	3/22	2:23am
♑	3/24	2:25pm
♒	3/26	11:11pm
♓	3/29	3:45am
♈	3/31	4:57am
♉	4/2	4:40am
♊	4/4	4:56am
♋	4/6	7:23am
♌	4/8	12:48pm
♍	4/10	9:07pm
♎	4/13	7:43am
♏	4/15	7:54pm
♐	4/18	8:52am
♑	4/20	9:14pm
♒	4/23	7:09am
♓	4/25	1:17pm
♈	4/27	3:40pm
♉	4/29	3:36pm
♊	5/1	3:00pm
♋	5/3	3:51pm
♌	5/5	7:38pm
♍	5/8	3:01am
♎	5/10	1:32pm
♏	5/13	1:57am
♐	5/15	2:54pm
♑	5/18	3:06am
♒	5/20	1:23pm
♓	5/22	8:45pm
♈	5/25	12:47am
♉	5/27	2:02am
♊	5/29	1:53am
♋	5/31	2:05am
♌	6/2	4:26am
♍	6/4	10:18am
♎	6/6	7:58pm
♏	6/9	8:15am
♐	6/11	9:12pm
♑	6/14	9:04am
♒	6/16	6:58pm
♓	6/19	2:31am
♈	6/21	7:38am
♉	6/23	10:29am
♊	6/25	11:42am
♋	6/27	12:28pm
♌	6/29	2:24pm
♍	7/1	7:06pm
♎	7/4	3:34am
♏	7/6	3:18pm
♐	7/9	4:13am
♑	7/11	3:56pm
♒	7/14	1:14am
♓	7/16	8:06am
♈	7/18	1:06pm
♉	7/20	4:43pm
♊	7/22	7:19pm
♋	7/24	9:25pm
♌	7/26	11:59pm
♍	7/29	4:28am
♎	7/31	12:06pm
♏	8/2	11:08pm
♐	8/5	11:57am
♑	8/7	11:52pm
♒	8/10	8:56am
♓	8/12	2:59pm
♈	8/14	6:59pm
♉	8/16	10:05pm
♊	8/19	1:03am
♋	8/21	4:14am
♌	8/23	8:00am
♍	8/25	1:08pm
♎	8/27	8:41pm
♏	8/30	7:15am
♐	9/1	7:58pm
♑	9/4	8:21am
♒	9/6	5:54pm
♓	9/8	11:45pm
♈	9/11	2:48am
♉	9/13	4:35am
♊	9/15	6:35am
♋	9/17	9:39am
♌	9/19	2:08pm
♍	9/21	8:15pm
♎	9/24	4:24am
♏	9/26	2:59pm
♐	9/29	3:36am
♑	10/1	4:28pm
♒	10/4	3:03am
♓	10/6	9:44am
♈	10/8	12:44pm
♉	10/10	1:32pm
♊	10/12	1:59pm
♋	10/14	3:39pm
♌	10/16	7:32pm
♍	10/19	1:58am
♎	10/21	10:51am
♏	10/23	9:52pm
♐	10/26	10:31am
♑	10/28	11:34pm
♒	10/31	11:08am
♓	11/2	7:19pm
♈	11/4	11:30pm
♉	11/7	12:31am
♊	11/9	12:03am
♋	11/11	12:03am
♌	11/13	2:14am
♍	11/15	7:41am
♎	11/17	4:32pm
♏	11/20	3:58am
♐	11/22	4:47pm
♑	11/25	5:45am
♒	11/27	5:37pm
♓	11/30	3:03am
♈	12/2	9:02am
♉	12/4	11:33am
♊	12/6	11:36am
♋	12/8	10:54am
♌	12/10	11:28am
♍	12/12	3:06pm
♎	12/14	10:47pm
♏	12/17	10:01am
♐	12/19	10:59pm
♑	12/22	11:49am
♒	12/24	11:20pm
♓	12/27	8:55am
♈	12/29	4:06pm
♉	12/31	8:28pm
1920		
♊	1/2	10:13pm
♋	1/4	10:19pm
♌	1/6	10:30pm
♍	1/9	12:46am
♎	1/11	6:47am
♏	1/13	4:57pm
♐	1/16	5:43am
♑	1/18	6:34pm
♒	1/21	5:39am
♓	1/23	2:34pm
♈	1/25	9:32pm
♉	1/28	2:43am
♊	1/30	6:05am
♋	2/1	7:54am
♌	2/3	9:05am
♍	2/5	11:18am
♎	2/7	4:19pm
♏	2/10	1:13am
♐	2/12	1:21pm
♑	2/15	2:14am
♒	2/17	1:20pm
♓	2/19	9:39pm
♈	2/22	3:36am
♉	2/24	8:06am
♊	2/26	11:42am
♋	2/28	2:40pm
♌	3/1	5:22pm
♍	3/3	8:40pm
♎	3/6	1:53am
♏	3/8	10:10am
♐	3/10	9:35pm
♑	3/13	10:25am
♒	3/15	9:58pm
♓	3/18	6:25am
♈	3/20	11:43am
♉	3/22	2:58pm
♊	3/24	5:25pm
♋	3/26	8:02pm
♌	3/28	11:20pm
♍	3/31	3:48am
♎	4/2	9:59am
♏	4/4	6:34pm
♐	4/7	5:42am
♑	4/9	6:25pm
♒	4/12	6:31am
♓	4/14	3:50pm
♈	4/16	9:29pm
♉	4/19	12:08am
♊	4/21	1:14am
♋	4/23	2:22am
♌	4/25	4:49am
♍	4/27	9:21am
♎	4/29	4:18pm
♏	5/2	1:37am
♐	5/4	12:59pm
♑	5/7	1:39am
♒	5/9	2:09pm
♓	5/12	12:32am
♈	5/14	7:23am
♉	5/16	10:35am
♊	5/18	11:13am
♋	5/20	11:01am
♌	5/22	11:49am
♍	5/24	3:10pm
♎	5/26	9:50pm
♏	5/29	7:32am
♐	5/31	7:20pm
♑	6/3	8:05am
♒	6/5	8:38pm
♓	6/8	7:43am
♈	6/10	3:57pm
♉	6/12	8:35pm
♊	6/14	9:57pm
♋	6/16	9:26pm
♌	6/18	9:01pm
♍	6/20	10:44pm
♎	6/23	4:05am
♏	6/25	1:19pm
♐	6/28	1:15am
♑	6/30	2:06pm
♒	7/3	2:30am
♓	7/5	1:37pm
♈	7/7	10:38pm
♉	7/10	4:45am
♊	7/12	7:40am
♋	7/14	8:03am
♌	7/16	7:32am
♍	7/18	8:12am
♎	7/20	12:02pm
♏	7/22	8:03pm
♐	7/25	7:31am
♑	7/27	8:22pm
♒	7/30	8:37am
♓	8/1	7:18pm
♈	8/4	4:10am
♉	8/6	10:56am
♊	8/8	3:15pm
♋	8/10	5:11pm
♌	8/12	5:41pm
♍	8/14	6:27pm
♎	8/16	9:28pm
♏	8/19	4:12am
♐	8/21	2:45pm
♑	8/24	3:22am
♒	8/26	3:36pm
♓	8/29	1:55am
♈	8/31	10:03am
♉	9/2	4:19pm
♊	9/4	8:58pm
♋	9/7	12:04am
♌	9/9	2:02am
♍	9/11	3:54am
♎	9/13	7:10am
♏	9/15	1:19pm
♐	9/17	10:58pm
♑	9/20	11:09am
♒	9/22	11:33pm
♓	9/25	9:57am
♈	9/27	5:35pm

Moon Sign Changes 1900-2005

♉ 9/29 10:49pm	♊ 2/16 12:54am	♌ 7/6 4:33pm	♎ 11/24 3:31pm	♏ 4/12 11:07am	♑ 8/31 8:53am
♊ 10/2 2:32am	♋ 2/18 3:58am	♍ 7/8 4:26pm	♏ 11/26 7:37pm	♐ 4/14 1:25pm	♒ 9/2 6:12pm
♋ 10/4 5:29am	♌ 2/20 4:34am	♎ 7/10 6:28pm	♐ 11/29 1:03am	♑ 4/16 7:01pm	♓ 9/5 5:41am
♌ 10/6 8:14am	♍ 2/22 4:20am	♏ 7/12 11:43pm	♑ 12/1 8:32am	♒ 4/19 4:28am	♈ 9/7 6:29pm
♍ 10/8 11:23am	♎ 2/24 5:21am	♐ 7/15 8:05am	♒ 12/3 6:41pm	♓ 4/21 4:44pm	♉ 9/10 7:24am
♎ 10/10 3:44pm	♏ 2/26 9:28am	♑ 7/17 6:43pm	♓ 12/6 7:03am	♈ 4/24 5:37am	♊ 9/12 6:50pm
♏ 10/12 10:14pm	♐ 2/28 5:36pm	♒ 7/20 6:43am	♈ 12/8 7:37pm	♉ 4/26 5:08pm	♋ 9/15 3:13am
♐ 10/15 7:30am	♑ 3/3 5:03am	♓ 7/22 7:23pm	♉ 12/11 5:46am	♊ 4/29 2:19am	♌ 9/17 7:48am
♑ 10/17 7:16pm	♒ 3/5 5:46pm	♈ 7/25 7:42am	♊ 12/13 12:07pm	♋ 5/1 9:12am	♍ 9/19 9:08am
♒ 10/20 7:52am	♓ 3/8 5:44am	♉ 7/27 5:58pm	♋ 12/15 3:11pm	♌ 5/3 2:05pm	♎ 9/21 8:43am
♓ 10/22 6:57pm	♈ 3/10 3:58pm	♊ 7/30 12:37am	♌ 12/17 4:34pm	♍ 5/5 5:19pm	♏ 9/23 8:27am
♈ 10/25 2:52am	♉ 3/13 12:15am	♋ 8/1 3:18am	♍ 12/19 6:02pm	♎ 5/7 7:21pm	♐ 9/25 10:11am
♉ 10/27 7:33am	♊ 3/15 6:29am	♌ 8/3 3:11am	♎ 12/21 8:52pm	♏ 5/9 9:00pm	♑ 9/27 3:15pm
♊ 10/29 9:59am	♋ 3/17 10:36am	♍ 8/5 2:18am	♏ 12/24 1:33am	♐ 5/11 11:32pm	♒ 9/30 12:02am
♋ 10/31 11:35am	♌ 3/19 12:52pm	♎ 8/7 2:51am	♐ 12/26 8:01am	♑ 5/14 4:25am	♓ 10/2 11:40am
♌ 11/2 1:37pm	♍ 3/21 2:07pm	♏ 8/9 6:33am	♑ 12/28 4:16pm	♒ 5/16 12:46pm	♈ 10/5 12:36am
♍ 11/4 5:03pm	♎ 3/23 3:49pm	♐ 8/11 1:59pm	♒ 12/31 2:31am	♓ 5/19 12:21am	♉ 10/7 1:20pm
♎ 11/6 10:23pm	♏ 3/25 7:33pm	♑ 8/14 12:30am	**1922**	♈ 5/21 1:13pm	♊ 10/10 12:44am
♏ 11/9 5:49am	♐ 3/28 2:34am	♒ 8/16 12:42pm	♓ 1/2 2:44pm	♉ 5/24 12:46am	♋ 10/12 9:52am
♐ 11/11 3:26pm	♑ 3/30 12:58pm	♓ 8/19 1:20am	♈ 1/5 3:42am	♊ 5/26 9:29am	♌ 10/14 4:01pm
♑ 11/14 3:03am	♒ 4/2 1:22am	♈ 8/21 1:30pm	♉ 1/7 2:58pm	♋ 5/28 3:26pm	♍ 10/16 7:04pm
♒ 11/16 3:44pm	♓ 4/4 1:28pm	♉ 8/24 12:07am	♊ 1/9 10:27pm	♌ 5/30 7:34pm	♎ 10/18 7:43pm
♓ 11/19 3:39am	♈ 4/6 11:31pm	♊ 8/26 7:58am	♋ 1/12 1:47am	♍ 6/1 10:48pm	♏ 10/20 7:26pm
♈ 11/21 12:45pm	♉ 4/9 7:00am	♋ 8/28 12:17pm	♌ 1/14 2:21am	♎ 6/4 1:43am	♐ 10/22 8:05pm
♉ 11/23 6:02pm	♊ 4/11 12:16pm	♌ 8/30 1:30pm	♍ 1/16 2:13am	♏ 6/6 4:42am	♑ 10/24 11:33pm
♊ 11/25 8:00pm	♋ 4/13 3:58pm	♍ 9/1 1:06pm	♎ 1/18 3:21am	♐ 6/8 8:18am	♒ 10/27 7:00am
♋ 11/27 8:12pm	♌ 4/15 6:47pm	♎ 9/3 1:05pm	♏ 1/20 7:02am	♑ 6/10 1:30pm	♓ 10/29 6:07pm
♌ 11/29 8:33pm	♍ 4/17 9:21pm	♏ 9/5 3:24pm	♐ 1/22 1:33pm	♒ 6/12 9:25pm	♈ 11/1 7:04am
♍ 12/1 10:45pm	♎ 4/20 12:24am	♐ 9/7 9:20pm	♑ 1/24 10:28pm	♓ 6/15 8:25am	♉ 11/3 7:40pm
♎ 12/4 3:50am	♏ 4/22 4:54am	♑ 9/10 6:58am	♒ 1/27 9:16am	♈ 6/17 9:12pm	♊ 11/6 6:33am
♏ 12/6 11:51am	♐ 4/24 11:45am	♒ 9/12 7:01pm	♓ 1/29 9:34pm	♉ 6/20 9:09am	♋ 11/8 3:23pm
♐ 12/8 10:09pm	♑ 4/26 9:27pm	♓ 9/15 7:39am	♈ 2/1 10:35am	♊ 6/22 6:02pm	♌ 11/10 10:05pm
♑ 12/11 9:59am	♒ 4/29 9:26am	♈ 9/17 7:29pm	♉ 2/3 10:41pm	♋ 6/24 11:27pm	♍ 11/13 2:36am
♒ 12/13 10:39pm	♓ 5/1 9:46pm	♉ 9/20 5:41am	♊ 2/6 7:41am	♌ 6/27 2:28am	♎ 11/15 5:01am
♓ 12/16 11:03am	♈ 5/4 8:14am	♊ 9/22 1:41pm	♋ 2/8 12:30pm	♍ 6/29 4:36am	♏ 11/17 5:59am
♈ 12/18 9:30pm	♉ 5/6 3:31pm	♋ 9/24 7:06pm	♌ 2/10 1:39pm	♎ 7/1 7:04am	♐ 11/19 6:53am
♉ 12/21 4:22am	♊ 5/8 7:51pm	♌ 9/26 9:57pm	♍ 2/12 12:58pm	♏ 7/3 10:29am	♑ 11/21 9:31am
♊ 12/23 7:15am	♋ 5/10 10:19pm	♍ 9/28 11:01pm	♎ 2/14 12:34pm	♐ 7/5 3:05pm	♒ 11/23 3:36pm
♋ 12/25 7:13am	♌ 5/13 12:16am	♎ 9/30 11:41pm	♏ 2/16 2:23pm	♑ 7/7 9:12pm	♓ 11/26 1:39am
♌ 12/27 6:16am	♍ 5/15 2:51am	♏ 10/3 1:37am	♐ 2/18 7:32pm	♒ 7/10 5:27am	♈ 11/28 2:20pm
♍ 12/29 6:37am	♎ 5/17 6:46am	♐ 10/5 6:22am	♑ 2/21 4:05am	♓ 7/12 4:16pm	♉ 12/1 3:00am
♎ 12/31 10:06am	♏ 5/19 12:21pm	♑ 10/7 2:45pm	♒ 2/23 3:12pm	♈ 7/15 4:59am	♊ 12/3 1:34pm
1921	♐ 5/21 7:53pm	♒ 10/10 2:12am	♓ 2/26 3:45am	♉ 7/17 5:28pm	♋ 12/5 9:34pm
♏ 1/2 5:27pm	♑ 5/24 5:34am	♓ 10/12 2:51pm	♈ 2/28 4:41pm	♊ 7/20 3:10am	♌ 12/8 3:33am
♐ 1/5 3:58am	♒ 5/26 5:17pm	♈ 10/15 2:34am	♉ 3/3 4:52am	♋ 7/22 8:56am	♍ 12/10 8:09am
♑ 1/7 4:10pm	♓ 5/29 5:50am	♉ 10/17 12:08pm	♊ 3/5 2:49pm	♌ 7/24 11:26am	♎ 12/12 11:39am
♒ 1/10 4:50am	♈ 5/31 5:05pm	♊ 10/19 7:21pm	♋ 3/7 9:19pm	♍ 7/26 12:21pm	♏ 12/14 2:14pm
♓ 1/12 5:10pm	♉ 6/3 1:03am	♋ 10/22 12:32am	♌ 3/10 12:09am	♎ 7/28 1:26pm	♐ 12/16 4:28pm
♈ 1/15 4:15am	♊ 6/5 5:17am	♌ 10/24 4:08am	♍ 3/12 12:22am	♏ 7/30 3:59pm	♑ 12/18 7:34pm
♉ 1/17 12:40pm	♋ 6/7 6:46am	♍ 10/26 6:40am	♎ 3/13 11:44pm	♐ 8/1 8:35pm	♒ 12/21 1:08am
♊ 1/19 5:23pm	♌ 6/9 7:18am	♎ 10/28 8:49am	♏ 3/16 12:13am	♑ 8/4 3:22am	♓ 12/23 10:14am
♋ 1/21 6:35pm	♍ 6/11 8:41am	♏ 10/30 11:33am	♐ 3/18 3:33am	♒ 8/6 12:19pm	♈ 12/25 10:22pm
♌ 1/23 5:45pm	♎ 6/13 12:10pm	♐ 11/1 4:08pm	♑ 3/20 10:41am	♓ 8/8 11:23pm	♉ 12/28 11:13am
♍ 1/25 5:04pm	♏ 6/15 6:10pm	♑ 11/3 11:38pm	♒ 3/22 9:18pm	♈ 8/11 12:05pm	♊ 12/30 10:02pm
♎ 1/27 6:46pm	♐ 6/18 2:28am	♒ 11/6 10:18am	♓ 3/25 9:56am	♉ 8/14 12:57am	**1923**
♏ 1/30 12:25am	♑ 6/20 12:39pm	♓ 11/8 10:51pm	♈ 3/27 10:49pm	♊ 8/16 11:42am	♋ 1/2 5:39am
♐ 2/1 10:04am	♒ 6/23 12:24am	♈ 11/11 10:52am	♉ 3/30 10:38am	♋ 8/18 6:40pm	♌ 1/4 10:34am
♑ 2/3 10:14pm	♓ 6/25 1:04pm	♉ 11/13 8:19pm	♊ 4/1 8:29pm	♌ 8/20 9:45pm	♍ 1/6 1:59pm
♒ 2/6 10:59am	♈ 6/28 1:02am	♊ 11/16 2:41am	♋ 4/4 3:46am	♍ 8/22 10:16pm	♎ 1/8 4:59pm
♓ 2/8 11:03pm	♉ 6/30 10:14am	♋ 11/18 6:41am	♌ 4/6 8:13am	♎ 8/24 10:05pm	♏ 1/10 8:04pm
♈ 2/11 9:51am	♊ 7/2 3:23pm	♌ 11/20 9:32am	♍ 4/8 10:09am	♏ 8/26 11:02pm	♐ 1/12 11:34pm
♉ 2/13 6:45pm	♋ 7/4 4:55pm	♍ 11/22 12:17pm	♎ 4/10 10:36am	♐ 8/29 2:26am	♑ 1/15 3:56am

Moon Sign Changes 1900-2005

♒	1/17	10:05am
♓	1/19	6:57pm
♈	1/22	6:37am
♉	1/24	7:34pm
♊	1/27	7:07am
♋	1/29	3:19pm
♌	1/31	7:57pm
♍	2/2	10:12pm
♎	2/4	11:38pm
♏	2/7	1:37am
♐	2/9	4:59am
♑	2/11	10:08am
♒	2/13	5:18pm
♓	2/16	2:43am
♈	2/18	2:20pm
♉	2/21	3:15am
♊	2/23	3:31pm
♋	2/26	12:57am
♌	2/28	6:30am
♍	3/2	8:41am
♎	3/4	9:00am
♏	3/6	9:16am
♐	3/8	11:05am
♑	3/10	3:34pm
♒	3/12	11:02pm
♓	3/15	9:08am
♈	3/17	9:06pm
♉	3/20	10:00am
♊	3/22	10:33pm
♋	3/25	9:05am
♌	3/27	4:13pm
♍	3/29	7:36pm
♎	3/31	8:06pm
♏	4/2	7:26pm
♐	4/4	7:33pm
♑	4/6	10:19pm
♒	4/9	4:48am
♓	4/11	2:51pm
♈	4/14	3:08am
♉	4/16	4:07pm
♊	4/19	4:33am
♋	4/21	3:28pm
♌	4/23	11:51pm
♍	4/26	4:56am
♎	4/28	6:48am
♏	4/30	6:32am
♐	5/2	5:59am
♑	5/4	7:14am
♒	5/6	12:05pm
♓	5/8	9:06pm
♈	5/11	9:12am
♉	5/13	10:14pm
♊	5/16	10:27am
♋	5/18	9:03pm
♌	5/21	5:40am
♍	5/23	11:54am
♎	5/25	3:25pm
♏	5/27	4:35pm
♐	5/29	4:37pm
♑	5/31	5:27pm
♒	6/2	9:04pm
♓	6/5	4:43am
♈	6/7	4:02pm
♉	6/10	4:56am
♊	6/12	5:03pm
♋	6/15	3:10am
♌	6/17	11:12am
♍	6/19	5:22pm
♎	6/21	9:44pm
♏	6/24	12:20am
♐	6/26	1:46am
♑	6/28	3:20am
♒	6/30	6:44am
♓	7/2	1:28pm
♈	7/4	11:51pm
♉	7/7	12:25pm
♊	7/10	12:37am
♋	7/12	10:34am
♌	7/14	5:53pm
♍	7/16	11:10pm
♎	7/19	3:05am
♏	7/21	6:08am
♐	7/23	8:43am
♑	7/25	11:32am
♒	7/27	3:42pm
♓	7/29	10:23pm
♈	8/1	8:11am
♉	8/3	8:22pm
♊	8/6	8:47am
♋	8/8	7:08pm
♌	8/11	2:19am
♍	8/13	6:44am
♎	8/15	9:27am
♏	8/17	11:38am
♐	8/19	2:12pm
♑	8/21	5:49pm
♒	8/23	11:03pm
♓	8/26	6:25am
♈	8/28	4:15pm
♉	8/31	4:12am
♊	9/2	4:50pm
♋	9/5	3:59am
♌	9/7	11:54am
♍	9/9	4:16pm
♎	9/11	6:03pm
♏	9/13	6:47pm
♐	9/15	8:05pm
♑	9/17	11:14pm
♒	9/20	4:53am
♓	9/22	1:03pm
♈	9/24	11:23pm
♉	9/27	11:22am
♊	9/30	12:06am
♋	10/2	12:00pm
♌	10/4	9:14pm
♍	10/7	2:41am
♎	10/9	4:35am
♏	10/11	4:25am
♐	10/13	4:08am
♑	10/15	5:43am
♒	10/17	10:29am
♓	10/19	6:43pm
♈	10/22	5:33am
♉	10/24	5:48pm
♊	10/27	6:29am
♋	10/29	6:39pm
♌	11/1	5:00am
♍	11/3	12:07pm
♎	11/5	3:24pm
♏	11/7	3:37pm
♐	11/9	2:37pm
♑	11/11	2:37pm
♒	11/13	5:40pm
♓	11/16	12:46am
♈	11/18	11:25am
♉	11/20	11:53pm
♊	11/23	12:32pm
♋	11/26	12:28am
♌	11/28	11:01am
♍	11/30	7:19pm
♎	12/3	12:24am
♏	12/5	2:14am
♐	12/7	1:57am
♑	12/9	1:31am
♒	12/11	3:10am
♓	12/13	8:35am
♈	12/15	6:08pm
♉	12/18	6:21am
♊	12/20	7:03pm
♋	12/23	6:40am
♌	12/25	4:40pm
♍	12/28	12:51am
♎	12/30	6:51am
	1924	
♏	1/1	10:23am
♐	1/3	11:48am
♑	1/5	12:22pm
♒	1/7	1:54pm
♓	1/9	6:13pm
♈	1/12	2:22am
♉	1/14	1:48pm
♊	1/17	2:28am
♋	1/19	2:05pm
♌	1/21	11:33pm
♍	1/24	6:49am
♎	1/26	12:14pm
♏	1/28	4:09pm
♐	1/30	6:52pm
♑	2/1	9:03pm
♒	2/3	11:43pm
♓	2/6	4:12am
♈	2/8	11:36am
♉	2/10	10:09pm
♊	2/13	10:35am
♋	2/15	10:34pm
♌	2/18	8:09am
♍	2/20	2:45pm
♎	2/22	6:57pm
♏	2/24	9:47pm
♐	2/27	12:16am
♑	2/29	3:12am
♒	3/2	7:11am
♓	3/4	12:44pm
♈	3/6	8:26pm
♉	3/9	6:35am
♊	3/11	6:44pm
♋	3/14	7:08am
♌	3/16	5:31pm
♍	3/19	12:27am
♎	3/21	4:00am
♏	3/23	5:27am
♐	3/25	6:29am
♑	3/27	8:37am
♒	3/29	12:47pm
♓	3/31	7:13pm
♈	4/3	3:45am
♉	4/5	2:11pm
♊	4/8	2:13am
♋	4/10	2:53pm
♌	4/13	2:15am
♍	4/15	10:21am
♎	4/17	2:27pm
♏	4/19	3:24pm
♐	4/21	3:04pm
♑	4/23	3:33pm
♒	4/25	6:30pm
♓	4/28	12:39am
♈	4/30	9:39am
♉	5/2	8:37pm
♊	5/5	8:48am
♋	5/7	9:31pm
♌	5/10	9:30am
♍	5/12	6:57pm
♎	5/15	12:28am
♏	5/17	2:10am
♐	5/19	1:33am
♑	5/21	12:48am
♒	5/23	2:04am
♓	5/25	6:49am
♈	5/27	3:16pm
♉	5/30	2:23am
♊	6/1	2:47pm
♋	6/4	3:27am
♌	6/6	3:29pm
♍	6/9	1:41am
♎	6/11	8:41am
♏	6/13	11:57am
♐	6/15	12:17pm
♑	6/17	11:28am
♒	6/19	11:42am
♓	6/21	2:52pm
♈	6/23	9:56pm
♉	6/26	8:27am
♊	6/28	8:51pm
♋	7/1	9:28am
♌	7/3	9:11pm
♍	7/6	7:15am
♎	7/8	2:55pm
♏	7/10	7:36pm
♐	7/12	9:32pm
♑	7/14	9:49pm
♒	7/16	10:11pm
♓	7/19	12:30am
♈	7/21	6:12am
♉	7/23	3:36pm
♊	7/26	3:36am
♋	7/28	4:11pm
♌	7/31	3:38am
♍	8/2	1:05pm
♎	8/4	8:20pm
♏	8/7	1:24am
♐	8/9	4:32am
♑	8/11	6:20am
♒	8/13	7:52am
♓	8/15	10:28am
♈	8/17	3:32pm
♉	8/19	11:54pm
♊	8/22	11:14am
♋	8/24	11:48pm
♌	8/27	11:19am
♍	8/29	8:19pm
♎	9/1	2:38am
♏	9/3	6:54am
♐	9/5	10:00am
♑	9/7	12:41pm
♒	9/9	3:33pm
♓	9/11	7:17pm
♈	9/14	12:42am
♉	9/16	8:39am
♊	9/18	7:24pm
♋	9/21	7:54am
♌	9/23	7:52pm
♍	9/26	5:06am
♎	9/28	10:53am
♏	9/30	2:00pm
♐	10/2	3:54pm
♑	10/4	6:02pm
♒	10/6	9:19pm
♓	10/9	2:06am
♈	10/11	8:31am
♉	10/13	4:50pm
♊	10/16	3:23am
♋	10/18	3:48pm
♌	10/21	4:21am
♍	10/23	2:33pm
♎	10/25	8:49pm
♏	10/27	11:26pm
♐	10/30	12:03am
♑	11/1	12:39am
♒	11/3	2:53am
♓	11/5	7:34am
♈	11/7	2:39pm
♉	11/9	11:44pm
♊	11/12	10:34am
♋	11/14	10:57pm
♌	11/17	11:51am
♍	11/19	11:11pm
♎	11/22	6:51am
♏	11/24	10:17am
♐	11/26	10:38am
♑	11/28	9:57am
♒	11/30	10:26am
♓	12/2	1:38pm
♈	12/4	8:10pm
♉	12/7	5:33am
♊	12/9	4:52pm
♋	12/12	5:21am
♌	12/14	6:13pm
♍	12/17	6:07am
♎	12/19	3:15pm
♏	12/21	8:26pm
♐	12/23	9:55pm
♑	12/25	9:18pm
♒	12/27	8:41pm
♓	12/29	10:06pm
	1925	
♈	1/1	2:57am
♉	1/3	11:31am
♊	1/5	10:52pm
♋	1/8	11:32am
♌	1/11	12:14am
♍	1/13	11:55am
♎	1/15	9:33pm
♏	1/18	4:11am
♐	1/20	7:34am
♑	1/22	8:22am
♒	1/24	8:09am
♓	1/26	8:46am
♈	1/28	11:59am
♉	1/30	6:58pm
♊	2/2	5:32am
♋	2/4	6:11pm
♌	2/7	6:50am
♍	2/9	6:01pm
♎	2/12	3:06am
♏	2/14	9:54am
♐	2/16	2:28pm
♑	2/18	5:02pm
♒	2/20	6:21pm
♓	2/22	7:36pm
♈	2/24	10:21pm
♉	2/27	4:04am
♊	3/1	1:26pm
♋	3/4	1:38am
♌	3/6	2:22pm
♍	3/9	1:24am
♎	3/11	9:44am
♏	3/13	3:37pm
♐	3/15	7:51pm
♑	3/17	11:07pm
♒	3/20	1:51am
♓	3/22	4:33am
♈	3/24	8:04am
♉	3/26	1:34pm
♊	3/28	10:08pm
♋	3/31	9:42am
♌	4/2	10:32pm
♍	4/5	9:55am
♎	4/7	6:04pm
♏	4/9	11:04pm
♐	4/12	2:05am
♑	4/14	4:32am
♒	4/16	7:23am
♓	4/18	11:02am
♈	4/20	3:45pm
♉	4/22	10:00pm
♊	4/25	6:33am
♋	4/27	5:45pm
♌	4/30	6:37am
♍	5/2	6:38pm
♎	5/5	3:26am
♏	5/7	8:22am

Moon Sign Changes 1900-2005

♐ 5/9 10:27am	♒ 9/27 11:29am	♓ 2/13 3:57am	♉ 7/3 11:59pm	♋ 11/22 2:54am	♌ 4/9 11:00pm
♑ 5/11 11:30am	♓ 9/29 1:19pm	♈ 2/15 3:47am	♊ 7/6 5:57am	♌ 11/24 11:10am	♍ 4/12 10:19am
♒ 5/13 1:08pm	♈ 10/1 3:06pm	♉ 2/17 6:09am	♋ 7/8 2:16pm	♍ 11/26 10:36pm	♎ 4/14 10:53pm
♓ 5/15 4:23pm	♉ 10/3 6:20pm	♊ 2/19 12:22pm	♌ 7/11 12:50am	♎ 11/29 11:14am	♏ 4/17 11:20am
♈ 5/17 9:34pm	♊ 10/6 12:35am	♋ 2/21 10:28pm	♍ 7/13 1:08pm	♏ 12/1 10:39pm	♐ 4/19 10:49pm
♉ 5/20 4:41am	♋ 10/8 10:33am	♌ 2/24 11:00am	♎ 7/16 1:52am	♐ 12/4 7:32am	♑ 4/22 8:35am
♊ 5/22 1:50pm	♌ 10/10 11:09pm	♍ 2/26 11:59pm	♏ 7/18 1:08pm	♑ 12/6 1:52pm	♒ 4/24 3:43pm
♋ 5/25 1:08am	♍ 10/13 11:43am	♎ 3/1 12:03pm	♐ 7/20 9:10pm	♒ 12/8 6:22pm	♓ 4/26 7:37pm
♌ 5/27 1:59pm	♎ 10/15 9:57pm	♏ 3/3 10:28pm	♑ 7/23 1:28am	♓ 12/10 9:44pm	♈ 4/28 8:43pm
♍ 5/30 2:35am	♏ 10/18 5:12am	♐ 3/6 6:40am	♒ 7/25 2:48am	♈ 12/13 12:33am	♉ 4/30 8:28pm
♎ 6/1 12:30pm	♐ 10/20 10:11am	♑ 3/8 12:06pm	♓ 7/27 2:46am	♉ 12/15 3:23am	♊ 5/2 8:52pm
♏ 6/3 6:21pm	♑ 10/22 1:57pm	♒ 3/10 2:40pm	♈ 7/29 3:13am	♊ 12/17 6:59am	♋ 5/4 11:51pm
♐ 6/5 8:33pm	♒ 10/24 5:12pm	♓ 3/12 3:03pm	♉ 7/31 5:47am	♋ 12/19 12:20pm	♌ 5/7 6:39am
♑ 6/7 8:45pm	♓ 10/26 8:14pm	♈ 3/14 2:52pm	♊ 8/2 11:24am	♌ 12/21 8:17pm	♍ 5/9 5:03pm
♒ 6/9 8:54pm	♈ 10/28 11:24pm	♉ 3/16 4:06pm	♋ 8/4 8:08pm	♍ 12/24 7:02am	♎ 5/12 5:27am
♓ 6/11 10:40pm	♉ 10/31 3:29am	♊ 3/18 8:42pm	♌ 8/7 7:12am	♎ 12/26 7:31pm	♏ 5/14 5:52pm
♈ 6/14 3:03am	♊ 11/2 9:44am	♋ 3/21 5:30am	♍ 8/9 7:39pm	♏ 12/29 7:28am	♐ 5/17 4:58am
♉ 6/16 10:15am	♋ 11/4 7:06pm	♌ 3/23 5:35pm	♎ 8/12 8:26am	♐ 12/31 4:50pm	♑ 5/19 2:11pm
♊ 6/18 7:57pm	♌ 11/7 7:16am	♍ 3/26 6:36am	♏ 8/14 8:18pm	**1927**	♒ 5/21 9:16pm
♋ 6/21 7:36am	♍ 11/9 8:07pm	♎ 3/28 6:27pm	♐ 8/17 5:39am	♑ 1/2 10:51pm	♓ 5/24 2:01am
♌ 6/23 8:31pm	♎ 11/12 6:52am	♏ 3/31 4:17am	♑ 8/19 11:23am	♒ 1/5 2:10am	♈ 5/26 4:37am
♍ 6/26 9:21am	♏ 11/14 2:05pm	♐ 4/2 12:08pm	♒ 8/21 1:31pm	♓ 1/7 4:05am	♉ 5/28 5:50am
♎ 6/28 8:15pm	♐ 11/16 6:13pm	♑ 4/4 6:04pm	♓ 8/23 1:14pm	♈ 1/9 6:00am	♊ 5/30 7:02am
♏ 7/1 3:32am	♑ 11/18 8:38pm	♒ 4/6 10:01pm	♈ 8/25 12:30pm	♉ 1/11 8:56am	♋ 6/1 9:50am
♐ 7/3 6:55am	♒ 11/20 10:48pm	♓ 4/9 12:03am	♉ 8/27 1:24pm	♊ 1/13 1:30pm	♌ 6/3 3:37pm
♑ 7/5 7:24am	♓ 11/23 1:37am	♈ 4/11 1:02am	♊ 8/29 5:39pm	♋ 1/15 7:59pm	♍ 6/6 12:55am
♒ 7/7 6:49am	♈ 11/25 5:31am	♉ 4/13 2:31am	♋ 9/1 1:48am	♌ 1/18 4:31am	♎ 6/8 12:49pm
♓ 7/9 7:06am	♉ 11/27 10:46am	♊ 4/15 6:20am	♌ 9/3 1:01pm	♍ 1/20 3:10pm	♏ 6/11 1:16am
♈ 7/11 9:53am	♊ 11/29 5:50pm	♋ 4/17 1:55pm	♍ 9/6 1:40am	♎ 1/23 3:27am	♐ 6/13 12:16pm
♉ 7/13 4:05pm	♋ 12/2 3:19am	♌ 4/20 1:07am	♎ 9/8 2:23pm	♏ 1/25 3:54pm	♑ 6/15 8:51pm
♊ 7/16 1:37am	♌ 12/4 3:13pm	♍ 4/22 1:59pm	♏ 9/11 2:15am	♐ 1/28 2:21am	♒ 6/18 3:05am
♋ 7/18 1:33pm	♍ 12/7 4:13am	♎ 4/25 1:52am	♐ 9/13 12:22pm	♑ 1/30 9:12am	♓ 6/20 7:25am
♌ 7/21 2:32am	♎ 12/9 3:52pm	♏ 4/27 11:19am	♑ 9/15 7:37pm	♒ 2/1 12:22pm	♈ 6/22 10:29am
♍ 7/23 3:17pm	♏ 12/12 12:03am	♐ 4/29 6:19pm	♒ 9/17 11:23pm	♓ 2/3 1:07pm	♉ 6/24 12:54pm
♎ 7/26 2:30am	♐ 12/14 4:23am	♑ 5/1 11:32pm	♓ 9/20 12:06am	♈ 2/5 1:19pm	♊ 6/26 3:26pm
♏ 7/28 10:56am	♑ 12/16 5:59am	♒ 5/4 3:31am	♈ 9/21 11:20pm	♉ 2/7 2:50pm	♋ 6/28 7:03pm
♐ 7/30 3:56pm	♒ 12/18 6:35am	♓ 5/6 6:32am	♉ 9/23 11:12pm	♊ 2/9 6:54pm	♌ 7/1 12:48am
♑ 8/1 5:46pm	♓ 12/20 7:51am	♈ 5/8 8:55am	♊ 9/26 1:50am	♋ 2/12 1:51am	♍ 7/3 9:27am
♒ 8/3 5:40pm	♈ 12/22 10:57am	♉ 5/10 11:33am	♋ 9/28 8:35am	♌ 2/14 11:11am	♎ 7/5 8:47pm
♓ 8/5 5:23pm	♉ 12/24 4:25pm	♊ 5/12 3:46pm	♌ 9/30 7:10pm	♍ 2/16 10:15pm	♏ 7/8 9:17am
♈ 8/7 6:46pm	♊ 12/27 12:18am	♋ 5/14 10:53pm	♍ 10/3 7:49am	♎ 2/19 10:31am	♐ 7/10 8:37pm
♉ 8/9 11:24pm	♋ 12/29 10:26am	♌ 5/17 9:20am	♎ 10/5 8:28pm	♏ 2/21 11:08pm	♑ 7/13 5:06am
♊ 8/12 7:57am	♌ 12/31 10:26pm	♍ 5/19 9:54pm	♏ 10/8 7:59am	♐ 2/24 10:35am	♒ 7/15 10:31am
♋ 8/14 7:39pm	**1926**	♎ 5/22 10:04am	♐ 10/10 5:54pm	♑ 2/26 6:56pm	♓ 7/17 1:43pm
♌ 8/17 8:41am	♍ 1/3 11:26am	♏ 5/24 7:41pm	♑ 10/13 1:47am	♒ 2/28 11:14pm	♈ 7/19 3:58pm
♍ 8/19 9:13pm	♎ 1/5 11:44pm	♐ 5/27 2:14am	♒ 10/15 7:02am	♓ 3/3 12:05am	♉ 7/21 6:24pm
♎ 8/22 8:05am	♏ 1/8 9:19am	♑ 5/29 6:24am	♓ 10/17 9:29am	♈ 3/4 11:19pm	♊ 7/23 9:46pm
♏ 8/24 4:44pm	♐ 1/10 3:01pm	♒ 5/31 9:19am	♈ 10/19 9:56am	♉ 3/6 11:07pm	♋ 7/26 2:31am
♐ 8/26 10:50pm	♑ 1/12 5:09pm	♓ 6/2 11:53am	♉ 10/21 10:01am	♊ 3/9 1:29am	♌ 7/28 9:00am
♑ 8/29 2:19am	♒ 1/14 5:07pm	♈ 6/4 2:45pm	♊ 10/23 11:50am	♋ 3/11 7:29am	♍ 7/30 5:42pm
♒ 8/31 3:41am	♓ 1/16 4:48pm	♉ 6/6 6:28pm	♋ 10/25 5:08pm	♌ 3/13 4:52pm	♎ 8/2 4:44am
♓ 9/2 4:02am	♈ 1/18 6:03pm	♊ 6/8 11:43pm	♌ 10/28 2:31am	♍ 3/16 4:22am	♏ 8/4 5:16pm
♈ 9/4 5:02am	♉ 1/20 10:16pm	♋ 6/11 7:15am	♍ 10/30 2:43pm	♎ 3/18 4:48pm	♐ 8/7 5:14am
♉ 9/6 8:27am	♊ 1/23 5:55am	♌ 6/13 5:29pm	♎ 11/2 3:22am	♏ 3/21 5:21am	♑ 8/9 2:23pm
♊ 9/8 3:39pm	♋ 1/25 4:30pm	♍ 6/16 5:48am	♏ 11/4 2:37pm	♐ 3/23 5:06pm	♒ 8/11 7:46pm
♋ 9/11 2:35am	♌ 1/28 4:52am	♎ 6/18 6:19pm	♐ 11/6 11:51pm	♑ 3/26 2:39am	♓ 8/13 10:04pm
♌ 9/13 3:30pm	♍ 1/30 5:49pm	♏ 6/21 4:40am	♑ 11/9 7:11am	♒ 3/28 8:39am	♈ 8/15 10:57pm
♍ 9/16 3:56am	♎ 2/2 6:11am	♐ 6/23 11:35am	♒ 11/11 12:42pm	♓ 3/30 10:52am	♉ 8/18 12:12am
♎ 9/18 2:18pm	♏ 2/4 4:39pm	♑ 6/25 3:18pm	♓ 11/13 4:22pm	♈ 4/1 10:30am	♊ 8/20 3:08am
♏ 9/20 10:18pm	♐ 2/7 12:02am	♒ 6/27 5:01pm	♈ 11/15 6:28pm	♉ 4/3 9:36am	♋ 8/22 8:19am
♐ 9/23 4:17am	♑ 2/9 3:49am	♓ 6/29 6:13pm	♉ 11/17 7:54pm	♊ 4/5 10:25am	♌ 8/24 3:39pm
♑ 9/25 8:37am	♒ 2/11 4:37am	♈ 7/1 8:14pm	♊ 11/19 10:10pm	♋ 4/7 2:42pm	♍ 8/27 12:55am

Moon Sign Changes 1900-2005

Sign	Date	Time
♎	8/29	12:02pm
♏	9/1	12:36am
♐	9/3	1:10pm
♑	9/5	11:28pm
♒	9/8	5:50am
♓	9/10	8:16am
♈	9/12	8:18am
♉	9/14	8:03am
♊	9/16	9:29am
♋	9/18	1:49pm
♌	9/20	9:13pm
♍	9/23	7:01am
♎	9/25	6:30pm
♏	9/28	7:05am
♐	9/30	7:54pm
♑	10/3	7:13am
♒	10/5	3:07pm
♓	10/7	6:50pm
♈	10/9	7:14pm
♉	10/11	6:17pm
♊	10/13	6:12pm
♋	10/15	8:50pm
♌	10/18	3:07am
♍	10/20	12:43pm
♎	10/23	12:28am
♏	10/25	1:08pm
♐	10/28	1:48am
♑	10/30	1:22pm
♒	11/1	10:26pm
♓	11/4	3:56am
♈	11/6	5:53am
♉	11/8	5:37am
♊	11/10	5:03am
♋	11/12	6:15am
♌	11/14	10:48am
♍	11/16	7:14pm
♎	11/19	6:41am
♏	11/21	7:26pm
♐	11/24	7:53am
♑	11/26	7:01pm
♒	11/29	4:06am
♓	12/1	10:37am
♈	12/3	2:20pm
♉	12/5	3:47pm
♊	12/7	4:10pm
♋	12/9	5:11pm
♌	12/11	8:31pm
♍	12/14	3:25am
♎	12/16	1:55pm
♏	12/19	2:31am
♐	12/21	2:59pm
♑	12/24	1:38am
♒	12/26	9:54am
♓	12/28	4:00pm
♈	12/30	8:19pm
1928		
♉	1/1	11:15pm
♊	1/4	1:20am
♋	1/6	3:28am
♌	1/8	6:52am
♍	1/10	12:53pm
♎	1/12	10:18pm
♏	1/15	10:26am
♐	1/17	11:06pm
♑	1/20	9:49am
♒	1/22	5:27pm
♓	1/24	10:24pm
♈	1/27	1:48am
♉	1/29	4:42am
♊	1/31	7:47am
♋	2/2	11:21am
♌	2/4	3:53pm
♍	2/6	10:09pm
♎	2/9	7:03am
♏	2/11	6:41pm
♐	2/14	7:32am
♑	2/16	6:54pm
♒	2/19	2:47am
♓	2/21	7:05am
♈	2/23	9:09am
♉	2/25	10:42am
♊	2/27	1:07pm
♋	2/29	5:04pm
♌	3/2	10:38pm
♍	3/5	5:51am
♎	3/7	3:04pm
♏	3/10	2:31am
♐	3/12	3:24pm
♑	3/15	3:33am
♒	3/17	12:31pm
♓	3/19	5:20pm
♈	3/21	6:54pm
♉	3/23	7:06pm
♊	3/25	7:53pm
♋	3/27	10:42pm
♌	3/30	4:04am
♍	4/1	11:53am
♎	4/3	9:47pm
♏	4/6	9:27am
♐	4/8	10:20pm
♑	4/11	10:56am
♒	4/13	9:07pm
♓	4/16	3:19am
♈	4/18	5:40am
♉	4/20	5:36am
♊	4/22	5:09am
♋	4/24	6:14am
♌	4/26	10:12am
♍	4/28	5:28pm
♎	5/1	3:36am
♏	5/3	3:38pm
♐	5/6	4:32am
♑	5/8	5:09pm
♒	5/11	3:58am
♓	5/13	11:35am
♈	5/15	3:30pm
♉	5/17	4:25pm
♊	5/19	3:56pm
♋	5/21	3:57pm
♌	5/23	6:17pm
♍	5/26	12:07am
♎	5/28	9:36am
♏	5/30	9:40pm
♐	6/2	10:38am
♑	6/4	11:00pm
♒	6/7	9:41am
♓	6/9	5:54pm
♈	6/11	11:13pm
♉	6/14	1:46am
♊	6/16	2:24am
♋	6/18	2:34am
♌	6/20	4:02am
♍	6/22	8:27am
♎	6/24	4:43pm
♏	6/27	4:17am
♐	6/29	5:13pm
♑	7/2	5:23am
♒	7/4	3:32pm
♓	7/6	11:23pm
♈	7/9	5:04am
♉	7/11	8:49am
♊	7/13	10:59am
♋	7/15	12:20pm
♌	7/17	2:06pm
♍	7/19	5:53pm
♎	7/22	1:02am
♏	7/24	11:47am
♐	7/27	12:34am
♑	7/29	12:47pm
♒	7/31	10:33pm
♓	8/3	5:35am
♈	8/5	10:33am
♉	8/7	2:19pm
♊	8/9	5:22pm
♋	8/11	8:03pm
♌	8/13	10:57pm
♍	8/16	3:07am
♎	8/18	9:53am
♏	8/20	7:57pm
♐	8/23	8:29am
♑	8/25	8:59pm
♒	8/28	6:57am
♓	8/30	1:31pm
♈	9/1	5:26pm
♉	9/3	8:07pm
♊	9/5	10:43pm
♋	9/8	1:51am
♌	9/10	5:49am
♍	9/12	11:01am
♎	9/14	6:12pm
♏	9/17	4:05am
♐	9/19	4:23pm
♑	9/22	5:16am
♒	9/24	4:01pm
♓	9/26	11:01pm
♈	9/29	2:31am
♉	10/1	3:59am
♊	10/3	5:09am
♋	10/5	7:21am
♌	10/7	11:18am
♍	10/9	5:13pm
♎	10/12	1:14am
♏	10/14	11:29am
♐	10/16	11:44pm
♑	10/19	12:50pm
♒	10/22	12:33am
♓	10/24	8:50am
♈	10/26	1:04pm
♉	10/28	2:16pm
♊	10/30	2:11pm
♋	11/1	2:40pm
♌	11/3	5:14pm
♍	11/5	10:41pm
♎	11/8	7:05am
♏	11/10	5:53pm
♐	11/13	6:20am
♑	11/15	7:25pm
♒	11/18	7:40am
♓	11/20	5:19pm
♈	11/22	11:14pm
♉	11/25	1:30am
♊	11/27	1:23am
♋	11/29	12:43am
♌	12/1	1:29am
♍	12/3	5:16am
♎	12/5	12:52pm
♏	12/7	11:46pm
♐	12/10	12:29pm
♑	12/13	1:29am
♒	12/15	1:36pm
♓	12/17	11:49pm
♈	12/20	7:15am
♉	12/22	11:25am
♊	12/24	12:40pm
♋	12/26	12:17pm
♌	12/28	12:07pm
♍	12/30	2:12pm
1929		
♎	1/1	8:08pm
♏	1/4	6:10am
♐	1/6	6:50pm
♑	1/9	7:51am
♒	1/11	7:33pm
♓	1/14	5:21am
♈	1/16	1:07pm
♉	1/18	6:37pm
♊	1/20	9:43pm
♋	1/22	10:52pm
♌	1/24	11:16pm
♍	1/27	12:47am
♎	1/29	5:19am
♏	1/31	1:57pm
♐	2/3	1:59am
♑	2/5	3:00pm
♒	2/8	2:34am
♓	2/10	11:43am
♈	2/12	6:41pm
♉	2/15	12:02am
♊	2/17	4:01am
♋	2/19	6:45am
♌	2/21	8:41am
♍	2/23	10:58am
♎	2/25	3:15pm
♏	2/27	10:54pm
♐	3/2	10:03am
♑	3/4	10:55pm
♒	3/7	10:44am
♓	3/9	7:44pm
♈	3/12	1:51am
♉	3/14	6:05am
♊	3/16	9:23am
♋	3/18	12:24pm
♌	3/20	3:27pm
♍	3/22	7:05pm
♎	3/25	12:11am
♏	3/27	7:50am
♐	3/29	6:26pm
♑	4/1	7:03am
♒	4/3	7:18pm
♓	4/6	4:52am
♈	4/8	10:57am
♉	4/10	2:17pm
♊	4/12	4:13pm
♋	4/14	6:04pm
♌	4/16	8:50pm
♍	4/19	1:05am
♎	4/21	7:13am
♏	4/23	3:35pm
♐	4/26	2:16am
♑	4/28	2:43pm
♒	5/1	3:19am
♓	5/3	1:51pm
♈	5/5	8:51pm
♉	5/8	12:18am
♊	5/10	1:22am
♋	5/12	1:44am
♌	5/14	3:03am
♍	5/16	6:33am
♎	5/18	12:52pm
♏	5/20	9:54pm
♐	5/23	9:04am
♑	5/25	9:34pm
♒	5/28	10:17am
♓	5/30	9:37pm
♈	6/2	5:58am
♉	6/4	10:34am
♊	6/6	11:57am
♋	6/8	11:35am
♌	6/10	11:25am
♍	6/12	1:20pm
♎	6/14	6:39pm
♏	6/17	3:32am
♐	6/19	3:03pm
♑	6/22	3:45am
♒	6/24	4:24pm
♓	6/27	3:59am
♈	6/29	1:22pm
♉	7/1	7:31pm
♊	7/3	10:14pm
♋	7/5	10:21pm
♌	7/7	9:37pm
♍	7/9	10:10pm
♎	7/12	1:54am
♏	7/14	9:44am
♐	7/16	9:00pm
♑	7/19	9:47am
♒	7/21	10:20pm
♓	7/24	9:39am
♈	7/26	7:13pm
♉	7/29	2:25am
♊	7/31	6:43am
♋	8/2	8:15am
♌	8/4	8:11am
♍	8/6	8:23am
♎	8/8	10:56am
♏	8/10	5:22pm
♐	8/13	3:44am
♑	8/15	4:21pm
♒	8/18	4:50am
♓	8/20	3:46pm
♈	8/23	12:47am
♉	8/25	7:55am
♊	8/27	1:03pm
♋	8/29	4:04pm
♌	8/31	5:26pm
♍	9/2	6:27pm
♎	9/4	8:51pm
♏	9/7	2:20am
♐	9/9	11:38am
♑	9/11	11:45pm
♒	9/14	12:17pm
♓	9/16	11:07pm
♈	9/19	7:30am
♉	9/21	1:45pm
♊	9/23	6:25pm
♋	9/25	9:52pm
♌	9/28	12:28am
♍	9/30	2:52am
♎	10/2	6:10am
♏	10/4	11:40am
♐	10/6	8:18pm
♑	10/9	7:49am
♒	10/11	8:25pm
♓	10/14	7:40am
♈	10/16	4:02pm
♉	10/18	9:29pm
♊	10/21	12:54am
♋	10/23	3:24am
♌	10/25	5:55am
♍	10/27	9:08am
♎	10/29	1:39pm
♏	10/31	8:02pm
♐	11/3	4:47am
♑	11/5	3:57pm
♒	11/8	4:33am
♓	11/10	4:30pm
♈	11/13	1:43am
♉	11/15	7:19am
♊	11/17	9:53am
♋	11/19	10:53am
♌	11/21	11:58am
♍	11/23	2:32pm
♎	11/25	7:23pm
♏	11/28	2:40am
♐	11/30	12:08pm
♑	12/2	11:25pm
♒	12/5	11:57am
♓	12/8	12:27am
♈	12/10	10:57am
♉	12/12	5:50pm
♊	12/14	8:49pm
♋	12/16	9:05pm

Moon Sign Changes 1900-2005

♌ 12/18 8:34pm
♍ 12/20 9:22pm
♎ 12/23 1:03am
♏ 12/25 8:12am
♐ 12/27 6:12pm
♑ 12/30 5:56am

1930

♒ 1/1 6:29pm
♓ 1/4 7:05am
♈ 1/6 6:27pm
♉ 1/9 2:59am
♊ 1/11 7:34am
♋ 1/13 8:35am
♌ 1/15 7:37am
♍ 1/17 6:57am
♎ 1/19 8:44am
♏ 1/21 2:25pm
♐ 1/23 11:56pm
♑ 1/26 11:53am
♒ 1/29 12:35am
♓ 1/31 12:59pm
♈ 2/3 12:23am
♉ 2/5 9:49am
♊ 2/7 4:08pm
♋ 2/9 6:55pm
♌ 2/11 7:00pm
♍ 2/13 6:14pm
♎ 2/15 6:50pm
♏ 2/17 10:45pm
♐ 2/20 6:49am
♑ 2/22 6:13pm
♒ 2/25 6:57am
♓ 2/27 7:13pm
♈ 3/2 6:08am
♉ 3/4 3:19pm
♊ 3/6 10:16pm
♋ 3/9 2:34am
♌ 3/11 4:25am
♍ 3/13 4:54am
♎ 3/15 5:43am
♏ 3/17 8:46am
♐ 3/19 3:24pm
♑ 3/22 1:40am
♒ 3/24 2:05pm
♓ 3/27 2:24am
♈ 3/29 1:00pm
♉ 3/31 9:24pm
♊ 4/3 3:42am
♋ 4/5 8:11am
♌ 4/7 11:09am
♍ 4/9 1:11pm
♎ 4/11 3:17pm
♏ 4/13 6:45pm
♐ 4/16 12:49am
♑ 4/18 10:07am
♒ 4/20 9:58pm
♓ 4/23 10:23am
♈ 4/25 9:10pm
♉ 4/28 5:08am
♊ 4/30 10:26am
♋ 5/2 1:54pm
♌ 5/4 4:32pm
♍ 5/6 7:11pm
♎ 5/8 10:30pm
♏ 5/11 3:06am
♐ 5/13 9:39am
♑ 5/15 6:39pm
♒ 5/18 6:04am
♓ 5/20 6:34pm
♈ 5/23 5:56am
♉ 5/25 2:15pm
♊ 5/27 7:07pm
♋ 5/29 9:26pm
♌ 5/31 10:45pm
♍ 6/3 12:37am
♎ 6/5 4:04am
♏ 6/7 9:30am
♐ 6/9 4:56pm
♑ 6/12 2:20am
♒ 6/14 1:39pm
♓ 6/17 2:12am
♈ 6/19 2:15pm
♉ 6/21 11:35pm
♊ 6/24 5:00am
♋ 6/26 6:57am
♌ 6/28 7:06am
♍ 6/30 7:28am
♎ 7/2 9:47am
♏ 7/4 2:56pm
♐ 7/6 10:49pm
♑ 7/9 8:49am
♒ 7/11 8:23pm
♓ 7/14 8:57am
♈ 7/16 9:26pm
♉ 7/19 7:54am
♊ 7/21 2:39pm
♋ 7/23 5:22pm
♌ 7/25 5:19pm
♍ 7/27 4:34pm
♎ 7/29 5:18pm
♏ 7/31 9:05pm
♐ 8/3 4:24am
♑ 8/5 2:34pm
♒ 8/8 2:26am
♓ 8/10 3:03pm
♈ 8/13 3:32am
♉ 8/15 2:38pm
♊ 8/17 10:46pm
♋ 8/20 3:02am
♌ 8/22 3:58am
♍ 8/24 3:13am
♎ 8/26 2:58am
♏ 8/28 5:11am
♐ 8/30 11:04am
♑ 9/1 8:35pm
♒ 9/4 8:27am
♓ 9/6 9:06pm
♈ 9/9 9:21am
♉ 9/11 8:18pm
♊ 9/14 5:01am
♋ 9/16 10:42am
♌ 9/18 1:18pm
♍ 9/20 1:45pm
♎ 9/22 1:43pm
♏ 9/24 3:07pm
♐ 9/26 7:34pm
♑ 9/29 3:48am
♒ 10/1 3:09pm
♓ 10/4 3:48am
♈ 10/6 3:52pm
♉ 10/9 2:14am
♊ 10/11 10:29am
♋ 10/13 4:29pm
♌ 10/15 8:19pm
♍ 10/17 10:26pm
♎ 10/19 11:43pm
♏ 10/22 1:32am
♐ 10/24 5:23am
♑ 10/26 12:27pm
♒ 10/28 10:54pm
♓ 10/31 11:23am
♈ 11/2 11:34pm
♉ 11/5 9:37am
♊ 11/7 4:58pm
♋ 11/9 10:05pm
♌ 11/12 1:45am
♍ 11/14 4:42am
♎ 11/16 7:27am
♏ 11/18 10:36am
♐ 11/20 3:00pm
♑ 11/22 9:42pm
♒ 11/25 7:23am
♓ 11/27 7:33pm
♈ 11/30 8:06am
♉ 12/2 6:32pm
♊ 12/5 1:32am
♋ 12/7 5:31am
♌ 12/9 7:53am
♍ 12/11 10:04am
♎ 12/13 1:05pm
♏ 12/15 5:19pm
♐ 12/17 10:54pm
♑ 12/20 6:11am
♒ 12/22 3:44pm
♓ 12/25 3:35am
♈ 12/27 4:29pm
♉ 12/30 3:52am

1931

♊ 1/1 11:34am
♋ 1/3 3:21pm
♌ 1/5 4:32pm
♍ 1/7 5:06pm
♎ 1/9 6:48pm
♏ 1/11 10:40pm
♐ 1/14 4:51am
♑ 1/16 1:02pm
♒ 1/18 11:04pm
♓ 1/21 10:55am
♈ 1/23 11:55pm
♉ 1/26 12:10pm
♊ 1/28 9:18pm
♋ 1/31 2:09am
♌ 2/2 3:24am
♍ 2/4 2:57am
♎ 2/6 2:54am
♏ 2/8 5:04am
♐ 2/10 10:21am
♑ 2/12 6:39pm
♒ 2/15 5:14am
♓ 2/17 5:23pm
♈ 2/20 6:21am
♉ 2/22 6:54pm
♊ 2/25 5:13am
♋ 2/27 11:47am
♌ 3/1 2:25pm
♍ 3/3 2:21pm
♎ 3/5 1:32pm
♏ 3/7 2:03pm
♐ 3/9 5:30pm
♑ 3/12 12:39am
♒ 3/14 11:03am
♓ 3/16 11:26pm
♈ 3/19 12:24pm
♉ 3/22 12:44am
♊ 3/24 11:19am
♋ 3/26 7:04pm
♌ 3/28 11:29pm
♍ 3/31 12:58am
♎ 4/2 12:49am
♏ 4/4 12:50am
♐ 4/6 2:52am
♑ 4/8 8:20am
♒ 4/10 5:40pm
♓ 4/13 5:49am
♈ 4/15 6:48pm
♉ 4/18 6:50am
♊ 4/20 4:56pm
♋ 4/23 12:42am
♌ 4/25 6:04am
♍ 4/27 9:10am
♎ 4/29 10:35am
♏ 5/1 11:26am
♐ 5/3 1:14pm
♑ 5/5 5:35pm
♒ 5/8 1:37am
♓ 5/10 1:02pm
♈ 5/13 1:57am
♉ 5/15 1:54pm
♊ 5/17 11:26pm
♋ 5/20 6:26am
♌ 5/22 11:27am
♍ 5/24 3:07pm
♎ 5/26 5:51pm
♏ 5/28 8:08pm
♐ 5/30 10:48pm
♑ 6/2 3:07am
♒ 6/4 10:23am
♓ 6/6 9:01pm
♈ 6/9 9:44am
♉ 6/11 9:54pm
♊ 6/14 7:22am
♋ 6/16 1:38pm
♌ 6/18 5:36pm
♍ 6/20 8:32pm
♎ 6/22 11:23pm
♏ 6/25 2:34am
♐ 6/27 6:26am
♑ 6/29 11:35am
♒ 7/1 6:56pm
♓ 7/4 5:10am
♈ 7/6 5:40pm
♉ 7/9 6:14am
♊ 7/11 4:14pm
♋ 7/13 10:30pm
♌ 7/16 1:41am
♍ 7/18 3:22am
♎ 7/20 5:06am
♏ 7/22 7:56am
♐ 7/24 12:18pm
♑ 7/26 6:22pm
♒ 7/29 2:24am
♓ 7/31 12:45pm
♈ 8/3 1:10am
♉ 8/5 2:05pm
♊ 8/8 1:01am
♋ 8/10 8:10am
♌ 8/12 11:31am
♍ 8/14 12:25pm
♎ 8/16 12:45pm
♏ 8/18 2:10pm
♐ 8/20 5:47pm
♑ 8/22 11:58pm
♒ 8/25 8:38am
♓ 8/27 7:27pm
♈ 8/30 7:56am
♉ 9/1 8:59pm
♊ 9/4 8:43am
♋ 9/6 5:15pm
♌ 9/8 9:47pm
♍ 9/10 11:04pm
♎ 9/12 10:43pm
♏ 9/14 10:40pm
♐ 9/17 12:39am
♑ 9/19 5:48am
♒ 9/21 2:18pm
♓ 9/24 1:28am
♈ 9/26 2:09pm
♉ 9/29 3:07am
♊ 10/1 3:03pm
♋ 10/4 12:38am
♌ 10/6 6:49am
♍ 10/8 9:34am
♎ 10/10 9:50am
♏ 10/12 9:17am
♐ 10/14 9:51am
♑ 10/16 1:18pm
♒ 10/18 8:39pm
♓ 10/21 7:32am
♈ 10/23 8:21pm
♉ 10/26 9:12am
♊ 10/28 8:48pm
♋ 10/31 6:26am
♌ 11/2 1:39pm
♍ 11/4 6:08pm
♎ 11/6 8:03pm
♏ 11/8 8:21pm
♐ 11/10 8:39pm
♑ 11/12 10:52pm
♒ 11/15 4:40am
♓ 11/17 2:32pm
♈ 11/20 3:08am
♉ 11/22 4:00pm
♊ 11/25 3:12am
♋ 11/27 12:09pm
♌ 11/29 7:06pm
♍ 12/2 12:16am
♎ 12/4 3:44am
♏ 12/6 5:43am
♐ 12/8 7:04am
♑ 12/10 9:18am
♒ 12/12 2:10pm
♓ 12/14 10:50pm
♈ 12/17 10:49am
♉ 12/19 11:45pm
♊ 12/22 10:59am
♋ 12/24 7:22pm
♌ 12/27 1:16am
♍ 12/29 5:41am
♎ 12/31 9:17am

1932

♏ 1/2 12:24pm
♐ 1/4 3:15pm
♑ 1/6 6:37pm
♒ 1/8 11:44pm
♓ 1/11 7:49am
♈ 1/13 7:07pm
♉ 1/16 8:02am
♊ 1/18 7:47pm
♋ 1/21 4:22am
♌ 1/23 9:39am
♍ 1/25 12:47pm
♎ 1/27 3:07pm
♏ 1/29 5:43pm
♐ 1/31 9:07pm
♑ 2/3 1:39am
♒ 2/5 7:48am
♓ 2/7 4:15pm
♈ 2/10 3:17am
♉ 2/12 4:05pm
♊ 2/15 4:27am
♋ 2/17 2:02pm
♌ 2/19 7:49pm
♍ 2/21 10:25pm
♎ 2/23 11:22pm
♏ 2/26 12:20am
♐ 2/28 2:39am
♑ 3/1 7:06am
♒ 3/3 2:00pm
♓ 3/5 11:15pm
♈ 3/8 10:35am
♉ 3/10 11:19pm
♊ 3/13 12:03pm
♋ 3/15 10:46pm
♌ 3/18 5:56am
♍ 3/20 9:18am
♎ 3/22 9:56am
♏ 3/24 9:35am
♐ 3/26 10:07am
♑ 3/28 1:08pm
♒ 3/30 7:30pm
♓ 4/2 5:05am
♈ 4/4 4:53pm

Moon Sign Changes 1900-2005

Sign	Date	Time
♉	4/7	5:44am
♊	4/9	6:27pm
♋	4/12	5:47am
♌	4/14	2:22pm
♍	4/16	7:21pm
♎	4/18	9:00pm
♏	4/20	8:33pm
♐	4/22	7:57pm
♑	4/24	9:15pm
♒	4/27	2:04am
♓	4/29	10:55am
♈	5/1	10:46pm
♉	5/4	11:46am
♊	5/7	12:20am
♋	5/9	11:34am
♌	5/11	8:47pm
♍	5/14	3:13am
♎	5/16	6:32am
♏	5/18	7:15am
♐	5/20	6:48am
♑	5/22	7:12am
♒	5/24	10:31am
♓	5/26	5:57pm
♈	5/29	5:09am
♉	5/31	6:05pm
♊	6/3	6:32am
♋	6/5	5:21pm
♌	6/8	2:14am
♍	6/10	9:06am
♎	6/12	1:41pm
♏	6/14	4:00pm
♐	6/16	4:45pm
♑	6/18	5:31pm
♒	6/20	8:12pm
♓	6/23	2:25am
♈	6/25	12:34pm
♉	6/28	1:08am
♊	6/30	1:35pm
♋	7/3	12:07am
♌	7/5	8:18am
♍	7/7	2:33pm
♎	7/9	7:12pm
♏	7/11	10:27pm
♐	7/14	12:38am
♑	7/16	2:35am
♒	7/18	5:44am
♓	7/20	11:34am
♈	7/22	8:52pm
♉	7/25	8:54am
♊	7/27	9:26pm
♋	7/30	8:07am
♌	8/1	3:57pm
♍	8/3	9:15pm
♎	8/6	12:56am
♏	8/8	3:49am
♐	8/10	6:32am
♑	8/12	9:38am
♒	8/14	1:54pm
♓	8/16	8:13pm
♈	8/19	5:18am
♉	8/21	4:56pm
♊	8/24	5:33am
♋	8/26	4:50pm
♌	8/29	1:03am
♍	8/31	5:58am
♎	9/2	8:32am
♏	9/4	10:06am
♐	9/6	12:00pm
♑	9/8	3:11pm
♒	9/10	8:16pm
♓	9/13	3:31am
♈	9/15	1:01pm
♉	9/18	12:34am
♊	9/20	1:14pm
♋	9/23	1:13am
♌	9/25	10:32am
♍	9/27	4:07pm
♎	9/29	6:22pm
♏	10/1	6:44pm
♐	10/3	7:02pm
♑	10/5	9:00pm
♒	10/8	1:44am
♓	10/10	9:26am
♈	10/12	7:36pm
♉	10/15	7:24am
♊	10/17	8:03pm
♋	10/20	8:26am
♌	10/22	6:57pm
♍	10/25	2:03am
♎	10/27	5:15am
♏	10/29	5:30am
♐	10/31	4:40am
♑	11/2	4:54am
♒	11/4	8:06am
♓	11/6	3:06pm
♈	11/9	1:24am
♉	11/11	1:33pm
♊	11/14	2:13am
♋	11/16	2:32pm
♌	11/19	1:35am
♍	11/21	10:08am
♎	11/23	3:08pm
♏	11/25	4:38pm
♐	11/27	3:58pm
♑	11/29	3:16pm
♒	12/1	4:46pm
♓	12/3	10:08pm
♈	12/6	7:35am
♉	12/8	7:41pm
♊	12/11	8:26am
♋	12/13	8:28pm
♌	12/16	7:13am
♍	12/18	4:09pm
♎	12/20	10:32pm
♏	12/23	1:53am
♐	12/25	2:42am
♑	12/27	2:31am
♒	12/29	3:23am
♓	12/31	7:16am
1933		
♈	1/2	3:13pm
♉	1/5	2:36am
♊	1/7	3:19pm
♋	1/10	3:16am
♌	1/12	1:27pm
♍	1/14	9:42pm
♎	1/17	4:03am
♏	1/19	8:24am
♐	1/21	10:54am
♑	1/23	12:18pm
♒	1/25	1:57pm
♓	1/27	5:31pm
♈	1/30	12:21am
♉	2/1	10:40am
♊	2/3	11:05pm
♋	2/6	11:13am
♌	2/8	9:16pm
♍	2/11	4:43am
♎	2/13	9:59am
♏	2/15	1:46pm
♐	2/17	4:42pm
♑	2/19	7:22pm
♒	2/21	10:29pm
♓	2/24	2:56am
♈	2/26	9:42am
♉	2/28	7:20pm
♊	3/3	7:18am
♋	3/5	7:43pm
♌	3/8	6:18am
♍	3/10	1:42pm
♎	3/12	6:03pm
♏	3/14	8:27pm
♐	3/16	10:18pm
♑	3/19	12:47am
♒	3/21	4:39am
♓	3/23	10:16am
♈	3/25	5:49pm
♉	3/28	3:32am
♊	3/30	3:13pm
♋	4/2	3:50am
♌	4/4	3:16pm
♍	4/6	11:33pm
♎	4/9	4:00am
♏	4/11	5:32am
♐	4/13	5:52am
♑	4/15	6:54am
♒	4/17	10:02am
♓	4/19	3:54pm
♈	4/22	12:14am
♉	4/24	10:31am
♊	4/26	10:18pm
♋	4/29	10:58am
♌	5/1	11:06pm
♍	5/4	8:41am
♎	5/6	2:17pm
♏	5/8	4:07pm
♐	5/10	3:43pm
♑	5/12	3:15pm
♒	5/14	4:46pm
♓	5/16	9:34pm
♈	5/19	5:45am
♉	5/21	4:26pm
♊	5/24	4:31am
♋	5/26	5:12pm
♌	5/29	5:33am
♍	5/31	4:06pm
♎	6/2	11:15pm
♏	6/5	2:25am
♐	6/7	2:32am
♑	6/9	1:33am
♒	6/11	1:41am
♓	6/13	4:50am
♈	6/15	11:51am
♉	6/17	10:12pm
♊	6/20	10:25am
♋	6/22	11:07pm
♌	6/25	11:17am
♍	6/27	10:01pm
♎	6/30	6:11am
♏	7/2	10:57am
♐	7/4	12:32pm
♑	7/6	12:15pm
♒	7/8	12:05pm
♓	7/10	2:01pm
♈	7/12	7:31pm
♉	7/15	4:49am
♊	7/17	4:44pm
♋	7/20	5:25am
♌	7/22	5:19pm
♍	7/25	3:36am
♎	7/27	11:44am
♏	7/29	5:21pm
♐	7/31	8:27pm
♑	8/2	9:40pm
♒	8/4	10:22pm
♓	8/7	12:10am
♈	8/9	4:41am
♉	8/11	12:45pm
♊	8/13	11:57pm
♋	8/16	12:32pm
♌	8/19	12:22am
♍	8/21	10:07am
♎	8/23	5:29pm
♏	8/25	10:45pm
♐	8/28	2:21am
♑	8/30	4:52am
♒	9/1	7:00am
♓	9/3	9:44am
♈	9/5	2:15pm
♉	9/7	9:35pm
♊	9/10	8:01am
♋	9/12	8:25pm
♌	9/15	8:30am
♍	9/17	6:13pm
♎	9/20	12:51am
♏	9/22	5:00am
♐	9/24	7:49am
♑	9/26	10:23am
♒	9/28	1:27pm
♓	9/30	5:27pm
♈	10/2	10:51pm
♉	10/5	6:18am
♊	10/7	4:18pm
♋	10/10	4:29am
♌	10/12	5:02pm
♍	10/15	3:24am
♎	10/17	10:07am
♏	10/19	1:27pm
♐	10/21	2:54pm
♑	10/23	4:13pm
♒	10/25	6:48pm
♓	10/27	11:17pm
♈	10/30	5:40am
♉	11/1	1:53pm
♊	11/4	12:02am
♋	11/6	12:05pm
♌	11/9	12:58am
♍	11/11	12:24pm
♎	11/13	8:13pm
♏	11/15	11:52pm
♐	11/18	12:34am
♑	11/20	12:24am
♒	11/22	1:21am
♓	11/24	4:50am
♈	11/26	11:13am
♉	11/28	8:03pm
♊	12/1	6:45am
♋	12/3	6:53pm
♌	12/6	7:49am
♍	12/8	8:00pm
♎	12/11	5:19am
♏	12/13	10:27am
♐	12/15	11:49am
♑	12/17	11:08am
♒	12/19	10:37am
♓	12/21	12:15pm
♈	12/23	5:15pm
♉	12/26	1:43am
♊	12/28	12:43pm
♋	12/31	1:07am
1934		
♌	1/2	1:56pm
♍	1/5	2:09am
♎	1/7	12:20pm
♏	1/9	7:11pm
♐	1/11	10:18pm
♑	1/13	10:37pm
♒	1/15	9:56pm
♓	1/17	10:17pm
♈	1/20	1:28am
♉	1/22	8:26am
♊	1/24	6:54pm
♋	1/27	7:24am
♌	1/29	8:12pm
♍	2/1	8:00am
♎	2/3	6:00pm
♏	2/6	1:31am
♐	2/8	6:14am
♑	2/10	8:23am
♒	2/12	8:57am
♓	2/14	9:27am
♈	2/16	11:39am
♉	2/18	5:03pm
♊	2/21	2:16am
♋	2/23	2:22pm
♌	2/26	3:13am
♍	2/28	2:46pm
♎	3/3	12:02am
♏	3/5	6:59am
♐	3/7	11:58am
♑	3/9	3:22pm
♒	3/11	5:36pm
♓	3/13	7:25pm
♈	3/15	10:00pm
♉	3/18	2:46am
♊	3/20	10:51am
♋	3/22	10:13pm
♌	3/25	11:03am
♍	3/27	10:44pm
♎	3/30	7:37am
♏	4/1	1:35pm
♐	4/3	5:37pm
♑	4/5	8:45pm
♒	4/7	11:43pm
♓	4/10	2:52am
♈	4/12	6:40am
♉	4/14	11:56am
♊	4/16	7:41pm
♋	4/19	6:26am
♌	4/21	7:10pm
♍	4/24	7:20am
♎	4/26	4:32pm
♏	4/28	10:07pm
♐	5/1	1:02am
♑	5/3	2:53am
♒	5/5	5:06am
♓	5/7	8:26am
♈	5/9	1:09pm
♉	5/11	7:24pm
♊	5/14	3:38am
♋	5/16	2:17pm
♌	5/19	2:55am
♍	5/21	3:35pm
♎	5/24	1:43am
♏	5/26	7:52am
♐	5/28	10:28am
♑	5/30	11:12am
♒	6/1	11:55am
♓	6/3	2:06pm
♈	6/5	6:31pm
♉	6/8	1:17am
♊	6/10	10:14am
♋	6/12	9:14pm
♌	6/15	9:53am
♍	6/17	10:51pm
♎	6/20	9:59am
♏	6/22	5:25pm
♐	6/24	8:49pm
♑	6/26	9:24pm
♒	6/28	9:02pm
♓	6/30	9:38pm
♈	7/3	12:39am
♉	7/5	6:47am
♊	7/7	3:55pm
♋	7/10	3:20am
♌	7/12	4:07pm
♍	7/15	5:07am
♎	7/17	4:47pm
♏	7/20	1:31am
♐	7/22	6:28am
♑	7/24	8:03am
♒	7/26	7:43am

Moon Sign Changes 1900-2005

♓	7/28	7:20am
♈	7/30	8:46am
♉	8/1	1:25pm
♊	8/3	9:48pm
♋	8/6	9:13am
♌	8/8	10:08pm
♍	8/11	10:59am
♎	8/13	10:33pm
♏	8/16	7:51am
♐	8/18	2:12pm
♑	8/20	5:27pm
♒	8/22	6:18pm
♓	8/24	6:08pm
♈	8/26	6:44pm
♉	8/28	9:55pm
♊	8/31	4:55am
♋	9/2	3:40pm
♌	9/5	4:32am
♍	9/7	5:16pm
♎	9/10	4:23am
♏	9/12	1:19pm
♐	9/14	8:03pm
♑	9/17	12:36am
♒	9/19	3:06am
♓	9/21	4:14am
♈	9/23	5:13am
♉	9/25	7:47am
♊	9/27	1:33pm
♋	9/29	11:14pm
♌	10/2	11:44am
♍	10/5	12:31am
♎	10/7	11:20am
♏	10/9	7:31pm
♐	10/12	1:32am
♑	10/14	6:04am
♒	10/16	9:32am
♓	10/18	12:10pm
♈	10/20	2:28pm
♉	10/22	5:34pm
♊	10/24	10:58pm
♋	10/27	7:46am
♌	10/29	7:42pm
♍	11/1	8:36am
♎	11/3	7:41pm
♏	11/6	3:32am
♐	11/8	8:33am
♑	11/10	11:57am
♒	11/12	2:52pm
♓	11/14	5:56pm
♈	11/16	9:26pm
♉	11/19	1:46am
♊	11/21	7:47am
♋	11/23	4:25pm
♌	11/26	3:54am
♍	11/28	4:52pm
♎	12/1	4:39am
♏	12/3	1:06pm
♐	12/5	5:53pm
♑	12/7	8:09pm
♒	12/9	9:34pm
♓	12/11	11:31pm
♈	12/14	2:51am

♉	12/16	7:56am
♊	12/18	2:58pm
♋	12/21	12:11am
♌	12/23	11:37am
♍	12/26	12:32am
♎	12/28	12:59pm
♏	12/30	10:41pm
	1935	
♐	1/2	4:27am
♑	1/4	6:44am
♒	1/6	7:04am
♓	1/8	7:17am
♈	1/10	9:03am
♉	1/12	1:25pm
♊	1/14	8:43pm
♋	1/17	6:37am
♌	1/19	6:27pm
♍	1/22	7:19am
♎	1/24	7:59pm
♏	1/27	6:46am
♐	1/29	2:11pm
♑	1/31	5:47pm
♒	2/2	6:26pm
♓	2/4	5:47pm
♈	2/6	5:49pm
♉	2/8	8:22pm
♊	2/11	2:35am
♋	2/13	12:24pm
♌	2/16	12:35am
♍	2/18	1:33pm
♎	2/21	2:02am
♏	2/23	1:04pm
♐	2/25	9:40pm
♑	2/28	3:05am
♒	3/2	5:16am
♓	3/4	5:13am
♈	3/6	4:40am
♉	3/8	5:43am
♊	3/10	10:11am
♋	3/12	6:52pm
♌	3/15	6:48am
♍	3/17	7:51pm
♎	3/20	8:08am
♏	3/22	6:44pm
♐	3/25	3:24am
♑	3/27	9:49am
♒	3/29	1:41pm
♓	3/31	3:14pm
♈	4/2	3:31pm
♉	4/4	4:18pm
♊	4/6	7:35pm
♋	4/9	2:49am
♌	4/11	1:52pm
♍	4/14	2:47am
♎	4/16	3:01pm
♏	4/19	1:09am
♐	4/21	9:06am
♑	4/23	3:13pm
♒	4/25	7:43pm
♓	4/27	10:40pm
♈	4/30	12:26am
♉	5/2	2:09am

♊	5/4	5:26am
♋	5/6	11:50am
♌	5/8	9:55pm
♍	5/11	10:26am
♎	5/13	10:48pm
♏	5/16	8:54am
♐	5/18	4:13pm
♑	5/20	9:20pm
♒	5/23	1:08am
♓	5/25	4:13am
♈	5/27	6:59am
♉	5/29	9:59am
♊	5/31	2:11pm
♋	6/2	8:44pm
♌	6/5	6:19am
♍	6/7	6:26pm
♎	6/10	7:00am
♏	6/12	5:35pm
♐	6/15	12:57am
♑	6/17	5:21am
♒	6/19	7:56am
♓	6/21	9:56am
♈	6/23	12:21pm
♉	6/25	3:54pm
♊	6/27	9:06pm
♋	6/30	4:26am
♌	7/2	2:13pm
♍	7/5	2:08am
♎	7/7	2:52pm
♏	7/10	2:15am
♐	7/12	10:27am
♑	7/14	3:03pm
♒	7/16	4:53pm
♓	7/18	5:30pm
♈	7/20	6:33pm
♉	7/22	9:21pm
♊	7/25	2:42am
♋	7/27	10:43am
♌	7/29	9:04pm
♍	8/1	9:07am
♎	8/3	9:55pm
♏	8/6	9:57am
♐	8/8	7:25pm
♑	8/11	1:10am
♒	8/13	3:22am
♓	8/15	3:19am
♈	8/17	2:55am
♉	8/19	4:07am
♊	8/21	8:25am
♋	8/23	4:17pm
♌	8/26	3:00am
♍	8/28	3:20pm
♎	8/31	4:08am
♏	9/2	4:22pm
♐	9/5	2:48am
♑	9/7	10:08am
♒	9/9	1:44pm
♓	9/11	2:15pm
♈	9/13	1:20pm
♉	9/15	1:10pm
♊	9/17	3:48pm
♋	9/19	10:27pm

♌	9/22	8:50am
♍	9/24	9:18pm
♎	9/27	10:05am
♏	9/29	10:06pm
♐	10/2	8:41am
♑	10/4	5:02pm
♒	10/6	10:20pm
♓	10/9	12:27am
♈	10/11	12:20am
♉	10/12	11:53pm
♊	10/15	1:17am
♋	10/17	6:21am
♌	10/19	3:35pm
♍	10/22	3:44am
♎	10/24	4:31pm
♏	10/27	4:15am
♐	10/29	2:17pm
♑	10/31	10:31pm
♒	11/3	4:38am
♓	11/5	8:20am
♈	11/7	9:54am
♉	11/9	10:29am
♊	11/11	11:52am
♋	11/13	3:56pm
♌	11/15	11:51pm
♍	11/18	11:10am
♎	11/20	11:52pm
♏	11/23	11:36am
♐	11/25	9:08pm
♑	11/28	4:28am
♒	11/30	10:00am
♓	12/2	2:03pm
♈	12/4	4:53pm
♉	12/6	7:03pm
♊	12/8	9:36pm
♋	12/11	1:54am
♌	12/13	9:07am
♍	12/15	7:33pm
♎	12/18	7:58am
♏	12/20	8:03pm
♐	12/23	5:45am
♑	12/25	12:27pm
♒	12/27	4:46pm
♓	12/29	7:42pm
♈	12/31	10:15pm
	1936	
♉	1/3	1:11am
♊	1/5	5:04am
♋	1/7	10:29am
♌	1/9	6:02pm
♍	1/12	4:05am
♎	1/14	4:10pm
♏	1/17	4:38am
♐	1/19	3:11pm
♑	1/21	10:19pm
♒	1/24	2:02am
♓	1/26	3:35am
♈	1/28	4:36am
♉	1/30	6:37am
♊	2/1	10:39am
♋	2/3	4:58pm
♌	2/6	1:26am

♍	2/8	11:48am
♎	2/10	11:45pm
♏	2/13	12:24pm
♐	2/15	11:56pm
♑	2/18	8:21am
♒	2/20	12:46pm
♓	2/22	1:55pm
♈	2/24	1:35pm
♉	2/26	1:51pm
♊	2/28	4:30pm
♋	3/1	10:25pm
♌	3/4	7:20am
♍	3/6	6:18pm
♎	3/9	6:26am
♏	3/11	7:03pm
♐	3/14	7:06am
♑	3/16	4:51pm
♒	3/18	10:52pm
♓	3/21	12:59am
♈	3/23	12:31am
♉	3/24	11:37pm
♊	3/27	12:31am
♋	3/29	4:52am
♌	3/31	1:04pm
♍	4/3	12:07am
♎	4/5	12:31pm
♏	4/8	1:05am
♐	4/10	1:03pm
♑	4/12	11:23pm
♒	4/15	6:49am
♓	4/17	10:37am
♈	4/19	11:20am
♉	4/21	10:37am
♊	4/23	10:37am
♋	4/25	1:22pm
♌	4/27	8:03pm
♍	4/30	6:22am
♎	5/2	6:43pm
♏	5/5	7:16am
♐	5/7	6:54pm
♑	5/10	4:57am
♒	5/12	12:47pm
♓	5/14	5:52pm
♈	5/16	8:14pm
♉	5/18	8:47pm
♊	5/20	9:12pm
♋	5/22	11:19pm
♌	5/25	4:41am
♍	5/27	1:48pm
♎	5/30	1:38am
♏	6/1	2:11pm
♐	6/4	1:37am
♑	6/6	11:03am
♒	6/8	6:17pm
♓	6/10	11:27pm
♈	6/13	2:46am
♉	6/15	4:48am
♊	6/17	6:30am
♋	6/19	9:09am
♌	6/21	2:06pm
♍	6/23	10:15pm
♎	6/26	9:23am

♏	6/28	9:53pm
♐	7/1	9:27am
♑	7/3	6:34pm
♒	7/6	12:56am
♓	7/8	5:10am
♈	7/10	8:10am
♉	7/12	10:46am
♊	7/14	1:38pm
♋	7/16	5:28pm
♌	7/18	10:58pm
♍	7/21	6:54am
♎	7/23	5:31pm
♏	7/26	5:54am
♐	7/28	5:56pm
♑	7/31	3:24am
♒	8/2	9:25am
♓	8/4	12:36pm
♈	8/6	2:21pm
♉	8/8	4:11pm
♊	8/10	7:12pm
♋	8/12	11:52pm
♌	8/15	6:20am
♍	8/17	2:44pm
♎	8/20	1:17am
♏	8/22	1:36pm
♐	8/25	2:09am
♑	8/27	12:35pm
♒	8/29	7:12pm
♓	8/31	10:06pm
♈	9/2	10:43pm
♉	9/4	11:04pm
♊	9/7	12:54am
♋	9/9	5:16am
♌	9/11	12:13pm
♍	9/13	9:20pm
♎	9/16	8:12am
♏	9/18	8:32pm
♐	9/21	9:24am
♑	9/23	8:53pm
♒	9/26	4:53am
♓	9/28	8:39am
♈	9/30	9:10am
♉	10/2	8:25am
♊	10/4	8:37am
♋	10/6	11:29am
♌	10/8	5:45pm
♍	10/11	3:01am
♎	10/13	2:19pm
♏	10/16	2:47am
♐	10/18	3:38pm
♑	10/21	3:37am
♒	10/23	1:00pm
♓	10/25	6:28pm
♈	10/27	8:09pm
♉	10/29	7:34pm
♊	10/31	6:49pm
♋	11/2	8:00pm
♌	11/5	12:37am
♍	11/7	9:00am
♎	11/9	8:15pm
♏	11/12	8:52am
♐	11/14	9:33pm

Moon Sign Changes 1900-2005

♑ 11/17 9:20am
♒ 11/19 7:11pm
♓ 11/22 2:04am
♈ 11/24 5:37am
♉ 11/26 6:29am
♊ 11/28 6:11am
♋ 11/30 6:40am
♌ 12/2 9:43am
♍ 12/4 4:31pm
♎ 12/7 2:55am
♏ 12/9 3:28pm
♐ 12/12 4:07am
♑ 12/14 3:25pm
♒ 12/17 12:42am
♓ 12/19 7:43am
♈ 12/21 12:26pm
♉ 12/23 3:05pm
♊ 12/25 4:24pm
♋ 12/27 5:36pm
♌ 12/29 8:14pm

1937

♍ 1/1 1:45am
♎ 1/3 10:55am
♏ 1/5 10:58pm
♐ 1/8 11:43am
♑ 1/10 10:53pm
♒ 1/13 7:25am
♓ 1/15 1:28pm
♈ 1/17 5:48pm
♉ 1/19 9:07pm
♊ 1/21 11:54pm
♋ 1/24 2:38am
♌ 1/26 6:08am
♍ 1/28 11:30am
♎ 1/30 7:49pm
♏ 2/2 7:10am
♐ 2/4 7:59pm
♑ 2/7 7:34am
♒ 2/9 4:00pm
♓ 2/11 9:10pm
♈ 2/14 12:12am
♉ 2/16 2:34am
♊ 2/18 5:22am
♋ 2/20 9:04am
♌ 2/22 1:51pm
♍ 2/24 8:04pm
♎ 2/27 4:26am
♏ 3/1 3:23pm
♐ 3/4 4:08am
♑ 3/6 4:23pm
♒ 3/9 1:36am
♓ 3/11 6:50am
♈ 3/13 9:00am
♉ 3/15 9:54am
♊ 3/17 11:19am
♋ 3/19 2:25pm
♌ 3/21 7:35pm
♍ 3/24 2:44am
♎ 3/26 11:47am
♏ 3/28 10:51pm
♐ 3/31 11:32am
♑ 4/3 12:16am
♒ 4/5 10:38am
♓ 4/7 4:59pm
♈ 4/9 7:28pm
♉ 4/11 7:39pm
♊ 4/13 7:34pm
♋ 4/15 9:02pm
♌ 4/18 1:11am
♍ 4/20 8:16am
♎ 4/22 5:51pm
♏ 4/25 5:21am
♐ 4/27 6:05pm
♑ 4/30 6:56am
♒ 5/2 6:08pm
♓ 5/5 1:57am
♈ 5/7 5:47am
♉ 5/9 6:32am
♊ 5/11 5:56am
♋ 5/13 6:00am
♌ 5/15 8:27am
♍ 5/17 2:19pm
♎ 5/19 11:34pm
♏ 5/22 11:18am
♐ 5/25 12:10am
♑ 5/27 12:53pm
♒ 5/30 12:13am
♓ 6/1 8:58am
♈ 6/3 2:22pm
♉ 6/5 4:36pm
♊ 6/7 4:46pm
♋ 6/9 4:31pm
♌ 6/11 5:44pm
♍ 6/13 10:01pm
♎ 6/16 6:08am
♏ 6/18 5:31pm
♐ 6/21 6:25am
♑ 6/23 6:58pm
♒ 6/26 5:54am
♓ 6/28 2:37pm
♈ 6/30 8:50pm
♉ 7/3 12:34am
♊ 7/5 2:15am
♋ 7/7 2:53am
♌ 7/9 3:59am
♍ 7/11 7:15am
♎ 7/13 2:04pm
♏ 7/16 12:36am
♐ 7/18 1:20pm
♑ 7/21 1:50am
♒ 7/23 12:20pm
♓ 7/25 8:21pm
♈ 7/28 2:15am
♉ 7/30 6:31am
♊ 8/1 9:29am
♋ 8/3 11:34am
♌ 8/5 1:35pm
♍ 8/7 4:54pm
♎ 8/9 10:58pm
♏ 8/12 8:37am
♐ 8/14 8:59pm
♑ 8/17 9:37am
♒ 8/19 8:05pm
♓ 8/22 3:28am
♈ 8/24 8:23am
♉ 8/26 11:57am
♊ 8/28 3:01pm
♋ 8/30 6:03pm
♌ 9/1 9:21pm
♍ 9/4 1:34am
♎ 9/6 7:48am
♏ 9/8 4:59pm
♐ 9/11 4:59am
♑ 9/13 5:52pm
♒ 9/16 4:51am
♓ 9/18 12:19pm
♈ 9/20 4:31pm
♉ 9/22 6:49pm
♊ 9/24 8:46pm
♋ 9/26 11:24pm
♌ 9/29 3:14am
♍ 10/1 8:29am
♎ 10/3 3:31pm
♏ 10/6 12:55am
♐ 10/8 12:44pm
♑ 10/11 1:47am
♒ 10/13 1:37pm
♓ 10/15 10:03pm
♈ 10/18 2:32am
♉ 10/20 4:09am
♊ 10/22 4:40am
♋ 10/24 5:47am
♌ 10/26 8:42am
♍ 10/28 2:01pm
♎ 10/30 9:47pm
♏ 11/2 7:48am
♐ 11/4 7:46pm
♑ 11/7 8:50am
♒ 11/9 9:19pm
♓ 11/12 7:07am
♈ 11/14 12:59pm
♉ 11/16 3:12pm
♊ 11/18 3:10pm
♋ 11/20 2:47pm
♌ 11/22 3:55pm
♍ 11/24 7:56pm
♎ 11/27 3:22am
♏ 11/29 1:46pm
♐ 12/2 2:05am
♑ 12/4 3:07pm
♒ 12/7 3:40am
♓ 12/9 2:21pm
♈ 12/11 9:55pm
♉ 12/14 1:50am
♊ 12/16 2:42am
♋ 12/18 2:03am
♌ 12/20 1:48am
♍ 12/22 3:57am
♎ 12/24 9:53am
♏ 12/26 7:45pm
♐ 12/29 8:12am
♑ 12/31 9:17pm

1938

♒ 1/3 9:31am
♓ 1/5 8:07pm
♈ 1/8 4:29am
♉ 1/10 10:06am
♊ 1/12 12:50pm
♋ 1/14 1:21pm
♌ 1/16 1:09pm
♍ 1/18 2:13pm
♎ 1/20 6:27pm
♏ 1/23 2:55am
♐ 1/25 2:51pm
♑ 1/28 3:58am
♒ 1/30 4:00pm
♓ 2/2 1:58am
♈ 2/4 9:54am
♉ 2/6 3:58pm
♊ 2/8 8:08pm
♋ 2/10 10:26pm
♌ 2/12 11:33pm
♍ 2/15 12:57am
♎ 2/17 4:28am
♏ 2/19 11:37am
♐ 2/21 10:33pm
♑ 2/24 11:28am
♒ 2/26 11:36pm
♓ 3/1 9:13am
♈ 3/3 4:16pm
♉ 3/5 9:29pm
♊ 3/8 1:33am
♋ 3/10 4:46am
♌ 3/12 7:23am
♍ 3/14 10:05am
♎ 3/16 2:08pm
♏ 3/18 8:53pm
♐ 3/21 7:01am
♑ 3/23 7:32pm
♒ 3/26 7:56am
♓ 3/28 5:52pm
♈ 3/31 12:33am
♉ 4/2 4:43am
♊ 4/4 7:33am
♋ 4/6 10:07am
♌ 4/8 1:04pm
♍ 4/10 4:51pm
♎ 4/12 10:02pm
♏ 4/15 5:21am
♐ 4/17 3:19pm
♑ 4/20 3:31am
♒ 4/22 4:11pm
♓ 4/25 2:53am
♈ 4/27 10:08am
♉ 4/29 2:01pm
♊ 5/1 3:45pm
♋ 5/3 4:51pm
♌ 5/5 6:42pm
♍ 5/7 10:17pm
♎ 5/10 4:06am
♏ 5/12 12:16pm
♐ 5/14 10:40pm
♑ 5/17 10:51am
♒ 5/19 11:37pm
♓ 5/22 11:08am
♈ 5/24 7:35pm
♉ 5/27 12:17am
♊ 5/29 1:52am
♋ 5/31 1:52am
♌ 6/2 2:09am
♍ 6/4 4:21am
♎ 6/6 9:35am
♏ 6/8 6:01pm
♐ 6/11 4:57am
♑ 6/13 5:21pm
♒ 6/16 6:07am
♓ 6/18 6:02pm
♈ 6/21 3:40am
♉ 6/23 9:50am
♊ 6/25 12:25pm
♋ 6/27 12:27pm
♌ 6/29 11:45am
♍ 7/1 12:24pm
♎ 7/3 4:09pm
♏ 7/5 11:49pm
♐ 7/8 10:45am
♑ 7/10 11:22pm
♒ 7/13 12:05pm
♓ 7/15 11:55pm
♈ 7/18 10:02am
♉ 7/20 5:31pm
♊ 7/22 9:43pm
♋ 7/24 10:54pm
♌ 7/26 10:26pm
♍ 7/28 10:17pm
♎ 7/31 12:35am
♏ 8/2 6:49am
♐ 8/4 5:02pm
♑ 8/7 5:33am
♒ 8/9 6:15pm
♓ 8/12 5:45am
♈ 8/14 3:34pm
♉ 8/16 11:25pm
♊ 8/19 4:51am
♋ 8/21 7:39am
♌ 8/23 8:27am
♍ 8/25 8:43am
♎ 8/27 10:26am
♏ 8/29 3:26pm
♐ 9/1 12:28am
♑ 9/3 12:30pm
♒ 9/6 1:10am
♓ 9/8 12:28pm
♈ 9/10 9:40pm
♉ 9/13 4:54am
♊ 9/15 10:23am
♋ 9/17 2:09pm
♌ 9/19 4:26pm
♍ 9/21 6:01pm
♎ 9/23 8:19pm
♏ 9/26 12:57am
♐ 9/28 9:02am
♑ 9/30 8:20pm
♒ 10/3 8:58am
♓ 10/5 8:27pm
♈ 10/8 5:22am
♉ 10/10 11:43am
♊ 10/12 4:10pm
♋ 10/14 7:31pm
♌ 10/16 10:19pm
♍ 10/19 1:09am
♎ 10/21 4:43am
♏ 10/23 10:00am
♐ 10/25 5:54pm
♑ 10/28 4:39am
♒ 10/30 5:08pm
♓ 11/2 5:09am
♈ 11/4 2:35pm
♉ 11/6 8:41pm
♊ 11/9 12:03am
♋ 11/11 1:59am
♌ 11/13 3:50am
♍ 11/15 6:38am
♎ 11/17 11:03am
♏ 11/19 5:26pm
♐ 11/22 1:56am
♑ 11/24 12:38pm
♒ 11/27 12:58am
♓ 11/29 1:30pm
♈ 12/2 12:02am
♉ 12/4 7:01am
♊ 12/6 10:18am
♋ 12/8 11:07am
♌ 12/10 11:17am
♍ 12/12 12:37pm
♎ 12/14 4:27pm
♏ 12/16 11:13pm
♐ 12/19 8:31am
♑ 12/21 7:39pm
♒ 12/24 7:59am
♓ 12/26 8:41pm
♈ 12/29 8:14am
♉ 12/31 4:47pm

1939

♊ 1/2 9:19pm
♋ 1/4 10:20pm
♌ 1/6 9:32pm
♍ 1/8 9:08pm
♎ 1/10 11:11pm
♏ 1/13 4:54am
♐ 1/15 2:10pm
♑ 1/18 1:44am
♒ 1/20 2:15pm
♓ 1/23 2:51am
♈ 1/25 2:42pm
♉ 1/28 12:29am
♊ 1/30 6:50am
♋ 2/1 9:22am
♌ 2/3 9:06am
♍ 2/5 8:02am
♎ 2/7 8:29am
♏ 2/9 12:22pm
♐ 2/11 8:24pm
♑ 2/14 7:41am
♒ 2/16 8:22am
♓ 2/19 8:52am
♈ 2/21 8:23pm
♉ 2/24 6:19am
♊ 2/26 1:47pm
♋ 2/28 6:06pm
♌ 3/2 7:30pm
♍ 3/4 7:17pm

Moon Sign Changes 1900-2005

Sign	Date	Time	Sign	Date	Time	Sign	Date	Time	Sign	Date	Time	Sign	Date	Time	Sign	Date	Time
♎	3/6	7:26pm	♐	7/25	7:10pm	♒	12/14	4:42am	♓	5/1	1:56am	♉	9/19	4:45pm	♊	2/5	5:09pm
♏	3/8	10:00pm	♑	7/28	4:51am	♓	12/16	4:14pm	♈	5/3	2:52pm	♊	9/22	5:05am	♋	2/8	2:57am
♐	3/11	4:23am	♒	7/30	4:15pm	♈	12/19	5:03am	♉	5/6	3:12am	♋	9/24	2:57pm	♌	2/10	9:07am
♑	3/13	2:35pm	♓	8/2	4:41am	♉	12/21	4:32pm	♊	5/8	1:34pm	♌	9/26	9:09pm	♍	2/12	12:21pm
♒	3/16	3:01am	♈	8/4	5:22pm	♊	12/24	12:37am	♋	5/10	9:33pm	♍	9/28	11:41pm	♎	2/14	2:07pm
♓	3/18	3:31pm	♉	8/7	4:47am	♋	12/26	5:03am	♌	5/13	3:22am	♎	9/30	11:46pm	♏	2/16	3:52pm
♈	3/21	2:41am	♊	8/9	1:06pm	♌	12/28	7:05am	♍	5/15	7:18am	♏	10/2	11:12pm	♐	2/18	6:37pm
♉	3/23	11:58am	♋	8/11	5:21pm	♍	12/30	8:29am	♎	5/17	9:40am	♐	10/4	11:54pm	♑	2/20	10:54pm
♊	3/25	7:15pm	♌	8/13	6:09pm		**1940**		♏	5/19	11:12am	♑	10/7	3:28am	♒	2/23	5:02am
♋	3/28	12:19am	♍	8/15	5:19pm	♎	1/1	10:44am	♐	5/21	1:00pm	♒	10/9	10:44am	♓	2/25	1:18pm
♌	3/30	3:15am	♎	8/17	5:04pm	♏	1/3	2:36pm	♑	5/23	4:35pm	♓	10/11	9:18pm	♈	2/27	11:54pm
♍	4/1	4:39am	♏	8/19	7:20pm	♐	1/5	8:12pm	♒	5/25	11:19pm	♈	10/14	9:50am	♉	3/2	12:23pm
♎	4/3	5:48am	♐	8/22	1:14am	♑	1/8	3:30am	♓	5/28	9:39am	♉	10/16	10:49pm	♊	3/5	1:12am
♏	4/5	8:21am	♑	8/24	10:33am	♒	1/10	12:42pm	♈	5/30	10:18pm	♊	10/19	10:59am	♋	3/7	12:04pm
♐	4/7	1:47pm	♒	8/26	10:09pm	♓	1/13	12:03am	♉	6/2	10:44am	♋	10/21	9:18pm	♌	3/9	7:19pm
♑	4/9	10:47pm	♓	8/29	10:42am	♈	1/15	12:56pm	♊	6/4	8:49pm	♌	10/24	4:51am	♍	3/11	10:51pm
♒	4/12	10:33am	♈	8/31	11:15pm	♉	1/18	1:15am	♋	6/7	4:02am	♍	10/26	9:10am	♎	3/13	11:51pm
♓	4/14	11:04pm	♉	9/3	10:47am	♊	1/20	10:32am	♌	6/9	9:00am	♎	10/28	10:37am	♏	3/16	12:03am
♈	4/17	10:13am	♊	9/5	8:02pm	♋	1/22	3:35pm	♍	6/11	12:41pm	♏	10/30	10:25am	♐	3/18	1:08am
♉	4/19	6:57pm	♋	9/8	1:52am	♌	1/24	5:10pm	♎	6/13	3:43pm	♐	11/1	10:21am	♑	3/20	4:25am
♊	4/22	1:16am	♌	9/10	4:11am	♍	1/26	5:12pm	♏	6/15	6:31pm	♑	11/3	12:22pm	♒	3/22	10:34am
♋	4/24	5:43am	♍	9/12	4:09am	♎	1/28	5:43pm	♐	6/17	9:34pm	♒	11/5	6:03pm	♓	3/24	7:30pm
♌	4/26	8:55am	♎	9/14	3:39am	♏	1/30	8:17pm	♑	6/20	1:44am	♓	11/8	3:46am	♈	3/27	6:39am
♍	4/28	11:26am	♏	9/16	4:43am	♐	2/2	1:36am	♒	6/22	8:15am	♈	11/10	4:13pm	♉	3/29	7:14pm
♎	4/30	2:02pm	♐	9/18	9:02am	♑	2/4	9:27am	♓	6/24	5:55pm	♉	11/13	5:13am	♊	4/1	8:06am
♏	5/2	5:36pm	♑	9/20	5:11pm	♒	2/6	7:21pm	♈	6/27	6:13am	♊	11/15	5:00pm	♋	4/3	7:44pm
♐	5/4	11:11pm	♒	9/23	4:24am	♓	2/9	6:58am	♉	6/29	6:52pm	♋	11/18	2:52am	♌	4/6	4:26am
♑	5/7	7:34am	♓	9/25	5:00pm	♈	2/11	7:49pm	♊	7/2	5:15am	♌	11/20	10:38am	♍	4/8	9:21am
♒	5/9	6:41pm	♈	9/28	5:22am	♉	2/14	8:36am	♋	7/4	12:10pm	♍	11/22	4:11pm	♎	4/10	10:54am
♓	5/12	7:09am	♉	9/30	4:29pm	♊	2/16	7:10pm	♌	7/6	4:12pm	♎	11/24	7:25pm	♏	4/12	10:31am
♈	5/14	6:41pm	♊	10/3	1:38am	♋	2/19	1:46am	♍	7/8	6:44pm	♏	11/26	8:44pm	♐	4/14	10:07am
♉	5/17	3:28am	♋	10/5	8:16am	♌	2/21	4:19am	♎	7/10	9:07pm	♐	11/28	9:18pm	♑	4/16	11:38am
♊	5/19	9:06am	♌	10/7	12:10pm	♍	2/23	4:11am	♏	7/13	12:07am	♑	11/30	10:50pm	♒	4/18	4:31pm
♋	5/21	12:23pm	♍	10/9	1:46pm	♎	2/25	3:29am	♐	7/15	4:05am	♒	12/3	3:12am	♓	4/21	1:07am
♌	5/23	2:33pm	♎	10/11	2:15pm	♏	2/27	4:13am	♑	7/17	9:17am	♓	12/5	11:35am	♈	4/23	12:34pm
♍	5/25	4:51pm	♏	10/13	3:18pm	♐	2/29	7:54am	♒	7/19	4:22pm	♈	12/7	11:26pm	♉	4/26	1:23am
♎	5/27	8:06pm	♐	10/15	6:36pm	♑	3/2	3:02pm	♓	7/22	1:58am	♉	12/10	12:27pm	♊	4/28	2:11pm
♏	5/30	12:47am	♑	10/18	1:22am	♒	3/5	1:07am	♈	7/24	2:02pm	♊	12/13	12:08am	♋	5/1	1:56am
♐	6/1	7:15am	♒	10/20	11:40am	♓	3/7	1:07pm	♉	7/27	2:56am	♋	12/15	9:20am	♌	5/3	11:34am
♑	6/3	3:50pm	♓	10/23	12:05am	♈	3/10	2:01am	♊	7/29	2:04pm	♌	12/17	4:16pm	♍	5/5	6:06pm
♒	6/6	2:40am	♈	10/25	12:28pm	♉	3/12	2:44pm	♋	7/31	9:32pm	♍	12/19	9:35pm	♎	5/7	9:11pm
♓	6/8	3:05pm	♉	10/27	11:09pm	♊	3/15	1:53am	♌	8/3	1:20am	♎	12/22	1:37am	♏	5/9	9:34pm
♈	6/11	3:10am	♊	10/30	7:31am	♋	3/17	9:57am	♍	8/5	2:50am	♏	12/24	4:30am	♐	5/11	8:49pm
♉	6/13	12:43pm	♋	11/1	1:41pm	♌	3/19	2:15pm	♎	8/7	3:50am	♐	12/26	6:36am	♑	5/13	9:03pm
♊	6/15	6:32pm	♌	11/3	6:01pm	♍	3/21	3:20pm	♏	8/9	5:46am	♑	12/28	8:58am	♒	5/16	12:15am
♋	6/17	9:06pm	♍	11/5	8:57pm	♎	3/23	2:47pm	♐	8/11	9:29am	♒	12/30	1:09pm	♓	5/18	7:33am
♌	6/19	9:58pm	♎	11/7	11:03pm	♏	3/25	2:33pm	♑	8/13	3:15pm		**1941**		♈	5/20	6:34pm
♍	6/21	10:56pm	♏	11/10	1:14am	♐	3/27	4:31pm	♒	8/15	11:07pm	♓	1/1	8:35pm	♉	5/23	7:26am
♎	6/24	1:30am	♐	11/12	4:41am	♑	3/29	10:00pm	♓	8/18	9:10am	♈	1/4	7:34am	♊	5/25	8:10pm
♏	6/26	6:25am	♑	11/14	10:42am	♒	4/1	7:13am	♈	8/20	9:14pm	♉	1/6	8:28pm	♋	5/28	7:36am
♐	6/28	1:39pm	♒	11/16	8:00pm	♓	4/3	7:11pm	♉	8/23	10:17am	♊	1/9	8:27am	♌	5/30	5:15pm
♑	6/30	10:53pm	♓	11/19	8:00am	♈	4/6	8:10am	♊	8/25	10:13pm	♋	1/11	5:33pm	♍	6/2	12:38am
♒	7/3	9:54am	♈	11/21	8:36pm	♉	4/8	8:39pm	♋	8/28	6:53am	♌	1/13	11:39pm	♎	6/4	5:17am
♓	7/5	10:17pm	♉	11/24	7:23am	♊	4/11	7:32am	♌	8/30	11:31am	♍	1/16	3:45am	♏	6/6	7:13am
♈	7/8	10:50am	♊	11/26	3:09pm	♋	4/13	4:04pm	♍	9/1	12:57pm	♎	1/18	7:00am	♐	6/8	7:24am
♉	7/10	9:27pm	♋	11/28	8:11pm	♌	4/15	9:44pm	♎	9/3	12:54pm	♏	1/20	10:04am	♑	6/10	7:32am
♊	7/13	4:20am	♌	11/30	11:34pm	♍	4/18	12:34am	♏	9/5	1:16pm	♐	1/22	1:16pm	♒	6/12	9:41am
♋	7/15	7:16am	♍	12/3	2:23am	♎	4/20	1:23am	♐	9/7	3:36pm	♑	1/24	5:01pm	♓	6/14	3:33pm
♌	7/17	7:30am	♎	12/5	5:22am	♏	4/22	1:33am	♑	9/9	8:45pm	♒	1/26	10:06pm	♈	6/17	1:30am
♍	7/19	7:07am	♏	12/7	8:57am	♐	4/24	2:48am	♒	9/12	4:51am	♓	1/29	5:34am	♉	6/19	2:03pm
♎	7/21	8:10am	♐	12/9	1:32pm	♑	4/26	6:50am	♓	9/14	3:25pm	♈	1/31	4:02pm	♊	6/22	2:44am
♏	7/23	12:04pm	♑	12/11	7:51pm	♒	4/28	2:39pm	♈	9/17	3:43am	♉	2/3	4:41am	♋	6/24	1:51pm

Moon Sign Changes 1900-2005

Sign	Date	Time
♌	6/26	10:55pm
♍	6/29	6:03am
♎	7/1	11:17am
♏	7/3	2:34pm
♐	7/5	4:13pm
♑	7/7	5:21pm
♒	7/9	7:36pm
♓	7/12	12:42am
♈	7/14	9:35am
♉	7/16	9:30pm
♊	7/19	10:10am
♋	7/21	9:15pm
♌	7/24	5:48am
♍	7/26	12:03pm
♎	7/28	4:41pm
♏	7/30	8:09pm
♐	8/1	10:49pm
♑	8/4	1:17am
♒	8/6	4:32am
♓	8/8	9:51am
♈	8/10	6:13pm
♉	8/13	5:32am
♊	8/15	6:09pm
♋	8/18	5:37am
♌	8/20	2:15pm
♍	8/22	7:53pm
♎	8/24	11:21pm
♏	8/27	1:49am
♐	8/29	4:13am
♑	8/31	7:18am
♒	9/2	11:39am
♓	9/4	5:52pm
♈	9/7	2:28am
♉	9/9	1:32pm
♊	9/12	2:06am
♋	9/14	2:09pm
♌	9/16	11:36pm
♍	9/19	5:29am
♎	9/21	8:17am
♏	9/23	9:24am
♐	9/25	10:24am
♑	9/27	12:44pm
♒	9/29	5:17pm
♓	10/2	12:18am
♈	10/4	9:37am
♉	10/6	8:52pm
♊	10/9	9:23am
♋	10/11	9:53pm
♌	10/14	8:29am
♍	10/16	3:36pm
♎	10/18	6:54pm
♏	10/20	7:25pm
♐	10/22	7:00pm
♑	10/24	7:40pm
♒	10/26	11:02pm
♓	10/29	5:51am
♈	10/31	3:38pm
♉	11/3	3:19am
♊	11/5	3:52pm
♋	11/8	4:26am
♌	11/10	3:49pm
♍	11/13	12:29am
♎	11/15	5:22am
♏	11/17	6:40am
♐	11/19	5:53am
♑	11/21	5:11am
♒	11/23	6:46am
♓	11/25	12:09pm
♈	11/27	9:26pm
♉	11/30	9:18am
♊	12/2	10:00pm
♋	12/5	10:22am
♌	12/7	9:43pm
♍	12/10	7:12am
♎	12/12	1:46pm
♏	12/14	4:51pm
♐	12/16	5:10pm
♑	12/18	4:26pm
♒	12/20	4:53pm
♓	12/22	8:33pm
♈	12/25	4:24am
♉	12/27	3:43pm
♊	12/30	4:27am
	1942	
♋	1/1	4:42pm
♌	1/4	3:32am
♍	1/6	12:42pm
♎	1/8	7:48pm
♏	1/11	12:24am
♐	1/13	2:31am
♑	1/15	3:07am
♒	1/17	3:52am
♓	1/19	6:43am
♈	1/21	1:08pm
♉	1/23	11:18pm
♊	1/26	11:44am
♋	1/29	12:03am
♌	1/31	10:37am
♍	2/2	6:57pm
♎	2/5	1:18am
♏	2/7	5:56am
♐	2/9	9:06am
♑	2/11	11:19am
♒	2/13	1:27pm
♓	2/15	4:50pm
♈	2/17	10:46pm
♉	2/20	7:57am
♊	2/22	7:47pm
♋	2/25	8:15am
♌	2/27	7:06pm
♍	3/2	3:06am
♎	3/4	8:23am
♏	3/6	11:50am
♐	3/8	2:28pm
♑	3/10	5:08pm
♒	3/12	8:30pm
♓	3/15	1:09am
♈	3/17	7:41am
♉	3/19	4:39pm
♊	3/22	4:00am
♋	3/24	4:33pm
♌	3/27	4:04am
♍	3/29	12:36pm
♎	3/31	5:36pm
♏	4/2	7:54pm
♐	4/4	9:04pm
♑	4/6	10:41pm
♒	4/9	1:56am
♓	4/11	7:19am
♈	4/13	2:49pm
♉	4/16	12:18am
♊	4/18	11:37am
♋	4/21	12:10am
♌	4/23	12:21pm
♍	4/25	10:02pm
♎	4/28	3:50am
♏	4/30	5:59am
♐	5/2	6:03am
♑	5/4	6:04am
♒	5/6	7:56am
♓	5/8	12:44pm
♈	5/10	8:31pm
♉	5/13	6:37am
♊	5/15	6:15pm
♋	5/18	6:49am
♌	5/20	7:21pm
♍	5/23	6:07am
♎	5/25	1:22pm
♏	5/27	4:32pm
♐	5/29	4:39pm
♑	5/31	3:43pm
♒	6/2	3:59pm
♓	6/4	7:14pm
♈	6/7	2:11am
♉	6/9	12:16pm
♊	6/12	12:11am
♋	6/14	12:50pm
♌	6/17	1:19am
♍	6/19	12:33pm
♎	6/21	9:04pm
♏	6/24	1:50am
♐	6/26	3:09am
♑	6/28	2:30am
♒	6/30	2:00am
♓	7/2	3:46am
♈	7/4	9:10am
♉	7/6	6:22pm
♊	7/9	6:10am
♋	7/11	6:51pm
♌	7/14	7:08am
♍	7/16	6:08pm
♎	7/19	3:02am
♏	7/21	9:02am
♐	7/23	11:58am
♑	7/25	12:38pm
♒	7/27	12:37pm
♓	7/29	1:49pm
♈	7/31	5:55pm
♉	8/3	1:47am
♊	8/5	12:54pm
♋	8/8	1:30am
♌	8/10	1:39pm
♍	8/13	12:09am
♎	8/15	8:31am
♏	8/17	2:38pm
♐	8/19	6:35pm
♑	8/21	8:46pm
♒	8/23	10:07pm
♓	8/25	11:55pm
♈	8/28	3:39am
♉	8/30	10:29am
♊	9/1	8:40pm
♋	9/4	9:00am
♌	9/6	9:15pm
♍	9/9	7:31am
♎	9/11	3:05pm
♏	9/13	8:19pm
♐	9/15	11:58pm
♑	9/18	2:48am
♒	9/20	5:27am
♓	9/22	8:34am
♈	9/24	12:57pm
♉	9/26	7:34pm
♊	9/29	5:05am
♋	10/1	5:03pm
♌	10/4	5:35am
♍	10/6	4:13pm
♎	10/8	11:33pm
♏	10/11	3:46am
♐	10/13	6:10am
♑	10/15	8:13am
♒	10/17	11:01am
♓	10/19	3:05pm
♈	10/21	8:37pm
♉	10/24	3:52am
♊	10/26	1:18pm
♋	10/29	1:00am
♌	10/31	1:48pm
♍	11/3	1:19am
♎	11/5	9:21am
♏	11/7	1:27pm
♐	11/9	2:47pm
♑	11/11	3:18pm
♒	11/13	4:48pm
♓	11/15	8:28pm
♈	11/18	2:30am
♉	11/20	10:38am
♊	11/22	8:35pm
♋	11/25	8:17am
♌	11/27	9:09pm
♍	11/30	9:29am
♎	12/2	6:55pm
♏	12/5	12:06am
♐	12/7	1:34am
♑	12/9	1:07am
♒	12/11	12:57am
♓	12/13	2:56am
♈	12/15	8:04am
♉	12/17	4:16pm
♊	12/20	2:46am
♋	12/22	2:46pm
♌	12/25	3:35am
♍	12/27	4:10pm
♎	12/30	2:44am
	1943	
♏	1/1	9:40am
♐	1/3	12:34pm
♑	1/5	12:35pm
♒	1/7	11:42am
♓	1/9	12:03pm
♈	1/11	3:21pm
♉	1/13	10:22pm
♊	1/16	8:39am
♋	1/18	8:53pm
♌	1/21	9:44am
♍	1/23	10:03pm
♎	1/26	8:47am
♏	1/28	4:51pm
♐	1/30	9:34pm
♑	2/1	11:15pm
♒	2/3	11:10pm
♓	2/5	11:07pm
♈	2/8	1:00am
♉	2/10	6:17am
♊	2/12	3:25pm
♋	2/15	3:24am
♌	2/17	4:18pm
♍	2/20	4:20am
♎	2/22	2:30pm
♏	2/24	10:25pm
♐	2/27	3:59am
♑	3/1	7:19am
♒	3/3	8:56am
♓	3/5	9:54am
♈	3/7	11:41am
♉	3/9	3:53pm
♊	3/11	11:39pm
♋	3/14	10:51am
♌	3/16	11:41pm
♍	3/19	11:43am
♎	3/21	9:21pm
♏	3/24	4:23am
♐	3/26	9:23am
♑	3/28	1:05pm
♒	3/30	3:57pm
♓	4/1	6:27pm
♈	4/3	9:17pm
♉	4/6	1:37am
♊	4/8	8:41am
♋	4/10	7:03pm
♌	4/13	7:39am
♍	4/15	7:59pm
♎	4/18	5:41am
♏	4/20	12:04pm
♐	4/22	3:56pm
♑	4/24	6:40pm
♒	4/26	9:21pm
♓	4/29	12:36am
♈	5/1	4:39am
♉	5/3	9:57am
♊	5/5	5:16pm
♋	5/8	3:17am
♌	5/10	3:39pm
♍	5/13	4:21am
♎	5/15	2:44pm
♏	5/17	9:19pm
♐	5/20	12:33am
♑	5/22	2:00am
♒	5/24	3:23am
♓	5/26	5:58am
♈	5/28	10:16am
♉	5/30	4:25pm
♊	6/2	12:29am
♋	6/4	10:45am
♌	6/6	11:03pm
♍	6/9	12:03pm
♎	6/11	11:22pm
♏	6/14	6:59am
♐	6/16	10:36am
♑	6/18	11:30am
♒	6/20	11:33am
♓	6/22	12:36pm
♈	6/24	3:52pm
♉	6/26	9:52pm
♊	6/29	6:27am
♋	7/1	5:13pm
♌	7/4	5:39am
♍	7/6	6:45pm
♎	7/9	6:44am
♏	7/11	3:40pm
♐	7/13	8:37pm
♑	7/15	10:07pm
♒	7/17	9:46pm
♓	7/19	9:30pm
♈	7/21	11:08pm
♉	7/24	3:53am
♊	7/26	12:04pm
♋	7/28	11:04pm
♌	7/31	11:43am
♍	8/3	12:45am
♎	8/5	12:51pm
♏	8/7	10:40pm
♐	8/10	5:08am
♑	8/12	8:09am
♒	8/14	8:36am
♓	8/16	8:06am
♈	8/18	8:32am
♉	8/20	11:40am
♊	8/22	6:34pm
♋	8/25	5:07am
♌	8/27	5:49pm
♍	8/30	6:47am
♎	9/1	6:33pm
♏	9/4	4:20am
♐	9/6	11:38am
♑	9/8	4:13pm
♒	9/10	6:18pm
♓	9/12	6:46pm
♈	9/14	7:09pm
♉	9/16	9:14pm
♊	9/19	2:42am
♋	9/21	12:10pm
♌	9/24	12:34am
♍	9/26	1:30pm
♎	9/29	12:56am
♏	10/1	10:04am
♐	10/3	5:03pm
♑	10/5	10:11pm
♒	10/8	1:39am
♓	10/10	3:44am
♈	10/12	5:12am
♉	10/14	7:26am

Moon Sign Changes 1900-2005

Sign	Date	Time
♊	10/16	12:07pm
♋	10/18	8:28pm
♌	10/21	8:12am
♍	10/23	9:10pm
♎	10/26	8:38am
♏	10/28	5:14pm
♐	10/30	11:14pm
♑	11/2	3:37am
♒	11/4	7:10am
♓	11/6	10:16am
♈	11/8	1:10pm
♉	11/10	4:32pm
♊	11/12	9:31pm
♋	11/15	5:22am
♌	11/17	4:27pm
♍	11/20	5:21am
♎	11/22	5:19pm
♏	11/25	2:09am
♐	11/27	7:35am
♑	11/29	10:43am
♒	12/1	1:01pm
♓	12/3	3:36pm
♈	12/5	7:00pm
♉	12/7	11:30pm
♊	12/10	5:32am
♋	12/12	1:46pm
♌	12/15	12:37am
♍	12/17	1:22pm
♎	12/20	1:55am
♏	12/22	11:46am
♐	12/24	5:44pm
♑	12/26	8:24pm
♒	12/28	9:21pm
♓	12/30	10:17pm
	1944	
♈	1/2	12:34am
♉	1/4	4:58am
♊	1/6	11:44am
♋	1/8	8:48pm
♌	1/11	7:58am
♍	1/13	8:38pm
♎	1/16	9:29am
♏	1/18	8:27pm
♐	1/21	3:53am
♑	1/23	7:26am
♒	1/25	8:09am
♓	1/27	7:48am
♈	1/29	8:15am
♉	1/31	11:07am
♊	2/2	5:17pm
♋	2/5	2:40am
♌	2/7	2:20pm
♍	2/10	3:08am
♎	2/12	3:54pm
♏	2/15	3:24am
♐	2/17	12:15pm
♑	2/19	5:33pm
♒	2/21	7:27pm
♓	2/23	7:09pm
♈	2/25	6:31pm
♉	2/27	7:36pm
♊	3/1	12:06am
♋	3/3	8:38am
♌	3/5	8:19pm
♍	3/8	9:18am
♎	3/10	9:55pm
♏	3/13	9:12am
♐	3/15	6:31pm
♑	3/18	1:13am
♒	3/20	4:55am
♓	3/22	5:59am
♈	3/24	5:42am
♉	3/26	6:01am
♊	3/28	8:58am
♋	3/30	3:59pm
♌	4/2	2:54am
♍	4/4	3:49pm
♎	4/7	4:22am
♏	4/9	3:12pm
♐	4/12	12:02am
♑	4/14	6:56am
♒	4/16	11:46am
♓	4/18	2:28pm
♈	4/20	3:35pm
♉	4/22	4:29pm
♊	4/24	6:59pm
♋	4/27	12:49am
♌	4/29	10:36am
♍	5/1	11:04pm
♎	5/4	11:40am
♏	5/6	10:18pm
♐	5/9	6:27am
♑	5/11	12:33pm
♒	5/13	5:10pm
♓	5/15	8:35pm
♈	5/17	11:03pm
♉	5/20	1:15am
♊	5/22	4:26am
♋	5/24	10:04am
♌	5/26	7:04pm
♍	5/29	6:58am
♎	5/31	7:37pm
♏	6/3	6:32am
♐	6/5	2:27pm
♑	6/7	7:41pm
♒	6/9	11:12pm
♓	6/12	1:58am
♈	6/14	4:41am
♉	6/16	7:52am
♊	6/18	12:11pm
♋	6/20	6:28pm
♌	6/23	3:25am
♍	6/25	2:58pm
♎	6/28	3:40am
♏	6/30	3:10pm
♐	7/2	11:38pm
♑	7/5	4:42am
♒	7/7	7:14am
♓	7/9	8:39am
♈	7/11	10:18am
♉	7/13	1:16pm
♊	7/15	6:11pm
♋	7/18	1:21am
♌	7/20	10:51am
♍	7/22	10:24pm
♎	7/25	11:08am
♏	7/27	11:16pm
♐	7/30	8:50am
♑	8/1	2:42pm
♒	8/3	5:10pm
♓	8/5	5:35pm
♈	8/7	5:43pm
♉	8/9	7:19pm
♊	8/11	11:38pm
♋	8/14	7:03am
♌	8/16	5:08pm
♍	8/19	5:01am
♎	8/21	5:45pm
♏	8/24	6:13am
♐	8/26	4:52pm
♑	8/29	12:12am
♒	8/31	3:44am
♓	9/2	4:14am
♈	9/4	3:27am
♉	9/6	3:28am
♊	9/8	6:14am
♋	9/10	12:47pm
♌	9/12	10:50pm
♍	9/15	11:00am
♎	9/17	11:48pm
♏	9/20	12:11pm
♐	9/22	11:16pm
♑	9/25	7:55am
♒	9/27	1:10pm
♓	9/29	2:58pm
♈	10/1	2:30pm
♉	10/3	1:46pm
♊	10/5	2:59pm
♋	10/7	7:56pm
♌	10/10	5:03am
♍	10/12	5:04pm
♎	10/15	5:55am
♏	10/17	6:03pm
♐	10/20	4:50am
♑	10/22	1:48pm
♒	10/24	8:19pm
♓	10/26	11:53pm
♈	10/29	12:54am
♉	10/31	12:45am
♊	11/2	1:28am
♋	11/4	5:04am
♌	11/6	12:44pm
♍	11/8	11:59pm
♎	11/11	12:45pm
♏	11/14	12:48am
♐	11/16	11:02am
♑	11/18	7:20pm
♒	11/21	1:47am
♓	11/23	6:18am
♈	11/25	8:57am
♉	11/27	10:22am
♊	11/29	11:55am
♋	12/1	3:17pm
♌	12/3	9:53pm
♍	12/6	8:04am
♎	12/8	8:28pm
♏	12/11	8:42am
♐	12/13	6:50pm
♑	12/16	2:22am
♒	12/18	7:44am
♓	12/20	11:39am
♈	12/22	2:42pm
♉	12/24	5:24pm
♊	12/26	8:26pm
♋	12/29	12:44am
♌	12/31	7:19am
	1945	
♍	1/2	4:49pm
♎	1/5	4:44am
♏	1/7	5:13pm
♐	1/10	3:55am
♑	1/12	11:28am
♒	1/14	3:57pm
♓	1/16	6:27pm
♈	1/18	8:21pm
♉	1/20	10:48pm
♊	1/23	2:35am
♋	1/25	8:05am
♌	1/27	3:33pm
♍	1/30	1:09am
♎	2/1	12:46pm
♏	2/4	1:22am
♐	2/6	12:57pm
♑	2/8	9:29pm
♒	2/11	2:12am
♓	2/13	3:52am
♈	2/15	4:12am
♉	2/17	5:05am
♊	2/19	8:01am
♋	2/21	1:42pm
♌	2/23	9:58pm
♍	2/26	8:13am
♎	2/28	7:57pm
♏	3/3	8:32am
♐	3/5	8:45pm
♑	3/8	6:37am
♒	3/10	12:40pm
♓	3/12	2:50pm
♈	3/14	2:32pm
♉	3/16	1:54pm
♊	3/18	3:04pm
♋	3/20	7:31pm
♌	3/23	3:32am
♍	3/25	2:11pm
♎	3/28	2:15am
♏	3/30	2:50pm
♐	4/2	3:08am
♑	4/4	1:51pm
♒	4/6	9:28pm
♓	4/9	1:10am
♈	4/11	1:38am
♉	4/13	12:40am
♊	4/15	12:31am
♋	4/17	3:14am
♌	4/19	9:52am
♍	4/21	8:03pm
♎	4/24	8:15am
♏	4/26	8:52pm
♐	4/29	8:56am
♑	5/1	7:40pm
♒	5/4	4:06am
♓	5/6	9:21am
♈	5/8	11:25am
♉	5/10	11:24am
♊	5/12	11:12am
♋	5/14	12:51pm
♌	5/16	5:57pm
♍	5/19	2:56am
♎	5/21	2:43pm
♏	5/24	3:21am
♐	5/26	3:11pm
♑	5/29	1:24am
♒	5/31	9:35am
♓	6/2	3:25pm
♈	6/4	6:51pm
♉	6/6	8:23pm
♊	6/8	9:15pm
♋	6/10	11:02pm
♌	6/13	3:20am
♍	6/15	11:07am
♎	6/17	10:06pm
♏	6/20	10:36am
♐	6/22	10:27pm
♑	6/25	8:14am
♒	6/27	3:36pm
♓	6/29	8:51pm
♈	7/2	12:29am
♉	7/4	3:04am
♊	7/6	5:20am
♋	7/8	8:10am
♌	7/10	12:43pm
♍	7/12	7:58pm
♎	7/15	6:13am
♏	7/17	6:29pm
♐	7/20	6:36am
♑	7/22	4:29pm
♒	7/24	11:16pm
♓	7/27	3:27am
♈	7/29	6:07am
♉	7/31	8:29am
♊	8/2	11:23am
♋	8/4	3:23pm
♌	8/6	8:53pm
♍	8/9	4:24am
♎	8/11	2:21pm
♏	8/14	2:24am
♐	8/16	2:56pm
♑	8/19	1:31am
♒	8/21	8:32am
♓	8/23	12:05pm
♈	8/25	1:30pm
♉	8/27	2:34pm
♊	8/29	4:47pm
♋	8/31	9:00pm
♌	9/3	3:20am
♍	9/5	11:36am
♎	9/7	9:48pm
♏	9/10	9:48am
♐	9/12	10:37pm
♑	9/15	10:11am
♒	9/17	6:19pm
♓	9/19	10:19pm
♈	9/21	11:11pm
♉	9/23	10:53pm
♊	9/25	11:32pm
♋	9/28	2:38am
♌	9/30	8:47am
♍	10/2	5:34pm
♎	10/5	4:17am
♏	10/7	4:24pm
♐	10/10	5:17am
♑	10/12	5:33pm
♒	10/15	3:07am
♓	10/17	8:34am
♈	10/19	10:09am
♉	10/21	9:30am
♊	10/23	8:49am
♋	10/25	10:11am
♌	10/27	2:55pm
♍	10/29	11:12pm
♎	11/1	10:08am
♏	11/3	10:29pm
♐	11/6	11:18am
♑	11/8	11:35pm
♒	11/11	9:59am
♓	11/13	5:05pm
♈	11/15	8:24pm
♉	11/17	8:48pm
♊	11/19	8:02pm
♋	11/21	8:14pm
♌	11/23	11:12pm
♍	11/26	5:59am
♎	11/28	4:18pm
♏	12/1	4:43am
♐	12/3	5:30pm
♑	12/6	5:23am
♒	12/8	3:34pm
♓	12/10	11:20pm
♈	12/13	4:15am
♉	12/15	6:30am
♊	12/17	7:03am
♋	12/19	7:27am
♌	12/21	9:30am
♍	12/23	2:44pm
♎	12/25	11:45pm
♏	12/28	11:43am
♐	12/31	12:32am
	1946	
♑	1/2	12:11pm
♒	1/4	9:38pm
♓	1/7	4:47am
♈	1/9	9:56am
♉	1/11	1:25pm
♊	1/13	3:42pm
♋	1/15	5:32pm
♌	1/17	8:04pm
♍	1/20	12:40am
♎	1/22	8:31am
♏	1/24	7:40pm
♐	1/27	8:27am
♑	1/29	8:18pm
♒	2/1	5:23am

Moon Sign Changes 1900-2005

♓	2/3	11:32am
♈	2/5	3:38pm
♉	2/7	6:47pm
♊	2/9	9:45pm
♋	2/12	12:59am
♌	2/14	4:50am
♍	2/16	10:03am
♎	2/18	5:36pm
♏	2/21	4:05am
♐	2/23	4:41pm
♑	2/26	5:01am
♒	2/28	2:34pm
♓	3/2	8:25pm
♈	3/4	11:23pm
♉	3/7	1:08am
♊	3/9	3:12am
♋	3/11	6:29am
♌	3/13	11:14am
♍	3/15	5:32pm
♎	3/18	1:40am
♏	3/20	12:04pm
♐	3/23	12:30am
♑	3/25	1:18pm
♒	3/27	11:51pm
♓	3/30	6:26am
♈	4/1	9:16am
♉	4/3	9:56am
♊	4/5	10:25am
♋	4/7	12:21pm
♌	4/9	4:37pm
♍	4/11	11:20pm
♎	4/14	8:13am
♏	4/16	7:03pm
♐	4/19	7:30am
♑	4/21	8:28pm
♒	4/24	7:56am
♓	4/26	3:54pm
♈	4/28	7:45pm
♉	4/30	8:31pm
♊	5/2	8:03pm
♋	5/4	8:23pm
♌	5/6	11:04pm
♍	5/9	4:57am
♎	5/11	1:53pm
♏	5/14	1:08am
♐	5/16	1:46pm
♑	5/19	2:42am
♒	5/21	2:31pm
♓	5/23	11:39pm
♈	5/26	5:05am
♉	5/28	7:03am
♊	5/30	6:54am
♋	6/1	6:29am
♌	6/3	7:39am
♍	6/5	11:57am
♎	6/7	7:57pm
♏	6/10	7:04am
♐	6/12	7:50pm
♑	6/15	8:39am
♒	6/17	8:16pm
♓	6/20	5:43am
♈	6/22	12:19pm

♉	6/24	3:56pm
♊	6/26	5:07pm
♋	6/28	5:10pm
♌	6/30	5:47pm
♍	7/2	8:45pm
♎	7/5	3:21am
♏	7/7	1:41pm
♐	7/10	2:20am
♑	7/12	3:05pm
♒	7/15	2:17am
♓	7/17	11:15am
♈	7/19	5:59pm
♉	7/21	10:35pm
♊	7/24	1:18am
♋	7/26	2:44am
♌	7/28	3:57am
♍	7/30	6:32am
♎	8/1	12:05pm
♏	8/3	9:23pm
♐	8/6	9:36am
♑	8/8	10:23pm
♒	8/11	9:23am
♓	8/13	5:41pm
♈	8/15	11:37pm
♉	8/18	3:59am
♊	8/20	7:22am
♋	8/22	10:06am
♌	8/24	12:38pm
♍	8/26	3:54pm
♎	8/28	9:15pm
♏	8/31	5:49am
♐	9/2	5:31pm
♑	9/5	6:24am
♒	9/7	5:41pm
♓	9/10	1:46am
♈	9/12	6:49am
♉	9/14	10:03am
♊	9/16	12:45pm
♋	9/18	3:42pm
♌	9/20	7:13pm
♍	9/22	11:38pm
♎	9/25	5:40am
♏	9/27	2:12pm
♐	9/30	1:32am
♑	10/2	2:29pm
♒	10/5	2:27am
♓	10/7	11:09am
♈	10/9	4:05pm
♉	10/11	6:20pm
♊	10/13	7:37pm
♋	10/15	9:23pm
♌	10/18	12:35am
♍	10/20	5:35am
♎	10/22	12:33pm
♏	10/24	9:41pm
♐	10/27	9:03am
♑	10/29	9:59pm
♒	11/1	10:36am
♓	11/3	8:32pm
♈	11/6	2:28am
♉	11/8	4:49am
♊	11/10	5:07am

♋	11/12	5:15am
♌	11/14	6:53am
♍	11/16	11:05am
♎	11/18	6:12pm
♏	11/21	3:58am
♐	11/23	3:44pm
♑	11/26	4:40am
♒	11/28	5:30pm
♓	12/1	4:30am
♈	12/3	12:05pm
♉	12/5	3:48pm
♊	12/7	4:30pm
♋	12/9	3:50pm
♌	12/11	3:46pm
♍	12/13	6:09pm
♎	12/16	12:07am
♏	12/18	9:43am
♐	12/20	9:48pm
♑	12/23	10:50am
♒	12/25	11:29pm
♓	12/28	10:43am
♈	12/30	7:31pm
	1947	
♉	1/2	1:06am
♊	1/4	3:26am
♋	1/6	3:28am
♌	1/8	2:53am
♍	1/10	3:45am
♎	1/12	7:54am
♏	1/14	4:15pm
♐	1/17	4:03am
♑	1/19	5:10pm
♒	1/22	5:37am
♓	1/24	4:23pm
♈	1/27	1:10am
♉	1/29	7:45am
♊	1/31	11:52am
♋	2/2	1:38pm
♌	2/4	2:01pm
♍	2/6	2:42pm
♎	2/8	5:39pm
♏	2/11	12:28am
♐	2/13	11:15am
♑	2/16	12:12am
♒	2/18	12:38pm
♓	2/20	10:57pm
♈	2/23	6:58am
♉	2/25	1:08pm
♊	2/27	5:47pm
♋	3/1	8:59pm
♌	3/3	11:00pm
♍	3/6	12:46am
♎	3/8	3:51am
♏	3/10	9:51am
♐	3/12	7:34pm
♑	3/15	8:00am
♒	3/17	8:35pm
♓	3/20	6:57am
♈	3/22	2:23pm
♉	3/24	7:29pm
♊	3/26	11:16pm
♋	3/29	2:26am

♌	3/31	5:22am
♍	4/2	8:30am
♎	4/4	12:39pm
♏	4/6	6:56pm
♐	4/9	4:12am
♑	4/11	4:08pm
♒	4/14	4:51am
♓	4/16	3:47pm
♈	4/18	11:26pm
♉	4/21	3:56am
♊	4/23	6:28am
♋	4/25	8:22am
♌	4/27	10:44am
♍	4/29	2:15pm
♎	5/1	7:24pm
♏	5/4	2:35am
♐	5/6	12:09pm
♑	5/8	11:55pm
♒	5/11	12:41pm
♓	5/14	12:20am
♈	5/16	8:56am
♉	5/18	1:51pm
♊	5/20	3:51pm
♋	5/22	4:27pm
♌	5/24	5:18pm
♍	5/26	7:50pm
♎	5/29	12:54am
♏	5/31	8:42am
♐	6/2	6:54pm
♑	6/5	6:51am
♒	6/7	7:38pm
♓	6/10	7:47am
♈	6/12	5:34pm
♉	6/14	11:45pm
♊	6/17	2:21am
♋	6/19	2:32am
♌	6/21	2:06am
♍	6/23	3:01am
♎	6/25	6:51am
♏	6/27	2:17pm
♐	6/30	12:46am
♑	7/2	1:03pm
♒	7/5	1:50am
♓	7/7	2:03pm
♈	7/10	12:34am
♉	7/12	8:12am
♊	7/14	12:17pm
♋	7/16	1:14pm
♌	7/18	12:34pm
♍	7/20	12:19pm
♎	7/22	2:33pm
♏	7/24	8:41pm
♐	7/27	6:40am
♑	7/29	7:01pm
♒	8/1	7:50am
♓	8/3	7:49pm
♈	8/6	6:20am
♉	8/8	2:43pm
♊	8/10	8:17pm
♋	8/12	10:49pm
♌	8/14	11:06pm
♍	8/16	10:49pm

♎	8/19	12:04am
♏	8/21	4:44am
♐	8/23	1:34pm
♑	8/26	1:31am
♒	8/28	2:18pm
♓	8/31	2:03am
♈	9/2	12:03pm
♉	9/4	8:10pm
♊	9/7	2:18am
♋	9/9	6:12am
♌	9/11	8:03am
♍	9/13	8:51am
♎	9/15	10:16am
♏	9/17	2:11pm
♐	9/19	9:49pm
♑	9/22	8:58am
♒	9/24	9:38pm
♓	9/27	9:24am
♈	9/29	6:58pm
♉	10/2	2:15am
♊	10/4	7:44am
♋	10/6	11:47am
♌	10/8	2:41pm
♍	10/10	4:57pm
♎	10/12	7:31pm
♏	10/14	11:45pm
♐	10/17	6:53am
♑	10/19	5:14pm
♒	10/22	5:39am
♓	10/24	5:45pm
♈	10/27	3:31am
♉	10/29	10:16am
♊	10/31	2:36pm
♋	11/2	5:32pm
♌	11/4	8:03pm
♍	11/6	10:55pm
♎	11/9	2:42am
♏	11/11	8:03am
♐	11/13	3:33pm
♑	11/16	1:37am
♒	11/18	1:45pm
♓	11/21	2:16am
♈	11/23	12:53pm
♉	11/25	8:06pm
♊	11/27	11:55pm
♋	11/30	1:31am
♌	12/2	2:30am
♍	12/4	4:23am
♎	12/6	8:14am
♏	12/8	2:24pm
♐	12/10	10:49pm
♑	12/13	9:14am
♒	12/15	9:16pm
♓	12/18	9:59am
♈	12/20	9:37pm
♉	12/23	6:11am
♊	12/25	10:47am
♋	12/27	12:03pm
♌	12/29	11:41am
♍	12/31	11:47am
	1948	
♎	1/2	2:10pm

♏	1/4	7:51pm
♐	1/7	4:41am
♑	1/9	3:41pm
♒	1/12	3:54am
♓	1/14	4:35pm
♈	1/17	4:44am
♉	1/19	2:42pm
♊	1/21	9:01pm
♋	1/23	11:23pm
♌	1/25	11:00pm
♍	1/27	9:56pm
♎	1/29	10:29pm
♏	2/1	2:27am
♐	2/3	10:26am
♑	2/5	9:30pm
♒	2/8	9:59am
♓	2/10	10:37pm
♈	2/13	10:37am
♉	2/15	9:08pm
♊	2/18	4:56am
♋	2/20	9:09am
♌	2/22	10:07am
♍	2/24	9:22am
♎	2/26	9:05am
♏	2/28	11:24am
♐	3/1	5:41pm
♑	3/4	3:50am
♒	3/6	4:14pm
♓	3/9	4:53am
♈	3/11	4:33pm
♉	3/14	2:40am
♊	3/16	10:45am
♋	3/18	4:14pm
♌	3/20	6:58pm
♍	3/22	7:42pm
♎	3/24	8:01pm
♏	3/26	9:49pm
♐	3/29	2:46am
♑	3/31	11:34am
♒	4/2	11:18pm
♓	4/5	11:56am
♈	4/7	11:28pm
♉	4/10	8:58am
♊	4/12	4:20pm
♋	4/14	9:41pm
♌	4/17	1:16am
♍	4/19	3:30am
♎	4/21	5:16am
♏	4/23	7:49am
♐	4/25	12:31pm
♑	4/27	8:22pm
♒	4/30	7:16am
♓	5/2	7:44pm
♈	5/5	7:28am
♉	5/7	4:48pm
♊	5/9	11:20pm
♋	5/12	3:38am
♌	5/14	6:39am
♍	5/16	9:14am
♎	5/18	12:07pm
♏	5/20	3:56pm
♐	5/22	9:22pm

Moon Sign Changes 1900-2005

Sign	Date	Time
♑	5/25	5:08am
♒	5/27	3:31pm
♓	5/30	3:46am
♈	6/1	3:55pm
♉	6/4	1:43am
♊	6/6	8:06am
♋	6/8	11:28am
♌	6/10	1:11pm
♍	6/12	2:49pm
♎	6/14	5:33pm
♏	6/16	10:03pm
♐	6/19	4:28am
♑	6/21	12:51pm
♒	6/23	11:15pm
♓	6/26	11:23am
♈	6/28	11:56pm
♉	7/1	10:40am
♊	7/3	5:48pm
♋	7/5	9:07pm
♌	7/7	9:53pm
♍	7/9	10:03pm
♎	7/11	11:31pm
♏	7/14	3:28am
♐	7/16	10:11am
♑	7/18	7:13pm
♒	7/21	6:02am
♓	7/23	6:13pm
♈	7/26	6:57am
♉	7/28	6:34pm
♊	7/31	3:01am
♋	8/2	7:20am
♌	8/4	8:13am
♍	8/6	7:32am
♎	8/8	7:30am
♏	8/10	9:57am
♐	8/12	3:49pm
♑	8/15	12:51am
♒	8/17	12:02pm
♓	8/20	12:23am
♈	8/22	1:05pm
♉	8/25	1:03am
♊	8/27	10:40am
♋	8/29	4:34pm
♌	8/31	6:41pm
♍	9/2	6:20pm
♎	9/4	5:35pm
♏	9/6	6:34pm
♐	9/8	10:52pm
♑	9/11	6:56am
♒	9/13	5:58pm
♓	9/16	6:27am
♈	9/18	7:02pm
♉	9/21	6:45am
♊	9/23	4:40pm
♋	9/25	11:46pm
♌	9/28	3:35am
♍	9/30	4:40am
♎	10/2	4:30am
♏	10/4	4:58am
♐	10/6	7:55am
♑	10/8	2:31pm
♒	10/11	12:42am
♓	10/13	1:03pm
♈	10/16	1:36am
♉	10/18	12:54pm
♊	10/20	10:15pm
♋	10/23	5:21am
♌	10/25	10:10am
♍	10/27	12:53pm
♎	10/29	2:16pm
♏	10/31	3:31pm
♐	11/2	6:10pm
♑	11/4	11:39pm
♒	11/7	8:41am
♓	11/9	8:34pm
♈	11/12	9:12am
♉	11/14	8:24pm
♊	11/17	5:02am
♋	11/19	11:11am
♌	11/21	3:32pm
♍	11/23	6:48pm
♎	11/25	9:33pm
♏	11/28	12:19am
♐	11/30	3:52am
♑	12/2	9:16am
♒	12/4	5:32pm
♓	12/7	4:46am
♈	12/9	5:30pm
♉	12/12	5:09am
♊	12/14	1:44pm
♋	12/16	7:01pm
♌	12/18	10:03pm
♍	12/21	12:19am
♎	12/23	2:59am
♏	12/25	6:39am
♐	12/27	11:29am
♑	12/29	5:47pm
	1949	
♒	1/1	2:07am
♓	1/3	12:58pm
♈	1/6	1:40am
♉	1/8	2:03pm
♊	1/10	11:31pm
♋	1/13	4:57am
♌	1/15	7:08am
♍	1/17	7:52am
♎	1/19	9:03am
♏	1/21	11:59am
♐	1/23	5:09pm
♑	1/26	12:22am
♒	1/28	9:26am
♓	1/30	8:26pm
♈	2/2	9:04am
♉	2/4	9:57pm
♊	2/7	8:40am
♋	2/9	3:22pm
♌	2/11	6:00pm
♍	2/13	6:05pm
♎	2/15	5:44pm
♏	2/17	6:53pm
♐	2/19	10:49pm
♑	2/22	5:50am
♒	2/24	3:26pm
♓	2/27	2:54am
♈	3/1	3:36pm
♉	3/4	4:33am
♊	3/6	4:05pm
♋	3/9	12:21am
♌	3/11	4:33am
♍	3/13	5:24am
♎	3/15	4:40am
♏	3/17	4:25am
♐	3/19	6:31am
♑	3/21	12:04pm
♒	3/23	9:10pm
♓	3/26	8:50am
♈	3/28	9:41pm
♉	3/31	10:29am
♊	4/2	10:03pm
♋	4/5	7:10am
♌	4/7	12:59pm
♍	4/9	3:32pm
♎	4/11	3:48pm
♏	4/13	3:27pm
♐	4/15	4:23pm
♑	4/17	8:16pm
♒	4/20	3:59am
♓	4/22	3:08pm
♈	4/25	4:01am
♉	4/27	4:41pm
♊	4/30	3:48am
♋	5/2	12:43pm
♌	5/4	7:11pm
♍	5/6	11:11pm
♎	5/9	1:07am
♏	5/11	1:54am
♐	5/13	2:57am
♑	5/15	5:57am
♒	5/17	12:19pm
♓	5/19	10:26pm
♈	5/22	11:02am
♉	5/24	11:42pm
♊	5/27	10:27am
♋	5/29	6:39pm
♌	6/1	12:36am
♍	6/3	4:53am
♎	6/5	7:57am
♏	6/7	10:13am
♐	6/9	12:24pm
♑	6/11	3:40pm
♒	6/13	9:26pm
♓	6/16	6:38am
♈	6/18	6:45pm
♉	6/21	7:30am
♊	6/23	6:20pm
♋	6/26	2:01am
♌	6/28	7:01am
♍	6/30	10:27am
♎	7/2	1:22pm
♏	7/4	4:22pm
♐	7/6	7:45pm
♑	7/9	12:02am
♒	7/11	6:09am
♓	7/13	3:01pm
♈	7/16	2:43am
♉	7/18	3:36pm
♊	7/21	2:57am
♋	7/23	10:52am
♌	7/25	3:19pm
♍	7/27	5:36pm
♎	7/29	7:20pm
♏	7/31	9:44pm
♐	8/3	1:25am
♑	8/5	6:36am
♒	8/7	1:34pm
♓	8/9	10:45pm
♈	8/12	10:20am
♉	8/14	11:18pm
♊	8/17	11:23am
♋	8/19	8:15pm
♌	8/22	1:08am
♍	8/24	2:56am
♎	8/26	3:24am
♏	8/28	4:20am
♐	8/30	7:00am
♑	9/1	12:05pm
♒	9/3	7:37pm
♓	9/6	5:26am
♈	9/8	5:13pm
♉	9/11	6:12am
♊	9/13	6:47pm
♋	9/16	4:52am
♌	9/18	11:04am
♍	9/20	1:34pm
♎	9/22	1:41pm
♏	9/24	1:20pm
♐	9/26	2:21pm
♑	9/28	6:07pm
♒	10/1	1:13am
♓	10/3	11:19am
♈	10/5	11:27pm
♉	10/8	12:26pm
♊	10/11	1:02am
♋	10/13	11:51am
♌	10/15	7:35pm
♍	10/17	11:42pm
♎	10/20	12:48am
♏	10/22	12:18am
♐	10/24	12:08am
♑	10/26	2:10am
♒	10/28	7:50am
♓	10/30	5:21pm
♈	11/2	5:34am
♉	11/4	6:37pm
♊	11/7	6:55am
♋	11/9	5:35pm
♌	11/12	2:00am
♍	11/14	7:42am
♎	11/16	10:35am
♏	11/18	11:18am
♐	11/20	11:15am
♑	11/22	12:19pm
♒	11/24	4:24pm
♓	11/27	12:35am
♈	11/29	12:18pm
♉	12/2	1:22am
♊	12/4	1:28pm
♋	12/6	11:31pm
♌	12/9	7:28am
♍	12/11	1:31pm
♎	12/13	5:45pm
♏	12/15	8:13pm
♐	12/17	9:32pm
♑	12/19	11:00pm
♒	12/22	2:24am
♓	12/24	9:20am
♈	12/26	8:05pm
♉	12/29	8:58am
♊	12/31	9:13pm
	1950	
♋	1/3	6:56am
♌	1/5	1:58pm
♍	1/7	7:06pm
♎	1/9	11:08pm
♏	1/12	2:28am
♐	1/14	5:16am
♑	1/16	8:06am
♒	1/18	12:07pm
♓	1/20	6:41pm
♈	1/23	4:37am
♉	1/25	5:08pm
♊	1/28	5:43am
♋	1/30	3:50pm
♌	2/1	10:34pm
♍	2/4	2:37am
♎	2/6	5:19am
♏	2/8	7:50am
♐	2/10	10:51am
♑	2/12	2:45pm
♒	2/14	7:57pm
♓	2/17	3:11am
♈	2/19	1:01pm
♉	2/22	1:12am
♊	2/24	2:03pm
♋	2/27	1:03am
♌	3/1	8:30am
♍	3/3	12:24pm
♎	3/5	2:00pm
♏	3/7	2:55pm
♐	3/9	4:37pm
♑	3/11	8:07pm
♒	3/14	1:52am
♓	3/16	9:59am
♈	3/18	8:21pm
♉	3/21	8:32am
♊	3/23	9:28pm
♋	3/26	9:17am
♌	3/28	6:04pm
♍	3/30	11:01pm
♎	4/2	12:41am
♏	4/4	12:35am
♐	4/6	12:37am
♑	4/8	2:29am
♒	4/10	7:24am
♓	4/12	3:38pm
♈	4/15	2:32am
♉	4/17	3:00pm
♊	4/20	3:54am
♋	4/22	4:02pm
♌	4/25	1:57am
♍	4/27	8:30am
♎	4/29	11:25am
♏	5/1	11:37am
♐	5/3	10:50am
♑	5/5	11:08am
♒	5/7	2:22pm
♓	5/9	9:34pm
♈	5/12	8:18am
♉	5/14	8:59pm
♊	5/17	9:52am
♋	5/19	9:50pm
♌	5/22	8:06am
♍	5/24	3:50pm
♎	5/26	8:26pm
♏	5/28	10:01pm
♐	5/30	9:43pm
♑	6/1	9:27pm
♒	6/3	11:18pm
♓	6/6	4:57am
♈	6/8	2:44pm
♉	6/11	3:12am
♊	6/13	4:05pm
♋	6/16	3:45am
♌	6/18	1:37pm
♍	6/20	9:31pm
♎	6/23	3:09am
♏	6/25	6:19am
♐	6/27	7:26am
♑	6/29	7:48am
♒	7/1	9:19am
♓	7/3	1:51pm
♈	7/5	10:24pm
♉	7/8	10:13am
♊	7/10	11:02pm
♋	7/13	10:34am
♌	7/15	7:52pm
♍	7/18	3:05am
♎	7/20	8:34am
♏	7/22	12:27pm
♐	7/24	2:55pm
♑	7/26	4:39pm
♒	7/28	6:55pm
♓	7/30	11:19pm
♈	8/2	7:03am
♉	8/4	6:06pm
♊	8/7	6:44am
♋	8/9	6:27pm
♌	8/12	3:36am
♍	8/14	10:03am
♎	8/16	2:31pm
♏	8/18	5:49pm
♐	8/20	8:36pm
♑	8/22	11:23pm
♒	8/25	2:53am
♓	8/27	8:02am
♈	8/29	3:45pm
♉	9/1	2:19am
♊	9/3	2:45pm
♋	9/6	2:54am
♌	9/8	12:34pm
♍	9/10	6:55pm
♎	9/12	10:28pm

Moon Sign Changes 1900-2005

♏ 9/15 12:27am	♐ 2/1 1:16am	♒ 6/21 4:04pm	♈ 11/9 5:52pm	♉ 3/27 3:05pm	♋ 8/15 6:52pm
♐ 9/17 2:12am	♑ 2/3 2:52am	♓ 6/23 5:49pm	♉ 11/12 1:07am	♊ 3/29 9:36pm	♌ 8/18 7:19am
♑ 9/19 4:49am	♒ 2/5 4:04am	♈ 6/25 11:13pm	♊ 11/14 10:15am	♋ 4/1 7:39am	♍ 8/20 8:22pm
♒ 9/21 8:59am	♓ 2/7 6:29am	♉ 6/28 8:17am	♋ 11/16 9:27pm	♌ 4/3 8:10pm	♎ 8/23 8:42am
♓ 9/23 3:09pm	♈ 2/9 11:43am	♊ 6/30 7:51pm	♌ 11/19 10:12am	♍ 4/6 8:40am	♏ 8/25 7:10pm
♈ 9/25 11:32pm	♉ 2/11 8:33pm	♋ 7/3 8:27am	♍ 11/21 10:35pm	♎ 4/8 6:56pm	♐ 8/28 2:53am
♉ 9/28 10:08am	♊ 2/14 8:18am	♌ 7/5 9:00pm	♎ 11/24 8:09am	♏ 4/11 2:13am	♑ 8/30 7:24am
♊ 9/30 10:26pm	♋ 2/16 8:51pm	♍ 7/8 8:36am	♏ 11/26 1:32pm	♐ 4/13 7:08am	♒ 9/1 9:03am
♋ 10/3 10:59am	♌ 2/19 8:01am	♎ 7/10 6:04pm	♐ 11/28 3:20pm	♑ 4/15 10:41am	♓ 9/3 9:00am
♌ 10/5 9:40pm	♍ 2/21 4:43pm	♏ 7/13 12:19am	♑ 11/30 3:22pm	♒ 4/17 1:43pm	♈ 9/5 8:57am
♍ 10/8 4:54am	♎ 2/23 11:01pm	♐ 7/15 3:03am	♒ 12/2 3:45pm	♓ 4/19 4:40pm	♉ 9/7 10:48am
♎ 10/10 8:29am	♏ 2/26 3:31am	♑ 7/17 3:14am	♓ 12/4 6:08pm	♈ 4/21 7:56pm	♊ 9/9 4:06pm
♏ 10/12 9:31am	♐ 2/28 6:49am	♒ 7/19 2:41am	♈ 12/6 11:18pm	♉ 4/24 12:15am	♋ 9/12 1:24am
♐ 10/14 9:44am	♑ 3/2 9:29am	♓ 7/21 3:29am	♉ 12/9 7:04am	♊ 4/26 6:40am	♌ 9/14 1:38pm
♑ 10/16 10:55am	♒ 3/4 12:11pm	♈ 7/23 7:21am	♊ 12/11 4:54pm	♋ 4/28 4:06pm	♍ 9/17 2:42am
♒ 10/18 2:27pm	♓ 3/6 3:45pm	♉ 7/25 3:07pm	♋ 12/14 4:22am	♌ 5/1 4:12am	♎ 9/19 2:41pm
♓ 10/20 8:53pm	♈ 3/8 9:16pm	♊ 7/28 2:08am	♌ 12/16 5:05pm	♍ 5/3 4:57pm	♏ 9/22 12:43am
♈ 10/23 5:59am	♉ 3/11 5:33am	♋ 7/30 2:42pm	♍ 12/19 5:52am	♎ 5/6 3:39am	♐ 9/24 8:33am
♉ 10/25 5:03pm	♊ 3/13 4:36pm	♌ 8/2 3:08am	♎ 12/21 4:41pm	♏ 5/8 10:49am	♑ 9/26 2:06pm
♊ 10/28 5:22am	♋ 3/16 5:06am	♍ 8/4 2:18pm	♏ 12/23 11:38pm	♐ 5/10 2:50pm	♒ 9/28 5:24pm
♋ 10/30 6:03pm	♌ 3/18 4:44pm	♎ 8/6 11:34pm	♐ 12/26 2:27am	♑ 5/12 5:09pm	♓ 9/30 6:52pm
♌ 11/2 5:38am	♍ 3/21 1:39am	♏ 8/9 6:24am	♑ 12/28 2:24am	♒ 5/14 7:14pm	♈ 10/2 7:34pm
♍ 11/4 2:21pm	♎ 3/23 7:21am	♐ 8/11 10:31am	♒ 12/30 1:36am	♓ 5/16 10:05pm	♉ 10/4 9:05pm
♎ 11/6 7:10pm	♏ 3/25 10:36am	♑ 8/13 12:18pm	**1952**	♈ 5/19 2:07am	♊ 10/7 1:15am
♏ 11/8 8:29pm	♐ 3/27 12:40pm	♒ 8/15 12:53pm	♓ 1/1 2:10am	♉ 5/21 7:29am	♋ 10/9 9:16am
♐ 11/10 7:51pm	♑ 3/29 2:51pm	♓ 8/17 1:52pm	♈ 1/3 5:42am	♊ 5/23 2:37pm	♌ 10/11 8:50pm
♑ 11/12 7:25pm	♒ 3/31 6:02pm	♈ 8/19 4:58pm	♉ 1/5 12:43pm	♋ 5/26 12:06am	♍ 10/14 9:51am
♒ 11/14 9:14pm	♓ 4/2 10:44pm	♉ 8/21 11:26pm	♊ 1/7 10:42pm	♌ 5/28 11:59am	♎ 10/16 9:44pm
♓ 11/17 2:38am	♈ 4/5 5:16am	♊ 8/24 9:27am	♋ 1/10 10:34am	♍ 5/31 12:57am	♏ 10/19 7:10am
♈ 11/19 11:39am	♉ 4/7 1:52pm	♋ 8/26 9:44pm	♌ 1/12 11:19pm	♎ 6/2 12:26pm	♐ 10/21 2:12pm
♉ 11/21 11:08pm	♊ 4/10 12:41am	♌ 8/29 10:10am	♍ 1/15 12:00pm	♏ 6/4 8:19pm	♑ 10/23 7:28pm
♊ 11/24 11:38am	♋ 4/12 1:04pm	♍ 8/31 9:00pm	♎ 1/17 11:19pm	♐ 6/7 12:21am	♒ 10/25 11:28pm
♋ 11/27 12:13am	♌ 4/15 1:18am	♎ 9/3 5:32am	♏ 1/20 7:44am	♑ 6/9 1:46am	♓ 10/28 2:23am
♌ 11/29 12:02pm	♍ 4/17 11:07am	♏ 9/5 11:49am	♐ 1/22 12:22pm	♒ 6/11 2:27am	♈ 10/30 4:34am
♍ 12/1 9:53pm	♎ 4/19 5:13pm	♐ 9/7 4:11pm	♑ 1/24 1:39pm	♓ 6/13 4:00am	♉ 11/1 6:58am
♎ 12/4 4:29am	♏ 4/21 7:55pm	♑ 9/9 7:06pm	♒ 1/26 1:06pm	♈ 6/15 7:29am	♊ 11/3 11:02am
♏ 12/6 7:19am	♐ 4/23 8:40pm	♒ 9/11 9:11pm	♓ 1/28 12:45pm	♉ 6/17 1:11pm	♋ 11/5 6:12pm
♐ 12/8 7:17am	♑ 4/25 9:20pm	♓ 9/13 11:21pm	♈ 1/30 2:33pm	♊ 6/19 9:03pm	♌ 11/8 4:56am
♑ 12/10 6:16am	♒ 4/27 11:32pm	♈ 9/16 2:47am	♉ 2/1 7:51pm	♋ 6/22 7:04am	♍ 11/10 5:47pm
♒ 12/12 6:34am	♓ 4/30 4:13am	♉ 9/18 8:41am	♊ 2/4 4:55am	♌ 6/24 7:02pm	♎ 11/13 5:57am
♓ 12/14 10:11am	♈ 5/2 11:26am	♊ 9/20 5:47pm	♋ 2/6 4:44pm	♍ 6/27 8:06am	♏ 11/15 3:18pm
♈ 12/16 5:58pm	♉ 5/4 8:47pm	♋ 9/23 5:34am	♌ 2/9 5:36am	♎ 6/29 8:18pm	♐ 11/17 9:33pm
♉ 12/19 5:10am	♊ 5/7 7:51am	♌ 9/25 6:08pm	♍ 2/11 6:02pm	♏ 7/2 5:25am	♑ 11/20 1:40am
♊ 12/21 5:49pm	♋ 5/9 8:13pm	♍ 9/28 5:05am	♎ 2/14 5:00am	♐ 7/4 10:27am	♒ 11/22 4:52am
♋ 12/24 6:18am	♌ 5/12 8:49am	♎ 9/30 1:08pm	♏ 2/16 1:45pm	♑ 7/6 12:02pm	♓ 11/24 7:55am
♌ 12/26 5:45pm	♍ 5/14 7:44pm	♏ 10/2 6:23pm	♐ 2/18 7:42pm	♒ 7/8 11:54am	♈ 11/26 11:09am
♍ 12/29 3:41am	♎ 5/17 3:05am	♐ 10/4 9:48pm	♑ 2/20 10:49pm	♓ 7/10 11:59am	♉ 11/28 2:54pm
♎ 12/31 11:20am	♏ 5/19 6:23am	♑ 10/7 12:30am	♒ 2/22 11:48pm	♈ 7/12 1:56pm	♊ 11/30 7:53pm
1951	♐ 5/21 6:44am	♒ 10/9 3:19am	♓ 2/25 12:01am	♉ 7/14 6:45pm	♋ 12/3 3:09am
♏ 1/2 3:58pm	♑ 5/23 6:07am	♓ 10/11 6:46am	♈ 2/27 1:11am	♊ 7/17 2:37am	♌ 12/5 1:23pm
♐ 1/4 5:38pm	♒ 5/25 6:41am	♈ 10/13 11:19am	♉ 2/29 5:02am	♋ 7/19 1:05pm	♍ 12/8 1:57am
♑ 1/6 5:32pm	♓ 5/27 10:05am	♉ 10/15 5:37pm	♊ 3/2 12:36pm	♌ 7/22 1:20am	♎ 12/10 2:35pm
♒ 1/8 5:35pm	♈ 5/29 4:53pm	♊ 10/18 2:22am	♋ 3/4 11:40pm	♍ 7/24 2:25pm	♏ 12/13 12:39am
♓ 1/10 7:56pm	♉ 6/1 2:33am	♋ 10/20 1:43pm	♌ 3/7 12:30pm	♎ 7/27 2:54am	♐ 12/15 7:00am
♈ 1/13 2:05am	♊ 6/3 2:03pm	♌ 10/23 2:25am	♍ 3/10 12:51am	♏ 7/29 1:04pm	♑ 12/17 10:17am
♉ 1/15 12:10pm	♋ 6/6 2:31am	♍ 10/25 2:01pm	♎ 3/12 11:16am	♐ 7/31 7:37pm	♒ 12/19 12:02pm
♊ 1/18 12:36am	♌ 6/8 3:12pm	♎ 10/27 10:25pm	♏ 3/14 7:20pm	♑ 8/2 10:27pm	♓ 12/21 1:45pm
♋ 1/20 1:06pm	♍ 6/11 2:47am	♏ 10/30 3:09am	♐ 3/17 1:15am	♒ 8/4 10:41pm	♈ 12/23 4:30pm
♌ 1/23 12:12am	♎ 6/13 11:31am	♐ 11/1 5:20am	♑ 3/19 5:19am	♓ 8/6 10:05pm	♉ 12/25 8:46pm
♍ 1/25 9:26am	♏ 6/15 4:17pm	♑ 11/3 6:40am	♒ 3/21 7:55am	♈ 8/8 10:33pm	♊ 12/28 2:48am
♎ 1/27 4:46pm	♐ 6/17 5:26pm	♒ 11/5 8:43am	♓ 3/23 9:39am	♉ 8/11 1:46am	♋ 12/30 10:53am
♏ 1/29 10:04pm	♑ 6/19 4:38pm	♓ 11/7 12:23pm	♈ 3/25 11:34am	♊ 8/13 8:36am	

Moon Sign Changes 1900-2005

	1953		♍	5/20	7:31pm	♏	10/9	7:56am	♐	2/25	10:00am	♒	7/16	1:19pm	♈	12/4	7:35pm
♌	1/1	9:17pm	♎	5/23	8:16am	♐	10/11	7:19pm	♑	2/27	7:58pm	♓	7/18	6:33pm	♉	12/6	9:23pm
♍	1/4	9:41am	♏	5/25	7:32pm	♑	10/14	4:51am	♒	3/2	2:07am	♈	7/20	10:07pm	♊	12/8	9:16pm
♎	1/6	10:36pm	♐	5/28	4:08am	♒	10/16	11:34am	♓	3/4	4:32am	♉	7/23	12:52am	♋	12/10	9:06pm
♏	1/9	9:44am	♑	5/30	10:17am	♓	10/18	2:55pm	♈	3/6	4:40am	♊	7/25	3:30am	♌	12/12	10:48pm
♐	1/11	5:14pm	♒	6/1	2:45pm	♈	10/20	3:27pm	♉	3/8	4:32am	♋	7/27	6:41am	♍	12/15	3:54am
♑	1/13	8:55pm	♓	6/3	6:12pm	♉	10/22	2:47pm	♊	3/10	6:06am	♌	7/29	11:10am	♎	12/17	12:51pm
♒	1/15	9:57pm	♈	6/5	9:01pm	♊	10/24	3:04pm	♋	3/12	10:37am	♍	7/31	5:50pm	♏	12/20	12:43am
♓	1/17	10:07pm	♉	6/7	11:41pm	♋	10/26	6:24pm	♌	3/14	6:17pm	♎	8/3	3:14am	♐	12/22	1:35pm
♈	1/19	11:08pm	♊	6/10	3:03am	♌	10/29	1:55am	♍	3/17	4:21am	♏	8/5	3:03pm	♑	12/25	1:40am
♉	1/22	2:20am	♋	6/12	8:17am	♍	10/31	1:04pm	♎	3/19	3:57pm	♐	8/8	3:32am	♒	12/27	12:00pm
♊	1/24	8:21am	♌	6/14	4:27pm	♎	11/3	1:51am	♏	3/22	4:26am	♑	8/10	2:20pm	♓	12/29	8:09pm
♋	1/26	5:07pm	♍	6/17	3:37am	♏	11/5	2:12pm	♐	3/24	4:56pm	♒	8/12	9:54pm		1955	
♌	1/29	4:06am	♎	6/19	4:16pm	♐	11/8	1:06am	♑	3/27	3:55am	♓	8/15	2:17am	♈	1/1	1:56am
♍	1/31	4:35pm	♏	6/22	3:57am	♑	11/10	10:18am	♒	3/29	11:37am	♈	8/17	4:37am	♉	1/3	5:24am
♎	2/3	5:31am	♐	6/24	12:48pm	♒	11/12	5:31pm	♓	3/31	3:16pm	♉	8/19	6:26am	♊	1/5	7:04am
♏	2/5	5:21pm	♑	6/26	6:29pm	♓	11/14	10:17pm	♈	4/2	3:40pm	♊	8/21	8:56am	♋	1/7	8:00am
♐	2/8	2:20am	♒	6/28	9:51pm	♈	11/17	12:35am	♉	4/4	2:43pm	♋	8/23	12:50pm	♌	1/9	9:41am
♑	2/10	7:32am	♓	7/1	12:08am	♉	11/19	1:15am	♊	4/6	2:40pm	♌	8/25	6:22pm	♍	1/11	1:43pm
♒	2/12	9:17am	♈	7/3	2:23am	♊	11/21	1:55am	♋	4/8	5:29pm	♍	8/28	1:44am	♎	1/13	9:15pm
♓	2/14	8:58am	♉	7/5	5:23am	♋	11/23	4:32am	♌	4/11	12:05am	♎	8/30	11:12am	♏	1/16	8:15am
♈	2/16	8:31am	♊	7/7	9:42am	♌	11/25	10:40am	♍	4/13	10:03am	♏	9/1	10:49pm	♐	1/18	9:01pm
♉	2/18	9:51am	♋	7/9	3:54pm	♍	11/27	8:41pm	♎	4/15	9:58pm	♐	9/4	11:32am	♑	1/21	9:09am
♊	2/20	2:27pm	♌	7/12	12:28am	♎	11/30	9:06am	♏	4/18	10:32am	♑	9/6	11:10pm	♒	1/23	6:58pm
♋	2/22	10:48pm	♍	7/14	11:28am	♏	12/2	9:30pm	♐	4/20	10:55pm	♒	9/9	7:31am	♓	1/26	2:11am
♌	2/25	10:05am	♎	7/17	12:04am	♐	12/5	8:09am	♑	4/23	10:11am	♓	9/11	11:55am	♈	1/28	7:19am
♍	2/27	10:51pm	♏	7/19	12:17pm	♑	12/7	4:33pm	♒	4/25	7:02pm	♈	9/13	1:22pm	♉	1/30	11:06am
♎	3/2	11:41am	♐	7/21	9:59pm	♒	12/9	10:59pm	♓	4/28	12:21am	♉	9/15	1:44pm	♊	2/1	2:02pm
♏	3/4	11:31pm	♑	7/24	4:06am	♓	12/12	3:46am	♈	4/30	2:08am	♊	9/17	2:55pm	♋	2/3	4:36pm
♐	3/7	9:20am	♒	7/26	7:03am	♈	12/14	7:06am	♉	5/2	1:42am	♋	9/19	6:13pm	♌	2/5	7:28pm
♑	3/9	4:10pm	♓	7/28	8:07am	♉	12/16	9:22am	♊	5/4	1:06am	♌	9/22	12:04am	♍	2/7	11:43pm
♒	3/11	7:37pm	♈	7/30	8:56am	♊	12/18	11:27am	♋	5/6	2:30am	♍	9/24	8:11am	♎	2/10	6:33am
♓	3/13	8:17pm	♉	8/1	10:57am	♋	12/20	2:40pm	♌	5/8	7:29am	♎	9/26	6:11pm	♏	2/12	4:38pm
♈	3/15	7:39pm	♊	8/3	3:10pm	♌	12/22	8:23pm	♍	5/10	4:23pm	♏	9/29	5:52am	♐	2/15	5:07am
♉	3/17	7:44pm	♋	8/5	9:59pm	♍	12/25	5:24am	♎	5/13	4:03am	♐	10/1	6:41pm	♑	2/17	5:34pm
♊	3/19	10:35pm	♌	8/8	7:16am	♎	12/27	5:11pm	♏	5/15	4:42pm	♑	10/4	7:04am	♒	2/20	3:33am
♋	3/22	5:29am	♍	8/10	6:33pm	♏	12/30	5:43am	♐	5/18	4:53am	♒	10/6	4:45pm	♓	2/22	10:09am
♌	3/24	4:14pm	♎	8/13	7:08am		1954		♑	5/20	3:49pm	♓	10/8	10:17pm	♈	2/24	2:06pm
♍	3/27	5:04am	♏	8/15	7:43pm	♐	1/1	4:39pm	♒	5/23	12:48am	♈	10/10	11:58pm	♉	2/26	4:46pm
♎	3/29	5:51pm	♐	8/18	6:30am	♑	1/4	12:45am	♓	5/25	7:08am	♉	10/12	11:32pm	♊	2/28	7:24pm
♏	4/1	5:19am	♑	8/20	1:53pm	♒	1/6	6:09am	♈	5/27	10:32am	♊	10/14	11:10pm	♋	3/2	10:40pm
♐	4/3	2:58pm	♒	8/22	5:29pm	♓	1/8	9:43am	♉	5/29	11:33am	♋	10/17	12:50am	♌	3/5	2:48am
♑	4/5	10:29pm	♓	8/24	6:12pm	♈	1/10	12:27pm	♊	5/31	11:41am	♌	10/19	5:41am	♍	3/7	8:09am
♒	4/8	3:27am	♈	8/26	5:46pm	♉	1/12	3:10pm	♋	6/2	12:46pm	♍	10/21	1:44pm	♎	3/9	3:20pm
♓	4/10	5:49am	♉	8/28	6:10pm	♊	1/14	6:29pm	♌	6/4	4:34pm	♎	10/24	12:12am	♏	3/12	1:04am
♈	4/12	6:19am	♊	8/30	9:07pm	♋	1/16	11:01pm	♍	6/7	12:06am	♏	10/26	12:11pm	♐	3/14	1:13pm
♉	4/14	6:31am	♋	9/2	3:30am	♌	1/19	5:24am	♎	6/9	10:59am	♐	10/29	12:59am	♑	3/17	2:01am
♊	4/16	8:27am	♌	9/4	1:05pm	♍	1/21	2:14pm	♏	6/11	11:30pm	♑	10/31	1:36pm	♒	3/19	12:47pm
♋	4/18	1:53pm	♍	9/7	12:47am	♎	1/24	1:30am	♐	6/14	11:37am	♒	11/3	12:22am	♓	3/21	7:45pm
♌	4/20	11:27pm	♎	9/9	1:27pm	♏	1/26	2:03pm	♑	6/16	10:05pm	♓	11/5	7:34am	♈	3/23	11:09pm
♍	4/23	11:53am	♏	9/12	2:05am	♐	1/29	1:42am	♒	6/19	6:26am	♈	11/7	10:42am	♉	3/26	12:31am
♎	4/26	12:40am	♐	9/14	1:32pm	♑	1/31	10:26am	♓	6/21	12:37pm	♉	11/9	10:48am	♊	3/28	1:42am
♏	4/28	11:52am	♑	9/16	10:21pm	♒	2/2	3:38pm	♈	6/23	4:43pm	♊	11/11	9:50am	♋	3/30	4:05am
♐	4/30	8:52pm	♒	9/19	3:30am	♓	2/4	6:03pm	♉	6/25	7:09pm	♋	11/13	9:59am	♌	4/1	8:20am
♑	5/3	3:55am	♓	9/21	5:06am	♈	2/6	7:14pm	♊	6/27	8:41pm	♌	11/15	1:03pm	♍	4/3	2:31pm
♒	5/5	9:12am	♈	9/23	4:30am	♉	2/8	8:47pm	♋	6/29	10:35pm	♍	11/17	7:52pm	♎	4/5	10:34pm
♓	5/7	12:46pm	♉	9/25	3:45am	♊	2/10	11:54pm	♌	7/2	2:16am	♎	11/20	6:02am	♏	4/8	8:38am
♈	5/9	2:49pm	♊	9/27	5:01am	♋	2/13	5:10am	♍	7/4	8:56am	♏	11/22	6:13pm	♐	4/10	8:41pm
♉	5/11	4:12pm	♋	9/29	9:56am	♌	2/15	12:35pm	♎	7/6	6:53pm	♐	11/25	7:01am	♑	4/13	9:40am
♊	5/13	6:27pm	♌	10/1	6:53pm	♍	2/17	10:00pm	♏	7/9	7:04am	♑	11/27	7:24pm	♒	4/15	9:20pm
♋	5/15	11:16pm	♍	10/4	6:40am	♎	2/20	9:14am	♐	7/11	7:19pm	♒	11/30	6:19am	♓	4/18	5:28am
♌	5/18	7:47am	♎	10/6	7:28pm	♏	2/22	9:43pm	♑	7/14	5:40am	♓	12/2	2:38pm	♈	4/20	9:29am

Moon Sign Changes 1900-2005

♉	4/22	10:29am
♊	4/24	10:24am
♋	4/26	11:09am
♌	4/28	2:09pm
♍	4/30	7:58pm
♎	5/3	4:26am
♏	5/5	3:04pm
♐	5/8	3:19am
♑	5/10	4:19pm
♒	5/13	4:29am
♓	5/15	1:53pm
♈	5/17	7:21pm
♉	5/19	9:12pm
♊	5/21	8:56pm
♋	5/23	8:33pm
♌	5/25	9:52pm
♍	5/28	2:16am
♎	5/30	10:08am
♏	6/1	8:54pm
♐	6/4	9:24am
♑	6/6	10:21pm
♒	6/9	10:30am
♓	6/11	8:32pm
♈	6/14	3:24am
♉	6/16	6:50am
♊	6/18	7:36am
♋	6/20	7:15am
♌	6/22	7:36am
♍	6/24	10:26am
♎	6/26	4:55pm
♏	6/29	3:04am
♐	7/1	3:34pm
♑	7/4	4:29am
♒	7/6	4:18pm
♓	7/9	2:09am
♈	7/11	9:33am
♉	7/13	2:20pm
♊	7/15	4:43pm
♋	7/17	5:30pm
♌	7/19	6:03pm
♍	7/21	8:06pm
♎	7/24	1:16am
♏	7/26	10:19am
♐	7/28	10:24pm
♑	7/31	11:18am
♒	8/2	10:52pm
♓	8/5	8:04am
♈	8/7	3:00pm
♉	8/9	8:03pm
♊	8/11	11:33pm
♋	8/14	1:50am
♌	8/16	3:34am
♍	8/18	5:57am
♎	8/20	10:34am
♏	8/22	6:37pm
♐	8/25	6:03am
♑	8/27	6:57pm
♒	8/30	6:35am
♓	9/1	3:23pm
♈	9/3	9:24pm
♉	9/6	1:36am
♊	9/8	4:58am
♋	9/10	8:01am
♌	9/12	11:02am
♍	9/14	2:33pm
♎	9/16	7:35pm
♏	9/19	3:18am
♐	9/21	2:11pm
♑	9/24	3:01am
♒	9/26	3:07pm
♓	9/29	12:12am
♈	10/1	5:46am
♉	10/3	8:52am
♊	10/5	10:59am
♋	10/7	1:23pm
♌	10/9	4:41pm
♍	10/11	9:11pm
♎	10/14	3:13am
♏	10/16	11:23am
♐	10/18	10:07pm
♑	10/21	10:52am
♒	10/23	11:33pm
♓	10/26	9:37am
♈	10/28	3:46pm
♉	10/30	6:30pm
♊	11/1	7:23pm
♋	11/3	8:11pm
♌	11/5	10:20pm
♍	11/8	2:36am
♎	11/10	9:15am
♏	11/12	6:12pm
♐	11/15	5:17am
♑	11/17	5:59pm
♒	11/20	6:58am
♓	11/22	6:10pm
♈	11/25	1:47am
♉	11/27	5:27am
♊	11/29	6:11am
♋	12/1	5:46am
♌	12/3	6:07am
♍	12/5	8:50am
♎	12/7	2:48pm
♏	12/9	11:59pm
♐	12/12	11:34am
♑	12/15	12:23am
♒	12/17	1:19pm
♓	12/20	1:02am
♈	12/22	10:05am
♉	12/24	3:33pm
♊	12/26	5:33pm
♋	12/28	5:17pm
♌	12/30	4:36pm
	1956	
♍	1/1	5:31pm
♎	1/3	9:44pm
♏	1/6	6:00am
♐	1/8	5:32pm
♑	1/11	6:33am
♒	1/13	7:19pm
♓	1/16	6:47am
♈	1/18	4:17pm
♉	1/20	11:11pm
♊	1/23	3:06am
♋	1/25	4:20am
♌	1/27	4:06am
♍	1/29	4:17am
♎	1/31	6:56am
♏	2/2	1:33pm
♐	2/5	12:13am
♑	2/7	1:08pm
♒	2/10	1:52am
♓	2/12	12:52pm
♈	2/14	9:48pm
♉	2/17	4:48am
♊	2/19	9:50am
♋	2/21	12:50pm
♌	2/23	2:10pm
♍	2/25	3:05pm
♎	2/27	5:20pm
♏	2/29	10:45pm
♐	3/3	8:09am
♑	3/5	8:32pm
♒	3/8	9:19am
♓	3/10	8:11pm
♈	3/13	4:26am
♉	3/15	10:32am
♊	3/17	3:12pm
♋	3/19	6:47pm
♌	3/21	9:31pm
♍	3/23	11:53pm
♎	3/26	3:00am
♏	3/28	8:19am
♐	3/30	4:56pm
♑	4/2	4:37am
♒	4/4	5:24pm
♓	4/7	4:37am
♈	4/9	12:46pm
♉	4/11	6:03pm
♊	4/13	9:30pm
♋	4/16	12:15am
♌	4/18	3:00am
♍	4/20	6:17am
♎	4/22	10:36am
♏	4/24	4:44pm
♐	4/27	1:25am
♑	4/29	12:44pm
♒	5/2	1:27am
♓	5/4	1:15pm
♈	5/6	10:05pm
♉	5/9	3:24am
♊	5/11	6:00am
♋	5/13	7:21am
♌	5/15	8:52am
♍	5/17	11:40am
♎	5/19	4:25pm
♏	5/21	11:26pm
♐	5/24	8:46am
♑	5/26	8:11pm
♒	5/29	8:52am
♓	5/31	9:09pm
♈	6/3	7:04am
♉	6/5	1:22pm
♊	6/7	4:09pm
♋	6/9	4:42pm
♌	6/11	4:45pm
♍	6/13	6:03pm
♎	6/15	9:58pm
♏	6/18	5:03am
♐	6/20	2:55pm
♑	6/23	2:43am
♒	6/25	3:26pm
♓	6/28	3:54am
♈	6/30	2:43pm
♉	7/2	10:26pm
♊	7/5	2:26am
♋	7/7	3:20am
♌	7/9	2:42am
♍	7/11	2:34am
♎	7/13	4:54am
♏	7/15	10:56am
♐	7/17	8:38pm
♑	7/20	8:40am
♒	7/22	9:28pm
♓	7/25	9:50am
♈	7/27	8:54pm
♉	7/30	5:40am
♊	8/1	11:16am
♋	8/3	1:32pm
♌	8/5	1:27pm
♍	8/7	12:50pm
♎	8/9	1:50pm
♏	8/11	6:20pm
♐	8/14	3:00am
♑	8/16	2:47pm
♒	8/19	3:38am
♓	8/21	3:47pm
♈	8/24	2:30am
♉	8/26	11:23am
♊	8/28	5:59pm
♋	8/30	9:51pm
♌	9/1	11:14pm
♍	9/3	11:20pm
♎	9/6	12:04am
♏	9/8	3:27am
♐	9/10	10:46am
♑	9/12	9:46pm
♒	9/15	10:28am
♓	9/17	10:34pm
♈	9/20	8:47am
♉	9/22	5:01pm
♊	9/24	11:25pm
♋	9/27	4:00am
♌	9/29	6:49am
♍	10/1	8:24am
♎	10/3	10:01am
♏	10/5	1:19pm
♐	10/7	7:46pm
♑	10/10	5:48am
♒	10/12	6:09pm
♓	10/15	6:25am
♈	10/17	4:35pm
♉	10/20	12:07am
♊	10/22	5:29am
♋	10/24	9:23am
♌	10/26	12:27pm
♍	10/28	3:09pm
♎	10/30	6:10pm
♏	11/1	10:24pm
♐	11/4	4:56am
♑	11/6	2:24pm
♒	11/9	2:19am
♓	11/11	2:51pm
♈	11/14	1:36am
♉	11/16	9:12am
♊	11/18	1:45pm
♋	11/20	4:18pm
♌	11/22	6:10pm
♍	11/24	8:32pm
♎	11/27	12:11am
♏	11/29	5:34am
♐	12/1	12:59pm
♑	12/3	10:36pm
♒	12/6	10:16am
♓	12/8	10:57pm
♈	12/11	10:37am
♉	12/13	7:15pm
♊	12/16	12:06am
♋	12/18	1:52am
♌	12/20	2:11am
♍	12/22	2:56am
♎	12/24	5:39am
♏	12/26	11:09am
♐	12/28	7:20pm
♑	12/31	5:37am
	1957	
♒	1/2	5:25pm
♓	1/5	6:04am
♈	1/7	6:23pm
♉	1/10	4:27am
♊	1/12	10:44am
♋	1/14	1:05pm
♌	1/16	12:50pm
♍	1/18	12:03pm
♎	1/20	12:55pm
♏	1/22	5:02pm
♐	1/25	12:52am
♑	1/27	11:32am
♒	1/29	11:42pm
♓	2/1	12:20pm
♈	2/4	12:42am
♉	2/6	11:37am
♊	2/8	7:34pm
♋	2/10	11:39pm
♌	2/13	12:19am
♍	2/14	11:17pm
♎	2/16	10:50pm
♏	2/19	1:06am
♐	2/21	7:23am
♑	2/23	5:27pm
♒	2/26	5:42am
♓	2/28	6:25pm
♈	3/3	6:31am
♉	3/5	5:20pm
♊	3/8	2:03am
♋	3/10	7:45am
♌	3/12	10:12am
♍	3/14	10:20am
♎	3/16	9:59am
♏	3/18	11:15am
♐	3/20	3:54pm
♑	3/23	12:34am
♒	3/25	12:17pm
♓	3/28	1:00am
♈	3/30	12:55pm
♉	4/1	11:11pm
♊	4/4	7:30am
♋	4/6	1:37pm
♌	4/8	5:24pm
♍	4/10	7:13pm
♎	4/12	8:08pm
♏	4/14	9:45pm
♐	4/17	1:43am
♑	4/19	9:08am
♒	4/21	7:53pm
♓	4/24	8:23am
♈	4/26	8:22pm
♉	4/29	6:18am
♊	5/1	1:47pm
♋	5/3	7:08pm
♌	5/5	10:54pm
♍	5/8	1:37am
♎	5/10	3:57am
♏	5/12	6:48am
♐	5/14	11:13am
♑	5/16	6:13pm
♒	5/19	4:12am
♓	5/21	4:20pm
♈	5/24	4:34am
♉	5/26	2:43pm
♊	5/28	9:47pm
♋	5/31	2:05am
♌	6/2	4:45am
♍	6/4	6:59am
♎	6/6	9:45am
♏	6/8	1:41pm
♐	6/10	7:09pm
♑	6/13	2:36am
♒	6/15	12:23pm
♓	6/18	12:15am
♈	6/20	12:46pm
♉	6/22	11:38pm
♊	6/25	7:07am
♋	6/27	11:00am
♌	6/29	12:31pm
♍	7/1	1:23pm
♎	7/3	3:16pm
♏	7/5	7:10pm
♐	7/8	1:20am
♑	7/10	9:35am
♒	7/12	7:43pm
♓	7/15	7:32am
♈	7/17	8:14pm
♉	7/20	7:58am
♊	7/22	4:34pm
♋	7/24	9:05pm
♌	7/26	10:16pm
♍	7/28	9:59pm
♎	7/30	10:20pm
♏	8/2	1:01am
♐	8/4	6:47am
♑	8/6	3:23pm
♒	8/9	2:01am

Moon Sign Changes 1900-2005

♓ 8/11 2:02pm	♉ 12/31 2:37am	♊ 5/19 12:14am	♌ 10/7 9:50am	♍ 2/23 2:06am	♏ 7/14 4:33am
♈ 8/14 2:46am	**1958**	♋ 5/21 9:23am	♍ 10/9 1:49pm	♎ 2/25 4:29am	♐ 7/16 6:42am
♉ 8/16 3:00pm	♊ 1/2 12:21pm	♌ 5/23 4:14pm	♎ 10/11 2:44pm	♏ 2/27 6:15am	♑ 7/18 7:42am
♊ 8/19 12:51am	♋ 1/4 6:22pm	♍ 5/25 9:00pm	♏ 10/13 2:11pm	♐ 3/1 8:33am	♒ 7/20 9:05am
♋ 8/21 6:48am	♌ 1/6 9:21pm	♎ 5/27 11:55pm	♐ 10/15 2:09pm	♑ 3/3 12:06pm	♓ 7/22 12:41pm
♌ 8/23 8:51am	♍ 1/8 10:59pm	♏ 5/30 1:33am	♑ 10/17 4:23pm	♒ 3/5 5:16pm	♈ 7/24 7:53pm
♍ 8/25 8:26am	♎ 1/11 12:52am	♐ 6/1 2:54am	♒ 10/19 10:04pm	♓ 3/8 12:25am	♉ 7/27 6:43am
♎ 8/27 7:41am	♏ 1/13 4:02am	♑ 6/3 5:23am	♓ 10/22 7:19am	♈ 3/10 9:54am	♊ 7/29 7:23pm
♏ 8/29 8:45am	♐ 1/15 8:49am	♒ 6/5 10:34am	♈ 10/24 7:10pm	♉ 3/12 9:37pm	♋ 8/1 7:24am
♐ 8/31 1:07pm	♑ 1/17 3:13pm	♓ 6/7 7:24pm	♉ 10/27 8:07am	♊ 3/15 10:31am	♌ 8/3 5:09pm
♑ 9/2 9:05pm	♒ 1/19 11:22pm	♈ 6/10 7:20am	♊ 10/29 8:49pm	♋ 3/17 10:28pm	♍ 8/6 12:29am
♒ 9/5 7:50am	♓ 1/22 9:42am	♉ 6/12 8:12pm	♋ 11/1 8:09am	♌ 3/20 7:22am	♎ 8/8 5:56am
♓ 9/7 8:04pm	♈ 1/24 10:03pm	♊ 6/15 7:31am	♌ 11/3 5:02pm	♍ 3/22 12:28pm	♏ 8/10 10:00am
♈ 9/10 8:45am	♉ 1/27 10:56am	♋ 6/17 4:04pm	♍ 11/5 10:45pm	♎ 3/24 2:27pm	♐ 8/12 12:58pm
♉ 9/12 8:57pm	♊ 1/29 9:47pm	♌ 6/19 10:04pm	♎ 11/8 1:16am	♏ 3/26 2:54pm	♑ 8/14 3:18pm
♊ 9/15 7:26am	♋ 2/1 4:41am	♍ 6/22 2:22am	♏ 11/10 1:30am	♐ 3/28 3:31pm	♒ 8/16 5:53pm
♋ 9/17 2:49pm	♌ 2/3 7:37am	♎ 6/24 5:42am	♐ 11/12 1:03am	♑ 3/30 5:49pm	♓ 8/18 9:59pm
♌ 9/19 6:31pm	♍ 2/5 8:11am	♏ 6/26 8:30am	♑ 11/14 1:54am	♒ 4/1 10:41pm	♈ 8/21 4:51am
♍ 9/21 7:11pm	♎ 2/7 8:23am	♐ 6/28 11:11am	♒ 11/16 5:53am	♓ 4/4 6:23am	♉ 8/23 2:58pm
♎ 9/23 6:33pm	♏ 2/9 10:03am	♑ 6/30 2:32pm	♓ 11/18 1:56pm	♈ 4/6 4:33pm	♊ 8/26 3:18am
♏ 9/25 6:40pm	♐ 2/11 2:11pm	♒ 7/2 7:44pm	♈ 11/21 1:28am	♉ 4/9 4:32am	♋ 8/28 3:33pm
♐ 9/27 9:27pm	♑ 2/13 8:55pm	♓ 7/5 3:57am	♉ 11/23 2:30pm	♊ 4/11 5:25pm	♌ 8/31 1:33am
♑ 9/30 3:59am	♒ 2/16 5:51am	♈ 7/7 3:18pm	♊ 11/26 3:00am	♋ 4/14 5:48am	♍ 9/2 8:31am
♒ 10/2 2:04pm	♓ 2/18 4:39pm	♉ 7/10 4:09am	♋ 11/28 1:51pm	♌ 4/16 3:55pm	♎ 9/4 12:56pm
♓ 10/5 2:17am	♈ 2/21 5:02am	♊ 7/12 3:46pm	♌ 11/30 10:41pm	♍ 4/18 10:27pm	♏ 9/6 3:53pm
♈ 10/7 2:57pm	♉ 2/23 6:05pm	♋ 7/15 12:15am	♍ 12/3 5:18am	♎ 4/21 1:19am	♐ 9/8 6:20pm
♉ 10/10 2:48am	♊ 2/26 5:52am	♌ 7/17 5:31am	♎ 12/5 9:31am	♏ 4/23 1:34am	♑ 9/10 9:04pm
♊ 10/12 1:01pm	♋ 2/28 2:17pm	♍ 7/19 8:42am	♏ 12/7 11:28am	♐ 4/25 12:59am	♒ 9/13 12:43am
♋ 10/14 8:54pm	♌ 3/2 6:27pm	♎ 7/21 11:12am	♐ 12/9 12:02pm	♑ 4/27 1:32am	♓ 9/15 5:54am
♌ 10/17 1:59am	♍ 3/4 7:15pm	♏ 7/23 1:57pm	♑ 12/11 12:46pm	♒ 4/29 4:55am	♈ 9/17 1:16pm
♍ 10/19 4:23am	♎ 3/6 6:35pm	♐ 7/25 5:25pm	♒ 12/13 3:38pm	♓ 5/1 11:58am	♉ 9/19 11:12pm
♎ 10/21 5:03am	♏ 3/8 6:34pm	♑ 7/27 9:53pm	♓ 12/15 10:12pm	♈ 5/3 10:19pm	♊ 9/22 11:16am
♏ 10/23 5:31am	♐ 3/10 8:56pm	♒ 7/30 3:52am	♈ 12/18 8:45am	♉ 5/6 10:39am	♋ 9/24 11:49pm
♐ 10/25 7:33am	♑ 3/13 2:36am	♓ 8/1 12:11pm	♉ 12/20 9:38pm	♊ 5/8 11:34pm	♌ 9/27 10:36am
♑ 10/27 12:41pm	♒ 3/15 11:28am	♈ 8/3 11:14pm	♊ 12/23 10:09am	♋ 5/11 11:57am	♍ 9/29 6:04pm
♒ 10/29 9:32pm	♓ 3/17 10:41pm	♉ 8/6 12:04pm	♋ 12/25 8:33pm	♌ 5/13 10:40pm	♎ 10/1 10:08pm
♓ 11/1 9:18am	♈ 3/20 11:17am	♊ 8/9 12:16am	♌ 12/28 4:33am	♍ 5/16 6:38am	♏ 10/3 11:54pm
♈ 11/3 10:00pm	♉ 3/23 12:16am	♋ 8/11 9:25am	♍ 12/30 10:41am	♎ 5/18 11:06am	♐ 10/6 12:54am
♉ 11/6 9:38am	♊ 3/25 12:20pm	♌ 8/13 2:43pm	**1959**	♏ 5/20 12:24pm	♑ 10/8 2:38am
♊ 11/8 7:09pm	♋ 3/27 9:53pm	♍ 8/15 5:07pm	♎ 1/1 3:21pm	♐ 5/22 11:51am	♒ 10/10 6:12am
♋ 11/11 2:24am	♌ 3/30 3:45am	♎ 8/17 6:17pm	♏ 1/3 6:42pm	♑ 5/24 11:24am	♓ 10/12 12:06pm
♌ 11/13 7:36am	♍ 4/1 6:01am	♏ 8/19 7:50pm	♐ 1/5 8:56pm	♒ 5/26 1:09pm	♈ 10/14 8:20pm
♍ 11/15 11:07am	♎ 4/3 5:54am	♐ 8/21 10:48pm	♑ 1/7 10:50pm	♓ 5/28 6:42pm	♉ 10/17 6:40am
♎ 11/17 1:25pm	♏ 4/5 5:16am	♑ 8/24 3:38am	♒ 1/10 1:52am	♈ 5/31 4:18am	♊ 10/19 6:40pm
♏ 11/19 3:17pm	♐ 4/7 6:07am	♒ 8/26 10:28am	♓ 1/12 7:39am	♉ 6/2 4:37pm	♋ 10/22 7:22am
♐ 11/21 5:52pm	♑ 4/9 10:01am	♓ 8/28 7:25pm	♈ 1/14 5:09pm	♊ 6/5 5:35am	♌ 10/24 7:03pm
♑ 11/23 10:29pm	♒ 4/11 5:41pm	♈ 8/31 6:35am	♉ 1/17 5:33am	♋ 6/7 5:44pm	♍ 10/27 3:48am
♒ 11/26 6:16am	♓ 4/14 4:38am	♉ 9/2 7:24pm	♊ 1/19 6:16pm	♌ 6/10 4:19am	♎ 10/29 8:41am
♓ 11/28 5:16pm	♈ 4/16 5:23pm	♊ 9/5 8:07am	♋ 1/22 4:47am	♍ 6/12 12:50pm	♏ 10/31 10:14am
♈ 12/1 5:56am	♉ 4/19 6:16am	♋ 9/7 6:22pm	♌ 1/24 12:13pm	♎ 6/14 6:42pm	♐ 11/2 10:02am
♉ 12/3 5:48pm	♊ 4/21 6:03pm	♌ 9/10 12:42am	♍ 1/26 5:13pm	♏ 6/16 9:38pm	♑ 11/4 10:05am
♊ 12/6 3:00am	♋ 4/24 3:46am	♍ 9/12 3:19am	♎ 1/28 8:54pm	♐ 6/18 10:14pm	♒ 11/6 12:14pm
♋ 12/8 9:16am	♌ 4/26 10:44am	♎ 9/14 3:44am	♏ 1/31 12:05am	♑ 6/20 10:01pm	♓ 11/8 5:35pm
♌ 12/10 1:23pm	♍ 4/28 2:40pm	♏ 9/16 3:49am	♐ 2/2 3:11am	♒ 6/22 11:00pm	♈ 11/11 2:10am
♍ 12/12 4:28pm	♎ 4/30 4:06pm	♐ 9/18 5:16am	♑ 2/4 6:29am	♓ 6/25 3:09am	♉ 11/13 1:04pm
♎ 12/14 7:23pm	♏ 5/2 4:14pm	♑ 9/20 9:13am	♒ 2/6 10:40am	♈ 6/27 11:28am	♊ 11/16 1:16am
♏ 12/16 10:35pm	♐ 5/4 4:43pm	♒ 9/22 4:03pm	♓ 2/8 4:50pm	♉ 6/29 11:11pm	♋ 11/18 1:57pm
♐ 12/19 2:30am	♑ 5/6 7:21pm	♓ 9/25 1:33am	♈ 2/11 1:55am	♊ 7/2 12:05pm	♌ 11/21 2:04am
♑ 12/21 7:47am	♒ 5/9 1:29am	♈ 9/27 1:07pm	♉ 2/13 1:47pm	♋ 7/5 12:03am	♍ 11/23 12:08pm
♒ 12/23 3:19pm	♓ 5/11 11:27am	♉ 9/30 1:58am	♊ 2/16 2:39am	♌ 7/7 10:08am	♎ 11/25 6:41pm
♓ 12/26 1:41am	♈ 5/13 11:58pm	♊ 10/2 2:50pm	♋ 2/18 1:50pm	♍ 7/9 6:15pm	♏ 11/27 9:21pm
♈ 12/28 2:13pm	♉ 5/16 12:50pm	♋ 10/5 2:00am	♌ 2/20 9:38pm	♎ 7/12 12:26am	♐ 11/29 9:12pm

Moon Sign Changes 1900-2005

♑	12/1	8:11pm
♒	12/3	8:35pm
♓	12/6	12:16am
♈	12/8	7:59am
♉	12/10	6:56pm
♊	12/13	7:24am
♋	12/15	8:00pm
♌	12/18	7:58am
♍	12/20	6:29pm
♎	12/23	2:29am
♏	12/25	7:01am
♐	12/27	8:15am
♑	12/29	7:38am
♒	12/31	7:15am
	1960	
♓	1/2	9:19am
♈	1/4	3:21pm
♉	1/7	1:22am
♊	1/9	1:45pm
♋	1/12	2:23am
♌	1/14	1:59pm
♍	1/17	12:03am
♎	1/19	8:14am
♏	1/21	1:59pm
♐	1/23	5:02pm
♑	1/25	5:59pm
♒	1/27	6:19pm
♓	1/29	7:56pm
♈	2/1	12:39am
♉	2/3	9:16am
♊	2/5	8:58pm
♋	2/8	9:37am
♌	2/10	9:08pm
♍	2/13	6:35am
♎	2/15	1:55pm
♏	2/17	7:24pm
♐	2/19	11:12pm
♑	2/22	1:39am
♒	2/24	3:32am
♓	2/26	6:04am
♈	2/28	10:38am
♉	3/1	6:18pm
♊	3/4	5:08am
♋	3/6	5:37pm
♌	3/9	5:25am
♍	3/11	2:47pm
♎	3/13	9:19pm
♏	3/16	1:37am
♐	3/18	4:37am
♑	3/20	7:14am
♒	3/22	10:10am
♓	3/24	2:02pm
♈	3/26	7:29pm
♉	3/29	3:13am
♊	3/31	1:32pm
♋	4/3	1:46am
♌	4/5	2:01pm
♍	4/8	12:02am
♎	4/10	6:35am
♏	4/12	10:01am
♐	4/14	11:37am
♑	4/16	1:01pm
♒	4/18	3:32pm
♓	4/20	7:55pm
♈	4/23	2:23am
♉	4/25	10:50am
♊	4/27	9:16pm
♋	4/30	9:22am
♌	5/2	9:59pm
♍	5/5	8:59am
♎	5/7	4:30pm
♏	5/9	8:07pm
♐	5/11	8:55pm
♑	5/13	8:50pm
♒	5/15	9:51pm
♓	5/18	1:23am
♈	5/20	7:55am
♉	5/22	5:00pm
♊	5/25	3:55am
♋	5/27	4:06pm
♌	5/30	4:50am
♍	6/1	4:38pm
♎	6/4	1:31am
♏	6/6	6:20am
♐	6/8	7:31am
♑	6/10	6:48am
♒	6/12	6:23am
♓	6/14	8:17am
♈	6/16	1:42pm
♉	6/18	10:33pm
♊	6/21	9:46am
♋	6/23	10:10pm
♌	6/26	10:51am
♍	6/28	10:53pm
♎	7/1	8:46am
♏	7/3	3:08pm
♐	7/5	5:42pm
♑	7/7	5:34pm
♒	7/9	4:43pm
♓	7/11	5:19pm
♈	7/13	9:07pm
♉	7/16	4:48am
♊	7/18	3:40pm
♋	7/21	4:09am
♌	7/23	4:46pm
♍	7/26	4:31am
♎	7/28	2:33pm
♏	7/30	9:55pm
♐	8/2	2:04am
♑	8/4	3:25am
♒	8/6	3:21am
♓	8/8	3:42am
♈	8/10	6:21am
♉	8/12	12:36pm
♊	8/14	10:29pm
♋	8/17	10:43am
♌	8/19	11:18pm
♍	8/22	10:41am
♎	8/24	8:09pm
♏	8/27	3:24am
♐	8/29	8:19am
♑	8/31	11:09am
♒	9/2	12:35pm
♓	9/4	1:51pm
♈	9/6	4:26pm
♉	9/8	9:44pm
♊	9/11	6:31am
♋	9/13	6:10pm
♌	9/16	6:46am
♍	9/18	6:07pm
♎	9/21	2:58am
♏	9/23	9:18am
♐	9/25	1:42pm
♑	9/27	4:54pm
♒	9/29	7:32pm
♓	10/1	10:14pm
♈	10/4	1:46am
♉	10/6	7:09am
♊	10/8	3:16pm
♋	10/11	2:18am
♌	10/13	2:55pm
♍	10/16	2:40am
♎	10/18	11:32am
♏	10/20	5:06pm
♐	10/22	8:16pm
♑	10/24	10:28pm
♒	10/27	12:57am
♓	10/29	4:26am
♈	10/31	9:11am
♉	11/2	3:27pm
♊	11/4	11:44pm
♋	11/7	10:26am
♌	11/9	10:59pm
♍	11/12	11:24am
♎	11/14	9:07pm
♏	11/17	2:53am
♐	11/19	5:17am
♑	11/21	6:02am
♒	11/23	7:04am
♓	11/25	9:49am
♈	11/27	2:51pm
♉	11/29	10:00pm
♊	12/2	7:01am
♋	12/4	5:52pm
♌	12/7	6:21am
♍	12/9	7:13pm
♎	12/12	6:10am
♏	12/14	1:13pm
♐	12/16	4:07pm
♑	12/18	4:16pm
♒	12/20	3:49pm
♓	12/22	4:47pm
♈	12/24	8:34pm
♉	12/27	3:30am
♊	12/29	1:01pm
	1961	
♋	1/1	12:22am
♌	1/3	12:54pm
♍	1/6	1:48am
♎	1/8	1:31pm
♏	1/10	10:09pm
♐	1/13	2:40am
♑	1/15	3:41am
♒	1/17	2:55am
♓	1/19	2:32am
♈	1/21	4:26am
♉	1/23	9:51am
♊	1/25	6:50pm
♋	1/28	6:22am
♌	1/30	7:05pm
♍	2/2	7:48am
♎	2/4	7:27pm
♏	2/7	4:51am
♐	2/9	11:01am
♑	2/11	1:50pm
♒	2/13	2:14pm
♓	2/15	1:53pm
♈	2/17	2:41pm
♉	2/19	6:21pm
♊	2/22	1:51am
♋	2/24	12:49pm
♌	2/27	1:34am
♍	3/1	2:12pm
♎	3/4	1:21am
♏	3/6	10:24am
♐	3/8	5:04pm
♑	3/10	9:19pm
♒	3/12	11:29pm
♓	3/15	12:26am
♈	3/17	1:32am
♉	3/19	4:25am
♊	3/21	10:32am
♋	3/23	8:22pm
♌	3/26	8:48am
♍	3/28	9:30pm
♎	3/31	8:21am
♏	4/2	4:36pm
♐	4/4	10:34pm
♑	4/7	2:52am
♒	4/9	6:03am
♓	4/11	8:31am
♈	4/13	10:55am
♉	4/15	2:16pm
♊	4/17	7:55pm
♋	4/20	4:50am
♌	4/22	4:43pm
♍	4/25	5:31am
♎	4/27	4:34pm
♏	4/30	12:27am
♐	5/2	5:25am
♑	5/4	8:40am
♒	5/6	11:24am
♓	5/8	2:23pm
♈	5/10	5:56pm
♉	5/12	10:25pm
♊	5/15	4:34am
♋	5/17	1:17pm
♌	5/20	12:45am
♍	5/22	1:38pm
♎	5/25	1:18am
♏	5/27	9:34am
♐	5/29	2:11pm
♑	5/31	4:20pm
♒	6/2	5:45pm
♓	6/4	7:50pm
♈	6/6	11:23pm
♉	6/9	4:38am
♊	6/11	11:40am
♋	6/13	8:50pm
♌	6/16	8:16am
♍	6/18	9:12pm
♎	6/21	9:32am
♏	6/23	6:51pm
♐	6/26	12:05am
♑	6/28	2:00am
♒	6/30	2:18am
♓	7/2	2:52am
♈	7/4	5:12am
♉	7/6	10:01am
♊	7/8	5:27pm
♋	7/11	3:13am
♌	7/13	2:56pm
♍	7/16	3:55am
♎	7/18	4:39pm
♏	7/21	3:04am
♐	7/23	9:42am
♑	7/25	12:28pm
♒	7/27	12:41pm
♓	7/29	12:13pm
♈	7/31	12:56pm
♉	8/2	4:19pm
♊	8/4	11:04pm
♋	8/7	8:56am
♌	8/9	8:59pm
♍	8/12	10:00am
♎	8/14	10:44pm
♏	8/17	9:44am
♐	8/19	5:44pm
♑	8/21	10:07pm
♒	8/23	11:25pm
♓	8/25	11:02pm
♈	8/27	10:49pm
♉	8/30	12:37am
♊	9/1	5:53am
♋	9/3	3:00pm
♌	9/6	3:01am
♍	9/8	4:05pm
♎	9/11	4:33am
♏	9/13	3:23pm
♐	9/15	11:54pm
♑	9/18	5:42am
♒	9/20	8:43am
♓	9/22	9:36am
♈	9/24	9:40am
♉	9/26	10:42am
♊	9/28	2:31pm
♋	9/30	10:19pm
♌	10/3	9:43am
♍	10/5	10:45pm
♎	10/8	11:04am
♏	10/10	9:19pm
♐	10/13	5:21am
♑	10/15	11:24am
♒	10/17	3:37pm
♓	10/19	6:10pm
♈	10/21	7:36pm
♉	10/23	9:07pm
♊	10/26	12:24am
♋	10/28	7:03am
♌	10/30	5:30pm
♍	11/2	6:17am
♎	11/4	6:42pm
♏	11/7	4:40am
♐	11/9	11:51am
♑	11/11	4:59pm
♒	11/13	8:59pm
♓	11/16	12:18am
♈	11/18	3:10am
♉	11/20	6:03am
♊	11/22	9:59am
♋	11/24	4:20pm
♌	11/27	2:01am
♍	11/29	2:25pm
♎	12/2	3:08am
♏	12/4	1:30pm
♐	12/6	8:25pm
♑	12/9	12:31am
♒	12/11	3:11am
♓	12/13	5:41am
♈	12/15	8:44am
♉	12/17	12:39pm
♊	12/19	5:47pm
♋	12/22	12:50am
♌	12/24	10:26am
♍	12/26	10:29pm
♎	12/29	11:26am
♏	12/31	10:42pm
	1962	
♐	1/3	6:23am
♑	1/5	10:24am
♒	1/7	12:00pm
♓	1/9	12:53pm
♈	1/11	2:34pm
♉	1/13	6:01pm
♊	1/15	11:42pm
♋	1/18	7:39am
♌	1/20	5:50pm
♍	1/23	5:53am
♎	1/25	6:52pm
♏	1/28	6:54am
♐	1/30	3:59pm
♑	2/1	9:09pm
♒	2/3	10:57pm
♓	2/5	10:53pm
♈	2/7	10:50pm
♉	2/10	12:35am
♊	2/12	5:18am
♋	2/14	1:20pm
♌	2/17	12:04am
♍	2/19	12:27pm
♎	2/22	1:22am
♏	2/24	1:36pm
♐	2/26	11:46pm
♑	3/1	6:38am
♒	3/3	9:52am
♓	3/5	10:16am
♈	3/7	9:32am
♉	3/9	9:40am
♊	3/11	12:35pm
♋	3/13	7:25pm
♌	3/16	5:56am
♍	3/18	6:33pm

Moon Sign Changes 1900-2005

Sign	Date	Time
♎	3/21	7:28am
♏	3/23	7:29pm
♐	3/26	5:49am
♑	3/28	1:46pm
♒	3/30	6:43pm
♓	4/1	8:42pm
♈	4/3	8:41pm
♉	4/5	8:25pm
♊	4/7	10:00pm
♋	4/10	3:12am
♌	4/12	12:36pm
♍	4/15	12:57am
♎	4/17	1:54pm
♏	4/20	1:37am
♐	4/22	11:27am
♑	4/24	7:20pm
♒	4/27	1:08am
♓	4/29	4:40am
♈	5/1	6:12am
♉	5/3	6:49am
♊	5/5	8:16am
♋	5/7	12:28pm
♌	5/9	8:35pm
♍	5/12	8:11am
♎	5/14	9:03pm
♏	5/17	8:43am
♐	5/19	6:02pm
♑	5/22	1:08am
♒	5/24	6:31am
♓	5/26	10:29am
♈	5/28	1:15pm
♉	5/30	3:17pm
♊	6/1	5:40pm
♋	6/3	9:56pm
♌	6/6	5:23am
♍	6/8	4:12pm
♎	6/11	4:51am
♏	6/13	4:45pm
♐	6/16	2:03am
♑	6/18	8:30am
♒	6/20	12:49pm
♓	6/22	3:59pm
♈	6/24	6:43pm
♉	6/26	9:34pm
♊	6/29	1:09am
♋	7/1	6:19am
♌	7/3	1:55pm
♍	7/6	12:22am
♎	7/8	12:48pm
♏	7/11	1:05am
♐	7/13	11:00am
♑	7/15	5:32pm
♒	7/17	9:07pm
♓	7/19	11:00pm
♈	7/22	12:34am
♉	7/24	2:57am
♊	7/26	6:57am
♋	7/28	1:00pm
♌	7/30	9:21pm
♍	8/2	7:57am
♎	8/4	8:17pm
♏	8/7	8:56am
♐	8/9	7:48pm
♑	8/12	3:18am
♒	8/14	7:07am
♓	8/16	8:17am
♈	8/18	8:25am
♉	8/20	9:20am
♊	8/22	12:28pm
♋	8/24	6:34pm
♌	8/27	3:30am
♍	8/29	2:36pm
♎	9/1	3:01am
♏	9/3	3:46pm
♐	9/6	3:26am
♑	9/8	12:20pm
♒	9/10	5:26pm
♓	9/12	7:02pm
♈	9/14	6:33pm
♉	9/16	6:01pm
♊	9/18	7:29pm
♋	9/21	12:26am
♌	9/23	9:07am
♍	9/25	8:31pm
♎	9/28	9:08am
♏	9/30	9:49pm
♐	10/3	9:40am
♑	10/5	7:35pm
♒	10/8	2:22am
♓	10/10	5:29am
♈	10/12	5:40am
♉	10/14	4:43am
♊	10/16	4:50am
♋	10/18	8:05am
♌	10/20	3:30pm
♍	10/23	2:31am
♎	10/25	3:13pm
♏	10/28	3:49am
♐	10/30	3:19pm
♑	11/2	1:17am
♒	11/4	9:02am
♓	11/6	1:52pm
♈	11/8	3:45pm
♉	11/10	3:45pm
♊	11/12	3:43pm
♋	11/14	5:49pm
♌	11/16	11:40pm
♍	11/19	9:33am
♎	11/21	9:58pm
♏	11/24	10:33am
♐	11/26	9:43pm
♑	11/29	7:00am
♒	12/1	2:26pm
♓	12/3	7:53pm
♈	12/5	11:17pm
♉	12/8	12:59am
♊	12/10	2:07am
♋	12/12	4:21am
♌	12/14	9:20am
♍	12/16	5:59pm
♎	12/19	5:41am
♏	12/21	6:18pm
♐	12/24	5:33am
♑	12/26	2:19pm
♒	12/28	8:42pm
♓	12/31	1:20am
	1963	
♈	1/2	4:48am
♉	1/4	7:33am
♊	1/6	10:14am
♋	1/8	1:41pm
♌	1/10	7:01pm
♍	1/13	3:07am
♎	1/15	2:05pm
♏	1/18	2:35am
♐	1/20	2:20pm
♑	1/22	11:23pm
♒	1/25	5:14am
♓	1/27	8:35am
♈	1/29	10:44am
♉	1/31	12:55pm
♊	2/2	4:03pm
♋	2/4	8:40pm
♌	2/7	3:06am
♍	2/9	11:36am
♎	2/11	10:18pm
♏	2/14	10:38am
♐	2/16	10:57pm
♑	2/19	9:00am
♒	2/21	3:23pm
♓	2/23	6:17pm
♈	2/25	7:05pm
♉	2/27	7:38pm
♊	3/1	9:39pm
♋	3/4	2:08am
♌	3/6	9:15am
♍	3/8	6:34pm
♎	3/11	5:35am
♏	3/13	5:51pm
♐	3/16	6:27am
♑	3/18	5:35pm
♒	3/21	1:21am
♓	3/23	5:04am
♈	3/25	5:38am
♉	3/27	4:57am
♊	3/29	5:13am
♋	3/31	8:14am
♌	4/2	2:45pm
♍	4/5	12:20am
♎	4/7	11:49am
♏	4/10	12:14am
♐	4/12	12:48pm
♑	4/15	12:27am
♒	4/17	9:34am
♓	4/19	2:53pm
♈	4/21	4:30pm
♉	4/23	3:51pm
♊	4/25	3:06pm
♋	4/27	4:27pm
♌	4/29	9:25pm
♍	5/2	6:13am
♎	5/4	5:42pm
♏	5/7	6:16am
♐	5/9	6:42pm
♑	5/12	6:13am
♒	5/14	3:51pm
♓	5/16	10:32pm
♈	5/19	1:48am
♉	5/21	2:21am
♊	5/23	1:53am
♋	5/25	2:29am
♌	5/27	5:59am
♍	5/29	1:22pm
♎	6/1	12:09am
♏	6/3	12:38pm
♐	6/6	1:01am
♑	6/8	12:07pm
♒	6/10	9:22pm
♓	6/13	4:21am
♈	6/15	8:46am
♉	6/17	10:54am
♊	6/19	11:44am
♋	6/21	12:46pm
♌	6/23	3:44pm
♍	6/25	9:56pm
♎	6/28	7:41am
♏	6/30	7:48pm
♐	7/3	8:11am
♑	7/5	7:03pm
♒	7/8	3:36am
♓	7/10	9:53am
♈	7/12	2:16pm
♉	7/14	5:15pm
♊	7/16	7:27pm
♋	7/18	9:45pm
♌	7/21	1:15am
♍	7/23	7:06am
♎	7/25	4:02pm
♏	7/28	3:38am
♐	7/30	4:08pm
♑	8/2	3:12am
♒	8/4	11:25am
♓	8/6	4:46pm
♈	8/8	8:07pm
♉	8/10	10:37pm
♊	8/13	1:16am
♋	8/15	4:39am
♌	8/17	9:17am
♍	8/19	3:40pm
♎	8/22	12:25am
♏	8/24	11:39am
♐	8/27	12:15am
♑	8/29	11:57am
♒	8/31	8:37pm
♓	9/3	1:37am
♈	9/5	3:52am
♉	9/7	5:02am
♊	9/9	6:46am
♋	9/11	10:08am
♌	9/13	3:30pm
♍	9/15	10:47pm
♎	9/18	8:00am
♏	9/20	7:10pm
♐	9/23	7:50am
♑	9/25	8:15pm
♒	9/28	6:03am
♓	9/30	11:46am
♈	10/2	1:48pm
♉	10/4	1:50pm
♊	10/6	1:58pm
♋	10/8	4:01pm
♌	10/10	8:54pm
♍	10/13	4:34am
♎	10/15	2:24pm
♏	10/18	1:53am
♐	10/20	2:32pm
♑	10/23	3:21am
♒	10/25	2:20pm
♓	10/27	9:36pm
♈	10/30	12:40am
♉	11/1	12:42am
♊	11/2	11:48pm
♋	11/5	12:08am
♌	11/7	3:24am
♍	11/9	10:14am
♎	11/11	8:07pm
♏	11/14	7:57am
♐	11/16	8:40pm
♑	11/19	9:23am
♒	11/21	8:51pm
♓	11/24	5:32am
♈	11/26	10:25am
♉	11/28	11:49am
♊	11/30	11:14am
♋	12/2	10:45am
♌	12/4	12:20pm
♍	12/6	5:26pm
♎	12/9	2:21am
♏	12/11	2:04pm
♐	12/14	2:53am
♑	12/16	3:21pm
♒	12/19	2:29am
♓	12/21	11:28am
♈	12/23	5:41pm
♉	12/25	8:57pm
♊	12/27	9:58pm
♋	12/29	10:07pm
♌	12/31	11:09pm
	1964	
♍	1/3	2:48am
♎	1/5	10:10am
♏	1/7	9:04pm
♐	1/10	9:49am
♑	1/12	10:14pm
♒	1/15	8:48am
♓	1/17	5:04pm
♈	1/19	11:10pm
♉	1/22	3:23am
♊	1/24	6:05am
♋	1/26	7:51am
♌	1/28	9:45am
♍	1/30	1:09pm
♎	2/1	7:25pm
♏	2/4	5:12am
♐	2/6	5:35pm
♑	2/9	6:11am
♒	2/11	4:39pm
♓	2/14	12:09am
♈	2/16	5:10am
♉	2/18	8:45am
♊	2/20	11:48am
♋	2/22	2:49pm
♌	2/24	6:11pm
♍	2/26	10:30pm
♎	2/29	4:46am
♏	3/2	1:54pm
♐	3/5	1:47am
♑	3/7	2:35pm
♒	3/10	1:35am
♓	3/12	9:05am
♈	3/14	1:15pm
♉	3/16	3:30pm
♊	3/18	5:26pm
♋	3/20	8:11pm
♌	3/23	12:15am
♍	3/25	5:42am
♎	3/27	12:48pm
♏	3/29	10:03pm
♐	4/1	9:41am
♑	4/3	10:36pm
♒	4/6	10:24am
♓	4/8	6:47pm
♈	4/10	11:08pm
♉	4/13	12:37am
♊	4/15	1:06am
♋	4/17	2:23am
♌	4/19	5:40am
♍	4/21	11:17am
♎	4/23	7:08pm
♏	4/26	5:01am
♐	4/28	4:46pm
♑	5/1	5:42am
♒	5/3	6:06pm
♓	5/6	3:43am
♈	5/8	9:15am
♉	5/10	11:09am
♊	5/12	11:01am
♋	5/14	10:53am
♌	5/16	12:31pm
♍	5/18	5:02pm
♎	5/21	12:41am
♏	5/23	10:58am
♐	5/25	11:03pm
♑	5/28	12:00pm
♒	5/31	12:32am
♓	6/2	11:01am
♈	6/4	6:03pm
♉	6/6	9:20pm
♊	6/8	9:50pm
♋	6/10	9:16pm
♌	6/12	9:35pm
♍	6/15	12:27am
♎	6/17	6:54am
♏	6/19	4:49pm
♐	6/22	5:03am
♑	6/24	6:02pm
♒	6/27	6:22am
♓	6/29	4:56pm
♈	7/2	12:52am
♉	7/4	5:42am
♊	7/6	7:43am
♋	7/8	7:57am

Moon Sign Changes 1900-2005

♌	7/10	8:01am
♍	7/12	9:44am
♎	7/14	2:41pm
♏	7/16	11:32pm
♐	7/19	11:28am
♑	7/22	12:27am
♒	7/24	12:30pm
♓	7/26	10:36pm
♈	7/29	6:25am
♉	7/31	12:00pm
♊	8/2	3:28pm
♋	8/4	5:13pm
♌	8/6	6:11pm
♍	8/8	7:50pm
♎	8/10	11:51pm
♏	8/13	7:31am
♐	8/15	6:44pm
♑	8/18	7:38am
♒	8/20	7:39pm
♓	8/23	5:13am
♈	8/25	12:15pm
♉	8/27	5:24pm
♊	8/29	9:16pm
♋	9/1	12:13am
♌	9/3	2:36am
♍	9/5	5:12am
♎	9/7	9:19am
♏	9/9	4:20pm
♐	9/12	2:47am
♑	9/14	3:30pm
♒	9/17	3:47am
♓	9/19	1:22pm
♈	9/21	7:44pm
♉	9/23	11:46pm
♊	9/26	2:46am
♋	9/28	5:39am
♌	9/30	8:52am
♍	10/2	12:42pm
♎	10/4	5:44pm
♏	10/7	12:57am
♐	10/9	11:02am
♑	10/11	11:32pm
♒	10/14	12:15pm
♓	10/16	10:33pm
♈	10/19	5:05am
♉	10/21	8:24am
♊	10/23	10:03am
♋	10/25	11:37am
♌	10/27	2:14pm
♍	10/29	6:25pm
♎	11/1	12:24am
♏	11/3	8:25am
♐	11/5	6:43pm
♑	11/8	7:06am
♒	11/10	8:08pm
♓	11/13	7:28am
♈	11/15	3:10pm
♉	11/17	6:57pm
♊	11/19	7:58pm
♋	11/21	8:04pm
♌	11/23	8:59pm
♍	11/26	12:02am
♎	11/28	5:54am
♏	11/30	2:31pm
♐	12/3	1:24am
♑	12/5	1:53pm
♒	12/8	2:57am
♓	12/10	3:00pm
♈	12/13	12:12am
♉	12/15	5:33am
♊	12/17	7:21am
♋	12/19	7:02am
♌	12/21	6:31am
♍	12/23	7:42am
♎	12/25	12:04pm
♏	12/27	8:11pm
♐	12/30	7:20am
1965		
♑	1/1	8:06pm
♒	1/4	9:04am
♓	1/6	9:06pm
♈	1/9	7:08am
♉	1/11	2:10pm
♊	1/13	5:48pm
♋	1/15	6:35pm
♌	1/17	5:57pm
♍	1/19	5:55pm
♎	1/21	8:28pm
♏	1/24	3:01am
♐	1/26	1:32pm
♑	1/29	2:21am
♒	1/31	3:17pm
♓	2/3	2:56am
♈	2/5	12:43pm
♉	2/7	8:24pm
♊	2/10	1:36am
♋	2/12	4:14am
♌	2/14	4:54am
♍	2/16	5:05am
♎	2/18	6:45am
♏	2/20	11:45am
♐	2/22	8:57pm
♑	2/25	9:17am
♒	2/27	10:14pm
♓	3/2	9:38am
♈	3/4	6:45pm
♉	3/7	1:49am
♊	3/9	7:14am
♋	3/11	11:03am
♌	3/13	1:23pm
♍	3/15	2:55pm
♎	3/17	5:04pm
♏	3/19	9:32pm
♐	3/22	5:37am
♑	3/24	5:07pm
♒	3/27	5:59am
♓	3/29	5:32pm
♈	4/1	2:19am
♉	4/3	8:29am
♊	4/5	12:55pm
♋	4/7	4:24pm
♌	4/9	7:23pm
♍	4/11	10:14pm
♎	4/14	1:38am
♏	4/16	6:42am
♐	4/18	2:31pm
♑	4/21	1:24am
♒	4/23	2:04pm
♓	4/26	2:02am
♈	4/28	11:12am
♉	4/30	5:03pm
♊	5/2	8:26pm
♋	5/4	10:39pm
♌	5/7	12:50am
♍	5/9	3:47am
♎	5/11	8:04am
♏	5/13	2:10pm
♐	5/15	10:32pm
♑	5/18	9:20am
♒	5/20	9:50pm
♓	5/23	10:14am
♈	5/25	8:19pm
♉	5/28	2:48am
♊	5/30	5:58am
♋	6/1	7:05am
♌	6/3	7:47am
♍	6/5	9:33am
♎	6/7	1:29pm
♏	6/9	8:04pm
♐	6/12	5:10am
♑	6/14	4:20pm
♒	6/17	4:51am
♓	6/19	5:29pm
♈	6/22	4:29am
♉	6/24	12:16pm
♊	6/26	4:18pm
♋	6/28	5:20pm
♌	6/30	4:59pm
♍	7/2	5:11pm
♎	7/4	7:43pm
♏	7/7	1:38am
♐	7/9	10:53am
♑	7/11	10:29pm
♒	7/14	11:08am
♓	7/16	11:45pm
♈	7/19	11:13am
♉	7/21	8:14pm
♊	7/24	1:48am
♋	7/26	3:53am
♌	7/28	3:37am
♍	7/30	2:55am
♎	8/1	3:54am
♏	8/3	8:20am
♐	8/5	4:49pm
♑	8/8	4:22am
♒	8/10	5:09pm
♓	8/13	5:37am
♈	8/15	4:57pm
♉	8/18	2:27am
♊	8/20	9:20am
♋	8/22	1:04pm
♌	8/24	2:01pm
♍	8/26	1:36pm
♎	8/28	1:52pm
♏	8/30	4:54pm
♐	9/1	11:59pm
♑	9/4	10:51am
♒	9/6	11:34pm
♓	9/9	11:56am
♈	9/11	10:50pm
♉	9/14	7:56am
♊	9/16	3:06pm
♋	9/18	8:01pm
♌	9/20	10:35pm
♍	9/22	11:30pm
♎	9/25	12:15am
♏	9/27	2:47am
♐	9/29	8:42am
♑	10/1	6:29pm
♒	10/4	6:48am
♓	10/6	7:14pm
♈	10/9	5:54am
♉	10/11	2:16pm
♊	10/13	8:40pm
♋	10/16	1:27am
♌	10/18	4:51am
♍	10/20	7:13am
♎	10/22	9:21am
♏	10/24	12:31pm
♐	10/26	6:09pm
♑	10/29	3:05am
♒	10/31	2:49pm
♓	11/3	3:23am
♈	11/5	2:21pm
♉	11/7	10:29pm
♊	11/10	3:54am
♋	11/12	7:29am
♌	11/14	10:13am
♍	11/16	12:55pm
♎	11/18	4:10pm
♏	11/20	8:37pm
♐	11/23	2:57am
♑	11/25	11:45am
♒	11/27	11:03pm
♓	11/30	11:40am
♈	12/2	11:22pm
♉	12/5	8:11am
♊	12/7	1:27pm
♋	12/9	3:57pm
♌	12/11	5:08pm
♍	12/13	6:35pm
♎	12/15	9:33pm
♏	12/18	2:40am
♐	12/20	10:01am
♑	12/22	7:27pm
♒	12/25	6:44am
♓	12/27	7:17pm
♈	12/30	7:40am
1966		
♉	1/1	5:46pm
♊	1/4	12:06am
♋	1/6	2:40am
♌	1/8	2:50am
♍	1/10	2:34am
♎	1/12	3:53am
♏	1/14	8:08am
♐	1/16	3:39pm
♑	1/19	1:45am
♒	1/21	1:26pm
♓	1/24	1:58am
♈	1/26	2:33pm
♉	1/29	1:43am
♊	1/31	9:43am
♋	2/2	1:41pm
♌	2/4	2:14pm
♍	2/6	1:11pm
♎	2/8	12:50pm
♏	2/10	3:15pm
♐	2/12	9:33pm
♑	2/15	7:26am
♒	2/17	7:25pm
♓	2/20	8:05am
♈	2/22	8:30pm
♉	2/25	7:53am
♊	2/27	5:03pm
♋	3/1	10:48pm
♌	3/4	12:57am
♍	3/6	12:36am
♎	3/7	11:48pm
♏	3/10	12:47am
♐	3/12	5:18am
♑	3/14	1:55pm
♒	3/17	1:35am
♓	3/19	2:19pm
♈	3/22	2:33am
♉	3/24	1:32pm
♊	3/26	10:41pm
♋	3/29	5:23am
♌	3/31	9:12am
♍	4/2	10:31am
♎	4/4	10:40am
♏	4/6	11:30am
♐	4/8	2:54pm
♑	4/10	10:02pm
♒	4/13	8:42am
♓	4/15	9:13pm
♈	4/18	9:27am
♉	4/20	8:00pm
♊	4/23	4:27am
♋	4/25	10:48am
♌	4/27	3:09pm
♍	4/29	5:50pm
♎	5/1	7:31pm
♏	5/3	9:23pm
♐	5/6	12:52am
♑	5/8	7:12am
♒	5/10	4:52pm
♓	5/13	4:55am
♈	5/15	5:15pm
♉	5/18	3:49am
♊	5/20	11:40am
♋	5/22	5:00pm
♌	5/24	8:37pm
♍	5/26	11:22pm
♎	5/29	2:00am
♏	5/31	5:11am
♐	6/2	9:38am
♑	6/4	4:10pm
♒	6/7	1:21am
♓	6/9	12:57pm
♈	6/12	1:26am
♉	6/14	12:29pm
♊	6/16	8:26pm
♋	6/19	1:05am
♌	6/21	3:29am
♍	6/23	5:08am
♎	6/25	7:23am
♏	6/27	11:04am
♐	6/29	4:31pm
♑	7/1	11:51pm
♒	7/4	9:14am
♓	7/6	8:39pm
♈	7/9	9:16am
♉	7/11	9:03pm
♊	7/14	5:51am
♋	7/16	10:44am
♌	7/18	12:27pm
♍	7/20	12:47pm
♎	7/22	1:38pm
♏	7/24	4:32pm
♐	7/26	10:04pm
♑	7/29	6:04am
♒	7/31	4:02pm
♓	8/3	3:36am
♈	8/5	4:15pm
♉	8/8	4:38am
♊	8/10	2:38pm
♋	8/12	8:41pm
♌	8/14	10:50pm
♍	8/16	10:35pm
♎	8/18	10:05pm
♏	8/20	11:24pm
♐	8/23	3:51am
♑	8/25	11:37am
♒	8/27	9:56pm
♓	8/30	9:48am
♈	9/1	10:27pm
♉	9/4	10:59am
♊	9/6	9:52pm
♋	9/9	5:26am
♌	9/11	9:01am
♍	9/13	9:25am
♎	9/15	8:33am
♏	9/17	8:34am
♐	9/19	11:21am
♑	9/21	5:52pm
♒	9/24	3:48am
♓	9/26	3:48pm
♈	9/29	4:29am
♉	10/1	4:47pm
♊	10/4	3:43am
♋	10/6	12:12pm
♌	10/8	5:25pm
♍	10/10	7:27pm
♎	10/12	7:29pm
♏	10/14	7:21pm
♐	10/16	8:59pm
♑	10/19	1:55am
♒	10/21	10:41am
♓	10/23	10:20pm
♈	10/26	11:03am
♉	10/28	11:05pm

Moon Sign Changes 1900-2005

♊ 10/31 9:28am	♋ 3/19 12:10pm	♍ 8/7 7:36am	♏ 12/26 10:36am	♐ 5/13 1:53am	♒ 9/30 10:11pm
♋ 11/2 5:43pm	♌ 3/21 6:04pm	♎ 8/9 9:34am	♐ 12/28 12:09pm	♑ 5/15 1:31am	♓ 10/3 3:21am
♌ 11/4 11:36pm	♍ 3/23 8:08pm	♏ 8/11 11:44am	♑ 12/30 1:11pm	♒ 5/17 3:22am	♈ 10/5 10:35am
♍ 11/7 3:10am	♎ 3/25 7:50pm	♐ 8/13 2:52pm	**1968**	♓ 5/19 8:53am	♉ 10/7 8:07pm
♎ 11/9 4:54am	♏ 3/27 7:10pm	♑ 8/15 7:18pm	♒ 1/1 3:24pm	♈ 5/21 6:14pm	♊ 10/10 7:43am
♏ 11/11 5:53am	♐ 3/29 8:08pm	♒ 8/18 1:17am	♓ 1/3 8:35pm	♉ 5/24 6:15am	♋ 10/12 8:23pm
♐ 11/13 7:36am	♑ 4/1 12:11am	♓ 8/20 9:18am	♈ 1/6 5:45am	♊ 5/26 7:12pm	♌ 10/15 8:08am
♑ 11/15 11:37am	♒ 4/3 7:49am	♈ 8/22 7:47pm	♉ 1/8 6:02pm	♋ 5/29 7:43am	♍ 10/17 4:58pm
♒ 11/17 7:03pm	♓ 4/5 6:29pm	♉ 8/25 8:21am	♊ 1/11 6:54am	♌ 5/31 6:53pm	♎ 10/19 10:05pm
♓ 11/20 5:53am	♈ 4/8 6:57am	♊ 8/27 9:08pm	♋ 1/13 5:54pm	♍ 6/3 3:52am	♏ 10/22 12:05am
♈ 11/22 6:31pm	♉ 4/10 7:56pm	♋ 8/30 7:34am	♌ 1/16 2:09am	♎ 6/5 9:49am	♐ 10/24 12:32am
♉ 11/25 6:37am	♊ 4/13 8:15am	♌ 9/1 2:08pm	♍ 1/18 8:11am	♏ 6/7 12:30pm	♑ 10/26 1:13am
♊ 11/27 4:31pm	♋ 4/15 6:37pm	♍ 9/3 5:07pm	♎ 1/20 12:47pm	♐ 6/9 12:42pm	♒ 10/28 3:43am
♋ 11/29 11:50pm	♌ 4/18 1:54am	♎ 9/5 6:03pm	♏ 1/22 4:28pm	♑ 6/11 12:05pm	♓ 10/30 8:54am
♌ 12/2 5:02am	♍ 4/20 5:42am	♏ 9/7 6:44pm	♐ 1/24 7:23pm	♒ 6/13 12:46pm	♈ 11/1 4:51pm
♍ 12/4 8:48am	♎ 4/22 6:41am	♐ 9/9 8:40pm	♑ 1/26 9:57pm	♓ 6/15 4:42pm	♉ 11/4 3:01am
♎ 12/6 11:43am	♏ 4/24 6:19am	♑ 9/12 12:43am	♒ 1/29 1:06am	♈ 6/18 12:50am	♊ 11/6 2:48pm
♏ 12/8 2:18pm	♐ 4/26 6:27am	♒ 9/14 7:08am	♓ 1/31 6:16am	♉ 6/20 12:25pm	♋ 11/9 3:26am
♐ 12/10 5:13pm	♑ 4/28 8:54am	♓ 9/16 3:53pm	♈ 2/2 2:39pm	♊ 6/23 1:22am	♌ 11/11 3:45pm
♑ 12/12 9:30pm	♒ 4/30 2:57pm	♈ 9/19 2:46am	♉ 2/5 2:15am	♋ 6/25 1:43pm	♍ 11/14 1:55am
♒ 12/15 4:19am	♓ 5/3 12:47am	♉ 9/21 3:20pm	♊ 2/7 3:09pm	♌ 6/28 12:30am	♎ 11/16 8:26am
♓ 12/17 2:17pm	♈ 5/5 1:10pm	♊ 9/24 4:21am	♋ 2/10 2:34am	♍ 6/30 9:26am	♏ 11/18 11:06am
♈ 12/20 2:39am	♉ 5/8 2:09am	♋ 9/26 3:45pm	♌ 2/12 10:50am	♎ 7/2 4:10pm	♐ 11/20 11:04am
♉ 12/22 3:07pm	♊ 5/10 2:08pm	♌ 9/28 11:41pm	♍ 2/14 4:02pm	♏ 7/4 8:20pm	♑ 11/22 10:20am
♊ 12/25 1:14am	♋ 5/13 12:11am	♍ 10/1 3:38am	♎ 2/16 7:21pm	♐ 7/6 10:05pm	♒ 11/24 11:02am
♋ 12/27 7:58am	♌ 5/15 7:49am	♎ 10/3 4:34am	♏ 2/18 10:00pm	♑ 7/8 10:24pm	♓ 11/26 2:52pm
♌ 12/29 11:57am	♍ 5/17 12:52pm	♏ 10/5 4:14am	♐ 2/21 12:48am	♒ 7/10 11:03pm	♈ 11/28 10:26pm
♍ 12/31 2:33pm	♎ 5/19 3:31pm	♐ 10/7 4:32am	♑ 2/23 4:12am	♓ 7/13 2:03am	♉ 12/1 8:58am
1967	♏ 5/21 4:30pm	♑ 10/9 7:04am	♒ 2/25 8:37am	♈ 7/15 8:51am	♊ 12/3 9:06pm
♎ 1/2 5:04pm	♐ 5/23 5:06pm	♒ 10/11 12:45pm	♓ 2/27 2:42pm	♉ 7/17 7:30pm	♋ 12/6 9:43am
♏ 1/4 8:16pm	♑ 5/25 6:58pm	♓ 10/13 9:38pm	♈ 2/29 11:14pm	♊ 7/20 8:13am	♌ 12/8 10:02pm
♐ 1/7 12:28am	♒ 5/27 11:44pm	♈ 10/16 8:58am	♉ 3/3 10:28am	♋ 7/22 8:31pm	♍ 12/11 8:59am
♑ 1/9 5:53am	♓ 5/30 8:18am	♉ 10/18 9:41pm	♊ 3/5 11:17pm	♌ 7/25 6:55am	♎ 12/13 5:08pm
♒ 1/11 1:05pm	♈ 6/1 8:07pm	♊ 10/21 10:38am	♋ 3/8 11:21am	♍ 7/27 3:10pm	♏ 12/15 9:31pm
♓ 1/13 10:45pm	♉ 6/4 9:04am	♋ 10/23 10:27pm	♌ 3/10 8:27pm	♎ 7/29 9:32pm	♐ 12/17 10:27pm
♈ 1/16 10:48am	♊ 6/6 8:52pm	♌ 10/26 7:40am	♍ 3/13 1:51am	♏ 8/1 2:11am	♑ 12/19 9:32pm
♉ 1/18 11:39pm	♋ 6/9 6:18am	♍ 10/28 1:19pm	♎ 3/15 4:23am	♐ 8/3 5:11am	♒ 12/21 8:59pm
♊ 1/21 10:38am	♌ 6/11 1:19pm	♎ 10/30 3:31pm	♏ 3/17 5:33am	♑ 8/5 6:57am	♓ 12/23 11:01pm
♋ 1/23 5:51pm	♍ 6/13 6:24pm	♏ 11/1 3:26pm	♐ 3/19 6:54am	♒ 8/7 8:37am	♈ 12/26 5:02am
♌ 1/25 9:20pm	♎ 6/15 9:58pm	♐ 11/3 2:51pm	♑ 3/21 9:34am	♓ 8/9 11:46am	♉ 12/28 2:57pm
♍ 1/27 10:36pm	♏ 6/18 12:25am	♑ 11/5 3:44pm	♒ 3/23 2:16pm	♈ 8/11 5:53pm	♊ 12/31 3:11am
♎ 1/29 11:33pm	♐ 6/20 2:20am	♒ 11/7 7:45pm	♓ 3/25 9:15pm	♉ 8/14 3:36am	**1969**
♏ 2/1 1:44am	♑ 6/22 4:46am	♓ 11/10 3:42am	♈ 3/28 6:32am	♊ 8/16 3:51pm	♋ 1/2 3:53pm
♐ 2/3 5:55am	♒ 6/24 9:11am	♈ 11/12 2:58pm	♉ 3/30 5:55pm	♋ 8/19 4:15am	♌ 1/5 3:55am
♑ 2/5 12:10pm	♓ 6/26 4:49pm	♉ 11/15 3:52am	♊ 4/2 6:40am	♌ 8/21 2:40pm	♍ 1/7 2:42pm
♒ 2/7 8:17pm	♈ 6/29 3:53am	♊ 11/17 4:40pm	♋ 4/4 7:13pm	♍ 8/23 10:21pm	♎ 1/9 11:32pm
♓ 2/10 6:19am	♉ 7/1 4:43pm	♋ 11/20 4:13am	♌ 4/7 5:28am	♎ 8/26 3:45am	♏ 1/12 5:32am
♈ 2/12 6:17pm	♊ 7/4 4:39am	♌ 11/22 1:47pm	♍ 4/9 12:04pm	♏ 8/28 7:38am	♐ 1/14 8:19am
♉ 2/15 7:19am	♋ 7/6 1:47pm	♍ 11/24 8:46pm	♎ 4/11 3:01pm	♐ 8/30 10:40am	♑ 1/16 8:39am
♊ 2/17 7:16pm	♌ 7/8 7:58pm	♎ 11/27 12:48am	♏ 4/13 3:32pm	♑ 9/1 1:22pm	♒ 1/18 8:17am
♋ 2/20 3:48am	♍ 7/11 12:07am	♏ 11/29 2:13am	♐ 4/15 3:23pm	♒ 9/3 4:19pm	♓ 1/20 9:21am
♌ 2/22 8:04am	♎ 7/13 3:20am	♐ 12/1 2:10am	♑ 4/17 4:23pm	♓ 9/5 8:27pm	♈ 1/22 1:43pm
♍ 2/24 9:04am	♏ 7/15 6:17am	♑ 12/3 2:25am	♒ 4/19 7:57pm	♈ 9/8 2:49am	♉ 1/24 10:13pm
♎ 2/26 8:44am	♐ 7/17 9:22am	♒ 12/5 4:57am	♓ 4/22 2:46am	♉ 9/10 12:06pm	♊ 1/27 9:53am
♏ 2/28 9:09am	♑ 7/19 12:59pm	♓ 12/7 11:19am	♈ 4/24 12:32pm	♊ 9/12 11:54pm	♋ 1/29 10:36pm
♐ 3/2 11:53am	♒ 7/21 5:59pm	♈ 12/9 9:43pm	♉ 4/27 12:22am	♋ 9/15 12:28pm	♌ 2/1 10:29am
♑ 3/4 5:35pm	♓ 7/24 1:28am	♉ 12/12 10:32am	♊ 4/29 1:11pm	♌ 9/17 11:25pm	♍ 2/3 8:40pm
♒ 3/7 2:03am	♈ 7/26 12:00pm	♊ 12/14 11:18pm	♋ 5/2 1:50am	♍ 9/20 7:15am	♎ 2/6 5:00am
♓ 3/9 12:41pm	♉ 7/29 12:40am	♋ 12/17 10:23am	♌ 5/4 12:54pm	♎ 9/22 12:00pm	♏ 2/8 11:18am
♈ 3/12 12:53am	♊ 7/31 1:00pm	♌ 12/19 7:21pm	♍ 5/6 8:58pm	♏ 9/24 2:39pm	♐ 2/10 3:23pm
♉ 3/14 1:54pm	♋ 8/2 10:32pm	♍ 12/22 2:21am	♎ 5/9 1:21am	♐ 9/26 4:30pm	♑ 2/12 5:28pm
♊ 3/17 2:19am	♌ 8/5 4:26am	♎ 12/24 7:27am	♏ 5/11 2:30am	♑ 9/28 6:44pm	♒ 2/14 6:30pm

Moon Sign Changes 1900-2005

Sign	Date	Time
♓	2/16	8:03pm
♈	2/18	11:48pm
♉	2/21	7:02am
♊	2/23	5:41pm
♋	2/26	6:11am
♌	2/28	6:12pm
♍	3/3	4:07am
♎	3/5	11:34am
♏	3/7	4:56pm
♐	3/9	8:48pm
♑	3/11	11:40pm
♒	3/14	2:09am
♓	3/16	5:04am
♈	3/18	9:27am
♉	3/20	4:20pm
♊	3/23	2:12am
♋	3/25	2:18pm
♌	3/28	2:37am
♍	3/30	12:54pm
♎	4/1	8:03pm
♏	4/4	12:22am
♐	4/6	2:57am
♑	4/8	5:04am
♒	4/10	7:46am
♓	4/12	11:41am
♈	4/14	5:13pm
♉	4/17	12:43am
♊	4/19	10:28am
♋	4/21	10:17pm
♌	4/24	10:51am
♍	4/26	9:57pm
♎	4/29	5:43am
♏	5/1	9:49am
♐	5/3	11:19am
♑	5/5	11:57am
♒	5/7	1:28pm
♓	5/9	5:04pm
♈	5/11	11:09pm
♉	5/14	7:28am
♊	5/16	5:41pm
♋	5/19	5:30am
♌	5/21	6:12pm
♍	5/24	6:07am
♎	5/26	3:07pm
♏	5/28	8:05pm
♐	5/30	9:30pm
♑	6/1	9:07pm
♒	6/3	9:03pm
♓	6/5	11:13pm
♈	6/8	4:36am
♉	6/10	1:06pm
♊	6/12	11:48pm
♋	6/15	11:52am
♌	6/18	12:35am
♍	6/20	12:53pm
♎	6/22	11:03pm
♏	6/25	5:31am
♐	6/27	8:00am
♑	6/29	7:44am
♒	7/1	6:49am
♓	7/3	7:26am
♈	7/5	11:16am
♉	7/7	6:53pm
♊	7/10	5:31am
♋	7/12	5:47pm
♌	7/15	6:29am
♍	7/17	6:42pm
♎	7/20	5:20am
♏	7/22	1:04pm
♐	7/24	5:10pm
♑	7/26	6:09pm
♒	7/28	5:34pm
♓	7/30	5:30pm
♈	8/1	7:55pm
♉	8/4	2:02am
♊	8/6	11:49am
♋	8/8	11:57pm
♌	8/11	12:38pm
♍	8/14	12:32am
♎	8/16	10:51am
♏	8/18	6:54pm
♐	8/21	12:12am
♑	8/23	2:49am
♒	8/25	3:36am
♓	8/27	4:03am
♈	8/29	5:57am
♉	8/31	10:50am
♊	9/2	7:23pm
♋	9/5	6:57am
♌	9/7	7:36pm
♍	9/10	7:20am
♎	9/12	5:01pm
♏	9/15	12:25am
♐	9/17	5:42am
♑	9/19	9:14am
♒	9/21	11:31am
♓	9/23	1:22pm
♈	9/25	3:55pm
♉	9/27	8:29pm
♊	9/30	4:05am
♋	10/2	2:52pm
♌	10/5	3:25am
♍	10/7	3:21pm
♎	10/10	12:48am
♏	10/12	7:19am
♐	10/14	11:33am
♑	10/16	2:35pm
♒	10/18	5:21pm
♓	10/20	8:26pm
♈	10/23	12:17am
♉	10/25	5:32am
♊	10/27	1:00pm
♋	10/29	11:13pm
♌	11/1	11:35am
♍	11/4	12:00am
♎	11/6	9:59am
♏	11/8	4:18pm
♐	11/10	7:30pm
♑	11/12	9:08pm
♒	11/14	10:53pm
♓	11/17	1:52am
♈	11/19	6:32am
♉	11/21	12:52pm
♊	11/23	8:59pm
♋	11/26	7:10am
♌	11/28	7:22pm
♍	12/1	8:14am
♎	12/3	7:17pm
♏	12/6	2:30am
♐	12/8	5:43am
♑	12/10	6:20am
♒	12/12	6:27am
♓	12/14	7:56am
♈	12/16	11:56am
♉	12/18	6:35pm
♊	12/21	3:28am
♋	12/23	2:09pm
♌	12/26	2:21am
♍	12/28	3:20pm
♎	12/31	3:18am
1970		
♏	1/2	12:03pm
♐	1/4	4:33pm
♑	1/6	5:30pm
♒	1/8	4:47pm
♓	1/10	4:37pm
♈	1/12	6:48pm
♉	1/15	12:20am
♊	1/17	9:07am
♋	1/19	8:13pm
♌	1/22	8:40am
♍	1/24	9:33pm
♎	1/27	9:42am
♏	1/29	7:34pm
♐	2/1	1:50am
♑	2/3	4:21am
♒	2/5	4:19am
♓	2/7	3:37am
♈	2/9	4:17am
♉	2/11	7:59am
♊	2/13	3:29pm
♋	2/16	2:17am
♌	2/18	2:53pm
♍	2/21	3:42am
♎	2/23	3:30pm
♏	2/26	1:23am
♐	2/28	8:38am
♑	3/2	12:54pm
♒	3/4	2:34pm
♓	3/6	2:49pm
♈	3/8	3:16pm
♉	3/10	5:43pm
♊	3/12	11:37pm
♋	3/15	9:18am
♌	3/17	9:40pm
♍	3/20	10:30am
♎	3/22	9:56pm
♏	3/25	7:10am
♐	3/27	2:07pm
♑	3/29	7:00pm
♒	3/31	10:08pm
♓	4/3	12:01am
♈	4/5	1:32am
♉	4/7	4:02am
♊	4/9	9:02am
♋	4/11	5:33pm
♌	4/14	5:16am
♍	4/16	6:07pm
♎	4/19	5:35am
♏	4/21	2:15pm
♐	4/23	8:15pm
♑	4/26	12:26am
♒	4/28	3:43am
♓	4/30	6:37am
♈	5/2	9:32am
♉	5/4	1:05pm
♊	5/6	6:17pm
♋	5/9	2:17am
♌	5/11	1:22pm
♍	5/14	2:10am
♎	5/16	2:02pm
♏	5/18	10:49pm
♐	5/21	4:11am
♑	5/23	7:13am
♒	5/25	9:25am
♓	5/27	11:59am
♈	5/29	3:27pm
♉	5/31	8:03pm
♊	6/3	2:10am
♋	6/5	10:25am
♌	6/7	9:17pm
♍	6/10	10:02am
♎	6/12	10:28pm
♏	6/15	8:01am
♐	6/17	1:39pm
♑	6/19	4:04pm
♒	6/21	5:00pm
♓	6/23	6:11pm
♈	6/25	8:52pm
♉	6/28	1:35am
♊	6/30	8:24am
♋	7/2	5:21pm
♌	7/5	4:26am
♍	7/7	5:11pm
♎	7/10	6:02am
♏	7/12	4:41pm
♐	7/14	11:26pm
♑	7/17	2:19am
♒	7/19	2:44am
♓	7/21	2:36am
♈	7/23	3:42am
♉	7/25	7:18am
♊	7/27	1:53pm
♋	7/29	11:14pm
♌	8/1	10:44am
♍	8/3	11:34pm
♎	8/6	12:33pm
♏	8/8	11:57pm
♐	8/11	8:07am
♑	8/13	12:25pm
♒	8/15	1:31pm
♓	8/17	1:01pm
♈	8/19	12:50pm
♉	8/21	2:46pm
♊	8/23	8:03pm
♋	8/26	4:58am
♌	8/28	4:38pm
♍	8/31	5:36am
♎	9/2	6:25pm
♏	9/5	5:54am
♐	9/7	2:58pm
♑	9/9	8:51pm
♒	9/11	11:34pm
♓	9/13	11:57pm
♈	9/15	11:35pm
♉	9/18	12:21am
♊	9/20	4:02am
♋	9/22	11:41am
♌	9/24	10:54pm
♍	9/27	11:53am
♎	9/30	12:33am
♏	10/2	11:35am
♐	10/4	8:31pm
♑	10/7	3:10am
♒	10/9	7:26am
♓	10/11	9:30am
♈	10/13	10:12am
♉	10/15	11:00am
♊	10/17	1:43pm
♋	10/19	7:59pm
♌	10/22	6:12am
♍	10/24	6:57pm
♎	10/27	7:37am
♏	10/29	6:15pm
♐	11/1	2:24am
♑	11/3	8:32am
♒	11/5	1:11pm
♓	11/7	4:33pm
♈	11/9	6:52pm
♉	11/11	8:50pm
♊	11/13	11:48pm
♋	11/16	5:23am
♌	11/18	2:36pm
♍	11/21	2:50am
♎	11/23	3:39pm
♏	11/26	2:25am
♐	11/28	10:02am
♑	11/30	3:05pm
♒	12/2	6:45pm
♓	12/4	9:55pm
♈	12/7	1:03am
♉	12/9	4:24am
♊	12/11	8:33am
♋	12/13	2:32pm
♌	12/15	11:21pm
♍	12/18	11:04am
♎	12/21	12:01am
♏	12/23	11:27am
♐	12/25	7:27pm
♑	12/28	12:01am
♒	12/30	2:24am
1971		
♓	1/1	4:08am
♈	1/3	6:26am
♉	1/5	10:00am
♊	1/7	3:08pm
♋	1/9	10:09pm
♌	1/12	7:24am
♍	1/14	6:57pm
♎	1/17	7:53am
♏	1/19	8:04pm
♐	1/22	5:15am
♑	1/24	10:32am
♒	1/26	12:36pm
♓	1/28	1:02pm
♈	1/30	1:36pm
♉	2/1	3:49pm
♊	2/3	8:34pm
♋	2/6	4:07am
♌	2/8	2:06pm
♍	2/11	1:58am
♎	2/13	2:50pm
♏	2/16	3:22am
♐	2/18	1:45pm
♑	2/20	8:37pm
♒	2/22	11:43pm
♓	2/25	12:05am
♈	2/26	11:30pm
♉	2/28	11:54pm
♊	3/3	3:01am
♋	3/5	9:47am
♌	3/7	7:55pm
♍	3/10	8:10am
♎	3/12	9:06pm
♏	3/15	9:31am
♐	3/17	8:23pm
♑	3/20	4:37am
♒	3/22	9:28am
♓	3/24	11:07am
♈	3/26	10:45am
♉	3/28	10:16am
♊	3/30	11:44am
♋	4/1	4:51pm
♌	4/4	2:05am
♍	4/6	2:16pm
♎	4/9	3:17am
♏	4/11	3:28pm
♐	4/14	2:03am
♑	4/16	10:38am
♒	4/18	4:46pm
♓	4/20	8:07pm
♈	4/22	9:08pm
♉	4/24	9:06pm
♊	4/26	9:58pm
♋	4/29	1:43am
♌	5/1	9:34am
♍	5/3	9:03pm
♎	5/6	9:59am
♏	5/8	10:03pm
♐	5/11	8:08am
♑	5/13	4:09pm
♒	5/15	10:19pm
♓	5/18	2:39am
♈	5/20	5:11am
♉	5/22	6:31am
♊	5/24	8:01am
♋	5/26	11:26am
♌	5/28	6:16pm
♍	5/31	4:48am
♎	6/2	5:26pm
♏	6/5	5:36am
♐	6/7	3:28pm

Moon Sign Changes 1900-2005

♑	6/9	10:45pm
♒	6/12	4:03am
♓	6/14	8:01am
♈	6/16	11:06am
♉	6/18	1:39pm
♊	6/20	4:24pm
♋	6/22	8:30pm
♌	6/25	3:12am
♍	6/27	1:06pm
♎	6/30	1:22am
♏	7/2	1:46pm
♐	7/4	11:59pm
♑	7/7	7:03am
♒	7/9	11:26am
♓	7/11	2:14pm
♈	7/13	4:32pm
♉	7/15	7:10pm
♊	7/17	10:47pm
♋	7/20	3:56am
♌	7/22	11:16am
♍	7/24	9:09pm
♎	7/27	9:12am
♏	7/29	9:50pm
♐	8/1	8:49am
♑	8/3	4:32pm
♒	8/5	8:46pm
♓	8/7	10:34pm
♈	8/9	11:27pm
♉	8/12	12:55am
♊	8/14	4:11am
♋	8/16	9:50am
♌	8/18	5:57pm
♍	8/21	4:19am
♎	8/23	4:22pm
♏	8/26	5:09am
♐	8/28	4:56pm
♑	8/31	1:54am
♒	9/2	7:04am
♓	9/4	8:51am
♈	9/6	8:43am
♉	9/8	8:37am
♊	9/10	10:25am
♋	9/12	3:21pm
♌	9/14	11:38pm
♍	9/17	10:29am
♎	9/19	10:47pm
♏	9/22	11:33am
♐	9/24	11:43pm
♑	9/27	9:52am
♒	9/29	4:39pm
♓	10/1	7:36pm
♈	10/3	7:40pm
♉	10/5	6:42pm
♊	10/7	6:53pm
♋	10/9	10:10pm
♌	10/12	5:30am
♍	10/14	4:16pm
♎	10/17	4:47am
♏	10/19	5:31pm
♐	10/22	5:31am
♑	10/24	4:05pm
♒	10/27	12:11am
♓	10/29	4:57am
♈	10/31	6:26am
♉	11/2	5:55am
♊	11/4	5:27am
♋	11/6	7:15am
♌	11/8	12:56pm
♍	11/10	10:44pm
♎	11/13	11:05am
♏	11/15	11:49pm
♐	11/18	11:30am
♑	11/20	9:36pm
♒	11/23	5:52am
♓	11/25	11:48am
♈	11/27	3:03pm
♉	11/29	4:08pm
♊	12/1	4:25pm
♋	12/3	5:51pm
♌	12/5	10:17pm
♍	12/8	6:40am
♎	12/10	6:19pm
♏	12/13	7:01am
♐	12/15	6:37pm
♑	12/18	4:07am
♒	12/20	11:32am
♓	12/22	5:10pm
♈	12/24	9:09pm
♉	12/26	11:45pm
♊	12/29	1:38am
♋	12/31	4:01am
1972		
♌	1/2	8:22am
♍	1/4	3:50pm
♎	1/7	2:33am
♏	1/9	3:03pm
♐	1/12	2:57am
♑	1/14	12:26pm
♒	1/16	7:04pm
♓	1/18	11:28pm
♈	1/21	2:35am
♉	1/23	5:17am
♊	1/25	8:14am
♋	1/27	12:01pm
♌	1/29	5:21pm
♍	2/1	12:56am
♎	2/3	11:07am
♏	2/5	11:18pm
♐	2/8	11:38am
♑	2/10	9:50pm
♒	2/13	4:36am
♓	2/15	8:11am
♈	2/17	9:51am
♉	2/19	11:11am
♊	2/21	1:35pm
♋	2/23	5:52pm
♌	2/26	12:15am
♍	2/28	8:39am
♎	3/1	7:00pm
♏	3/4	7:00am
♐	3/6	7:36pm
♑	3/9	6:49am
♒	3/11	2:42pm
♓	3/13	6:39pm
♈	3/15	7:37pm
♉	3/17	7:27pm
♊	3/19	8:12pm
♋	3/21	11:26pm
♌	3/24	5:46am
♍	3/26	2:48pm
♎	3/29	1:42am
♏	3/31	1:48pm
♐	4/3	2:27am
♑	4/5	2:20pm
♒	4/7	11:37pm
♓	4/10	4:58am
♈	4/12	6:32am
♉	4/14	5:54am
♊	4/16	5:16am
♋	4/18	6:46am
♌	4/20	11:47am
♍	4/22	8:24pm
♎	4/25	7:34am
♏	4/27	7:56pm
♐	4/30	8:31am
♑	5/2	8:29pm
♒	5/5	6:35am
♓	5/7	1:28pm
♈	5/9	4:35pm
♉	5/11	4:47pm
♊	5/13	3:57pm
♋	5/15	4:16pm
♌	5/17	7:38pm
♍	5/20	2:56am
♎	5/22	1:36pm
♏	5/25	2:01am
♐	5/27	2:33pm
♑	5/30	2:13am
♒	6/1	12:15pm
♓	6/3	7:52pm
♈	6/6	12:27am
♉	6/8	2:15am
♊	6/10	2:24am
♋	6/12	2:45am
♌	6/14	5:10am
♍	6/16	11:03am
♎	6/18	8:39pm
♏	6/21	8:43am
♐	6/23	9:14pm
♑	6/26	8:36am
♒	6/28	6:02pm
♓	7/1	1:18am
♈	7/3	6:22am
♉	7/5	9:25am
♊	7/7	11:05am
♋	7/9	12:29pm
♌	7/11	3:05pm
♍	7/13	8:16pm
♎	7/16	4:49am
♏	7/18	4:15pm
♐	7/21	4:46am
♑	7/23	4:10pm
♒	7/26	1:07am
♓	7/28	7:29am
♈	7/30	11:50am
♉	8/1	2:57pm
♊	8/3	5:33pm
♋	8/5	8:18pm
♌	8/7	11:56pm
♍	8/10	5:23am
♎	8/12	1:27pm
♏	8/15	12:19am
♐	8/17	12:49pm
♑	8/20	12:38am
♒	8/22	9:43am
♓	8/24	3:28pm
♈	8/26	6:40pm
♉	8/28	8:43pm
♊	8/30	10:56pm
♋	9/2	2:11am
♌	9/4	6:54am
♍	9/6	1:15pm
♎	9/8	9:36pm
♏	9/11	8:15am
♐	9/13	8:42pm
♑	9/16	9:07am
♒	9/18	7:04pm
♓	9/21	1:09am
♈	9/23	3:44am
♉	9/25	4:27am
♊	9/27	5:14am
♋	9/29	7:39am
♌	10/1	12:25pm
♍	10/3	7:31pm
♎	10/6	4:35am
♏	10/8	3:27pm
♐	10/11	3:52am
♑	10/13	4:44pm
♒	10/16	3:51am
♓	10/18	11:12am
♈	10/20	2:22pm
♉	10/22	2:37pm
♊	10/24	2:02pm
♋	10/26	2:44pm
♌	10/28	6:14pm
♍	10/31	12:59am
♎	11/2	10:27am
♏	11/4	9:46pm
♐	11/7	10:16am
♑	11/9	11:11pm
♒	11/12	11:02am
♓	11/14	7:56pm
♈	11/17	12:44am
♉	11/19	1:53am
♊	11/21	1:05am
♋	11/23	12:31am
♌	11/25	2:12am
♍	11/27	7:24am
♎	11/29	4:15pm
♏	12/2	3:42am
♐	12/4	4:22pm
♑	12/7	5:06am
♒	12/9	4:53pm
♓	12/12	2:33am
♈	12/14	8:59am
♉	12/16	11:59am
♊	12/18	12:24pm
♋	12/20	11:57am
♌	12/22	12:34pm
♍	12/24	4:03pm
♎	12/26	11:21pm
♏	12/29	10:10am
♐	12/31	10:51pm
1973		
♑	1/3	11:30am
♒	1/5	10:47pm
♓	1/8	8:03am
♈	1/10	2:57pm
♉	1/12	7:24pm
♊	1/14	9:41pm
♋	1/16	10:39pm
♌	1/18	11:40pm
♍	1/21	2:24am
♎	1/23	8:16am
♏	1/25	5:52pm
♐	1/28	6:10am
♑	1/30	6:54pm
♒	2/2	5:55am
♓	2/4	2:22pm
♈	2/6	8:29pm
♉	2/9	12:53am
♊	2/11	4:10am
♋	2/13	6:44am
♌	2/15	9:12am
♍	2/17	12:31pm
♎	2/19	5:58pm
♏	2/22	2:35am
♐	2/24	2:14pm
♑	2/27	3:04am
♒	3/1	2:22pm
♓	3/3	10:31pm
♈	3/6	3:37am
♉	3/8	6:51am
♊	3/10	9:31am
♋	3/12	12:29pm
♌	3/14	4:07pm
♍	3/16	8:42pm
♎	3/19	2:48am
♏	3/21	11:15am
♐	3/23	10:26pm
♑	3/26	11:16am
♒	3/28	11:12pm
♓	3/31	7:55am
♈	4/2	12:48pm
♉	4/4	2:58pm
♊	4/6	4:12pm
♋	4/8	6:04pm
♌	4/10	9:31pm
♍	4/13	2:47am
♎	4/15	9:50am
♏	4/17	6:51pm
♐	4/20	6:02am
♑	4/22	6:49pm
♒	4/25	7:21am
♓	4/27	5:09pm
♈	4/29	10:53pm
♉	5/2	1:01am
♊	5/4	1:16am
♋	5/6	1:35am
♌	5/8	3:36am
♍	5/10	8:13am
♎	5/12	3:31pm
♏	5/15	1:09am
♐	5/17	12:41pm
♑	5/20	1:30am
♒	5/22	2:17pm
♓	5/25	1:05am
♈	5/27	8:14am
♉	5/29	11:28am
♊	5/31	11:53am
♋	6/2	11:21am
♌	6/4	11:49am
♍	6/6	2:51pm
♎	6/8	9:16pm
♏	6/11	6:52am
♐	6/13	6:43pm
♑	6/16	7:37am
♒	6/18	8:19pm
♓	6/21	7:29am
♈	6/23	3:48pm
♉	6/25	8:37pm
♊	6/27	10:18pm
♋	6/29	10:08pm
♌	7/1	9:55pm
♍	7/3	11:31pm
♎	7/6	4:23am
♏	7/8	1:05pm
♐	7/11	12:48am
♑	7/13	1:45pm
♒	7/16	2:15am
♓	7/18	1:07pm
♈	7/20	9:43pm
♉	7/23	3:41am
♊	7/25	6:58am
♋	7/27	8:10am
♌	7/29	8:29am
♍	7/31	9:35am
♎	8/2	1:12pm
♏	8/4	8:35pm
♐	8/7	7:37am
♑	8/9	8:30pm
♒	8/12	8:52am
♓	8/14	7:14pm
♈	8/17	3:16am
♉	8/19	9:14am
♊	8/21	1:26pm
♋	8/23	4:08pm
♌	8/25	5:49pm
♍	8/27	7:33pm
♎	8/29	10:52pm
♏	9/1	5:17am
♐	9/3	3:24pm
♑	9/6	4:01am
♒	9/8	4:30pm
♓	9/11	2:40am
♈	9/13	9:56am
♉	9/15	2:59pm
♊	9/17	6:48pm
♋	9/19	10:01pm
♌	9/22	12:56am
♍	9/24	3:58am
♎	9/26	8:00am

Moon Sign Changes 1900-2005

♏ 9/28 2:18pm
♐ 9/30 11:47pm
♑ 10/3 12:02pm
♒ 10/6 12:49am
♓ 10/8 11:23am
♈ 10/10 6:29pm
♉ 10/12 10:36pm
♊ 10/15 1:09am
♋ 10/17 3:28am
♌ 10/19 6:25am
♍ 10/21 10:19am
♎ 10/23 3:28pm
♏ 10/25 10:28pm
♐ 10/28 7:58am
♑ 10/30 7:57pm
♒ 11/2 8:58am
♓ 11/4 8:26pm
♈ 11/7 4:19am
♉ 11/9 8:25am
♊ 11/11 9:59am
♋ 11/13 10:46am
♌ 11/15 12:20pm
♍ 11/17 3:41pm
♎ 11/19 9:15pm
♏ 11/22 5:06am
♐ 11/24 3:11pm
♑ 11/27 3:13am
♒ 11/29 4:17pm
♓ 12/2 4:32am
♈ 12/4 1:50pm
♉ 12/6 7:08pm
♊ 12/8 8:58pm
♋ 12/10 8:52pm
♌ 12/12 8:44pm
♍ 12/14 10:20pm
♎ 12/17 2:53am
♏ 12/19 10:44am
♐ 12/21 9:20pm
♑ 12/24 9:41am
♒ 12/26 10:43pm
♓ 12/29 11:10am
♈ 12/31 9:34pm

1974

♉ 1/3 4:38am
♊ 1/5 8:00am
♋ 1/7 8:28am
♌ 1/9 7:42am
♍ 1/11 7:41am
♎ 1/13 10:21am
♏ 1/15 4:54pm
♐ 1/18 3:12am
♑ 1/20 3:47pm
♒ 1/23 4:50am
♓ 1/25 5:00pm
♈ 1/28 3:32am
♉ 1/30 11:41am
♊ 2/1 4:53pm
♋ 2/3 7:05pm
♌ 2/5 7:11pm
♍ 2/7 6:52pm
♎ 2/9 8:10pm
♏ 2/12 12:58am
♐ 2/14 10:01am
♑ 2/16 10:16pm
♒ 2/19 11:21am
♓ 2/21 11:15pm
♈ 2/24 9:12am
♉ 2/26 5:11pm
♊ 2/28 11:10pm
♋ 3/3 2:59am
♌ 3/5 4:49am
♍ 3/7 5:33am
♎ 3/9 6:52am
♏ 3/11 10:40am
♐ 3/13 6:20pm
♑ 3/16 5:41am
♒ 3/18 6:38pm
♓ 3/21 6:33am
♈ 3/23 4:02pm
♉ 3/25 11:09pm
♊ 3/28 4:33am
♋ 3/30 8:40am
♌ 4/1 11:40am
♍ 4/3 1:56pm
♎ 4/5 4:22pm
♏ 4/7 8:25pm
♐ 4/10 3:27am
♑ 4/12 1:56pm
♒ 4/15 2:34am
♓ 4/17 2:44pm
♈ 4/20 12:20am
♉ 4/22 6:53am
♊ 4/24 11:11am
♋ 4/26 2:17pm
♌ 4/28 5:03pm
♍ 4/30 8:00pm
♎ 5/2 11:39pm
♏ 5/5 4:43am
♐ 5/7 12:05pm
♑ 5/9 10:15pm
♒ 5/12 10:34am
♓ 5/14 11:03pm
♈ 5/17 9:20am
♉ 5/19 4:10pm
♊ 5/21 7:54pm
♋ 5/23 9:46pm
♌ 5/25 11:12pm
♍ 5/28 1:25am
♎ 5/30 5:16am
♏ 6/1 11:10am
♐ 6/3 7:21pm
♑ 6/6 5:48am
♒ 6/8 6:02pm
♓ 6/11 6:43am
♈ 6/13 5:52pm
♉ 6/16 1:46am
♊ 6/18 5:59am
♋ 6/20 7:21am
♌ 6/22 7:30am
♍ 6/24 8:11am
♎ 6/26 10:57am
♏ 6/28 4:40pm
♐ 7/1 1:20am
♑ 7/3 12:19pm
♒ 7/6 12:41am
♓ 7/8 1:25pm
♈ 7/11 1:10am
♉ 7/13 10:21am
♊ 7/15 3:54pm
♋ 7/17 5:56pm
♌ 7/19 5:43pm
♍ 7/21 5:10pm
♎ 7/23 6:19pm
♏ 7/25 10:45pm
♐ 7/28 7:00am
♑ 7/30 6:11pm
♒ 8/2 6:46am
♓ 8/4 7:26pm
♈ 8/7 7:15am
♉ 8/9 5:13pm
♊ 8/12 12:15am
♋ 8/14 3:49am
♌ 8/16 4:26am
♍ 8/18 3:43am
♎ 8/20 3:45am
♏ 8/22 6:37am
♐ 8/24 1:34pm
♑ 8/27 12:15am
♒ 8/29 12:52pm
♓ 9/1 1:29am
♈ 9/3 12:58pm
♉ 9/5 10:50pm
♊ 9/8 6:36am
♋ 9/10 11:39am
♌ 9/12 1:54pm
♍ 9/14 2:12pm
♎ 9/16 2:17pm
♏ 9/18 4:14pm
♐ 9/20 9:46pm
♑ 9/23 7:22am
♒ 9/25 7:38pm
♓ 9/28 8:14am
♈ 9/30 7:25pm
♉ 10/3 4:39am
♊ 10/5 12:00pm
♋ 10/7 5:30pm
♌ 10/9 9:03pm
♍ 10/11 10:56pm
♎ 10/14 12:11am
♏ 10/16 2:23am
♐ 10/18 7:14am
♑ 10/20 3:44pm
♒ 10/23 3:20am
♓ 10/25 3:57pm
♈ 10/28 3:13am
♉ 10/30 12:00pm
♊ 11/1 6:23pm
♋ 11/3 11:01pm
♌ 11/6 2:30am
♍ 11/8 5:18am
♎ 11/10 7:58am
♏ 11/12 11:23am
♐ 11/14 4:39pm
♑ 11/17 12:42am
♒ 11/19 11:39am
♓ 11/22 12:11am
♈ 11/24 11:59am
♉ 11/26 9:05pm
♊ 11/29 2:58am
♋ 12/1 6:22am
♌ 12/3 8:31am
♍ 12/5 10:40am
♎ 12/7 1:42pm
♏ 12/9 6:13pm
♐ 12/12 12:34am
♑ 12/14 9:04am
♒ 12/16 7:48pm
♓ 12/19 8:12am
♈ 12/21 8:35pm
♉ 12/24 6:45am
♊ 12/26 1:15pm
♋ 12/28 4:15pm
♌ 12/30 5:05pm

1975

♍ 1/1 5:32pm
♎ 1/3 7:21pm
♏ 1/5 11:39pm
♐ 1/8 6:39am
♑ 1/10 3:58pm
♒ 1/13 3:03am
♓ 1/15 3:23pm
♈ 1/18 4:03am
♉ 1/20 3:21pm
♊ 1/22 11:23pm
♋ 1/25 3:20am
♌ 1/27 4:00am
♍ 1/29 3:14am
♎ 1/31 3:13am
♏ 2/2 5:53am
♐ 2/4 12:10pm
♑ 2/6 9:42pm
♒ 2/9 9:16am
♓ 2/11 9:45pm
♈ 2/14 10:22am
♉ 2/16 10:09pm
♊ 2/19 7:35am
♋ 2/21 1:18pm
♌ 2/23 3:13pm
♍ 2/25 2:37pm
♎ 2/27 1:38pm
♏ 3/1 2:33pm
♐ 3/3 7:05pm
♑ 3/6 3:39am
♒ 3/8 3:09pm
♓ 3/11 3:49am
♈ 3/13 4:18pm
♉ 3/16 3:52am
♊ 3/18 1:43pm
♋ 3/20 8:48pm
♌ 3/23 12:31am
♍ 3/25 1:21am
♎ 3/27 12:51am
♏ 3/29 1:08am
♐ 3/31 4:10am
♑ 4/2 11:08am
♒ 4/4 9:45pm
♓ 4/7 10:17am
♈ 4/9 10:44pm
♉ 4/12 9:53am
♊ 4/14 7:14pm
♋ 4/17 2:27am
♌ 4/19 7:14am
♍ 4/21 9:42am
♎ 4/23 10:41am
♏ 4/25 11:39am
♐ 4/27 2:20pm
♑ 4/29 8:08pm
♒ 5/2 5:34am
♓ 5/4 5:34pm
♈ 5/7 6:03am
♉ 5/9 5:03pm
♊ 5/12 1:44am
♋ 5/14 8:08am
♌ 5/16 12:38pm
♍ 5/18 3:45pm
♎ 5/20 6:05pm
♏ 5/22 8:25pm
♐ 5/24 11:51pm
♑ 5/27 5:31am
♒ 5/29 2:09pm
♓ 6/1 1:32am
♈ 6/3 2:01pm
♉ 6/6 1:19am
♊ 6/8 9:49am
♋ 6/10 3:21pm
♌ 6/12 6:45pm
♍ 6/14 9:11pm
♎ 6/16 11:41pm
♏ 6/19 2:59am
♐ 6/21 7:34am
♑ 6/23 1:56pm
♒ 6/25 10:33pm
♓ 6/28 9:33am
♈ 6/30 10:02pm
♉ 7/3 9:54am
♊ 7/5 6:58pm
♋ 7/8 12:23am
♌ 7/10 2:50am
♍ 7/12 3:55am
♎ 7/14 5:21am
♏ 7/16 8:23am
♐ 7/18 1:32pm
♑ 7/20 8:46pm
♒ 7/23 5:56am
♓ 7/25 4:58pm
♈ 7/28 5:27am
♉ 7/30 5:53pm
♊ 8/2 4:02am
♋ 8/4 10:17am
♌ 8/6 12:44pm
♍ 8/8 12:53pm
♎ 8/10 12:51pm
♏ 8/12 2:30pm
♐ 8/14 6:59pm
♑ 8/17 2:25am
♒ 8/19 12:09pm
♓ 8/21 11:32pm
♈ 8/24 12:02pm
♉ 8/27 12:45am
♊ 8/29 11:53am
♋ 8/31 7:35pm
♌ 9/2 11:08pm
♍ 9/4 11:29pm
♎ 9/6 10:38pm
♏ 9/8 10:46pm
♐ 9/11 1:41am
♑ 9/13 8:11am
♒ 9/15 5:51pm
♓ 9/18 5:32am
♈ 9/20 6:07pm
♉ 9/23 6:43am
♊ 9/25 6:13pm
♋ 9/28 3:07am
♌ 9/30 8:20am
♍ 10/2 10:03am
♎ 10/4 9:39am
♏ 10/6 9:09am
♐ 10/8 10:36am
♑ 10/10 3:29pm
♒ 10/13 12:10am
♓ 10/15 11:40am
♈ 10/18 12:20am
♉ 10/20 12:43pm
♊ 10/22 11:51pm
♋ 10/25 8:57am
♌ 10/27 3:20pm
♍ 10/29 6:47pm
♎ 10/31 7:55pm
♏ 11/2 8:07pm
♐ 11/4 9:10pm
♑ 11/7 12:45am
♒ 11/9 7:59am
♓ 11/11 6:42pm
♈ 11/14 7:17am
♉ 11/16 7:38pm
♊ 11/19 6:14am
♋ 11/21 2:36pm
♌ 11/23 8:48pm
♍ 11/26 1:04am
♎ 11/28 3:48am
♏ 11/30 5:37am
♐ 12/2 7:33am
♑ 12/4 10:58am
♒ 12/6 5:12pm
♓ 12/9 2:52am
♈ 12/11 3:06pm
♉ 12/14 3:39am
♊ 12/16 2:12pm
♋ 12/18 9:49pm
♌ 12/21 2:54am
♍ 12/23 6:28am
♎ 12/25 9:27am
♏ 12/27 12:28pm
♐ 12/29 3:53pm
♑ 12/31 8:16pm

1976

♒ 1/3 2:33am
♓ 1/5 11:35am
♈ 1/7 11:21pm
♉ 1/10 12:10pm
♊ 1/12 11:19pm
♋ 1/15 7:00am

Moon Sign Changes 1900-2005

Sign	Date	Time
♌	1/17	11:15am
♍	1/19	1:25pm
♎	1/21	3:11pm
♏	1/23	5:48pm
♐	1/25	9:51pm
♑	1/28	3:24am
♒	1/30	10:34am
♓	2/1	7:47pm
♈	2/4	7:17am
♉	2/6	8:13pm
♊	2/9	8:16am
♋	2/11	4:59pm
♌	2/13	9:32pm
♍	2/15	10:59pm
♎	2/17	11:14pm
♏	2/20	12:14am
♐	2/22	3:18am
♑	2/24	8:54am
♒	2/26	4:48pm
♓	2/29	2:42am
♈	3/2	2:22pm
♉	3/5	3:18am
♊	3/7	3:56pm
♋	3/10	1:59am
♌	3/12	7:55am
♍	3/14	9:59am
♎	3/16	9:44am
♏	3/18	9:18am
♐	3/20	10:34am
♑	3/22	2:48pm
♒	3/24	10:19pm
♓	3/27	8:34am
♈	3/29	8:37pm
♉	4/1	9:34am
♊	4/3	10:15pm
♋	4/6	9:06am
♌	4/8	4:36pm
♍	4/10	8:16pm
♎	4/12	8:54pm
♏	4/14	8:14pm
♐	4/16	8:15pm
♑	4/18	10:43pm
♒	4/21	4:47am
♓	4/23	2:28pm
♈	4/26	2:37am
♉	4/28	3:37pm
♊	5/1	4:05am
♋	5/3	2:53pm
♌	5/5	11:09pm
♍	5/8	4:21am
♎	5/10	6:39am
♏	5/12	7:03am
♐	5/14	7:04am
♑	5/16	8:31am
♒	5/18	1:02pm
♓	5/20	9:27pm
♈	5/23	9:07am
♉	5/25	10:07pm
♊	5/28	10:22am
♋	5/30	8:39pm
♌	6/2	4:37am
♍	6/4	10:21am
♎	6/6	2:00pm
♏	6/8	3:58pm
♐	6/10	5:07pm
♑	6/12	6:45pm
♒	6/14	10:31pm
♓	6/17	5:43am
♈	6/19	4:32pm
♉	6/22	5:21am
♊	6/24	5:37pm
♋	6/27	3:29am
♌	6/29	10:39am
♍	7/1	3:46pm
♎	7/3	7:34pm
♏	7/5	10:33pm
♐	7/8	1:05am
♑	7/10	3:49am
♒	7/12	7:53am
♓	7/14	2:36pm
♈	7/17	12:40am
♉	7/19	1:11pm
♊	7/22	1:40am
♋	7/24	11:39am
♌	7/26	6:18pm
♍	7/28	10:23pm
♎	7/31	1:13am
♏	8/2	3:55am
♐	8/4	7:03am
♑	8/6	10:54am
♒	8/8	3:57pm
♓	8/10	11:00pm
♈	8/13	8:49am
♉	8/15	9:05pm
♊	8/18	9:54am
♋	8/20	8:34pm
♌	8/23	3:31am
♍	8/25	7:03am
♎	8/27	8:42am
♏	8/29	10:05am
♐	8/31	12:28pm
♑	9/2	4:29pm
♒	9/4	10:20pm
♓	9/7	6:11am
♈	9/9	4:18pm
♉	9/12	4:30am
♊	9/14	5:32pm
♋	9/17	5:07am
♌	9/19	1:10pm
♍	9/21	5:16pm
♎	9/23	6:28pm
♏	9/25	6:34pm
♐	9/27	7:21pm
♑	9/29	10:13pm
♒	10/2	3:49am
♓	10/4	12:10pm
♈	10/6	10:50pm
♉	10/9	11:11am
♊	10/12	12:14am
♋	10/14	12:24pm
♌	10/16	9:49pm
♍	10/19	3:25am
♎	10/21	5:26am
♏	10/23	5:17am
♐	10/25	4:49am
♑	10/27	5:55am
♒	10/29	10:05am
♓	10/31	5:53pm
♈	11/3	4:46am
♉	11/5	5:23pm
♊	11/8	6:21am
♋	11/10	6:28pm
♌	11/13	4:36am
♍	11/15	11:46am
♎	11/17	3:34pm
♏	11/19	4:31pm
♐	11/21	4:03pm
♑	11/23	4:03pm
♒	11/25	6:30pm
♓	11/28	12:47am
♈	11/30	11:01am
♉	12/2	11:41pm
♊	12/5	12:38pm
♋	12/8	12:21am
♌	12/10	10:12am
♍	12/12	5:55pm
♎	12/14	11:13pm
♏	12/17	2:01am
♐	12/19	2:54am
♑	12/21	3:12am
♒	12/23	4:48am
♓	12/25	9:36am
♈	12/27	6:32pm
♉	12/30	6:43am
1977		
♊	1/1	7:43pm
♋	1/4	7:12am
♌	1/6	4:20pm
♍	1/8	11:23pm
♎	1/11	4:48am
♏	1/13	8:44am
♐	1/15	11:18am
♑	1/17	1:02pm
♒	1/19	3:12pm
♓	1/21	7:30pm
♈	1/24	3:20am
♉	1/26	2:41pm
♊	1/29	3:37am
♋	1/31	3:20pm
♌	2/3	12:11am
♍	2/5	6:17am
♎	2/7	10:36am
♏	2/9	2:04pm
♐	2/11	5:11pm
♑	2/13	8:14pm
♒	2/15	11:45pm
♓	2/18	4:45am
♈	2/20	12:22pm
♉	2/22	11:06pm
♊	2/25	11:50am
♋	2/28	12:02am
♌	3/2	9:25am
♍	3/4	3:19pm
♎	3/6	6:34pm
♏	3/8	8:37pm
♐	3/10	10:42pm
♑	3/13	1:40am
♒	3/15	6:00am
♓	3/17	12:06pm
♈	3/19	8:23pm
♉	3/22	7:05am
♊	3/24	7:39pm
♋	3/27	8:16am
♌	3/29	6:40pm
♍	4/1	1:25am
♎	4/3	4:39am
♏	4/5	5:40am
♐	4/7	6:09am
♑	4/9	7:40am
♒	4/11	11:24am
♓	4/13	5:49pm
♈	4/16	2:52am
♉	4/18	2:02pm
♊	4/21	2:37am
♋	4/23	3:25pm
♌	4/26	2:43am
♍	4/28	10:52am
♎	4/30	3:12pm
♏	5/2	4:23pm
♐	5/4	3:59pm
♑	5/6	3:54pm
♒	5/8	6:00pm
♓	5/10	11:29pm
♈	5/13	8:29am
♉	5/15	8:04pm
♊	5/18	8:50am
♋	5/20	9:35pm
♌	5/23	9:13am
♍	5/25	6:31pm
♎	5/28	12:28am
♏	5/30	2:57am
♐	6/1	2:54am
♑	6/3	2:07am
♒	6/5	2:44am
♓	6/7	6:35am
♈	6/9	2:34pm
♉	6/12	1:56am
♊	6/14	2:50pm
♋	6/17	3:28am
♌	6/19	2:53pm
♍	6/22	12:29am
♎	6/24	7:35am
♏	6/26	11:42am
♐	6/28	1:02pm
♑	6/30	12:48pm
♒	7/2	12:56pm
♓	7/4	3:31pm
♈	7/6	10:03pm
♉	7/9	8:33am
♊	7/11	9:15pm
♋	7/14	9:50am
♌	7/16	8:51pm
♍	7/19	5:58am
♎	7/21	1:09pm
♏	7/23	6:13pm
♐	7/25	9:04pm
♑	7/27	10:15pm
♒	7/29	11:04pm
♓	8/1	1:23am
♈	8/3	6:54am
♉	8/5	4:18pm
♊	8/8	4:29am
♋	8/10	5:04pm
♌	8/13	3:57am
♍	8/15	12:26pm
♎	8/17	6:49pm
♏	8/19	11:35pm
♐	8/22	3:03am
♑	8/24	5:30am
♒	8/26	7:41am
♓	8/28	10:46am
♈	8/30	4:11pm
♉	9/2	12:52am
♊	9/4	12:27pm
♋	9/7	1:03am
♌	9/9	12:14pm
♍	9/11	8:34pm
♎	9/14	2:07am
♏	9/16	5:45am
♐	9/18	8:28am
♑	9/20	11:04am
♒	9/22	2:12pm
♓	9/24	6:30pm
♈	9/27	12:40am
♉	9/29	9:21am
♊	10/1	8:33pm
♋	10/4	9:09am
♌	10/6	8:58pm
♍	10/9	5:59am
♎	10/11	11:29am
♏	10/13	2:11pm
♐	10/15	3:27pm
♑	10/17	4:51pm
♒	10/19	7:36pm
♓	10/22	12:26am
♈	10/24	7:34am
♉	10/26	4:53pm
♊	10/29	4:08am
♋	10/31	4:40pm
♌	11/3	5:03am
♍	11/5	3:17pm
♎	11/7	9:51pm
♏	11/10	12:42am
♐	11/12	1:03am
♑	11/14	12:50am
♒	11/16	2:00am
♓	11/18	5:58am
♈	11/20	1:13pm
♉	11/22	11:09pm
♊	11/25	10:48am
♋	11/27	11:20pm
♌	11/30	11:53am
♍	12/2	11:05pm
♎	12/5	7:17am
♏	12/7	11:33am
♐	12/9	12:22pm
♑	12/11	11:26am
♒	12/13	10:59am
♓	12/15	1:09pm
♈	12/17	7:11pm
♉	12/20	4:54am
♊	12/22	4:51pm
♋	12/25	5:30am
♌	12/27	5:52pm
♍	12/30	5:13am
1978		
♎	1/1	2:31pm
♏	1/3	8:35pm
♐	1/5	11:03pm
♑	1/7	10:55pm
♒	1/9	10:05pm
♓	1/11	10:50pm
♈	1/14	3:05am
♉	1/16	11:30am
♊	1/18	11:06pm
♋	1/21	11:50am
♌	1/24	12:02am
♍	1/26	10:56am
♎	1/28	8:08pm
♏	1/31	3:04am
♐	2/2	7:13am
♑	2/4	8:50am
♒	2/6	9:04am
♓	2/8	9:47am
♈	2/10	12:56pm
♉	2/12	7:50pm
♊	2/15	6:24am
♋	2/17	6:56pm
♌	2/20	7:09am
♍	2/22	5:39pm
♎	2/25	2:03am
♏	2/27	8:28am
♐	3/1	1:02pm
♑	3/3	3:58pm
♒	3/5	5:51pm
♓	3/7	7:46pm
♈	3/9	11:08pm
♉	3/12	5:18am
♊	3/14	2:48pm
♋	3/17	2:49am
♌	3/19	3:12pm
♍	3/22	1:49am
♎	3/24	9:41am
♏	3/26	3:01pm
♐	3/28	6:37pm
♑	3/30	9:23pm
♒	4/2	12:05am
♓	4/4	3:20am
♈	4/6	7:51am
♉	4/8	2:21pm
♊	4/10	11:27pm
♋	4/13	10:59am
♌	4/15	11:30pm
♍	4/18	10:44am
♎	4/20	6:53pm
♏	4/22	11:39pm
♐	4/25	2:00am
♑	4/27	3:28am
♒	4/29	5:28am
♓	5/1	9:00am
♈	5/3	2:27pm
♉	5/5	9:52pm

Moon Sign Changes 1900-2005

♊	5/8	7:18am	♌	9/26	4:02pm	♍	2/12	5:18pm	♏	7/4	5:57am	♑	11/22	6:01am	♒	4/9	8:00am
♋	5/10	6:41pm	♍	9/29	4:11am	♎	2/15	5:37am	♐	7/6	12:55pm	♒	11/24	10:37am	♓	4/11	11:07am
♌	5/13	7:17am	♎	10/1	2:17pm	♏	2/17	4:12pm	♑	7/8	4:07pm	♓	11/26	2:17pm	♈	4/13	11:40am
♍	5/15	7:15pm	♏	10/3	9:48pm	♐	2/19	11:51pm	♒	7/10	4:59pm	♈	11/28	5:17pm	♉	4/15	11:11am
♎	5/18	4:24am	♐	10/6	3:07am	♑	2/22	4:00am	♓	7/12	5:23pm	♉	11/30	7:54pm	♊	4/17	11:41am
♏	5/20	9:39am	♑	10/8	6:52am	♒	2/24	5:12am	♈	7/14	6:57pm	♊	12/2	11:02pm	♋	4/19	3:11pm
♐	5/22	11:31am	♒	10/10	9:42am	♓	2/26	4:52am	♉	7/16	10:43pm	♋	12/5	4:01am	♌	4/21	10:52pm
♑	5/24	11:41am	♓	10/12	12:12pm	♈	2/28	4:54am	♊	7/19	5:00am	♌	12/7	12:09pm	♍	4/24	10:12am
♒	5/26	12:10pm	♈	10/14	3:06pm	♉	3/2	7:09am	♋	7/21	1:40pm	♍	12/9	11:33pm	♎	4/26	11:09pm
♓	5/28	2:37pm	♉	10/16	7:22pm	♊	3/4	12:58pm	♌	7/24	12:30am	♎	12/12	12:29pm	♏	4/29	11:35am
♈	5/30	7:52pm	♊	10/19	2:05am	♋	3/6	10:34pm	♍	7/26	1:01pm	♏	12/15	12:08am	♐	5/1	10:22pm
♉	6/2	3:50am	♋	10/21	11:52am	♌	3/9	10:47am	♎	7/29	2:06am	♐	12/17	8:36am	♑	5/4	7:14am
♊	6/4	1:53pm	♌	10/24	12:04am	♍	3/11	11:42pm	♏	7/31	1:46pm	♑	12/19	1:54pm	♒	5/6	2:03pm
♋	6/7	1:30am	♍	10/26	12:32pm	♎	3/14	11:42am	♐	8/2	10:05pm	♒	12/21	5:13pm	♓	5/8	6:33pm
♌	6/9	2:07pm	♎	10/28	10:51pm	♏	3/16	9:49pm	♑	8/5	2:23am	♓	12/23	7:50pm	♈	5/10	8:44pm
♍	6/12	2:35am	♏	10/31	5:52am	♐	3/19	5:38am	♒	8/7	3:28am	♈	12/25	10:40pm	♉	5/12	9:24pm
♎	6/14	12:55pm	♐	11/2	10:03am	♑	3/21	10:56am	♓	8/9	3:05am	♉	12/28	2:08am	♊	5/14	10:07pm
♏	6/16	7:28pm	♑	11/4	12:40pm	♒	3/23	1:52pm	♈	8/11	3:10am	♊	12/30	6:32am	♋	5/17	12:52am
♐	6/18	10:01pm	♒	11/6	3:04pm	♓	3/25	3:04pm	♉	8/13	5:21am		**1980**		♌	5/19	7:14am
♑	6/20	9:52pm	♓	11/8	6:06pm	♈	3/27	3:47pm	♊	8/15	10:41am	♋	1/1	12:29pm	♍	5/21	5:32pm
♒	6/22	9:07pm	♈	11/10	10:11pm	♉	3/29	5:36pm	♋	8/17	7:17pm	♌	1/3	8:47pm	♎	5/24	6:11am
♓	6/24	9:57pm	♉	11/13	3:35am	♊	3/31	10:08pm	♌	8/20	6:28am	♍	1/6	7:48am	♏	5/26	6:37pm
♈	6/27	1:53am	♊	11/15	10:45am	♋	4/3	6:24am	♍	8/22	7:11pm	♎	1/8	8:38pm	♐	5/29	5:05am
♉	6/29	9:21am	♋	11/17	8:16pm	♌	4/5	5:58pm	♎	8/25	8:13am	♏	1/11	8:55am	♑	5/31	1:14pm
♊	7/1	7:37pm	♌	11/20	8:09am	♍	4/8	6:52am	♏	8/27	8:12pm	♐	1/13	6:17pm	♒	6/2	7:29pm
♋	7/4	7:33am	♍	11/22	8:57pm	♎	4/10	6:45pm	♐	8/30	5:39am	♑	1/15	11:51pm	♓	6/5	12:10am
♌	7/6	8:13pm	♎	11/25	8:07am	♏	4/13	4:16am	♑	9/1	11:33am	♒	1/18	2:25am	♈	6/7	3:23am
♍	7/9	8:44am	♏	11/27	3:38pm	♐	4/15	11:18am	♒	9/3	1:59pm	♓	1/20	3:33am	♉	6/9	5:29am
♎	7/11	7:48pm	♐	11/29	7:23pm	♑	4/17	4:23pm	♓	9/5	2:03pm	♈	1/22	4:52am	♊	6/11	7:22am
♏	7/14	3:47am	♑	12/1	8:44pm	♒	4/19	8:02pm	♈	9/7	1:29pm	♉	1/24	7:31am	♋	6/13	10:29am
♐	7/16	7:50am	♒	12/3	9:35pm	♓	4/21	10:41pm	♉	9/9	2:12pm	♊	1/26	12:11pm	♌	6/15	4:22pm
♑	7/18	8:33am	♓	12/5	11:36pm	♈	4/24	12:51am	♊	9/11	5:54pm	♋	1/28	7:02pm	♍	6/18	1:47am
♒	7/20	7:41am	♈	12/8	3:40am	♉	4/26	3:27am	♋	9/14	1:27am	♌	1/31	4:08am	♎	6/20	1:55pm
♓	7/22	7:26am	♉	12/10	9:50am	♊	4/28	7:49am	♌	9/16	12:25pm	♍	2/2	3:21pm	♏	6/23	2:26am
♈	7/24	9:46am	♊	12/12	5:54pm	♋	4/30	3:11pm	♍	9/19	1:15am	♎	2/5	4:04am	♐	6/25	1:02pm
♉	7/26	3:50pm	♋	12/15	3:50am	♌	5/3	1:56am	♎	9/21	2:11pm	♏	2/7	4:46pm	♑	6/27	8:46pm
♊	7/29	1:31am	♌	12/17	3:37pm	♍	5/5	2:41pm	♏	9/24	1:54am	♐	2/10	3:19am	♒	6/30	2:04am
♋	7/31	1:28pm	♍	12/20	4:34am	♎	5/8	2:47am	♐	9/26	11:36am	♑	2/12	10:12am	♓	7/2	5:48am
♌	8/3	2:10am	♎	12/22	4:40pm	♏	5/10	12:10pm	♑	9/28	6:40pm	♒	2/14	1:19pm	♈	7/4	8:46am
♍	8/5	2:29pm	♏	12/25	1:32am	♐	5/12	6:25pm	♒	9/30	10:49pm	♓	2/16	1:54pm	♉	7/6	11:30am
♎	8/8	1:30am	♐	12/27	6:07am	♑	5/14	10:25pm	♓	10/3	12:23am	♈	2/18	1:43pm	♊	7/8	2:33pm
♏	8/10	10:11am	♑	12/29	7:15am	♒	5/17	1:26am	♈	10/5	12:28am	♉	2/20	2:35pm	♋	7/10	6:44pm
♐	8/12	3:43pm	♒	12/31	6:53am	♓	5/19	4:18am	♉	10/7	12:45am	♊	2/22	5:58pm	♌	7/13	1:03am
♑	8/14	6:03pm		**1979**		♈	5/21	7:30am	♊	10/9	3:07am	♋	2/25	12:34am	♍	7/15	10:11am
♒	8/16	6:15pm	♓	1/2	7:08am	♉	5/23	11:20am	♋	10/11	9:09am	♌	2/27	10:10am	♎	7/17	9:55pm
♓	8/18	6:04pm	♈	1/4	9:41am	♊	5/25	4:28pm	♌	10/13	7:12pm	♍	2/29	9:53pm	♏	7/20	10:33am
♈	8/20	7:29pm	♉	1/6	3:17pm	♋	5/27	11:51pm	♍	10/16	7:51am	♎	3/3	10:40am	♐	7/22	9:42am
♉	8/23	12:06am	♊	1/8	11:42pm	♌	5/30	10:08am	♎	10/18	8:44pm	♏	3/5	11:22pm	♑	7/25	5:45am
♊	8/25	8:31am	♋	1/11	10:14am	♍	6/1	10:41pm	♏	10/21	8:02am	♐	3/8	10:38am	♒	7/27	10:34am
♋	8/27	7:59pm	♌	1/13	10:16pm	♎	6/4	11:12am	♐	10/23	5:09pm	♑	3/10	7:02pm	♓	7/29	1:11pm
♌	8/30	8:40am	♍	1/16	11:10am	♏	6/6	9:05pm	♑	10/26	12:11am	♒	3/12	11:45pm	♈	7/31	2:53pm
♍	9/1	8:46pm	♎	1/18	11:40pm	♐	6/9	3:15am	♒	10/28	5:16am	♓	3/15	1:10am	♉	8/2	4:55pm
♎	9/4	7:15am	♏	1/21	9:51am	♑	6/11	6:23am	♓	10/30	8:29am	♈	3/17	12:41am	♊	8/4	8:10pm
♏	9/6	3:38pm	♐	1/23	4:08pm	♒	6/13	8:06am	♈	11/1	10:09am	♉	3/19	12:13am	♋	8/7	1:12am
♐	9/8	9:39pm	♑	1/25	6:27pm	♓	6/15	9:56am	♉	11/3	11:16am	♊	3/21	1:47am	♌	8/9	8:23am
♑	9/11	1:20am	♒	1/27	6:12pm	♈	6/17	12:52pm	♊	11/5	1:26pm	♋	3/23	6:55am	♍	8/11	5:54pm
♒	9/13	3:09am	♓	1/29	5:25pm	♉	6/19	5:18pm	♋	11/7	6:24pm	♌	3/25	3:58pm	♎	8/14	5:32am
♓	9/15	4:09am	♈	1/31	6:11pm	♊	6/21	11:23pm	♌	11/10	3:14am	♍	3/28	3:52am	♏	8/16	6:15pm
♈	9/17	5:50am	♉	2/2	10:03pm	♋	6/24	7:25am	♍	11/12	3:20pm	♎	3/30	4:49pm	♐	8/19	6:08am
♉	9/19	9:43am	♊	2/5	5:33am	♌	6/26	5:47pm	♎	11/15	4:16am	♏	4/2	5:21am	♑	8/21	3:11pm
♊	9/21	4:56pm	♋	2/7	4:06pm	♍	6/29	6:14am	♏	11/17	3:29pm	♐	4/4	4:35pm	♒	8/23	8:32pm
♋	9/24	3:31am	♌	2/10	4:25am	♎	7/1	7:08pm	♐	11/19	11:56pm	♑	4/7	1:43am	♓	8/25	10:43pm

Moon Sign Changes 1900-2005

♈	8/27	11:11pm
♉	8/29	11:41pm
♊	9/1	1:50am
♋	9/3	6:39am
♌	9/5	2:22pm
♍	9/8	12:31am
♎	9/10	12:22pm
♏	9/13	1:06am
♐	9/15	1:28pm
♑	9/17	11:45pm
♒	9/20	6:30am
♓	9/22	9:27am
♈	9/24	9:37am
♉	9/26	8:53am
♊	9/28	9:21am
♋	9/30	12:46pm
♌	10/2	7:57pm
♍	10/5	6:19am
♎	10/7	6:30pm
♏	10/10	7:15am
♐	10/12	7:37pm
♑	10/15	6:37am
♒	10/17	2:54pm
♓	10/19	7:31pm
♈	10/21	8:43pm
♉	10/23	7:55pm
♊	10/25	7:17pm
♋	10/27	9:00pm
♌	10/30	2:38am
♍	11/1	12:18pm
♎	11/4	12:31am
♏	11/6	1:19pm
♐	11/9	1:25am
♑	11/11	12:15pm
♒	11/13	9:10pm
♓	11/16	3:21am
♈	11/18	6:22am
♉	11/20	6:51am
♊	11/22	6:27am
♋	11/24	7:19am
♌	11/26	11:23am
♍	11/28	7:37pm
♎	12/1	7:13am
♏	12/3	8:00pm
♐	12/6	7:57am
♑	12/8	6:12pm
♒	12/11	2:36am
♓	12/13	9:03am
♈	12/15	1:21pm
♉	12/17	3:36pm
♊	12/19	4:39pm
♋	12/21	6:03pm
♌	12/23	9:34pm
♍	12/26	4:32am
♎	12/28	3:05pm
♏	12/31	3:36am
	1981	
♐	1/2	3:42pm
♑	1/5	1:41am
♒	1/7	9:12am
♓	1/9	2:42pm
♈	1/11	6:43pm
♉	1/13	9:45pm
♊	1/16	12:17am
♋	1/18	3:08am
♌	1/20	7:21am
♍	1/22	2:02pm
♎	1/24	11:45pm
♏	1/27	11:49am
♐	1/30	12:12am
♑	2/1	10:37am
♒	2/3	5:55pm
♓	2/5	10:21pm
♈	2/8	1:01am
♉	2/10	3:11am
♊	2/12	5:51am
♋	2/14	9:43am
♌	2/16	3:10pm
♍	2/18	10:34pm
♎	2/21	8:12am
♏	2/23	7:54pm
♐	2/26	8:29am
♑	2/28	7:46pm
♒	3/3	3:51am
♓	3/5	8:12am
♈	3/7	9:48am
♉	3/9	10:22am
♊	3/11	11:42am
♋	3/13	3:06pm
♌	3/15	9:02pm
♍	3/18	5:20am
♎	3/20	3:31pm
♏	3/23	3:14am
♐	3/25	3:51pm
♑	3/28	3:52am
♒	3/30	1:15pm
♓	4/1	6:41pm
♈	4/3	8:25pm
♉	4/5	8:04pm
♊	4/7	7:47pm
♋	4/9	9:34pm
♌	4/12	2:36am
♍	4/14	10:56am
♎	4/16	9:38pm
♏	4/19	9:39am
♐	4/21	10:15pm
♑	4/24	10:31am
♒	4/26	8:57pm
♓	4/29	3:56am
♈	5/1	6:57am
♉	5/3	6:59am
♊	5/5	6:01am
♋	5/7	6:18am
♌	5/9	9:40am
♍	5/11	4:55pm
♎	5/14	3:24am
♏	5/16	3:37pm
♐	5/19	4:14am
♑	5/21	4:20pm
♒	5/24	3:01am
♓	5/26	11:05am
♈	5/28	3:44pm
♉	5/30	5:10pm
♊	6/1	4:48pm
♋	6/3	4:38pm
♌	6/5	6:43pm
♍	6/8	12:25am
♎	6/10	9:55am
♏	6/12	9:54pm
♐	6/15	10:31am
♑	6/17	10:21pm
♒	6/20	8:36am
♓	6/22	4:44pm
♈	6/24	10:18pm
♉	6/27	1:16am
♊	6/29	2:21am
♋	7/1	2:57am
♌	7/3	4:47am
♍	7/5	9:26am
♎	7/7	5:42pm
♏	7/10	5:02am
♐	7/12	5:35pm
♑	7/15	5:19am
♒	7/17	3:02pm
♓	7/19	10:26pm
♈	7/22	3:43am
♉	7/24	7:18am
♊	7/26	9:42am
♋	7/28	11:41am
♌	7/30	2:20pm
♍	8/1	6:54pm
♎	8/4	2:24am
♏	8/6	12:58pm
♐	8/9	1:22am
♑	8/11	1:20pm
♒	8/13	10:56pm
♓	8/16	5:34am
♈	8/18	9:49am
♉	8/20	12:43pm
♊	8/22	3:18pm
♋	8/24	6:17pm
♌	8/26	10:10pm
♍	8/29	3:32am
♎	8/31	11:02am
♏	9/2	9:10pm
♐	9/5	9:24am
♑	9/7	9:48pm
♒	9/10	7:58am
♓	9/12	2:34pm
♈	9/14	5:55pm
♉	9/16	7:30pm
♊	9/18	8:59pm
♋	9/20	11:39pm
♌	9/23	4:08am
♍	9/25	10:29am
♎	9/27	6:40pm
♏	9/30	4:53am
♐	10/2	5:00pm
♑	10/5	5:49am
♒	10/7	5:01pm
♓	10/10	12:32am
♈	10/12	4:01am
♉	10/14	4:43am
♊	10/16	4:41am
♋	10/18	5:52am
♌	10/20	9:34am
♍	10/22	4:05pm
♎	10/25	12:56am
♏	10/27	11:38am
♐	10/29	11:48pm
♑	11/1	12:46pm
♒	11/4	12:51am
♓	11/6	9:52am
♈	11/8	2:38pm
♉	11/10	3:44pm
♊	11/12	2:59pm
♋	11/14	2:37pm
♌	11/16	4:33pm
♍	11/18	9:53pm
♎	11/21	6:33am
♏	11/23	5:36pm
♐	11/26	6:00am
♑	11/28	6:53pm
♒	12/1	7:09am
♓	12/3	5:16pm
♈	12/5	11:49pm
♉	12/8	2:31am
♊	12/10	2:30am
♋	12/12	1:40am
♌	12/14	2:08am
♍	12/16	5:38am
♎	12/18	12:58pm
♏	12/20	11:39pm
♐	12/23	12:11pm
♑	12/26	12:59am
♒	12/28	12:54pm
♓	12/30	11:01pm
	1982	
♈	1/2	6:33am
♉	1/4	11:02am
♊	1/6	12:48pm
♋	1/8	1:01pm
♌	1/10	1:21pm
♍	1/12	3:37pm
♎	1/14	9:17pm
♏	1/17	6:46am
♐	1/19	7:00pm
♑	1/22	7:51am
♒	1/24	7:25pm
♓	1/27	4:49am
♈	1/29	11:58am
♉	1/31	5:03pm
♊	2/2	8:20pm
♋	2/4	10:18pm
♌	2/6	11:50pm
♍	2/9	2:15am
♎	2/11	7:02am
♏	2/13	3:16pm
♐	2/16	2:45am
♑	2/18	3:36pm
♒	2/21	3:15am
♓	2/23	12:09pm
♈	2/25	6:17pm
♉	2/27	10:32pm
♊	3/2	1:50am
♋	3/4	4:48am
♌	3/6	7:50am
♍	3/8	11:27am
♎	3/10	4:34pm
♏	3/13	12:17am
♐	3/15	11:03am
♑	3/17	11:47pm
♒	3/20	11:53am
♓	3/22	9:01pm
♈	3/25	2:37am
♉	3/27	5:39am
♊	3/29	7:44am
♋	3/31	10:09am
♌	4/2	1:36pm
♍	4/4	6:18pm
♎	4/7	12:26am
♏	4/9	8:33am
♐	4/11	7:07pm
♑	4/14	7:41am
♒	4/16	8:18pm
♓	4/19	6:20am
♈	4/21	12:23pm
♉	4/23	2:59pm
♊	4/25	3:48pm
♋	4/27	4:43pm
♌	4/29	7:09pm
♍	5/1	11:45pm
♎	5/4	6:32am
♏	5/6	3:24pm
♐	5/9	2:17am
♑	5/11	2:50pm
♒	5/14	3:44am
♓	5/16	2:46pm
♈	5/18	10:04pm
♉	5/21	1:22am
♊	5/23	1:54am
♋	5/25	1:38am
♌	5/27	2:27am
♍	5/29	5:43am
♎	5/31	12:02pm
♏	6/2	9:12pm
♐	6/5	8:31am
♑	6/7	9:12pm
♒	6/10	10:08am
♓	6/12	9:44pm
♈	6/15	6:20am
♉	6/17	11:07am
♊	6/19	12:34pm
♋	6/21	12:13pm
♌	6/23	11:57am
♍	6/25	1:36pm
♎	6/27	6:30pm
♏	6/30	3:02am
♐	7/2	2:25pm
♑	7/5	3:15am
♒	7/7	4:03pm
♓	7/10	3:35am
♈	7/12	12:49pm
♉	7/14	7:00pm
♊	7/16	10:03pm
♋	7/18	10:46pm
♌	7/20	10:35pm
♍	7/22	11:20pm
♎	7/25	2:45am
♏	7/27	9:58am
♐	7/29	8:48pm
♑	8/1	9:36am
♒	8/3	10:17pm
♓	8/6	9:23am
♈	8/8	6:21pm
♉	8/11	1:00am
♊	8/13	5:22am
♋	8/15	7:40am
♌	8/17	8:40am
♍	8/19	9:40am
♎	8/21	12:22pm
♏	8/23	6:21pm
♐	8/26	4:11am
♑	8/28	4:42pm
♒	8/31	5:23am
♓	9/2	4:11pm
♈	9/5	12:24am
♉	9/7	6:27am
♊	9/9	10:57am
♋	9/11	2:18pm
♌	9/13	4:46pm
♍	9/15	6:57pm
♎	9/17	10:03pm
♏	9/20	3:32am
♐	9/22	12:30pm
♑	9/25	12:31am
♒	9/27	1:21pm
♓	9/30	12:18am
♈	10/2	8:06am
♉	10/4	1:09pm
♊	10/6	4:39pm
♋	10/8	7:39pm
♌	10/10	10:44pm
♍	10/13	2:09am
♎	10/15	6:23am
♏	10/17	12:21pm
♐	10/19	9:02pm
♑	10/22	8:38am
♒	10/24	9:36pm
♓	10/27	9:12am
♈	10/29	5:25pm
♉	10/31	10:04pm
♊	11/3	12:23am
♋	11/5	1:59am
♌	11/7	4:10am
♍	11/9	7:40am
♎	11/11	12:46pm
♏	11/13	7:42pm
♐	11/16	4:52am
♑	11/18	4:21pm
♒	11/21	5:20am
♓	11/23	5:43pm
♈	11/26	3:07am
♉	11/28	8:31am
♊	11/30	10:36am
♋	12/2	10:58am
♌	12/4	11:26am
♍	12/6	1:32pm
♎	12/8	6:11pm
♏	12/11	1:34am
♐	12/13	11:27am
♑	12/15	11:15pm

Moon Sign Changes 1900-2005

♒	12/18	12:12pm
♓	12/21	12:56am
♈	12/23	11:34am
♉	12/25	6:37pm
♊	12/27	9:49pm
♋	12/29	10:12pm
♌	12/31	9:33pm
	1983	
♍	1/2	9:49pm
♎	1/5	12:44am
♏	1/7	7:16am
♐	1/9	5:14pm
♑	1/12	5:26am
♒	1/14	6:26pm
♓	1/17	7:02am
♈	1/19	6:08pm
♉	1/22	2:36am
♊	1/24	7:40am
♋	1/26	9:28am
♌	1/28	9:10am
♍	1/30	8:35am
♎	2/1	9:47am
♏	2/3	2:32pm
♐	2/5	11:28pm
♑	2/8	11:33am
♒	2/11	12:40am
♓	2/13	1:02pm
♈	2/15	11:46pm
♉	2/18	8:31am
♊	2/20	2:52pm
♋	2/22	6:31pm
♌	2/24	7:47pm
♍	2/26	7:49pm
♎	2/28	8:30pm
♏	3/2	11:51pm
♐	3/5	7:15am
♑	3/7	6:29pm
♒	3/10	7:30am
♓	3/12	7:47pm
♈	3/15	6:00am
♉	3/17	2:04pm
♊	3/19	8:20pm
♋	3/22	12:52am
♌	3/24	3:43am
♍	3/26	5:18am
♎	3/28	6:48am
♏	3/30	9:57am
♐	4/1	4:20pm
♑	4/4	2:30am
♒	4/6	3:06pm
♓	4/9	3:30am
♈	4/11	1:37pm
♉	4/13	8:59pm
♊	4/16	2:15am
♋	4/18	6:14am
♌	4/20	9:26am
♍	4/22	12:12pm
♎	4/24	3:04pm
♏	4/26	7:04pm
♐	4/29	1:28am
♑	5/1	11:01am
♒	5/3	11:09pm
♓	5/6	11:43am
♈	5/8	10:16pm
♉	5/11	5:36am
♊	5/13	10:03am
♋	5/15	12:48pm
♌	5/17	3:01pm
♍	5/19	5:37pm
♎	5/21	9:11pm
♏	5/24	2:17am
♐	5/26	9:27am
♑	5/28	7:07pm
♒	5/31	7:00am
♓	6/2	7:42pm
♈	6/5	6:59am
♉	6/7	3:05pm
♊	6/9	7:37pm
♋	6/11	9:32pm
♌	6/13	10:21pm
♍	6/15	11:38pm
♎	6/18	2:36am
♏	6/20	7:59am
♐	6/22	3:55pm
♑	6/25	2:08am
♒	6/27	2:07pm
♓	6/30	2:52am
♈	7/2	2:47pm
♉	7/5	12:05am
♊	7/7	5:41am
♋	7/9	7:50am
♌	7/11	7:54am
♍	7/13	7:43am
♎	7/15	9:10am
♏	7/17	1:38pm
♐	7/19	9:31pm
♑	7/22	8:11am
♒	7/24	8:26pm
♓	7/27	9:11am
♈	7/29	9:21pm
♉	8/1	7:37am
♊	8/3	2:43pm
♋	8/5	6:09pm
♌	8/7	6:37pm
♍	8/9	5:49pm
♎	8/11	5:51pm
♏	8/13	8:44pm
♐	8/16	3:33am
♑	8/18	1:59pm
♒	8/21	2:25am
♓	8/23	3:10pm
♈	8/26	3:08am
♉	8/28	1:38pm
♊	8/30	9:49pm
♋	9/2	2:53am
♌	9/4	4:47am
♍	9/6	4:36am
♎	9/8	4:13am
♏	9/10	5:49am
♐	9/12	11:08am
♑	9/14	8:34pm
♒	9/17	8:45am
♓	9/19	9:30pm
♈	9/22	9:10am
♉	9/24	7:12pm
♊	9/27	3:24am
♋	9/29	9:24am
♌	10/1	12:54pm
♍	10/3	2:15pm
♎	10/5	2:42pm
♏	10/7	4:06pm
♐	10/9	8:21pm
♑	10/12	4:30am
♒	10/14	4:00pm
♓	10/17	4:41am
♈	10/19	4:18pm
♉	10/22	1:47am
♊	10/24	9:10am
♋	10/26	2:47pm
♌	10/28	6:50pm
♍	10/30	9:33pm
♎	11/1	11:31pm
♏	11/4	1:53am
♐	11/6	6:09am
♑	11/8	1:31pm
♒	11/11	12:10am
♓	11/13	12:41pm
♈	11/16	12:36am
♉	11/18	10:06am
♊	11/20	4:45pm
♋	11/22	9:10pm
♌	11/25	12:19am
♍	11/27	3:02am
♎	11/29	5:57am
♏	12/1	9:41am
♐	12/3	2:56pm
♑	12/5	10:28pm
♒	12/8	8:39am
♓	12/10	8:53pm
♈	12/13	9:17am
♉	12/15	7:33pm
♊	12/18	2:23am
♋	12/20	6:02am
♌	12/22	7:44am
♍	12/24	9:01am
♎	12/26	11:18am
♏	12/28	3:27pm
♐	12/30	9:44pm
	1984	
♑	1/2	6:07am
♒	1/4	4:30pm
♓	1/7	4:34am
♈	1/9	5:15pm
♉	1/12	4:36am
♊	1/14	12:40pm
♋	1/16	4:47pm
♌	1/18	5:49pm
♍	1/20	5:35pm
♎	1/22	6:07pm
♏	1/24	9:04pm
♐	1/27	3:12am
♑	1/29	12:12pm
♒	1/31	11:11pm
♓	2/3	11:22am
♈	2/6	12:04am
♉	2/8	12:05pm
♊	2/10	9:39pm
♋	2/13	3:20am
♌	2/15	5:09am
♍	2/17	4:32am
♎	2/19	3:39am
♏	2/21	4:44am
♐	2/23	9:22am
♑	2/25	5:49pm
♒	2/28	5:02am
♓	3/1	5:29pm
♈	3/4	6:07am
♉	3/6	6:09pm
♊	3/9	4:30am
♋	3/11	11:48am
♌	3/13	3:21pm
♍	3/15	3:47pm
♎	3/17	2:51pm
♏	3/19	2:49pm
♐	3/21	5:41pm
♑	3/24	12:36am
♒	3/26	11:09am
♓	3/28	11:37pm
♈	3/31	12:14pm
♉	4/2	11:55pm
♊	4/5	10:04am
♋	4/7	5:59pm
♌	4/9	11:01pm
♍	4/12	1:11am
♎	4/14	1:29am
♏	4/16	1:41am
♐	4/18	3:44am
♑	4/20	9:10am
♒	4/22	6:27pm
♓	4/25	6:26am
♈	4/27	7:02pm
♉	4/30	6:30am
♊	5/2	4:02pm
♋	5/4	11:26pm
♌	5/7	4:43am
♍	5/9	8:02am
♎	5/11	9:54am
♏	5/13	11:22am
♐	5/15	1:50pm
♑	5/17	6:43pm
♒	5/20	2:55am
♓	5/22	2:09pm
♈	5/25	2:39am
♉	5/27	2:13pm
♊	5/29	11:23pm
♋	6/1	5:53am
♌	6/3	10:19am
♍	6/5	1:27pm
♎	6/7	4:03pm
♏	6/9	6:48pm
♐	6/11	10:26pm
♑	6/14	3:48am
♒	6/16	11:41am
♓	6/18	10:18pm
♈	6/21	10:40am
♉	6/23	10:38pm
♊	6/26	8:04am
♋	6/28	2:09pm
♌	6/30	5:30pm
♍	7/2	7:28pm
♎	7/4	9:27pm
♏	7/7	12:28am
♐	7/9	5:03am
♑	7/11	11:23am
♒	7/13	7:41pm
♓	7/16	6:10am
♈	7/18	6:26pm
♉	7/21	6:52am
♊	7/23	5:10pm
♋	7/25	11:44pm
♌	7/28	2:41am
♍	7/30	3:29am
♎	8/1	4:03am
♏	8/3	6:04am
♐	8/5	10:30am
♑	8/7	5:24pm
♒	8/10	2:25am
♓	8/12	1:13pm
♈	8/15	1:28am
♉	8/17	2:13pm
♊	8/20	1:31am
♋	8/22	9:20am
♌	8/24	1:00pm
♍	8/26	1:32pm
♎	8/28	12:57pm
♏	8/30	1:23pm
♐	9/1	4:30pm
♑	9/3	10:55pm
♒	9/6	8:11am
♓	9/8	7:24pm
♈	9/11	7:47am
♉	9/13	8:33pm
♊	9/16	8:26am
♋	9/18	5:36pm
♌	9/20	10:49pm
♍	9/23	12:19am
♎	9/24	11:41pm
♏	9/26	11:04pm
♐	9/29	12:32am
♑	10/1	5:28am
♒	10/3	2:03pm
♓	10/6	1:19am
♈	10/8	1:51pm
♉	10/11	2:28am
♊	10/13	2:14pm
♋	10/16	12:00am
♌	10/18	6:41am
♍	10/20	9:56am
♎	10/22	10:32am
♏	10/24	10:08am
♐	10/26	10:43am
♑	10/28	2:05pm
♒	10/30	9:13pm
♓	11/2	7:50am
♈	11/4	8:20pm
♉	11/7	8:53am
♊	11/9	8:10pm
♋	11/12	5:31am
♌	11/14	12:34pm
♍	11/16	5:08pm
♎	11/18	7:29pm
♏	11/20	8:30pm
♐	11/22	9:34pm
♑	11/25	12:17am
♒	11/27	6:06am
♓	11/29	3:33pm
♈	12/2	3:42am
♉	12/4	4:20pm
♊	12/7	3:24am
♋	12/9	11:56am
♌	12/11	6:08pm
♍	12/13	10:35pm
♎	12/16	1:52am
♏	12/18	4:27am
♐	12/20	6:58am
♑	12/22	10:21am
♒	12/24	3:47pm
♓	12/27	12:18am
♈	12/29	11:49am
	1985	
♉	1/1	12:36am
♊	1/3	12:00pm
♋	1/5	8:18pm
♌	1/8	1:28am
♍	1/10	4:40am
♎	1/12	7:13am
♏	1/14	10:07am
♐	1/16	1:48pm
♑	1/18	6:29pm
♒	1/21	12:38am
♓	1/23	9:02am
♈	1/25	8:05pm
♉	1/28	8:53am
♊	1/30	9:01pm
♋	2/2	5:59am
♌	2/4	11:02am
♍	2/6	1:09pm
♎	2/8	2:10pm
♏	2/10	3:49pm
♐	2/12	7:09pm
♑	2/15	12:27am
♒	2/17	7:36am
♓	2/19	4:38pm
♈	2/22	3:43am
♉	2/24	4:27pm
♊	2/27	5:11am
♋	3/1	3:23pm
♌	3/3	9:28pm
♍	3/5	11:43pm
♎	3/7	11:47pm
♏	3/9	11:47pm
♐	3/12	1:29am
♑	3/14	5:55am
♒	3/16	1:11pm
♓	3/18	10:50pm
♈	3/21	10:20am
♉	3/23	11:06pm
♊	3/26	12:02pm
♋	3/28	11:13pm
♌	3/31	6:51am
♍	4/2	10:25am
♎	4/4	10:54am

Moon Sign Changes 1900-2005

♏	4/6	10:10am
♐	4/8	10:18am
♑	4/10	12:57pm
♒	4/12	7:04pm
♓	4/15	4:30am
♈	4/17	4:18pm
♉	4/20	5:12am
♊	4/22	6:01pm
♋	4/25	5:26am
♌	4/27	2:10pm
♍	4/29	7:24pm
♎	5/1	9:22pm
♏	5/3	9:17pm
♐	5/5	8:56pm
♑	5/7	10:11pm
♒	5/10	2:38am
♓	5/12	10:56am
♈	5/14	10:25pm
♉	5/17	11:23am
♊	5/20	12:01am
♋	5/22	11:05am
♌	5/24	7:54pm
♍	5/27	2:06am
♎	5/29	5:40am
♏	5/31	7:07am
♐	6/2	7:33am
♑	6/4	8:34am
♒	6/6	11:52am
♓	6/8	6:46pm
♈	6/11	5:24am
♉	6/13	6:11pm
♊	6/16	6:45am
♋	6/18	5:22pm
♌	6/21	1:32am
♍	6/23	7:32am
♎	6/25	11:48am
♏	6/27	2:37pm
♐	6/29	4:30pm
♑	7/1	6:22pm
♒	7/3	9:36pm
♓	7/6	3:40am
♈	7/8	1:20pm
♉	7/11	1:44am
♊	7/13	2:23pm
♋	7/16	12:54am
♌	7/18	8:25am
♍	7/20	1:29pm
♎	7/22	5:10pm
♏	7/24	8:16pm
♐	7/26	11:12pm
♑	7/29	2:21am
♒	7/31	6:25am
♓	8/2	12:33pm
♈	8/4	9:43pm
♉	8/7	9:41am
♊	8/9	10:31pm
♋	8/12	9:28am
♌	8/14	4:57pm
♍	8/16	9:15pm
♎	8/18	11:44pm
♏	8/21	1:51am
♐	8/23	4:36am

♑	8/25	8:24am
♒	8/27	1:31pm
♓	8/29	8:25pm
♈	9/1	5:42am
♉	9/3	5:28pm
♊	9/6	6:27am
♋	9/8	6:10pm
♌	9/11	2:27am
♍	9/13	6:52am
♎	9/15	8:34am
♏	9/17	9:17am
♐	9/19	10:40am
♑	9/21	1:49pm
♒	9/23	7:11pm
♓	9/26	2:50am
♈	9/28	12:43pm
♉	10/1	12:35am
♊	10/3	1:36pm
♋	10/6	1:59am
♌	10/8	11:33am
♍	10/10	5:09pm
♎	10/12	7:12pm
♏	10/14	7:13pm
♐	10/16	7:05pm
♑	10/18	8:35pm
♒	10/21	12:54am
♓	10/23	8:27am
♈	10/25	6:47pm
♉	10/28	6:59am
♊	10/30	7:59pm
♋	11/2	8:31am
♌	11/4	7:04pm
♍	11/7	2:18am
♎	11/9	5:52am
♏	11/11	6:31am
♐	11/13	5:52am
♑	11/15	5:53am
♒	11/17	8:25am
♓	11/19	2:42pm
♈	11/22	12:42am
♉	11/24	1:07pm
♊	11/27	2:08am
♋	11/29	2:23pm
♌	12/2	12:59am
♍	12/4	9:14am
♎	12/6	2:33pm
♏	12/8	4:56pm
♐	12/10	5:13pm
♑	12/12	4:59pm
♒	12/14	6:15pm
♓	12/16	10:50pm
♈	12/19	7:37am
♉	12/21	7:41pm
♊	12/24	8:45am
♋	12/26	8:44pm
♌	12/29	6:44am
♍	12/31	2:43pm
	1986	
♎	1/2	8:45pm
♏	1/5	12:44am
♐	1/7	2:47am
♑	1/9	3:42am

♒	1/11	5:01am
♓	1/13	8:39am
♈	1/15	4:03pm
♉	1/18	3:14am
♊	1/20	4:12pm
♋	1/23	4:14am
♌	1/25	1:47pm
♍	1/27	8:51pm
♎	1/30	2:10am
♏	2/1	6:19am
♐	2/3	9:31am
♑	2/5	12:01pm
♒	2/7	2:35pm
♓	2/9	6:32pm
♈	2/12	1:21am
♉	2/14	11:38am
♊	2/17	12:17am
♋	2/19	12:39pm
♌	2/21	10:25pm
♍	2/24	4:58am
♎	2/26	9:07am
♏	2/28	12:06pm
♐	3/2	2:51pm
♑	3/4	5:56pm
♒	3/6	9:42pm
♓	3/9	2:48am
♈	3/11	10:03am
♉	3/13	8:04pm
♊	3/16	8:23am
♋	3/18	9:04pm
♌	3/21	7:38am
♍	3/23	2:39pm
♎	3/25	6:22pm
♏	3/27	8:05pm
♐	3/29	9:20pm
♑	3/31	11:25pm
♒	4/3	3:11am
♓	4/5	9:03am
♈	4/7	5:12pm
♉	4/10	3:36am
♊	4/12	3:51pm
♋	4/15	4:42am
♌	4/17	4:10pm
♍	4/20	12:24am
♎	4/22	4:50am
♏	4/24	6:15am
♐	4/26	6:16am
♑	4/28	6:41am
♒	4/30	9:06am
♓	5/2	2:30pm
♈	5/4	11:01pm
♉	5/7	9:59am
♊	5/9	10:26pm
♋	5/12	11:18am
♌	5/14	11:15pm
♍	5/17	8:45am
♎	5/19	2:41pm
♏	5/21	5:02pm
♐	5/23	4:57pm
♑	5/25	4:15pm
♒	5/27	5:00pm
♓	5/29	8:54pm

♈	6/1	4:43am
♉	6/3	3:45pm
♊	6/6	4:26am
♋	6/8	5:16pm
♌	6/11	5:11am
♍	6/13	3:18pm
♎	6/15	10:38pm
♏	6/18	2:36am
♐	6/20	3:36am
♑	6/22	3:00am
♒	6/24	2:50am
♓	6/26	5:13am
♈	6/28	11:35am
♉	6/30	9:54pm
♊	7/3	10:32am
♋	7/5	11:19pm
♌	7/8	10:56am
♍	7/10	8:50pm
♎	7/13	4:40am
♏	7/15	9:58am
♐	7/17	12:34pm
♑	7/19	1:10pm
♒	7/21	1:17pm
♓	7/23	2:59pm
♈	7/25	8:02pm
♉	7/28	5:11am
♊	7/30	5:19pm
♋	8/2	6:04am
♌	8/4	5:26pm
♍	8/7	2:44am
♎	8/9	10:05am
♏	8/11	3:36pm
♐	8/13	7:17pm
♑	8/15	9:22pm
♒	8/17	10:44pm
♓	8/20	12:52am
♈	8/22	5:27am
♉	8/24	1:36pm
♊	8/27	1:00am
♋	8/29	1:40pm
♌	9/1	1:08am
♍	9/3	10:06am
♎	9/5	4:33pm
♏	9/7	9:12pm
♐	9/10	12:40am
♑	9/12	3:28am
♒	9/14	6:07am
♓	9/16	9:27am
♈	9/18	2:33pm
♉	9/20	10:25pm
♊	9/23	9:13am
♋	9/25	9:44pm
♌	9/28	9:39am
♍	9/30	6:57pm
♎	10/3	1:03am
♏	10/5	4:35am
♐	10/7	6:48am
♑	10/9	8:52am
♒	10/11	11:45am
♓	10/13	4:03pm
♈	10/15	10:13pm
♉	10/18	6:35am

♊	10/20	5:15pm
♋	10/23	5:37am
♌	10/25	6:02pm
♍	10/28	4:20am
♎	10/30	11:04am
♏	11/1	2:19pm
♐	11/3	3:19pm
♑	11/5	3:49pm
♒	11/7	5:29pm
♓	11/9	9:30pm
♈	11/12	4:14am
♉	11/14	1:24pm
♊	11/17	12:26am
♋	11/19	12:46pm
♌	11/22	1:25am
♍	11/24	12:46pm
♎	11/26	8:59pm
♏	11/29	1:13am
♐	12/1	2:08am
♑	12/3	1:28am
♒	12/5	1:23am
♓	12/7	3:48am
♈	12/9	9:49am
♉	12/11	7:10pm
♊	12/14	6:41am
♋	12/16	7:09pm
♌	12/19	7:44am
♍	12/21	7:30pm
♎	12/24	5:05am
♏	12/26	11:06am
♐	12/28	1:19pm
♑	12/30	12:54pm
	1987	
♒	1/1	11:54am
♓	1/3	12:36pm
♈	1/5	4:51pm
♉	1/8	1:13am
♊	1/10	12:39pm
♋	1/13	1:18am
♌	1/15	1:45pm
♍	1/18	1:15am
♎	1/20	11:09am
♏	1/22	6:30pm
♐	1/24	10:35pm
♑	1/26	11:42pm
♒	1/28	11:17pm
♓	1/30	11:24pm
♈	2/2	2:09am
♉	2/4	8:53am
♊	2/6	7:23pm
♋	2/9	7:55am
♌	2/11	8:21pm
♍	2/14	7:26am
♎	2/16	4:44pm
♏	2/19	12:04am
♐	2/21	5:09am
♑	2/23	7:57am
♒	2/25	9:08am
♓	2/27	10:07am
♈	3/1	12:37pm
♉	3/3	6:11pm
♊	3/6	3:26am

♋	3/8	3:24pm
♌	3/11	3:54am
♍	3/13	2:55pm
♎	3/15	11:34pm
♏	3/18	5:57am
♐	3/20	10:32am
♑	3/22	1:48pm
♒	3/24	4:18pm
♓	3/26	6:46pm
♈	3/28	10:12pm
♉	3/31	3:46am
♊	4/2	12:16pm
♋	4/4	11:33pm
♌	4/7	12:04pm
♍	4/9	11:28pm
♎	4/12	8:06am
♏	4/14	1:41pm
♐	4/16	5:01pm
♑	4/18	7:21pm
♒	4/20	9:45pm
♓	4/23	1:02am
♈	4/25	5:41am
♉	4/27	12:06pm
♊	4/29	8:43pm
♋	5/2	7:39am
♌	5/4	8:06pm
♍	5/7	8:07am
♎	5/9	5:29pm
♏	5/11	11:09pm
♐	5/14	1:41am
♑	5/16	2:37am
♒	5/18	3:42am
♓	5/20	6:24am
♈	5/22	11:23am
♉	5/24	6:39pm
♊	5/27	3:55am
♋	5/29	2:59pm
♌	6/1	3:25am
♍	6/3	3:56pm
♎	6/6	2:24am
♏	6/8	9:06am
♐	6/10	11:53am
♑	6/12	12:05pm
♒	6/14	11:45am
♓	6/16	12:54pm
♈	6/18	4:56pm
♉	6/21	12:09am
♊	6/23	9:54am
♋	6/25	9:22pm
♌	6/28	9:52am
♍	6/30	10:34pm
♎	7/3	9:55am
♏	7/5	6:03pm
♐	7/7	10:05pm
♑	7/9	10:43pm
♒	7/11	9:49pm
♓	7/13	9:36pm
♈	7/16	12:00am
♉	7/18	6:04am
♊	7/20	3:33pm
♋	7/23	3:13am
♌	7/25	3:50pm

Moon Sign Changes 1900-2005

♍	7/28	4:26am
♎	7/30	3:59pm
♏	8/2	1:09am
♐	8/4	6:47am
♑	8/6	8:51am
♒	8/8	8:37am
♓	8/10	8:01am
♈	8/12	9:09am
♉	8/14	1:38pm
♊	8/16	9:59pm
♋	8/19	9:19am
♌	8/21	9:58pm
♍	8/24	10:23am
♎	8/26	9:35pm
♏	8/29	6:49am
♐	8/31	1:24pm
♑	9/2	5:04pm
♒	9/4	6:22pm
♓	9/6	6:37pm
♈	9/8	7:34pm
♉	9/10	10:57pm
♊	9/13	5:55am
♋	9/15	4:22pm
♌	9/18	4:50am
♍	9/20	5:13pm
♎	9/23	3:58am
♏	9/25	12:30pm
♐	9/27	6:49pm
♑	9/29	11:08pm
♒	10/2	1:51am
♓	10/4	3:39am
♈	10/6	5:35am
♉	10/8	8:57am
♊	10/10	3:03pm
♋	10/13	12:31am
♌	10/15	12:34pm
♍	10/18	1:06am
♎	10/20	11:50am
♏	10/22	7:41pm
♐	10/25	12:57am
♑	10/27	4:33am
♒	10/29	7:27am
♓	10/31	10:19am
♈	11/2	1:40pm
♉	11/4	6:02pm
♊	11/7	12:16am
♋	11/9	9:10am
♌	11/11	8:45pm
♍	11/14	9:29am
♎	11/16	8:48pm
♏	11/19	4:47am
♐	11/21	9:16am
♑	11/23	11:32am
♒	11/25	1:13pm
♓	11/27	3:40pm
♈	11/29	7:36pm
♉	12/2	1:06am
♊	12/4	8:13am
♋	12/6	5:20pm
♌	12/9	4:40am
♍	12/11	5:30pm
♎	12/14	5:40am

♏	12/16	2:41pm
♐	12/18	7:33pm
♑	12/20	9:07pm
♒	12/22	9:20pm
♓	12/24	10:10pm
♈	12/27	1:05am
♉	12/29	6:37am
♊	12/31	2:29pm
	1988	
♋	1/3	12:17am
♌	1/5	11:47am
♍	1/8	12:35am
♎	1/10	1:17pm
♏	1/12	11:39pm
♐	1/15	5:58am
♑	1/17	8:15am
♒	1/19	8:02am
♓	1/21	7:27am
♈	1/23	8:31am
♉	1/25	12:36pm
♊	1/27	8:02pm
♋	1/30	6:11am
♌	2/1	6:06pm
♍	2/4	6:54am
♎	2/6	7:36pm
♏	2/9	6:42am
♐	2/11	2:36pm
♑	2/13	6:36pm
♒	2/15	7:25pm
♓	2/17	6:44pm
♈	2/19	6:35pm
♉	2/21	8:50pm
♊	2/24	2:42am
♋	2/26	12:12pm
♌	2/29	12:12am
♍	3/2	1:06pm
♎	3/5	1:32am
♏	3/7	12:27pm
♐	3/9	8:59pm
♑	3/12	2:31am
♒	3/14	5:08am
♓	3/16	5:42am
♈	3/18	5:45am
♉	3/20	7:05am
♊	3/22	11:21am
♋	3/24	7:27pm
♌	3/27	6:54am
♍	3/29	7:49pm
♎	4/1	8:05am
♏	4/3	6:26pm
♐	4/6	2:29am
♑	4/8	8:19am
♒	4/10	12:10pm
♓	4/12	2:24pm
♈	4/14	3:47pm
♉	4/16	5:31pm
♊	4/18	9:10pm
♋	4/21	4:04am
♌	4/23	2:34pm
♍	4/26	3:16am
♎	4/28	3:37pm
♏	5/1	1:39am

♐	5/3	8:52am
♑	5/5	1:54pm
♒	5/7	5:37pm
♓	5/9	8:39pm
♈	5/11	11:23pm
♉	5/14	2:22am
♊	5/16	6:31am
♋	5/18	1:05pm
♌	5/20	10:51pm
♍	5/23	11:12am
♎	5/25	11:49pm
♏	5/28	10:06am
♐	5/30	4:57pm
♑	6/1	8:58pm
♒	6/3	11:34pm
♓	6/6	2:00am
♈	6/8	5:04am
♉	6/10	9:02am
♊	6/12	2:14pm
♋	6/14	9:19pm
♌	6/17	6:57am
♍	6/19	7:03pm
♎	6/22	7:57am
♏	6/24	6:58pm
♐	6/27	2:18am
♑	6/29	6:00am
♒	7/1	7:30am
♓	7/3	8:33am
♈	7/5	10:37am
♉	7/7	2:27pm
♊	7/9	8:16pm
♋	7/12	4:08am
♌	7/14	2:11pm
♍	7/17	2:17am
♎	7/19	3:22pm
♏	7/22	3:13am
♐	7/24	11:42am
♑	7/26	4:07pm
♒	7/28	5:25pm
♓	7/30	5:23pm
♈	8/1	5:53pm
♉	8/3	8:24pm
♊	8/6	1:43am
♋	8/8	9:52am
♌	8/10	8:26pm
♍	8/13	8:46am
♎	8/15	9:52pm
♏	8/18	10:12am
♐	8/20	7:55pm
♑	8/23	1:49am
♒	8/25	4:05am
♓	8/27	4:01am
♈	8/29	3:29am
♉	8/31	4:22am
♊	9/2	8:11am
♋	9/4	3:37pm
♌	9/7	2:14am
♍	9/9	2:48pm
♎	9/12	3:51am
♏	9/14	4:07pm
♐	9/17	2:25am
♑	9/19	9:45am

♒	9/21	1:43pm
♓	9/23	2:51pm
♈	9/25	2:29pm
♉	9/27	2:29pm
♊	9/29	4:43pm
♋	10/1	10:39pm
♌	10/4	8:31am
♍	10/6	9:01pm
♎	10/9	10:03am
♏	10/11	9:58pm
♐	10/14	7:58am
♑	10/16	3:44pm
♒	10/18	9:05pm
♓	10/20	11:58pm
♈	10/23	12:59am
♉	10/25	1:22am
♊	10/27	2:55am
♋	10/29	7:28am
♌	10/31	4:03pm
♍	11/3	4:02am
♎	11/5	5:04pm
♏	11/8	4:46am
♐	11/10	2:06pm
♑	11/12	9:12pm
♒	11/15	2:36am
♓	11/17	6:34am
♈	11/19	9:12am
♉	11/21	11:02am
♊	11/23	1:12pm
♋	11/25	5:20pm
♌	11/28	12:52am
♍	11/30	12:00pm
♎	12/3	12:56am
♏	12/5	12:51pm
♐	12/7	9:55pm
♑	12/10	4:07am
♒	12/12	8:25am
♓	12/14	11:53am
♈	12/16	3:03pm
♉	12/18	6:11pm
♊	12/20	9:43pm
♋	12/23	2:35am
♌	12/25	9:57am
♍	12/27	8:27pm
♎	12/30	9:09am
	1989	
♏	1/1	9:34pm
♐	1/4	7:12am
♑	1/6	1:14pm
♒	1/8	4:31pm
♓	1/10	6:31pm
♈	1/12	8:36pm
♉	1/14	11:36pm
♊	1/17	3:57am
♋	1/19	9:57am
♌	1/21	6:02pm
♍	1/24	4:32am
♎	1/26	5:01pm
♏	1/29	5:49am
♐	1/31	4:30pm
♑	2/2	11:30pm
♒	2/5	2:51am

♓	2/7	3:52am
♈	2/9	4:18am
♉	2/11	5:45am
♊	2/13	9:22am
♋	2/15	3:40pm
♌	2/18	12:33am
♍	2/20	11:34am
♎	2/23	12:05am
♏	2/25	12:57pm
♐	2/28	12:29am
♑	3/2	8:58am
♒	3/4	1:36pm
♓	3/6	2:59pm
♈	3/8	2:36pm
♉	3/10	2:25pm
♊	3/12	4:16pm
♋	3/14	9:27pm
♌	3/17	6:13am
♍	3/19	5:39pm
♎	3/22	6:24am
♏	3/24	7:10pm
♐	3/27	6:54am
♑	3/29	4:25pm
♒	3/31	10:45pm
♓	4/3	1:37am
♈	4/5	1:51am
♉	4/7	1:07am
♊	4/9	1:31am
♋	4/11	4:58am
♌	4/13	12:31pm
♍	4/15	11:39pm
♎	4/18	12:31pm
♏	4/21	1:13am
♐	4/23	12:38pm
♑	4/25	10:15pm
♒	4/28	5:33am
♓	4/30	10:03am
♈	5/2	11:50am
♉	5/4	11:55am
♊	5/6	12:03pm
♋	5/8	2:19pm
♌	5/10	8:23pm
♍	5/13	6:30am
♎	5/15	7:07pm
♏	5/18	7:48am
♐	5/20	6:52pm
♑	5/23	3:54am
♒	5/25	11:01am
♓	5/27	4:13pm
♈	5/29	7:25pm
♉	5/31	8:59pm
♊	6/2	10:02pm
♋	6/5	12:17am
♌	6/7	5:28am
♍	6/9	2:29pm
♎	6/12	2:31am
♏	6/14	3:11pm
♐	6/17	2:12am
♑	6/19	10:41am
♒	6/21	4:57pm
♓	6/23	9:36pm
♈	6/26	1:06am

♉	6/28	3:45am
♊	6/30	6:08am
♋	7/2	9:19am
♌	7/4	2:37pm
♍	7/6	11:04pm
♎	7/9	10:30am
♏	7/11	11:09pm
♐	7/14	10:31am
♑	7/16	7:01pm
♒	7/19	12:35am
♓	7/21	4:07am
♈	7/23	6:41am
♉	7/25	9:10am
♊	7/27	12:15pm
♋	7/29	4:32pm
♌	7/31	10:41pm
♍	8/3	7:19am
♎	8/5	6:28pm
♏	8/8	7:05am
♐	8/10	7:02pm
♑	8/13	4:16am
♒	8/15	9:59am
♓	8/17	12:45pm
♈	8/19	1:59pm
♉	8/21	3:10pm
♊	8/23	5:39pm
♋	8/25	10:13pm
♌	8/28	5:12am
♍	8/30	2:29pm
♎	9/2	1:47am
♏	9/4	2:23pm
♐	9/7	2:51am
♑	9/9	1:13pm
♒	9/11	8:02pm
♓	9/13	11:08pm
♈	9/15	11:38pm
♉	9/17	11:22pm
♊	9/20	12:16am
♋	9/22	3:50am
♌	9/24	10:44am
♍	9/26	8:32pm
♎	9/29	8:15am
♏	10/1	8:53pm
♐	10/4	9:29am
♑	10/6	8:45pm
♒	10/9	5:06am
♓	10/11	9:37am
♈	10/13	10:41am
♉	10/15	9:52am
♊	10/17	9:19am
♋	10/19	11:09am
♌	10/21	4:47pm
♍	10/24	2:15am
♎	10/26	2:11pm
♏	10/29	2:56am
♐	10/31	3:23pm
♑	11/3	2:46am
♒	11/5	12:09pm
♓	11/7	6:25pm
♈	11/9	9:08pm
♉	11/11	9:09pm
♊	11/13	8:19pm

Moon Sign Changes 1900-2005

Sign	Date	Time
♋	11/15	8:51pm
♌	11/18	12:45am
♍	11/20	8:54am
♎	11/22	8:25pm
♏	11/25	9:13am
♐	11/27	9:30pm
♑	11/30	8:26am
♒	12/2	5:42pm
♓	12/5	12:48am
♈	12/7	5:11am
♉	12/9	6:59am
♊	12/11	7:15am
♋	12/13	7:49am
♌	12/15	10:41am
♍	12/17	5:19pm
♎	12/20	3:45am
♏	12/22	4:18pm
♐	12/25	4:37am
♑	12/27	3:10pm
♒	12/29	11:38pm
1990		
♓	1/1	6:10am
♈	1/3	10:56am
♉	1/5	2:04pm
♊	1/7	4:02pm
♋	1/9	5:52pm
♌	1/11	9:02pm
♍	1/14	2:57am
♎	1/16	12:18pm
♏	1/19	12:16am
♐	1/21	12:44pm
♑	1/23	11:27pm
♒	1/26	7:25am
♓	1/28	12:51pm
♈	1/30	4:34pm
♉	2/1	7:27pm
♊	2/3	10:12pm
♋	2/6	1:27am
♌	2/8	5:51am
♍	2/10	12:13pm
♎	2/12	9:09pm
♏	2/15	8:34am
♐	2/17	9:07pm
♑	2/20	8:30am
♒	2/22	4:52pm
♓	2/24	9:49pm
♈	2/27	12:16am
♉	3/1	1:43am
♊	3/3	3:37am
♋	3/5	7:02am
♌	3/7	12:24pm
♍	3/9	7:47pm
♎	3/12	5:09am
♏	3/14	4:25pm
♐	3/17	4:56am
♑	3/19	5:01pm
♒	3/22	2:31am
♓	3/24	8:08am
♈	3/26	10:15am
♉	3/28	10:26am
♊	3/30	10:42am
♋	4/1	12:50pm
♌	4/3	5:50pm
♍	4/6	1:42am
♎	4/8	11:44am
♏	4/10	11:18pm
♐	4/13	11:48am
♑	4/16	12:15am
♒	4/18	10:53am
♓	4/20	5:57pm
♈	4/22	8:58pm
♉	4/24	9:03pm
♊	4/26	8:12pm
♋	4/28	8:39pm
♌	5/1	12:08am
♍	5/3	7:18am
♎	5/5	5:28pm
♏	5/8	5:22am
♐	5/10	5:56pm
♑	5/13	6:21am
♒	5/15	5:30pm
♓	5/18	1:54am
♈	5/20	6:31am
♉	5/22	7:42am
♊	5/24	7:00am
♋	5/26	6:34am
♌	5/28	8:29am
♍	5/30	2:08pm
♎	6/1	11:31pm
♏	6/4	11:21am
♐	6/6	11:59pm
♑	6/9	12:12pm
♒	6/11	11:09pm
♓	6/14	8:00am
♈	6/16	1:55pm
♉	6/18	4:43pm
♊	6/20	5:14pm
♋	6/22	5:10pm
♌	6/24	6:25pm
♍	6/26	10:42pm
♎	6/29	6:47am
♏	7/1	6:01pm
♐	7/4	6:35am
♑	7/6	6:39pm
♒	7/9	5:07am
♓	7/11	1:29pm
♈	7/13	7:36pm
♉	7/15	11:29pm
♊	7/18	1:32am
♋	7/20	2:44am
♌	7/22	4:29am
♍	7/24	8:17am
♎	7/26	3:19pm
♏	7/29	1:39am
♐	7/31	2:00pm
♑	8/3	2:08am
♒	8/5	12:19pm
♓	8/7	7:54pm
♈	8/10	1:13am
♉	8/12	4:55am
♊	8/14	7:41am
♋	8/16	10:12am
♌	8/18	1:11pm
♍	8/20	5:33pm
♎	8/23	12:17am
♏	8/25	9:56am
♐	8/27	9:57pm
♑	8/30	10:23am
♒	9/1	8:51pm
♓	9/4	4:06am
♈	9/6	8:23am
♉	9/8	10:55am
♊	9/10	1:05pm
♋	9/12	3:53pm
♌	9/14	7:52pm
♍	9/17	1:19am
♎	9/19	8:34am
♏	9/21	6:06pm
♐	9/24	5:52am
♑	9/26	6:36pm
♒	9/29	5:54am
♓	10/1	1:42pm
♈	10/3	5:42pm
♉	10/5	7:06pm
♊	10/7	7:47pm
♋	10/9	9:29pm
♌	10/12	1:16am
♍	10/14	7:21am
♎	10/16	3:26pm
♏	10/19	1:24am
♐	10/21	1:09pm
♑	10/24	2:03am
♒	10/26	2:14pm
♓	10/28	11:22pm
♈	10/31	4:14am
♉	11/2	5:31am
♊	11/4	5:06am
♋	11/6	5:07am
♌	11/8	7:24am
♍	11/10	12:48pm
♎	11/12	9:08pm
♏	11/15	7:39am
♐	11/17	7:39pm
♑	11/20	8:32am
♒	11/22	9:07pm
♓	11/25	7:32am
♈	11/27	2:06pm
♉	11/29	4:37pm
♊	12/1	4:22pm
♋	12/3	3:27pm
♌	12/5	4:00pm
♍	12/7	7:39pm
♎	12/10	3:00am
♏	12/12	1:28pm
♐	12/15	1:44am
♑	12/17	2:35pm
♒	12/20	2:59am
♓	12/22	1:48pm
♈	12/24	9:45pm
♉	12/27	2:09am
♊	12/29	3:26am
♋	12/31	3:02am
1991		
♌	1/2	2:54am
♍	1/4	4:57am
♎	1/6	10:33am
♏	1/8	7:59pm
♐	1/11	8:06am
♑	1/13	9:00pm
♒	1/16	9:04am
♓	1/18	7:23pm
♈	1/21	3:28am
♉	1/23	9:01am
♊	1/25	12:06pm
♋	1/27	1:23pm
♌	1/29	2:03pm
♍	1/31	3:44pm
♎	2/2	8:02pm
♏	2/5	4:01am
♐	2/7	3:23pm
♑	2/10	4:16am
♒	2/12	4:16pm
♓	2/15	1:59am
♈	2/17	9:11am
♉	2/19	2:24pm
♊	2/21	6:10pm
♋	2/23	8:56pm
♌	2/25	11:13pm
♍	2/28	1:50am
♎	3/2	6:03am
♏	3/4	1:08pm
♐	3/6	11:35pm
♑	3/9	12:14pm
♒	3/12	12:31am
♓	3/14	10:11am
♈	3/16	4:37pm
♉	3/18	8:40pm
♊	3/20	11:37pm
♋	3/23	2:27am
♌	3/25	5:43am
♍	3/27	9:41am
♎	3/29	2:49pm
♏	3/31	10:01pm
♐	4/3	7:59am
♑	4/5	8:20pm
♒	4/8	9:00am
♓	4/10	7:18pm
♈	4/13	1:49am
♉	4/15	5:06am
♊	4/17	6:41am
♋	4/19	8:17am
♌	4/21	11:04am
♍	4/23	3:29pm
♎	4/25	9:36pm
♏	4/28	5:34am
♐	4/30	3:42pm
♑	5/3	3:55am
♒	5/5	4:51pm
♓	5/8	4:04am
♈	5/10	11:34am
♉	5/12	3:07pm
♊	5/14	4:02pm
♋	5/16	4:14pm
♌	5/18	5:30pm
♍	5/20	9:00pm
♎	5/23	3:08am
♏	5/25	11:41am
♐	5/27	10:21pm
♑	5/30	10:40am
♒	6/1	11:42pm
♓	6/4	11:36am
♈	6/6	8:25pm
♉	6/9	1:13am
♊	6/11	2:36am
♋	6/13	2:16am
♌	6/15	2:10am
♍	6/17	4:03am
♎	6/19	9:01am
♏	6/21	5:18pm
♐	6/24	4:16am
♑	6/26	4:49pm
♒	6/29	5:47am
♓	7/1	5:51pm
♈	7/4	3:33am
♉	7/6	9:52am
♊	7/8	12:42pm
♋	7/10	1:03pm
♌	7/12	12:35pm
♍	7/14	1:12pm
♎	7/16	4:34pm
♏	7/18	11:41pm
♐	7/21	10:16am
♑	7/23	10:55pm
♒	7/26	11:49am
♓	7/28	11:35pm
♈	7/31	9:20am
♉	8/2	4:32pm
♊	8/4	8:54pm
♋	8/6	10:47pm
♌	8/8	11:09pm
♍	8/10	11:35pm
♎	8/13	1:52am
♏	8/15	7:34am
♐	8/17	5:11pm
♑	8/20	5:34am
♒	8/22	6:27pm
♓	8/25	5:51am
♈	8/27	3:01pm
♉	8/29	10:00pm
♊	9/1	3:02am
♋	9/3	6:19am
♌	9/5	8:13am
♍	9/7	9:35am
♎	9/9	11:52am
♏	9/11	4:42pm
♐	9/14	1:14am
♑	9/16	1:04pm
♒	9/19	1:58am
♓	9/21	1:20pm
♈	9/23	9:56pm
♉	9/26	3:59am
♊	9/28	8:25am
♋	9/30	11:58am
♌	10/2	2:58pm
♍	10/4	5:45pm
♎	10/6	9:00pm
♏	10/9	2:00am
♐	10/11	9:58am
♑	10/13	9:10pm
♒	10/16	10:04am
♓	10/18	9:53pm
♈	10/21	6:33am
♉	10/23	11:55am
♊	10/25	3:09pm
♋	10/27	5:37pm
♌	10/29	8:20pm
♍	10/31	11:47pm
♎	11/3	4:13am
♏	11/5	10:09am
♐	11/7	6:21pm
♑	11/10	5:16am
♒	11/12	6:06pm
♓	11/15	6:33am
♈	11/17	4:08pm
♉	11/19	9:49pm
♊	11/22	12:22am
♋	11/24	1:25am
♌	11/26	2:37am
♍	11/28	5:12am
♎	11/30	9:47am
♏	12/2	4:33pm
♐	12/5	1:32am
♑	12/7	12:41pm
♒	12/10	1:27am
♓	12/12	2:19pm
♈	12/15	1:06am
♉	12/17	8:10am
♊	12/19	11:21am
♋	12/21	11:54am
♌	12/23	11:38am
♍	12/25	12:24pm
♎	12/27	3:37pm
♏	12/29	10:03pm
1992		
♐	1/1	7:30am
♑	1/3	7:09pm
♒	1/6	7:59am
♓	1/8	8:52pm
♈	1/11	8:22am
♉	1/13	5:00pm
♊	1/15	9:55pm
♋	1/17	11:26pm
♌	1/19	10:57pm
♍	1/21	10:22pm
♎	1/23	11:42pm
♏	1/26	4:32am
♐	1/28	1:20pm
♑	1/31	1:07am
♒	2/2	2:09pm
♓	2/5	2:51am
♈	2/7	2:15pm
♉	2/9	11:36pm
♊	2/12	6:08am
♋	2/14	9:31am
♌	2/16	10:15am
♍	2/18	9:47am
♎	2/20	10:05am
♏	2/22	1:11pm
♐	2/24	8:26pm
♑	2/27	7:33am
♒	2/29	8:34pm
♓	3/3	9:11am

Moon Sign Changes 1900-2005

♈	3/5	8:07pm
♉	3/8	5:05am
♊	3/10	12:03pm
♋	3/12	4:50pm
♌	3/14	7:20pm
♍	3/16	8:13pm
♎	3/18	8:55pm
♏	3/20	11:20pm
♐	3/23	5:13am
♑	3/25	3:08pm
♒	3/28	3:44am
♓	3/30	4:23pm
♈	4/2	3:04am
♉	4/4	11:18am
♊	4/6	5:33pm
♋	4/8	10:18pm
♌	4/11	1:46am
♍	4/13	4:09am
♎	4/15	6:10am
♏	4/17	9:10am
♐	4/19	2:40pm
♑	4/21	11:40pm
♒	4/24	11:38am
♓	4/27	12:20am
♈	4/29	11:13am
♉	5/1	7:09pm
♊	5/4	12:28am
♋	5/6	4:09am
♌	5/8	7:07am
♍	5/10	9:56am
♎	5/12	1:05pm
♏	5/14	5:15pm
♐	5/16	11:22pm
♑	5/19	8:13am
♒	5/21	7:43pm
♓	5/24	8:25am
♈	5/26	7:52pm
♉	5/29	4:16am
♊	5/31	9:19am
♋	6/2	11:58am
♌	6/4	1:35pm
♍	6/6	3:28pm
♎	6/8	6:33pm
♏	6/10	11:27pm
♐	6/13	6:29am
♑	6/15	3:50pm
♒	6/18	3:19am
♓	6/20	4:00pm
♈	6/23	4:03am
♉	6/25	1:28pm
♊	6/27	7:14pm
♋	6/29	9:42pm
♌	7/1	10:15pm
♍	7/3	10:37pm
♎	7/6	12:27am
♏	7/8	4:53am
♐	7/10	12:17pm
♑	7/12	10:16pm
♒	7/15	10:03am
♓	7/17	10:44pm
♈	7/20	11:07am
♉	7/22	9:36pm
♊	7/25	4:44am
♋	7/27	8:08am
♌	7/29	8:39am
♍	7/31	8:01am
♎	8/2	8:17am
♏	8/4	11:16am
♐	8/6	5:57pm
♑	8/9	4:00am
♒	8/11	4:06pm
♓	8/14	4:51am
♈	8/16	5:11pm
♉	8/19	4:10am
♊	8/21	12:36pm
♋	8/23	5:36pm
♌	8/25	7:15pm
♍	8/27	6:46pm
♎	8/29	6:11pm
♏	8/31	7:38pm
♐	9/3	12:50am
♑	9/5	10:06am
♒	9/7	10:08pm
♓	9/10	10:56am
♈	9/12	11:02pm
♉	9/15	9:47am
♊	9/17	6:40pm
♋	9/20	12:59am
♌	9/22	4:19am
♍	9/24	5:08am
♎	9/26	4:55am
♏	9/28	5:44am
♐	9/30	9:33am
♑	10/2	5:29pm
♒	10/5	4:53am
♓	10/7	5:38pm
♈	10/10	5:36am
♉	10/12	3:48pm
♊	10/15	12:08am
♋	10/17	6:36am
♌	10/19	11:01am
♍	10/21	1:27pm
♎	10/23	2:39pm
♏	10/25	4:04pm
♐	10/27	7:29pm
♑	10/30	2:18am
♒	11/1	12:43pm
♓	11/4	1:13am
♈	11/6	1:19pm
♉	11/8	11:19pm
♊	11/11	6:49am
♋	11/13	12:19pm
♌	11/15	4:23pm
♍	11/17	7:28pm
♎	11/19	10:03pm
♏	11/22	12:52am
♐	11/24	5:01am
♑	11/26	11:38am
♒	11/28	9:19pm
♓	12/1	9:23am
♈	12/3	9:49pm
♉	12/6	8:16am
♊	12/8	3:37pm
♋	12/10	8:05pm
♌	12/12	10:47pm
♍	12/15	12:56am
♎	12/17	3:33am
♏	12/19	7:20am
♐	12/21	12:42pm
♑	12/23	8:04pm
♒	12/26	5:43am
♓	12/28	5:28pm
♈	12/31	6:07am
	1993	
♉	1/2	5:30pm
♊	1/5	1:42am
♋	1/7	6:10am
♌	1/9	7:49am
♍	1/11	8:20am
♎	1/13	9:30am
♏	1/15	12:42pm
♐	1/17	6:30pm
♑	1/20	2:46am
♒	1/22	1:00pm
♓	1/25	12:47am
♈	1/27	1:28pm
♉	1/30	1:37am
♊	2/1	11:14am
♋	2/3	4:56pm
♌	2/5	6:51pm
♍	2/7	6:29pm
♎	2/9	5:58pm
♏	2/11	7:23pm
♐	2/14	12:08am
♑	2/16	8:20am
♒	2/18	7:05pm
♓	2/21	7:12am
♈	2/23	7:50pm
♉	2/26	8:11am
♊	2/28	6:52pm
♋	3/3	2:16am
♌	3/5	5:40am
♍	3/7	5:52am
♎	3/9	4:46am
♏	3/11	4:40am
♐	3/13	7:33am
♑	3/15	2:28pm
♒	3/18	12:52am
♓	3/20	1:11pm
♈	3/23	1:51am
♉	3/25	1:59pm
♊	3/28	12:48am
♋	3/30	9:14am
♌	4/1	2:21pm
♍	4/3	4:10pm
♎	4/5	3:54pm
♏	4/7	3:32pm
♐	4/9	5:10pm
♑	4/11	10:24pm
♒	4/14	7:36am
♓	4/16	7:32pm
♈	4/19	8:14am
♉	4/21	8:08pm
♊	4/24	6:27am
♋	4/26	2:45pm
♌	4/28	8:39pm
♍	4/30	11:59pm
♎	5/3	1:20am
♏	5/5	1:57am
♐	5/7	3:34am
♑	5/9	7:51am
♒	5/11	3:44pm
♓	5/14	2:50am
♈	5/16	3:24pm
♉	5/19	3:16am
♊	5/21	1:07pm
♋	5/23	8:38pm
♌	5/26	2:03am
♍	5/28	5:46am
♎	5/30	8:18am
♏	6/1	10:22am
♐	6/3	1:01pm
♑	6/5	5:26pm
♒	6/8	12:39am
♓	6/10	10:57am
♈	6/12	11:14pm
♉	6/15	11:19am
♊	6/17	9:12pm
♋	6/20	4:05am
♌	6/22	8:26am
♍	6/24	11:18am
♎	6/26	1:45pm
♏	6/28	4:37pm
♐	6/30	8:28pm
♑	7/3	1:49am
♒	7/5	9:14am
♓	7/7	7:10pm
♈	7/10	7:11am
♉	7/12	7:37pm
♊	7/15	6:07am
♋	7/17	1:08pm
♌	7/19	4:47pm
♍	7/21	6:24pm
♎	7/23	7:39pm
♏	7/25	10:00pm
♐	7/28	2:13am
♑	7/30	8:27am
♒	8/1	4:36pm
♓	8/4	2:44am
♈	8/6	2:39pm
♉	8/9	3:22am
♊	8/11	2:47pm
♋	8/13	10:46pm
♌	8/16	2:43am
♍	8/18	3:41am
♎	8/20	3:35am
♏	8/22	4:27am
♐	8/24	7:45am
♑	8/26	1:58pm
♒	8/28	10:42pm
♓	8/31	9:18am
♈	9/2	9:21pm
♉	9/5	10:09am
♊	9/7	10:16pm
♋	9/10	7:37am
♌	9/12	12:51pm
♍	9/14	2:20pm
♎	9/16	1:44pm
♏	9/18	1:15pm
♐	9/20	2:53pm
♑	9/22	7:54pm
♒	9/25	4:19am
♓	9/27	3:13pm
♈	9/30	3:29am
♉	10/2	4:13pm
♊	10/5	4:27am
♋	10/7	2:42pm
♌	10/9	9:34pm
♍	10/12	12:36am
♎	10/14	12:47am
♏	10/16	12:01am
♐	10/18	12:23am
♑	10/20	3:42am
♒	10/22	10:49am
♓	10/24	9:17pm
♈	10/27	9:39am
♉	10/29	10:20pm
♊	11/1	10:13am
♋	11/3	8:25pm
♌	11/6	4:06am
♍	11/8	8:47am
♎	11/10	10:42am
♏	11/12	11:00am
♐	11/14	11:20am
♑	11/16	1:34pm
♒	11/18	7:08pm
♓	11/21	4:27am
♈	11/23	4:30pm
♉	11/26	5:14am
♊	11/28	4:48pm
♋	12/1	2:17am
♌	12/3	9:33am
♍	12/5	2:43pm
♎	12/7	6:03pm
♏	12/9	8:04pm
♐	12/11	9:39pm
♑	12/14	12:06am
♒	12/16	4:51am
♓	12/18	12:59pm
♈	12/21	12:19am
♉	12/23	1:05pm
♊	12/26	12:46am
♋	12/28	9:46am
♌	12/30	3:59pm
	1994	
♍	1/1	8:15pm
♎	1/3	11:31pm
♏	1/6	2:29am
♐	1/8	5:34am
♑	1/10	9:16am
♒	1/12	2:25pm
♓	1/14	10:04pm
♈	1/17	8:42am
♉	1/19	9:22pm
♊	1/22	9:34am
♋	1/24	6:55pm
♌	1/27	12:38am
♍	1/29	3:39am
♎	1/31	5:34am
♏	2/2	7:49am
♐	2/4	11:14am
♑	2/6	4:02pm
♒	2/8	10:16pm
♓	2/11	6:23am
♈	2/13	4:49pm
♉	2/16	5:20am
♊	2/18	6:05pm
♋	2/21	4:27am
♌	2/23	10:47am
♍	2/25	1:27pm
♎	2/27	2:06pm
♏	3/1	2:43pm
♐	3/3	4:54pm
♑	3/5	9:24pm
♒	3/8	4:15am
♓	3/10	1:09pm
♈	3/12	11:59pm
♉	3/15	12:27am
♊	3/18	1:29am
♋	3/20	12:54pm
♌	3/22	8:39pm
♍	3/25	12:14am
♎	3/27	12:46am
♏	3/29	12:15am
♐	3/31	12:41am
♑	4/2	3:38am
♒	4/4	9:45am
♓	4/6	6:51pm
♈	4/9	6:09am
♉	4/11	6:48pm
♊	4/14	7:48am
♋	4/16	7:41pm
♌	4/19	4:45am
♍	4/21	9:58am
♎	4/23	11:40am
♏	4/25	11:18am
♐	4/27	10:48am
♑	4/29	12:05pm
♒	5/1	4:34pm
♓	5/4	12:47am
♈	5/6	12:01pm
♉	5/9	12:50am
♊	5/11	1:43pm
♋	5/14	1:27am
♌	5/16	10:58am
♍	5/18	5:31pm
♎	5/20	8:54pm
♏	5/22	9:51pm
♐	5/24	9:43pm
♑	5/26	10:17pm
♒	5/29	1:19am
♓	5/31	8:03am
♈	6/2	6:31pm
♉	6/5	7:14am
♊	6/7	8:03pm
♋	6/10	7:22am
♌	6/12	4:29pm
♍	6/14	11:16pm
♎	6/17	3:48am
♏	6/19	6:20am
♐	6/21	7:32am
♑	6/23	8:37am

Moon Sign Changes 1900-2005

Sign	Date	Time
♒	6/25	11:10am
♓	6/27	4:44pm
♈	6/30	2:07am
♉	7/2	2:23pm
♊	7/5	3:12am
♋	7/7	2:17pm
♌	7/9	10:43pm
♍	7/12	4:48am
♎	7/14	9:15am
♏	7/16	12:35pm
♐	7/18	3:09pm
♑	7/20	5:30pm
♒	7/22	8:38pm
♓	7/25	1:56am
♈	7/27	10:31am
♉	7/29	10:13pm
♊	8/1	11:05am
♋	8/3	10:22pm
♌	8/6	6:31am
♍	8/8	11:42am
♎	8/10	3:07pm
♏	8/12	5:56pm
♐	8/14	8:53pm
♑	8/17	12:18am
♒	8/19	4:34am
♓	8/21	10:27am
♈	8/23	6:55pm
♉	8/26	6:13am
♊	8/28	7:07pm
♋	8/31	7:00am
♌	9/2	3:37pm
♍	9/4	8:33pm
♎	9/6	10:57pm
♏	9/9	12:26am
♐	9/11	2:25am
♑	9/13	5:44am
♒	9/15	10:42am
♓	9/17	5:31pm
♈	9/20	2:30am
♉	9/22	1:47pm
♊	9/25	2:41am
♋	9/27	3:12pm
♌	9/30	12:55am
♍	10/2	6:39am
♎	10/4	8:56am
♏	10/6	9:22am
♐	10/8	9:47am
♑	10/10	11:44am
♒	10/12	4:09pm
♓	10/14	11:18pm
♈	10/17	8:56am
♉	10/19	8:34pm
♊	10/22	9:28am
♋	10/24	10:15pm
♌	10/27	9:05am
♍	10/29	4:21pm
♎	10/31	7:46pm
♏	11/2	8:19pm
♐	11/4	7:46pm
♑	11/6	8:02pm
♒	11/8	10:48pm
♓	11/11	5:04am
♈	11/13	2:44pm
♉	11/16	2:44am
♊	11/18	3:41pm
♋	11/21	4:21am
♌	11/23	3:33pm
♍	11/26	12:09am
♎	11/28	5:22am
♏	11/30	7:21am
♐	12/2	7:13am
♑	12/4	6:42am
♒	12/6	7:52am
♓	12/8	12:24pm
♈	12/10	9:03pm
♉	12/13	8:56am
♊	12/15	10:00pm
♋	12/18	10:25am
♌	12/20	9:13pm
♍	12/23	6:01am
♎	12/25	12:27pm
♏	12/27	4:17pm
♐	12/29	5:45pm
♑	12/31	5:57pm
	1995	
♒	1/2	6:39pm
♓	1/4	9:49pm
♈	1/7	4:56am
♉	1/9	3:58pm
♊	1/12	4:57am
♋	1/14	5:20pm
♌	1/17	3:36am
♍	1/19	11:39am
♎	1/21	5:54pm
♏	1/23	10:32pm
♐	1/26	1:37am
♑	1/28	3:26am
♒	1/30	5:03am
♓	2/1	8:05am
♈	2/3	2:12pm
♉	2/6	12:08am
♊	2/8	12:44pm
♋	2/11	1:17am
♌	2/13	11:31am
♍	2/15	6:52pm
♎	2/18	12:00am
♏	2/20	3:55am
♐	2/22	7:13am
♑	2/24	10:11am
♒	2/26	1:14pm
♓	2/28	5:16pm
♈	3/2	11:30pm
♉	3/5	8:50am
♊	3/7	8:55pm
♋	3/10	9:40am
♌	3/12	8:28pm
♍	3/15	3:54am
♎	3/17	8:18am
♏	3/19	10:52am
♐	3/21	12:57pm
♑	3/23	3:31pm
♒	3/25	7:10pm
♓	3/28	12:18am
♈	3/30	7:26am
♉	4/1	4:59pm
♊	4/4	4:49am
♋	4/6	5:40pm
♌	4/9	5:15am
♍	4/11	1:39pm
♎	4/13	6:20pm
♏	4/15	8:13pm
♐	4/17	8:51pm
♑	4/19	9:54pm
♒	4/22	12:38am
♓	4/24	5:50am
♈	4/26	1:41pm
♉	4/28	11:53pm
♊	5/1	11:53am
♋	5/4	12:45am
♌	5/6	12:55pm
♍	5/8	10:33pm
♎	5/11	4:30am
♏	5/13	6:53am
♐	5/15	6:58am
♑	5/17	6:36am
♒	5/19	7:39am
♓	5/21	11:40am
♈	5/23	7:13pm
♉	5/26	5:46am
♊	5/28	6:07pm
♋	5/31	6:59am
♌	6/2	7:17pm
♍	6/5	5:46am
♎	6/7	1:13pm
♏	6/9	5:03pm
♐	6/11	5:50pm
♑	6/13	5:05pm
♒	6/15	4:52pm
♓	6/17	7:13pm
♈	6/20	1:29am
♉	6/22	11:35am
♊	6/25	12:02am
♋	6/27	12:56pm
♌	6/30	1:02am
♍	7/2	11:35am
♎	7/4	7:55pm
♏	7/7	1:19am
♐	7/9	3:37am
♑	7/11	3:43am
♒	7/13	3:21am
♓	7/15	4:37am
♈	7/17	9:23am
♉	7/19	6:20pm
♊	7/22	6:23am
♋	7/24	7:16pm
♌	7/27	7:07am
♍	7/29	5:12pm
♎	8/1	1:23am
♏	8/3	7:29am
♐	8/5	11:14am
♑	8/7	12:52pm
♒	8/9	1:28pm
♓	8/11	2:46pm
♈	8/13	6:41pm
♉	8/16	2:25am
♊	8/18	1:40pm
♋	8/21	2:24am
♌	8/23	2:13pm
♍	8/25	11:50pm
♎	8/28	7:15am
♏	8/30	12:51pm
♐	9/1	4:57pm
♑	9/3	7:45pm
♒	9/5	9:47pm
♓	9/8	12:08am
♈	9/10	4:14am
♉	9/12	11:21am
♊	9/14	9:48pm
♋	9/17	10:16am
♌	9/19	10:19pm
♍	9/22	8:01am
♎	9/24	2:50pm
♏	9/26	7:20pm
♐	9/28	10:30pm
♑	10/1	1:10am
♒	10/3	3:59am
♓	10/5	7:35am
♈	10/7	12:41pm
♉	10/9	8:05pm
♊	10/12	6:10am
♋	10/14	6:20pm
♌	10/17	6:46am
♍	10/19	5:11pm
♎	10/22	12:15am
♏	10/24	4:06am
♐	10/26	5:56am
♑	10/28	7:15am
♒	10/30	9:23am
♓	11/1	1:17pm
♈	11/3	7:21pm
♉	11/6	3:35am
♊	11/8	1:55pm
♋	11/11	1:57am
♌	11/13	2:37pm
♍	11/16	2:02am
♎	11/18	10:18am
♏	11/20	2:40pm
♐	11/22	3:56pm
♑	11/24	3:48pm
♒	11/26	4:15pm
♓	11/28	6:59pm
♈	12/1	12:51am
♉	12/3	9:40am
♊	12/5	8:35pm
♋	12/8	8:44am
♌	12/10	9:24pm
♍	12/13	9:26am
♎	12/15	7:09pm
♏	12/18	1:07am
♐	12/20	3:13am
♑	12/22	2:46am
♒	12/24	1:52am
♓	12/26	2:45am
♈	12/28	7:06am
♉	12/30	3:21pm
	1996	
♊	1/2	2:29am
♋	1/4	2:56pm
♌	1/7	3:30am
♍	1/9	3:29pm
♎	1/12	1:55am
♏	1/14	9:30am
♐	1/16	1:25pm
♑	1/18	2:07pm
♒	1/20	1:15pm
♓	1/22	1:02pm
♈	1/24	3:37pm
♉	1/26	10:16pm
♊	1/29	8:42am
♋	1/31	9:11pm
♌	2/3	9:46am
♍	2/5	9:22pm
♎	2/8	7:30am
♏	2/10	3:35pm
♐	2/12	8:58pm
♑	2/14	11:29pm
♒	2/16	11:59pm
♓	2/19	12:09am
♈	2/21	1:58am
♉	2/23	7:08am
♊	2/25	4:14pm
♋	2/28	4:10am
♌	3/1	4:47pm
♍	3/4	4:13am
♎	3/6	1:40pm
♏	3/8	9:05pm
♐	3/11	2:32am
♑	3/13	6:08am
♒	3/15	8:15am
♓	3/17	9:50am
♈	3/19	12:15pm
♉	3/21	4:59pm
♊	3/24	12:59am
♋	3/26	12:06pm
♌	3/29	12:37am
♍	3/31	12:14pm
♎	4/2	9:26pm
♏	4/5	3:57am
♐	4/7	8:21am
♑	4/9	11:30am
♒	4/11	2:09pm
♓	4/13	5:00pm
♈	4/15	8:42pm
♉	4/18	2:05am
♊	4/20	9:54am
♋	4/22	8:25pm
♌	4/25	8:44am
♍	4/27	8:49pm
♎	4/30	6:27am
♏	5/2	12:42pm
♐	5/4	4:05pm
♑	5/6	5:54pm
♒	5/8	7:39pm
♓	5/10	10:29pm
♈	5/13	3:00am
♉	5/15	9:25am
♊	5/17	5:48pm
♋	5/20	4:16am
♌	5/22	4:28pm
♍	5/25	4:58am
♎	5/27	3:33pm
♏	5/29	10:30pm
♐	6/1	1:43am
♑	6/3	2:29am
♒	6/5	2:45am
♓	6/7	4:19am
♈	6/9	8:23am
♉	6/11	3:11pm
♊	6/14	12:16am
♋	6/16	11:08am
♌	6/18	11:22pm
♍	6/21	12:07pm
♎	6/23	11:37pm
♏	6/26	7:53am
♐	6/28	12:01pm
♑	6/30	12:47pm
♒	7/2	12:05pm
♓	7/4	12:07pm
♈	7/6	2:42pm
♉	7/8	8:43pm
♊	7/11	5:52am
♋	7/13	5:08pm
♌	7/16	5:31am
♍	7/18	6:16pm
♎	7/21	6:14am
♏	7/23	3:43pm
♐	7/25	9:24pm
♑	7/27	11:17pm
♒	7/29	10:47pm
♓	7/31	10:00pm
♈	8/2	11:05pm
♉	8/5	3:33am
♊	8/7	11:49am
♋	8/9	10:57pm
♌	8/12	11:29am
♍	8/15	12:07am
♎	8/17	11:55am
♏	8/19	9:50pm
♐	8/22	4:48am
♑	8/24	8:22am
♒	8/26	9:10am
♓	8/28	8:49am
♈	8/30	9:15am
♉	9/1	12:19pm
♊	9/3	7:08pm
♋	9/6	5:29am
♌	9/8	5:54pm
♍	9/11	6:28am
♎	9/13	5:51pm
♏	9/16	3:20am
♐	9/18	10:31am
♑	9/20	3:12pm
♒	9/22	5:39pm
♓	9/24	6:43pm
♈	9/26	7:46pm
♉	9/28	10:24pm
♊	10/1	4:01am
♋	10/3	1:14pm
♌	10/6	1:12am
♍	10/8	1:49pm
♎	10/11	1:00am
♏	10/13	9:46am

Moon Sign Changes 1900-2005

♐	10/15	4:07pm
♑	10/17	8:37pm
♒	10/19	11:51pm
♓	10/22	2:22am
♈	10/24	4:50am
♉	10/26	8:11am
♊	10/28	1:35pm
♋	10/30	9:56pm
♌	11/2	9:16am
♍	11/4	9:57pm
♎	11/7	9:29am
♏	11/9	6:02pm
♐	11/11	11:26pm
♑	11/14	2:44am
♒	11/16	5:14am
♓	11/18	8:00am
♈	11/20	11:34am
♉	11/22	4:12pm
♊	11/24	10:20pm
♋	11/27	6:37am
♌	11/29	5:30pm
♍	12/2	6:11am
♎	12/4	6:23pm
♏	12/7	3:38am
♐	12/9	8:58am
♑	12/11	11:14am
♒	12/13	12:14pm
♓	12/15	1:44pm
♈	12/17	4:55pm
♉	12/19	10:09pm
♊	12/22	5:17am
♋	12/24	2:14pm
♌	12/27	1:09am
♍	12/29	1:45pm
1997		
♎	1/1	2:32am
♏	1/3	1:02pm
♐	1/5	7:27pm
♑	1/7	9:55pm
♒	1/9	10:00pm
♓	1/11	9:51pm
♈	1/13	11:22pm
♉	1/16	3:40am
♊	1/18	10:53am
♋	1/20	8:29pm
♌	1/23	7:50am
♍	1/25	8:26pm
♎	1/28	9:21am
♏	1/30	8:48pm
♐	2/2	4:51am
♑	2/4	8:44am
♒	2/6	9:21am
♓	2/8	8:34am
♈	2/10	8:29am
♉	2/12	10:56am
♊	2/14	4:53pm
♋	2/17	2:13am
♌	2/19	1:52pm
♍	2/22	2:38am
♎	2/24	3:23pm
♏	2/27	2:57am
♐	3/1	12:01pm
♑	3/3	5:38pm
♒	3/5	7:54pm
♓	3/7	7:57pm
♈	3/9	7:33pm
♉	3/11	8:37pm
♊	3/14	12:48am
♋	3/16	8:51am
♌	3/18	8:08pm
♍	3/21	8:59am
♎	3/23	9:35pm
♏	3/26	8:42am
♐	3/28	5:40pm
♑	3/31	12:07am
♒	4/2	3:59am
♓	4/4	5:42am
♈	4/6	6:19am
♉	4/8	7:20am
♊	4/10	10:28am
♋	4/12	5:03pm
♌	4/15	3:22am
♍	4/17	4:00pm
♎	4/20	4:36am
♏	4/22	3:19pm
♐	4/24	11:32pm
♑	4/27	5:32am
♒	4/29	9:50am
♓	5/1	12:50pm
♈	5/3	2:59pm
♉	5/5	5:04pm
♊	5/7	8:21pm
♋	5/10	2:13am
♌	5/12	11:33am
♍	5/14	11:43pm
♎	5/17	12:27pm
♏	5/19	11:11pm
♐	5/22	6:51am
♑	5/24	11:51am
♒	5/26	3:20pm
♓	5/28	6:18pm
♈	5/30	9:18pm
♉	6/2	12:39am
♊	6/4	4:55am
♋	6/6	11:02am
♌	6/8	7:58pm
♍	6/11	7:43am
♎	6/13	8:35pm
♏	6/16	7:51am
♐	6/18	3:39pm
♑	6/20	8:02pm
♒	6/22	10:20pm
♓	6/25	12:09am
♈	6/27	2:38am
♉	6/29	6:23am
♊	7/1	11:35am
♋	7/3	6:33pm
♌	7/6	3:45am
♍	7/8	3:22pm
♎	7/11	4:21am
♏	7/13	4:20pm
♐	7/16	1:02am
♑	7/18	5:45am
♒	7/20	7:29am
♓	7/22	8:00am
♈	7/24	9:03am
♉	7/26	11:53am
♊	7/28	5:04pm
♋	7/31	12:38am
♌	8/2	10:27am
♍	8/4	10:15pm
♎	8/7	11:17am
♏	8/9	11:50pm
♐	8/12	9:45am
♑	8/14	3:42pm
♒	8/16	5:58pm
♓	8/18	6:01pm
♈	8/20	5:45pm
♉	8/22	6:57pm
♊	8/24	10:56pm
♋	8/27	6:10am
♌	8/29	4:19pm
♍	9/1	4:27am
♎	9/3	5:30pm
♏	9/6	6:10am
♐	9/8	4:54pm
♑	9/11	12:23am
♒	9/13	4:10am
♓	9/15	4:59am
♈	9/17	4:25am
♉	9/19	4:21am
♊	9/21	6:39am
♋	9/23	12:33pm
♌	9/25	10:12pm
♍	9/28	10:27am
♎	9/30	11:32pm
♏	10/3	11:57am
♐	10/5	10:43pm
♑	10/8	7:04am
♒	10/10	12:29pm
♓	10/12	2:59pm
♈	10/14	3:25pm
♉	10/16	3:16pm
♊	10/18	4:26pm
♋	10/20	8:45pm
♌	10/23	5:10am
♍	10/25	4:59pm
♎	10/28	6:05am
♏	10/30	6:15pm
♐	11/2	4:27am
♑	11/4	12:31pm
♒	11/6	6:33pm
♓	11/8	10:34pm
♈	11/11	12:44am
♉	11/13	1:45am
♊	11/15	3:05am
♋	11/17	6:32am
♌	11/19	1:38pm
♍	11/22	12:33am
♎	11/24	1:29pm
♏	11/27	1:43am
♐	11/29	11:28am
♑	12/1	6:38pm
♒	12/3	11:58pm
♓	12/6	4:07am
♈	12/8	7:24am
♉	12/10	10:00am
♊	12/12	12:35pm
♋	12/14	4:25pm
♌	12/16	10:58pm
♍	12/19	9:00am
♎	12/21	9:35pm
♏	12/24	10:07am
♐	12/26	8:07pm
♑	12/29	2:48am
♒	12/31	6:58am
1998		
♓	1/2	9:56am
♈	1/4	12:43pm
♉	1/6	3:52pm
♊	1/8	7:42pm
♋	1/11	12:43am
♌	1/13	7:45am
♍	1/15	5:31pm
♎	1/18	5:44am
♏	1/20	6:34pm
♐	1/23	5:25am
♑	1/25	12:39pm
♒	1/27	4:27pm
♓	1/29	6:08pm
♈	1/31	7:21pm
♉	2/2	9:25pm
♊	2/5	1:09am
♋	2/7	6:57am
♌	2/9	2:57pm
♍	2/12	1:09am
♎	2/14	1:17pm
♏	2/17	2:13am
♐	2/19	1:56pm
♑	2/21	10:29pm
♒	2/24	3:10am
♓	2/26	4:42am
♈	2/28	4:42am
♉	3/2	5:00am
♊	3/4	7:15am
♋	3/6	12:27pm
♌	3/8	8:46pm
♍	3/11	7:35am
♎	3/13	7:58pm
♏	3/16	8:51am
♐	3/18	8:56pm
♑	3/21	6:43am
♒	3/23	1:01pm
♓	3/25	3:43pm
♈	3/27	3:49pm
♉	3/29	3:06pm
♊	3/31	3:37pm
♋	4/2	7:10pm
♌	4/5	2:36am
♍	4/7	1:25pm
♎	4/10	2:04am
♏	4/12	2:55pm
♐	4/15	2:52am
♑	4/17	1:05pm
♒	4/19	8:41pm
♓	4/22	1:06am
♈	4/24	2:30am
♉	4/26	2:09am
♊	4/28	1:55am
♋	4/30	3:57am
♌	5/2	9:49am
♍	5/4	7:47pm
♎	5/7	8:19am
♏	5/9	9:10pm
♐	5/12	8:48am
♑	5/14	6:39pm
♒	5/17	2:30am
♓	5/19	8:03am
♈	5/21	11:06am
♉	5/23	12:06pm
♊	5/25	12:25pm
♋	5/27	1:58pm
♌	5/29	6:38pm
♍	6/1	3:21am
♎	6/3	3:17pm
♏	6/6	4:06am
♐	6/8	3:34pm
♑	6/11	12:50am
♒	6/13	8:03am
♓	6/15	1:31pm
♈	6/17	5:23pm
♉	6/19	7:47pm
♊	6/21	9:26pm
♋	6/23	11:39pm
♌	6/26	4:04am
♍	6/28	11:54am
♎	6/30	11:05pm
♏	7/3	11:45am
♐	7/5	11:24pm
♑	7/8	8:27am
♒	7/10	2:52pm
♓	7/12	7:22pm
♈	7/14	10:45pm
♉	7/17	1:33am
♊	7/19	4:18am
♋	7/21	7:43am
♌	7/23	12:48pm
♍	7/25	8:34pm
♎	7/28	7:14am
♏	7/30	7:44pm
♐	8/2	7:48am
♑	8/4	5:18pm
♒	8/6	11:31pm
♓	8/9	3:04am
♈	8/11	5:10am
♉	8/13	7:04am
♊	8/15	9:46am
♋	8/17	1:55pm
♌	8/19	8:00pm
♍	8/22	4:21am
♎	8/24	3:02pm
♏	8/27	3:25am
♐	8/29	3:55pm
♑	9/1	2:23am
♒	9/3	9:21am
♓	9/5	12:48pm
♈	9/7	1:52pm
♉	9/9	2:16pm
♊	9/11	3:40pm
♋	9/13	7:20pm
♌	9/16	1:48am
♍	9/18	10:52am
♎	9/20	9:57pm
♏	9/23	10:22am
♐	9/25	11:05pm
♑	9/28	10:30am
♒	9/30	6:53pm
♓	10/2	11:23pm
♈	10/5	12:32am
♉	10/6	11:57pm
♊	10/8	11:43pm
♋	10/11	1:48am
♌	10/13	7:25am
♍	10/15	4:32pm
♎	10/18	4:02am
♏	10/20	4:36pm
♐	10/23	5:16am
♑	10/25	5:05pm
♒	10/28	2:44am
♓	10/30	8:58am
♈	11/1	11:27am
♉	11/3	11:12am
♊	11/5	10:11am
♋	11/7	10:39am
♌	11/9	2:33pm
♍	11/11	10:37pm
♎	11/14	9:57am
♏	11/16	10:41pm
♐	11/19	11:13am
♑	11/21	10:45pm
♒	11/24	8:43am
♓	11/26	4:14pm
♈	11/28	8:34pm
♉	11/30	9:52pm
♊	12/2	9:29pm
♋	12/4	9:28pm
♌	12/6	11:55pm
♍	12/9	6:21am
♎	12/11	4:43pm
♏	12/14	5:16am
♐	12/16	5:47pm
♑	12/19	4:55am
♒	12/21	2:17pm
♓	12/23	9:45pm
♈	12/26	3:03am
♉	12/28	6:05am
♊	12/30	7:22am
1999		
♋	1/1	8:15am
♌	1/3	10:31am
♍	1/5	3:49pm
♎	1/8	12:53am
♏	1/10	12:49pm
♐	1/13	1:23am
♑	1/15	12:28pm
♒	1/17	9:11pm
♓	1/20	3:40am
♈	1/22	8:25am
♉	1/24	11:52am
♊	1/26	2:29pm
♋	1/28	4:57pm
♌	1/30	8:16pm

Moon Sign Changes 1900-2005

♍	2/2	1:37am
♎	2/4	9:56am
♏	2/6	9:06pm
♐	2/9	9:38am
♑	2/11	9:10pm
♒	2/14	5:57am
♓	2/16	11:40am
♈	2/18	3:06pm
♉	2/20	5:29pm
♊	2/22	7:54pm
♋	2/24	11:09pm
♌	2/27	3:44am
♍	3/1	10:04am
♎	3/3	6:34pm
♏	3/6	5:22am
♐	3/8	5:46pm
♑	3/11	5:54am
♒	3/13	3:32pm
♓	3/15	9:30pm
♈	3/18	12:13am
♉	3/20	1:09am
♊	3/22	2:05am
♋	3/24	4:33am
♌	3/26	9:22am
♍	3/28	4:34pm
♎	3/31	1:49am
♏	4/2	12:49pm
♐	4/5	1:07am
♑	4/7	1:39pm
♒	4/10	12:24am
♓	4/12	7:35am
♈	4/14	10:46am
♉	4/16	11:07am
♊	4/18	10:39am
♋	4/20	11:27am
♌	4/22	3:06pm
♍	4/24	10:04pm
♎	4/27	7:46am
♏	4/29	7:12pm
♐	5/2	7:36am
♑	5/4	8:12pm
♒	5/7	7:40am
♓	5/9	4:16pm
♈	5/11	8:53pm
♉	5/13	9:56pm
♊	5/15	9:07pm
♋	5/17	8:39pm
♌	5/19	10:37pm
♍	5/22	4:15am
♎	5/24	1:29pm
♏	5/27	1:05am
♐	5/29	1:37pm
♑	6/1	2:05am
♒	6/3	1:37pm
♓	6/5	11:00pm
♈	6/8	5:08am
♉	6/10	7:43am
♊	6/12	7:48am
♋	6/14	7:14am
♌	6/16	8:07am
♍	6/18	12:12pm
♎	6/20	8:10pm
♏	6/23	7:18am
♐	6/25	7:51pm
♑	6/28	8:12am
♒	6/30	7:19pm
♓	7/3	4:34am
♈	7/5	11:21am
♉	7/7	3:22pm
♊	7/9	5:00pm
♋	7/11	5:27pm
♌	7/13	6:26pm
♍	7/15	9:39pm
♎	7/18	4:19am
♏	7/20	2:30pm
♐	7/23	2:48am
♑	7/25	3:08pm
♒	7/28	1:54am
♓	7/30	10:27am
♈	8/1	4:47pm
♉	8/3	9:09pm
♊	8/5	11:57pm
♋	8/8	1:52am
♌	8/10	3:55am
♍	8/12	7:22am
♎	8/14	1:24pm
♏	8/16	10:40pm
♐	8/19	10:31am
♑	8/21	10:59pm
♒	8/24	9:49am
♓	8/26	5:50pm
♈	8/28	11:09pm
♉	8/31	2:41am
♊	9/2	5:25am
♋	9/4	8:09am
♌	9/6	11:29am
♍	9/8	3:57pm
♎	9/10	10:16pm
♏	9/13	7:08am
♐	9/15	6:35pm
♑	9/18	7:13am
♒	9/20	6:38pm
♓	9/23	2:51am
♈	9/25	7:34am
♉	9/27	9:51am
♊	9/29	11:21am
♋	10/1	1:31pm
♌	10/3	5:13pm
♍	10/5	10:40pm
♎	10/8	5:52am
♏	10/10	3:01pm
♐	10/13	2:18am
♑	10/15	3:04pm
♒	10/18	3:17am
♓	10/20	12:33pm
♈	10/22	5:41pm
♉	10/24	7:25pm
♊	10/26	7:33pm
♋	10/28	8:09pm
♌	10/30	10:47pm
♍	11/2	4:07am
♎	11/4	11:57am
♏	11/6	9:46pm
♐	11/9	9:15am
♑	11/11	10:00pm
♒	11/14	10:46am
♓	11/16	9:21pm
♈	11/19	3:57am
♉	11/21	6:26am
♊	11/23	6:13am
♋	11/25	5:29am
♌	11/27	6:19am
♍	11/29	10:11am
♎	12/1	5:29pm
♏	12/4	3:35am
♐	12/6	3:27pm
♑	12/9	4:14am
♒	12/11	4:59pm
♓	12/14	4:18am
♈	12/16	12:30pm
♉	12/18	4:45pm
♊	12/20	5:39pm
♋	12/22	4:52pm
♌	12/24	4:32pm
♍	12/26	6:34pm
♎	12/29	12:14am
♏	12/31	9:36am
	2000	
♐	1/2	9:32pm
♑	1/5	10:24am
♒	1/7	10:53pm
♓	1/10	9:59am
♈	1/12	6:48pm
♉	1/15	12:38am
♊	1/17	3:25am
♋	1/19	4:01am
♌	1/21	3:58am
♍	1/23	5:07am
♎	1/25	9:09am
♏	1/27	5:01pm
♐	1/30	4:17am
♑	2/1	5:10pm
♒	2/4	5:31am
♓	2/6	4:02pm
♈	2/9	12:17am
♉	2/11	6:21am
♊	2/13	10:23am
♋	2/15	12:45pm
♌	2/17	2:11pm
♍	2/19	3:53pm
♎	2/21	7:21pm
♏	2/24	1:58am
♐	2/26	12:10pm
♑	2/29	12:45am
♒	3/2	1:14pm
♓	3/4	11:30pm
♈	3/7	6:54am
♉	3/9	12:01pm
♊	3/11	3:46pm
♋	3/13	6:51pm
♌	3/15	9:43pm
♍	3/18	12:48am
♎	3/20	4:57am
♏	3/22	11:17am
♐	3/24	8:43pm
♑	3/27	8:51am
♒	3/29	9:34pm
♓	4/1	8:12am
♈	4/3	3:22pm
♉	4/5	7:29pm
♊	4/7	9:58pm
♋	4/10	12:16am
♌	4/12	3:16am
♍	4/14	7:19am
♎	4/16	12:36pm
♏	4/18	7:35pm
♐	4/21	4:58am
♑	4/23	4:47pm
♒	4/26	5:42am
♓	4/28	5:06pm
♈	5/1	12:55am
♉	5/3	4:54am
♊	5/5	6:23am
♋	5/7	7:14am
♌	5/9	9:01am
♍	5/11	12:41pm
♎	5/13	6:27pm
♏	5/16	2:16am
♐	5/18	12:09pm
♑	5/21	12:01am
♒	5/23	1:00pm
♓	5/26	1:07am
♈	5/28	10:08am
♉	5/30	3:02pm
♊	6/1	4:34pm
♋	6/3	4:30pm
♌	6/5	4:45pm
♍	6/7	6:57pm
♎	6/9	11:59pm
♏	6/12	7:55am
♐	6/14	6:18pm
♑	6/17	6:26am
♒	6/19	7:26pm
♓	6/22	7:52am
♈	6/24	5:55pm
♉	6/27	12:19am
♊	6/29	2:59am
♋	7/1	3:09am
♌	7/3	2:38am
♍	7/5	3:19am
♎	7/7	6:47am
♏	7/9	1:48pm
♐	7/12	12:06am
♑	7/14	12:28pm
♒	7/17	1:27am
♓	7/19	1:44pm
♈	7/22	12:09am
♉	7/24	7:44am
♊	7/26	12:01pm
♋	7/28	1:30pm
♌	7/30	1:23pm
♍	8/1	1:27pm
♎	8/3	3:31pm
♏	8/5	9:04pm
♐	8/8	6:30am
♑	8/10	6:44pm
♒	8/13	7:43am
♓	8/15	7:41pm
♈	8/18	5:44am
♉	8/20	1:31pm
♊	8/22	6:55pm
♋	8/24	10:00pm
♌	8/26	11:17pm
♍	8/28	11:55pm
♎	8/31	1:33am
♏	9/2	5:55am
♐	9/4	2:08pm
♑	9/7	1:47am
♒	9/9	2:44pm
♓	9/12	2:34am
♈	9/14	12:00pm
♉	9/16	7:05pm
♊	9/19	12:22am
♋	9/21	4:16am
♌	9/23	7:00am
♍	9/25	9:02am
♎	9/27	11:22am
♏	9/29	3:30pm
♐	10/1	10:50pm
♑	10/4	9:42am
♒	10/6	10:33pm
♓	10/9	10:36am
♈	10/11	7:51pm
♉	10/14	2:06am
♊	10/16	6:19am
♋	10/18	9:37am
♌	10/20	12:42pm
♍	10/22	3:52pm
♎	10/24	7:30pm
♏	10/27	12:23am
♐	10/29	7:40am
♑	10/31	6:02pm
♒	11/3	6:41am
♓	11/5	7:13pm
♈	11/8	5:02am
♉	11/10	11:12am
♊	11/12	2:27pm
♋	11/14	4:21pm
♌	11/16	6:19pm
♍	11/18	9:15pm
♎	11/21	1:35am
♏	11/23	7:33am
♐	11/25	3:33pm
♑	11/28	1:57am
♒	11/30	2:26pm
♓	12/3	3:23am
♈	12/5	2:17pm
♉	12/7	9:27pm
♊	12/10	12:50am
♋	12/12	1:48am
♌	12/14	2:09am
♍	12/16	3:30am
♎	12/18	7:01am
♏	12/20	1:12pm
♐	12/22	9:57pm
♑	12/25	8:54am
♒	12/27	9:25pm
♓	12/30	10:27am
	2001	
♈	1/1	10:14pm
♉	1/4	6:57am
♊	1/6	11:44am
♋	1/8	1:09pm
♌	1/10	12:44pm
♍	1/12	12:26pm
♎	1/14	2:05pm
♏	1/16	7:02pm
♐	1/19	3:36am
♑	1/21	2:57pm
♒	1/24	3:43am
♓	1/26	4:39pm
♈	1/29	4:35am
♉	1/31	2:21pm
♊	2/2	8:56pm
♋	2/5	12:00am
♌	2/7	12:21am
♍	2/8	11:35pm
♎	2/10	11:46pm
♏	2/13	2:51am
♐	2/15	10:02am
♑	2/17	8:59pm
♒	2/20	9:53am
♓	2/22	10:45pm
♈	2/25	10:20am
♉	2/27	8:06pm
♊	3/2	3:36am
♋	3/4	8:24am
♌	3/6	10:30am
♍	3/8	10:44am
♎	3/10	10:47am
♏	3/12	12:43pm
♐	3/14	6:17pm
♑	3/17	4:02am
♒	3/19	4:36pm
♓	3/22	5:28am
♈	3/24	4:44pm
♉	3/27	1:51am
♊	3/29	9:01am
♋	3/31	2:23pm
♌	4/2	5:54pm
♍	4/4	7:46pm
♎	4/6	8:57pm
♏	4/8	11:01pm
♐	4/11	3:47am
♑	4/13	12:21pm
♒	4/16	12:11am
♓	4/18	1:00pm
♈	4/21	12:18am
♉	4/23	8:56am
♊	4/25	3:11pm
♋	4/27	7:49pm
♌	4/29	11:25pm
♍	5/2	2:16am
♎	5/4	4:50am
♏	5/6	8:01am
♐	5/8	1:05pm
♑	5/10	9:10pm
♒	5/13	8:20am
♓	5/15	9:01pm
♈	5/18	8:41am
♉	5/20	5:29pm
♊	5/22	11:12pm

Moon Sign Changes 1900-2005

♋	5/25	2:42am
♌	5/27	5:12am
♍	5/29	7:38am
♎	5/31	10:41am
♏	6/2	2:56pm
♐	6/4	8:58pm
♑	6/7	5:23am
♒	6/9	4:20pm
♓	6/12	4:53am
♈	6/14	5:03pm
♉	6/17	2:39am
♊	6/19	8:42am
♋	6/21	11:41am
♌	6/23	12:55pm
♍	6/25	1:58pm
♎	6/27	4:11pm
♏	6/29	8:28pm
♐	7/2	3:13am
♑	7/4	12:21pm
♒	7/6	11:33pm
♓	7/9	12:05pm
♈	7/12	12:36am
♉	7/14	11:13am
♊	7/16	6:26pm
♋	7/18	9:56pm
♌	7/20	10:43pm
♍	7/22	10:29pm
♎	7/24	11:08pm
♏	7/27	2:17am
♐	7/29	8:44am
♑	7/31	6:16pm
♒	8/3	5:53am
♓	8/5	6:30pm
♈	8/8	7:05am
♉	8/10	6:23pm
♊	8/13	2:59am
♋	8/15	7:55am
♌	8/17	9:25am
♍	8/19	8:53am
♎	8/21	8:19am
♏	8/23	9:50am
♐	8/25	2:59pm
♑	8/28	12:02am
♒	8/30	11:48am
♓	9/2	12:32am
♈	9/4	12:58pm
♉	9/7	12:18am
♊	9/9	9:41am
♋	9/11	4:09pm
♌	9/13	7:16pm
♍	9/15	7:39pm
♎	9/17	7:00pm
♏	9/19	7:27pm
♐	9/21	11:02pm
♑	9/24	6:48am
♒	9/26	6:05pm
♓	9/29	6:50am
♈	10/1	7:08pm
♉	10/4	6:01am
♊	10/6	3:12pm
♋	10/8	10:19pm
♌	10/11	2:54am
♍	10/13	4:58am
♎	10/15	5:26am
♏	10/17	6:03am
♐	10/19	8:47am
♑	10/21	3:11pm
♒	10/24	1:26am
♓	10/26	1:56pm
♈	10/29	2:15am
♉	10/31	12:48pm
♊	11/2	9:12pm
♋	11/5	3:44am
♌	11/7	8:34am
♍	11/9	11:49am
♎	11/11	1:53pm
♏	11/13	3:44pm
♐	11/15	6:51pm
♑	11/18	12:40am
♒	11/20	9:55am
♓	11/22	9:52pm
♈	11/25	10:21am
♉	11/27	9:06pm
♊	11/30	5:04am
♋	12/2	10:30am
♌	12/4	2:15pm
♍	12/6	5:11pm
♎	12/8	7:57pm
♏	12/10	11:09pm
♐	12/13	3:30am
♑	12/15	9:48am
♒	12/17	6:43pm
♓	12/20	6:09am
♈	12/22	6:45pm
♉	12/25	6:12am
♊	12/27	2:39pm
♋	12/29	7:40pm
♌	12/31	10:09pm
	2002	
♍	1/2	11:34pm
♎	1/5	1:23am
♏	1/7	4:41am
♐	1/9	9:57am
♑	1/11	5:18pm
♒	1/14	2:41am
♓	1/16	2:00pm
♈	1/19	2:35am
♉	1/21	2:47pm
♊	1/24	12:28am
♋	1/26	6:17am
♌	1/28	8:31am
♍	1/30	8:40am
♎	2/1	8:44am
♏	2/3	10:35am
♐	2/5	3:21pm
♑	2/7	11:08pm
♒	2/10	9:15am
♓	2/12	8:53pm
♈	2/15	9:26am
♉	2/17	9:58pm
♊	2/20	8:50am
♋	2/22	4:16pm
♌	2/24	7:36pm
♍	2/26	7:47pm
♎	2/28	6:47pm
♏	3/2	6:51pm
♐	3/4	9:55pm
♑	3/7	4:48am
♒	3/9	2:56pm
♓	3/12	2:56am
♈	3/14	3:34pm
♉	3/17	4:01am
♊	3/19	3:20pm
♋	3/22	12:06am
♌	3/24	5:12am
♍	3/26	6:44am
♎	3/28	6:04am
♏	3/30	5:21am
♐	4/1	6:48am
♑	4/3	11:58am
♒	4/5	9:07pm
♓	4/8	8:57am
♈	4/10	9:40pm
♉	4/13	9:55am
♊	4/15	8:56pm
♋	4/18	6:01am
♌	4/20	12:20pm
♍	4/22	3:35pm
♎	4/24	4:22pm
♏	4/26	4:15pm
♐	4/28	5:13pm
♑	4/30	9:03pm
♒	5/3	4:43am
♓	5/5	3:46pm
♈	5/8	4:22am
♉	5/10	4:32pm
♊	5/13	3:04am
♋	5/15	11:33am
♌	5/17	5:52pm
♍	5/19	10:01pm
♎	5/22	12:19am
♏	5/24	1:38am
♐	5/26	3:20am
♑	5/28	6:54am
♒	5/30	1:35pm
♓	6/1	11:37pm
♈	6/4	11:51am
♉	6/7	12:07am
♊	6/9	10:29am
♋	6/11	6:15pm
♌	6/13	11:39pm
♍	6/16	3:23am
♎	6/18	6:11am
♏	6/20	8:42am
♐	6/22	11:42am
♑	6/24	4:01pm
♒	6/26	10:36pm
♓	6/29	8:00am
♈	7/1	7:49pm
♉	7/4	8:16am
♊	7/6	7:01pm
♋	7/9	2:36am
♌	7/11	7:08am
♍	7/13	9:41am
♎	7/15	11:39am
♏	7/17	2:13pm
♐	7/19	6:02pm
♑	7/21	11:26pm
♒	7/24	6:40am
♓	7/26	4:04pm
♈	7/29	3:39am
♉	7/31	4:17pm
♊	8/3	3:46am
♋	8/5	12:02pm
♌	8/7	4:27pm
♍	8/9	6:03pm
♎	8/11	6:38pm
♏	8/13	8:01pm
♐	8/15	11:25pm
♑	8/18	5:15am
♒	8/20	1:16pm
♓	8/22	11:11pm
♈	8/25	10:48am
♉	8/27	11:32pm
♊	8/30	11:45am
♋	9/1	9:14pm
♌	9/4	2:36am
♍	9/6	4:16am
♎	9/8	3:57am
♏	9/10	3:48am
♐	9/12	5:44am
♑	9/14	10:47am
♒	9/16	6:54pm
♓	9/19	5:18am
♈	9/21	5:11pm
♉	9/24	5:55am
♊	9/26	6:26pm
♋	9/29	5:01am
♌	10/1	11:58am
♍	10/3	2:52pm
♎	10/5	2:51pm
♏	10/7	1:57pm
♐	10/9	2:21pm
♑	10/11	5:45pm
♒	10/14	12:51am
♓	10/16	11:07am
♈	10/18	11:13pm
♉	10/21	11:57am
♊	10/24	12:17am
♋	10/26	11:10am
♌	10/28	7:20pm
♍	10/30	11:59pm
♎	11/2	1:28am
♏	11/4	1:10am
♐	11/6	1:01am
♑	11/8	2:59am
♒	11/10	8:27am
♓	11/12	5:42pm
♈	11/15	5:38am
♉	11/17	6:23pm
♊	11/20	6:25am
♋	11/22	4:48pm
♌	11/25	1:00am
♍	11/27	6:42am
♎	11/29	9:54am
♏	12/1	11:15am
♐	12/3	11:58am
♑	12/5	1:39pm
♒	12/7	5:54pm
♓	12/10	1:46am
♈	12/12	12:58pm
♉	12/15	1:43am
♊	12/17	1:43pm
♋	12/19	11:30pm
♌	12/22	6:48am
♍	12/24	12:05pm
♎	12/26	3:53pm
♏	12/28	6:41pm
♐	12/30	9:01pm
	2003	
♑	1/1	11:42pm
♒	1/4	3:56am
♓	1/6	10:57am
♈	1/8	9:15pm
♉	1/11	9:48am
♊	1/13	10:08pm
♋	1/16	7:56am
♌	1/18	2:29pm
♍	1/20	6:32pm
♎	1/22	9:23pm
♏	1/25	12:09am
♐	1/27	3:26am
♑	1/29	7:30am
♒	1/31	12:44pm
♓	2/2	7:55pm
♈	2/5	5:44am
♉	2/7	5:59pm
♊	2/10	6:45am
♋	2/12	5:19pm
♌	2/15	12:04am
♍	2/17	3:22am
♎	2/19	4:48am
♏	2/21	6:09am
♐	2/23	8:46am
♑	2/25	1:11pm
♒	2/27	7:24pm
♓	3/2	3:26am
♈	3/4	1:30pm
♉	3/7	1:36am
♊	3/9	2:38pm
♋	3/12	2:12am
♌	3/14	10:06am
♍	3/16	1:52pm
♎	3/18	2:43pm
♏	3/20	2:38pm
♐	3/22	3:33pm
♑	3/24	6:48pm
♒	3/27	12:51am
♓	3/29	9:26am
♈	3/31	8:04pm
♉	4/3	8:20am
♊	4/5	9:24pm
♋	4/8	9:36am
♌	4/10	6:54pm
♍	4/13	12:07am
♎	4/15	1:42am
♏	4/17	1:16am
♐	4/19	12:51am
♑	4/21	2:20am
♒	4/23	6:58am
♓	4/25	3:02pm
♈	4/28	1:54am
♉	4/30	2:26pm
♊	5/3	3:27am
♋	5/5	3:42pm
♌	5/8	1:46am
♍	5/10	8:31am
♎	5/12	11:42am
♏	5/14	12:14pm
♐	5/16	11:43am
♑	5/18	12:03pm
♒	5/20	3:01pm
♓	5/22	9:41pm
♈	5/25	7:59am
♉	5/27	8:32pm
♊	5/30	9:32am
♋	6/1	9:27pm
♌	6/4	7:25am
♍	6/6	2:51pm
♎	6/8	7:30pm
♏	6/10	9:39pm
♐	6/12	10:12pm
♑	6/14	10:38pm
♒	6/17	12:41am
♓	6/19	5:57am
♈	6/21	3:06pm
♉	6/24	3:15am
♊	6/26	4:13pm
♋	6/29	3:52am
♌	7/1	1:13pm
♍	7/3	8:16pm
♎	7/6	1:20am
♏	7/8	4:43am
♐	7/10	6:48am
♑	7/12	8:21am
♒	7/14	10:38am
♓	7/16	3:14pm
♈	7/18	11:20pm
♉	7/21	10:48am
♊	7/23	11:42pm
♋	7/26	11:23am
♌	7/28	8:17pm
♍	7/31	2:27am
♎	8/2	6:48am
♏	8/4	10:12am
♐	8/6	1:11pm
♑	8/8	4:02pm
♒	8/10	7:23pm
♓	8/13	12:19am
♈	8/15	8:00am
♉	8/17	6:52pm
♊	8/20	7:41am
♋	8/22	7:44pm
♌	8/25	4:48am
♍	8/27	10:27am
♎	8/29	1:41pm
♏	8/31	4:00pm
♐	9/2	6:32pm
♑	9/4	9:51pm
♒	9/7	2:15am
♓	9/9	8:07am
♈	9/11	4:09pm

Moon Sign Changes 1900-2005

♉	9/14	2:50am
♊	9/16	3:32pm
♋	9/19	4:07am
♌	9/21	2:02pm
♍	9/23	8:04pm
♎	9/25	10:49pm
♏	9/27	11:52pm
♐	9/30	12:57am
♑	10/2	3:21am
♒	10/4	7:45am
♓	10/6	2:20pm
♈	10/8	11:07pm
♉	10/11	10:05am
♊	10/13	10:45pm
♋	10/16	11:41am
♌	10/18	10:41pm
♍	10/21	6:01am
♎	10/23	9:27am
♏	10/25	10:08am
♐	10/27	9:55am
♑	10/29	10:37am
♒	10/31	1:41pm
♓	11/2	7:52pm
♈	11/5	5:02am
♉	11/7	4:29pm
♊	11/10	5:14am
♋	11/12	6:10pm
♌	11/15	5:48am
♍	11/17	2:36pm
♎	11/19	7:42pm
♏	11/21	9:24pm
♐	11/23	9:02pm
♑	11/25	8:31pm
♒	11/27	9:48pm
♓	11/30	2:25am
♈	12/2	10:56am
♉	12/4	10:30pm
♊	12/7	11:26am
♋	12/10	12:11am
♌	12/12	11:40am
♍	12/14	9:07pm
♎	12/17	3:46am
♏	12/19	7:20am
♐	12/21	8:16am
♑	12/23	7:55am
♒	12/25	8:13am
♓	12/27	11:10am
♈	12/29	6:08pm
2004		
♉	1/1	5:02am
♊	1/3	5:58pm
♋	1/6	6:38am
♌	1/8	5:38pm
♍	1/11	2:37am
♎	1/13	9:38am
♏	1/15	2:33pm
♐	1/17	5:18pm
♑	1/19	6:24pm
♒	1/21	7:11pm
♓	1/23	9:29pm
♈	1/26	3:06am
♉	1/28	12:46pm
♊	1/31	1:18am
♋	2/2	2:03pm
♌	2/5	12:50am
♍	2/7	9:03am
♎	2/9	3:12pm
♏	2/11	7:58pm
♐	2/13	11:35pm
♑	2/16	2:14am
♒	2/18	4:27am
♓	2/20	7:27am
♈	2/22	12:45pm
♉	2/24	9:30pm
♊	2/27	9:22am
♋	2/29	10:12pm
♌	3/3	9:18am
♍	3/5	5:18pm
♎	3/7	10:31pm
♏	3/10	2:03am
♐	3/12	4:57am
♑	3/14	7:51am
♒	3/16	11:10am
♓	3/18	3:26pm
♈	3/20	9:29pm
♉	3/23	6:10am
♊	3/25	5:35pm
♋	3/28	6:23am
♌	3/30	6:07pm
♍	4/2	2:45am
♎	4/4	7:52am
♏	4/6	10:24am
♐	4/8	11:50am
♑	4/10	1:33pm
♒	4/12	4:33pm
♓	4/14	9:24pm
♈	4/17	4:24am
♉	4/19	1:43pm
♊	4/22	1:10am
♋	4/24	1:56pm
♌	4/27	2:14am
♍	4/29	12:00pm
♎	5/1	6:03pm
♏	5/3	8:38pm
♐	5/5	9:08pm
♑	5/7	9:17pm
♒	5/9	10:46pm
♓	5/12	2:52am
♈	5/14	10:02am
♉	5/16	7:57pm
♊	5/19	7:47am
♋	5/21	8:35pm
♌	5/24	9:07am
♍	5/26	7:52pm
♎	5/29	3:22am
♏	5/31	7:08am
♐	6/2	7:52am
♑	6/4	7:12am
♒	6/6	7:10am
♓	6/8	9:38am
♈	6/10	3:49pm
♉	6/13	1:37am
♊	6/15	1:44pm
♋	6/18	2:37am
♌	6/20	3:05pm
♍	6/23	2:10am
♎	6/25	10:50am
♏	6/27	4:13pm
♐	6/29	6:15pm
♑	7/1	6:01pm
♒	7/3	5:22pm
♓	7/5	6:26pm
♈	7/7	11:03pm
♉	7/10	7:51am
♊	7/12	7:45pm
♋	7/15	8:40am
♌	7/17	8:56pm
♍	7/20	7:44am
♎	7/22	4:39pm
♏	7/24	11:08pm
♐	7/27	2:48am
♑	7/29	3:57am
♒	7/31	3:54am
♓	8/2	4:34am
♈	8/4	7:59am
♉	8/6	3:26pm
♊	8/9	2:33am
♋	8/11	3:20pm
♌	8/14	3:30am
♍	8/16	1:49pm
♎	8/18	10:09pm
♏	8/21	4:37am
♐	8/23	9:08am
♑	8/25	11:46am
♒	8/27	1:08pm
♓	8/29	2:33pm
♈	8/31	5:46pm
♉	9/3	12:16am
♊	9/5	10:24am
♋	9/7	10:50pm
♌	9/10	11:06am
♍	9/12	9:16pm
♎	9/15	4:54am
♏	9/17	10:25am
♐	9/19	2:30pm
♑	9/21	5:35pm
♒	9/23	8:10pm
♓	9/25	10:55pm
♈	9/28	2:57am
♉	9/30	9:24am
♊	10/2	6:55pm
♋	10/5	6:54am
♌	10/7	7:23pm
♍	10/10	6:00am
♎	10/12	1:32pm
♏	10/14	6:10pm
♐	10/16	8:58pm
♑	10/18	11:07pm
♒	10/21	1:38am
♓	10/23	5:13am
♈	10/25	10:24am
♉	10/27	5:37pm
♊	10/30	3:11am
♋	11/1	2:53pm
♌	11/4	3:32am
♍	11/6	3:00pm
♎	11/8	11:23pm
♏	11/11	4:05am
♐	11/13	5:56am
♑	11/15	6:33am
♒	11/17	7:39am
♓	11/19	10:38am
♈	11/21	4:11pm
♉	11/24	12:16am
♊	11/26	10:25am
♋	11/28	10:10pm
♌	12/1	10:50am
♍	12/3	11:00pm
♎	12/6	8:46am
♏	12/8	2:43pm
♐	12/10	4:54pm
♑	12/12	4:42pm
♒	12/14	4:10pm
♓	12/16	5:24pm
♈	12/18	9:52pm
♉	12/21	5:52am
♊	12/23	4:32pm
♋	12/26	4:38am
♌	12/28	5:14pm
♍	12/31	5:33am
2005		
♎	1/2	4:19pm
♏	1/4	11:59pm
♐	1/7	3:44am
♑	1/9	4:11am
♒	1/11	3:07am
♓	1/13	2:50am
♈	1/15	5:27am
♉	1/17	12:06pm
♊	1/19	10:24pm
♋	1/22	10:42am
♌	1/24	11:21pm
♍	1/27	11:24am
♎	1/29	10:13pm
♏	2/1	6:51am
♐	2/3	12:21pm
♑	2/5	2:32pm
♒	2/7	2:26pm
♓	2/9	1:59pm
♈	2/11	3:21pm
♉	2/13	8:18pm
♊	2/16	5:18am
♋	2/18	5:13pm
♌	2/21	5:54am
♍	2/23	5:44pm
♎	2/26	3:59am
♏	2/28	12:21pm
♐	3/2	6:29pm
♑	3/4	10:12pm
♒	3/6	11:49pm
♓	3/9	12:32am
♈	3/11	2:03am
♉	3/13	6:05am
♊	3/15	1:44pm
♋	3/18	12:44am
♌	3/20	1:17pm
♍	3/23	1:10am
♎	3/25	11:00am
♏	3/27	6:29pm
♐	3/29	11:56pm
♑	4/1	3:48am
♒	4/3	6:31am
♓	4/5	8:45am
♈	4/7	11:28am
♉	4/9	3:50pm
♊	4/11	10:55pm
♋	4/14	9:03am
♌	4/16	9:17pm
♍	4/19	9:27am
♎	4/21	7:27pm
♏	4/24	2:25am
♐	4/26	6:46am
♑	4/28	9:33am
♒	4/30	11:54am
♓	5/2	2:43pm
♈	5/4	6:36pm
♉	5/7	12:01am
♊	5/9	7:29am
♋	5/11	5:20pm
♌	5/14	5:17am
♍	5/16	5:46pm
♎	5/19	4:30am
♏	5/21	11:49am
♐	5/23	3:38pm
♑	5/25	5:11pm
♒	5/27	6:10pm
♓	5/29	8:09pm
♈	6/1	12:07am
♉	6/3	6:20am
♊	6/5	2:36pm
♋	6/8	12:46am
♌	6/10	12:39pm
♍	6/13	1:22am
♎	6/15	12:59pm
♏	6/17	9:23pm
♐	6/20	1:45am
♑	6/22	2:52am
♒	6/24	2:36am
♓	6/26	3:03am
♈	6/28	5:51am
♉	6/30	11:45am
♊	7/2	8:26pm
♋	7/5	7:07am
♌	7/7	7:11pm
♍	7/10	7:57am
♎	7/12	8:09pm
♏	7/15	5:51am
♐	7/17	11:35am
♑	7/19	1:26pm
♒	7/21	12:55pm
♓	7/23	12:12pm
♈	7/25	1:23pm
♉	7/27	5:54pm
♊	7/30	2:02am
♋	8/1	12:52pm
♌	8/4	1:10am
♍	8/6	1:54pm
♎	8/9	2:08am
♏	8/11	12:35pm
♐	8/13	7:47pm
♑	8/15	11:13pm
♒	8/17	11:39pm
♓	8/19	10:52pm
♈	8/21	11:01pm
♉	8/24	1:58am
♊	8/26	8:43am
♋	8/28	6:57pm
♌	8/31	7:14am
♍	9/2	7:56pm
♎	9/5	7:52am
♏	9/7	6:10pm
♐	9/10	2:03am
♑	9/12	6:56am
♒	9/14	9:02am
♓	9/16	9:24am
♈	9/18	9:43am
♉	9/20	11:47am
♊	9/22	5:07pm
♋	9/25	2:10am
♌	9/27	2:03pm
♍	9/30	2:44am
♎	10/2	2:24pm
♏	10/5	12:03am
♐	10/7	7:28am
♑	10/9	12:43pm
♒	10/11	4:05pm
♓	10/13	6:05pm
♈	10/15	7:39pm
♉	10/17	10:04pm
♊	10/20	2:44am
♋	10/22	10:41am
♌	10/24	9:48pm
♍	10/27	10:28am
♎	10/29	10:15pm
♏	11/1	7:29am
♐	11/3	1:55pm
♑	11/5	6:17pm
♒	11/7	9:31pm
♓	11/10	12:22am
♈	11/12	3:22am
♉	11/14	7:02am
♊	11/16	12:10pm
♋	11/18	7:42pm
♌	11/21	6:10am
♍	11/23	6:41pm
♎	11/26	6:58am
♏	11/28	4:33pm
♐	11/30	10:32pm
♑	12/3	1:42am
♒	12/5	3:36am
♓	12/7	5:44am
♈	12/9	9:02am
♉	12/11	1:46pm
♊	12/13	7:59pm
♋	12/16	4:01am
♌	12/18	2:18pm
♍	12/21	2:39am
♎	12/23	3:26pm
♏	12/26	2:04am
♐	12/28	8:43am
♑	12/30	11:35am

Mercury Sign Changes 1900-2005

Sign	Date	Time
1900		
♑	1/9	2:10am
♒	1/28	5:11pm
♓	2/15	12:04am
♈	3/3	9:21pm
♓	3/29	11:07pm
♈	4/17	1:05am
♉	5/11	12:14am
♊	5/26	10:51am
♋	6/9	9:23am
♌	6/27	9:13am
♍	9/3	12:39am
♎	9/18	11:18pm
♏	10/7	8:22am
♐	10/30	6:29am
♏	11/18	8:38pm
♐	12/12	3:03pm
1901		
♑	1/2	12:27pm
♒	1/21	6:30am
♓	2/7	10:35am
♈	4/15	5:10pm
♉	5/3	1:58pm
♊	5/17	8:08pm
♋	6/1	11:35pm
♌	8/10	4:45am
♍	8/25	10:24pm
♎	9/11	6:21am
♏	10/1	4:35am
♐	12/6	11:38pm
♑	12/26	9:31am
1902		
♒	1/13	7:35pm
♓	2/1	3:58pm
♒	2/18	7:09am
♓	3/19	3:04am
♈	4/9	12:07pm
♉	4/25	8:41am
♊	5/9	12:09pm
♋	5/29	8:28am
♊	6/26	6:27am
♋	7/13	9:32am
♌	8/2	9:22pm
♍	8/17	4:34pm
♎	9/4	2:30am
♏	9/28	7:22am
♎	10/15	11:38pm
♏	11/10	3:08pm
♐	11/30	1:30am
♑	12/19	3:01am
1903		
♒	1/6	7:31pm
♓	3/14	9:52pm
♈	4/2	12:25am
♉	4/16	9:51pm
♊	5/2	1:36pm
♋	7/10	1:08pm
♌	7/25	12:11pm
♍	8/9	5:51pm
♎	8/29	5:36am
♏	11/4	4:56am
♐	11/22	7:22pm
♑	12/12	12:14am
1904		
♒	1/2	9:24am
♑	1/14	3:47am
♒	2/15	10:59am
♓	3/7	8:05am
♈	3/23	11:34pm
♉	4/7	7:13pm
♊	6/14	6:23am
♋	7/1	10:14pm
♌	7/16	12:26am
♍	8/1	1:25pm
♎	8/28	8:17am
♍	9/7	8:25pm
♎	10/9	1:51am
♏	10/26	8:16pm
♐	11/14	1:47pm
♑	12/4	2:14pm
1905		
♒	2/9	5:35am
♓	2/27	10:07pm
♈	3/15	7:33pm
♉	4/1	6:19pm
♈	4/28	12:43pm
♉	5/15	8:06pm
♊	6/8	6:00pm
♋	6/23	9:54am
♌	7/7	10:07pm
♍	7/27	6:51am
♎	10/1	11:17pm
♏	10/19	7:45am
♐	11/7	4:27pm
♑	12/2	4:46am
♐	12/10	12:57am
1906		
♑	1/12	8:56pm
♒	2/2	12:04pm
♓	2/20	3:32am
♈	3/8	2:10am
♉	5/15	3:10am
♊	5/31	10:49pm
♋	6/14	7:24pm
♌	6/30	9:27pm
♍	9/7	9:54pm
♎	9/24	3:26am
♏	10/11	11:37pm
♐	11/1	7:33pm
♏	12/6	10:06pm
♐	12/12	11:49pm
1907		
♑	1/7	12:55am
♒	1/26	5:00am
♓	2/12	8:38am
♈	3/3	8:52pm
♓	3/14	4:59am
♈	4/18	10:42am
♉	5/8	3:23pm
♊	5/23	10:39am
♋	6/6	4:43pm
♌	6/27	8:05am
♋	7/26	2:36pm
♌	8/12	4:20pm
♍	8/31	6:54am
♎	9/16	6:56am
♏	10/5	4:36am
♐	12/11	3:37am
♑	12/31	3:57am
1908		
♒	1/18	5:22pm
♓	2/5	4:24am
♈	4/12	10:48pm
♉	4/29	7:00pm
♊	5/13	8:52pm
♋	5/30	4:34am
♌	8/6	11:47pm
♍	8/22	1:31am
♎	9/7	6:14pm
♏	9/28	7:36pm
♎	11/1	10:44pm
♏	11/11	5:53pm
♐	12/3	5:54pm
♑	12/22	10:31pm
1909		
♒	1/10	9:00am
♓	3/17	11:31am
♈	4/6	1:27am
♉	4/21	10:00am
♊	5/5	9:46pm
♋	7/13	6:04am
♌	7/30	12:39am
♍	8/13	9:32pm
♎	9/1	12:05am
♏	11/7	6:06pm
♐	11/26	2:59pm
♑	12/15	4:33pm
1910		
♒	1/3	9:27pm
♑	1/31	2:44am
♒	2/15	1:10pm
♓	3/11	9:34pm
♈	3/29	6:52am
♉	4/13	12:28am
♊	4/30	3:54pm
♉	6/1	11:39pm
♊	6/12	12:14am
♋	7/7	3:28am
♌	7/21	12:38pm
♍	8/6	4:37am
♎	8/27	6:42am
♍	9/28	1:20pm
♎	10/12	4:36am
♏	10/31	6:09pm
♐	11/19	8:12am
♑	12/8	6:22pm
1911		
♒	2/13	4:03am
♓	3/4	9:14pm
♈	3/21	3:30am
♉	4/5	9:04am
♊	6/13	1:26am
♋	6/28	11:59pm
♌	7/13	3:20am
♍	7/30	1:41pm
♎	10/6	8:49pm
♏	10/24	6:33am
♐	11/12	4:56am
♑	12/3	1:44am
♐	12/27	4:35pm
1912		
♑	1/15	7:15am
♒	2/7	2:24am
♓	2/25	6:32am
♈	3/12	1:26am
♉	5/16	7:54pm
♊	6/5	5:10am
♋	6/19	9:00am
♌	7/4	9:00am
♍	7/26	8:13am
♌	8/21	3:21am
♍	9/10	5:07pm
♎	9/28	7:27am
♏	10/15	6:58pm
♐	11/4	2:46pm
1913		
♑	1/10	5:20am
♒	1/30	1:44am
♓	2/16	10:43am
♈	3/4	10:35pm
♓	4/7	3:02pm
♈	4/14	2:49am
♉	5/12	6:15am
♊	5/28	12:30am
♋	6/10	9:31pm
♌	6/28	5:37am
♍	9/4	10:58am
♎	9/20	10:03am
♏	10/8	2:53pm
♐	10/30	6:07pm
♏	11/23	12:26pm
♐	12/13	8:51am
1914		
♑	1/3	7:20pm
♒	1/22	3:51pm
♓	2/8	7:11pm
♈	4/16	4:06pm
♉	5/5	12:58am
♊	5/19	10:03am
♋	6/3	5:53am
♌	8/11	6:30am
♍	8/27	10:46am
♎	9/12	3:47pm
♏	10/2	5:54am
♐	12/8	4:53am
♑	12/27	5:40pm
1915		
♒	1/15	4:28am
♓	2/2	10:33am
♒	2/23	3:04pm
♓	3/19	8:46am
♈	4/10	7:22pm
♉	4/26	9:40pm
♊	5/10	11:47pm
♋	5/29	10:34am
♌	8/4	9:00am
♍	8/19	4:38am
♎	9/5	9:02am
♏	9/28	8:11am
♎	10/21	1:13am
♏	11/11	2:08pm
♐	12/1	9:18am
♑	12/20	11:14am
1916		
♒	1/8	1:22am
♓	3/15	12:08am
♈	4/2	11:00am
♉	4/17	11:00am
♊	5/2	4:14pm
♋	7/10	6:17pm
♌	7/26	1:42am
♍	8/10	4:04am
♎	8/29	4:52am
♏	11/4	12:25pm
♐	11/23	3:40am
♑	12/12	7:13am
1917		
♒	1/1	5:07pm
♑	1/18	4:29am
♒	2/15	3:21am
♓	3/8	3:34pm
♈	3/25	11:35am
♉	4/9	5:43am
♊	6/14	6:14pm
♋	7/3	10:27am
♌	7/17	1:26pm
♍	8/2	7:31pm
♎	8/26	10:50pm
♍	9/14	12:12pm
♎	10/10	4:48am
♏	10/28	5:23am
♐	11/15	9:29pm
♑	12/5	4:57pm
1918		
♒	2/10	9:24am
♓	3/1	7:52am
♈	3/17	7:24am
♉	4/2	1:15pm
♊	6/10	1:22am
♋	6/24	11:50pm
♌	7/9	8:39am
♍	7/28	1:27am
♎	10/3	8:59am
♏	10/20	4:47pm
♐	11/8	10:06pm
♑	12/1	4:19pm
♐	12/15	1:03pm
1919		
♑	1/13	6:13pm
♒	2/3	7:27pm
♓	2/21	2:10pm
♈	3/9	10:42am
♉	5/16	2:25am
♊	6/2	11:06am
♋	6/16	8:44am
♌	7/2	2:02am
♍	9/9	3:43am
♎	9/25	2:16pm
♏	10/13	7:25am
♐	11/2	7:07pm
1920		
♑	1/8	5:55am
♒	1/27	1:49pm
♓	2/13	6:41pm
♈	3/2	7:25pm
♓	3/19	4:26pm
♈	4/17	6:06pm
♉	5/8	11:55pm
♊	5/24	12:32am
♋	6/7	3:02am
♌	6/26	12:30pm
♋	8/2	10:10pm
♌	8/10	9:13am
♍	8/31	6:29pm
♎	9/16	5:13pm
♏	10/5	9:27am
♐	10/30	12:40pm
♏	11/10	7:45pm
♐	12/11	4:37am
♑	12/31	11:22am
1921		
♒	1/19	2:28am
♓	2/5	10:14am
♈	4/14	2:12am
♉	5/1	7:03am
♊	5/15	10:09am
♋	5/31	5:12am
♌	8/8	7:42am
♍	8/23	1:54pm
♎	9/9	2:37am
♏	9/29	4:01pm
♐	12/5	12:28am
♑	12/24	6:45am
1922		
♒	1/11	4:58pm
♓	2/1	5:43pm
♒	2/9	4:25am
♓	3/18	6:32am
♈	4/7	10:22am
♉	4/22	11:19pm
♊	5/7	7:03am
♋	6/1	3:08am
♊	6/10	10:13pm
♋	7/13	8:04pm
♌	7/31	1:25pm
♍	8/15	8:59am
♎	9/2	4:20am
♏	10/1	9:14am
♎	10/5	1:45am
♏	11/8	10:32pm
♐	11/27	11:05pm
♑	12/17	12:27am
1923		
♒	1/4	11:40pm
♑	2/6	3:36pm
♒	2/13	11:24pm
♓	3/13	2:36am
♈	3/30	6:09pm
♉	4/14	12:58pm
♊	5/1	5:18am
♋	7/8	12:47pm
♌	7/23	2:07am

Mercury Sign Changes 1900-2005

♍ 8/7 1:33pm
♎ 8/27 10:30pm
♍ 10/4 11:53am
♎ 10/11 10:23pm
♏ 11/2 2:47am
♐ 11/20 4:26pm
♑ 12/10 12:18am

1924

♒ 2/14 3:18am
♓ 3/5 5:53am
♈ 3/21 3:37pm
♉ 4/5 4:23pm
♊ 6/13 1:42am
♋ 6/29 1:22pm
♌ 7/13 3:38pm
♍ 7/30 4:48pm
♎ 10/7 4:12am
♏ 10/24 3:59pm
♐ 11/12 12:08pm
♑ 12/2 11:41pm
♐ 12/31 3:52pm

1925

♑ 1/14 7:16am
♒ 2/7 8:12am
♓ 2/25 4:53pm
♈ 3/13 12:36pm
♉ 4/1 3:21pm
♈ 4/15 11:12pm
♉ 5/17 1:32am
♊ 6/6 3:23pm
♋ 6/20 11:07pm
♌ 7/5 5:52pm
♍ 7/26 11:46am
♌ 8/27 6:28am
♍ 9/11 5:09am
♎ 9/29 6:04pm
♏ 10/17 3:52am
♐ 11/5 6:54pm

1926

♑ 1/11 7:27am
♒ 1/31 10:04am
♓ 2/17 9:30pm
♈ 3/6 2:57am
♉ 5/13 10:53am
♊ 5/29 1:51pm
♋ 6/12 10:08am
♌ 6/29 5:01am
♍ 9/5 8:33pm
♎ 9/21 8:57pm
♏ 10/9 9:58pm
♐ 10/31 11:01am
♏ 11/28 5:05am
♐ 12/13 8:38pm

1927

♑ 1/5 1:58am
♒ 1/24 1:13am
♓ 2/10 4:28am
♈ 4/17 12:24pm
♉ 5/6 11:28am
♊ 5/21 12:03am
♋ 6/4 1:38pm
♌ 6/28 7:33pm
♋ 7/14 4:08am
♌ 8/12 3:43am
♍ 8/28 11:07pm
♎ 9/14 1:37am
♏ 10/3 8:38am
♐ 12/9 9:26am
♑ 12/29 1:48am

1928

♒ 1/16 1:35pm
♓ 2/3 10:22am
♒ 2/29 6:00am
♓ 3/18 2:45am
♈ 4/11 1:55am
♉ 4/27 10:35am
♊ 5/11 12:08pm
♋ 5/28 11:03pm
♌ 8/4 8:00pm
♍ 8/19 4:59pm
♎ 9/5 4:20pm
♏ 9/27 6:12pm
♎ 10/24 9:43pm
♏ 11/11 9:05am
♐ 12/1 4:57pm
♑ 12/20 7:37pm

1929

♒ 1/8 8:09am
♓ 3/16 1:07am
♈ 4/3 9:21pm
♉ 4/19 12:23am
♊ 5/3 9:34pm
♋ 7/11 9:07pm
♌ 7/27 3:12pm
♍ 8/11 2:48pm
♎ 8/30 6:01am
♏ 11/5 7:29pm
♐ 11/24 12:06pm
♑ 12/13 2:42pm

1930

♒ 1/2 10:25am
♑ 1/23 12:30am
♒ 2/15 3:08pm
♓ 3/9 10:39pm
♈ 3/26 11:36pm
♉ 4/10 5:05pm
♊ 5/1 5:31am
♉ 5/17 11:06am
♊ 6/14 8:09pm
♋ 7/4 10:10pm
♌ 7/19 2:44am
♍ 8/4 2:38am
♎ 8/26 6:04pm
♍ 9/20 2:16am
♎ 10/11 4:45am
♏ 10/29 2:35pm
♐ 11/17 5:31am
♑ 12/6 8:57pm

1931

♒ 2/11 12:27pm
♓ 3/2 5:28pm
♈ 3/18 7:31pm
♉ 4/3 1:38pm
♊ 6/11 7:27am
♋ 6/26 1:49pm
♌ 7/10 7:56pm
♍ 7/28 11:24pm
♎ 10/4 6:27pm
♏ 10/22 2:08am
♐ 11/10 4:27am
♑ 12/2 12:00am
♐ 12/20 7:59am

1932

♑ 1/14 12:47pm
♒ 2/5 2:36am
♓ 2/23 12:50am
♈ 3/9 8:21pm
♉ 5/15 10:49pm
♊ 6/2 11:05pm
♋ 6/16 10:30pm
♌ 7/2 8:16am
♍ 7/27 8:38pm
♌ 8/10 7:31am
♍ 9/9 7:20am
♎ 9/26 1:15am
♏ 10/13 3:41pm
♐ 11/2 8:28pm

1933

♑ 1/8 10:25am
♒ 1/27 10:39pm
♓ 2/14 5:06am
♈ 3/3 10:49am
♓ 3/25 9:49pm
♈ 4/17 3:27pm
♉ 5/10 7:42am
♊ 5/25 2:27pm
♋ 6/8 2:12pm
♌ 6/27 1:12am
♍ 9/2 5:44am
♎ 9/18 3:48am
♏ 10/6 3:04pm
♐ 10/30 4:27am
♏ 11/16 2:07am
♐ 12/12 3:43am

1934

♑ 1/1 6:40pm
♒ 1/20 11:44am
♓ 2/6 5:24pm
♈ 4/15 4:14am
♉ 5/2 6:45pm
♊ 5/16 11:43pm
♋ 6/1 8:22am
♌ 8/9 1:49pm
♍ 8/25 2:18am
♎ 9/10 11:29am
♏ 9/30 2:46pm
♐ 12/6 6:42am
♑ 12/25 2:59pm

1935

♒ 1/13 1:20am
♓ 2/1 11:16am
♒ 2/15 3:02am
♓ 3/18 9:53pm
♈ 4/8 6:40pm
♉ 4/24 12:29pm
♊ 5/8 5:20pm
♋ 5/29 7:26pm
♊ 6/20 5:58pm
♋ 7/13 10:22pm
♌ 8/2 1:48am
♍ 8/16 8:39pm
♎ 9/3 9:33am
♏ 9/28 3:52pm
♎ 10/12 6:03pm
♏ 11/10 1:24am
♐ 11/29 7:05am
♑ 12/18 8:28am

1936

♒ 1/6 3:32am
♓ 3/13 6:40am
♈ 3/31 5:08am
♉ 4/15 1:45am
♊ 5/1 1:30am
♋ 7/8 8:47pm
♌ 7/23 3:39pm
♍ 8/7 10:59pm
♎ 8/27 5:43pm
♏ 11/2 11:00am
♐ 11/21 12:39am
♑ 12/10 6:40am

1937

♒ 1/1 4:41pm
♑ 1/9 9:28pm
♒ 2/14 12:26am
♓ 3/6 2:06pm
♈ 3/23 3:41am
♉ 4/7 1:09am
♊ 6/13 10:28pm
♋ 7/1 2:21am
♌ 7/15 4:11am
♍ 7/31 9:07pm
♎ 10/8 10:12am
♏ 10/26 1:14am
♐ 11/13 7:25pm
♑ 12/3 11:51pm

1938

♐ 1/6 9:37pm
♑ 1/12 10:30pm
♒ 2/8 1:17pm
♓ 2/27 3:01am
♈ 3/15 12:02am
♉ 4/1 1:24pm
♈ 4/23 1:56pm
♉ 5/16 5:46pm
♊ 6/8 12:32am
♋ 6/22 1:09pm
♌ 7/7 3:21am
♍ 7/26 10:55pm
♌ 9/3 2:58am
♍ 9/10 3:38pm
♎ 10/1 4:19am
♏ 10/18 12:43pm
♐ 11/6 11:33pm

1939

♑ 1/12 7:57am
♒ 2/1 5:57pm
♓ 2/19 8:09am
♈ 3/7 9:14am
♉ 5/14 1:43pm
♊ 5/31 2:45am
♋ 6/13 11:01pm
♌ 6/30 6:41am
♍ 9/7 4:58am
♎ 9/23 7:48am
♏ 10/11 5:20am
♐ 11/1 7:03am
♏ 12/3 7:22am
♐ 12/13 7:16pm

1940

♑ 1/6 7:56am
♒ 1/25 10:14am
♓ 2/11 2:01pm
♈ 3/4 10:09am
♓ 3/8 1:25am
♈ 4/17 4:56am
♉ 5/6 9:14pm
♊ 5/21 1:59pm
♋ 6/4 10:29pm
♌ 6/26 2:32pm
♋ 7/21 1:39am
♌ 8/11 5:06pm
♍ 8/29 11:11am
♎ 9/14 11:34am
♏ 10/3 12:14pm
♐ 12/9 12:45pm
♑ 12/29 9:35am

1941

♒ 1/16 10:36pm
♓ 2/3 1:08pm
♒ 3/7 2:22am
♓ 3/16 12:26pm
♈ 4/12 7:19am
♉ 4/28 11:09pm
♊ 5/13 12:50am
♋ 5/29 5:32pm
♌ 8/6 5:57am
♍ 8/21 5:18am
♎ 9/6 11:58pm
♏ 9/28 9:21am
♎ 10/29 8:34pm
♏ 11/11 8:11pm
♐ 12/3 12:11am
♑ 12/22 3:54am

1942

♒ 1/9 3:24pm
♓ 3/17 12:10am
♈ 4/5 7:06am
♉ 4/20 1:42pm
♊ 5/5 4:37am
♋ 7/12 8:24pm
♌ 7/29 4:24am
♍ 8/13 1:48am
♎ 8/31 8:27am
♏ 11/7 1:44am
♐ 11/25 8:26pm
♑ 12/14 10:21pm

1943

♒ 1/3 8:27am
♑ 1/27 11:42pm
♒ 2/15 7:00pm
♓ 3/11 4:59am
♈ 3/28 11:19am
♉ 4/12 4:56am
♊ 4/30 3:56pm
♉ 5/26 10:04am
♊ 6/14 12:46am
♋ 7/6 9:05am
♌ 7/20 4:08pm
♍ 8/5 10:33am
♎ 8/27 12:36am
♍ 9/25 9:56am
♎ 10/11 11:27pm
♏ 10/30 11:37pm
♐ 11/18 1:39pm
♑ 12/8 1:47am

1944

♒ 2/12 2:17pm
♓ 3/3 2:45am
♈ 3/19 7:43am
♉ 4/3 5:29pm
♊ 6/11 11:46am
♋ 6/27 3:40am
♌ 7/11 7:41am
♍ 7/28 11:44pm
♎ 10/5 3:17am
♏ 10/22 11:33am
♐ 11/10 11:09am
♑ 12/1 3:31pm
♐ 12/23 11:21pm

1945

♑ 1/14 3:04am
♒ 2/5 9:20am
♓ 2/23 11:25am
♈ 3/11 6:45am
♉ 5/16 3:21pm
♊ 6/4 10:30am
♋ 6/18 12:27pm
♌ 7/3 3:39pm
♍ 7/26 2:48pm
♌ 8/17 8:50am
♍ 9/10 7:21am
♎ 9/27 12:08pm
♏ 10/15 12:13am
♐ 11/3 11:06pm

1946

♑ 1/9 2:09pm
♒ 1/29 7:22am
♓ 2/15 3:43pm
♈ 3/4 9:26am
♓ 4/1 6:16pm
♈ 4/16 2:54pm
♉ 5/11 2:29pm
♊ 5/27 4:13am
♋ 6/10 2:00am
♌ 6/27 7:07pm
♍ 9/3 4:29pm
♎ 9/19 2:34pm
♏ 10/7 9:21pm
♐ 10/30 11:23am
♏ 11/20 8:16pm
♐ 12/13 12:03am

Mercury Sign Changes 1900-2005

1947	♑ 12/5 1:57am	♏ 11/11 10:25am	♏ 10/16 8:52am	♑ 12/12 8:51pm	♏ 10/5 10:03pm
♑ 1/3 1:46am	**1951**	♐ 12/4 7:02am	♐ 11/5 2:36am	**1963**	♐ 10/30 7:38am
♒ 1/21 9:06pm	♒ 2/9 5:50pm	♑ 12/23 12:10pm	**1959**	♒ 1/2 1:10am	♏ 11/13 3:26am
♓ 2/8 1:31am	♓ 2/28 1:04pm	**1955**	♑ 1/10 4:48pm	♑ 1/20 4:59am	♐ 12/11 3:27pm
♈ 4/16 4:31am	♈ 3/16 11:53am	♒ 1/10 11:05pm	♒ 1/30 3:41pm	♒ 2/15 10:08am	**1967**
♉ 5/4 6:03am	♉ 4/2 3:27am	♓ 3/17 8:49pm	♓ 2/17 2:15am	♓ 3/9 5:26am	♑ 1/1 12:52am
♊ 5/18 1:33pm	♈ 5/1 9:25pm	♈ 4/6 4:15pm	♈ 3/5 11:52am	♈ 3/26 3:52am	♒ 1/19 5:05pm
♋ 6/2 1:40pm	♉ 5/15 1:40am	♉ 4/22 2:57am	♉ 5/12 7:48pm	♉ 4/9 10:03pm	♓ 2/6 12:38am
♌ 8/10 5:40pm	♊ 6/9 8:43am	♊ 5/6 1:05pm	♊ 5/28 5:35pm	♊ 5/3 4:17am	♈ 4/14 2:38pm
♍ 8/26 2:50pm	♋ 6/24 3:13am	♋ 7/13 2:44pm	♋ 6/11 2:11pm	♉ 5/10 8:39pm	♉ 5/1 11:26pm
♎ 9/11 8:54pm	♌ 7/8 1:39pm	♌ 7/30 5:22pm	♌ 6/28 4:31pm	♊ 6/14 11:21pm	♊ 5/16 3:27am
♏ 10/1 3:26pm	♍ 7/27 3:24pm	♍ 8/14 1:08pm	♍ 9/5 2:28am	♋ 7/4 3:00am	♋ 5/31 6:02pm
♐ 12/7 12:32pm	♎ 10/2 2:25pm	♎ 9/1 12:06pm	♎ 9/21 1:20am	♌ 7/18 6:19am	♌ 8/8 10:09pm
♑ 12/26 11:17pm	♏ 10/19 9:52pm	♏ 11/8 6:57am	♏ 10/9 4:02am	♍ 8/3 9:20am	♍ 8/24 6:17am
1948	♐ 11/8 4:59am	♐ 11/27 4:34am	♐ 10/31 1:16am	♎ 8/26 8:33pm	♎ 9/9 4:53pm
♒ 1/14 10:06am	♑ 12/1 8:41pm	♑ 12/16 6:06am	♏ 11/25 11:53am	♍ 9/16 8:29pm	♏ 9/30 1:46am
♓ 2/2 12:46am	♐ 12/12 12:39pm	**1956**	♐ 12/13 3:42pm	♎ 10/10 4:44pm	♐ 12/5 1:41pm
♒ 2/20 11:08am	**1952**	♒ 1/4 9:16am	**1960**	♏ 10/28 7:54pm	♑ 12/24 8:33pm
♓ 3/18 8:14am	♑ 1/13 6:44am	♑ 2/2 12:18pm	♑ 1/4 8:24am	♐ 11/16 11:07am	**1968**
♈ 4/9 2:26am	♒ 2/3 1:38am	♒ 2/15 6:34am	♒ 1/23 6:16am	♑ 12/6 5:17am	♒ 1/12 7:19am
♉ 4/25 1:38am	♓ 2/20 6:55pm	♓ 3/11 10:27am	♓ 2/9 10:13am	**1964**	♓ 2/1 12:57pm
♊ 5/9 4:38am	♈ 3/7 5:10pm	♈ 3/28 10:41pm	♈ 4/16 2:22am	♒ 2/10 9:30pm	♒ 2/11 6:54pm
♋ 5/28 10:50am	♉ 5/14 2:43pm	♉ 4/12 5:10pm	♉ 5/4 4:45pm	♓ 2/29 10:50pm	♓ 3/17 2:45pm
♊ 6/28 5:57pm	♊ 5/31 3:26pm	♊ 4/29 10:41pm	♊ 5/19 3:27am	♈ 3/16 11:54pm	♈ 4/7 1:01am
♋ 7/11 8:56pm	♋ 6/14 12:22pm	♋ 7/6 7:02pm	♋ 6/2 8:31pm	♉ 4/2 12:57am	♉ 4/22 4:18pm
♌ 8/2 1:54pm	♌ 6/30 10:27am	♌ 7/21 5:35am	♌ 7/1 1:14am	♊ 6/9 3:45pm	♊ 5/6 10:56pm
♍ 8/17 8:44am	♍ 9/7 12:02pm	♍ 8/5 7:06pm	♋ 7/6 1:22am	♋ 6/24 5:17pm	♋ 5/29 10:44pm
♎ 9/3 3:47pm	♎ 9/23 6:45pm	♎ 8/26 1:30pm	♌ 8/10 5:49pm	♌ 7/9 12:38am	♊ 6/13 10:32pm
♏ 9/27 7:19am	♏ 10/11 1:05pm	♍ 9/29 9:25pm	♍ 8/27 3:11am	♍ 7/27 11:35am	♋ 7/13 1:30am
♎ 10/17 3:33am	♐ 11/1 5:34am	♎ 10/11 7:30am	♎ 9/12 6:29am	♎ 10/3 12:12am	♌ 7/31 6:11am
♏ 11/10 2:19am	**1953**	♏ 10/31 8:19am	♏ 10/1 5:17pm	♏ 10/20 7:11am	♍ 8/15 12:53am
♐ 11/29 3:09pm	♑ 1/6 1:24pm	♐ 11/18 9:42pm	♐ 12/7 5:30pm	♐ 11/8 11:02am	♎ 9/1 4:59pm
♑ 12/18 4:46pm	♒ 1/25 7:10pm	♑ 12/8 7:11am	♑ 12/27 7:21am	♑ 11/30 7:30pm	♏ 9/28 2:40pm
1949	♓ 2/11 11:57pm	**1957**	**1961**	♐ 12/16 2:31pm	♎ 10/7 10:46pm
♒ 1/6 8:53am	♈ 3/2 7:21pm	♒ 2/12 2:30pm	♒ 1/14 6:58pm	**1965**	♏ 11/8 11:00am
♓ 3/14 9:52am	♓ 3/15 9:16pm	♓ 3/4 11:34am	♓ 2/1 9:39pm	♑ 1/13 3:12am	♐ 11/27 12:47pm
♈ 4/1 4:02pm	♈ 4/17 4:48pm	♈ 3/20 7:48pm	♒ 2/24 8:22pm	♒ 2/3 9:02am	♑ 12/16 2:11pm
♉ 4/16 2:55pm	♉ 5/8 6:24am	♉ 4/4 11:37pm	♓ 3/18 10:16am	♓ 2/21 5:40am	**1969**
♊ 5/2 2:19am	♊ 5/23 3:58am	♊ 6/12 1:40pm	♈ 4/10 9:22am	♈ 3/9 2:19am	♒ 1/4 12:18pm
♋ 7/10 3:19am	♋ 6/6 8:23am	♋ 6/28 5:08pm	♉ 4/26 2:34pm	♉ 5/15 1:19pm	♓ 3/12 3:19pm
♌ 7/25 5:20am	♌ 6/26 11:01am	♌ 7/12 7:41pm	♊ 5/10 4:34pm	♊ 6/2 3:47am	♈ 3/30 9:59am
♍ 8/9 9:04am	♋ 7/28 1:40pm	♍ 7/30 1:44am	♋ 5/28 5:23pm	♋ 6/16 2:04am	♉ 4/14 5:55am
♎ 8/28 3:48pm	♌ 8/11 2:04pm	♎ 10/6 11:09am	♌ 8/4 1:15am	♌ 7/1 3:55pm	♊ 4/30 3:18pm
♏ 11/3 6:58pm	♍ 8/30 10:59pm	♏ 10/23 8:50pm	♍ 8/18 8:52pm	♍ 7/31 11:24am	♋ 7/8 3:58am
♐ 11/22 9:06am	♎ 9/15 9:45pm	♐ 11/11 6:00pm	♎ 9/4 10:32pm	♌ 8/3 8:09am	♌ 7/22 7:11pm
♑ 12/11 1:37pm	♏ 10/4 4:40pm	♑ 12/2 11:19am	♏ 9/27 12:16pm	♍ 9/8 5:14pm	♍ 8/7 4:21am
1950	♐ 10/31 3:49pm	♐ 12/28 5:30pm	♎ 10/22 2:29am	♎ 9/25 5:49am	♎ 8/27 6:50am
♒ 1/1 12:39pm	♏ 11/6 10:18pm	**1958**	♏ 11/10 11:53pm	♏ 10/12 9:15pm	♍ 10/7 2:57am
♑ 1/15 7:35am	♐ 12/10 2:48pm	♑ 1/14 10:03am	♐ 11/30 10:54pm	♐ 11/2 6:04am	♎ 10/9 4:56pm
♒ 2/14 7:12pm	♑ 12/30 5:14pm	♒ 2/6 3:21pm	♑ 12/20 1:04am	**1966**	♏ 11/1 4:53pm
♓ 3/7 10:04pm	**1954**	♓ 2/24 9:44pm	**1962**	♑ 1/7 6:26pm	♐ 11/20 6:00am
♈ 3/24 3:52pm	♒ 1/18 7:43am	♈ 3/12 5:31pm	♒ 1/7 3:08pm	♒ 1/27 4:10am	♑ 12/9 1:21pm
♉ 4/8 11:13am	♓ 2/4 6:03pm	♉ 4/2 7:17pm	♓ 3/15 11:43am	♓ 2/13 10:17am	**1970**
♊ 6/14 2:33pm	♈ 4/13 11:34am	♈ 4/10 1:51pm	♈ 4/3 2:32am	♈ 3/3 2:57am	♒ 2/13 1:08pm
♋ 7/2 2:57pm	♉ 4/30 11:26am	♉ 5/17 1:53am	♉ 4/18 4:10am	♓ 3/22 2:34am	♓ 3/5 8:10pm
♌ 7/16 5:08pm	♊ 5/14 1:57pm	♊ 6/5 8:59pm	♊ 5/3 6:05am	♈ 4/17 9:31pm	♈ 3/22 7:59am
♍ 8/2 2:44am	♋ 5/30 4:13pm	♋ 6/20 2:20am	♋ 7/11 7:36am	♉ 5/9 2:48pm	♉ 4/6 7:40am
♎ 8/27 2:17pm	♌ 8/7 2:44pm	♌ 7/4 11:46pm	♌ 7/26 6:50pm	♊ 5/24 5:59pm	♊ 6/13 12:46pm
♍ 9/10 7:16pm	♍ 8/22 5:42pm	♍ 7/26 10:08am	♍ 8/10 7:29pm	♋ 6/7 7:11pm	♋ 6/30 6:22am
♎ 10/9 2:40pm	♎ 9/8 8:05am	♌ 8/23 2:31pm	♎ 8/29 3:48pm	♌ 6/26 7:05pm	♌ 7/14 8:06am
♏ 10/27 10:36am	♏ 9/29 4:06am	♍ 9/11 1:10am	♏ 11/5 2:20am	♍ 9/1 10:35am	♍ 7/31 5:21am
♐ 11/15 3:10am	♎ 11/4 12:37pm	♎ 9/28 10:45pm	♐ 11/23 5:31pm	♎ 9/17 8:19am	♎ 10/7 6:04pm

Mercury Sign Changes 1900-2005

Sign	Date	Time
♏	10/25	6:16am
♐	11/13	1:16am
♑	12/3	10:14am
1971		
♐	1/2	11:36pm
♑	1/14	2:16am
♒	2/7	8:51pm
♓	2/26	7:57am
♈	3/14	4:46am
♉	4/1	2:11pm
♈	4/18	9:52pm
♉	5/17	3:32am
♊	6/7	6:45am
♋	6/21	4:25pm
♌	7/6	8:53am
♍	7/26	5:03pm
♌	8/29	8:42pm
♍	9/11	6:45am
♎	9/30	9:19am
♏	10/17	5:49pm
♐	11/6	6:59am
1972		
♑	1/11	6:18pm
♒	1/31	11:46pm
♓	2/18	12:53pm
♈	3/5	4:59pm
♉	5/12	11:45pm
♊	5/29	6:46am
♋	6/12	2:56am
♌	6/28	4:52pm
♍	9/5	11:36am
♎	9/21	12:11pm
♏	10/9	11:11am
♐	10/30	7:27pm
♏	11/29	7:08am
♐	12/12	11:20pm
1973		
♑	1/4	2:41pm
♒	1/23	3:23pm
♓	2/9	7:30pm
♈	4/16	9:17pm
♉	5/6	2:55am
♊	5/20	5:24pm
♋	6/4	4:42am
♌	6/27	6:42am
♋	7/16	8:03am
♌	8/11	12:21pm
♍	8/28	3:22pm
♎	9/13	4:16pm
♏	10/2	8:12pm
♐	12/8	9:29pm
♑	12/28	3:14pm
1974		
♒	1/16	3:56am
♓	2/2	10:42pm
♒	3/2	5:49pm
♓	3/17	8:11pm
♈	4/11	3:20pm
♉	4/28	3:10am
♊	5/12	4:55am
♋	5/29	8:03am
♌	8/5	11:42am
♍	8/20	9:04am
♎	9/6	5:48am
♏	9/28	12:20am
♎	10/26	11:21pm
♏	11/11	4:05pm
♐	12/2	6:17am
♑	12/21	9:16am
1975		
♒	1/8	9:58pm
♓	3/16	11:50am
♈	4/4	12:28pm
♉	4/19	5:20pm
♊	5/4	11:55am
♋	7/12	8:56am
♌	7/28	8:05am
♍	8/12	6:12am
♎	8/30	5:20pm
♏	11/6	8:58am
♐	11/25	1:44am
♑	12/14	4:10am
1976		
♒	1/2	8:22pm
♑	1/25	1:30am
♒	2/15	7:03pm
♓	3/9	12:02pm
♈	3/26	3:36pm
♉	4/10	9:29am
♊	4/29	11:11pm
♉	5/19	7:21pm
♊	6/13	7:20pm
♋	7/4	2:18pm
♌	7/18	7:35pm
♍	8/3	4:41pm
♎	8/25	8:52pm
♍	9/21	7:15am
♎	10/10	2:47pm
♏	10/29	4:55am
♐	11/16	7:02pm
♑	12/6	9:25am
1977		
♒	2/10	11:55pm
♓	3/2	8:09am
♈	3/18	11:56am
♉	4/3	2:46am
♊	6/10	9:07pm
♋	6/26	7:07am
♌	7/10	12:00pm
♍	7/28	10:15am
♎	10/4	9:16am
♏	10/21	4:23pm
♐	11/9	5:20pm
♑	12/1	6:43am
♐	12/21	7:18am
1978		
♑	1/13	8:07pm
♒	2/4	3:54pm
♓	2/22	4:11pm
♈	3/10	12:10pm
♉	5/16	8:20am
♊	6/3	3:26pm
♋	6/17	3:49pm
♌	7/2	10:28pm
♍	7/27	6:10am
♌	8/13	7:05am
♍	9/9	7:23pm
♎	9/26	4:40pm
♏	10/14	5:30am
♐	11/3	7:48am
1979		
♑	1/8	10:33pm
♒	1/28	12:49pm
♓	2/14	8:38pm
♈	3/3	9:32pm
♓	3/28	10:39am
♈	4/17	12:48pm
♉	5/10	10:03pm
♊	5/26	7:44am
♋	6/9	6:32am
♌	6/27	9:51am
♍	9/2	9:39pm
♎	9/18	6:59pm
♏	10/7	3:55am
♐	10/30	7:06am
♏	11/18	3:08am
♐	12/12	1:34pm
1980		
♑	1/2	8:02am
♒	1/21	2:18am
♓	2/7	8:07am
♈	4/14	3:58pm
♉	5/2	10:56am
♊	5/16	5:06pm
♋	5/31	10:05pm
♌	8/9	3:31am
♍	8/24	6:47pm
♎	9/10	2:00am
♏	9/30	1:16am
♐	12/5	7:45pm
♑	12/25	4:46am
1981		
♒	1/12	3:48pm
♓	1/31	5:35pm
♒	2/16	8:02am
♓	3/18	4:33am
♈	4/8	9:11am
♉	4/24	5:31am
♊	5/8	9:42am
♋	5/28	5:04pm
♊	6/22	10:51pm
♋	7/12	9:08pm
♌	8/1	6:30pm
♍	8/16	12:47pm
♎	9/2	10:40pm
♏	9/27	11:02am
♎	10/14	2:09am
♏	11/9	1:14pm
♐	11/28	8:52pm
♑	12/17	10:21pm
1982		
♒	1/5	4:49pm
♓	3/13	7:11pm
♈	3/31	8:59pm
♉	4/15	6:54pm
♊	5/1	1:29pm
♋	7/9	11:26am
♌	7/24	8:48am
♍	8/8	2:06pm
♎	8/28	3:22am
♏	11/3	1:10am
♐	11/21	2:28pm
♑	12/10	8:04pm
1983		
♒	1/1	1:32pm
♑	1/12	6:55am
♒	2/14	9:36am
♓	3/7	4:23am
♈	3/23	8:09pm
♉	4/7	5:04pm
♊	6/14	8:06am
♋	7/1	7:18pm
♌	7/15	8:57pm
♍	8/1	10:22am
♎	8/29	6:07am
♍	9/6	2:30am
♎	10/8	11:44pm
♏	10/26	3:47pm
♐	11/14	8:56am
♑	12/4	11:22am
1984		
♒	2/9	1:50am
♓	2/27	6:07pm
♈	3/14	4:27pm
♉	3/31	8:25pm
♈	4/25	11:49am
♉	5/15	12:33pm
♊	6/7	3:45pm
♋	6/22	6:39am
♌	7/6	6:56pm
♍	7/26	6:49am
♎	9/30	7:44pm
♏	10/18	3:01am
♐	11/6	12:09pm
♑	12/1	4:29pm
♐	12/7	9:46pm
1985		
♑	1/11	6:25pm
♒	2/1	7:43am
♓	2/18	11:41pm
♈	3/7	12:07am
♉	5/14	2:10am
♊	5/30	7:44pm
♋	6/13	4:11pm
♌	6/29	7:34pm
♍	9/6	7:39pm
♎	9/22	11:13pm
♏	10/10	6:50pm
♐	10/31	4:44pm
♏	12/4	7:23pm
♐	12/12	11:05am
1986		
♑	1/5	8:42pm
♒	1/25	12:33am
♓	2/11	5:21am
♈	3/3	7:22am
♓	3/11	5:36pm
♈	4/17	12:33pm
♉	5/7	12:33pm
♊	5/22	7:26am
♋	6/5	2:06pm
♌	6/26	2:15pm
♋	7/23	9:51pm
♌	8/11	9:09pm
♍	8/30	3:28am
♎	9/15	2:28am
♏	10/4	12:19am
♐	12/10	12:34am
♑	12/29	11:09pm
1987		
♒	1/17	1:08pm
♓	2/4	2:31am
♒	3/11	9:55pm
♓	3/13	9:09pm
♈	4/12	8:23pm
♉	4/29	3:39pm
♊	5/13	5:50pm
♋	5/30	4:21am
♌	8/6	9:20pm
♍	8/21	9:36pm
♎	9/7	1:52pm
♏	9/28	5:21pm
♎	11/1	1:57am
♏	11/11	9:57pm
♐	12/3	1:33pm
♑	12/22	5:40pm
1988		
♒	1/10	5:28am
♓	3/16	10:09am
♈	4/4	10:04pm
♉	4/20	6:42am
♊	5/4	7:40pm
♋	7/12	6:42am
♌	7/28	9:19pm
♍	8/12	5:29pm
♎	8/30	8:25pm
♏	11/6	2:57pm
♐	11/25	10:04am
♑	12/14	11:53am
1989		
♒	1/2	7:41pm
♑	1/29	4:06am
♒	2/14	6:11pm
♓	3/10	6:07pm
♈	3/28	3:16am
♉	4/11	9:36pm
♊	4/29	7:53pm
♉	5/28	10:53pm
♊	6/12	8:56am
♋	7/6	12:55am
♌	7/20	9:04am
♍	8/5	12:54am
♎	8/26	6:14am
♍	9/26	3:28pm
♎	10/11	6:11am
♏	10/30	1:53pm
♐	11/18	3:10am
♑	12/7	2:30pm
1990		
♒	2/12	1:11am
♓	3/3	5:14pm
♈	3/20	12:04am
♉	4/4	7:35am
♊	6/12	12:29am
♋	6/27	8:46pm
♌	7/11	11:48pm
♍	7/29	11:10am
♎	10/5	5:44pm
♏	10/23	1:46am
♐	11/11	12:06am
♑	12/2	12:13am
♐	12/25	10:57pm
1991		
♑	1/14	8:02am
♒	2/5	10:20pm
♓	2/24	2:35am
♈	3/11	10:40pm
♉	5/16	10:45pm
♊	6/5	2:24am
♋	6/19	5:40am
♌	7/4	6:05am
♍	7/26	1:00pm
♌	8/19	9:40pm
♍	9/10	5:14pm
♎	9/28	3:26am
♏	10/15	2:01pm
♐	11/4	10:41am
1992		
♑	1/10	1:46am
♒	1/29	9:15pm
♓	2/16	7:04am
♈	3/3	9:45pm
♓	4/3	11:52pm
♈	4/14	5:35pm
♉	5/11	4:10am
♊	5/26	9:16pm
♋	6/9	6:27pm
♌	6/27	5:11am
♍	9/3	8:03am
♎	9/19	5:41am
♏	10/7	10:13am
♐	10/29	5:02pm
♏	11/21	7:44pm
♐	12/12	8:05am
1993		
♑	1/2	2:47pm
♒	1/21	11:25am
♓	2/7	4:19pm
♈	4/15	3:18pm
♉	5/3	9:54pm
♊	5/18	6:53am
♋	6/2	3:54am
♌	8/10	5:51am
♍	8/26	7:06am
♎	9/11	11:18am
♏	10/1	2:09am
♐	12/7	1:04am
♑	12/26	12:47pm
1994		
♒	1/14	12:25am
♓	2/1	10:28am
♒	2/21	3:15pm

Mercury Sign Changes 1900-2005

♓ 3/18 12:04pm	♓ 3/7 11:53am	♓ 2/20 10:22am	♓ 2/5 8:09am	♓ 3/11 11:34pm	♉ 4/1 2:27am
♈ 4/9 4:30pm	♈ 3/24 8:03am	♈ 3/8 8:28am	♈ 4/13 12:17am	♈ 3/29 2:44pm	♈ 4/13 1:23am
♉ 4/25 6:27pm	♉ 4/8 3:16am	♉ 5/15 2:10am	♉ 4/30 3:53am	♉ 4/13 10:10am	♉ 5/16 6:54am
♊ 5/9 9:08pm	♊ 6/13 9:45pm	♊ 6/1 8:07am	♊ 5/14 7:10am	♊ 4/30 7:15am	♊ 6/5 12:47pm
♋ 5/28 2:52pm	♋ 7/2 7:37am	♋ 6/15 5:33am	♋ 5/30 4:27am	♋ 7/7 10:35am	♋ 6/19 7:49pm
♊ 7/2 11:18pm	♌ 7/16 9:56am	♌ 6/30 11:52pm	♌ 8/7 5:42am	♌ 7/21 10:41pm	♌ 7/4 2:52pm
♋ 7/10 12:41pm	♍ 8/1 4:17pm	♍ 9/8 1:58am	♍ 8/22 10:11am	♍ 8/6 9:51am	♍ 7/25 1:58pm
♌ 8/3 6:09am	♎ 8/26 5:17am	♎ 9/24 10:13am	♎ 9/7 10:22pm	♎ 8/26 9:10pm	♌ 8/25 1:33am
♍ 8/18 12:44am	♍ 9/12 9:32am	♏ 10/12 2:44am	♏ 9/28 1:28pm	♍ 10/2 9:26am	♍ 9/10 7:38am
♎ 9/4 4:55am	♎ 10/9 3:13am	♐ 11/1 4:02pm	♎ 11/7 7:28am	♎ 10/11 5:56am	♎ 9/28 2:13pm
♏ 9/27 8:51am	♏ 10/27 1:01am	**1999**	♏ 11/8 7:55pm	♏ 10/31 10:43pm	♏ 10/15 10:57pm
♎ 10/19 6:19am	♐ 11/14 4:36pm	♑ 1/7 2:04am	♐ 12/3 8:26pm	♐ 11/19 11:29am	♐ 11/4 2:40pm
♏ 11/10 12:46pm	♑ 12/4 1:48pm	♒ 1/26 9:32am	♑ 12/23 2:03am	♑ 12/8 8:21pm	**2005**
♐ 11/30 4:38am	**1997**	♓ 2/12 3:28pm	**2001**	**2003**	♑ 1/10 4:09am
♑ 12/19 6:26am	♒ 2/9 5:53am	♈ 3/2 10:50pm	♒ 1/10 1:26pm	♒ 2/13 1:00am	♒ 1/30 5:37am
1995	♓ 2/28 3:54am	♓ 3/18 9:23am	♓ 2/1 7:13am	♓ 3/5 2:04am	♓ 2/16 5:46pm
♒ 1/6 10:17pm	♈ 3/16 4:13am	♈ 4/17 10:09pm	♒ 2/6 7:57pm	♈ 3/21 12:16pm	♈ 3/5 1:34am
♓ 3/14 9:35pm	♉ 4/1 1:45pm	♉ 5/8 9:22pm	♓ 3/17 6:05am	♉ 4/5 2:37pm	♉ 5/12 9:13am
♈ 4/2 7:29am	♈ 5/5 1:48am	♊ 5/23 9:22pm	♈ 4/6 7:14am	♊ 6/13 1:34am	♊ 5/28 10:44am
♉ 4/17 7:54am	♉ 5/12 10:25am	♋ 6/7 12:18am	♉ 4/21 8:08pm	♋ 6/29 10:17am	♋ 6/11 7:03am
♊ 5/2 3:18pm	♊ 6/8 11:25pm	♌ 6/26 3:39pm	♊ 5/6 4:53am	♌ 7/13 12:10pm	♌ 6/28 4:01am
♋ 7/10 4:58pm	♋ 6/23 8:41pm	♋ 7/31 6:44pm	♋ 7/12 10:47pm	♍ 7/30 2:05pm	♍ 9/4 5:52pm
♌ 7/25 10:19pm	♌ 7/8 5:28am	♌ 8/11 4:25am	♌ 7/30 10:18am	♎ 10/7 1:28am	♎ 9/20 4:40pm
♍ 8/10 12:13am	♍ 7/27 12:42am	♍ 8/31 3:15pm	♍ 8/14 5:04am	♏ 10/24 11:20am	♏ 10/8 5:15pm
♎ 8/29 2:07am	♎ 10/2 5:38am	♎ 9/16 12:53pm	♎ 9/1 12:37am	♐ 11/12 7:19am	♐ 10/30 9:02am
♏ 11/4 8:50am	♏ 10/19 12:08pm	♏ 10/5 5:12am	♏ 11/7 7:53pm	♑ 12/2 9:34pm	♏ 11/26 11:53am
♐ 11/22 10:46pm	♐ 11/7 5:42pm	♐ 10/30 8:08pm	♐ 11/26 6:23pm	♐ 12/30 7:52pm	♐ 12/12 9:19pm
♑ 12/12 2:57am	♑ 11/30 7:11pm	♏ 11/9 8:13pm	♑ 12/15 7:55pm	**2004**	
1996	♐ 12/13 6:06pm	♐ 12/11 2:09am	**2002**	♑ 1/14 11:02am	
♒ 1/1 6:06pm	**1998**	♑ 12/31 6:48am	♒ 1/3 9:38pm	♒ 2/7 4:20am	
♑ 1/17 9:37am	♑ 1/12 4:20pm	**2000**	♑ 2/4 4:19am	♓ 2/25 12:58pm	
♒ 2/15 2:44am	♒ 2/2 3:15pm	♒ 1/18 10:20pm	♒ 2/13 5:20pm	♈ 3/12 9:44am	

Venus Sign Changes 1900-2005

Sign	Date	Time
1900		
♓	1/20	1:39am
♈	2/13	2:08pm
♉	3/10	6:08pm
♊	4/6	4:15am
♋	5/5	3:46pm
♌	9/8	8:55pm
♍	10/8	1:36pm
♎	11/3	9:33pm
♏	11/28	9:55pm
♐	12/23	7:48am
1901		
♑	1/16	11:29am
♒	2/9	1:06pm
♓	3/5	2:51pm
♈	3/29	6:03pm
♉	4/22	11:34pm
♊	5/17	7:34am
♋	6/10	5:37pm
♌	7/5	5:22am
♍	7/29	7:13pm
♎	8/23	12:33pm
♏	9/17	11:29am
♐	10/12	7:15pm
♑	11/7	7:25pm
♒	12/5	1:32pm
1902		
♓	1/11	5:47pm
♒	2/6	10:55pm
♓	4/4	7:31pm
♈	5/7	7:05am
♉	6/3	11:59pm
♊	6/30	6:28am
♋	7/25	6:59pm
♌	8/19	6:28pm
♍	9/13	7:18am
♎	10/7	12:06pm
♏	10/31	11:51am
♐	11/24	9:06am
♑	12/18	5:32am
1903		
♒	1/11	2:18am
♓	2/4	12:47am
♈	2/28	3:03am
♉	3/24	11:53am
♊	4/18	6:41am
♋	5/13	4:23pm
♌	6/9	3:07am
♍	7/7	8:36pm
♎	8/17	9:51pm
♍	9/6	2:28am
♎	11/8	2:44pm
♏	12/9	2:42pm
1904		
♐	1/5	3:43am
♑	1/30	9:28am
♒	2/24	3:08am
♓	3/19	4:01pm
♈	4/13	3:27am
♉	5/7	2:52pm
♊	6/1	2:28am
♋	6/25	1:29pm
♌	7/19	11:01pm
♍	8/13	6:53am
♎	9/6	1:50pm
♏	9/30	9:04pm
♐	10/25	5:37am
♑	11/18	4:40pm
♒	12/13	9:08am
1905		
♓	1/7	2:38pm
♈	2/3	4:49am
♉	3/6	5:26am
♈	5/9	10:37am
♉	5/28	11:18am
♊	7/8	12:00pm
♋	8/6	8:18am
♌	9/1	8:16pm
♍	9/27	4:02am
♎	10/21	6:32pm
♏	11/14	10:40pm
♐	12/8	9:31pm
1906		
♑	1/1	6:23pm
♒	1/25	3:12pm
♓	2/18	1:13pm
♈	3/14	1:42pm
♉	4/7	5:59pm
♊	5/2	3:13am
♋	5/26	6:17pm
♌	6/20	4:36pm
♍	7/16	1:18am
♎	8/11	3:21am
♏	9/7	3:33pm
♐	10/9	10:31am
♏	12/15	11:42am
♐	12/25	11:49pm
1907		
♑	2/6	4:28pm
♒	3/6	8:44pm
♓	4/2	1:28am
♈	4/27	12:29pm
♉	5/22	3:18pm
♊	6/16	1:14pm
♋	7/11	6:42am
♌	8/4	7:08pm
♍	8/29	2:30am
♎	9/22	5:52am
♏	10/16	6:55am
♐	11/9	7:08am
♑	12/3	7:26am
♒	12/27	8:53am
1908		
♓	1/20	1:50pm
♈	2/14	2:55am
♉	3/10	8:06am
♊	4/5	8:57pm
♋	5/5	5:44pm
♌	9/8	10:32pm
♍	10/8	6:13am
♎	11/3	11:29am
♏	11/28	10:43am
♐	12/22	8:01pm
1909		
♑	1/15	11:20pm
♒	2/9	12:41am
♓	3/5	2:11am
♈	3/29	5:12am
♉	4/22	10:35am
♊	5/16	6:31pm
♋	6/10	4:37am
♌	7/4	4:32pm
♍	7/29	6:42am
♎	8/23	12:34am
♏	9/17	12:21am
♐	10/12	9:28am
♑	11/7	12:11pm
♒	12/5	1:01pm
1910		
♓	1/15	8:56pm
♒	1/29	9:12am
♓	4/5	9:53am
♈	5/7	2:27am
♉	6/3	2:58pm
♊	6/29	7:32pm
♋	7/25	7:01am
♌	8/19	5:56am
♍	9/12	6:29pm
♎	10/6	11:11pm
♏	10/30	10:53pm
♐	11/23	8:09pm
♑	12/17	4:38pm
1911		
♒	1/10	1:28pm
♓	2/3	12:03pm
♈	2/27	2:29pm
♉	3/23	11:35pm
♊	4/17	6:56pm
♋	5/13	5:42am
♌	6/8	6:48pm
♍	7/7	7:04pm
♎	11/9	12:55am
♏	12/9	9:23am
1912		
♐	1/4	6:38pm
♑	1/29	10:45pm
♒	2/23	3:29pm
♓	3/19	3:49am
♈	4/12	2:50pm
♉	5/7	1:57am
♊	5/31	1:19pm
♋	6/25	12:12am
♌	7/19	9:44am
♍	8/12	5:43pm
♎	9/6	12:53am
♏	9/30	8:26am
♐	10/24	5:25pm
♑	11/18	5:03am
♒	12/12	10:23pm
1913		
♓	1/7	5:27am
♈	2/2	11:22pm
♉	3/6	5:09pm
♈	5/2	5:12am
♉	5/31	9:45am
♊	7/8	9:16am
♋	8/5	11:33pm
♌	9/1	9:20am
♍	9/26	4:04pm
♎	10/21	6:02am
♏	11/14	9:55am
♐	12/8	8:38am
1914		
♑	1/1	5:25am
♒	1/25	2:09am
♓	2/18	12:05am
♈	3/14	12:30am
♉	4/7	4:48am
♊	5/1	2:11pm
♋	5/26	5:34am
♌	6/20	4:26am
♍	7/15	2:10pm
♎	8/10	6:11pm
♏	9/7	10:58am
♐	10/10	1:49am
♏	12/5	11:20pm
♐	12/30	11:15pm
1915		
♑	2/6	3:57pm
♒	3/6	1:15pm
♓	4/1	3:19pm
♈	4/27	12:56am
♉	5/22	2:56am
♊	6/16	12:21am
♋	7/10	5:31pm
♌	8/4	5:47am
♍	8/28	1:06pm
♎	9/21	4:31pm
♏	10/15	5:42pm
♐	11/8	6:07pm
♑	12/2	6:38pm
♒	12/26	8:21pm
1916		
♓	1/20	1:41am
♈	2/13	3:24pm
♉	3/9	9:49pm
♊	4/5	1:31pm
♋	5/5	8:37pm
♌	9/8	10:26pm
♍	10/7	10:11pm
♎	11/3	12:59am
♏	11/27	11:07pm
♐	12/22	7:50am
1917		
♑	1/15	10:46am
♒	2/8	11:51am
♓	3/4	1:09pm
♈	3/28	4:01pm
♉	4/21	9:17pm
♊	5/16	5:08am
♋	6/9	3:15pm
♌	7/4	3:20am
♍	7/28	5:52pm
♎	8/22	12:19pm
♏	9/16	1:00pm
♐	10/11	11:33pm
♑	11/7	5:01am
♒	12/5	1:14pm
1918		
♓	4/5	8:11pm
♈	5/6	8:58pm
♉	6/3	5:27am
♊	6/29	8:12am
♋	7/24	6:44pm
♌	8/18	5:06pm
♍	9/12	5:23am
♎	10/6	10:00am
♏	10/30	9:43am
♐	11/23	7:02am
♑	12/17	3:34am
1919		
♒	1/10	12:28am
♓	2/2	11:08pm
♈	2/27	1:43am
♉	3/23	11:08am
♊	4/17	7:03am
♋	5/12	6:59pm
♌	6/8	10:35am
♍	7/7	6:17pm
♎	11/9	8:05am
♏	12/9	3:29am
1920		
♐	1/4	9:20am
♑	1/29	11:55am
♒	2/23	3:47am
♓	3/18	3:31pm
♈	4/12	2:07am
♉	5/6	12:55pm
♊	5/31	12:05am
♋	6/24	10:53am
♌	7/18	8:25pm
♍	8/12	4:31am
♎	9/5	11:53am
♏	9/29	7:45pm
♐	10/24	5:11am
♑	11/17	5:28pm
♒	12/12	11:46am
1921		
♓	1/6	8:33pm
♈	2/2	6:35pm
♉	3/7	9:18am
♈	4/25	11:46pm
♉	6/2	4:21am
♊	7/8	5:57am
♋	8/5	2:42pm
♌	8/31	10:24pm
♍	9/26	4:08am
♎	10/20	5:35pm
♏	11/13	9:11pm
♐	12/7	7:47pm
♑	12/31	4:31pm
1922		
♒	1/24	1:13pm
♓	2/17	11:06am
♈	3/13	11:30am
♉	4/6	3:50pm
♊	5/1	1:22am
♋	5/25	5:04pm
♌	6/19	4:32pm
♍	7/15	3:22am
♎	8/10	9:30am
♏	9/7	7:15am
♐	10/10	10:33pm
♏	11/28	9:47pm
1923		
♐	1/2	7:27am
♑	2/6	2:34pm
♒	3/6	5:38am
♓	4/1	5:16am
♈	4/26	1:36pm
♉	5/21	2:50pm
♊	6/15	11:46am
♋	7/10	4:36am
♌	8/3	4:42pm
♍	8/27	11:59pm
♎	9/21	3:29am
♏	10/15	4:49am
♐	11/8	5:23am
♑	12/2	6:06am
♒	12/26	8:03am
1924		
♓	1/19	1:45pm
♈	2/13	4:10am
♉	3/9	11:55am
♊	4/5	6:46am
♋	5/6	1:49am
♌	9/8	9:43pm
♍	10/7	2:16pm
♎	11/2	2:44pm
♏	11/27	11:48am
♐	12/21	7:56pm
1925		
♑	1/14	10:28pm
♒	2/7	11:16pm
♓	3/4	12:21am
♈	3/28	3:04am
♉	4/21	8:14am
♊	5/15	4:04pm
♋	6/9	2:14am
♌	7/3	2:31pm
♍	7/28	5:25am
♎	8/22	12:28am
♏	9/16	2:05am
♐	10/11	2:10pm
♑	11/6	10:34pm
♒	12/5	3:09pm
1926		
♓	4/6	3:59am
♈	5/6	3:13pm
♉	6/2	7:59pm
♊	6/28	9:05pm
♋	7/24	6:42am
♌	8/18	4:35am
♍	9/11	4:37pm
♎	10/5	9:07pm
♏	10/29	8:50pm
♐	11/22	6:12pm
♑	12/16	2:48pm
1927		
♒	1/9	11:48am
♓	2/2	10:33am

Venus Sign Changes 1900-2005

Sign	Date	Time
♈	2/26	1:16pm
♉	3/22	10:56pm
♊	4/16	7:25pm
♋	5/12	8:33am
♌	6/8	2:51am
♍	7/7	6:55pm
♎	11/9	1:26pm
♏	12/8	9:26pm
1928		
♐	1/4	12:06am
♑	1/29	1:13am
♒	2/22	4:15pm
♓	3/18	3:25am
♈	4/11	1:35pm
♉	5/6	12:03am
♊	5/30	11:00am
♋	6/23	9:42pm
♌	7/18	7:16am
♍	8/11	3:29pm
♎	9/4	11:05pm
♏	9/29	7:18am
♐	10/23	5:12pm
♑	11/17	6:09am
♒	12/12	1:25am
1929		
♓	1/6	12:01pm
♈	2/2	2:34pm
♉	3/8	7:29am
♈	4/20	2:05am
♉	6/3	9:48am
♊	7/8	2:00am
♋	8/5	5:39am
♌	8/31	11:24am
♍	9/25	4:13pm
♎	10/20	5:12am
♏	11/13	8:35am
♐	12/7	7:03am
♑	12/31	3:44am
1930		
♒	1/24	12:22am
♓	2/16	10:11pm
♈	3/12	10:34pm
♉	4/6	2:57am
♊	4/30	12:37pm
♋	5/25	4:36am
♌	6/19	4:39am
♍	7/14	4:34pm
♎	8/10	12:54am
♏	9/7	4:05am
♐	10/12	2:45am
♏	11/22	7:44am
1931		
♐	1/3	8:03pm
♑	2/6	12:25pm
♒	3/5	9:46pm
♓	3/31	7:04pm
♈	4/26	2:10am
♉	5/21	2:38am
♊	6/14	11:04pm
♋	7/9	3:35pm
♌	8/3	3:29am
♍	8/27	10:42am
♎	9/20	2:15pm
♏	10/14	3:45pm
♐	11/7	4:32pm
♑	12/1	5:29pm
♒	12/25	7:44pm
1932		
♓	1/19	1:52am
♈	2/12	4:58pm
♉	3/9	2:07am
♊	4/5	12:19am
♋	5/6	9:04am
♊	7/13	10:33am
♋	7/28	12:36pm
♌	9/8	7:45pm
♍	10/7	5:46am
♎	11/2	4:01am
♏	11/27	12:06am
♐	12/21	7:43am
1933		
♑	1/14	9:56am
♒	2/7	10:30am
♓	3/3	11:24am
♈	3/27	1:58pm
♉	4/20	7:00pm
♊	5/15	2:47am
♋	6/8	1:01pm
♌	7/3	1:29am
♍	7/27	4:45pm
♎	8/21	12:23pm
♏	9/15	2:54pm
♐	10/11	4:32am
♑	11/6	4:02pm
♒	12/5	6:00pm
1934		
♓	4/6	9:23am
♈	5/6	8:54am
♉	6/2	10:11am
♊	6/28	9:38am
♋	7/23	6:22pm
♌	8/17	3:45pm
♍	9/11	3:32am
♎	10/5	7:56am
♏	10/29	7:37am
♐	11/22	4:59am
♑	12/16	1:39am
1935		
♒	1/8	10:44pm
♓	2/1	9:36pm
♈	2/26	12:30am
♉	3/22	10:29am
♊	4/16	7:37am
♋	5/11	10:01pm
♌	6/7	7:11pm
♍	7/7	8:33pm
♎	11/9	4:34pm
♏	12/8	2:36pm
1936		
♐	1/3	2:16pm
♑	1/28	2:00pm
♒	2/22	4:14am
♓	3/17	2:53pm
♈	4/11	12:41am
♉	5/5	10:53am
♊	5/29	9:39pm
♋	6/23	8:16am
♌	7/17	5:51pm
♍	8/11	2:11am
♎	9/4	10:02am
♏	9/28	6:36pm
♐	10/23	5:00am
♑	11/16	6:36pm
♒	12/11	2:51pm
1937		
♓	1/6	3:18am
♈	2/2	10:39am
♉	3/9	1:19pm
♈	4/14	4:19am
♉	6/4	6:41am
♊	7/7	9:13pm
♋	8/4	8:14pm
♌	8/31	12:08am
♍	9/25	4:03am
♎	10/19	4:33pm
♏	11/12	7:43pm
♐	12/6	6:06pm
♑	12/30	2:42pm
1938		
♒	1/23	11:16am
♓	2/16	9:00am
♈	3/12	9:20am
♉	4/5	1:46pm
♊	4/29	11:35pm
♋	5/24	3:56pm
♌	6/18	4:37pm
♍	7/14	5:44am
♎	8/9	4:26pm
♏	9/7	1:36am
♐	10/13	6:49pm
♏	11/15	4:07pm
1939		
♐	1/4	9:48pm
♑	2/6	9:20am
♒	3/5	1:29pm
♓	3/31	8:34am
♈	4/25	2:28pm
♉	5/20	2:13pm
♊	6/14	10:11am
♋	7/9	2:25am
♌	8/2	2:11pm
♍	8/26	9:24pm
♎	9/20	1:02am
♏	10/14	2:41am
♐	11/7	3:41am
♑	12/1	4:52am
♒	12/25	7:25am
1940		
♓	1/18	2:00pm
♈	2/12	5:51am
♉	3/8	4:25pm
♊	4/4	6:10pm
♋	5/6	6:47pm
♊	7/5	4:17pm
♋	8/1	2:20am
♌	9/8	4:59pm
♍	10/6	9:10pm
♎	11/1	5:24pm
♏	11/26	12:32pm
♐	12/20	7:36pm
1941		
♑	1/13	9:29pm
♒	2/6	9:49pm
♓	3/2	10:33pm
♈	3/27	12:58am
♉	4/20	5:53am
♊	5/14	1:36pm
♋	6/7	11:53pm
♌	7/2	12:33pm
♍	7/27	4:12am
♎	8/21	12:29am
♏	9/15	4:01am
♐	10/10	7:21pm
♑	11/6	10:17am
♒	12/5	11:04pm
1942		
♓	4/6	1:14pm
♈	5/6	2:26am
♉	6/2	12:26am
♊	6/27	10:18pm
♋	7/23	6:10am
♌	8/17	3:04am
♍	9/10	2:38pm
♎	10/4	6:58pm
♏	10/28	6:40pm
♐	11/21	4:07pm
♑	12/15	12:53pm
1943		
♒	1/8	10:03am
♓	2/1	9:02am
♈	2/25	12:04pm
♉	3/21	10:24pm
♊	4/15	8:12pm
♋	5/11	11:56am
♌	6/7	12:09pm
♍	7/7	11:56pm
♎	11/9	6:25pm
♏	12/8	7:45am
1944		
♐	1/3	4:43am
♑	1/28	3:11am
♒	2/21	4:40pm
♓	3/17	2:46am
♈	4/10	12:09pm
♉	5/4	10:04pm
♊	5/29	8:39am
♋	6/22	7:12pm
♌	7/17	4:47am
♍	8/10	1:13pm
♎	9/3	9:16pm
♏	9/28	6:12am
♐	10/22	5:07pm
♑	11/16	7:26am
♒	12/11	4:47am
1945		
♓	1/5	7:18pm
♈	2/2	8:07am
♉	3/11	11:17am
♈	4/7	7:15pm
♉	6/4	10:58pm
♊	7/7	4:20pm
♋	8/4	10:59am
♌	8/30	1:05pm
♍	9/24	4:06pm
♎	10/19	4:09am
♏	11/12	7:05am
♐	12/6	5:22am
♑	12/30	1:56am
1946		
♒	1/22	10:28pm
♓	2/15	8:11pm
♈	3/11	8:32pm
♉	4/5	1:01am
♊	4/29	10:59am
♋	5/24	3:39am
♌	6/18	5:00am
♍	7/13	7:22pm
♎	8/9	8:34am
♏	9/7	12:16am
♐	10/16	10:45am
♏	11/8	8:56am
1947		
♐	1/5	4:45pm
♑	2/6	5:41am
♒	3/5	5:09am
♓	3/30	10:14pm
♈	4/25	3:03am
♉	5/20	2:06am
♊	6/13	9:35pm
♋	7/8	1:30pm
♌	8/2	1:06am
♍	8/26	8:17am
♎	9/19	12:01pm
♏	10/13	1:49pm
♐	11/6	2:59pm
♑	11/30	4:23pm
♒	12/24	7:13pm
1948		
♓	1/18	2:14am
♈	2/11	6:51pm
♉	3/8	6:59am
♊	4/4	12:40pm
♋	5/7	8:27am
♊	6/29	7:58am
♋	8/3	2:15am
♌	9/8	1:40pm
♍	10/6	12:25pm
♎	11/1	6:42am
♏	11/26	12:55am
♐	12/20	7:28am
1949		
♑	1/13	9:01am
♒	2/6	9:05am
♓	3/2	9:38am
♈	3/26	11:54am
♉	4/19	4:44pm
♊	5/14	12:25am
♋	6/7	10:47am
♌	7/1	11:40pm
♍	7/26	3:43pm
♎	8/20	12:39pm
♏	9/14	5:12pm
♐	10/10	10:18am
♑	11/6	4:53am
♒	12/6	6:06am
1950		
♓	4/6	3:13pm
♈	5/5	7:19pm
♉	6/1	2:19pm
♊	6/27	10:45am
♋	7/22	5:50pm
♌	8/16	2:18pm
♍	9/10	1:37am
♎	10/4	5:51am
♏	10/28	5:33am
♐	11/21	3:03am
♑	12/14	11:54pm
1951		
♒	1/7	9:10pm
♓	1/31	8:14pm
♈	2/24	11:26pm
♉	3/21	10:05am
♊	4/15	8:33am
♋	5/11	1:41am
♌	6/7	5:10am
♍	7/8	4:54am
♎	11/9	6:48pm
♏	12/8	12:19am
1952		
♐	1/2	6:44pm
♑	1/27	3:58pm
♒	2/21	4:42am
♓	3/16	2:18pm
♈	4/9	11:17pm
♉	5/4	8:55am
♊	5/28	7:19pm
♋	6/22	5:46am
♌	7/16	3:23pm
♍	8/9	11:58pm
♎	9/3	8:17am
♏	9/27	5:36pm
♐	10/22	5:02am
♑	11/15	8:03pm
♒	12/10	6:30pm
1953		
♓	1/5	11:10am
♈	2/2	5:54am
♉	3/14	6:58pm
♈	3/31	5:17am
♉	6/5	10:34am
♊	7/7	10:30am
♋	8/4	1:08am
♌	8/30	1:35am
♍	9/24	3:48am
♎	10/18	3:27pm
♏	11/11	6:12pm
♐	12/5	4:24pm
♑	12/29	12:53pm
1954		
♒	1/22	9:20am
♓	2/15	7:01am
♈	3/11	7:22am

Venus Sign Changes 1900-2005

Sign	Date	Time
♉	4/4	11:55am
♊	4/28	10:03pm
♋	5/23	3:04pm
♌	6/17	5:04pm
♍	7/13	8:43am
♎	8/9	12:34am
♏	9/6	11:29pm
♐	10/23	10:07pm
♏	10/27	10:42am
1955		
♐	1/6	6:48am
♑	2/6	1:15am
♒	3/4	8:22pm
♓	3/30	11:30am
♈	4/24	3:13pm
♉	5/19	1:35pm
♊	6/13	8:38am
♋	7/8	12:15am
♌	8/1	11:43am
♍	8/25	6:52pm
♎	9/18	10:41pm
♏	10/13	12:39am
♐	11/6	2:02am
♑	11/30	3:42am
♒	12/24	6:52am
1956		
♓	1/17	2:22pm
♈	2/11	7:46am
♉	3/7	9:31pm
♊	4/4	7:23am
♋	5/8	2:17am
♊	6/23	12:10pm
♋	8/4	9:49am
♌	9/8	9:23am
♍	10/6	3:12am
♎	10/31	7:40pm
♏	11/25	1:01pm
♐	12/19	7:07pm
1957		
♑	1/12	8:23pm
♒	2/5	8:16pm
♓	3/1	8:39pm
♈	3/25	10:46pm
♉	4/19	3:28am
♊	5/13	11:08am
♋	6/6	9:35pm
♌	7/1	10:42am
♍	7/26	3:10am
♎	8/20	12:44am
♏	9/14	6:20am
♐	10/10	1:16am
♑	11/5	11:46pm
♒	12/6	3:26pm
1958		
♓	4/6	4:00pm
♈	5/5	11:59am
♉	6/1	4:07am
♊	6/26	11:08pm
♋	7/22	5:26am
♌	8/16	1:28am
♍	9/9	12:35pm
♎	10/3	4:44pm
♏	10/27	4:26pm
♐	11/20	1:59pm
♑	12/14	10:55am
1959		
♒	1/7	8:16am
♓	1/31	7:28am
♈	2/24	10:53am
♉	3/20	9:55pm
♊	4/14	9:08pm
♋	5/10	3:45pm
♌	6/6	10:43pm
♍	7/8	12:08pm
♌	9/20	3:01am
♍	9/25	8:15am
♎	11/9	6:11pm
♏	12/7	4:41pm
1960		
♐	1/2	8:43am
♑	1/27	4:46am
♒	2/20	4:47pm
♓	3/16	1:53am
♈	4/9	10:32am
♉	5/3	7:56pm
♊	5/28	6:11am
♋	6/21	4:34pm
♌	7/16	2:11am
♍	8/9	10:54am
♎	9/2	7:29pm
♏	9/27	5:13am
♐	10/21	5:12pm
♑	11/15	8:57am
♒	12/10	8:34am
1961		
♓	1/5	3:31am
♈	2/2	4:46am
♉	6/5	7:25pm
♊	7/7	4:32am
♋	8/3	3:28pm
♌	8/29	2:18pm
♍	9/23	3:43pm
♎	10/18	2:58am
♏	11/11	5:33am
♐	12/5	3:40am
♑	12/29	12:07am
1962		
♒	1/21	8:31pm
♓	2/14	6:09pm
♈	3/10	6:28pm
♉	4/3	11:05pm
♊	4/28	9:23am
♋	5/23	2:46am
♌	6/17	5:31am
♍	7/12	10:32pm
♎	8/8	5:13pm
♏	9/7	12:11am
1963		
♐	1/6	5:35pm
♑	2/5	8:36pm
♒	3/4	11:41am
♓	3/30	1:00am
♈	4/24	3:39am
♉	5/19	1:21am
♊	6/12	7:57pm
♋	7/7	11:18am
♌	7/31	10:38pm
♍	8/25	5:49am
♎	9/18	9:43am
♏	10/12	11:50am
♐	11/5	1:25pm
♑	11/29	3:21pm
♒	12/23	6:53pm
1964		
♓	1/17	2:54am
♈	2/10	9:09pm
♉	3/7	12:38pm
♊	4/4	3:03am
♋	5/9	3:16am
♊	6/17	6:17pm
♋	8/5	8:53am
♌	9/8	4:53am
♍	10/5	6:10pm
♎	10/31	8:54am
♏	11/25	1:25am
♐	12/19	7:02am
1965		
♑	1/12	8:00am
♒	2/5	7:41am
♓	3/1	7:55am
♈	3/25	9:54am
♉	4/18	2:31pm
♊	5/12	10:08pm
♋	6/6	8:39am
♌	6/30	9:59pm
♍	7/25	2:51pm
♎	8/19	1:06pm
♏	9/13	7:50pm
♐	10/9	4:46pm
♑	11/5	7:36pm
♒	12/7	4:37am
1966		
♑	2/6	12:46pm
♒	2/25	10:55am
♓	4/6	3:53pm
♈	5/5	4:33am
♉	5/31	6:00pm
♊	6/26	11:40am
♋	7/21	5:11pm
♌	8/15	12:47pm
♍	9/8	11:40pm
♎	10/3	3:44am
♏	10/27	3:28am
♐	11/20	1:06am
♑	12/13	10:09pm
1967		
♒	1/6	7:36pm
♓	1/30	6:53pm
♈	2/23	10:30pm
♉	3/20	9:56am
♊	4/14	9:54am
♋	5/10	6:05am
♌	6/6	4:48pm
♍	7/8	10:11pm
♌	9/9	11:58am
♍	10/1	6:07pm
♎	11/9	4:32pm
♏	12/7	8:48am
1968		
♐	1/1	10:37pm
♑	1/26	5:35pm
♒	2/20	4:55am
♓	3/15	1:32pm
♈	4/8	9:49pm
♉	5/3	6:56am
♊	5/27	5:02pm
♋	6/21	3:20am
♌	7/15	12:59pm
♍	8/8	9:49pm
♎	9/2	6:39am
♏	9/26	4:45pm
♐	10/21	5:16am
♑	11/14	9:48pm
♒	12/9	10:40pm
1969		
♓	1/4	8:07pm
♈	2/2	4:45am
♉	6/6	1:48am
♊	7/6	10:04pm
♋	8/3	5:30am
♌	8/29	2:48am
♍	9/23	3:26am
♎	10/17	2:17pm
♏	11/10	4:40pm
♐	12/4	2:41pm
♑	12/28	11:04am
1970		
♒	1/21	7:26am
♓	2/14	5:04am
♈	3/10	5:25am
♉	4/3	10:05am
♊	4/27	8:33pm
♋	5/22	2:19pm
♌	6/16	5:49pm
♍	7/12	12:16pm
♎	8/8	9:59am
♏	9/7	1:54am
1971		
♐	1/7	1:00am
♑	2/5	2:57pm
♒	3/4	2:24am
♓	3/29	2:02pm
♈	4/23	3:44pm
♉	5/18	12:48pm
♊	6/12	6:58am
♋	7/6	10:02pm
♌	7/31	9:15am
♍	8/24	4:25pm
♎	9/17	8:25pm
♏	10/11	10:43pm
♐	11/5	12:30am
♑	11/29	2:41am
♒	12/23	6:32am
1972		
♓	1/16	3:01pm
♈	2/10	10:08am
♉	3/7	3:25am
♊	4/3	10:48pm
♋	5/10	1:51pm
♊	6/11	8:08pm
♋	8/6	1:26am
♌	9/7	11:27pm
♍	10/5	8:33am
♎	10/30	9:40pm
♏	11/24	1:23pm
♐	12/18	6:34pm
1973		
♑	1/11	7:15pm
♒	2/4	6:43pm
♓	2/28	6:45pm
♈	3/24	8:34pm
♉	4/18	1:05am
♊	5/12	8:42am
♋	6/5	7:20pm
♌	6/30	8:55am
♍	7/25	2:13am
♎	8/19	1:10am
♏	9/13	9:05am
♐	10/9	8:08am
♑	11/5	3:39pm
♒	12/7	9:37pm
1974		
♑	1/29	7:51pm
♒	2/28	2:25pm
♓	4/6	2:17pm
♈	5/4	8:21pm
♉	5/31	7:19am
♊	6/25	11:44pm
♋	7/21	4:34am
♌	8/14	11:47pm
♍	9/8	10:28am
♎	10/2	2:27pm
♏	10/26	2:12pm
♐	11/19	11:56am
♑	12/13	9:06am
1975		
♒	1/6	6:39am
♓	1/30	6:05am
♈	2/23	9:53am
♉	3/19	9:42pm
♊	4/13	10:26pm
♋	5/9	8:11pm
♌	6/6	10:54am
♍	7/9	11:06am
♌	9/2	3:34pm
♍	10/4	5:19am
♎	11/9	1:52pm
♏	12/7	12:29am
1976		
♐	1/1	12:14pm
♑	1/26	6:09am
♒	2/19	4:50pm
♓	3/15	12:59am
♈	4/8	8:56am
♉	5/2	5:49pm
♊	5/27	3:43am
♋	6/20	1:56pm
♌	7/14	11:36pm
♍	8/8	8:36am
♎	9/1	5:44pm
♏	9/26	4:17am
♐	10/20	5:22pm
♑	11/14	10:42am
♒	12/9	12:53pm
1977		
♓	1/4	1:01pm
♈	2/2	5:54am
♉	6/6	6:10am
♊	7/6	3:09pm
♋	8/2	7:19pm
♌	8/28	3:09pm
♍	9/22	3:05pm
♎	10/17	1:37am
♏	11/10	3:52am
♐	12/4	1:49am
♑	12/27	10:09pm
1978		
♒	1/20	6:29pm
♓	2/13	4:07pm
♈	3/9	4:29pm
♉	4/2	9:14pm
♊	4/27	7:53am
♋	5/22	2:03am
♌	6/16	6:19am
♍	7/12	2:14am
♎	8/8	3:08am
♏	9/7	5:07am
1979		
♐	1/7	6:38am
♑	2/5	9:16am
♒	3/3	5:18pm
♓	3/29	3:18am
♈	4/23	4:02am
♉	5/18	12:29am
♊	6/11	6:13pm
♋	7/6	9:02am
♌	7/30	8:07pm
♍	8/24	3:16am
♎	9/17	7:21am
♏	10/11	9:48am
♐	11/4	11:50am
♑	11/28	2:20pm
♒	12/22	6:35pm
1980		
♓	1/16	3:37am
♈	2/9	11:39pm
♉	3/6	6:54pm
♊	4/3	7:46pm
♋	5/12	8:53pm
♊	6/5	5:44pm
♋	8/6	2:25pm
♌	9/7	5:57pm
♍	10/4	11:07pm
♎	10/30	10:38am
♏	11/24	1:35am
♐	12/18	6:21am
1981		
♑	1/11	6:48am
♒	2/4	6:07am
♓	2/28	6:01am
♈	3/24	7:43am
♉	4/17	12:08pm

Venus Sign Changes 1900-2005

Sign	Date	Time
♊	5/11	7:45pm
♋	6/5	6:29am
♌	6/29	8:20pm
♍	7/24	2:04pm
♎	8/18	1:44pm
♏	9/12	10:51pm
♐	10/9	12:04am
♑	11/5	12:39pm
♒	12/8	8:52pm
1982		
♑	1/23	2:56am
♒	3/2	11:25am
♓	4/6	12:20pm
♈	5/4	12:27pm
♉	5/30	9:02pm
♊	6/25	12:13pm
♋	7/20	4:21pm
♌	8/14	11:09am
♍	9/7	9:38pm
♎	10/2	1:32am
♏	10/26	1:19am
♐	11/18	11:07pm
♑	12/12	8:20pm
1983		
♒	1/5	5:58pm
♓	1/29	5:31pm
♈	2/22	9:35pm
♉	3/19	9:51am
♊	4/13	11:26am
♋	5/9	10:56am
♌	6/6	6:04am
♍	7/10	5:25am
♌	8/27	11:43am
♍	10/5	7:35pm
♎	11/9	10:52am
♏	12/6	4:15pm
1984		
♐	1/1	2:00am
♑	1/25	6:51pm
♒	2/19	4:53am
♓	3/14	12:35pm
♈	4/7	8:13pm
♉	5/2	4:53am
♊	5/26	2:40pm
♋	6/20	12:48am
♌	7/14	10:30am
♍	8/7	7:40pm
♎	9/1	5:07am
♏	9/25	4:05pm
♐	10/20	5:45am
♑	11/13	11:54pm
♒	12/9	3:26am
1985		
♓	1/4	6:23am
♈	2/2	8:29am
♉	6/6	8:53am
♊	7/6	8:01am
♋	8/2	9:10am
♌	8/28	3:39am
♍	9/22	2:53am
♎	10/16	1:04pm
♏	11/9	3:08pm
♐	12/3	1:00pm
♑	12/27	9:17am
1986		
♒	1/20	5:36am
♓	2/13	3:11am
♈	3/9	3:32am
♉	4/2	8:19am
♊	4/26	7:10pm
♋	5/21	1:46pm
♌	6/15	6:52pm
♍	7/11	4:23pm
♎	8/7	8:46pm
♏	9/7	10:15am
1987		
♐	1/7	10:20am
♑	2/5	3:03am
♒	3/3	7:55am
♓	3/28	4:20pm
♈	4/22	4:07pm
♉	5/17	11:56am
♊	6/11	5:15am
♋	7/5	7:50pm
♌	7/30	6:49am
♍	8/23	2:00pm
♎	9/16	6:12pm
♏	10/10	8:49pm
♐	11/3	11:04pm
♑	11/28	1:51am
♒	12/22	6:29am
1988		
♓	1/15	4:04pm
♈	2/9	1:04pm
♉	3/6	10:21am
♊	4/3	5:07pm
♋	5/17	4:26pm
♊	5/27	7:36am
♋	8/6	11:24pm
♌	9/7	11:37am
♍	10/4	1:15pm
♎	10/29	11:20pm
♏	11/23	1:34pm
♐	12/17	5:56pm
1989		
♑	1/10	6:08pm
♒	2/3	5:15pm
♓	2/27	4:59pm
♈	3/23	6:32pm
♉	4/16	10:52pm
♊	5/11	6:28am
♋	6/4	5:17pm
♌	6/29	7:21am
♍	7/24	1:31am
♎	8/18	1:58am
♏	9/12	12:22pm
♐	10/8	4:00pm
♑	11/5	10:13am
♒	12/10	4:54am
1990		
♑	1/16	3:23pm
♒	3/3	5:52pm
♓	4/6	9:13am
♈	5/4	3:52am
♉	5/30	10:13am
♊	6/25	12:14am
♋	7/20	3:41am
♌	8/13	10:05pm
♍	9/7	8:21am
♎	10/1	12:13pm
♏	10/25	12:03pm
♐	11/18	9:58am
♑	12/12	7:18am
1991		
♒	1/5	5:03am
♓	1/29	4:44am
♈	2/22	9:02am
♉	3/18	9:45pm
♊	4/13	12:10am
♋	5/9	1:28am
♌	6/6	1:16am
♍	7/11	5:06am
♌	8/21	3:06pm
♍	10/6	9:15pm
♎	11/9	6:37am
♏	12/6	7:21am
♐	12/31	3:19pm
1992		
♑	1/25	7:14am
♒	2/18	4:40pm
♓	3/13	11:57pm
♈	4/7	7:16am
♉	5/1	3:41pm
♊	5/26	1:18am
♋	6/19	11:22am
♌	7/13	9:07pm
♍	8/7	6:26am
♎	8/31	4:09pm
♏	9/25	3:31am
♐	10/19	5:47pm
♑	11/13	12:48pm
♒	12/8	5:49pm
1993		
♓	1/3	11:54pm
♈	2/2	12:37pm
♉	6/6	10:03am
♊	7/6	12:21am
♋	8/1	10:38pm
♌	8/27	3:48pm
♍	9/21	2:22pm
♎	10/16	12:13am
♏	11/9	2:07am
♐	12/2	11:54pm
♑	12/26	8:09pm
1994		
♒	1/19	4:28pm
♓	2/12	2:04pm
♈	3/8	2:28pm
♉	4/1	7:20pm
♊	4/26	6:24am
♋	5/21	1:26am
♌	6/15	7:23am
♍	7/11	6:33am
♎	8/7	2:36pm
♏	9/7	5:12pm
1995		
♐	1/7	12:07pm
♑	2/4	8:12pm
♒	3/2	10:10pm
♓	3/28	5:10am
♈	4/22	4:07am
♉	5/16	11:22pm
♊	6/10	4:18pm
♋	7/5	6:39am
♌	7/29	5:32pm
♍	8/23	12:43am
♎	9/16	5:01am
♏	10/10	7:48am
♐	11/3	10:18am
♑	11/27	1:23pm
♒	12/21	6:23pm
1996		
♓	1/15	4:30am
♈	2/9	2:30am
♉	3/6	2:01am
♊	4/3	3:26pm
♋	8/7	6:15am
♌	9/7	5:07am
♍	10/4	3:22am
♎	10/29	12:02pm
♏	11/23	1:34am
♐	12/17	5:34am
1997		
♑	1/10	5:32am
♒	2/3	4:28am
♓	2/27	4:01am
♈	3/23	5:26am
♉	4/16	9:43am
♊	5/10	5:20pm
♋	6/4	4:18am
♌	6/28	6:38pm
♍	7/23	1:16pm
♎	8/17	2:31pm
♏	9/12	2:17am
♐	10/8	8:25am
♑	11/5	8:50am
♒	12/12	4:39am
1998		
♑	1/9	9:03pm
♒	3/4	4:14pm
♓	4/6	5:38am
♈	5/3	7:16pm
♉	5/29	11:32pm
♊	6/24	12:27pm
♋	7/19	3:17pm
♌	8/13	9:19am
♍	9/6	7:24pm
♎	9/30	11:13pm
♏	10/24	11:06pm
♐	11/17	9:06pm
♑	12/11	6:33pm
1999		
♒	1/4	4:25pm
♓	1/28	4:17pm
♈	2/21	8:49pm
♉	3/18	9:59am
♊	4/12	1:17pm
♋	5/8	4:29pm
♌	6/5	9:25pm
♍	7/12	3:18pm
♌	8/15	2:12pm
♍	10/7	4:51pm
♎	11/9	2:19am
♏	12/5	10:41pm
♐	12/31	4:54am
2000		
♑	1/24	7:52pm
♒	2/18	4:43am
♓	3/13	11:36am
♈	4/6	6:37pm
♉	5/1	2:49am
♊	5/25	12:15pm
♋	6/18	10:15pm
♌	7/13	8:02am
♍	8/6	5:32pm
♎	8/31	3:35am
♏	9/24	3:26pm
♐	10/19	6:18am
♑	11/13	2:14am
♒	12/8	8:48am
2001		
♓	1/3	6:14pm
♈	2/2	7:14pm
♉	6/6	10:25am
♊	7/5	4:44pm
♋	8/1	12:18pm
♌	8/27	4:12am
♍	9/21	2:09am
♎	10/15	11:42am
♏	11/8	1:28pm
♐	12/2	11:11am
♑	12/26	7:25am
2002		
♒	1/19	3:42am
♓	2/12	1:18am
♈	3/8	1:42am
♉	4/1	6:39am
♊	4/25	5:57pm
♋	5/20	1:27pm
♌	6/14	8:16pm
♍	7/10	9:09pm
♎	8/7	9:09am
♏	9/8	3:05am
2003		
♐	1/7	1:07pm
♑	2/4	1:27pm
♒	3/2	12:40pm
♓	3/27	6:14pm
♈	4/21	4:18pm
♉	5/16	10:58am
♊	6/10	3:32am
♋	7/4	5:39pm
♌	7/29	4:25am
♍	8/22	11:35am
♎	9/15	3:58pm
♏	10/9	6:56pm
♐	11/2	9:42pm
♑	11/27	1:07am
♒	12/21	6:32am
2004		
♓	1/14	5:16pm
♈	2/8	4:20pm
♉	3/5	6:12pm
♊	4/3	2:57pm
♋	8/7	11:02am
♌	9/6	10:16pm
♍	10/3	5:20pm
♎	10/29	12:39am
♏	11/22	1:31pm
♐	12/16	5:10pm
2005		
♑	1/9	4:56pm
♒	2/2	3:42pm
♓	2/26	3:07pm
♈	3/22	4:25pm
♉	4/15	8:37pm
♊	5/10	4:14am
♋	6/3	3:18pm
♌	6/28	5:53am
♍	7/23	1:01am
♎	8/17	3:05am
♏	9/11	4:14pm
♐	10/8	1:00am
♑	11/5	8:10am
♒	12/15	3:57pm

Mars Sign Changes 1900-2005

1900
♒ 1/21 6:51pm
♓ 2/28 10:15pm
♈ 4/8 3:58am
♉ 5/17 9:05am
♊ 6/27 9:21am
♋ 8/10 1:15am
♌ 9/26 6:08pm
♍ 11/23 8:41am

1901
♌ 3/1 7:28pm
♍ 5/11 6:05am
♎ 7/13 7:59pm
♏ 8/31 6:13pm
♐ 10/14 12:48pm
♑ 11/24 4:44am

1902
♒ 1/1 11:54pm
♓ 2/8 11:54pm
♈ 3/19 4:31am
♉ 4/27 10:49am
♊ 6/7 11:20am
♋ 7/20 5:44pm
♌ 9/4 2:48pm
♍ 10/23 10:55pm
♎ 12/20 3:33am

1903
♍ 4/19 8:46pm
♎ 5/30 5:21pm
♏ 8/6 4:27pm
♐ 9/22 1:52pm
♑ 11/3 5:31am
♒ 12/12 9:56am

1904
♓ 1/19 3:50pm
♈ 2/27 3:12am
♉ 4/6 6:06pm
♊ 5/18 3:35am
♋ 6/30 2:56pm
♌ 8/15 3:22am
♍ 10/1 1:52pm
♎ 11/20 6:24am

1905
♏ 1/13 7:26pm
♐ 8/21 7:33pm
♑ 10/8 12:06am
♒ 11/18 4:15am
♓ 12/27 1:50pm

1906
♈ 2/4 11:45pm
♉ 3/17 11:54am
♊ 4/28 5:00pm
♋ 6/11 7:39pm
♌ 7/27 2:13pm
♍ 9/12 12:53pm
♎ 10/30 4:26am
♏ 12/17 12:07pm

1907
♐ 2/5 9:29am
♑ 4/1 6:33pm
♒ 10/13 2:29pm
♓ 11/29 4:30am

1908
♈ 1/11 4:39am
♉ 2/23 3:25am
♊ 4/7 4:06am
♋ 5/22 2:14pm
♌ 7/8 3:54am
♍ 8/24 6:44am
♎ 10/10 6:05am
♏ 11/25 2:18pm

1909
♐ 1/10 3:55am
♑ 2/24 2:13am
♒ 4/9 8:34pm
♓ 5/25 10:54pm
♈ 7/21 8:36am
♓ 9/26 9:19pm
♈ 11/20 8:48pm

1910
♉ 1/23 1:54am
♊ 3/14 7:17am
♋ 5/1 8:49pm
♌ 6/19 3:30am
♍ 8/6 12:58am
♎ 9/22 12:15am
♏ 11/6 1:39pm
♐ 12/20 12:16pm

1911
♑ 1/31 9:30pm
♒ 3/14 12:07am
♓ 4/23 8:28am
♈ 6/2 9:48pm
♉ 7/15 4:01pm
♊ 9/5 3:21pm
♉ 11/30 4:07am

1912
♊ 1/30 9:02pm
♋ 4/5 11:31am
♌ 5/28 8:16am
♍ 7/17 2:43am
♎ 9/2 5:04pm
♏ 10/18 2:39am
♐ 11/30 7:41am

1913
♑ 1/10 1:43pm
♒ 2/19 8:00am
♓ 3/30 5:53am
♈ 5/8 3:00am
♉ 6/17 12:38am
♊ 7/29 10:31am
♋ 9/15 5:18pm

1914
♌ 5/1 8:31pm
♍ 6/26 4:48am
♎ 8/14 2:10pm
♏ 9/29 10:38am
♐ 11/11 10:47am
♑ 12/22 3:49am

1915
♒ 1/30 6:12am
♓ 3/9 12:56pm
♈ 4/16 8:42pm
♉ 5/26 3:08am
♊ 7/6 6:23am
♋ 8/19 9:10am
♌ 10/7 8:48pm

1916
♍ 5/28 6:42pm
♎ 7/23 5:23am
♏ 9/8 5:44pm
♐ 10/22 2:58am
♑ 12/1 5:10pm

1917
♒ 1/9 12:55pm
♓ 2/16 1:33pm
♈ 3/26 5:40pm
♉ 5/4 10:14pm
♊ 6/14 8:58pm
♋ 7/28 4:00am
♌ 9/12 10:52am
♍ 11/2 11:00am

1918
♎ 1/11 8:55am
♍ 2/25 7:00pm
♎ 6/23 7:19pm
♏ 8/17 4:16am
♐ 10/1 7:42am
♑ 11/11 10:13am
♒ 12/20 9:05am

1919
♓ 1/27 11:20am
♈ 3/6 6:48pm
♉ 4/15 5:00am
♊ 5/26 9:38am
♋ 7/8 5:14pm
♌ 8/23 6:17am
♍ 10/10 3:53am
♎ 11/30 12:10pm

1920
♏ 1/31 11:18pm
♎ 4/23 8:29pm
♏ 7/10 6:14pm
♐ 9/4 8:27pm
♑ 10/18 1:22pm
♒ 11/27 1:38pm

1921
♓ 1/5 7:39am
♈ 2/13 5:21am
♉ 3/25 6:26am
♊ 5/6 1:45am
♋ 6/18 8:34pm
♌ 8/3 11:01am
♍ 9/19 11:40am
♎ 11/6 4:13pm
♏ 12/26 11:48am

1922
♐ 2/18 4:15pm
♑ 9/13 1:02pm
♒ 10/30 6:55pm
♓ 12/11 1:10pm

1923
♈ 1/21 10:07am
♉ 3/4 12:42am
♊ 4/16 2:54am
♋ 5/30 9:19pm
♌ 7/16 1:26am
♍ 9/1 12:57am
♎ 10/18 4:18am
♏ 12/4 2:11am

1924
♐ 1/19 7:06pm
♑ 3/6 7:02pm
♒ 4/24 3:58pm
♓ 6/24 4:27pm
♒ 8/24 3:38pm
♓ 10/19 6:42pm
♈ 12/19 11:09am

1925
♉ 2/5 10:17am
♊ 3/24 12:42am
♋ 5/9 10:44pm
♌ 6/26 9:08am
♍ 8/12 9:12pm
♎ 9/28 7:01pm
♏ 11/13 2:02pm
♐ 12/28 12:36am

1926
♑ 2/9 3:35am
♒ 3/23 4:39am
♓ 5/3 5:03pm
♈ 6/15 12:50am
♉ 8/1 9:14am

1927
♊ 2/22 12:43am
♋ 4/17 1:29am
♌ 6/6 11:36am
♍ 7/25 7:47am
♎ 9/10 2:19pm
♏ 10/26 12:20am
♐ 12/8 11:01am

1928
♑ 1/19 2:02am
♒ 2/28 6:30am
♓ 4/7 2:27pm
♈ 5/16 9:35pm
♉ 6/26 9:04am
♊ 8/9 4:10am
♋ 10/3 3:46am
♊ 12/20 5:23am

1929
♋ 3/10 11:18pm
♌ 5/13 2:33am
♍ 7/4 10:03am
♎ 8/21 9:52pm
♏ 10/6 12:27pm
♐ 11/18 1:29pm
♑ 12/29 10:45am

1930
♒ 2/6 6:21pm
♓ 3/17 5:55am
♈ 4/24 5:27pm
♉ 6/3 3:15am
♊ 7/14 12:54pm
♋ 8/28 11:27am
♌ 10/20 2:43pm

1931
♋ 2/16 2:27pm
♌ 3/30 3:48am
♍ 6/10 2:58pm
♎ 8/1 4:38pm
♏ 9/17 8:43am
♐ 10/30 12:46pm
♑ 12/10 3:11am

1932
♒ 1/18 12:35am
♓ 2/25 2:36am
♈ 4/3 7:02am
♉ 5/12 10:53am
♊ 6/22 9:19am
♋ 8/4 7:52pm
♌ 9/20 7:43pm
♍ 11/13 9:25pm

1933
♎ 7/6 10:03pm
♏ 8/26 6:34am
♐ 10/9 11:35am
♑ 11/19 7:18am
♒ 12/28 3:43am

1934
♓ 2/4 4:13am
♈ 3/14 9:09am
♉ 4/22 3:40pm
♊ 6/2 4:21pm
♋ 7/15 9:33pm
♌ 8/30 1:43pm
♍ 10/18 4:59am
♎ 12/11 9:32am

1935
♏ 7/29 5:32pm
♐ 9/16 12:59pm
♑ 10/28 6:22pm
♒ 12/7 4:34am

1936
♓ 1/14 1:59pm
♈ 2/22 4:09am
♉ 4/1 9:30pm
♊ 5/13 9:17am
♋ 6/25 9:53pm
♌ 8/10 9:43am
♍ 9/26 2:51pm
♎ 11/14 2:52pm

1937
♏ 1/5 8:39pm
♐ 3/13 3:16am
♏ 5/14 10:52pm
♐ 8/8 10:14pm
♑ 9/30 9:08am
♒ 11/11 6:31pm
♓ 12/21 5:46pm

1938
♈ 1/30 12:44pm
♉ 3/12 7:48am
♊ 4/23 6:39pm
♋ 6/7 1:28am
♌ 7/22 10:26pm
♍ 9/7 8:22pm
♎ 10/25 6:20am
♏ 12/11 11:25pm

1939
♐ 1/29 9:49am
♑ 3/21 7:25am
♒ 5/25 12:19am
♑ 7/21 7:31pm
♒ 9/24 1:13am
♓ 11/19 3:56pm

1940
♈ 1/4 12:05am
♉ 2/17 1:54am
♊ 4/1 6:41pm
♋ 5/17 2:45pm
♌ 7/3 10:32am
♍ 8/19 3:58pm
♎ 10/5 2:21pm
♏ 11/20 5:16pm

1941
♐ 1/4 7:42pm
♑ 2/17 11:32pm
♒ 4/2 11:46am
♓ 5/16 5:05am
♈ 7/2 5:17am

1942
♉ 1/11 10:21pm
♊ 3/7 8:04am
♋ 4/26 6:18am
♌ 6/14 3:56am
♍ 8/1 8:27am
♎ 9/17 10:11am
♏ 11/1 10:36pm
♐ 12/15 4:51pm

1943
♑ 1/26 7:10pm
♒ 3/8 12:42pm
♓ 4/17 10:25am
♈ 5/27 9:25am
♉ 7/7 11:05pm
♊ 8/23 11:58pm

1944
♋ 3/28 9:54am
♌ 5/22 2:16pm
♍ 7/12 2:54am
♎ 8/29 12:23am
♏ 10/13 12:09pm
♐ 11/25 4:11pm

1945
♑ 1/5 7:31pm
♒ 2/14 9:58am
♓ 3/25 3:43am
♈ 5/2 8:29pm
♉ 6/11 11:52am
♊ 7/23 8:59am
♋ 9/7 8:56pm
♌ 11/11 9:05pm
♋ 12/26 3:04pm

1946
♌ 4/22 7:31pm
♍ 6/20 8:31am
♎ 8/9 1:17pm
♏ 9/24 4:35pm
♐ 11/6 6:22pm
♑ 12/17 10:56am

Mars Sign Changes 1900-2005

1947
♒ 1/25 11:44am
♓ 3/4 4:46pm
♈ 4/11 11:03pm
♉ 5/21 3:40am
♊ 7/1 3:34am
♋ 8/13 9:26pm
♌ 10/1 2:31am
♍ 12/1 11:44am

1948
♌ 2/12 10:28am
♍ 5/18 8:54pm
♎ 7/17 5:25am
♏ 9/3 1:58pm
♐ 10/17 5:43am
♑ 11/26 9:59pm

1949
♒ 1/4 5:50pm
♓ 2/11 6:05pm
♈ 3/21 10:02pm
♉ 4/30 2:33am
♊ 6/10 12:57am
♋ 7/23 5:54am
♌ 9/7 4:51am
♍ 10/27 12:58am
♎ 12/26 5:23am

1950
♍ 3/28 11:05am
♎ 6/11 8:27pm
♏ 8/10 4:48pm
♐ 9/25 7:48pm
♑ 11/6 6:40am
♒ 12/15 8:59am

1951
♓ 1/22 1:05pm
♈ 3/1 10:03pm
♉ 4/10 9:37am
♊ 5/21 3:32pm
♋ 7/3 11:42pm
♌ 8/18 10:55am
♍ 10/5 12:20am
♎ 11/24 6:11am

1952
♏ 1/20 1:33am
♐ 8/27 6:53pm
♑ 10/12 4:45am
♒ 11/21 7:40pm
♓ 12/30 9:35pm

1953
♈ 2/8 1:07am
♉ 3/20 6:54am
♊ 5/1 6:08am
♋ 6/14 3:49am
♌ 7/29 7:25pm
♍ 9/14 5:59pm
♎ 11/1 2:19pm
♏ 12/20 11:22am

1954
♐ 2/9 7:18pm
♑ 4/12 4:28pm
♐ 7/3 7:23am
♑ 8/24 1:22pm
♒ 10/21 12:03pm
♓ 12/4 7:41am

1955
♈ 1/15 4:33am
♉ 2/26 10:22am
♊ 4/10 11:09pm
♋ 5/26 12:50am
♌ 7/11 9:22am
♍ 8/27 10:13am
♎ 10/13 11:20am
♏ 11/29 1:33am

1956
♐ 1/14 2:28am
♑ 2/28 8:05pm
♒ 4/14 11:40pm
♓ 6/3 7:51am
♈ 12/6 11:24am

1957
♉ 1/28 2:19pm
♊ 3/17 9:34pm
♋ 5/4 3:22pm
♌ 6/21 12:18pm
♍ 8/8 5:27am
♎ 9/24 4:31am
♏ 11/8 9:04pm
♐ 12/23 1:29am

1958
♑ 2/3 6:57pm
♒ 3/17 7:11am
♓ 4/27 2:31am
♈ 6/7 6:21am
♉ 7/21 7:03am
♊ 9/21 5:26am
♉ 10/29 12:00am

1959
♊ 2/10 1:57pm
♋ 4/10 9:46am
♌ 6/1 2:26am
♍ 7/20 11:03am
♎ 9/5 10:46pm
♏ 10/21 9:40am
♐ 12/3 6:09pm

1960
♑ 1/14 4:59am
♒ 2/23 4:11am
♓ 4/2 6:24am
♈ 5/11 7:19am
♉ 6/20 9:05am
♊ 8/2 4:32am
♋ 9/21 4:06am

1961
♊ 2/5 12:23am
♋ 2/7 5:25am
♌ 5/6 1:13am
♍ 6/28 11:47pm
♎ 8/17 12:41am
♏ 10/1 8:02pm
♐ 11/13 9:50pm
♑ 12/24 5:50pm

1962
♒ 2/1 11:06pm
♓ 3/12 7:58am
♈ 4/19 4:58pm
♉ 5/28 11:47pm
♊ 7/9 3:50am
♋ 8/22 11:37am
♌ 10/11 11:54pm

1963
♍ 6/3 6:30am
♎ 7/27 4:14am
♏ 9/12 9:11am
♐ 10/25 5:31pm
♑ 12/5 9:03am

1964
♒ 1/13 6:13am
♓ 2/20 7:33am
♈ 3/29 11:24am
♉ 5/7 2:41pm
♊ 6/17 11:43am
♋ 7/30 6:23pm
♌ 9/15 5:22am
♍ 11/6 3:20am

1965
♎ 6/29 1:12am
♏ 8/20 12:16pm
♐ 10/4 6:46am
♑ 11/14 7:19am
♒ 12/23 5:36am

1966
♓ 1/30 7:01am
♈ 3/9 12:55pm
♉ 4/17 8:35pm
♊ 5/28 10:07pm
♋ 7/11 3:15am
♌ 8/25 3:52pm
♍ 10/12 6:37pm
♎ 12/4 12:55am

1967
♏ 2/12 12:20pm
♎ 3/31 6:10am
♏ 7/19 10:56pm
♐ 9/10 1:44am
♑ 10/23 2:14am
♒ 12/1 8:12pm

1968
♓ 1/9 9:49am
♈ 2/17 3:18am
♉ 3/27 11:43pm
♊ 5/8 2:14pm
♋ 6/21 5:03am
♌ 8/5 5:07pm
♍ 9/21 6:39pm
♎ 11/9 6:10am
♏ 12/29 10:07pm

1969
♐ 2/25 6:21am
♑ 9/21 6:35am
♒ 11/4 6:51pm
♓ 12/15 2:22pm

1970
♈ 1/24 9:29pm
♉ 3/7 1:28am
♊ 4/18 6:59pm
♋ 6/2 6:50am
♌ 7/18 6:43am
♍ 9/3 4:57am
♎ 10/20 10:57am
♏ 12/6 4:34pm

1971
♐ 1/23 1:34am
♑ 3/12 10:11am
♒ 5/3 8:57pm
♓ 11/6 12:31pm
♈ 12/26 6:04pm

1972
♉ 2/10 2:04pm
♊ 3/27 4:30am
♋ 5/12 1:14pm
♌ 6/28 4:09pm
♍ 8/15 12:59am
♎ 9/30 11:23pm
♏ 11/15 10:17pm
♐ 12/30 4:12pm

1973
♑ 2/12 5:51am
♒ 3/26 8:59pm
♓ 5/8 4:09am
♈ 6/20 8:54pm
♉ 8/12 2:56pm
♈ 10/29 10:56pm
♉ 12/24 8:09am

1974
♊ 2/27 10:11am
♋ 4/20 8:18am
♌ 6/9 12:54am
♍ 7/27 2:04pm
♎ 9/12 7:08pm
♏ 10/28 7:05am
♐ 12/10 10:05pm

1975
♑ 1/21 6:49pm
♒ 3/3 5:32am
♓ 4/11 7:15pm
♈ 5/21 8:14am
♉ 7/1 3:53am
♊ 8/14 8:47pm
♋ 10/17 8:44am
♊ 11/25 6:30pm

1976
♋ 3/18 1:15pm
♌ 5/16 11:10am
♍ 7/6 11:27pm
♎ 8/24 5:55am
♏ 10/8 8:23pm
♐ 11/20 11:53pm

1977
♑ 1/1 12:42am
♒ 2/9 11:57am
♓ 3/20 2:19am
♈ 4/27 3:46pm
♉ 6/6 3:00am
♊ 7/17 3:13pm
♋ 9/1 12:20am
♌ 10/26 6:56pm

1978
♋ 1/26 1:59am
♌ 4/10 6:50pm
♍ 6/14 2:38am
♎ 8/4 9:07am
♏ 9/19 8:57pm
♐ 11/2 1:20am
♑ 12/12 5:39pm

1979
♒ 1/20 5:07pm
♓ 2/27 8:25pm
♈ 4/7 1:08am
♉ 5/16 4:25am
♊ 6/26 1:55am
♋ 8/8 1:28pm
♌ 9/24 9:21pm
♍ 11/19 9:36pm

1980
♌ 3/11 8:46pm
♍ 5/4 2:26am
♎ 7/10 5:59pm
♏ 8/29 5:50am
♐ 10/12 6:27am
♑ 11/22 1:42am
♒ 12/30 10:30pm

1981
♓ 2/6 10:48pm
♈ 3/17 2:40am
♉ 4/25 7:17am
♊ 6/5 5:26am
♋ 7/18 8:54am
♌ 9/2 1:52am
♍ 10/21 1:56am
♎ 12/16 12:14am

1982
♏ 8/3 11:45am
♐ 9/20 1:20am
♑ 10/31 11:05pm
♒ 12/10 6:17am

1983
♓ 1/17 1:10pm
♈ 2/25 12:19am
♉ 4/5 2:03pm
♊ 5/16 9:43pm
♋ 6/29 6:54am
♌ 8/13 4:54pm
♍ 9/30 12:12am
♎ 11/18 10:26am

1984
♏ 1/11 3:20am
♐ 8/17 7:50pm
♑ 10/5 6:02am
♒ 11/15 6:09pm
♓ 12/25 6:38am

1985
♈ 2/2 5:19pm
♉ 3/15 5:06am
♊ 4/26 9:13am
♋ 6/9 10:40am
♌ 7/25 4:04am
♍ 9/10 1:31am
♎ 10/27 3:16pm
♏ 12/14 6:59pm

1986
♐ 2/2 6:27am
♑ 3/28 3:47am
♒ 10/9 1:01am
♓ 11/26 2:35am

1987
♈ 1/8 12:20pm
♉ 2/20 2:44pm
♊ 4/5 4:37pm
♋ 5/21 3:01am
♌ 7/6 4:46pm
♍ 8/22 7:51pm
♎ 10/8 7:27pm
♏ 11/24 3:19am

1988
♐ 1/8 3:24pm
♑ 2/22 10:15am
♒ 4/6 9:44pm
♓ 5/22 7:42am
♈ 7/13 8:00pm
♓ 10/23 10:02pm
♈ 11/1 12:57pm

1989
♉ 1/19 8:11am
♊ 3/11 8:51am
♋ 4/29 4:37am
♌ 6/16 2:10pm
♍ 8/3 1:35pm
♎ 9/19 2:38pm
♏ 11/4 5:29am
♐ 12/18 4:57am

1990
♑ 1/29 2:10pm
♒ 3/11 3:54pm
♓ 4/20 10:09pm
♈ 5/31 7:11am
♉ 7/12 2:44pm
♊ 8/31 11:40am
♉ 12/14 7:46am

1991
♊ 1/21 1:15am
♋ 4/3 12:49am
♌ 5/26 12:19pm
♍ 7/15 12:36pm
♎ 9/1 6:38am
♏ 10/16 7:05pm
♐ 11/29 2:19am

1992
♑ 1/9 9:47am
♒ 2/18 4:38am
♓ 3/28 2:04am
♈ 5/5 9:36pm
♉ 6/14 3:56pm
♊ 7/26 6:59pm
♋ 9/12 6:05am

1993
♌ 4/27 11:40pm
♍ 6/23 7:42am
♎ 8/12 1:10am
♏ 9/27 2:15am
♐ 11/9 5:29am
♑ 12/20 12:34am

Mars Sign Changes 1900-2005

1994	**1996**	♒ 12/18 6:37am	♒ 11/26 6:56am	**2002**	**2004**
♒ 1/28 4:05am	♒ 1/ 8 11:02am	**1998**	**2000**	♈ 1/18 10:53pm	♉ 2/ 3 10:04am
♓ 3/ 7 11:01am	♓ 2/15 11:50am	♓ 1/25 9:26am	♓ 1/ 4 3:01am	♉ 3/ 1 3:05pm	♊ 3/21 7:39am
♈ 4/14 6:02pm	♈ 3/24 3:12pm	♈ 3/ 4 4:18pm	♈ 2/12 1:04am	♊ 4/13 5:36pm	♋ 5/ 7 8:45am
♉ 5/23 10:37pm	♉ 5/ 2 6:16pm	♉ 4/13 1:05am	♉ 3/23 1:25am	♋ 5/28 11:43am	♌ 6/23 8:50pm
♊ 7/ 3 10:30pm	♊ 6/12 2:42pm	♊ 5/24 3:42am	♊ 5/ 3 7:18pm	♌ 7/13 3:23pm	♍ 8/10 10:14am
♋ 8/16 7:15pm	♋ 7/25 6:32pm	♋ 7/ 6 9:00am	♋ 6/16 12:30pm	♍ 8/29 2:38pm	♎ 9/26 9:15am
♌ 10/ 4 3:48pm	♌ 9/ 9 8:02pm	♌ 8/20 7:16pm	♌ 8/ 1 1:21am	♎ 10/15 5:38pm	♏ 11/11 5:11am
♍ 12/12 11:32am	♍ 10/30 7:13am	♍ 10/ 7 12:28pm	♍ 9/17 12:19am	♏ 12/ 1 2:26pm	♐ 12/25 4:04pm
1995	**1997**	♎ 11/27 10:10am	♎ 11/ 4 2:00am	**2003**	**2005**
♌ 1/22 11:48pm	♎ 1/ 3 8:10am	**1999**	♏ 12/23 2:37pm	♐ 1/17 4:22am	♑ 2/ 6 6:32pm
♍ 5/25 4:09pm	♍ 3/ 8 7:49pm	♏ 1/26 11:59am	**2001**	♑ 3/ 4 9:17pm	♒ 3/20 6:02pm
♎ 7/21 9:21am	♎ 6/19 8:30am	♎ 5/ 5 9:32pm	♐ 2/14 8:06pm	♒ 4/21 11:48pm	♓ 5/ 1 2:58am
♏ 9/ 7 7:00am	♏ 8/14 8:42am	♏ 7/ 5 3:59am	♑ 9/ 8 5:51pm	♓ 6/17 2:25am	♈ 6/12 2:30am
♐ 10/20 9:02pm	♐ 9/28 10:22pm	♐ 9/ 2 7:29pm	♒ 10/27 5:19pm	♈ 12/16 1:24pm	♉ 7/28 5:12am
♑ 11/30 1:57pm	♑ 11/ 9 5:33am	♑ 10/17 1:35am	♓ 12/ 8 9:52pm		

Jupiter Sign Changes 1900-2005

1901	**1920**	♈ 12/20 5:03pm	♎ 8/7 2:11am	♏ 8/15 5:58pm	**1988**
♑ 1/19 8:33am	♍ 8/27 5:29am	**1940**	**1958**	**1971**	♉ 3/8 3:44pm
1902	**1921**	♉ 5/16 7:54am	♏ 1/13 12:52pm	♐ 1/14 8:49am	♊ 7/21 11:59pm
♒ 2/6 7:31pm	♎ 9/25 11:10pm	**1941**	♎ 3/20 7:13pm	♏ 6/5 2:12am	♉ 11/30 8:53pm
1903	**1922**	♊ 5/26 12:48pm	♏ 9/7 8:52am	♐ 9/11 3:33pm	**1989**
♓ 2/20 8:35am	♏ 10/26 7:16pm	**1942**	**1959**	**1972**	♊ 3/11 3:26am
1904	**1923**	♋ 6/10 10:36am	♐ 2/10 1:46pm	♑ 2/6 7:37pm	♋ 7/30 11:50pm
♈ 3/1 3:00am	♐ 11/24 5:31pm	**1943**	♏ 4/24 2:10pm	♐ 7/24 4:42pm	**1990**
♉ 8/8 8:11pm	**1924**	♌ 6/30 9:46pm	♐ 10/5 2:40pm	♑ 9/25 6:20pm	♌ 8/18 7:30am
♈ 8/31 1:54pm	♑ 12/18 6:25am	**1944**	**1960**	**1973**	**1991**
1905	**1926**	♍ 7/26 1:04am	♑ 3/1 1:10pm	♒ 2/23 9:28am	♍ 9/12 6:00am
♉ 3/7 6:28pm	♒ 1/6 1:01am	**1945**	♐ 6/10 1:52am	**1974**	**1992**
♊ 7/21 12:23am	**1927**	♎ 8/25 6:06am	♑ 10/26 3:01am	♓ 3/8 11:11am	♎ 10/10 1:26pm
♉ 12/4 10:31pm	♓ 1/18 11:44am	**1946**	**1961**	**1975**	**1993**
1906	♈ 6/6 10:14am	♏ 9/25 10:19am	♒ 3/15 8:01am	♈ 3/18 4:47pm	♏ 11/10 8:15am
♊ 3/9 9:48pm	♓ 9/11 3:43am	**1947**	♑ 8/12 8:54am	**1976**	**1994**
♋ 7/30 11:12pm	**1928**	♐ 10/24 3:00am	♒ 11/4 2:49am	♉ 3/26 10:25am	♐ 12/9 10:54am
1907	♈ 1/23 2:54am	**1948**	**1962**	♊ 8/23 10:24am	**1996**
♌ 8/18 11:15pm	♉ 6/4 4:51am	♑ 11/15 10:38am	♓ 3/25 10:07pm	♉ 10/16 8:24pm	♑ 1/3 7:22am
1908	**1929**	**1949**	**1963**	**1977**	**1997**
♍ 9/12 10:02am	♊ 6/12 12:20pm	♒ 4/12 7:18pm	♈ 4/4 3:19am	♊ 4/3 3:42pm	♒ 1/21 3:13pm
1909	**1930**	♑ 6/27 6:29pm	**1964**	♋ 8/20 12:43pm	**1998**
♎ 10/11 11:33pm	♋ 6/26 10:42pm	♒ 11/30 8:08pm	♉ 4/12 6:52am	♊ 12/30 11:50pm	♓ 2/4 10:52am
1910	**1931**	**1950**	**1965**	**1978**	**1999**
♏ 11/11 5:04pm	♌ 7/17 7:52am	♓ 4/15 8:58am	♊ 4/22 2:32pm	♋ 4/12 12:12am	♈ 2/13 1:23am
1911	**1932**	♒ 9/15 2:23am	♋ 9/21 4:40am	♌ 9/5 8:31am	♉ 6/28 9:29am
♐ 12/10 11:36am	♍ 8/11 7:16am	♓ 12/1 7:57pm	♊ 11/17 3:08am	**1979**	♈ 10/23 5:48am
1913	**1933**	**1951**	**1966**	♋ 2/28 11:35pm	**2000**
♑ 1/2 7:46pm	♎ 9/10 5:11am	♈ 4/21 2:57pm	♋ 5/5 2:52pm	♌ 4/20 8:30am	♉ 2/14 9:40pm
1914	**1934**	**1952**	♌ 9/27 1:19pm	♍ 9/29 10:23am	♊ 6/30 7:35am
♒ 1/21 3:13pm	♏ 10/11 4:55am	♉ 4/28 8:50pm	**1967**	**1980**	**2001**
1915	**1935**	**1953**	♋ 1/16 3:50am	♎ 10/27 10:10am	♋ 7/13 12:03am
♓ 2/4 12:44am	♐ 11/9 2:56am	♊ 5/9 3:33pm	♌ 5/23 8:21am	**1981**	**2002**
1916	**1936**	**1954**	♍ 10/19 10:51am	♏ 11/27 2:19am	♌ 8/1 5:20pm
♈ 2/12 7:11am	♑ 12/2 8:39am	♋ 5/24 4:43am	**1968**	**1982**	**2003**
♉ 6/26 1:32am	**1937**	**1955**	♌ 2/27 3:33am	♐ 12/26 1:57am	♍ 8/27 9:26am
♈ 10/26 2:53pm	♒ 12/20 4:06am	♌ 6/13 12:07am	♍ 6/15 2:44pm	**1984**	**2004**
1917	**1938**	♍ 11/17 3:59am	♎ 11/15 10:44pm	♑ 1/19 3:04pm	♎ 9/25 3:23am
♉ 2/12 3:58pm	♓ 5/14 7:46am	**1956**	**1969**	**1985**	**2005**
♊ 6/29 11:51pm	♒ 7/30 3:01am	♌ 1/18 2:04am	♍ 3/30 9:36pm	♒ 2/6 3:35pm	♏ 10/26 2:52am
1918	♓ 12/29 6:34pm	♍ 7/7 7:01pm	♎ 7/15 1:30pm	**1986**	
♋ 7/13 5:54am	**1939**	♎ 12/13 2:17am	♏ 12/16 3:55pm	♓ 2/20 4:05pm	
1919	♈ 5/11 2:08pm	**1957**	**1970**	**1987**	
♌ 8/2 8:39am	♓ 10/30 12:44am	♍ 2/19 3:37pm	♎ 4/30 6:43am	♈ 3/2 6:41pm	

Saturn Sign Changes 1900-2005

1900	**1915**	**1935**	**1951**	**1973**	♐ 6/10 5:22am
♑ 1/21 8:10am	♋ 5/11 9:23pm	♓ 2/14 2:08pm	♍ 3/7 12:12pm	♋ 8/1 10:20pm	♑ 11/12 9:26am
♐ 7/18 5:32pm	**1916**	**1937**	♎ 8/13 4:44pm	**1974**	**1991**
♑ 10/17 5:03am	♌ 10/17 3:36pm	♈ 4/25 6:29am	**1953**	♊ 1/7 8:26pm	♒ 2/6 6:51pm
1903	♋ 12/7 7:21pm	♓ 10/18 3:41am	♏ 10/22 3:36pm	♋ 4/18 10:34pm	**1993**
♒ 1/19 10:15pm	**1917**	**1938**	**1956**	**1975**	♓ 5/21 4:58am
1905	♌ 6/24 1:54pm	♈ 1/14 10:31am	♐ 1/12 6:46pm	♌ 9/17 4:57am	♒ 6/30 8:28am
♓ 4/13 8:39am	**1919**	**1939**	♏ 5/14 3:45am	**1976**	**1994**
♒ 8/17 12:41am	♍ 8/12 1:52pm	♉ 7/6 5:45am	♐ 10/10 3:11pm	♋ 1/14 1:16pm	♓ 1/28 11:43pm
1906	**1921**	♈ 9/22 5:18am	**1959**	♌ 6/5 5:09am	**1996**
♓ 1/8 12:47pm	♎ 10/7 5:22pm	**1940**	♑ 1/5 1:33pm	**1977**	♈ 4/7 8:49am
1908	**1923**	♉ 3/20 9:40am	**1962**	♍ 11/17 2:43am	**1998**
♈ 3/19 2:22pm	♏ 12/20 4:25am	**1942**	♒ 1/3 7:01pm	**1978**	♉ 6/9 6:07am
1910	**1924**	♊ 5/8 7:39pm	**1964**	♌ 1/5 12:44am	♈ 10/25 6:41pm
♉ 5/17 7:30am	♎ 4/6 8:35am	**1944**	♓ 3/24 4:18am	♍ 7/26 12:02pm	**1999**
♈ 12/14 11:09pm	♏ 9/13 10:00pm	♋ 6/20 7:48am	♒ 9/16 9:04pm	**1980**	♉ 3/1 1:26am
1911	**1926**	**1946**	♓ 12/16 5:39am	♎ 9/21 10:48am	**2000**
♉ 1/20 9:21am	♐ 12/2 10:35pm	♌ 8/2 2:42pm	**1967**	**1982**	♊ 8/10 2:26am
1912	**1929**	**1948**	♈ 3/3 9:32pm	♏ 11/29 10:29am	♉ 10/16 12:44am
♊ 7/7 6:13am	♑ 3/15 1:49pm	♍ 9/19 4:36am	**1969**	**1983**	**2001**
♉ 11/30 6:18pm	♐ 5/5 4:18am	**1949**	♉ 4/29 10:24pm	♎ 5/6 7:29pm	♊ 4/20 9:59pm
1913	♑ 11/30 4:22am	♌ 4/3 3:38am	**1971**	♏ 8/24 11:54am	**2003**
♊ 3/26 1:07pm	**1932**	♍ 5/29 12:59pm	♊ 6/18 4:09pm	**1985**	♋ 6/4 1:28am
1914	♒ 2/24 2:47am	**1950**	**1972**	♐ 11/17 2:10am	**2005**
♋ 8/24 5:28pm	♑ 8/13 11:14am	♎ 11/20 3:50pm	♉ 1/10 3:43am	**1988**	♌ 7/16 12:30pm
♊ 12/7 6:48am	♒ 11/20 2:10am		♊ 2/21 2:53pm	♑ 2/13 11:51pm	

Uranus Sign Changes 1900-2005

1904	**1927**	♉10/5 2:08am	♌ 6/10 1:48am	**1974**	♑12/2 3:35pm
♑12/20 1:37pm	♈ 3/31 5:26pm	**1942**	**1961**	♏11/21 9:32am	**1995**
1912	♓11/4 10:30am	♊ 5/15 4:04am	♍11/1 4:01pm	**1975**	♒ 4/1 12:11pm
♒ 1/30 10:42pm	**1928**	**1948**	**1962**	♎ 5/1 5:46pm	♑ 6/9 1:42am
♑ 9/4 4:47pm	♈ 1/13 8:47am	♋ 8/30 3:40pm	♌ 1/10 5:53am	♏ 9/8 5:16am	**1996**
♒11/12 8:45am	**1934**	♊11/12 1:27pm	♍ 8/10 1:19am	**1981**	♒ 1/12 7:13am
1919	♉ 6/6 3:41pm	**1949**	**1968**	♐ 2/17 9:02am	**2003**
♓ 4/1 1:48am	♈10/10 12:37am	♋ 6/10 4:08am	♎ 9/28 4:10pm	♏ 3/20 11:15pm	♓ 3/10 8:53pm
♒ 8/16 10:06pm	**1935**	**1955**	**1969**	♐11/16 12:05pm	♒ 9/15 3:47am
1920	♉ 3/28 2:57am	♌ 8/24 6:04pm	♍ 5/20 8:51pm	**1988**	♓12/30 9:14am
♓ 1/22 6:33pm	**1941**	**1956**	♎ 6/24 10:36am	♑ 2/15 12:11am	
	♊ 8/7 3:32pm	♋ 1/28 1:57am		♐ 5/27 1:17am	

Neptune Sign Changes 1900-2005

1901	**1915**	**1929**	**1955**	**1970**	**1998**
♋ 7/19 11:55pm	♌ 7/19 1:33pm	♌ 2/19 11:23am	♏12/24 3:22pm	♐ 1/4 7:55pm	♒ 1/29 2:52am
♊12/25 1:33pm	**1916**	♍ 7/24 3:04pm	**1956**	♏ 5/3 1:30am	♑ 8/23 12:13am
1902	♋ 3/19 3:24pm	**1942**	♎ 3/12 1:53am	♐11/6 4:32pm	♒11/28 1:19am
♋ 5/21 1:33pm	♌ 5/2 10:48am	♎10/3 5:01pm	♏10/19 9:27am	**1984**	
1914	**1928**	**1943**	**1957**	♑ 1/19 2:55am	
♌ 9/23 8:24pm	♍ 9/21 12:05pm	♍ 4/17 10:56am	♎ 6/15 8:07pm	♐ 6/23 1:10am	
♋12/14 8:38pm		♎ 8/2 7:10pm	♏ 8/6 8:25am	♑11/21 1:21pm	

Pluto Sign Changes 1900-2005

1912	**1914**	**1939**	♍ 8/19 4:23am	**1972**	♏ 8/28 4:44am
♋ 9/10 4:51pm	♋ 5/26 8:49pm	♋ 2/7 1:00pm	**1958**	♍ 4/17 7:49am	**1995**
♊10/20 7:57am	**1937**	♌ 6/14 4:46am	♌ 4/11 2:58pm	♎ 7/30 11:39am	♐ 1/17 9:16am
1913	♌10/7 12:08pm	**1956**	♍ 6/10 6:50pm	**1983**	♏ 4/21 2:56am
♋ 7/9 10:31pm	♋11/25 9:13am	♍10/20 6:12am	**1971**	♏11/5 9:07pm	♐11/10 7:11pm
♊12/28 4:10am	**1938**	**1957**	♎10/5 6:15am	**1984**	
	♌ 8/3 5:56pm	♌ 1/15 2:45am		♎ 5/18 2:35pm	

Suggested Reading

Arroyo, Stephen. *Astrology, Karma and Transformation.* Sebastopol, Calif.: CRCS Publications, 1978.

Bogart, Gregory. *Astrology and Spiritual Awakening.* Berkeley, Calif.: Dawn Mountain Press, 1994.

Forrest, Stephen. *The Inner Sky.* New York, N.Y.: Bantam Books, 1984.

Greene, Liz. *Relating.* New York, N.Y.: Samuel Weiser, 1978.

Hand, Robert. *Horoscope Symbols.* Atglen, Pa.: Whitford Press, 1981.

———. *Planets in Composite.* Gloucester, Mass.: Para Research, 1975.

Hanh, Thich Nhat. *Peace is Every Step.* New York, N.Y.: Bantam Books, 1991.

Oken, Alan. *As Above, So Below.* New York, N.Y.: Bantam Books, 1973.

Pond, David and Lucy Pond. *The Metaphysical Handbook.* Port Angeles, Wash.: Reflecting Pond Publications, 1984.

Robertson, Mark. *Sex, Mind and Habit.* Tempe, Ariz.: AFA, 1975.

Rogers-Gallagher, Kim. *Astrology for the Light Side of the Brain.* San Diego, Calif.: ACS, 1995.

Rudhyar, Dane. *Triptych.* Wassenaar, The Netherlands: Servire, 1968.

Salzberg, Sharon. *Lovingkindness.* Boston, Mass.: Shambhala, 1995.

Wickenburg, Joanne. *Journey Through the Birth Chart.* Seattle, Wash.: Search, 1981.

Index

Free Magazine

Read unique articles by Llewellyn authors, recommendations by experts, and information on new releases. To receive a **free** copy of Llewellyn's consumer magazine, *New Worlds of Mind & Spirit,* simply call 1-877-NEW-WRLD or visit our website at www.llewellyn.com and click on *New Worlds.*

Llewellyn Ordering Information

Order Online:

Visit our website at www.llewellyn.com, select your books, and order them on our secure server.

Order by Phone:

- Call toll-free within the U.S. at 1-877-NEW-WRLD (1-877-639-9753). Call toll-free within Canada at 1-866-NEW-WRLD (1-866-639-9753)
- We accept VISA, MasterCard, and American Express

Order by Mail:

Send the full price of your order (MN residents add 7% sales tax) in U.S. funds, plus postage & handling to:

Llewellyn Worldwide
2143 Wooddale Drive, Dept. 0-7387-0046-0
Woodbury, MN 55125-2989, U.S.A.

Postage & Handling:

Standard (U.S., Mexico, & Canada). If your order is:
$49.99 and under, add $3.00
$50.00 and over, FREE STANDARD SHIPPING

AK, HI, PR: $15.00 for one book plus $1.00 for each additional book.

International Orders (airmail only):
$16.00 for one book plus $3.00 for each additional book

Orders are processed within 2 business days. Please allow for normal shipping time. Postage and handling rates subject to change.

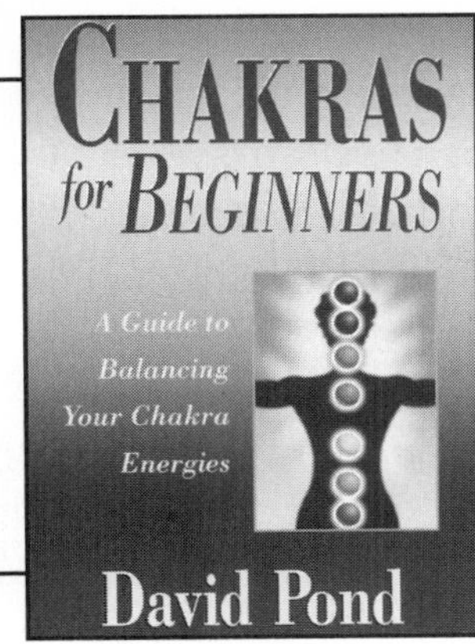

Chakras for Beginners

A Guide to Balancing Your Chakra Energies

DAVID POND

The chakras are spinning vortexes of energy located just in front of your spine and positioned from the tailbone to the crown of the head. They are a map of your inner world—your relationship to yourself and how you experience energy. They are also the batteries for the various levels of your life energy. The freedom with which energy can flow back and forth between you and the universe correlates directly to your total health and well-being.

Blocks or restrictions in this energy flow expresses itself as disease, discomfort, lack of energy, fear, or an emotional imbalance. By acquainting yourself with the chakra system, how they work and how they should operate optimally, you can perceive your own blocks and restrictions and develop guidelines for relieving entanglements.

The chakras stand out as the most useful model for you to identify how your energy is expressing itself. With *Chakras for Beginners* you will discover what is causing any imbalances, how to bring your energies back into alignment, and how to achieve higher levels of consciousness.

1-56718-537-1
216 pp., 5³⁄₁₆ x 8 **$9.95**

To order, call 1-877-NEW-WRLD

Prices subject to change without notice

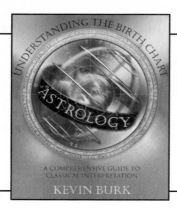